CHANGE AND CONTINUITY

RURAL SETTLEMENT IN NORTH-WEST LINCOLNSHIRE

Skegger Beck

Kettleby Thorpe township

former deer park

Kettleby
House

b

a

c

d

e

g

f

h

Metres
0   100   200

0
Feet
600

[1] *Bigby (1) Moated Site, Garden Remains, Ponds and Paddocks, (3) Deserted Village of Kettleby.*

ROYAL COMMISSION ON THE HISTORICAL MONUMENTS OF ENGLAND

CHANGE AND CONTINUITY

RURAL SETTLEMENT IN NORTH-WEST LINCOLNSHIRE

P. L. Everson, C. C. Taylor and C. J. Dunn

LONDON : HMSO

© Crown copyright 1991
First published 1991

ISBN 0 11 300024 3

British Library Cataloguing in Publication Data.
A CIP catalogue record for this book is
available from the British Library.

Printed in the United Kingdom for HMSO
Dd 240085 7/91 C5

FRONTISPIECE

[1] *Bigby (1) Moated Site, Garden Remains, Ponds and Paddocks, (3) Deserted Village of Kettleby. Kettleby House stands in the centre of the moated site of its predecessor, the medieval manor house of Kettleby. Also within the moat are the remains of a 16th or 17th-century garden with its associated decorative fishponds to the E. Other paddocks and enclosures of at least two periods surround the moat on the N, W and S. All these gardens, ponds and enclosures relate to the occupation of Kettleby House by the Tyrwhitt family between 1400 and c 1650. Partly underlying the gardens and enclosures, and almost completely destroyed by ploughing in the 1950s, are the faint traces of the village of Kettleby, cleared for sheep pasture by the Tyrwhitts soon after 1400.*

CONTENTS

ILLUSTRATIONS AND LIST OF PARISHES AND SITES INVESTIGATED   vi

COMMISSIONERS   xiv

CHAIRMAN'S PREFACE   xv

ACKNOWLEDGEMENTS   xvi

NOTES   xvii

INTRODUCTION   1
Methodology   1
Geology and Topography   2
Prehistoric and Roman Settlement   6
Post-Roman Settlement   8
Medieval Settlement   9
    The Economic and Tenurial Background   9
    Forms of Settlement   12
    The Origins of Settlement   13
    Settlement Change   28
    The Population of Villages   34
    The Desertion of Settlement   36
Manorial Sites   41
Churches   44
Religious Houses   46
Castles   48
Moated Sites   48
Fishponds   50
Water-mills and Windmills   51
Deer Parks   53
Garden Remains   54
Post-medieval and Undated Earthworks   55
Conclusions   56
Sites Most Worthy of Preservation   57

SELECT INVENTORY   61

SELECT BIBLIOGRAPHY AND ABBREVIATIONS   221

INDEX   225

ILLUSTRATIONS AND LIST OF PARISHES AND SITES INVESTIGATED

Sites published in the Inventory are entered in this list in bold type. Italic type indicates names which are no longer in current use and which derive from early documents. Illustrations included in this book are denoted by bold numbers in square brackets.

General

West Lindsey
  Relief and Drainage [3]
  Drift Geology [4]
  Settlements, Parishes and Townships [8]
  Land of Acrehouse in the parishes of Claxby and
    Normanby le Wold [2]

Village Plans [14–21]

Village Development [23–26]

Deer Parks: **Gainsborough (4), Goltho (3), Kettlethorpe (4), Stow (4)** [40]

Key to the drawings in the Select Inventory [46]

Parishes

1 AISTHORPE

  (1) Settlement Remains, formerly part of Aisthorpe
      (SK 847802). Destroyed 1952–3

2 APLEY

  (1) **Settlement Remains, formerly part of Apley
      (TF 108751)** [47]

  (2) Settlement Remains, formerly part of Kingthorpe
      (TF 129750)

3 BARDNEY

  (1) Mound (TF 12117069). Damaged between 1946 and
      1970

  (2) Site of Benedictine Abbey (TF 113706) [35]

  (3) Fishponds (TF 112704)

  (4) Canal (TF 105706–111708)

  (5) **Moated Site at Southrey (TF 134691)** [48]

  (6) Settlement Remains, formerly part of Bardney
      (TF 119697). Destroyed 1977 [20]

  (7) **Settlement Remains of Osgodby (TF 130726).**
      Greater part destroyed 1957 [10, 49]

  (8) Settlement Remains of *Butyate* (TF 133717).
      Destroyed 1959 [10]

  (9) Settlement of Southrey (TF 137664) [13, 15]

4 BARLINGS

  (1) **Site of Premonstratensian Abbey (TF 089734).**
      Peripheral destruction between 1946 and 1970 [50,
      51]

  (2) **Remains of post-medieval House and Gardens at
      Barlings Abbey (TF 089734)** [50]

  (3) **Enclosures (TF 080743).** Damaged [52]

  (4) Deer Park (centred TF 066750)

  (5) Settlement Remains, formerly part of Barlings
      (TF 076748). Destroyed after 1946

  (6) Settlement of Langworth (TF 063765) [20]

5 BIGBY

  (1) **Moated Site, Garden Remains, Fishponds and
      Paddocks at Kettleby (TA 033078).** Partly
      destroyed in mid 1980s [1, 53]

  (2) Deer Park (centred TA 040090) [1]

  (3) **Deserted Village of Kettleby (TA 032076).**
      Destroyed in 1950s [1, 53]

  (4) Deserted Village of Kettleby Thorpe (TA 042081).
      Destroyed 1964

  (5) Settlement of Bigby (TA 059074)

  (6) **Site of Lime-kiln (TA 03210738).** Damaged [1]

  (7) Enclosure (TA 019076). Destroyed 1962–3

6 BISHOP NORTON

  (1) Settlement of Bishop Norton (SK 984926) [14]

  (2) Settlement Remains, formerly part of Atterby
      (SK 981930). Destroyed 1977

  (3) Deserted Settlement of Crossholme (SK 993918).
      Destroyed after 1964

  (4) Settlement Remains, formerly part of Spital in the
      Street (SK 967903). Destroyed before 1945

  (5) Dam (SK 97559245)

7 BLYBOROUGH

(1) **Settlement Remains, formerly part of Blyborough (SK 933944)** [54]

(2) Site of medieval Building (SK 931941)

(3) Mill Dam (SK 960948)

8 BLYTON

(1) Settlement of Blyton (SK 853948) [**15**]

(2) Deserted Settlement of Wharton (SK 846936). Destroyed in mid 1960s

9 BRAMPTON

(1) Settlement of Brampton (SK 846795)

10 BRATTLEBY

(1) **Settlement Remains, formerly part of Brattleby (SK 947808)** [55, 56]

11 BROCKLESBY

(1) Site of Premonstratensian Abbey of Newsham (TA 129133). Peripheral destruction after 1946

(2) Site of Cistercian Priory of Nun Cotham, with post-medieval House and Gardens (TA 156112) [**36**]

(3) Settlement of Brocklesby (TA 139112)

(4) Deserted Village of *Cotham* (unlocated, perhaps TA 156112)

(5) Deserted Village of Little Limber (TA 123103). Destroyed between 1946 and 1971

(6) Deserted Village of Newsham (TA 130136). Destroyed in 1950s

(7) Windmill Mounds (TA 12701398 and 12591411). Destroyed in 1983

12 BROXHOLME

(1) **Settlement Remains, formerly part of Broxholme (SK 911781).** Partly destroyed in mid 1980s [**57, 58**]

13 BULLINGTON

(1) Site of Gilbertine Priory (TF 101767). Destroyed between 1953 and 1970

(2) Deserted Village of Bullington (unlocated)

(3) **Enclosure (TF 106764)** [59]

(4) Deer Park (centred approximately TF 100763)

14 BURTON

(1) **Settlement Remains, formerly part of Burton (SK 961744)** [60, 61]

(2) **Garden Remains and Park (SK 960743)** [60, 61]

(3) Medieval Settlement of *Haddow* (area SK 918751)

(4) Windmill Mound (SK 959752)

(5) Duck Decoy (SK 943745). Destroyed between 1848 and 1886

15 BUSLINGTHORPE

(1) **Moated Site (TF 080852).** Damaged 1969 [**62, 63**]

(2) **Deserted Village of Buslingthorpe (TF 080851)** [**62, 63**]

(3) **Pond (TF 081848)** [**62, 63**]

(4) Deer Park (TF 082852)

16 CABOURNE

(1) **Settlement Remains, formerly part of Cabourne (TA 143018).** Extensively damaged 1965 and 1968 and partly destroyed in mid 1980s [**64**]

17 CAENBY

(1) Settlement Remains, formerly part of Caenby, Moated Site and Ponds (TF 000897). Damaged in mid 1980s

18 CAISTOR

(1) Castle(?) (TA 115013)

(2) Settlement of Caistor (TA 118013)

(3) Settlement Remains of Hundon (area TA 115024)

(4) Settlement Remains of Audleby (area TA 110039). Damaged

(5) Settlement Remains of Fonaby (TA 112031)

(6) **Fishponds (TA 108012)** [65]

(7) Canal (TF 011989–073992)

19 CAMMERINGHAM

(1) Site of Alien Priory and post-medieval Garden Remains (area SK 949822)

(2) Settlement Remains, formerly part of Cammeringham (SK 948821)

20 CHERRY WILLINGHAM

(1) Settlement Remains, formerly part of Cherry Willingham (TF 030724). Destroyed between 1950 and 1980

(2) **Fishponds (TF 033724)** [66]

21 CLAXBY [6]

(1) **Settlement Remains, formerly part of Claxby (TF 112946)** [67]

(2) **Garden Remains (TF 112946)** [67]

(3) **Deserted Farmstead (TF 11039664)** [2, 68, 69]

22 COLD HANWORTH

(1) **Deserted Village of Cold Hanworth (TF 035831).** Extensively damaged between 1950 and 1960 [70]

23 CORRINGHAM

(1) Moated Site (SK 873919). Damaged 1976

(2) Settlement of Great Corringham (SK 871916)

(3) Settlement of Little Corringham (SK 869910)

23 CORRINGHAM—*continued*

(4) Settlement of Aisby (SK 872929) [**12, 18**]

(5) Deserted Village of Dunstall (SK 890938). Destroyed *c* 1979

(6) Deserted Settlement of Huckerby (area SK 902938)

(7) Deserted Village of Somerby (SK 847898). Destroyed 1957

(8) Farm of Woodhouse (SK 847906)

(9) Settlement Remains, formerly part of Yawthorpe (SK 897920). Destroyed after 1946

(10) Deer Park (centred SK 850890)

24 DUNHOLME

(1) Settlement Remains, formerly part of Dunholme (TF 027793). Destroyed in 1948 and later

(2) Site of Water-mill (TF 022796)

25 EAST FERRY

(1) Settlement of East Ferry (SK 814998) [**11, 15**]

26 EAST STOCKWITH

(1) Settlement of East Stockwith (SK 790946)

27 FALDINGWORTH

(1) Settlement Remains, formerly part of Faldingworth (TF 067848). Damaged [**18**]

(2) Monastic Grange (unlocated)

28 FENTON

(1) Settlement of Fenton (SK 847767)

29 FILLINGHAM

(1) Settlement Remains, formerly part of Fillingham (SK 948859). Damaged [**21**]

30 FISKERTON

(1) Settlement of Fiskerton (TF 048720)

31 FRIESTHORPE

(1) Settlement Remains, formerly part of Friesthorpe (TF 072834)

32 FULNETBY

(1) Garden Remains (TF 096794). Damaged

(2) Deserted Village of Fulnetby (TF 098795). Destroyed after 1953

(3) **Deserted Settlement of *Helethorpe* (TF 086787).** Destroyed after 1946 [**71**]

33 GAINSBOROUGH

(1) Moated Site (SK 813900)

(2) Settlement of Gainsborough (SK 815899)

(3) Moated Site (SK 836881). Destroyed between 1963 and 1967 [**40**]

(4) **Deer Park (centred SK 835885) [40, 41]**

(5) Gypsum Quarries (centred SK 816911)

34 GATE BURTON

(1) **Settlement Remains, formerly part of Gate Burton (SK 838829) [72]**

35 GLENTHAM

(1) Settlement Remains, formerly part of Glentham (TF 002905). Partly destroyed 1972 and later

36 GLENTWORTH

(1) Settlement Remains, formerly part of Glentworth (centred SK 946881). Destroyed after 1946

(2) Deserted Settlement of Thorpe (SK 934877)

(3) Moated Site (SK 929873). Destroyed 1963–4

(4) Deer Park (centred SK 935878)

(5) Garden Remains (SK 943881). Destroyed before 1960

37 GOLTHO

(1) Deserted Village of Goltho (TF 116774). Destroyed between 1960 and 1970

(2) **Moated Site and Garden Remains (TF 117766).** Damaged between 1964 and 1971 [**40, 73**]

(3) **Deer Park (centred TF 123765) [40, 73]**

38 GRANGE DE LINGS

(1) Site of Monastic Grange (SK 987773)

39 GRASBY

(1) Settlement of Grasby (TA 088049)

(2) Settlement Remains, formerly part of Clixby (TA 100044). Destroyed after 1946

(3) Garden Remains (TA 099043)

40 GRAYINGHAM

(1) Settlement Remains, formerly part of Grayingham (centred SK 935962). Destroyed 1969 and later

41 GREAT LIMBER

(1) **House Site (TA 138085) [74]**

(2) **Settlement Remains, formerly part of Great Limber (TA 137086).** Largely destroyed between 1969 and 1976 [**74, 75**]

42 GREETWELL

(1) **Deserted Village of Greetwell (TF 014716) [25, 76]**

(2) **Garden Remains (TF 014715) [25, 76]**

43 HACKTHORN

(1) Site of Monastic Grange and Settlement Remains, formerly part of Hackthorn (SK 995824). Partly destroyed before 1945 [**77**]

44 HARDWICK

(1) Settlement Remains, formerly part of Hardwick (SK 869̄757). Partly destroyed after 1946

(2) Settlement of Drinsey (SK 870748)

45 HARPSWELL

(1) Settlement Remains, formerly part of Harpswell (SK 933899). Greater part destroyed in 1980s [**78**]

(2) Garden Remains (SK 933899). Greater part destroyed in 1980s [**42, 78, 79, 80**]

46 HEAPHAM

(1) Moated Site and Settlement Remains, formerly part of Heapham (SK 881887) [**18, 34, 81**]

(2) Settlement of Heapham (SK 876882) [**34**]

47 HEMSWELL

(1) Site of Church (SK 93289113)

(2) Settlement Remains, formerly part of Hemswell St Helen and Hemswell All Saints (centred SK 928930). Destroyed after 1946 [**17**]

(3) Settlement Remains, formerly part of Spital in the Street (SK 966901). Destroyed after 1946

48 HOLTON CUM BECKERING

(1) Deserted Settlement of Beckering (TF 122807). Destroyed between 1963 and 1975

(2) Settlement Remains, formerly part of Holton (TF 116813). Damaged [**19**]

49 HOLTON LE MOOR

(1) Settlement Remains, formerly part of Holton (TF 081978)

50 INGHAM

(1) Site of Monastic Grange (?SK 948838)

(2) Settlement of Ingham (SK 946835)

51 KEELBY

(1) Settlement of Keelby (TA 165099) [**16**]

52 KETTLETHORPE

(1) Moated Site (SK 848756)

(2) Settlement Remains, formerly part of Kettlethorpe (SK 848758) [**40**]

(3) Settlement of Laughterton (SK 837758)

(4) Deer Park (centred SK 850753) [**40**]

(5) Enclosure (SK 851756) [**40, 82**]

53 KEXBY

(1) Settlement of Kexby (SK 873858)

54 KIRMOND LE MIRE

(1) Settlement Remains, formerly part of Kirmond le Mire (TF 188925). Destroyed in 1975 [**83**]

55 KNAITH

(1) Site of Cistercian Priory of Heynings (SK 846853). Damaged in mid 1980s [**84**]

(2) Settlement Remains, formerly part of Knaith (SK 829847) [**26, 85**]

(3) Garden and Park Remains (SK 828845) [**26, 85**]

(4) Deer Park (SK 839851)

56 LAUGHTON

(1) Settlement Remains, formerly part of Laughton (SK 850972). Destroyed [**21**]

57 LEA

(1) Settlement of Lea (SK 829866) [**21**]

(2) Moated Site (SK 843872) [**86**]

(3) Moated Site (SK 839871) [**86**]

(4) Deer Park (centred SK 840870)

(5) Garden Remains (SK 830863)

58 LEGSBY

(1) Moated Site at Bleasby (TF 131848) [**27, 87**]

(2) Deserted Village of Bleasby (TF 130848). Damaged in mid 1980s [**27, 87, 88**]

(3) Deserted Settlement of *Coldecotes* (TF 159848) [**89**]

(4) Site of Monastic Grange at Collow (TF 140837). Destroyed in mid 1980s [**90**]

(5) Deserted Village of East Torrington (TF 147835) [**91**]

(6) Moated Site, Site of Monastic Grange and Deserted Settlement of Holtham (TF 153863). Destroyed between 1963 and 1971 [**92**]

(7) Settlement Remains, formerly part of Legsby (TF 137856)

(8) Site of Chapel(?) (TF 15778392). Destroyed in mid 1980s [**93**]

(9) Windmill Mound (TF 13258397) [**94**]

(10) Tree Ring (TF 15838498) [**89**]

59 LINWOOD

(1) Moated Sites and Deserted Settlement, formerly part of Linwood (TF 115857). Destroyed 1962 and 1980 [**37, 95**]

(2) Settlement Remains, formerly part of Linwood (TF 112865). Partly destroyed between 1966 and 1969 [**95**]

(3) Deer Park (centred TF 112858)

60 LISSINGTON

(1) Settlement Remains, formerly part of Lissington (TF 108836). Destroyed 1977

61 MARKET RASEN

(1) Settlement of Market Rasen (TF 107892)

62 MARTON

(1) Settlement of Marton (SK 840818)

63 MIDDLE RASEN

(1) Site of Church (TF 09078943)

(2) Settlement Remains, formerly part of Middle Rasen Drax (area TF 090892). Largely destroyed after 1950 [17]

(3) Settlement of Middle Rasen Tupholme (TF 087895) [17]

64 MORTON

(1) Settlement of Morton (SK 808916)

65 NETTLEHAM

(1) **Site of Bishop's Palace (TF 006752) [18, 96]**

(2) Settlement of Nettleham (TF 008753) [**18**]

(3) Settlement Remains at Nettleham Field Farm (SK 993744)

66 NETTLETON

(1) Deserted Settlement of Draycote (TA 101003). Destroyed after 1946

(2) Deserted Settlement of Hardwick (TF 121983). Partly destroyed before 1964

(3) Settlement Remains, formerly part of Nettleton, and Site of Monastic Grange (TA 111001). Damaged [19, 30]

(4) Deserted Settlement of Wykeham (TF 120973)

(5) **Deserted Farmstead (TF 11189710) [69]**

67 NEWBALL

(1) **Settlement Remains, formerly part of Newball (TF 073764). Partly destroyed [97]**

(2) Deserted Settlement of East Langworth (TF 068768)

(3) **Enclosure (TF 084760). Damaged since 1945 [98]**

68 NEWTON ON TRENT

(1) Settlement of Newton on Trent (SK 832743) [**14**]

69 NORMANBY BY SPITAL

(1) Settlement of Normanby (TF 001881)

70 NORMANBY LE WOLD

(1) **Settlement Remains, formerly part of Normanby (TF 122951) [99]**

71 NORTH CARLTON

(1) **Settlement Remains, formerly part of North Carlton (SK 944776) [26, 100]**

(2) **Deserted Village of Middle Carlton (SK 948773). Destroyed since 1959 [100]**

(3) **Site of Monastic Grange and Rabbit Warren (SK 943774) [26, 100]**

(4) **Garden Remains (SK 943777) [100]**

(5) Deer Park (SK 941777)

72 NORTH KELSEY

(1) Settlement of North Kelsey (TA 044015)

(2) **Fishponds and Settlement Remains at North Kelsey Grange (TA 043010). Partly destroyed between 1945 and 1960 [38, 101]**

73 NORTHORPE

(1) **Deserted Village of Southorpe (SK 896952). Damaged 1966 [102]**

(2) **Settlement Remains, formerly part of Northorpe (SK 895971). Destroyed before 1950 [103, 104]**

(3) **Deserted Settlement (SK 893973). Destroyed between 1956 and 1969 [103, 104]**

74 NORTH WILLINGHAM

(1) Settlement Remains, formerly part of North Willingham (TF 164883). Damaged

75 OSGODBY

(1) **Moated Site (TF 068928) [105]**

(2) **Settlement Remains, formerly part of Osgodby (TF 074927). Partly destroyed in mid 1980s [105, 106]**

(3) **Moated Manor and Site of former Castle (TF 056928) [107, 108]**

(4) **Deserted Village of Kingerby (TF 055928).** Partly destroyed in mid 1980s [**28, 106, 108**]

(5) Settlement of Kirkby (TF 063928) [**106**]

(6) Settlement of Usselby (TF 095936)

(7) Deer Park (centred TF 055925)

76 OWERSBY

(1) **Settlement Remains, formerly parts of Owersby (TF 058956–064935). Destroyed between 1960 and mid 1980s [109, 110]**

(2) Settlement Remains, formerly part of Thornton le Moor (TF 050962). Destroyed in 1964 [**109**]

(3) Deserted Settlement of Beasthorpe (TF 048967). Destroyed after 1946 [**109**]

(4) Deserted Settlement of *Cauthorpe* (TF 057958). Damaged [**109**]

77 OWMBY

(1) Settlement of Owmby (TF 001874)

78 PILHAM

(1) Settlement of Pilham (SK 862938)

(2) **Deserted Village of Gilby (SK 864932) [111]**

79 RAND

(1) **Moated Site (TF 106791) [25, 33, 112]**

(2) **Deserted Village of Rand (TF 108791) [25, 33, 112]**

80 REEPHAM

(1) Settlement of Reepham (TF 038739)

81 RIBY

(1) **Settlement Remains, formerly part of Riby (TA 184073). Partly destroyed in mid 1980s [31, 113]**

82 RISEHOLME

(1) **Deserted Village of Riseholme (SK 982753) [114]**

(2) **Site of Monastic Grange (SK 984754) [114]**

83 ROTHWELL

(1) Settlement Remains, formerly part of Rothwell (TF 150994). Largely destroyed after 1946

84 SAXBY

(1) Settlement of Saxby (TF 005862)

(2) Deer Park (unlocated)

85 SAXILBY WITH INGLEBY

(1) Settlement of Saxilby (SK 892755) [18]

(2) **Moated Site and Deserted Village of North Ingleby (SK 893778). Partly destroyed in mid 1980s [26, 115]**

(3) **Moated Site and Deserted Village of South Ingleby (SK 893771). Partly destroyed in mid 1980s [26, 115]**

(4) Site of Monastic Grange (SK 870788). Destroyed 1962

(5) Moated Site, probable Monastic Grange (SK 876770). Destroyed between 1946 and 1966

86 SCAMPTON

(1) Sites of Monastic Granges and Settlement Remains (SK 949794)

(2) Site of post-medieval House, Gardens and Park (SK 945795)

87 SCOTHERN

(1) Settlement of Scothern (TF 034774) [19]

(2) Windmill Mound (TF 03407698). Destroyed in mid 1980s

88 SCOTTER

(1) Settlement of Scotter (SE 886009) [20]

(2) Settlement of Scotterthorpe (SE 876020) [15]

(3) Settlement of Susworth (SE 834022)

(4) Settlement of Cote Houses (SE 842017)

89 SCOTTON

(1) Settlement of Scotton (SK 890991) [16]

90 SEARBY CUM OWMBY

(1) Settlement of Searby (TA 072058)

(2) Settlement Remains, formerly part of Owmby (TA 078049). Damaged

91 SIXHILLS

(1) **Site of Gilbertine Priory and later Settlement (TF 163872). Partly destroyed before 1946 [116]**

(2) Settlement Remains, formerly part of Sixhills (TF 170870). Destroyed in 1960s

92 SNARFORD

(1) Deserted Village of Snarford (TF 051824). Destroyed 1954–6

(2) Sites of post-medieval Houses and Gardens (TF 051822 and 050824). Destroyed 1954–6

(3) Park (centred TF 051834)

93 SNELLAND

(1) Settlement Remains, formerly part of Snelland (TF 077805). Destroyed between 1946 and 1970

(2) **Deserted Settlement of Swinthorpe (TF 063805). Partly destroyed between 1946 and 1960 [117]**

94 SNITTERBY

(1) Settlement of Snitterby (SK 986947)

95 SOMERBY

(1) **Deserted Village of Somerby (TA 062063) [118]**

(2) **Garden Remains (TA 062063) [118, 119]**

96 SOUTH CARLTON

(1) **Site of Monastic Grange (SK 948764) [120]**

(2) **Manorial Enclosure and Fishponds (SK 951766) [120]**

(3) **Settlement Remains, formerly part of South Carlton (SK 951765) [120]**

(4) Duck Decoy (SK 931755). Destroyed before 1945 [43]

(5) Deer Park (centred SK 953767)

97 SOUTH KELSEY

(1) Site of Alien Priory of Winghale (TF 030970). Damaged in mid 1980s [**121**]

(2) Site of Church (TF 043988)

(3) Settlement Remains, formerly part of South Kelsey St Mary and South Kelsey St Nicholas (TF 042982). Damaged [**16**]

(4) Moated Site (TF 045976) [**16, 122**]

(5) Enclosure and Platform (TF 04429754 and 04399748) [**122**]

(6) Deer Park (centred TF 041973)

(7) Caistor Canal (TF 01079897–07089910)

98 SPRIDLINGTON

(1) Settlement Remains, formerly part of Spridlington St Albinus and Spridlington St Hilary (TF 008845). Damaged in mid 1980s [**123**]

99 SPRINGTHORPE

(1) Settlement of Springthorpe (SK 876897)

(2) Settlement of Sturgate (SK 880892) [**15**]

100 STAINFIELD

(1) Site of Benedictine Priory (TF 111732). Damaged in 1980 [**24, 124**]

(2) Deserted Village of Stainfield (TF 113729). Destroyed in 1980 [**24, 124**]

(3) Garden Remains (TF 112731). Partly destroyed in 1980 [**24, 124, 125**]

(4) Deer Park (centred TF 112731)

101 STAINTON BY LANGWORTH

(1) Settlement Remains, formerly part of Stainton (TF 062776)

(2) Moated Site and Deserted Settlement of Reasby (TF 067795). Destroyed after 1946

102 STAINTON LE VALE [**7**]

(1) Settlement Remains, formerly part of Stainton le Vale (TF 170944). Partly destroyed in mid 1980s [**126, 127**]

(2) Deserted Village of Orford (TF 198946) [**128**]

(3) Site of Premonstratensian Priory at Orford and post-medieval House and Garden (TF 195945) [**128**]

(4) Garden Remains at Orford House (TF 203947) [**129**]

103 STOW

(1) Settlement Remains, formerly part of Stow (SK 882820) [**20**]

(2) Moated Site (SK 881819). Damaged

(3) Moated Site of Bishop's Palace (SK 867809). Damaged [**40, 130**]

(4) Deer Park (centred SK 864798) [**40, 130**]

(5) Deserted Settlement of Stow Park (SK 867808). Partly destroyed [**40, 130**]

(6) Settlement Remains, formerly part of Normanby (SK 882830). Partly destroyed

(7) Deserted Village of Coates (SK 911833) [**25, 131, 132**]

104 STURTON

(1) Settlement of Sturton (SK 890804)

(2) Settlement Remains, formerly part of Bransby (SK 899791)

(3) Deserted Settlement of *Gorwick* (unlocated)

105 SUDBROOKE

(1) Settlement Remains, formerly part of Sudbrooke (TF 033758). Destroyed in 1978 [**133**]

(2) Deserted Settlement of Holme (area TF 043762)

106 SWALLOW

(1) Moated Site and Settlement Remains, formerly part of Swallow (TA 175030). Partly destroyed in mid 1980s [**134**]

(2) Settlement Remains, formerly part of Cuxwold (TA 172011). Destroyed before 1971

107 SWINHOPE

(1) Deserted Village of Swinhope (TF 218961). Destroyed in 1969 [**135**]

(2) Site of post-medieval House (TF 21569631). Destroyed between 1946 and 1963

(3) Enclosure (TF 231955). Damaged between 1946 and 1972

108 TEALBY

(1) Settlement Remains, formerly part of Tealby (centred TF 157909). Damaged [**17**]

(2) Settlement Remains, formerly part of Tealby Thorpe (centred TF 149899)

(3) Moated Site at Chapel Hill (TF 130894) [**136**]

109 THONOCK

(1) Ring and Baileys (SK 818915). Damaged in mid 1980s [**137**]

(2) Deer Parks (centred SK 815916 and 822915)

(3) Deserted Settlement of Thonock (unlocated)

(4) Deserted Settlement of *Havercroft* (unlocated)

110 THORESWAY

(1) Settlement Remains, formerly part of Thoresway (TF 169967). Partly destroyed in 1962 and further damaged in mid 1980s [**29, 138**]

110 THORESWAY—continued

   (2) **Site of Monastic Grange (TF 168963).** Partly destroyed after 1946 [**29, 138**]

   (3) **Deserted Village of Croxby (TF 192983).** Partly destroyed in mid 1980s [**139**]

   (4) **Garden Remains (TF 189981)** [**139**]

   (5) Duck Decoy (TF 194992). Destroyed in 1950s

111 THORGANBY

   (1) **Deserted Village of Thorganby (TF 208978).** Destroyed between 1946 and 1966 [**44, 45, 140**]

   (2) Ponds (TF 209980)

112 THORPE IN THE FALLOWS

   (1) **Deserted Village of Thorpe (SK 912807)** [**141**]

113 TOFT NEWTON

   (1) Site of Monastic Grange (TF 053870)

   (2) Settlement Remains, formerly part of Newton (TF 051872). Destroyed 1964

   (3) **Settlement Remains, formerly part of Toft (TF 043882).** Partly destroyed in mid 1980s [**142**]

114 TORKSEY

   (1) Site of Augustinian Priory (SK 837791). Destroyed 1950 and before

   (2) Site of Cistercian Nunnery (SK 836782). Destroyed

   (3) Settlement Remains, formerly part of the medieval town of Torksey (SK 837789)

115 UPTON

   (1) Settlement of Upton (SK 868868) [**14**]

116 WADDINGHAM

   (1) Settlement of Waddingham St Peter (SK 987963) [**16**]

   (2) Settlement of Waddingham St Mary (SK 982961) [**16**]

117 WALESBY

   (1) **Settlement Remains, formerly part of Walesby (TF 138923)** [**143, 144**]

   (2) **Deserted Settlement of Risby (TF 146918)** [**9, 145**]

   (3) **Deserted Settlement of Otby (TF 138936)** [**146**]

118 WALKERITH

   (1) Settlement of Walkerith (SK 788931)

119 WELTON

   (1) Settlement of Welton (TF 011798) [**19**]

   (2) Settlement of Ryland (TF 021800) [**14**]

   (3) Deserted Settlement of Rutton (area TF 018813)

   (4) **Fishponds (TF 009796)** [**147**]

120 WEST FIRSBY

   (1) **Deserted Village of Firsby (SK 990852).** Damaged [**22, 25, 32, 148**]

   (2) Alleged Deserted Village of East Firsby (?TF 022857)

121 WEST RASEN

   (1) **Settlement Remains, formerly part of West Rasen (TF 064893).** Partly destroyed in 1960s and early 1970s [**149**]

   (2) **Windmill Mound (TF 05618886)** [**39, 150**]

122 WICKENBY

   (1) Site of Monastic Grange at Westlaby (unlocated)

   (2) Deserted Settlement of Westlaby (unlocated)

   (3) **Settlement Remains, formerly part of Wickenby (TF 090820).** Largely destroyed between 1946 and 1970 [**151**]

123 WILDSWORTH

   (1) Settlement of Wildsworth (SK 808979) [**5, 15**]

124 WILLINGHAM BY STOW

   (1) Settlement of Willingham (SK 875845)

125 WILLOUGHTON

   (1) **Moated Site, Site of Grange of Alien Priory (SK 932931)** [**152**]

   (2) **Site of Preceptory of the Knights Templars and Hospitallers (SK 927932).** Damaged in mid 1980s [**153**]

   (3) Settlement of Willoughton (SK 930932) [**19**]

   (4) Settlement Remains, formerly part of *Helpesthorpe* (SK 933928). Destroyed

COMMISSIONERS

CHAIRMAN'S PREFACE

Lincolnshire has long been known for its large number of archaeological sites, broadly datable to the medieval period, and in particular for the exceptional nature and preservation of many deserted villages.

Yet with a few notable exceptions no full record or analysis has been made of any of these sites, in the face of an ever-increasing rate of destruction. The Royal Commission decided, therefore, to carry out a survey of medieval earthworks in Lincolnshire. The limited resources of the Commission, the large size of Lincolnshire and the numbers and complexity of the sites therein have meant that only one part of the county, the western part of the former division of Lindsey, could be covered and that only a selection of sites could be fully recorded and published here. All other medieval sites in the chosen area, as well as prehistoric and Roman sites and known archaeological material of all dates, have been noted and are contained in a full archive held in the National Monuments Record. The present publication also contains an Introduction analysing the evidence recovered.

The Royal Commission's intention in publishing the material in this way is four-fold. Firstly, we wish to draw attention to both the fragile nature of this type of archaeological material and the increasing rate of its destruction, not only in Lincolnshire but elsewhere. Secondly, we are providing the basis for an informed enhancement of the list of scheduled monuments of West Lindsey. Thirdly, our publication should enable scholars to use the results for research purposes, and lastly we intend the methodology to stand as an exemplar for future work of this kind, all over England. The analysis of medieval and later settlement forms in particular is intended to be an assessment of the current state of research and to act as a springboard for future exploration of the complex physical, social, economic and tenurial forces that together created the villages of this part of England.

The Commissioners wish to express their special thanks to the University of Nottingham for academic guidance and administrative help and to the Lincolnshire County Council for considerable practical assistance, and in particular the generous provision of accommodation and services. Without this help the project would not have been completed. They also desire to record their appreciation of the help given by occupiers and owners who have allowed access to the monuments in their charge. Many individuals and agencies within the county have freely supplied or made accessible information, finds and records, to the benefit of the work.

Finally, and not without considerable pride, they acknowledge the good work accomplished by their executive staff in the production of this volume and of the archive which lies behind it.

CHARLES THOMAS

Acting Chairman

ACKNOWLEDGEMENTS

The bulk of the fieldwork and documentary research, and the preparation of the Inventory accounts, both in this publication and in the archive, has been the work of Mr P. L. Everson, assisted by Mr C. J. Dunn. The introduction was written by Mr C. C. Taylor who was also responsible for the overall supervision of the work. The editing was carried out by Mrs S. E. Taylor. Other members of staff involved were Mr P. M. Sinton who produced all the line drawings and Mr D. Jones who helped with transcription of aerial photographs and with the documentary research. The ground photographs are the work of Mr A. D. Perry and that on the cover was taken by Mr R. Featherstone. Aerial photographs not taken by members of the Royal Commission's own staff are reproduced by permission of the Committee of Aerial Photography, University of Cambridge, and the Ministry of Defence (Air). The Royal Commission is also indebted to the following for permission to reproduce illustrations: [41] the Public Record Office; [51] Lincolnshire County Council, Recreational Services, Usher Gallery, Lincoln; [79, 107, 119] from the Local Studies Collection, Lincoln Library by courtesy of Lincolnshire Library Service.

Many other people have contributed in various ways, notably the executive staff of the Lincolnshire County Council, Miss F. N. Field (the Field Archaeologist for North Lincolnshire), Mr A. J. White and other staff of the Lincolnshire Museums Service, Mr K. Leahy at Scunthorpe Museum, successive County Archivists at the Lincolnshire Archives Office and their staff, the staff of the Reference and Local Studies section of Lincoln Central Library, Professor K. Cameron (Honorary Director of the English Place-Name Society), Dr John Sheail of the Institute of Terrestrial Ecology, the late Mrs E. H. Rudkin, Mrs J. Mostyn Lewis and Mr J. T. Hayes. Various students and temporary employees under schemes funded by the Manpower Services Commission have contributed to the survey work.

NOTES

The basis of the present publication lies in a study of the medieval and later settlement of 125 parishes in West Lindsey. The archive relating to this project is complete up to 1984 when work on it ceased and is available for public consultation in the National Monuments Record.

This archive consists of accounts of all the medieval and later archaeological sites, arranged by modern civil parish, together with a descriptive analysis of all existing villages and hamlets. Each of the 125 parishes has a brief account of its geology and topography together with reference to prehistoric and Roman sites and finds. Other information such as details of constituent townships and the dates of the enclosure of the common fields, where relevant or known, are also included.

The recording of the sites included in the archive was carried out at two levels and this has resulted in two different standards of information. The majority of the most notable surviving earthworks of medieval settlements were surveyed at 1:1000, considered in detail and recorded with full analytical descriptions. These include deserted and shrunken villages and the numerous manorial sites, granges, moats and fishponds which form part of these complexes of earthworks. Most other moated sites, castles and garden remains were also treated in the same way. Windmill mounds, fishponds, water-mills and other isolated sites were treated selectively and only the better examples were surveyed and analysed. Not all surviving monastic sites were fully recorded and only a selection was made to give a reasonable range of the religious orders found in the area under review, but with a bias to the smaller, less well known or problematic houses. All other sites including the numerous remains of deserted and shrunken villages now either totally or largely destroyed, other ploughed-out earthworks of various origins and most medieval deer parks, were treated summarily, often with minimum fieldwork, though the relevant air photographs were used to provide details of their original forms and layout. Notes on documented but unlocated sites have also been included in the archive. In the published Select Inventory most of the plans which were surveyed at 1:1000 are reproduced at a scale of 1:3000 but for reasons of economy the plans for a few very extensive sites have been reproduced at somewhat less than 1:3000. A few small sites were surveyed at 1:500 and are reproduced at 1:1500 and a number of plans where the archaeological detail is derived almost entirely from air photographs are reproduced at 1:5000. Air photographs are included in the publication where relevant. In the case of vertical air photographs the prints are arranged with north at the top of the page.

All existing villages were visited and the interpretation of their morphology was again included in the archive. No attempt was made to record ridge-and-furrow or other remains of medieval and later agriculture, except where it impinged directly on other sites.

The mere recording of archaeological sites of medieval and later date without some examination of the relevant historical documentation would have led to the loss of much of their significance. On the other hand the complete examination of every documentary source in both national and local archives was a task beyond the resources of the Royal Commission. As a result, documentary research has been limited to the more obvious and easily accessible material and further documentation was only pursued where fieldwork suggested it was justified. The sources consulted included the incomparable information contained in the extensive publications of the Lincolnshire Record Society, material in numerous other local and national archaeological and historical journals and the published calendars of the Public Record Office. Unpublished sources in both the Lincolnshire Archives Office and the Public Record Office have been used selectively but all known Estate, Tithe, Enclosure and OS maps and plans have been consulted.

In the description of deserted and existing settlements, in both the Select Inventory and the archive, consistent use has been made of Domesday Book and other medieval and later national taxation returns and population statistics. To avoid constant repetition of the bibliographical details of these sources they have been omitted from the accounts. The sources used are as follows:

1086   Domesday Book – *The Lincolnshire Domesday and the Lindsey Survey,* ed C. W. Foster and T. Longley, LRS 19 (1924) reprinted 1976

c 1115   Lindsey Survey – as above

1316   *Nomina Villarum – Feudal Aids* III, 177–87

1327/8   Lay Subsidy – PRO E179/135/11

1332/3   Lay Subsidy – PRO E179/135/16

1334   Lay Subsidy – R. E. Glasscock, The Lay Subsidy of 1334 for Lincolnshire, *LAASRP* **10** pt 2 (1964), 115–33, transcribed from PRO E179/135/24

1352   Lay Subsidy/Reliefs – PRO E179/135/58 extracted from MVRG files in NMR from transcription by E. Dodds

1377   Poll Tax – various sources including PRO E179/135/67, 70, 71 and 76, E179/196/40, E179/240/256–9

1428   Subsidy – *Feudal Aids* III, 310–35

1448   Lay Subsidy/Reliefs – PRO E179/136/233

1463   Lay Subsidy/Reliefs – PRO E179/136/293

1524/5   Lay Subsidy – transcribed data from PRO E179 files supplied by Dr John Sheail

1539   Lindsey Musters – *Calendar of Letters and Papers Foreign and Domestic, Henry VIII,* XIV pt 1 (1894), 276–9

1543/5   Lay Subsidy – transcribed data from PRO E179 files supplied by Dr John Sheail

1563   Diocesan Survey – *LNQ* **4** (1896), 247–52; **5** (1898), 8–10, 114–16

1603   Survey of Archdeaconry of Stow – *The State of the Church,* ed C. W. Foster, LRS 23 (1926), 337–53

1676   Religious Census – *LNQ* **16** (1920), 33–51

1705–23 *Speculum – Speculum Dioeceseos Lincolniensis,* ed R. E. G. Cole, LRS 4 (1913)

1801, 1841, 1901, 1951, Census – *Abstracts of Census Enumerators Returns* in LAO

In the absence of a county historian comparable to Bridges, Thoroton or Ormerod, and of VCH volumes dealing with individual parishes, the following sources were consulted to establish an outline tenurial descent where the nature of the field remains suggested that the tenure was a directly relevant matter:

1086   Domesday Book and *c* 1115 Lindsey Survey as above

1212   Book of Fees – *The Book of Fees* I (1921), 153–97

1242–3 Book of Fees – *The Book of Fees* II (1923), 1002–97

1303, 1346, 1401/2, 1428, 1431 – *Feudal Aids* III (1904)

Calendars of Inquisitions Post Mortem

Calendars of Inquisitions Miscellaneous

INTRODUCTION

Methodology

Though a wide range of medieval and later earthworks in West Lindsey is described in the following Inventory and in the archive, the majority of the sites recorded are those of medieval and later settlements. The greater part of this essay is therefore an attempt to place these monuments in a wider context.

The origin and development of nucleated villages in England have in recent years come under new scrutiny. It has become clear that the older and traditional views of the village as an early Saxon creation cannot be accepted without reservation, while at the same time it has emerged that even after their foundation all villages were subjected to continual change and alteration. It was partly to answer, or at least systematically to record information that may be used to elucidate, some of the problems arising from recent research, not only in West Lindsey itself but in England as a whole, that the Royal Commission undertook the present study.

The Royal Commission's survey in West Lindsey was concerned with the recording of three types of archaeological evidence associated with villages. These are the upstanding earthwork remains of former areas of settlement, the marks of earthworks now destroyed and only visible from the air, and occupation debris marking sites of habitation which can be recovered from modern arable land by field-walking. The Royal Commission believes that cartographic depiction of this evidence and analytical interpretation, especially when combined with research into the documentary history of the villages themselves, can play an important role in the understanding of the origins and development over time of both medieval and later settlements.

This work has been especially valuable because the earthwork remains and the other archaeological evidence often related to arrangements of settlements or parts of settlements which were abandoned sometimes quite early in medieval times. The analysis of such arrangements has thus helped in the recovery of information on the beginnings of and changes in settlement in a way that would not have been possible in those places where the evidence had either been destroyed by subsequent and often quite recent expansion, or distorted by later changes. Such studies may, therefore, help scholars to come closer to an understanding of the history of these villages in ways that no other method could achieve, except perhaps by total excavation. The results obtained from the examination of archaeological evidence relating to deserted or partly abandoned areas of occupation were compared to the layouts of existing settlements. As a result it has been possible to recognize in these settlements patterns which reflect similar origins and developments.

Analytical fieldwork on medieval and later settlement, important though it is, cannot stand alone. It requires support by historical documentation. Though the physical remains of former settlements are a primary source of information for understanding these places, without the historical background it would be impossible to explain these remains except at a very superficial level. Most of the major collections of both published and unpublished records have been examined albeit in a selective way and attempts made to relate the information to the recoverable archaeological and topographical evidence. On the whole, while it has been rare that specific questions have produced unequivocal answers, at least certain lines of enquiry have been opened up and aspects of settlement history have become clearer.

The value of combining analytical fieldwork with historical documentation will emerge in succeeding paragraphs but by way of illustration three examples may be noted here. The group of earthworks at Acrehouse (Claxby (3)) [2] might be interpreted as the site of a small deserted hamlet in a situation similar to those at Risby and Otby (Walesby (2, 3)). Examination of medieval documents shows that Newsham Abbey had a grange locally at the centre of a small estate founded in the 12th century: it would be natural to assume that the earthworks are the remains, but post-medieval records indicate that the site is most likely that of a post-Dissolution farmstead whose modern replacement stands only a few hundred metres away in the adjacent parish.

A more important example is at Cabourne (1) where extensive areas of complex earthworks suggest massive shrinkage of the village at some period. In fact the documentary record shows that the earthworks had nothing to do with the village itself or its fluctuating population but probably relate to the establishment of numerous monastic holdings mainly in the 12th century. The correct identification of the earthworks not only helps to gain a truer picture of Cabourne but, and more importantly, sheds much light on the impact of monastic landholding on the medieval landscape.

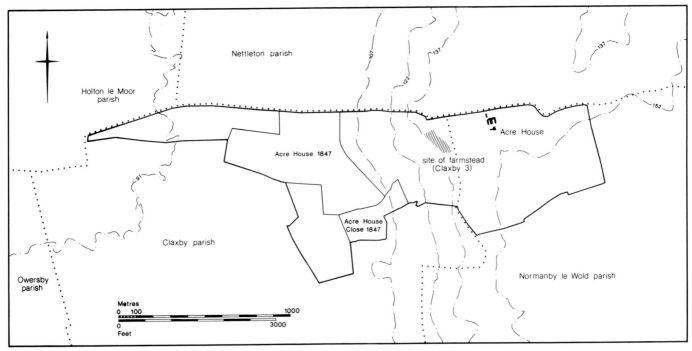

[2] *Land of Acrehouse in the parishes of Claxby and Normanby le Wold, based on Claxby Tithe Map of 1847.*

An even more interesting instance of the use of fieldwork and documentation from this part of Lincolnshire, with far-reaching implications, has been the reassessment of the excavations at Goltho (Goltho (1)) following the work carried out for this publication (Everson 1988). As a result not only has the actual identification of the village of 'Goltho' been questioned, but a radical reinterpretation of the surrounding landscape has been suggested.

Though the combination of fieldwork and historical documentation in the study of medieval settlement is therefore of great value, its limitations also have to be recognized. These include aspects such as the lack of documentation for long periods and the constraints resulting from the lack of archaeological material often over longer periods. But perhaps the most important limitation is in using historical and archaeological evidence to attempt to explain what is now seen to be the full complexity of settlement history and development. So many factors, geographical, tenurial, social, political and economic, have been recognized as playing a part in the origins and history of medieval settlement that it is often difficult, if not impossible, to isolate them and to assess their true significance at any individual place. All medieval settlements, even those which were abandoned at a relatively early date in the medieval period, have clearly been subject to continuous change, whatever their origins, and as a result, not only are the origins themselves usually lost, but most of the later changes are obscured too. The Royal Commission, in its survey of West Lindsey, has tried to extract what seem to be the most obvious indications of settlement beginnings and subsequent alterations and these are described in the following Select Inventory and more fully in the archive. Illustrations [24–26] are provisional attempts to indicate graphically some of the results. Nevertheless the Commission is well aware that all its conclusions are tentative and that, in the end, any attempt to unravel the exact development of most medieval villages is virtually impossible given that these villages, like their inhabitants, are and always have been living organisms continually adapting to changing circumstances.

Geology and Topography [3, 4]

The area under review is the western part of the ancient administrative division of Lincolnshire known as Lindsey. It covers some 1200 sq km of land extending from the River Trent in the W into the Lincolnshire Wolds in the E and from the River Witham in the S as far as the S boundary of the modern county of South Humberside in the N. It thus encompasses a wide variety of solid and drift geology with consequent differences in both soils and elevations.

The River Trent, here forming the W boundary of both Lindsey and the County of Lincoln, flows N to the Humber in a broad valley, carpeted by deposits of recent date overlying Keuper Marl and Jurassic clays. At present the river is cut into a narrow band of its own alluvium, edged on the E by gravel terraces laid down by an earlier course of the river. In places these river gravels are overlain by more recent deposits, notably Cover Sands, which occupy large areas to the S and NE of Gainsborough and which now give

2

rise to small patches of ancient woodland to the S of the town and to the extensive modern conifer plantations around Laughton and Scotter. In medieval times much of the latter area was low-lying unenclosed common land at less than 5 m above OD belonging to the parishes of Blyton, Scotter and Laughton. Within it, as well as the parochial centres, were the two smaller settlements of Scotterthorpe and Cote Houses (Scotter (2, 4)). In addition there is a line of settlements along the edge of the River Trent, mostly situated on river gravels and all of which have a close connection with the river as a main communication and trading route. Many of these villages appear to have layouts adapted to river trade as at Marton (1), Knaith (2) [26], Wildsworth (1) [5, 15], East Ferry (1) [11, 15] and Susworth (Scotter (3)) (Cf RCHME 1972, Horningsea (34, 35)). Two of these settlements were of more than local importance. Torksey (3) in the S, situated at the junction of the River Trent and the Roman Fosse Dyke was a major late Saxon trading centre. On its decline it was replaced by Gainsborough (2) 12 km to the N. The latter appears to have been a planned medieval town of the early 13th century and has remained as a local urban centre. More recently it became a minor railway junction. Torksey is now only a small village.

To the E of the main Trent valley is a broad undulating vale running N–S, almost all under 30 m above OD and mainly drained by the N-flowing River Eau and the S-flowing River Till and their tributaries. This vale falls into two distinct parts. The W section is floored by Liassic clays which, in medieval times, appear to have been well wooded. This led to the establishment of a number of deer parks as at Stow (4), Gainsborough (4), Lea (4), Knaith (4) and Thonock (2) as well as areas of managed woodland as at Lea and in Corringham. This clay region is edged by a line of villages from Saxilby in the S to Pilham in the N, beyond which, to the E, the clay is almost entirely overlain by glacial deposits, mainly Boulder Clay or Till, but including some Cover Sands. Though there are now no major settlements here a number of small villages or hamlets exist or once existed, including Thorpe in the Fallows (1), Broxholme (1), Coates (Stow (7)), Dunstall, Huckerby and Yawthorpe (Corringham (5, 6, 9)).

The E edge of this clay vale is marked by the steep W-facing edge of the Lincolnshire Limestone escarpment, for the most part 30 m to 40 m high and known as the Lincoln Cliff. At its S end it is cut through by the River Witham, at the point where the City of Lincoln is situated. The main scarp of the Cliff consists of Upper Lias Clay, overlain by the Lower Estuarine Beds and capped by Lincolnshire Limestone. This produces a spring-line near the base which has given rise to another line of villages from Burton in the S to Grayingham in the N.

From the crest of the Cliff itself, between 60 m and 70 m above OD, the land falls gently E across the dipslope to around 20 m above OD and is cut into by a series of small E-draining valleys. The rolling landscape thus formed, now characterized by limestone-walled fields, mainly of 18th and 19th-century date and resulting from parliamentary enclosure, is largely devoid of medieval settlement. Only in the larger and thus well-watered valleys are there, or were there, settlements, as at Riseholme (1), Hackthorn (1) and Firsby (West Firsby (1)) [22].

The limestone dipslope gives way to the Lincoln Clay Vale, whose W edge is marked by yet another line of villages which include Nettleham (2) [18], Welton (1) [19], Spridlington (1), Owmby (1), Glentham (1) and Waddingham (1, 2) [16]. The vale itself is based on soft Jurassic clays largely covered by later glacial deposits and eroded by the N-flowing River Ancholme and the S-flowing Barlings Eau (River Langworth) and their tributaries.

The S part of the vale is floored by deposits of Boulder Clay or Till which has given rise to extensive blocks of woodland, much of which was managed in medieval times. It also contains settlements that appear more scattered in the landscape, though locally related to slope and water supply. Some are medium to large, for example Bardney (6) [20], Goltho (1), Rand (2), Snarford (1), Faldingworth (1) [18], Buslingthorpe (2), Linwood (1, 2), Middle Rasen (2, 3) [17] and West Rasen (1); but distinctively there are many small settlements, commonly two or more to a parish, the majority of which are now either completely deserted or reduced to farmsteads. These include *Butyate* and Osgodby in Bardney (7, 8), Kingthorpe and Apley (Apley 1, 2), Newball (1) and Reasby (Stainton by Langworth (2)), *Helethorpe* and Fulnetby (Fulnetby 2, 3), Westlaby (Wickenby (2)), Swinthorpe (Snelland (2)), and Bleasby, *Coldecotes* and Holtham in Legsby (2, 3, 6). Further N the Boulder Clay or Till extends along the W side of the clay vale, but on the E, around and to the N of the small town of Market Rasen (1), are broad areas of Cover Sands. The N Boulder Clay is devoid of all but modern settlement, but along the junction between the clay and the sands is a line of villages including North Kelsey (1), South Kelsey (3) [16] and Owersby (1) as well as some largely or entirely deserted smaller settlements such as Beasthorpe and *Cauthorpe* in Owersby (3, 4). The Cover Sands are now occupied by extensive conifer plantations, but the common place-name 'Moor' as at Claxby Moor, Owersby Moor and even the settlement Holton le Moor (1), indicate the older land-use.

The clay vale is abruptly terminated on its E by the massive scarp face of the Lincolnshire Wolds. To the E and NE of Market Rasen this is between 100 m and 150 m high, though further N, beyond Caistor, it declines to 80 m to 90 m. Though the scarp is capped by chalk, the bulk of the exposed face is made up of outcrops of a variety of Lower Cretaceous rocks resting on Kimmeridge Clay. These include the Spilsby Sandstone, the Claxby Clay and ironstone beds and the Tealby Clay and Limestone, all mainly in thin beds. The result is that the scarp face is characterized by extensive soil slips, solifluction lobes and mud flows, as well as flat limestone benches just below the summit of the scarp face, through which minor streams have cut deep gullies [6].

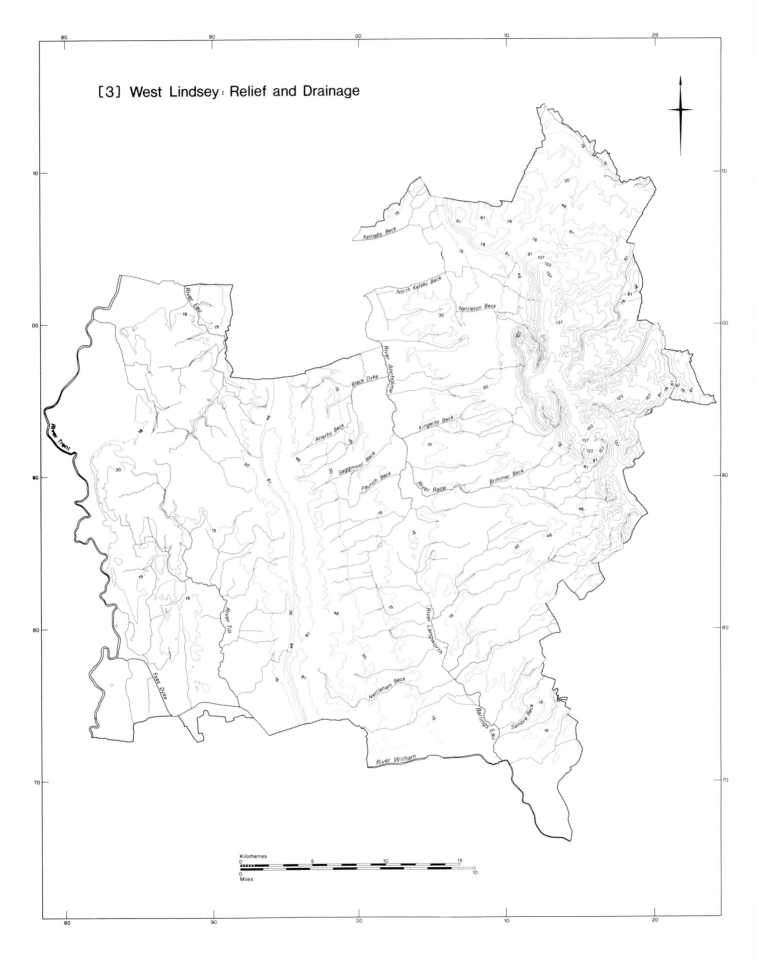

[3] West Lindsey: Relief and Drainage

River Eau

River Trent

Kettleby Beck

North Kelsey Beck

Nettleton Beck

River Ancholme

Black Dyke

Atterby Beck

Kingerby Beck

Brimmer Beck

Seggimoor Beck

Paunch Beck

River Rase

River Till

Foss Dyke

River Langworth

Nettleham Beck

Barlings Eau

Sambre Beck

River Witham

Kilometres

0   5   10   15

0   5   10

Miles

4

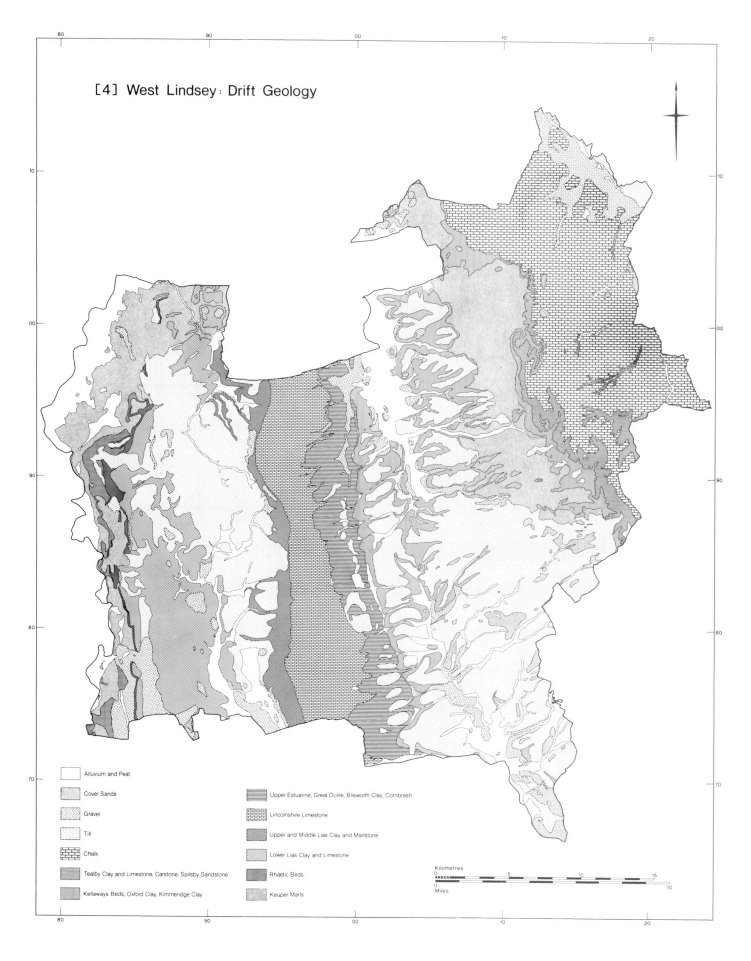

[4] West Lindsey: Drift Geology

Alluvium and Peat

Cover Sands

Gravel

Till

Chalk

Tealby Clay and Limestone, Carstone, Spilsby Sandstone

Kellaways Beds, Oxford Clay, Kimmeridge Clay

Upper Estuarine, Great Oolite, Blisworth Clay, Cornbrash

Lincolnshire Limestone

Upper and Middle Lias Clay and Marlstone

Lower Lias Clay and Limestone

Rhaetic Beds

Keuper Marls

Kilometres
0   5   10   15
0   10
Miles

Prehistoric and Roman Settlement

While a detailed analysis of the form, location and distribution of prehistoric and Roman settlement is not a direct concern of this study, it is likely that the existence of these settlements did have an effect on later occupation, particularly perhaps in terms of land-use rather than settlement position. The whole matter of early settlement in Lincolnshire is in need of review and most of the published works are now out of date. Certainly there has been no modern survey that takes account of recent fieldwork, excavation and aerial photography, all of which indicate extensive occupation and exploitation of almost the whole of West Lindsey in prehistoric and Roman times. Nevertheless little or none of this evidence survives in earthwork form. Given the area's land-use history of extensive arable during the high medieval period, special and specific conditions are required for such survival. A clear example is the occurrence of groups of mounds within the former peat fen areas of Barlings and Stainfield parishes. They appear to stand on an old ground surface below the peat and have been progressively revealed by modern arable cultivation and resulting wasting of the peat cover. Though undated except by their relationship to the peat, they are probably Bronze Age barrow cemeteries that are paralleled by similar groups along the Lincolnshire peat fen edge, for example at Washingborough, Heighington and Anwick. Another example may be a row of mounds on the fringe of the settlement remains at Normanby le Wold (1); another may be the enclosure at Newball (3), preserved in medieval managed woodland.

At present most published works suggest that the bulk of prehistoric occupation was largely confined to the chalk and limestone areas. While it is true that there was indeed massive occupation of the Wolds especially, now amply confirmed by the results of recent air photography in particular and summarized briefly in the Royal Commission's archive, recent research shows that many other parts of the area were settled and cultivated during most of the later prehistoric period (Jones 1988).

The material evidence for this occupation has been collected in a totally unsystematic way largely by local amateur archaeologists and much of it is undated. As a result the overall distribution of the material is hardly meaningful in terms of understanding the detailed pattern of settlement. Nevertheless the resulting picture, however incomplete, is impressive in total.

On the chalk Wolds the well-known Neolithic earthen long barrows, such as those at Swinhope, Bronze Age barrows and extensive scatters of Neolithic and Bronze Age flint tools can now be seen as merely part of extensive occupation. Several oval or elongated enclosures, possibly also Neolithic in date, and notably at Stainton le Vale, and crop-marks of ring ditches, linear ditches and field systems as well as large

[5] *Wildsworth (1) from the N, 9 October 1980. A typical Trent-side settlement, it is first documented at the end of the 12th century. In plan it exemplifies both the dependence of the string of small settlements N of Gainsborough upon the river on which they are sited and, in its regularity, their probable deliberate creation.*

The major settlements of this area lie along the spring-line at the foot of the scarp as at Nettleton (3) [19], Claxby (1) and Tealby (1) [17]. In addition, however, there are a number of smaller settlements which are, or were, located either on the limestone benches or on the chalk summit of the scarp. These include Normanby le Wold (1), Otby and Risby (Walesby (2, 3)) and part of Walesby (1) itself.

To the E of the scarp face the Wolds extend to well beyond the edge of the area under review. They form a well-dissected chalk dipslope sloping gently E between 170 m and 120 m above OD, cut into by small streams draining generally E and NE. All the major medieval settlements such as Thoresway (2) [29], Stainton le Vale (1) and Swallow (1), lie within these deep valleys. The plateau tops, in an area generally of parliamentary enclosure, are occupied only by post-enclosure or relatively modern farmsteads.

settlement complexes as at Great Limber, Kirmond le Mire and Cabourne, all testify to early activity.

On the limestone dipslope, the recent increase in information on prehistoric and probably Roman activity has been even more remarkable. Most of it is in the form of crop and soil-marks recorded by aerial photography. In parishes such as Bishop Norton many ring ditches, pit alignments and settlement enclosures are now known and at Nettleham, Grayingham and Cammeringham, where linear ditches have been noted, the understanding of early land-use in these places has been revolutionized.

Perhaps the most remarkable advances in knowledge have been made in the Cover Sand areas in the NW and NE of the study area. In parishes such as Scotter, Scotton, Holton le Moor, Claxby and Caistor, large quantities of material ranging from Mesolithic to Bronze Age in date have been recovered from field-walking and this evidence has been complemented by air photographs of enclosures, ring ditches and linear features.

Even on the clay areas finds and crop-marks indicate early occupation of some form. At Snelland and Welton in the Lincoln Clay Vale crop-marks of settlements are known from a gravel area along the Barlings Eau, while at Lea in the W clay vale early prehistoric flintwork has been recorded in profusion.

During the Roman period, the density of settlement appears to have increased considerably. There is now a substantial quantity of material, much of it unpublished, which suggests that Roman occupation of some form or other existed in most parts of the area. The majority of parishes here have two or three Roman sites within their boundaries. These range from villa sites such as those at Kirmond le Mire on the Wolds and Sturton by Stow in the W clay vale to numerous ill-defined occupation sites, perhaps mainly small farmsteads, which have been recorded on the Cover Sand areas as at Blyton, along the River Trent as at Marton, or within the clay valleys as at Lea and Linwood. They also include extensive areas of occupation of village-like size as at Stainton le Vale [7], Glentworth and Barlings.

The question of continuity of settlement, at least from Roman times through to the Saxon period, is one that cannot be answered satisfactorily. There is little evidence that is even reasonably acceptable in deciding the matter either way. Certainly there are numerous instances of Roman material having been found within both existing and deserted villages. These include Cherry Willingham (1), Somerby (Corringham (7)), East Torrington (Legsby (5)), Burton (1), Great Limber (2), Claxby (1) and Glentworth Thorpe (Glentworth (2)). However, at none of these places is there any evidence for Saxon occupation. At most of them there are other Roman sites elsewhere in the parish which equally have no evidence of later occupation. It could thus be argued that the existence of Roman material at all these places is entirely fortuitous. Yet the standard of fieldwork which recovered this type of information is usually of an order which precludes any certainty that later Saxon material did not exist on the site. It is probable that only excavation could produce the true answer.

There are a few Roman sites where occupation, of some kind, seems to have continued into the Saxon period. At Fillingham two of the three known Roman settlements have produced early Saxon material as has another at Scotton. An early Saxon brooch has been found on the site of the presumed Roman villa at Glentham. At the deserted medieval village of Kettleby (Bigby (3)) early Saxon as well as Roman material has been discovered, but nothing datable to the later Saxon period. Elsewhere a handful of sites have definite Roman occupation, but then nothing except mid to late Saxon or even later material. The best instance is at Goltho (1) where excavations have indicated some Roman occupation, and no further evidence until mid Saxon times. The same picture, albeit recovered from field-walking, has been revealed at Linwood (2) and at Newton (Toft Newton (2)).

[6] *Scarp face of The Wolds near Acrehouse, Claxby parish, here distorted by massive landslips, soil creep and slumping, 19 October 1948. (RAF)*

7

[7] *Stainton le Vale from the SW, 19 March 1966. Cropmarks of an extensive 'ladder' settlement, probably of Roman date, on chalk, NW of Priory Farm, Orford. (Cambridge University Collection: copyright reserved).*

Post-Roman Settlement

The centuries between the formal end of Roman rule and the Norman Conquest are perhaps the most difficult period to understand in the history of settlement in West Lindsey as elsewhere. There is abundant material available, including place-names, burials, and historical documentation, as well as a little occupation evidence. Yet it is difficult if not impossible to reconcile it all and to produce a satisfactory picture of settlement development. As noted above, continuity of occupation from the Roman period into early Saxon times has been found in a few places, but apparently did not occur at many others. At some sites, though occupation extended into the post-Roman period, it seems to have failed often after a short time. On the other hand, new settlements certainly came into existence on hitherto empty sites in the early, mid and later Saxon periods and many of these survived into medieval times. Lissington (1) has produced a range of Saxon material of all dates, while at Kirmond le Mire (1), Somerby (Corringham (7)), Kettleby Thorpe (Bigby (4)), and at an unnamed settlement in Northorpe (3), the recognized sequence of occupation appears to begin only in the late Saxon period. At Willoughton, extensive spreads of early Saxon pottery discovered by field-walking and the limited excavation of a sunken-featured building to the S of the village suggest a later movement of settlement or at least a less concentrated or organized form of settlement straggling along the spring-line. Similar discoveries of early and mid Saxon material on the fringe of later villages have been reported, for example, at Nettleham (1), Cherry Willingham (1) and Middle Carlton (North Carlton (2)), though nowhere in the area has systematic whole-parish field-walking taken place. On the other hand, at Normanby le Wold a mid Saxon site appears not to have survived into later Saxon times while at the site of the later alien priory of Winghale (South Kelsey (1)) there is again only mid Saxon occupation debris, following earlier Iron Age settlement. In view of this kind of conflicting evidence it is no longer possible to be certain that all of those places which were to be medieval villages were actually in existence by the 6th or 7th centuries. And even if they were, these settlements did not have the layout of their medieval successors as the excavations at Goltho (1) have indicated.

It is also impossible to use the multitude of Scandinavian place-names, so common in the area under review, to explain the sequence of settlement development. In some cases the earliest recognized occupation certainly pre-dates the

Scandinavian invasions, as at Kettleby (Bigby (3)), while in other places, for example at Somerby (Corringham (7)), it is much later. Certainly the simple hypothesis such as that which assumes that English and Anglo-Scandinavian place-names indicate earlier settlement than those with place-names of pure Scandinavian origin is no longer tenable.

All that can be said is that it is likely that by the late 11th century or early 12th century, most of the major later settlements of West Lindsey were in existence but these were not necessarily very old at that date, nor on the site nor in the form of the later medieval villages.

Medieval Settlement

The Economic and Tenurial Background [8]

In medieval times the parish was the basic unit of ecclesiastical administration, but certainly by the 12th century, and probably for long before, the economic basis of settlement in West Lindsey was the township. Although in many places parish and township were synonymous, as for example at Cabourne, Greetwell and Cammeringham, many ecclesiastical parishes were made up of more than one township. Thus Bishop Norton was divided into the land of Bishop Norton, Atterby and Crossholme while Swallow contained the township of Cuxwold as well as Swallow itself. Some modern administrative parishes were also townships in neighbouring medieval parishes as with Kexby, formerly a township of Upton, and Brampton whose township was once part of Torksey parish.

The arrangement of these townships is such that they seem to produce a neat subdivision giving the associated settlements a representative share of the available resources in the area and often in proportion to their early medieval size. This was not always the case, however, and at Bigby, for instance, the township of Bigby spanned the Wolds scarp and so extended across a variety of soils, while the townships of Kettleby, Kettleby Thorpe and Westrum (now in South Humberside) were confined to the lower-lying land in the W of the parish. In most cases the resulting townships also contained a single, common or open-field system worked by the inhabitants of the major or only settlements.

Exactly how and when these townships were established is not known. Some scholars have seen them as the result of early Saxon settlement and land allotment; others would explain them as arising from a tenurial and economic reorganization in late Saxon times. It has even been suggested that the origins of some townships lie in Roman agricultural estates or even earlier ones. It is likely that all these theories are too simplistic in seeing a monocausal origin for townships and that the townships, as they finally emerge in the medieval period, are the result of a whole series of interrelated factors.

In some cases where townships would certainly be expected there is no evidence for them, in spite of a multiplicity of settlements. Thus the parish of Nettleton contained the settlements of Hardwick, Wykeham and Draycote (Nettleton (2, 4, 1)) as well as Nettleton (3) itself yet there is no indication that any of these places had separate townships or field systems. It may be that as all except Nettleton were always very small, they never reached the point at which separate townships and field systems developed, thus implying a relatively late date for township origin.

Even more complicated is Corringham. The present and medieval parish contained the villages of Great and Little Corringham (now physically one), and Aisby, together with the hamlets of Dunstall, Huckerby, Somerby, Yawthorpe and Woodhouse (Corringham (2–9)). The field systems and townships of all these settlements can be reconstructed from early maps which indicate that while most had separate fields and townships, Aisby shared its fields with Great Corringham, though perhaps this was not always so, and that parts of the common fields of Little Corringham were shared by the adjacent settlement of Springthorpe (1), to the S, now and in medieval times a separate parish. This latter situation demonstrates that Springthorpe was once in some way part of Corringham as the configuration of its boundaries would suggest.

The same pattern of boundaries also indicates that other medieval parishes were once part of larger blocks. Sudbrooke parish appears as if it has been cut out of Scothern parish, and Cold Hanworth seems to have once been part of Hackthorn. The strong tenurial and economic links between the last two places throughout the medieval period also suggest that this was so.

These links, also seen at Aisthorpe, Brattleby and Thorpe in the Fallows, might suggest that some of these settlements are secondary to a primary village. However this may not necessarily be so and may merely indicate that the main block had some kind of unified tenurial origin with administrative control over other dependent settlements. Nevertheless these almost always had their own economic independence in the form of separate field systems.

This type of administrative grouping above and beyond the economic basis is often recoverable from the evidence of fiscal arrangements listed in Domesday Book. Aisthorpe, Brattleby and Thorpe in the Fallows also made up a neat twelve carucate fiscal unit in 1086. In contrast, there were some large areas which, however subdivided, always retained rights of a common economic or agricultural nature which extended far beyond the parish or township boundaries. The parishes of Buslingthorpe, Faldingworth, Friesthorpe and Snarford also form a geographically compact block. In medieval times the first three places shared an interest in an extra-parochial area of common meadow called Lissingleys, most of which is now in Buslingthorpe parish. In addition, up until the 19th century, the parishes of Lissington, Wickenby, Linwood and Market Rasen, to the E and S also retained interests in Lissingleys. Other extensive former common areas for which residual evidence survives are

Blyton, Scotton and Scotter Commons N of Gainsborough, Madgin Moor in the western clay vale, and Caistor Moor at the N end of the Lincoln Clay Vale.

Other large blocks of land seem to relate to late Saxon ecclesiastical administration, if not to an even earlier administrative pattern. The most notable of these is the area attributable to the *parochia* of the Saxon minster church at Stow. The modern parish of Stow now includes Coates (Stow (7)), but this was once a separate parish which had close connections with Ingham to its E. Medieval Stow comprised not only Stow, Stow Park and Normanby by Stow (Stow (1, 5, 6)), all still within its boundaries, but also the modern parish of Sturton by Stow. Sturton itself is made up of the townships of Sturton and Bransby (Sturton (1, 2)) and may have included a further farm or settlement of *Gorwick* perhaps with its own land unit. Similarly the Saxon minster of Wragby (outside the study area) originally included among its dependencies the area of land which later became the medieval parish of Rand. Yet even here it is not clear what the significance of Wragby as a minster parish was, for in 1086 Rand was also part of a major secular estate which included most of the Wragby *parochia*.

Elsewhere the definition of some townships and even parishes was apparently not an early feature. Caenby and Glentham were both medieval parishes, but the curious dividing boundary between them looks as if it was a late division, a situation which is implied by the tenurial and ecclesiastical history of both places. The multitude of monastic foundations and land grants, particularly in the 12th century, also led to the creation of townships or estates. Some of these were no more than the taking over of townships by new monastic houses which were planted on the sites of existing settlement. Thus the demesne lands of Newsham Abbey and Nun Cotham Priory, both in Brocklesby parish (Brocklesby (1, 2)), were effectively the townships of earlier villages. The demesne land of Bardney Abbey (Bardney (2)) appears to have been partly cut out of land which had earlier been a section of the township of Bardney village, but it also included the lands and settlements of *Butyate* and Osgodby, both of which were probably earlier separate townships (Bardney (6–8)).

In contrast, the land and grange of Acrehouse, in Claxby parish, granted to Newsham in the mid 12th century, was a separate block, within the open fields of Claxby, but extending E into Normanby parish, itself once apparently linked to Claxby in some way [2]. Likewise the origins of the modern civil parish of Grange de Lings, formerly an extra-parochial area, may lie in the presumably 12th-century grant of sheep-walks to Barlings Abbey and the subsequent establishment of a grange there. The creation of a similar block of land is implied by the surviving documentation of the monastic grange at Collow (Legsby (4)). There, various gifts of land in the fields of Bleasby, Torrington and Lissington, to the Cistercian abbey of Louth Park may have perhaps created the land unit that survived to be traceable as

the township of Collow on the Legsby Tithe Map of 1846.

This latter point is of wider interest. Whenever these townships were created and for whatever reason, once they were in being they tended to resist further change and become permanent fixtures in the landscape. By the end of the 12th century at the latest, most major settlements in West Lindsey lay within clearly defined blocks of land, usually farmed by the inhabitants of those settlements as a single agricultural unit. Thus such units were always or had become primarily economic or agricultural in purpose. They were not necessarily tenurial or administrative units. Some of these land blocks were also ecclesiastical parishes and a few were single manorial holdings. But the great majority were grouped together to form parishes, and were multi-manorial, or formed parts of greater landed estates. While the tenurial and administrative arrangements changed, as a result of sub-infeudation, marriage settlements, confiscations, grants and endowments, both the parish structure and the agricultural township structure once fixed tended to remain so. The townships, in particular, thus survived largely intact, despite tenurial changes and more importantly massive alterations to the settlements within them. They thus continued to be the economic basis of most occupation of West Lindsey until at least the 19th century.

The individual settlements associated with these townships could theoretically at least have been sited almost anywhere within them, depending on the physical conditions therein, or indeed the desires or demands of the intended inhabitants or their lords. On a broad scale, the choice of sites for medieval settlements in West Lindsey does reflect the basic physical determinants of the region. Most of the larger settlements, at least, produce a repetitive pattern of river-edge, scarp-foot, spring-line, clay-edge or wold-valley positions, their sites clearly conditioned by access to water or the availability of dry land.

In some cases this basic geographical determinism is emphasized by what, at first sight, appear to be unusual situations. For example, Firsby (West Firsby (1)) [22], Riseholme (1) and Hackthorn (1) all lie on the limestone dipslope, well to the W of and considerably higher than their near neighbours which are situated along the clay–limestone junction. Yet all apparently owe their existence to major streams which break out as springs high on the dipslope. On the other hand there are settlements whose siting seems to defy all logical explanation and certainly simple geographical determinants. The most notable of these are the hamlets of Risby and Otby (Walesby (2, 3)) as well as the E part of Walesby (1) itself, all of which are situated on the scarp face of the Wolds, on limestone benches which are and always have been subject to massive landslips and spring-head sapping [9]. These phenomena reduce much of the area of settlement to waterlogged and unstable ground. A possible explanation for these locations may be that the arable fields of these settlements lay entirely on the Wolds top, and therefore such a position ensured direct access to these fields

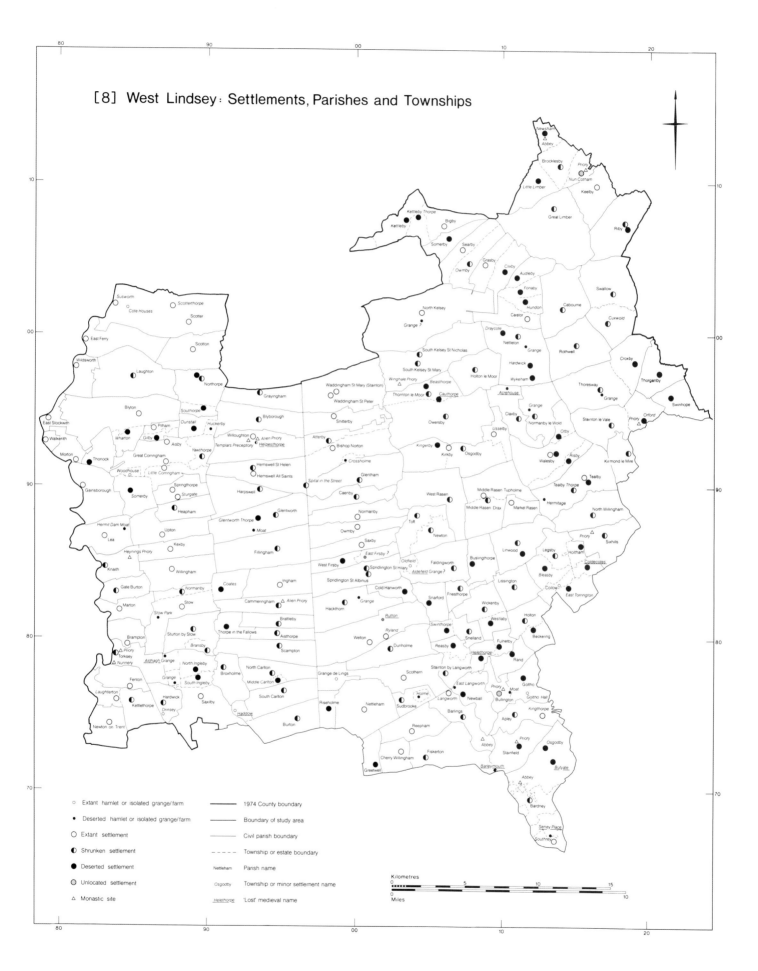

[8] West Lindsey: Settlements, Parishes and Townships

Newsham
Abbey
Brocklesby
Priory
Nun Cotham
Little Limber
Keelby
Great Limber
Kettleby Thorpe
Kettleby
Bigby
Riby
Somerby
Searby
Grasby
Cixby
Swallow
Owmby
Audleby
Fonaby
Cabourne
Cuxwold
North Kelsey
Hundon
Caistor
Grange ?
Draycote
Nettleton
Grange
Rothwell
Croxby
East Ferry
Scotton
South Kelsey St Nicholas
Thorganby
Wildsworth
South Kelsey St Mary
Beasthorpe
Hardwick
Grange
Swinhope
Susworth
Scotterthorpe
Cote Houses
Scotter
Holton le Moor
Wykeham
Thoresway
Laughton
Northorpe
Waddingham St Mary (Stainton)
Winghale Priory
Cauthorpe
Acrehouse
Grange
Stainton le Vale
Grayingham
Waddingham St Peter
Thornton le Moor
Priory
Orford
East Stockwith
Blyton
Southorpe
Blyborough
Snitterby
Owersby
Claxby
Normanby le Wold
Otby
Walkerith
Dunstall
Huckerby
Bishop Norton
Usselby
Morton
Pilham
Gilby
Aisby
Willoughton
Alien Priory
Atterby
Kingerby
Krkby
Osgodby
Walesby
Risby
Kirmond le Mire
Thonock
Wharton
Yawthorpe
Templars Preceptory
Helpesthorpe
Hemswell St Helen
Crossholme
Tealby
Woodhouse
Great Corringham
Glentham
Tealby Thorpe
Gainsborough
Little Corringham
Hemswell All Saints
Spital in the Street
Caenby
West Rasen
Middle Rasen Tupholme
Hermitage
Somerby
Springthorpe
Sturgate
Harpswell
Middle Rasen Drax
Market Rasen
North Willingham
Heapham
Normanby
Hermit Dam Moat
Glentworth Thorpe
Glentworth
Owmby
Toft
Priory
Sixhills
Upton
Moat
Newton
Linwood
Legsby
Hotham
Lea
Kexby
Saxby
Buslingthorpe
Coldecotes
Heynings Priory
Filingham
East Firsby ?
Oldfield
Lissington
Bleasby
Knaith
Willingham
West Firsby
Spridlington St Hilary
Faldingworth
Collow
Spridlington St Albinus
Aldefeld Grange ?
East Torrington
Gate Burton
Normanby
Coates
Ingham
Grange
Snarford
Freesthorpe
Wickenby
Holton
Marton
Stow
Cammenngham
Alien Priory
Hackthorn
Rutton
Cold Hanworth
Westlaby
Stow Park
Brattleby
Swinthorpe
Sturton by Stow
Bransby
Thorpe in the Fallows
Aisthorpe
Welton
Ryland
Reasby
Sneiland
Fulnetby
Beckering
Brampton
Scampton
Dunholme
Helethorpe
Rand
Priory
Torksey
Aldhagh Grange
North Ingleby
Grange
Broxholme
North Carlton
Scothern
Stainton by Langworth
Nunnery
Grange
South Ingleby
Middle Carlton
Grange de Lings
East Langworth
Gotho
Fenton
Priory
Moat
Laughterton
Hardwick
Saxilby
South Carlton
Holme
Langworth
Newball
Bullington
Gotho Hall
Kettlethorpe
Drinsey
Riseholme
Barlings
Apley
Kingthorpe
Newton on Trent
Haddow
Burton
Nettleham
Sudbrooke
Reepham
Abbey
Priory
Osgodby
Stainfield
Cherry Willingham
Fiskerton
Greetwell
Barleymouth
Butyate
Abbey
Bardney
Seney Place
Southrey

○ Extant hamlet or isolated grange/farm
● Deserted hamlet or isolated grange/farm
◯ Extant settlement
◐ Shrunken settlement
● Deserted settlement
⊕ Unlocated settlement
△ Monastic site

1974 County boundary
Boundary of study area
Civil parish boundary
Township or estate boundary
Nettleham Parish name
Osgodby Township or minor settlement name
Helethorpe 'Lost' medieval name

Kilometres
0   5   10   15
0
Miles
10

[9] *Walesby (2), deserted settlement of Risby, 30 October 1980. The earthworks are hardly distinguishable from the landslips and mud flows which they overlie. Despite the apparently inhospitable nature of the site, Risby was certainly in existence in 1086 and survived until at least the 16th century.*

as well as to fresh water and some shelter. Even so the sites seem far from ideal. At a more local level, the surviving earthworks of the former village of Somerby (1) occupy land which is still almost permanently waterlogged and which has defied all attempts to drain it. Here also it is not clear why the settlement was placed on such apparently unsuitable ground. It is particularly difficult to interpret the history of Somerby in view of this. The extant earthworks may be part of the original village, though they more likely represent a deliberate movement of the earlier village from its much better site near the parish church. If this is so, the unsatisfactory position could be the result of an arbitrary decision by a lord who had scant regard for the disadvantage of the new site for its occupants. Tealby Thorpe (Tealby (2)) has at least part of its main street set in a stream (cf RCHME 1975, Luddington (3)), yet another instance of the apparent disregard for the unsatisfactory aspects of a site.

A similar lack of respect for topographical features, though in a different context, is apparently visible at Croxby (Thoresway (3)). There, what may be a planned extension to the earlier village was laid out across the chalk valley in a way that totally ignored the existence of its stream. Particularly

relevant in this context is the site of the deserted village of Stainfield (2). It is sited not on the gravel-lined valley bottom of a small stream, but on the heavy clay land of the valley side. Yet here the unsuitable situation is explicable. The regular, presumably planned arrangement of the village, together with the documented history of the Benedictine priory (Stainfield (1)) which occupied the favoured site, indicates that the village of Stainfield was moved bodily from its original position to its present one, probably in the 12th century, to make way for the new monastic establishment [24]. It is possible that other less well-documented sites have similar histories that are largely irrecoverable.

Forms of Settlement

A consideration of relevance both to the preceding discussion of economic units and to the subsequent discussion of origins and change in settlement is that of settlement form. It is perhaps too readily assumed that in this lowland Midland area at the heart of the belt of champion lands all settlements are characteristically and uniformly substantial nucleated villages. The extensive list of 'deserted' or 'shrunken' medieval villages for a county like Lincolnshire tends to reinforce and fossilize this view. One effect of a study such as this in West Lindsey is to throw light on this pre-conception. While it is clear that, on the whole, many nucleated villages and their associated open or common-field systems did indeed exist there were also other forms of settlement in the area, including in particular individual farms or specialist holdings. A good example is *Haddow* (Burton (3)) in the far W low-lying end of Burton parish, with its definable associated land unit that is reflected in the configuration of the parish boundary. Another may be Crossholme (Bishop Norton (3)), that has conventionally been regarded as a deserted village; others are Drinsey in Hardwick (2) or Woodhouse in Corringham (8) or perhaps Westrum in Bigby. Such sites are typically poorly documented, are rarely mentioned at an early date, and create little field evidence, which makes them difficult to deal with satisfactorily in the present study with its prime focus on earthwork survey. More probably remain to be identified, such as may be hinted at by the name *Gorwick* in Sturton by Stow, by the lost farm called Randy Lea in Thorpe in the Fallows, by the farm names Hornsbeck in Blyborough, Turpin Farm in Fillingham and Cold Harbour in Cammeringham (each in the W low-lying end of these parishes), by the names *Alfletby* in Willingham by Stow, Thorncroft Farm in Snitterby, Coldstead and *Gippetoft* in Newball, Havercroft, *Bondemannescroft* and *Simundescroft* in Thonock, Bonsdale, *Wheatbear* and *Cotegarthe* in Corringham. Some of these may, of course, not have medieval origins, be topographical names only, or be constituent parts of larger settlements. If distinct medieval farms they are likely to have resembled monastic granges – some of which clearly bore just such names as Collow in Legsby (4), *Aldhagh* in Saxilby

(4) and *Aldefeld* in Faldingworth (2): some may indeed prove to have been monastic holdings.

The distinction between such places and those better-documented settlements which perhaps warrant the term 'hamlet' rather than 'village' is not always clear. The latter are especially common in the southern central clay vale but include the three subsidiary settlements in Nettleton (1, 2, 4) and Beasthorpe and *Cauthorpe* in Owersby (3, 4). The distinction is finer still in circumstances of changing status, as with those small settlements taken over as monastic granges, like Osgodby and *Butyate* in Bardney (7, 8) [**10**]. Overall, however, though there is none of the dispersed or attenuated roadside pattern, visible for example on the Lindsey Marshlands, the picture is of a more mixed and dynamic pattern of settlement size, form and function than might have been presumed.

The Origins of Settlement

The limited archaeological material for the periods when the medieval villages of West Lindsey took on their medieval form, as well as the unsatisfactory nature of place-name evidence have already been outlined. The documentary record is, for the most part, even more limited. The first recorded date for the existence of most settlements is not until 1086, when the majority of places are listed as landholdings in Domesday Book. A few places have an earlier mention in late Saxon documents, but all these date from the period just prior to the Norman Conquest. The late Saxon town of Torksey is one such, as is Gainsborough, which was used as a base for the Danish army in 1013–14.

In a large number of instances there is no record of the existence of many smaller settlements until the 13th century. This is not to suggest that these smaller places did not exist at an earlier period, but merely that they were usually subsumed in the documentary record under the names of larger neighbours with which they were usually tenurially or economically linked. In some cases archaeological evidence clearly indicates that these smaller settlements are often older than their first documented mention. For example, *Helethorpe* (Fultnetby (3)) is first recorded by its name in 1212, yet finds from field-walking on its now destroyed site indicate that it was in existence for at least a hundred years before then.

On the other hand if, as seems likely, a large number of settlements did at least acquire their present form in the 10th to 12th centuries, historical documentation which becomes common at that time can be extremely valuable. This aspect is dealt with below.

By its nature analytical fieldwork cannot produce exact dates for the origin of settlement. The work involves, at least in part, the establishment of the relative chronology of individual parts of settlements to each other or to other non-habitative features in the surrounding landscape. Such relationships are important but do not give an absolute chronology. Thus the two adjacent settlements of

Waddingham St Peter and Waddingham St Mary (Waddingham (1, 2)) each consist of a compact nucleus [**16**]. Yet close as they are together the two street systems do not align suggesting that the plans are of different dates. Nevertheless there is one of these relationships which has value in understanding how if not when villages were established in West Lindsey. This is where medieval settlement remains overlie earlier fields or field systems. Such relationships have been found in many places in England notably in Northamptonshire (RCHME 1979, Pytchley (8), Walgrave (7); 1981, Lilbourne (3)).

In West Lindsey the Royal Commission's work has again indicated that a large number of now abandoned settlements or parts of abandoned settlements overlie ridge-and-furrow. All three sections of the deserted village of Firsby (West Firsby (1)), which in themselves are of different periods, overlie ridge-and-furrow and the largely abandoned

[**10**] *Bardney (7, 8), settlement remains of Osgodby, to N (at top), and Butyate, to S, air photograph taken 10 May 1946 before destruction. Both sites were apparently small hamlets in 1086 but were then granted to Bardney Abbey in the 12th century and perhaps became granges. (RAF)*

[11] *East Ferry (1), 31 July 1963. The settlement of East Ferry lies on either side of a N-S street which mirrors the curve of the River Trent. The properties on the E side of the street appear to have been developed over earlier arable. This suggests that the street was previously a back lane of a former main street set along the river bank as at Wildsworth (1) and Susworth (Scotter (3)). (RAF)*

settlement of Newball (1) also exhibits the same feature. *Helethorpe* (Fultnetby (3)) seems to have been fitted into pre-existing furlongs in the same way as the equally small hamlet of Charlock, Northants, has been (RCHME 1982, Abthorpe (5)). At other sites, only parts of the abandoned earthworks can be seen to be on top of ridge-and-furrow. What seems to be a second phase of development at Coates (Stow (7)) [25] appears to have been laid out over land which was earlier arable. At South Carlton (3) too the section of the village which is presumed to have been developed as part of a 12th-century reorganization also overlies ridge-and-furrow. The same situation is visible at West Rasen (1), East Torrington (Legsby (5)), Somerby (Corringham (7)) and at both North and South Ingleby (Saxilby with Ingleby (2, 3)) [26]. At Stainfield (2) [24], as already discussed, the existing earthworks relate to the village which had been moved to a new site in the 12th century. Thus, as might be expected, the field evidence shows that it overlies earlier arable.

The fact that there is good archaeological field evidence for deserted settlements being superimposed on earlier fields suggests that existing villages without surviving earthworks, if examined carefully, might produce similar evidence. This has been looked for both on the ground and on early topographical plans and there is no doubt that such evidence does exist and can be recognized. Part of the Trent-side village of East Stockwith (1) appears to be over an earlier field system and the same is true at another Trent-side village, East Ferry (1) [11]. At Sturgate (Springthorpe (2))

[15], Scotterthorpe (Scotter (2)) [15] and Southrey (Bardney (9)) [13] the highly regular layout seems to have been inserted into pre-existing fields and a similar situation is recognizable at the two parts of Heapham (1) [18].

As already noted these relationships are not datable, except at Stainfield where a 12th-century date for the establishment of the village is likely. Neither in West Lindsey, nor elsewhere in England, is there any direct documentary evidence to indicate that the process of laying out villages over fields was as common as the archaeological evidence suggests. This might mean that it, therefore, took place in the pre-Conquest period before detailed documentation on such developments began. On the other hand it may be that documentation does survive, but as yet has not been recognized. The Royal Commission's survey has discovered one piece of documentary evidence, albeit not directly related to a true village, but which does reveal that the concept of settlements being laid out over arable land was at least known and accepted.

A 13th-century grant of land at North Kelsey Grange (North Kelsey (2)) to the Gilbertine priory of North Ormsby specifically states that the donor gave '2 selions which lie to the North of their court – that they may make tofts of them or sow them'. The selions, or ridges, still survive on the ground N of North Kelsey Grange, truncated at their S ends by the boundary ditch of what are the tofts of a small settlement associated with the monastic grange.

This evidence indicates that the origin of many West Lindsey villages must be sought not in immediate post-Roman times but at a much later period. Such suggestions have already been made for villages in various parts of England, notably in North Yorkshire and Durham (Allerston 1970, 95–109; Roberts 1972, 33–56; Sheppard 1976, 3–20) and in Somerset (Ellison 1976). Indeed some scholars have gone further and postulated that deliberate planning of villages either *de novo* or by the total reorganization of existing sites was a common feature of the English landscape in late Saxon and early medieval times (Taylor 1984, 133–48). Further, it has been postulated that subsequent expansion of villages also often involved a degree of conscious planning.

One of the most important aspects of the Royal Commission's work in West Lindsey is the amount of evidence found for such 'planning' of villages in its widest sense. A large proportion of all the sites examined, both of totally deserted and merely shrunken villages, have their street systems, house sites and associated crofts or closes arranged in such a way as to indicate that the overall plan was the result of conscious and deliberate actions.

A particularly fine example is Riseholme (1), though it may be that the surviving earthworks only related to one section of a polyfocal village made up of two quite separate parts. The regular pattern of closes, arranged neatly along either side of the straight main street is difficult to explain in any other way than by deliberate planning. The fact that there is also evidence that the village was laid out over pre-existing ridge-and-furrow may strengthen this argument.

Elsewhere the same indicators of a planned beginning for what later became a medieval village are visible. Buslingthorpe (2), despite later alterations, shows a highly regular layout that may have included both the church and the manorial site, while Bleasby (Legsby (2)) though even more altered has traces of a grid-like arrangement. Stainfield (2) has already been mentioned as a 12th-century relocated village over former arable land and its plan too has elements of regularity including being laid out parallel to what is the precinct boundary of the adjacent priory [24].

A similar deserted village with an origin perhaps identical to Stainfield is Orford (Stainton le Vale (2)). It not only lies some distance from and unrelated to the ford which gives it its name, but it appears to have been regularly arranged along only one side of its main street which produces a plan form already noted elsewhere in West Lindsey, as at Newton on Trent (1) [14], and Gilby (Pilham (2)), and in Northamptonshire (RCHME 1981, xlv, Braunston (1)) and which is again perhaps indicative of planning. Orford too lies just outside the precinct of the small house of Premonstratensian nuns founded in the 12th century and it may be that it was relocated here when the priory took over the original site. Another example of an apparently planned settlement, now largely deserted, is the N part of Linwood (2) whose original rectangular plan is still dimly recognizable under the subsequent alterations. Brattleby (1), before it was entirely reorganized in the early 19th century, also had a grid plan, set askew to the adjacent through-communications pattern, which suggests a planned origin. Broxholme (1), too, appears to once have had a simple grid plan. Other places where there is evidence for a former ordered layout include Heapham (1) [18] where both parts overlie former fields, Burton (1), Upton (1) [14], Wildsworth (1) [15], Welton (1) [19], Toft (Toft Newton (3)), Otby (Walesby (3)) and East Torrington (Legsby (5)).

Clearer, though again what survives is the result of complex later changes, is the plan of the now largely deserted village of Knaith (2) [26]. There, what may be the elements of a regular settlement consisting of two or perhaps three parallel streets each terminating on the edge of the River Trent survive and could well reflect its former importance as a small riverside port. A similar plan is just recognizable at nearby Marton (1), a surviving village in an identical situation. Again it is possible to re-examine the arrangements of surviving villages and to see in them possible fragments of former planned or ordered layouts. The present W half of Walesby (1) has a basic form which, though distorted and partly obscured by subsequent change, has a grid-like appearance and the same is true at Bishop Norton (1) [14].

Southrey (Bardney (9)) [13, 15] is made up of two quite separate blocks, both of which are highly regular and overlie early fields, as is Sturgate (Springthorpe (2)) [15]. Scotterthorpe (Scotter (2)) [15] is a symmetrical two-row village, while Middle Rasen Tupholme (Middle Rasen (3)) [17] now the N part of Middle Rasen, also had a very regular plan.

Elsewhere care has to be exercised in the interpretation of such villages and sometimes a regular layout is not necessarily an early feature. Newton on Trent (1) [14] has an extremely well-ordered and indeed planned appearance, but though the E row may have always been of regular form, the long properties on the W side of the street are probably a recent addition as they lay outside the 'old enclosures' in the 19th century. Thus the village may have been a single-row village until then. On the other hand, if such single-row settlements were planned as has been suggested at Orford, then not only could Newton have a similar origin, but other places such as Aisby (Corringham (4)) [12, 18], Gilby (Pilham (2)) and perhaps the N part of Southorpe (Northorpe (1)) may be included in this list. Aisby is extremely unusual in having a small irregular loop bisected by an E–W street on the line of an old lane through the former open fields. It may be that this is the result of two phases of development whereby the loop has been superimposed on a simple single-row plan.

All this evidence, limited though it is at the individual site level, suggests that planning, in one form or another, is one way in which some villages in West Lindsey came to take on their present form. This then would support the conclusion reached from studies in other parts of England.

Nevertheless, though planning may be recognized as having taken place, it is much more difficult to assign a reason and date for the process. In North Yorkshire and Durham it has been postulated that many of the regular or 'planned' villages there came into being in the late 11th or early 12th century following the devastation caused by the 'Harrying of the North'. In those areas it seems that many villages were newly laid out by major landowners, perhaps as a deliberate policy of estate reorganization at that time. Lindsey, though it had a tradition of giving aid to

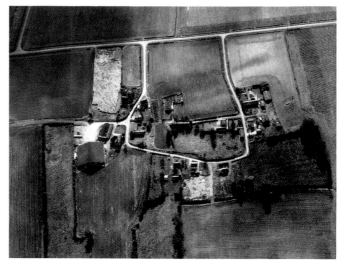

[12] *Corringham (4), settlement of Aisby from the N, 9 October 1980. It was never large and shows no clear decline or growth. The plan suggests a two-phase development in which the loop may have been superimposed upon a simpler single-street arrangement. The S side of the loop was obliterated after the new enclosure road altered access to the village in 1852.*

Scandinavian invaders and certainly drew the Conqueror's personal attention to make it militarily secure, escaped the 'Harrying' and there is therefore no obvious situation which could have led to a similar reorganization of settlement. Nor is the evidence of planning in West Lindsey so widespread as to suggest that it took place on the same scale as, for example, in the Vale of Pickering, North Yorkshire. On the other hand, studies elsewhere in England have suggested that the late 11th or 12th century is the period in which many settlements were planned or replanned, often following the consolidation of fragmented holdings in the late 11th century or soon after (Aston 1985, 84).

Yet if the date for such settlement planning can be tentatively assigned to the 11th and 12th centuries following the reorganization of estates or landholdings, there is still no certainty about the identification of the people involved in either the overall reorganization or the specific alteration to settlement form. Archaeologists and geographers have tended to stress the importance of lordly intervention on the assumption that only lords would have had the power, opportunity and desire to carry through the work. Some historians have also supported this (King 1986, 424–6). Others, however, have stressed the power of the peasant community at this time and by implication suggested that settlement change could be achieved by such communities acting alone (Reynolds 1984; Dyer 1985, 32; Fox 1986). The contradiction between these two approaches has been well summarized by P. D. A. Harvey (1982, 36; 1989, 31–44).

On the whole the inevitably limited evidence from West Lindsey tends to favour the theory of lordly intervention though much more work is required before there is conclusive proof. The two best examples are the settlements which appear to have been relocated following the establishment of monastic houses on or near the sites of existing villages, namely Stainfield (2) [24] and Orford (Stainton le Vale (2)). At both, the monastic precinct appears to occupy the site of the earlier settlements, both houses have an early 12th-century foundation date and the remains of the two villages indicate that they were probably planned, in the case of Stainfield over earlier ridge-and-furrow. Here it would seem most likely that the settlements did originate as 12th-century planned villages as a result of institutional intervention. Newsham (Brocklesby (6)) is perhaps another instance of 12th-century monastic planning following relocation.

Riseholme (1) is another possibility. The results of a very limited excavation show that the earliest occupation, in the centre of the village at least, was of the 12th century and may indicate that the regular plan dates from this time. If this was so, then the most likely person to have carried out the work was Hugh Bardolf I who in the mid 12th century was the major landlord there. This possibility is strengthened by the fact that Bardolf is known to have erected the castle at Castle Carlton in East Lindsey and to have laid out a new market village adjacent to it, in this period, in a small township cut out of the parish of Great Carlton.

As already noted Buslingthorpe (2) has good field evidence for a planned beginning. But the historical evidence for a 12th-century date is somewhat tenuous and rests only on the fact that the name of the village in the late 11th and early 12th century, *Esethorp*, was changed to the present one in the later 12th century, presumably soon after the arrival of a new tenant, by name *Buselinus*. It is again just possible that this person not only reorganized the settlement but created the moated manorial site and its associated paddocks, which form part of the overall plan.

Linwood (2) too, as noted above, retains in its arrangement the last vestiges of a planned origin. If such a plan did indeed stem from a 12th-century reorganization, the then holders of Linwood, the Malet family, may have been responsible. Elsewhere the evidence is equally unsatisfactory. If, for example, the regular plan of Brattleby (1) is indeed of 12th-century date then Robert de Haia, who by the early 12th century held the newly consolidated manor, might have created it. Similar evidence suggests that the village of Rand (2) [25] may have been formally laid out by the Burdet family when it took full possession of the manor in the late 12th century while at North Ingleby (Saxilby with Ingleby (2)) [26] the Ingleby family, resident there from the 12th century, perhaps imposed a regular plan on the settlement there. The Amundevilles at Kingerby (Osgodby (4)) [28] who held a substantial residence there from the 12th century could also have given the village its rectangular layout.

Both consolidation and manorialization may have led to the creation of planned settlements. At Bishop Norton (1) [14], for example, the Bishop's holding was inland and soke of Stow in 1086 with only one demesne plough team. The subsequent development into a fully manorialized holding may have been associated with the existing grid-like plan. The regulated forms of both the S sections of West Rasen (1) suggests a radical change in plan at some period. This may have been either before or shortly after 1086 when both parts were in separate ownership. On the other hand it could have occurred shortly after 1100 when the whole settlement was tenurially unified under the Paynels. These instances of presumed lordly intervention in village plans are of interest in that they all involved either persons who were usually resident, substantial tenants or local religious institutions. That is, the work seems to have been carried out, not by tenants-in-chief, operating at a multi-estate level, but by mesne lords at a local level. The same is true of those apparently engaged in creating planned additions to villages at this time (see below).

This type of evidence may not be totally convincing and indeed may be counterbalanced by evidence from elsewhere. Thus Burton (1), which appears to have a planned central core, has no indication of strong single tenure at any period between 1086 and the 16th century. It could be argued that the holders of the largest Domesday manor at Burton might have been responsible for the planning before it was sub-infeudated in the mid 12th century, but in other places there is not even evidence of this nature. Ingham (2) for example, has evidence of a regular plan, but nevertheless the medieval tenure was always fragmented. It is possible, of course, that the lack of 12th-century and indeed later evidence for planning merely indicates that the process of planning took place in pre-Conquest times, when detailed documentation is lacking. Certainly a 9th to 10th-century period of estate reorganization has been suggested for elsewhere in England, into which the replanning of at least some villages might well fit. On the other hand it may be that at such places there was indeed an 11th to 12th-century input from the community at large rather than from a single lord. Thus, while there is some evidence to suggest that the 12th century was a period during which some villages were being planned or reorganized, given the limited nature of this evidence, there can be no certainty that all planning relates to that period and there must be a strong possibility that some of it took place in late Saxon times.

The general hypothesis that some planning did indeed take place in the 12th century gains additional support from the evidence from a much larger number of village remains in West Lindsey where the surviving earthworks indicate that many settlements had planned additions, some of which can also be tentatively dated to the 12th century. Among the best are Coates (Stow (7)) [25], where two rectangular blocks of properties, on either side of a former street, appear to have been added to the E side of an earlier nucleus, and Cold Hanworth (1) where there seems to be another regular addition on the W side of the presumably earlier village. The E end of North Carlton (1) [26] also appears to be a planned two-row extension. At Thoresway (1) too, though any overall interpretation of the village remains is impossible, there can be little doubt that the N half and perhaps the W end of the village are the results of consciously planned additions [29]. The same feature is visible at the deserted village of Goltho (1) where the former earthworks, as the plan and the excavation there imply, are a later regulated addition.

A more spectacular example is at Croxby (Thoresway (3)) where a highly regulated arrangement of properties, adjacent to the church and the presumed earlier irregular core of the village, are arranged in a pattern that totally ignores the details of local topography. Less impressive, but equally interesting, is Broxholme (1) where a long single-row extension, perhaps of two phases, both planned, seems to have been added to the earlier centre, itself with a planned grid-form.

Similar features are visible in a number of surviving villages. A particularly good example is Blyton (1) [15]. Not only is there a presumed original core, consisting of a now partly infilled green, surrounded by at least four distinct elements made up of regular plots, but there is also a separate two-row block to the NE. Such a plan indicates a process of piecemeal planned accretion.

At Scotter (1) [20] there is also an apparently ancient core centred on a green with a regular two-row block to the NE and an apparently less regular two-row block to the W. The latter is, however, probably of two separate periods with its

[13] *Bardney (9), settlement of Southrey, exhibits a remarkably regular form based on two E–W streets parallel to the River Witham, 10 May 1946. (RAF)*

W half planned and the E a later growth joining it to the rest of the village. Stow (1) [20] also has two-row blocks to the N and S of the earlier rectangular core which may be additions, while Faldingworth (1) [18] though far from being completely explicable may have had two regular elements added to the W side of an older centre. Other villages having evidence of possible planned additions include Nettleton (3) [19], Middle Rasen Drax, now the S part of Middle Rasen (2) [17], Blyton (1) [15] and Welton (1) [19].

The dating of such additions as well as the reasons for their development, is again difficult to ascertain. Perhaps the primary reason for their existence, though not their form, was a large increase in the rural population of Lincolnshire in the 12th century, though this is almost completely undocumented. This problem is discussed later. There is some evidence that many of these planned additions, as with the totally planned settlements, do date from the 12th century, though others are certainly later and yet more may be of the late pre-Conquest period.

[14] *Village plans showing regular forms. Bishop Norton (1) and Upton (1) appear to be based on grids. Ryland (Welton (2)) has a regular two-row arrangement and though Newton on Trent (1) seems superficially similar the W half may have only developed after enclosure in 1766. Thus Newton was earlier a single-row settlement.*

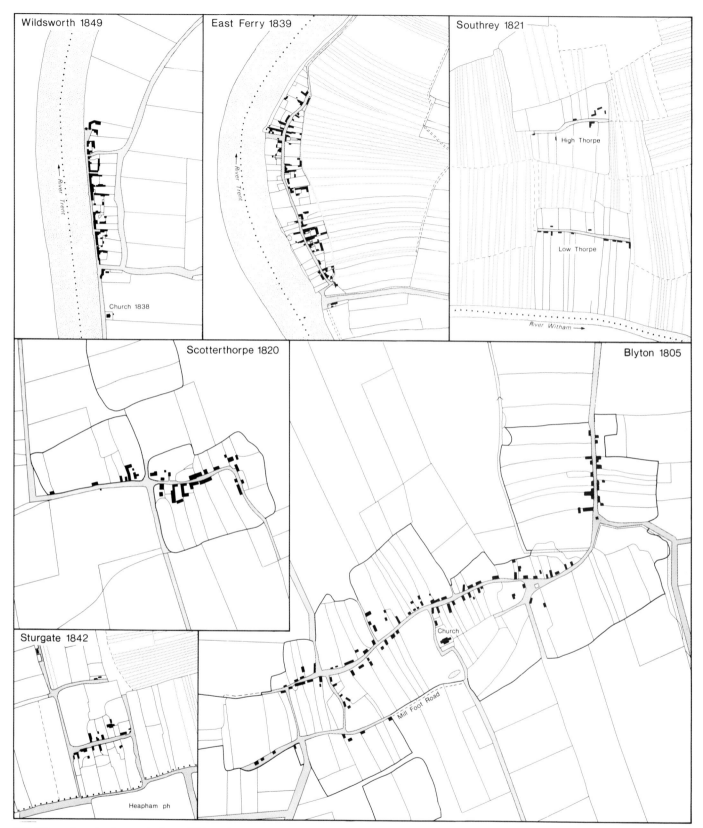

[15] *Village plans showing regular forms. Wildsworth (1) and East Ferry (1) are linear Trent-side settlements. Southrey (Bardney (9)) consists of two two-row settlements and is, in effect, polyfocal. Sturgate (Springthorpe (2)) and Scotterthorpe (Scotter (2)) are also regular two-row villages, perhaps inserted into former arable furlongs. Blyton (1) comprises a whole series of two-row blocks, perhaps of successive dates, centred on a green, now much reduced by encroachment.*

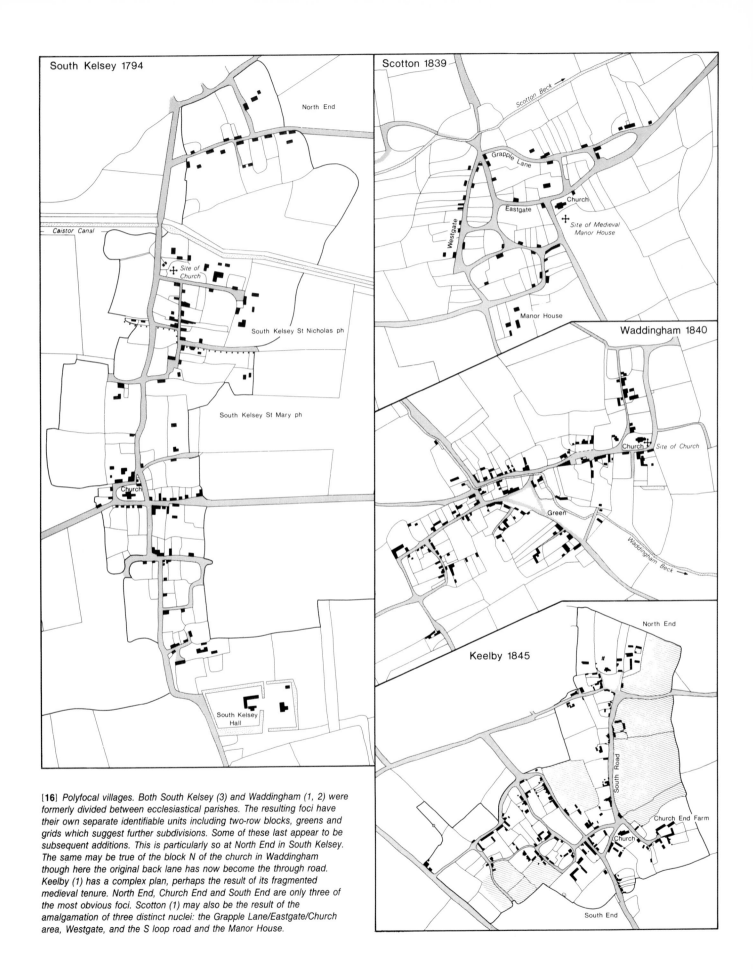

South Kelsey 1794

North End

Caistor Canal

Site of Church

South Kelsey St Nicholas ph

South Kelsey St Mary ph

Church

South Kelsey Hall

Scotton 1839

Scotton Beck

Grapple Lane

Church

Eastgate

Westgate

Site of Medieval Manor House

Manor House

Waddingham 1840

Church + Site of Church

Green

Waddingham Beck

Keelby 1845

North End

South Road

Church End Farm

Church

South End

[16] *Polyfocal villages. Both South Kelsey (3) and Waddingham (1, 2) were formerly divided between ecclesiastical parishes. The resulting foci have their own separate identifiable units including two-row blocks, greens and grids which suggest further subdivisions. Some of these last appear to be subsequent additions. This is particularly so at North End in South Kelsey. The same may be true of the block N of the church in Waddingham though here the original back lane has now become the through road. Keelby (1) has a complex plan, perhaps the result of its fragmented medieval tenure. North End, Church End and South End are only three of the most obvious foci. Scotton (1) may also be the result of the amalgamation of three distinct nuclei: the Grapple Lane/Eastgate/Church area, Westgate, and the S loop road and the Manor House.*

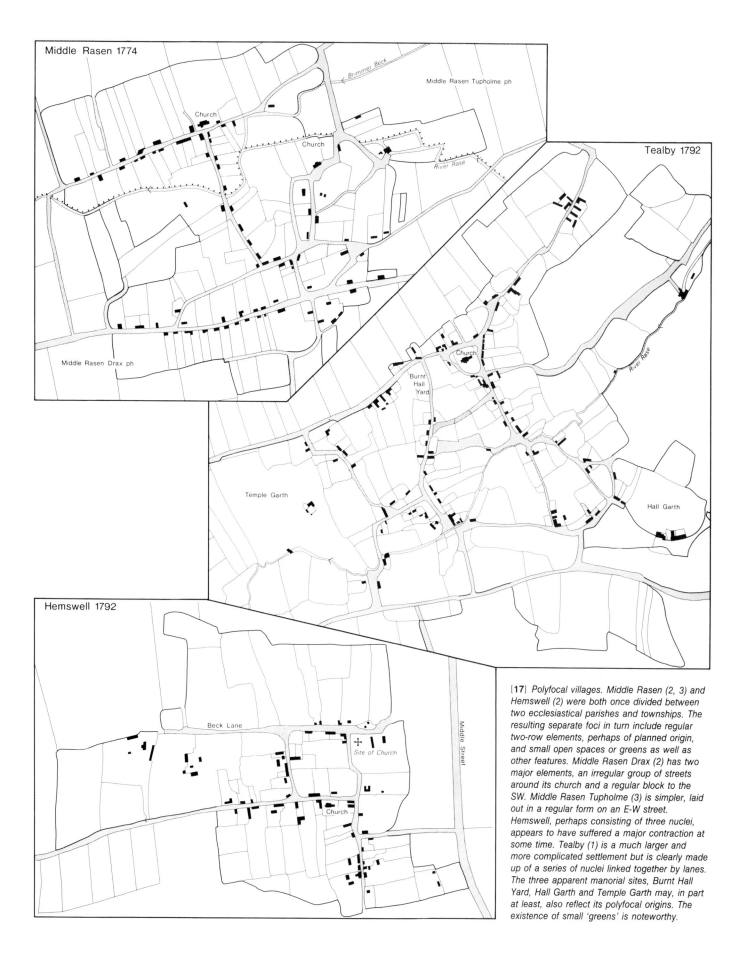

Middle Rasen 1774

Brimmer Beck

Middle Rasen Tupholme ph

Church

Church

River Rase

Tealby 1792

River Rase

Middle Rasen Drax ph

Church

Burnt
Hall
Yard

Temple Garth

Hall Garth

Hemswell 1792

Beck Lane

Site of Church

Church

Middle Street

[**17**] *Polyfocal villages. Middle Rasen (2, 3) and Hemswell (2) were both once divided between two ecclesiastical parishes and townships. The resulting separate foci in turn include regular two-row elements, perhaps of planned origin, and small open spaces or greens as well as other features. Middle Rasen Drax (2) has two major elements, an irregular group of streets around its church and a regular block to the SW. Middle Rasen Tupholme (3) is simpler, laid out in a regular form on an E-W street. Hemswell, perhaps consisting of three nuclei, appears to have suffered a major contraction at some time. Tealby (1) is a much larger and more complicated settlement but is clearly made up of a series of nuclei linked together by lanes. The three apparent manorial sites, Burnt Hall Yard, Hall Garth and Temple Garth may, in part at least, also reflect its polyfocal origins. The existence of small 'greens' is noteworthy.*

At Coates (Stow (7)) [25] the acquisition of most of the village by Welbeck Abbey, Notts, between 1173 and 1182 might have led to its reorganization by deliberate expansion.

Willoughton (3) [19] is especially interesting in both its plan and its probable instigators. The core of the village consists, superficially, of an irregular grid lying across a meandering E–W road. Closer examination reveals that this is actually made up of two blocks both of which may have had a planned origin. It is tempting to equate this duality with the two major manors recorded in Domesday Book which were perpetuated by the endowments of two religious foundations in the 12th century. Both these institutions seem to have acquired or added extensions to the village core. To the SW, the moated Preceptory of the Knights Templars, later the Hospitallers (2), has a regular pattern of closes attached to it which may mark former settlement. The surviving documentation suggests that they may have already been in existence when the Templars acquired the manor and thus may be an earlier addition to the village plan created by a previous owner. To the SE of the village lies the moated site (1) of the manor house or grange granted to the alien priory of St Nicholas of Angers. By the 14th century this moat was attached to a further settlement element (4), that may perhaps be identified with 'the hamlet of *Helpesthorpe*' whose tithes formed an adjunct to the priory's manor. It is likely that the settlement is to be identified with a rectangular block of properties S of the moat, now broken up by later development, but shown complete on the Enclosure Map of 1769. This settlement block is undoubtedly later than the lane to its N which narrows and curves around it. It is possible that this block represents a planned settlement created by the alien priory.

Though not perhaps strictly planning, the now abandoned part of South Carlton (3) laid out over ridge-and-furrow may well date from the 12th century when Hugh Bardolf seems to have reorganized the pre-existing polyfocal settlement there following a monastic grant.

A further possible factor in village planning, visible in West Lindsey is the existence of a medieval market grant. It has been suggested (Taylor 1982) that in some parts of England the acquisition of a market grant in the 12th to 14th centuries led to the deliberate creation of market places within or attached to settlements. In West Lindsey there are a number of villages whose lords received permission to hold fairs and markets and some of these appear to have had their morphology disrupted or added to by small market places [20]. At Bardney (6) the core of the present village is centred on a small open space which is now all that survives of a large triangular open area with a lane leading directly from its NW corner to Bardney Abbey. This area may have originally been a market place, related to the weekly market instituted by the Abbey by 1232. At Scotter (1) an annual fair and weekly market was granted to Peterborough Abbey who held Scotter at the end of the 12th century and 'markett shoppes in the markett place' formed part of the manor when leased

to Sir William Tyrwhitt in 1538. The principal element in the centre of the village is related to the church, probably with a manorial complex to its N. Alongside this is an open green, or market place, latterly a small triangle with an island of infill. Earlier, however, it appears to have been much larger and more rectangular.

At Stow (1) the importance of the village as the centre of a late Saxon estate as well as the existence of the Saxon minster church would perhaps suggest an early marketing function as well, a hypothesis supported by its description in Domesday Book. A formal market certainly existed by the later 12th century and may have been an old established feature by then. Though the morphology of the village has clearly been much altered, nevertheless on the S side of the church is a former open area, containing several islands of properties. This was perhaps a market place, now largely infilled. One completely new settlement which perhaps relates to this process of commercial exploitation is Langworth in Barlings parish (Barlings (6)). The place is not documented in Domesday Book and has all the characteristics of a secondary settlement. It is probably a planned settlement, perhaps an abortive 'new town' established at the N edge of the parish and alongside the main through road. A weekly market and an annual fair were granted to the abbot and convent of Barlings 'at their manor of Langworth' in 1270. The plan of Langworth is purely linear and has none of the features of other 'new' towns. Yet the section of the road on which it is situated is a local diversion of the Lincoln to Burgh-le-Marsh Roman road, here passing across land liable to flood. The establishment of Langworth may have involved the alteration of the road to accommodate new properties.

All the foregoing suggests that planning or replanning of villages was a phenomenon of the 10th to the 12th centuries. Yet this is not the whole story for there is much evidence from West Lindsey to show that planning and planned additions continued throughout later medieval times. This is well illustrated at the deserted village of Firsby (West Firsby (1)) [22, 25]. Firsby, one of the largest and most complex sites in the area, is made up of a number of separate units, all but one of which appear to be the result of conscious planning and all laid out on pre-existing arable land. It is probable that the regular manorial complex and the once separate rectangular arrangement of properties to its E, itself perhaps of two phases, relates to a 12th-century or earlier re-organization of the village. A second regular block of settlement to the S however may belong to the later 13th and 14th centuries when the demesne arable was being leased to bondsmen.

Whatever the date of all this reorganization of settlement, visible in both the earthworks and in the surviving arrangements of villages in West Lindsey, the influence of lordly power and estate exploitation seems obvious. The importance of tenure and the ability of lords to transform the layout of villages is also documented and visible in the later

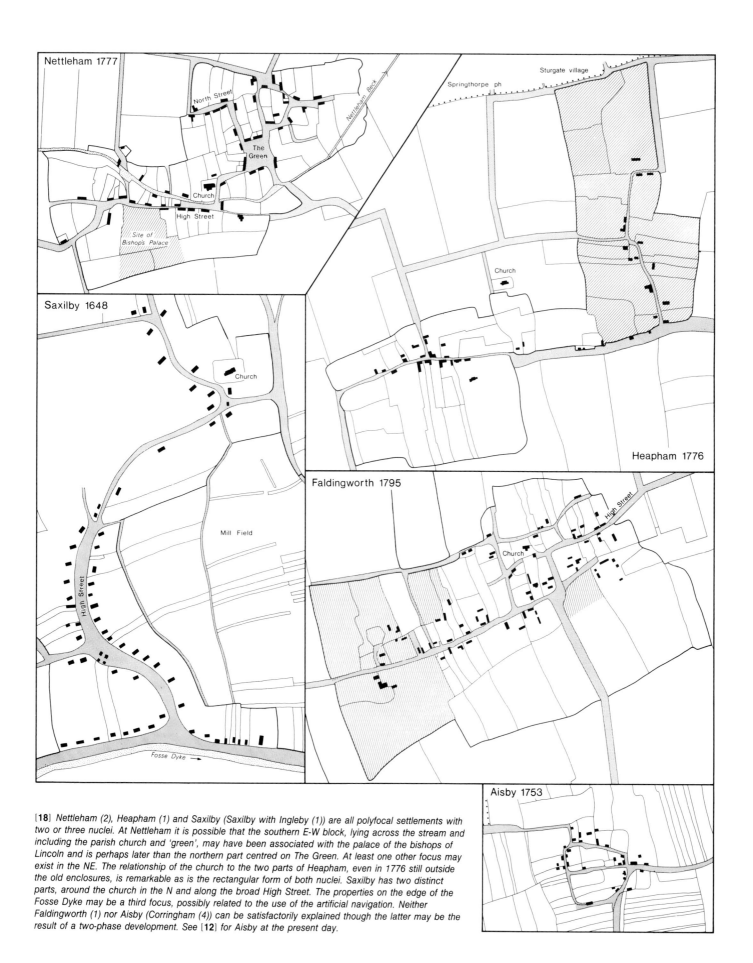

[**18**] *Nettleham (2), Heapham (1) and Saxilby (Saxilby with Ingleby (1)) are all polyfocal settlements with two or three nuclei. At Nettleham it is possible that the southern E-W block, lying across the stream and including the parish church and 'green', may have been associated with the palace of the bishops of Lincoln and is perhaps later than the northern part centred on The Green. At least one other focus may exist in the NE. The relationship of the church to the two parts of Heapham, even in 1776 still outside the old enclosures, is remarkable as is the rectangular form of both nuclei. Saxilby has two distinct parts, around the church in the N and along the broad High Street. The properties on the edge of the Fosse Dyke may be a third focus, possibly related to the use of the artificial navigation. Neither Faldingworth (1) nor Aisby (Corringham (4)) can be satisfactorily explained though the latter may be the result of a two-phase development. See [**12**] for Aisby at the present day.*

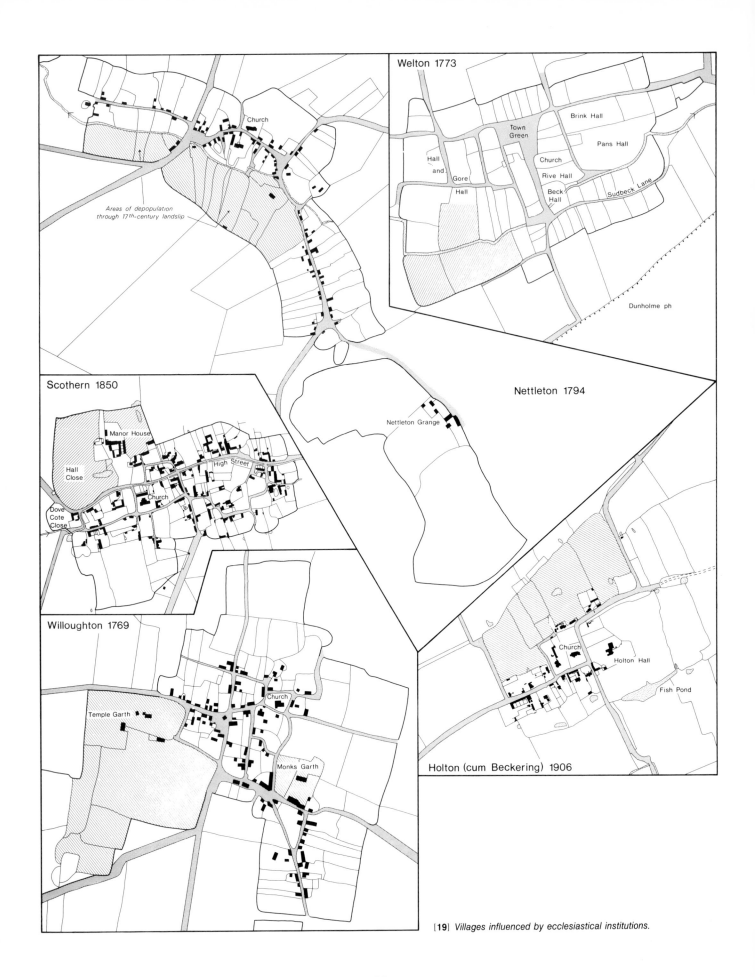

Welton 1773

Brink Hall

Town
Green

Pans Hall

Hall
and

Church

Gore
Hall

Rive Hall

Sudbeck Lane

Beck
Hall

Dunholme ph

Church

Nettleton 1794

Nettleton Grange

Scothern 1850

Manor House

Hall
Close

High Street

Church

Dove
Cote
Close

Areas of depopulation
through 17th-century landslip

Church

Holton Hall

Fish Pond

Willoughton 1769

Church

Temple Garth

Monks Garth

Holton (cum Beckering) 1906

[19] *Villages influenced by ecclesiastical institutions.*

medieval period, even if the process by then seems to have lost much of its earlier regularity. Perhaps the most impressive of these later alterations are to be seen at North and South Ingleby (Saxilby with Ingleby (2, 3)) [26] where the two adjacent and now deserted villages were both apparently reorganized together in a process that produced an almost unified area of occupation lying across the older township boundary that once separated the two villages. Documentary evidence suggests that this took place in the late 14th or early 15th centuries when, for the first time, both villages were held by the same lords. That planning of some form did continue to a relatively late date is suggested at Osgodby (2) where the regular form of the village may date from the later 14th century when the Tournay family seems to have finally acquired the whole lordship.

A common village form, recognized in West Lindsey, is the polyfocal or composite settlement, best seen in early cartographic form at Waddingham (1, 2) [16], Tealby (1) [17], South Kelsey (3) [16] and Saxilby (Saxilby with Ingleby (1)) [18]. The term polyfocal is usually only a descriptive one, used to identify settlements which are composed of two or more discrete units of occupation. The origins and date of such polyfocal villages are difficult to ascertain. Certainly many of the villages already described, especially those with planned additions, fall within the broad category of polyfocal settlements as at Southrey (Bardney (9)) [15], Blyton (1) [15], Scotter (1) [20] and Nettleton (3) [19]. There are many other places, however, which are made up of discrete foci whose origins cannot be readily explained by deliberately planned additions. Such foci might be the result of the expansion or agglomeration of earlier and broadly contemporary farmsteads or hamlets to form a single settlement, additions by later piecemeal growth to an original core, or even of redevelopment following shrinkage or partial desertion of a large compact settlement.

Polyfocal settlements, apparently resulting from all these processes, have been recognized in West Lindsey, though it is often impossible to be sure of the true sequence of any particular development. Even with villages with elements of

apparent planning this is so. Thus the existence of two foci, one planned and the other unplanned, may not necessarily prove that the former is a later addition. It could merely be the result of the replanning of an earlier focus, which in origin was contemporary with its neighbour. This is suggested in the Inventory for Firsby (West Firsby (1)) and at Scothern (1). Sometimes both foci appear to have had a planned origin as at Spridlington (1) and possibly Bleasby (Legsby (2)) [27], though in these examples both may be merely the later reorganization of units that were much older.

Often the lack of any documentation makes it difficult to distinguish between a true polyfocal village and a group of close-set but entirely independent settlements. One such is Owersby (1) where the name relates to a single parish probably divided, at least in later medieval times, into two townships, yet containing six separate settlement blocks. Here it is impossible to ascertain whether the recoverable pattern developed from one single settlement, two adjacent settlements or six settlements each with its own township land. All that can be reported is the physical appearance of the remains. Any interpretation is open to debate.

A related problem is that it is often impossible to be sure that a settlement is polyfocal from the surviving pattern where later changes have obscured or modified the earlier situation. The plan of Grasby (1) appears at first sight to consist of an irregular grid and thus to have had a possible planned origin. Yet the grid lacks any real coherence and may well be the result of the growing together of a number of closely bunched foci which the tenurial history there would suggest.

At other places, too, while the physical situation is clear, the origins remain elusive. Walesby (1) [144] in later medieval times certainly comprised two separate foci each the centre of a manor. The upper one, set around the parish church, is now deserted and the remains show no sign of a regular layout. The lower part, which still survives as Walesby village, has a simple grid, now much distorted, which suggests a planned origin. Yet both foci seem to have been in existence in the early medieval period. At both Northorpe (2) [104] and Southorpe (Northorpe (1)), the former partly abandoned and the latter entirely so, both villages seem to have had two foci, yet there is no documentary evidence for the origins or development of either of them.

The same is true of Corringham. There two villages, Great and Little Corringham (2) and (3), are recorded in documents, and the present village has usually been said to be Great Corringham while Little Corringham has been described as an unlocated deserted settlement. The Royal Commission's research has established that Little Corringham was in fact part of Great Corringham village but each had its own township land and field system. Willingham by Stow (1) is a similar example. There are indications from its surviving plan that it is polyfocal, and it is likely that one

[19] *Villages influenced by ecclesiastical institutions. Nettleton (3) exhibits many typical features such as apparently planned two-row extensions at its extreme ends. More unusual is the large detached block of old enclosures centred on Nettleton Grange. The grange belonged to Sixhills Priory but earlier the area may have been part of the village. Scothern (1), perhaps as a result of its early fragmented tenure a polyfocal village, also included a well-defined block of land surrounding the Manor House. This was the site of a grange held by Barlings Abbey. At Willoughton (3) the large area to the SW of the village was the site of the Preceptory of the Knights Templars and Hospitallers (2) while the regular two-row settlement block to the SE was the hamlet of Helpesthorpe (4) attached to and part of the appurtenances of the moated site (1) at Monks Garth. The diversion of the road around the park of Holton Hall, at Holton cum Beckering (2), may have been caused by the existence of a grange of Sixhills Priory. Welton (1) is exceptional. A central green, now much encroached upon, is surrounded by a complex pattern of closes and lanes. The two-row block along Sudbeck Lane and the row on the N side of the green may be planned elements, but most of the other closes relate to six medieval prebendal manors of Lincoln Cathedral.*

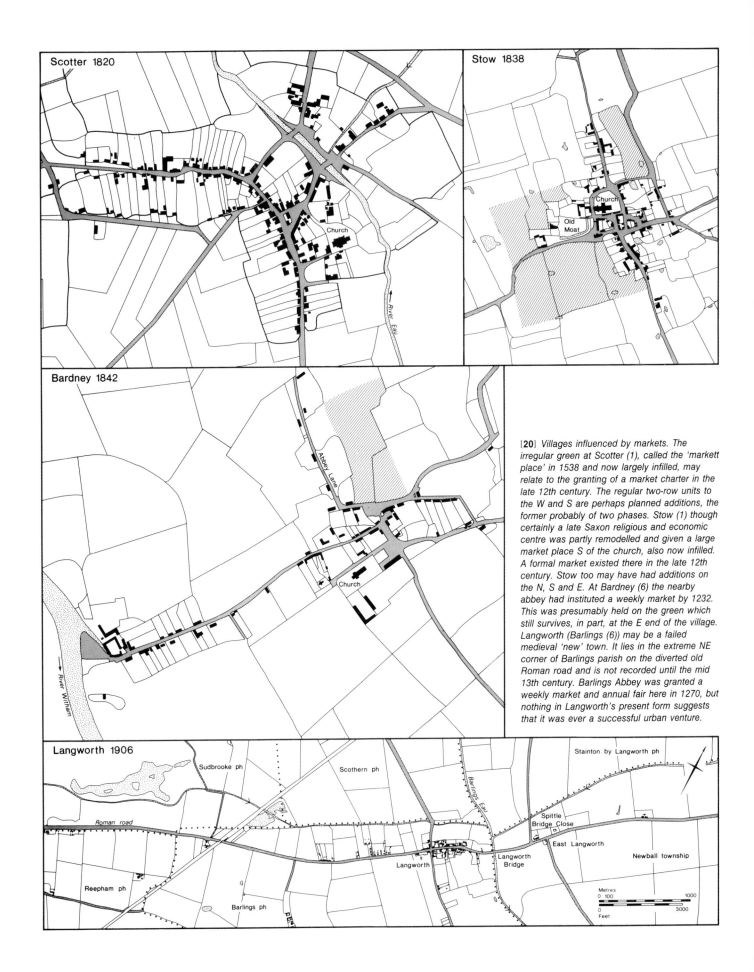

Scotter 1820

Stow 1838

Bardney 1842

Langworth 1906

[20] Villages influenced by markets. The irregular green at Scotter (1), called the 'markett place' in 1538 and now largely infilled, may relate to the granting of a market charter in the late 12th century. The regular two-row units to the W and S are perhaps planned additions, the former probably of two phases. Stow (1) though certainly a late Saxon religious and economic centre was partly remodelled and given a large market place S of the church, also now infilled. A formal market existed there in the late 12th century. Stow too may have had additions on the N, S and E. At Bardney (6) the nearby abbey had instituted a weekly market by 1232. This was presumably held on the green which still survives, in part, at the E end of the village. Langworth (Barlings (6)) may be a failed medieval 'new' town. It lies in the extreme NE corner of Barlings parish on the diverted old Roman road and is not recorded until the mid 13th century. Barlings Abbey was granted a weekly market and annual fair here in 1270, but nothing in Langworth's present form suggests that it was ever a successful urban venture.

[21] *Village plans which are difficult to interpret. At Fillingham (1) extensive earthworks now largely destroyed or submerged by the lake, archaeological evidence for a second undocumented church as well as a grid-like pattern are almost impossible to explain in a coherent way. The arrangement at Lea (1) may result from a partial reorientation from an early E to W street with a central green to a N to S road. Laughton (1) might once have been a polyfocal village. The former extensive earthworks at its E end, on a different axis to the rest of the settlement, perhaps mark the nucleus cleared in one of the county's 'great depopulations' recorded in 1607.*

of the two foci is the site of the otherwise lost settlement of *Alfletby.* Saxilby (Saxilby with Ingleby (1)) [**18**], though now impossible to interpret, is clearly depicted on a 1648 map as a polyfocal village, but no suggestion as to its origin is forthcoming.

In some cases it is not clear whether the remains are those of a polyfocal settlement at all. The documentary evidence at Somerby (1) suggests that the village may once have had two separate foci, a possibility supported by the relationship of the surviving earthworks to the parish church and the Hall. At the same time, however, the site could equally be interpreted as the result of the movement of a single unit either resulting from gradual shift or deliberate relocation.

At certain villages the identifiable foci may be of differing

dates and origins. Normanby le Wold (1) has three, or perhaps four nuclei, two or three of which may be ancient. But one, now utterly deserted, has some evidence that it was a hamlet associated with a holding of the Knights Templars and thus might be interpreted as a late development of the village. On the other hand the Templars' holding was based on grants of land which were parts of separate tenurial units in the late 11th century and which thus may have been based on the other foci or possibly all three. The position at Normanby is made even more confusing by the existence of a mid or late Saxon occupation area close by, discovered from excavation.

At Normanby, three of the foci are set close together while the fourth lies some distance away. This relationship poses the problem whether there is any real distinction between a polyfocal nucleated settlement and a dispersed settlement pattern. This is well seen at Walesby, where, in addition to the undoubted polyfocal settlement of Walesby (1) itself, the parish also contains the now abandoned settlements of Risby and Otby (Walesby (2) and (3)) [9], both situated in what can only be described as a hostile environment, on exposed limestone shelves high on the Wolds scarp face and subject to continuous landslips. Topographically both are classic secondary settlements yet both are recorded in Domesday Book and both have Scandinavian place-names and thus neither can be explained as the result of late medieval expansion. They might be regarded as representing part of a pre 11th-century, Scandinavian, development of settlement in the area, but the existence of at least one major Roman occupation site on the scarp top nearby may indicate an even older origin for such places.

A related form of settlement, though in an entirely different environment, is exemplified by Heapham (1, 2) [18]. The village there clearly has two distinct foci, both with some evidence of planning, yet with the parish church, set above a spring, quite isolated from both areas of medieval occupation. Have the two parts of the village always been where they now stand, with the parish church placed where it is for unknown, pre-Christian reasons, or are they the result of a later reorganization of settlement? No clear explanation is readily forthcoming.

Elsewhere there are excellent examples of polyfocal villages, all of which present various problems of interpretation. Scotton (1) [16] appears to consist of an amorphous muddle of loop roads, but it may be the result of the abutment of two quite separate elements. These may have belonged to the two documented manors, one based on an E–W axis including a manorial site and church and the other on a N–S axis with a small green at its S end including the present Manor House. Scothern (1) [19] is even more complex in its arrangement of streets and this may perhaps relate to the multiplicity of tenure there recorded throughout the medieval period. Even so, a number of separate foci can be recognized and that centred on the Manor House is likely to be that part of the village held by Barlings Abbey from the late 12th century.

The plan of Keelby (1) [16] may be the result of the amalgamation of small foci, relating to the early fragmented tenure there. The names of three of these foci, Church, North and South Ends, emphasize this pattern. Tealby (1) [17] is another highly complex village where it is also possible to distinguish a number of separate foci as is Riby (1). At South Carlton (3) the two quite separate parts which may relate to the 11th-century duality of tenure seem to have been joined together in the 12th century as a result of reorganization. Otby (Walesby (3)) might also owe its dual form to 12th-century division of the earlier single manor. Here it is probable that the one part was either then, or later, given a regular form.

Perhaps the most interesting of these polyfocal villages is Welton (1) [19] where there appears to be a documented reason for its form. There, each of the observable foci can be identified with separate medieval prebendal manors of Lincoln Cathedral whose separate existence and presumably management perhaps fossilizes an even older pattern.

Settlement Change

The foregoing long discussion on the origins of settlement has both implicitly and explicitly emphasized the difficulty of understanding the early forms of many of the villages in West Lindsey. There are a number of reasons for this, including the lack of documentation and archaeological excavation. But perhaps the most important reason is the continuous growth, decline and movement of villages throughout their lives which has effectively concealed, in most cases, any clear early pattern. Some of these alterations took place in post-medieval times and will be discussed later. Most of the observable change cannot however be dated but there is evidence for continuous change during the medieval period. The result of all this piecemeal expansion, decline or alteration can, as always, be recognized in some places, but rarely understood. In the end there are a large number of villages which are completely inexplicable and which must be the result of long-term and extensive changes; these include Thoresway (1) [29] and Reepham (1).

Some areas of occupation within villages can certainly be seen as amorphous, unplanned, expansion, presumably arising from an increase in population. One part of Firsby (West Firsby (1)) [22, 25], which lies over earlier arable and which is squeezed uncomfortably in between the rectangular manorial *curia* and the perhaps two-phase extension to the E, has been plausibly identified as the result of 13th and 14th-century estate reorganization, while at Scotton (1) [16] small irregular areas of settlement attached to the recognizable early foci may be the result of the same process. However, even here the lack of direct and firm evidence makes it impossible to be certain. At Bardney (6) [20] the evidence of a planned market place, perhaps relating to the mid 13th-century market grant and a regularly planned W extension to it, almost detached, would suggest that the area of former settlement earthworks to the N were an even later expansion. But the recovery of material from this destroyed settlement area, including pottery of 11th-century date, suggests that the apparent sequence of development might be reversed. Likewise, as already discussed, Somerby (1) has an amorphous plan which is open to a number of interpretations. The same is true at Kingerby (Osgodby (4)) [28], where the settlement remains at the E end of the village are most likely the result of expansion from the original core, though they might equally represent the site of an earlier part of the village before it was reorganized. At Greetwell (1) [25] the earthworks at the extreme N end of the former village may have been the site of a new area of settlement after the older village centre had been cleared in post-medieval times,

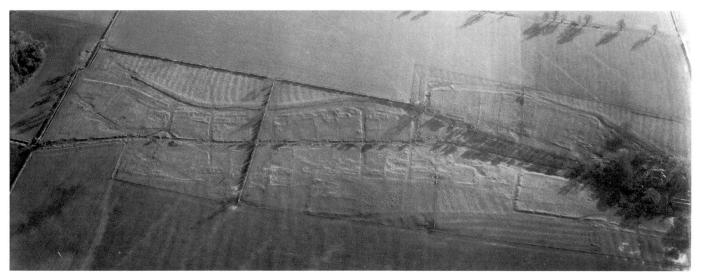

[22] *West Firsby (1), deserted village of Firsby from the N, 26 November 1980. The earthworks straddle the small stream which has been realigned in recent times. At the SW end, N of the stream, the rectangular manorial curia is visible. To the SE and NE are remains which indicate three stages of the development of the village, all of which overlie ridge-and-furrow.*

but a more acceptable interpretation is that they represent medieval expansion.

Alterations to the village layouts could also apparently take place with or without expansion. At North Ingleby (Saxilby with Ingleby (2)) [26] the regular presumed original core of the settlement is cut obliquely by a later hollow-way which appears to be part of a new street pattern.

There is also evidence that villages have moved in response to changing external communication patterns. Faldingworth (1) [18] is a possibility, for though most of the village plan there is inexplicable, the present concentration of occupation at its E end probably represents the growing importance of the Lincoln to Market Rasen road (A46). Another instance is Lea (1) [21]. Much of this process may relate to the post-medieval period as is indicated at Linwood (2), Lissington (1) and Middle Rasen (2, 3) [17]. Two of the Trent-side villages, Walkerith (1) and Wildsworth (1) [5], seem to have originated as single-row settlements along the river edge, but subsequently their back lanes have become the main streets, as a result of their changing relationship to through routes.

Other observable but undated changes to many villages include the destruction and infilling of former greens and market places. At Thorpe in the Fallows (1) and Southorpe (Northorpe (1)) the fact that the villages were already largely abandoned by the end of the medieval period suggests that the infilling of their conjectural greens took place well within medieval times. Elsewhere, however, as at Stow (1) [20], Blyton (1) [15], Bardney (6) [20], Dunholme (1), Nettleham (2) [18], Scotter (1) [20], West Rasen (1), Welton (1) [19] and Willingham by Stow (1) no date can be assigned to the process and it may well be that it took place over many centuries.

Another aspect of village development in West Lindsey, revealed by the examination of both earthworks and existing settlement areas, concerns manorial sites. Most village

remains have areas of earthworks which can be identified as manorial in function, including moated sites, associated paddocks and closes, ponds and mill sites. The details of such sites are discussed below, but here their relationships to the associated settlements are examined.

In many cases these manorial sites are more difficult to interpret than the associated village remains, for often the last surviving habitation still occupies these areas. Thus at Buslingthorpe (1) the moat is still occupied by the Manor Farm whose buildings have spread over much of the inner part of the manorial complex. Yet here, and elsewhere, enough remains to suggest that the manorial site has been planned as part of the overall layout of the adjacent village. At Buslingthorpe itself (2), the site, comprising moat, 'park', closes and indeed the church, all lie within a neat rectangular area surrounded on three sides by the equally regular village arrangement. At Firsby (West Firsby (1)) [25], though the modern farmhouse and its extensive outbuildings still occupy what was undoubtedly most of the medieval manorial site, the remains of the N part of the manorial enclosure, together with its fishponds, seem to have been part of a planned arrangement, perhaps associated with at least one part of the village.

At other places the chronological relationships between manorial complexes and village remains are identifiable. One of the most interesting is that at Bleasby (Legsby (1)) [27] where the construction of the moated manor seems to have blocked one of the original village roads. More certain is the blocking of the former main street of South Ingleby (Saxilby with Ingleby (3)) [26] by the construction of the moated site there while at Rand (1) [25] the presumed planned expansion of the manorial *curia* led to the incorporation of former village properties within it and the diversion of a village street around it. At Holton cum Beckering (2) [19] a large rectangular enclosure, the site of a manor or grange of

Sixhills Priory, has not only blocked the old village street, but led to the development of a diversion around it, thus completely distorting the presumed original village layout.

Not all the examples of this type of manorial layout necessarily imply an alteration to the adjacent settlement. A number of enlargements or alterations to earlier manorial complexes appear to have occurred after their associated settlements had already been abandoned. This certainly appears to be the case at Kettleby (Bigby (1)) [53] where the outer garden closes of the manor site overlie part of the site of the village of Kettleby and the same is true at Greetwell (1) [25] where the 17th-century garden remains (Greetwell (2)) are superimposed on part of the former village. Another, less certain, instance is at Goltho (2). In these last two cases the extensions are related to the construction of gardens in the early post-medieval period and are different in function from the medieval examples.

A special form of village earthworks, recognized in West Lindsey for the first time and closely related to manorial sites, is that of monastic demesne farms or granges. In economic terms there is perhaps little difference between monastic granges and lay manors and certainly the holdings of the older monastic orders are rarely termed granges. As would be expected such granges or monastic manorial sites occur both in isolated situations away from villages and in close association with the villages themselves. Both are dealt with in detail below, but the latter are so much part of village development that they are also considered here [19].

In many cases, as at Holton cum Beckering (2) discussed above, the earthworks are similar to those of manorial sites held by lay lords and their influence upon the village no different. In a few places, however, a more complex picture has been recognized. The situation is best exemplified at Cabourne (1) where the present small village is surrounded by extensive earthworks. The initial impression is that of a village, once of considerable size, which has suffered severe depopulation. Yet though some depopulation certainly occurred at Cabourne, notably in the 14th century, it appears unlikely that the large areas of earthworks could ever have been fully occupied at any one time. It might be suggested that the earthworks represent a movement of settlement, and it is certainly obvious that not all the remains are contemporary and that large parts overlie former arable land. On the other hand the earthworks have two important characteristics: they tend to be arranged in clearly identifiable blocks and though they consist of complex arrangements of paddocks and closes, there is little evidence of occupation within them except for the sites of what appear to be single small farmsteads or individual buildings. Thus a large proportion of the earthworks at Cabourne seem to be the sites of single farmsteads surrounded by large groups of closes, laid out at the extremities of the village on former arable land. The documentary record indicates that by at least the 13th century no less than six ecclesiastical institutions held small manors in Cabourne, all apparently emanating from 12th-century grants, and most of them

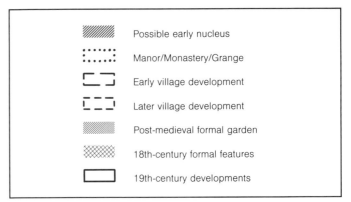

[23] *Key to village development plans.*

▨	Possible early nucleus
⁞⁞⁞⁞	Manor/Monastery/Grange
⌐ ¬	Early village development
⌐ ¬	Later village development
▦	Post-medieval formal garden
▧	18th-century formal features
▭	19th-century developments

probably based primarily on sheep-farming. Though no absolute proof is forthcoming at Cabourne, and certainly the individual blocks cannot be directly linked with the known tenurial arrangements, it seems at least a possibility that small demesne farms were deliberately added to the existing village following the breakup of larger estates by grants to ecclesiastical institutions in the 12th century. The growth of sheep-farms in the 13th and 14th centuries which demanded small paddocks for lambing, breeding and shearing may have produced the farmsteads and closes which now survive as earthworks.

A similar if less complex example is Swallow (1). There another farmstead, still in existence, is set within a clearly defined block of paddocks lying to the E of the village. It is possible that this is to be associated with the land held by either Wellow Abbey or Nun Cotham Priory. Another block, less obvious following later destruction, may represent the second holding.

While not directly part of the villages as such, the identification of these tenurial and agricultural units attached to villages in West Lindsey is of considerable interest, not only in the understanding of the history of medieval estate management but also of the history and development of the villages themselves.

[24] *Village development. Stainfield (2).*
A. *Presumed location of pre 12th-century village.*
B. *Sites of 12th-century monastery and relocated village.*
C. *Area of early 17th-century garden.*
D. *Area of early 18th-century gardens and park.*

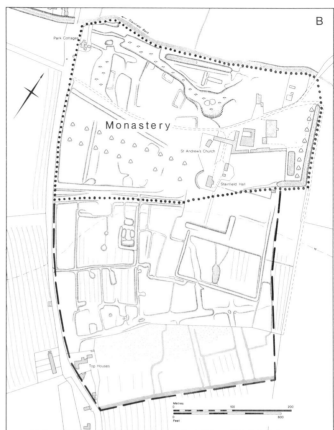

[**24**] *Village development. Stainfield (2).*

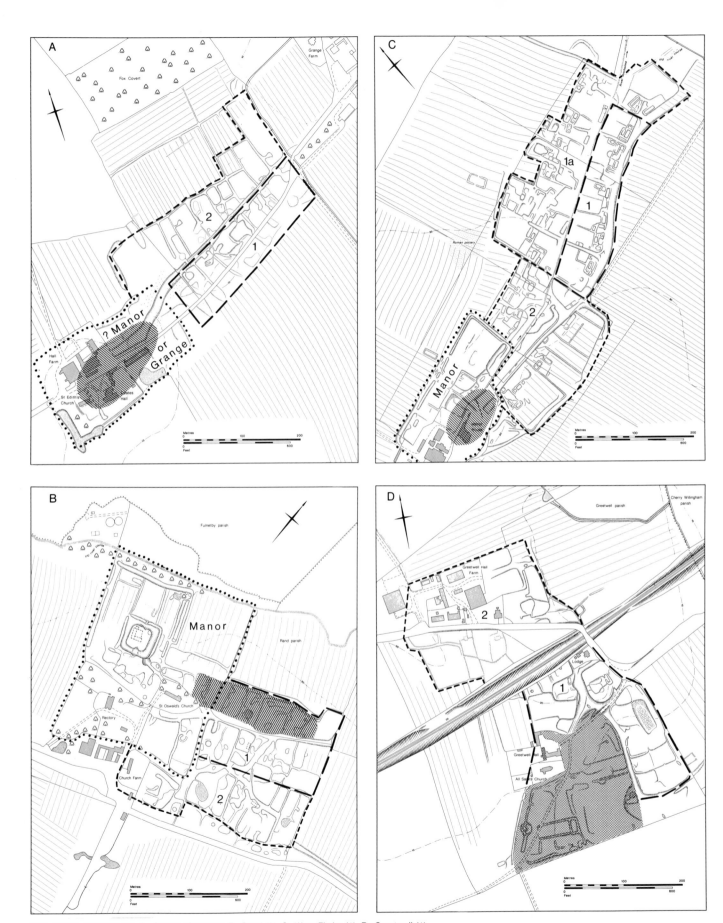

[25] *Village development.* **A.** *Coates (Stow (7)).* **B.** *Rand (2).* **C.** *West Firsby (1).* **D.** *Greetwell (1).*

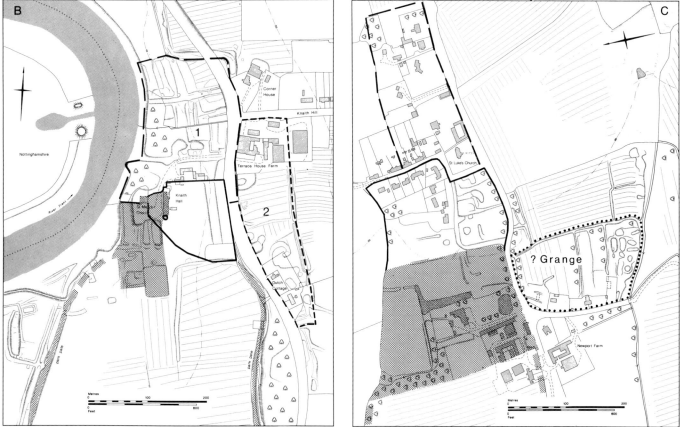

[26] *Village development.* **A.** *North and South Ingleby (Saxilby with Ingleby (2, 3)).* **B.** *Knaith (2).* **C.** *North Carlton (1).*

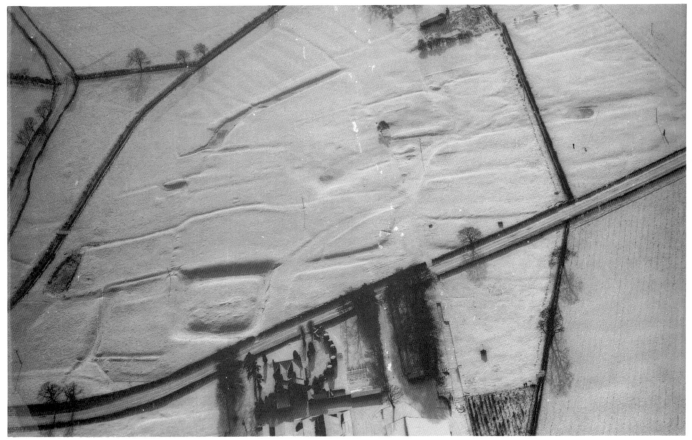

[27] *Legsby (1, 2), moated site and deserted village of Bleasby from the N, 11 February 1978. The S side of the well-marked moated manorial site cuts through an earlier E–W hollow-way. This and later post-desertion trackways have obscured the underlying regular nature of the settlement. (Cambridge University Collection: copyright reserved)*

The Population of Villages

The history of the development of any village is dependent on many interrelated aspects which include physical geography, social make-up, the pattern of tenure, economic forces and much else. As has already been made clear in the foregoing pages, the appearance of many West Lindsey villages can be considered the result of tenurial arrangements and estate management, especially in the 10th to 12th centuries. But in terms of physical size, expansion and decline, the other important factors are the levels of population and the economic and social pressures which led to their fluctuation.

For most of the villages described in the Inventory an attempt has been made to ascertain from local and national records their population at various periods. The basic national records, including Domesday Book, the 14th to 16th-century Lay Subsidies, the 1377 Poll Tax Returns, the 1428 Taxation, the 16th-century Muster Rolls and the 19th-century Census Returns have all been used. Local records examined include the early 17th-century lists of communicants and various medieval manorial accounts (see Notes).

The use of these sources, however, poses considerable problems of interpretation for various reasons which are well known. Except for the Census Returns none can be regarded as complete, all have different bases, and some are known to have involved widespread evasion. In addition, as many of the records were taken on a township or parish basis, in those parishes or townships with multiple settlements the figures are often combined into single entries. Thus, for example, no population figures for the deserted villages of North and South Ingleby (Saxilby with Ingleby (2) and (3)) are ascertainable. Both places were always returned explicitly or implicitly as members of Saxilby in whose parish they lay and which is, and always has been, a flourishing community. The same problem arises in places such as the abandoned settlements of Risby and Otby in Walesby (2, 3) where the situation is compounded by the fact that Walesby itself is partly deserted, and at Southorpe and Northorpe in Northorpe parish (1, 2). A further factor which distorts the evidence is the existence, from the 12th century onwards, of large monastic holdings, as at Croxby (Thoresway (3)), Stainton le Vale (1) and Swallow (1), whose possessions were exempt from the Lay Subsidies. This presumably reduced the numbers of taxpayers recorded. As a result it is difficult, if not impossible, to establish the levels of population from the available documentation of any individual place, especially in the medieval period.

An even more serious problem arises from the lack of any documentation for population between Domesday Book in 1086 and the early 14th-century Lay Subsidies. In many places, such as for example Croxby (Thoresway (3)), Buslingthorpe (2) and Kingerby (Osgodby (4)) [28], it appears that the late 11th-century population, as recorded in Domesday Book, was higher than at any time prior to the 18th or even the 19th centuries. Yet it is at precisely such villages that the surviving earthworks and other historical records indicate major planning, planned additions or piecemeal expansion, seemingly taking place in the 12th to 13th centuries. In effect, the archaeological and tenurial records suggest a considerable increase in population after the late 11th century which is not noted in any national taxation return. It is likely that, by the early 14th century, this trend had not only ceased, but was already in reverse.

Even the relatively recent records of population do not necessarily reflect the situation in the villages themselves. Many parishes show fluctuating population levels in the 18th and 19th centuries which result from the changing prosperity of agriculture, then being carried out from newly established outlying farmsteads and sometimes involving an attenuated pattern of new roadside properties as at Apley (1) or Snarford (1) away from the old village site. The best instance is Broxholme (1) where the parish population varied between 26 and 49 households in the period 1801 to 1851 and then remained steady to 1901. Yet cartographic evidence shows that the greater part of Broxholme was swept away some time between 1839 and 1870 following massive estate reorganization.

At other times, and in other places, major change in population or even permanent depopulation is hardly evident from the documentary record. It is certain, for example, that the major period of depopulation and abandonment at Owersby (1) from which it never recovered was in the 17th century, probably connected with conversion to pasture. But because of the constantly changing bases on which the existing records were compiled and the inadequate nature of other documentation, the real meaning of the earthworks on the ground is obscure.

[28] Osgodby (4), deserted village of Kingerby, 9 October 1980. This air photograph, taken from the N, emphasizes the remarkably regular arrangement of the W part of the village. The moated manorial site (3), earlier a castle, is obscured by the trees S of the church.

The Desertion of Settlement [8]

Many of the sites which the Commission has surveyed and which are described in the Inventory are perhaps not fully typical of the totality of medieval and later settlement in West Lindsey. By their very nature the Inventory sites tend to be those which, for a variety of reasons, failed to survive or suffered exceptional reductions of population. Nevertheless, it is clear from the overall picture of all the West Lindsey villages that a majority of them do contain evidence which indicates desertion or shrinkage of some form and it can be assumed that at others evidence of similar shrinkage has been totally destroyed or obliterated by later development. Thus an analysis of this form of settlement is perhaps worthwhile in the overall context of West Lindsey villages, as well as for its own sake.

Certain broad conclusions can be reached about the abandonment and shrinkage of villages in the area under review. The size of a settlement in the late 11th century when the first details are available, is apparently no guide to its future failure, survival or success. Many places with a large population recorded in Domesday Book either disappeared completely or have been reduced to a small hamlet or a single farmstead and some have only recovered marginally in the last century or so. Villages such as Croxby (Thoresway (3)), Kingerby (Osgodby (4)), Firsby (West Firsby (1)), Thoresway (1) and Stainton le Vale (1) all exhibit this feature. Nor was wealth, as expressed in the early 14th-century Lay Subsidies, a certain recipe for future prosperity. Harpswell (1) and Owersby (1) were very wealthy in the early 14th century but both declined greatly later on. On the other hand, some villages which were extremely small in the late 11th century have managed to survive in one form or another despite many changes and fluctuations in size. Knaith (2) [26] is one such place while another, Apley (1), even managed to grow in the 18th century, though not on its original site. As with the question of planned settlements the power and the influence of the manorial lords seem to have had the greatest effect on the success or failure of a village, often regardless of its size. Though a small settlement would, theoretically, be more vulnerable to the ruthless exercise of power or even to general economic decline or climatic deterioration this is not always borne out by the actuality. The fluctuations in the size and prosperity of Knaith (2) seem to be much more a reflection of the changing pattern of resident or non-resident medieval lords and their varying policies of estate management than of any general geographical or economic determinant. The failure of Riseholme (1) in the 17th century seems to result directly from estate management policies, while the growth of Apley (1) in the 18th century took place only when the absolute control of the Tyrwhitt family was removed. The population of the parish, though not the village, of Kingerby (Osgodby (4)) rose in the 19th century following the massive injection of capital into the farming there, while Greetwell (1) [25]

finally disappeared in the 18th century as a result of similar estate reorganization by the major owners there.

The reasons for and periods of abandonment and contraction of medieval settlement in England are well known, but not all are applicable to the villages of West Lindsey. Further, merely to list such reasons and periods, where they seem obvious, leads to the danger of inferring a series of simplistic and largely monocausal explanations. There can be little doubt that the true situation was usually far more complicated than appears from the evidence of surviving documents.

Nevertheless there are general periods and conditions which did help to reduce the size of settlements and in some cases led to their abandonment. These therefore can be usefully examined in the context of West Lindsey.

The earliest period of change which produced alteration in settlement location and morphology is largely undated and undocumented. This is the establishment of the pattern of nucleated villages at some time in the later Saxon period. There can no longer be any certainty that all the villages of West Lindsey were newly created in the 5th century following the English settlement. The available evidence, inadequate though it is, suggests that the major medieval nucleated settlements emerged over a long period of time, perhaps developing from an earlier pattern of dispersed settlement similar to the prehistoric and Roman ones. This hypothesis, if correct, presupposes the existence of abandoned mid to late Saxon settlements, perhaps in considerable numbers. As yet few such settlements have been discovered, though those at Normanby le Wold and Willoughton may be examples. The forces which brought about this change from dispersed to nucleated settlement whether economic, social, demographic, climatic or tenurial, are almost completely unknown and thus little can usefully be said at the present time. Once the major settlements were established, and certainly after the late 11th century, matters become somewhat clearer.

The first period of population contraction, arguably perhaps the most important, though completely undocumented and only suggested by inference, is that of the 13th and early 14th century. In a number of places there is a clear drop in population between 1086, when Domesday Book was compiled, and the early 14th century when the first Lay Subsidies recorded size and wealth of settlement. Croxby (Thoresway (3)), Firsby (West Firsby (1)), Kingerby (Osgodby (4)), Thoresway (1) [29], Cuxwold (Swallow (2)), Snitterby (1), Buslingthorpe (2) and perhaps Brattleby (1) and Dunstall (Corringham (5)) all show this feature. At some of these places and elsewhere, though the surviving figures for population are either unclear or defective, there is archaeological evidence to suggest that replanning or expansion took place in the 12th century on a scale that presupposes an increase in population at that time, but which had fallen again by the early 14th century. At Riseholme (1), though its 1086 size is not known, the 17 and 18 taxpayers recorded in the early 14th century suggest that the village was

[29] *Thoresway (1), 21 September 1946, a typical Wolds valley settlement now substantially reduced in size and exhibiting a complex sequence of development, not fully understood. To the S in the subsidiary valley is the site of Thoresway (2), a monastic grange of Revesby Abbey. (RAF)*

relatively small. Yet, apparently in the 12th century at least one half of the polyfocal village had been replanned, with at least 20 and possibly 25 new tofts and crofts in addition to the other half of the village whose form and size is unknown. Likewise at Buslingthorpe (2), the village was very small in 1086 and was much the same size in the early 14th century. But the archaeological evidence indicates that it was completely replanned, again probably in the 12th century, on a scale that might suggest that it was then larger than both earlier or later.

It is not clear why there should have been a 12th-century increase in population, nor a later fall. It may be that, as has recently been suggested, the population statistics in Domesday Book are extremely defective and thus the late 11th-century population was much higher than was actually recorded. On the other hand the general nation-wide prosperity of the 12th century which also produced numerous 'new' towns, may well have been a factor in causing population increase. Similarly the onset of more difficult economic conditions by the early 14th century could have led to the subsequent decline. But in West Lindsey, at least, this assumed decline was itself not universal. Some villages seem to have passed into the mid 14th century with no obvious reduction of population and so other and unknown factors must have been at work. Harpswell (1) and Spridlington (1), for example, both seem to have been considerably larger in the early 14th century than they were 250 years earlier, while Greetwell (1) and Somerby (1) seem to have been largely

unchanged. On the other hand the lack of documentation for the 12th and 13th centuries may be obscuring a rapid rise, fall and subsequent rise again even at these places.

One possible local reason for the 13th-century decline may have been the large-scale acquisition of land by monastic houses in West Lindsey and a subsequent development of sheep-farming. There is an apparent decline in the size of places such as Cabourne (1) and Audleby (Caistor (4)) by the early 14th century following a period of large-scale monastic land grants. Yet the fact that the early 14th-century Lay Subsidies specifically excluded ecclesiastical wealth may mean that the extant population figures are again misleading. In any case the existence of a former village or hamlet, later occupied by a monastic holding or isolated grange, does not necessarily imply that the clearance was carried out by the monastic owners. *Coldecotes* (Legsby (3)) was once a settlement with dwelling houses, gardens and orchards. But when this fact was recorded in 1322 the houses were already in ruins. Thus when the depleted manor was granted to the Gilbertine priory of Sixhills in 1407 it consisted of nothing but 50 acres of meadow and 300 acres of pasture. Clearly the demise of *Coldecotes* had nothing to do with the priory. The same may be true of Swinthorpe (Snelland (2)) which became a grange of Kirkstead Abbey. In addition it is possible that sheep-farming, the development of which is well documented on monastic estates, might have been just as important on lay estates although it is there largely unrecorded.

A much better recorded period of decline is that following the Black Death in 1348–9. As elsewhere in England there is no doubt that the arrival of the epidemic in West Lindsey had a devastating effect. In most villages the surviving documentation indicates a considerable fall in population, in some cases almost to extinction, yet all recovered to a lesser or greater degree. Cherry Willingham (1) was already very small in the early 14th century and was exempt from tax in 1342. Yet it survived the Black Death albeit with less than 10 householders in 1428 and continued on into the post-medieval period with 15 to 20 households. Incidentally, though it remained so small that in the mid 19th century the Manchester, Sheffield and Lincolnshire Railway Company thought it unnecessary to build a station there, it is now one of the largest villages around the fringes of Lincoln.

There is no indication that the Black Death was felt equally over the whole area of West Lindsey and no significance can be seen in the distribution of those settlements particularly affected by the epidemic. Places such as Swallow (1), Croxby (Thoresway (3)) and Owersby (1) were apparently almost completely depopulated. At others the disease seems to have been of little consequence, as at Harpswell (1), while in a few cases such as East Torrington (Legsby (5)) the Black Death had little or no impact. Nor was the size of a settlement any protection against the plague. Spridlington (1), one of the larger villages in the area, suffered badly but Cold Hanworth (1), already very small, emerged into the 15th century but little reduced in size. As elsewhere in England, the real impact of the Black Death was in its weakening effects on formerly prosperous places which paved the way for their abandonment or decline in succeeding centuries.

Two factors have been suggested as leading to depopulation and shrinkage of settlements in the 15th century: conversion to pasture for sheep or cattle and climatic deterioration. The former factor was important in West Lindsey and a whole group of settlements seems to have disappeared, probably as a result of sheep-farming. Snarford (1), always a small place, survived the Black Death but appears to have succumbed to conversion to grazing at this period, while at Kettleby Thorpe (Bigby (4)) the archaeological evidence of the now destroyed site indicates desertion by 1450, perhaps as a result of sheep-farming by the Tyrwhitt family. The site of Atterby (Bishop Norton (2)) has produced a long sequence of pottery which terminates abruptly in the early 15th century. Others, described in the Inventory, include Southorpe (Northorpe (1)), Firsby (West Firsby (1)) and perhaps Orford (Stainton le Vale (2)). There is also a large group of settlements whose abandonment is not firmly dated but which disappears at some time in the 15th or early 16th century. These include Wharton (Blyton (2)), Buslingthorpe (2), Audleby (Caistor (4)) and Somerby and Dunstall (Corringham (7), (5)).

Many villages, however, although much reduced in size by extensive conversion to pasture in their townships survived the 15th century. Somerby (1) certainly suffered some depopulation at this time, but nevertheless continued to exist. Snitterby (1) though in medieval times only a small settlement and township in Waddingham parish and further depleted in the 15th century, grew to achieve parochial status with its own church in the late 18th century.

The effect of 15th-century climatic change is more difficult to assess. Mr G. Beresford has used the results of excavations at Goltho (1) and elsewhere to support the thesis that increasingly wet conditions in the 15th century led to the abandonment of arable land, its replacement by pasture and a consequent desertion of settlement (Beresford 1975, 50–4). This theory has not been accepted universally and certainly further work at Goltho has indicated that the village there was probably not completely deserted in the 15th century but actually survived, albeit much smaller, for some time. That the arable land at Goltho was abandoned and pastoral farming introduced may be true, but whether the associated settlement disappeared is much more doubtful. In any case climatic deterioration, if it occurred at Goltho, was not apparently universal or contemporary. The village of Rand (2), an immediate neighbour of Goltho, was also largely deserted as a result of conversion to pasture but the process seems to have occurred a century or so later. Though waterlogging of soils may indeed have been a major factor in the abandonment of arable and thus in the reduction of settlement size, it is more likely that the real reasons lay in the increasing viability of grazing for the landowners involved. Given good returns on capital, even the most unsuitable land could be and was cultivated. Its abandonment likewise was probably more to do with profitability than with rainfall. In passing, it may be noted that contemporary documentation is not necessarily any more valid than excavational evidence when assessing the viability of agricultural land. The poverty of Knaith (2) in the late 14th century was ascribed to the sandy soils there. Yet as has already been noted, Knaith had a long history of fluctuating prosperity and decline which seems to have been more a result of its changing lords than any physical determinants.

The later 16th and 17th centuries were generally a time of rural population decline in the area of West Lindsey, as for much of the county, that was exacerbated by migration into towns and into the fen lands and by the periodic incidence of dearth and plague. This was coupled with continued conversion to pasture and rationalization of farming that gathered pace over the same period. All these factors had a great impact on the settlements of West Lindsey and led to the greatest amount of abandonment and shrinkage (Holmes 1980, 18–29; Hill 1956, 198). Many villages seem to have been affected to a greater or lesser degree by the process and the lack of detailed documentation may be concealing an even greater influence. Certainly some villages virtually disappeared at this time, though these had often been already much reduced. They include Riseholme (1), Stainfield (2), Kingerby (Osgodby (4)), Croxby (Thoresway (3)), one of the two parts of Walesby (1) and Little Limber (Brocklesby (5)). Other such as Owmby (1), Cold Hanworth (1), Riby (1),

Blyborough (1), Searby (Searby cum Owmby (1)) and Heapham (1) were all reduced in size. Some villages seemingly survived despite the most massive attempts to depopulate them. Cammeringham (2) was the scene of one of the 'great depopulations' recorded in 1607 and its population was reduced by a third. Yet it continued as a flourishing settlement.

Much of the conversion to pasture and subsequent depopulation was carried out by a new generation of great landowning families who, though they sometimes already held considerable estates by the early 16th century, grew rich or richer on the spoils of former monastic houses. Among the most notable were the Tyrwhitts. The family, originally from Northumberland, acquired the manor of Kettleby (Bigby (3)) in the late 14th or early 15th century and Sir William Tyrwhitt took up residence there. His son Robert, a justice of the King's Bench and of the Common Bench (d 1428), was also apparently a resident lord at Kettleby. Either father or son enclosed the bulk of the fields of Kettleby and Kettleby Thorpe and depopulated both villages. With scarcely an exception the Tyrwhitt heirs through the 15th and 16th centuries were publicly prominent as MPs or High Sheriffs for the county and in direct service of the Crown. Sir Robert Tyrwhitt (1482–1548) was notable as a Dissolution Commissioner and a grantee of a large amount of monastic property. Cadet branches of the family were established on a number of his acquisitions as at Cammeringham, Stainfield and Nun Cotham in Brocklesby. At all these places extensive depopulation seems to have taken place in the 16th and 17th centuries though there is no physical evidence for the process at Cammeringham. Another family were the Monsons who, in the 15th century, were resident at South Kelsey. In 1506–7 Sir John Monson bought South Carlton and the family moved there. They then began a policy of land acquisition which included the manor of Owersby in 1532, the former Barlings manor at South Carlton in 1544 and later in the 16th century the manors of North Carlton and Broxholme. They also acquired Burton which they made their main residence. At all these places the family enclosed land and carried out removal of tenants, mainly in the early 17th century. Amongst other early 17th-century depopulations were those carried out by Richard Rossiter at Somerby (1), Little Limber (Brocklesby (5)) and Searby (Searby cum Owmby (1)), by Sir William Pelham and others at Great Limber (2) and by Henry Ayscough at Blyborough (1).

Because of the localized nature of the acquisition of such estates, the evidence for the process of 16th and 17th-century depopulation is widespread but not geographically significant. Reduction in population, perhaps following on enclosure, continued sporadically throughout the 17th century. Hemswell (2) [17] suffered a considerable drop in size in the late 17th century, though recovery was very rapid and may even have led to the establishment anew of the southern section of the village. This recovery and subsequent reorganization of villages which follows late medieval or early post-medieval depopulation, and often led to further changes in settlement morphology, has also been noted elsewhere in West Lindsey. The single E–W street at Normanby by Spital (1) may well be the result of a simplification of its plan brought about by regrowth of population from the very low point in the late 16th century. More conclusive is Lissington (1) where the massive decline in the 17th century left settlement earthworks whose later destruction revealed occupation debris from the early Saxon period to the early 17th century. Its subsequent recovery led to the diversion of the village street to the S where the modern settlement still exists, leaving the earthworks totally divorced from the village. Marton (1) may also fall into this category. It is possible that the increase in its size after the very low levels of the early 15th century could have transformed it from a village with a single street running W to the River Trent into a N–S riverside two-row settlement. At Great Limber (2) the later 17th century also saw a massive change in the size and arrangement of the village.

One remarkable process of village abandonment which took place in the later 17th century was at Nettleton (3) [19, 30]. There, some 25 houses and 'garths' were engulfed by landslips and the area still remains largely vacant today.

[30] Nettleton (3), 9 October 1980. The empty closes lying between the village core and the main Wolds scarp to the S were occupied by buildings until the late 17th century when landslips overwhelmed some twenty-five houses.

[31] *Riby (1), 6 December 1946. The 18th-century landscaped park of Riby Grove has preserved the remains of the two separate nuclei of the former village, as well as its fields* [113]. *Yet the emparking was probably also partly responsible for the demise of Riby. (RAF)*

After the 17th century far fewer villages were completely abandoned, though a number were reduced in size or transformed. It is usually assumed that emparking was the main reason for 18th or 19th century total or partial clearance and this is certainly true in a few cases, for example Knaith (2) [26], Blyborough (1), Gate Burton (1), North Carlton (1) [26], Riby (1) [31] and the SE part of Tealby (1) [17]. More often, however, clearance or decline of villages in West Lindsey at this time appears to have been the result of estate management and changes in farming practices including the dispersal of farmsteads into newly enclosed fields. Thus at Greetwell (1) [25], while the remains of the former village lie mainly within the landscaped park there and would therefore seem, superficially, an excellent instance of emparking, the village was actually removed in the early 18th century before the park was conceived. Its decline was seemingly the result of changes in farm management. Broxholme (1) too was almost completely removed in the mid

19th century as part of an extensive scheme of estate re-organization and at Gilby (Pilham (2)), what remained of the village by the early 19th century had gone by 1850, though here the reasons are unclear. Clixby (Grasby (2)) was also finally deserted in the early 19th century after many vicissitudes. It was still a prosperous village in the 16th century, declined in the 17th century and increased in size in the 18th century. But its final clearance appears to have been the result of a deliberate policy by its lord, reacting apparently to provisions of the Poor Laws. The necessary labour for the estate was provided by workmen walking into Clixby from the adjacent 'open' villages.

Many other places seem to have declined dramatically in the last two centuries, though mostly their population merely moved to farmsteads elsewhere in the township, as at Thorpe in the Fallows (1), Kingerby (Osgodby (4)), Cold Hanworth (1) and Owersby (1). Yet other villages went through large reorganization or redevelopment often at the instigation of their lords. At some the results were spectacular as is the case with Brattleby (1) even though the initial work involved merely the insertion of new roads. At a less impressive level places such as Scampton (1) and Spridlington (1) demonstrate the impact of the 19th-century lords while at Newton on Trent (1) [14] enclosure of the common fields seems to have changed the village from a single-row settlement to a two-row one.

The last century and especially the last forty years has seen perhaps the greatest change in the rural settlements of West Lindsey in response to an increasing population, higher living standards and development in commuting. Most villages which lie close to the urban areas have been expanded out of all recognition, notably Nettleham and Cherry Willingham outside Lincoln, but all villages which have survived into the 20th century in a viable state have been altered. There has, in effect, been a post-war version of 'open/closed' villages operating through the planning process, often with local political dimensions behind it. Key villages have been selected in which, for example, primary schools were allowed to survive and expand, secondary schools established, sewerage works provided and shops encouraged or promoted. In addition such villages have been actively allowed to extend their areas of occupation.

Even so, some abandonment has continued in many places. The modern desertion of much of the parish as distinct from the settlement of Blyborough is largely the result of engrossment and the development of mechanized arable farming in the last few years though the planning processes outlined above have also played an important part. Blyborough is but the best example of a general decline in population and abandonment of newly established farmsteads in the area under review. Particularly interesting are the sites of two relatively recent farmsteads which have succumbed to agricultural changes. A farmstead at Nettleton (5), erected a little before 1824 following the enclosure of the parish in 1794, was abandoned only in recent years, while another at Claxby (3), probably built in the 18th century, was replaced by a new farmstead in the adjacent parish between 1856 and 1867.

Concentration by the Commission during its survey of West Lindsey on the discovery and recording of abandoned settlements and shrunken sites could result in a distorted view of settlement development. Thus in this essay every effort has been made to discuss the totality of rural settlement in the area in order to avoid the mistake of assuming that abandoned or shrunken settlements are the norm. For, taking the broader view, most settlements have survived the vicissitudes of the past 800 years. Even those which are said to have been abandoned or to have undergone large-scale decline, and are therefore described in the Inventory and discussed at length here, rarely suffered real desertion or shrinkage for long periods. At the level of individual settlements few have ever been totally deserted and many listed in the Inventory as such still have one or two farmsteads on or close to their sites with a population equal to, or in excess of, what was recorded centuries ago.

More important is the status of the vill, township or parish. Whatever happened to the principal settlement, there were almost always other settlements elsewhere in the township. This is most clearly seen in the 17th century and later though it certainly occurred earlier. The methods by which population was recorded, usually by townships, and thus including people living in outlying farmsteads and hamlets, often obscures the fact that the principal settlement was in decline or had been abandoned. While this is unfortunate for the study of the history of individual settlements, the fact that, even in medieval times, the township or vill was the unit of administration and taxation rather than any particular settlement within it, makes the point that it is the land, not the location of settlement, that was the most important basis of rural life. Individual settlements could appear or disappear, be removed or reorganized. Dispersed patterns could be changed to nucleated ones and in turn be replaced by renewed dispersal. Yet the land was still worked, within its ancient bounds. Where people lived in West Lindsey and what they, or more usually their lords, did to their settlements, is perhaps less important historically than the treatment of the farmland.

Manorial Sites

Within the area under review are numerous examples of what can generally be termed manorial sites, many now completely or partly abandoned. It is not always possible to distinguish between those belonging to lay lords and those held by the monastic orders and indeed in many respects no distinction ever existed. This is well seen at Stainton le Vale (1) where a large part of the alleged village remains appears to be the sites of discrete demesne farms, some of which were secular manors and others monastic holdings or granges. The

same situation may also have existed at Cabourne (1), Swallow (1) and elsewhere.

Yet despite this, certain topographical and historical aspects of a number of both lay and ecclesiastical manorial sites are of such importance that they should be discussed as separate types, while at the same time bearing in mind that the functions of lay manors and monastic holdings or granges were, in many respects, the same.

Lay Manorial Sites

In many settlements abandoned manorial sites are not readily identifiable. In certain villages this is because they never had resident lords of whatever status, and thus what survives are only the sites of peasant houses and closes. Sudbrooke (1) and Thorpe in the Fallows (1) are possible examples.

Many other presumed manorial sites are still occupied by modern farmsteads which, with their outbuildings, obscure any evidence that might allow them to be attributed to medieval manors, as at Newball (1). In other villages where there was also fragmented tenure or where extensive sub-infeudation took place, and thus where a large number of so-called manors are recorded, it is difficult to be sure of what the resulting manorial sites actually consisted. Certainly in such cases it is unlikely that the physical remains would easily be distinguishable from the dwellings of those of lesser status. On the whole the recognizable manorial sites are those which belong to the owners or tenants of relatively large landholdings whose position, or the demands of agriculture, required extensive paddocks, closes, moats and fishponds, all of which can be identified as surviving earthworks, or can be seen as topographically distinct elements in the overall village morphology.

Four types of manorial sites have been recognized in West Lindsey, based on their physical characteristics, location and relationship to their associated settlement. The first type comprises a group of manorial sites which might be termed 'normal' in that they are by far the most common and which lie within or close to their associated settlements, but with no clearly observable significance in their position or relationship to that settlement.

The site at Southorpe (Northorpe (1)) is a good example of this type, comprising a moated enclosure, paddocks and fishponds, situated and forming an integral part of the surrounding village remains. Caenby (1) is a variant of this type with two sites, one moated, situated at either end of the village. The moated site and the adjacent enclosures at Spridlington (1) also lie on one side of the southern nucleus of the village with which it was probably associated, as do the manorial sites at Osgodby (1), Scotterthorpe (Scotter (2)) [15], Kettleby Thorpe (Bigby (4)) and perhaps Glentham (1).

The second type of manorial site is where it is connected to a village of highly regular form and which was probably laid out as part of the village plan, perhaps in the 12th

[**32**] *West Firsby (1) from the N, 26 November 1980. At the W end of the deserted village of Firsby the now abandoned Manor Farm lies within the SW part of the rectangular curia of the manor of Firsby. To the E, on the N side of the stream, a huddle of former village properties overlies earlier ridge-and-furrow. To the S another, more regular, block of properties outlined by a hollow-way also overlies former fields.*

century. These manorial sites are fully integrated within the village layout and appear to be part of the overall settlement arrangement. Examples include the rectangular arrangement of paddocks and fishponds at Firsby (West Firsby (1)) [**25, 32**] and the closes, moated site and small 'park' at Buslingthorpe (1, 2, 4). The site now largely occupied by the existing Manor Farm at Linwood (1) [**37**], though having few identifiable earthworks, would come into this category as would the similar site at Brattleby (1) where the modern great house seems to stand on the site of an earlier manor house and *curia*, attached to the planned village there.

The third situation is where the manorial site appears to be an intrusion into a presumably long-established village arrangement, with consequent disruption of an existing street pattern or the incorporation into the *curia* of land formerly occupied by village houses and crofts. From field evidence alone it is not always possible to determine whether these encroachments took place when the adjacent settlement was still occupied or at a period when the settlement was already partly or completely abandoned. At South Ingleby

(Saxilby with Ingleby (3)) [**26**] what is certainly an extension of an earlier moated manor site blocks one of the main streets of the former village, though there are indications that this took place at a relatively late date when the adjacent part of the village had already been deserted. The moated manorial site at Bleasby (Legsby (1)) [**27**] also blocks an earlier street, but in addition, the associated closes may overlie earlier properties. Parts of the manorial complexes at both Wickenby (3) and Rand (1) [**25, 33**] have certainly encroached upon earlier village properties and have also disrupted former road systems. The same situation has been revealed by excavation at Goltho (1) (Beresford 1977).

A fourth type of manorial site includes those which lie some distance from their associated settlement. Among these are the moated sites at Goltho (2) and Lea (2). Neither is observably different from other isolated moated sites and it is only from documentary sources that their status and relationships can be established. Both sites seem to be in secondary locations and thus appear to be the result of the moving of the manorial centre from an earlier position within their associated villages. Yet even here there is no certainty, and at Goltho at least the site may also mark the position of an earlier hamlet, within the township, long abandoned.

Without excavation it is not possible to understand when most of the lay manorial sites of West Lindsey came into being. Some appear to be the centres of landholdings recorded in Domesday Book, and therefore already in existence in the late 11th century, while others may represent the result of sub-infeudation in succeeding centuries. A few at least seem to have developed as manorial or estate centres following the decline of earlier, perhaps largely defensive, functions. The site within the village of Goltho (1) has been excavated and a complex sequence of development discovered. This comprised a 9th-century defensive structure, rebuilt on a large scale in the first part of the 11th century, replaced by a small motte and bailey in the late 11th century and altered again in the mid 12th century to form a more elaborate manorial site before being abandoned. At Kingerby (Osgodby (4)) at least part of a similar sequence is visible where the slight remains of the documented castle are still recognizable around the later moated manor and its appurtenances. In contrast, at Thonock (1) the massive ringwork and double bailey seems to have survived its down-grading from a major strategic centre to a manorial one without major alterations.

[33] Rand (1, 2), 30 October 1980. The well-marked rectangular area on the W, containing the moated site, fishponds, church and rectory, is almost certainly the later medieval curia of the manor of Rand. However, this curia also includes within its boundaries former village properties both to the N and S of the church. This suggests that the village itself, once of very regular form, has been encroached upon by the curia at some time.

Ecclesiastical Estate Centres

A characteristic feature of the history of West Lindsey in the early medieval period is the large number of grants of land and other rights to monastic houses and related religious orders, both within and beyond the area under review. These were especially prevalent in the 12th century when houses of the new orders were being founded and endowed. The endowments ranged from land covering entire parishes, through individual manors to relatively small pieces of land. The latter, particularly, tended to be greatly enlarged by subsequent grants.

As has already been discussed, it is not easy to distinguish the centres of these holdings from those in lay hands, nor were there probably any major functional differences between them. Indeed many monastic holdings were later leased out and run as purely lay estates as at Riby (1) and Willoughton (1). In addition, the range of agricultural activities of these centres was just as wide as those of their lay counterparts. At the lowest level some operated, at least for a time, as no more than simple sheep-farms, as is likely at Cabourne (1). At others, to judge by the surviving remains which include large numbers of closes and sites of buildings, there were altogether more complex agricultural activities as at Riseholme (2) or perhaps at Collow (Legsby (4)) where fishponds, a possible water-mill and a large ditched enclosure as well as building platforms all survive. Elsewhere industrial activities of various kinds were carried out as at Thoresway (2). At the upper end of the scale is the site at Willoughton

(2), originally a preceptory of the Knights Templars and later the administrative centre of all the Hospitallers' Lincolnshire estates.

Any attempt to analyse the physical manifestations of such a broad range of sites is thus fraught with difficulties, but some aspects of their form and location are worth noting. In detail, most monastic manorial centres have the same physical features as lay sites, for obvious reasons: closes, building complexes, mills and moats all occur, as well as occasional evidence for associated hamlets, perhaps for farm workers. The grange at North Kelsey (2) belonging to Ormsby Priory has evidence for an adjacent settlement, overlying earlier ridge-and-furrow and another small hamlet is perhaps recognizable at Holtham (Legsby (6)). The Cistercian grange at Thoresway (2) [29] also seems to include the remains of some form of contemporary peasant occupation as does perhaps the Templars/Hospitallers holding at the N end of Normanby le Wold (1).

In terms of location there are four types of monastic estate centres. The first is where the site is quite isolated from older settlements as at Thoresway (2) and Collow (Legsby (4)), North Kelsey (2), Scampton (1) and Nettleton (3) [19] as well as the existing farmstead at Grange de Lings (1). Without excavation it is impossible to know whether such sites were founded anew on previously unoccupied places or whether they took over pre-existing settlements which had already been abandoned or which were removed by their monastic owners. Certainly the isolated holdings at *Coldecotes* (Legsby (3)), Osgodby (Bardney (7)) and Swinthorpe (Snelland (2)) all have either field or documentary evidence that they were situated on older settlements though only at *Coldecotes* is it clear that the earlier occupation had ended before the arrival of the grange. The site at Barlings (3) which became a grange of Barlings Abbey was perhaps earlier the original position of the abbey itself, though again whether this was founded on an empty site is not known.

Some isolated monastic holdings appear to have had separate 'townships' associated with them which might suggest that they had a pre-monastic origin as small settlements. Two granges in Saxilby with Ingleby (4, 5), one belonging to the Augustinian priory of Nocton Park and the other perhaps a holding of the Gilbertine priory of Catley, each had a small block of land which together occupied the NW part of the parish. Yet the archaeological evidence from both the now destroyed sites indicates that they had extremely short lives of little more than 200 years in the 13th and 14th centuries. They thus may have been located on previously unoccupied sites and granted a block of the surrounding land, which remained in separate tenure long enough to be recognizable as a form of township. A similar situation may be seen at Collow (Legsby (4)) which also had a recognizable 'township' recorded on the 19th-century Tithe Map. It certainly did not exist as an inhabited place until the late 12th century when it was founded as a grange of the Cistercian abbey of Louth Park. Its accompanying township seems to have evolved gradually from the granting of numerous small blocks of land in the surrounding area.

The second type of location is where the monastic centre lies close to, though still separate from, an existing settlement and where there seems to have been a close tenurial link with that settlement. Such sites may well have been chosen when there was no other available land within the village itself. A good example is that at South Carlton (1, 2, 3), perhaps following from the complex way in which the land there was granted to Barlings Abbey by Robert Bardolf, who retained parts of both the existing lay manors in his own hands and apparently continued to use the main manorial site after the grant to Barlings. Other examples include those at North Carlton (3) [26], Hackthorn (1), Thorganby (1) and Great Limber (1) and perhaps at Toft (Toft Newton (1)).

It is not always clear what the exact relationship of such sites to their villages really was. The site at Riseholme (2) lies almost equidistant from the main deserted part of the polyfocal village and the other nucleus which certainly survived until the 17th century and which is now occupied by the Hall and its outbuildings. The grange there may not have been established until the 14th century, by which time one section of the village had already been abandoned and its area perhaps reused as a sheep-walk.

The third position for an ecclesiastical estate centre is within the village with which it was tenurially linked. In some cases such centres are related to land held by the older orders, acquired in pre-Conquest times as at Scotter (1) [20] and

were presumably the result of the granting of an existing manor, including its administrative centre, to a religious institution. Not all these were pre-Conquest in date, however, and Scampton (1) and perhaps Snelland (1) are later instances.

The final position for ecclesiastical manors or granges is where they have been added to an existing village, thus producing a complex morphology which is not always easy to interpret. The best example is at Cabourne (1) where a series of blocks has been added to the village, laid out over earlier arable land, and perhaps worked as individual sheep-farms. It is not possible to correlate the blocks with the land held by various religious institutions at Cabourne and some blocks may have been in the hands of lay lords, particularly in the later medieval period. The same general picture is visible both on the ground and in terms of tenure at Stainton le Vale (1), yet only one of the identifiable blocks appears to have been in monastic hands.

Additions of a different kind exist at Willoughton (1) and (2). One site, the centre of the holding of an alien priory, is little more than a simple moat, though other evidence suggests that it had a planned hamlet (Willoughton (4)) attached to it. The other site, comprising a very large moat and associated enclosures and perhaps another settlement block, was a preceptory of the Knights Templars. Yet another variant may be the Templars' holding at Normanby le Wold (1) also with evidence of an attached settlement whose existence makes the interpretation of the polyfocal village there extremely difficult.

The establishment of a monastic manorial centre could also disrupt the overall plan of a village. This has occurred at Holton cum Beckering (2) [19] where the surviving rectangular area containing the Hall and park is almost certainly the site of a manor or grange of Sixhills Priory. The establishment of this blocked the original E–W road through the village and led to a long diversion around it.

At a few places the exact location of documented monastic holdings cannot be identified with certainty, often because existing buildings stand on the presumed site and have thus destroyed any identifiable remains. The grange at Toft (Toft Newton (1)), one of the most valuable possessions of Sixhills Priory, may have been on the site of the modern farmstead. A similar difficulty is the identification of the grange of Welbeck Abbey at Coates (Stow (7)) [25].

Churches

Though not directly the concern of this present survey by the Royal Commission the chronological and spatial relationships of churches to their associated settlements are important in the understanding of these settlements. Many villages described in the Inventory were parochial centres and thus had churches within or near them. In numerous cases the church is situated in an observable and significant relationship to either the village itself or to a manorial site.

The origins and development of the parochial system, as well as the establishment and growth of churches, are currently topics of major interest to archaeologists and historians. Though most aspects of the subject are outside the scope of this work, certain features noted during the Royal Commission's survey are worth some discussion.

In West Lindsey, as elsewhere, a few late Saxon minster churches apparently situated at the centres of once extensive estates have been identified. That at Stow with its remarkable surviving structure is perhaps the best known, but others such as those at Kirton and Wragby (both just outside the area under review) and Caistor had a similar status and were situated at places with a long history of settlement and often royal administration. How the almost ubiquitous parish church came into existence is less clear. Some may have been founded at an early date on older pagan sites, while others may have been set up in villages as dependent chapelries of the minster churches. Yet more may have been proprietorial churches established by lords at a relatively late date. None of these possibilities has been proved beyond question by the Commission's survey and only the observations of analytical fieldwork can be offered here.

The most characteristic relationship in West Lindsey is that between church and manorial sites. Often, as a result of later and sometimes quite recent activity, this relationship can only be observed as one of close proximity of the church and an adjacent manor house. This is well seen at Blyborough (1), Hackthorn (1), Knaith (2), Riseholme (1) and Holton le Moor (1) where 18th-century and later emparking and estate improvements have obliterated any evidence of other relationships. Elsewhere there is some additional evidence, often of a fragmentary nature, that the parish church was once associated with the appurtenances of a manorial site. At Brattleby (1) the position of the church and Hall, set to one side of the regularly laid out village, suggests that the primary connection of the church was with the medieval predecessors of the Hall rather than with the village. However as the village is perhaps a secondary replanning it remains a possibility that the present relationship was not the original one.

More important are those places where the correlation between church and manor site is direct, in that the parish church lies within a clearly defined manorial enclosure which may encompass not only the site of the manor house, but also fishponds, water-mills and various other features. Such relationships exist at Buslingthorpe (1), Rand (1) [25], Wickenby (3) and probably existed at Firsby (West Firsby (1)) [25]. Similar situations may be recognizable at Scampton (1), Toft (Toft Newton (3)) and Linwood (1) and also at villages where only existing topographical details or vague documentary references remain to hint at such relationships. The latter include Scotter (1) [20] and Rothwell (1). At these villages the origin of the church as a

[34] *Heapham (1, 2) from the N, 9 October 1980. The isolated parish church lies at a spring head. It stands almost equidistant from the tiny ordered hamlet which constitutes the bulk of modern Heapham to the E, and the even smaller hamlet to the W, part of whose abandoned closes are just visible.*

lordly proprietorial foundation seems likely. However, there is sometimes additional evidence which conflicts with this hypothesis.

Thus at Buslingthorpe (1, 2), while the surviving earthworks of both the village and the manorial site indicate that both were laid out as a coherent unit and the documentary record suggests a 12th-century date for such a planned beginning, the dedication of the church to St Michael hints that it may have existed there long before the 12th century. More convincing is the situation at Rand (1, 2) [25, 33]. There, the church lies within the regular *curia,* but field evidence indicates that at least part of the latter is a secondary feature as it blocks part of the adjacent village street system. Further, excavations have also shown that the church perhaps pre-dates the *curia* while the documentary records certainly point to the beginnings of the church as a dependent chapelry of the ancient minster at Wragby. These examples show that much work remains to be carried out before the true relationships between manorial sites, their lords and the associated churches can be established, and that first reading of the present appearance of the landscape may be over-simplistic.

A number of churches now stand almost isolated in the modern landscape, and at virtually every one field evidence has been recorded for the existence of a former settlement of some kind around it. Only the church at Heapham [18, 34] does not fall into this category. That stands quite alone, set above an important spring in a natural basin, with its

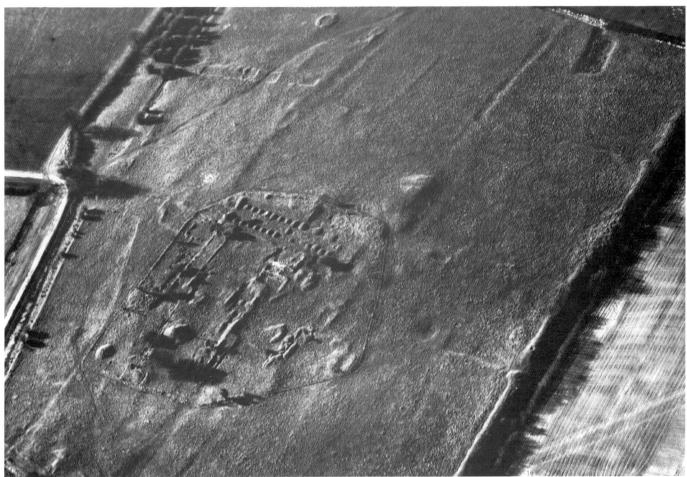

associated settlements (Heapham (1, 2)) arranged on the surrounding higher land. It may be that the church is on a much older pre-Christian ritual site, connected with water cults. Even here, however, there can be no certainty in the matter until excavation on the church can be carried out and the adjacent land, at present permanent pasture covered by ridge-and-furrow, examined archaeologically. Another possible instance may be the church at Harpswell, again with an ancient dedication. Though now situated within what remains of Harpswell village (1), it too stands on a spring, one of a number at the foot of the Jurassic Limestone scarp with saintly or ritual associations.

With the exception of Heapham already noted, the numerous polyfocal villages in West Lindsey almost all have their churches situated in one of the foci as at Normanby le Wold (1), and Walesby (1). It is possible that such a position indicates the relative age of the foci with the oldest being that which contains the church. The situation at Riseholme (1), where excavation, fieldwork and documents suggest that the southern focus is of planned 12th-century origin and perhaps later than the northern focus with the church, might support this. As always, however, the matter is far from clear and at a

number of polyfocal villages there is direct or indirect evidence of more than one church. Examples include Fillingham (1), Hemswell (1, 2), South Kelsey (2, 3) [16], Spridlington (1), Waddingham (1, 2) [16] and Glentworth (1).

Religious Houses

The area covered by the Commission's survey includes examples of the sites of almost all the major religious orders. Not all have been examined in detail, but of those that have, surprisingly limited conclusions have been reached. There are two reasons for this. First, and perhaps the most important, is the destruction of sites by modern agriculture over the last thirty to forty years even at places nominally protected by legislation. It is now often impossible to establish the outlines of many of the monastic precincts let alone interpret the former earthworks contained within them. Over half the site of the Gilbertine priory of Sixhills (1) has been destroyed and all the outer works at the

46

Premonstratensian abbey of Barlings (1) have now disappeared. The same is true at the Benedictine house of Bardney (2) [35] while the site of the Gilbertine priory of Bullington (1) was totally destroyed between 1953 and 1970 as was that of the Augustinian priory of St Leonard at Torksey (1) in 1950.

The second reason is the continued occupation of the sites, often within the area of the conventual buildings, which has effectively destroyed all evidence of the original arrangement. Sixhills Priory again falls into this category as does the Cistercian nunnery at Heynings (Knaith (1)), the Benedictine nunnery at Stainfield (1) and the alien priory of Winghale (South Kelsey (1)). Other sites which are now completely or largely abandoned have been found to have had large post-medieval residences erected on them which, though they have now in turn also been abandoned, have destroyed or obscured the evidence for the monastic layout. The priory of Premonstratensian nuns at Orford (Stainton le Vale (3)) and the Cistercian priory of Nun Cotham (Brocklesby (2)) [36] both show this feature. At the original site of Barlings Abbey (3) it is probable that after the removal and refoundation of the abbey in the late 12th century the land was occupied first by a monastic grange and then by a substantial post-medieval house.

A considerable 17th-century house and its formal gardens (Barlings (2)) also occupied much of the precinct of the second site of Barlings Abbey (1) but here the post-medieval activity lay outside the area of the main monastic buildings. The result is that here, alone of the surveyed sites, are there surviving earthworks to enable an understanding of the monastic church and its associated structures of conventual buildings to be reached.

The best preserved earthworks of the outer precincts of a monastic house are again those at Barlings and at Heynings (Knaith (1)), where much of the arrangement of fishponds, drains and buildings survives. They also include evidence of the expansion of a precinct over former arable. Well-preserved remains of other fishponds and perhaps mills also survive at Stainfield, Orford, Barlings and Winghale. Nothing remains of the Cistercian nunnery of Torksey (2).

The physical impact on the wider landscape of West Lindsey of the major religious houses was more extensive and perhaps more lasting than that of their actual sites. In some places, notably in the SE part of the area under review, where the core of the demesne lands of Stainfield, Bullington, Barlings and Bardney formed contiguous blocks, the outlines of the modern landscape are essentially monastic in origin. Much of the existing woodland was formerly managed by the monastic houses there and many of the streams flow in either wholly or partly artificial courses created by the abbeys. These include at least two formerly navigable canals at Bardney and at Stainfield, and others serving Barlings and Bullington. The construction of the latter is directly documented in 1195 × 1203 'for the easy transit of ships' from the river. Settlements such as Osgodby and *Butyate* (Bardney (7) and (8)) as well as Kingthorpe (Apley (2)) were at least in part influenced by their use as monastic granges

[36] *Brocklesby (2), 16 January 1973. Well-preserved earthworks on the site of Nun Cotham Priory, founded in the mid 12th century and dissolved in 1539. The complex pattern of remains in the centre which should be the site of the church and conventual buildings is at least in part the remains of a secular mansion erected soon after 1540 and probably demolished in the 17th century. Much if not most of the earthworks probably belong to this house and its associated gardens and closes. (Cambridge University Collection: copyright reserved)*

while the entire village of Langworth (Barlings (6)) is probably a monastic foundation, as was the replanting of the former villages of Stainfield (2) [24] and Orford (Stainton le Vale (2)).

Within the general category of religious houses is the site of Willoughton (2), a preceptory of the Templars and later the Hospitallers. For both it was the administrative centre of their extensive estates within the county and was therefore more than a local manorial site. Nevertheless, except perhaps for the unusually large moat, there is little that marks it out as being different from similar estate centres. Though not strictly religious houses, the sites of the palaces of the bishops of Lincoln at Stow (3) and Nettleham (1) are both worthy of note. The palace at Stow was contained by a massive moat, edged by an impressive array of fishponds at least partly positioned for appearance as well as for their functional aspects, and set within a large contemporary deer park. The isolated situation of this palace required a subsidiary settlement to provide accommodation for servants and this has been identified on the ground (5). At Nettleham the site is situated within the village, but still encompasses a group of paddocks, former barns and impressive approach drive and gatehouses. Though the greater part of the earthworks of the former palace themselves are well preserved, even more important and interesting is the small medieval walled and terraced garden there.

Castles

Only one major castle earthwork is extant in the area under review, Castle Hills, Thonock (1) situated at a place of considerable strategic significance and tactical strength. Its date is unknown but its form, a ring-motte and two baileys, would suggest an 11th to 12th-century origin. Though it has retained its defensive aspect, it is unlikely to have had a military function after the mid 12th century and its later history, at least until the 15th century, was as a local estate centre.

The only other castles are at Goltho (1) and Kingerby (Osgodby (3)). The present form of the latter, that of a moated manorial site, is the successor to an earlier castle, probably also a ringwork, deliberately destroyed by royal decree in 1218. In contrast a similar sequence at Goltho removed the moated successor to a location elsewhere in the parish (2).

The documented castle at Caistor (1), apparently referred to in 1143, has not been discovered and it may be that the site was merely a refurbishing of the Roman walls there. The area known as Castle Hill has no extant features though it is just possible that a change in the street alignment in the area may be significant.

Moated Sites

In respect of function, of course, the commonest category of moated sites, manorial enclosures, differ not at all from their unmoated counterparts on soils and in topographical situations that favour stone-built walls rather than ditched or water-filled boundaries. Within this study, the absence of a moat at Nettleham (1) makes it no less a palatial manor than Stow (3). Likewise the manorial complex at Firsby (West Firsby (1)) is no less a local lordly residence than Buslingthorpe (1) or North Ingleby (Saxilby with Ingleby (2)). Indeed the wider manorial *curia,* where it can be recognized, commonly has many points of similarity between moated and unmoated manors, that include associated paddocks, appurtenances such as fishponds, and significant relationship to churches.

Similar considerations apply to other functional categories, including most obviously granges and park lodges. Here too their moated or unmoated physical form cuts across these functions and over-emphasis on such form can obscure more important insights and understanding of land-use and settlement development. Nevertheless, archaeologists have usually studied moats as a category and some observations can be most usefully made within that tradition.

Numerous moated sites exist, or are known to have existed in West Lindsey, about thirty of which are recorded in detail in the Inventory. Most tend to be rectangular in plan, but there is a considerable range in the area enclosed by the moat itself. The latter is well illustrated at Willoughton (1) and (2) where two moated sites in the same village lie at opposite ends of the range of sizes.

In terms of earthworks, perhaps the most notable feature is that simple moated sites are rare. Most have only a single moated enclosure, though South Kelsey (4) and Linwood (1) [**37**] are exceptions in having outer moated courts. But in almost every instance field survey has indicated that there are, or were, associated earthworks, often very slight but forming an integral part of the site. Without the recognition of these earthworks large parts of the history and function of the moats would have been lost. For example the moated site of the Bishop of Lincoln's palace at Stow (3) is still preserved largely intact, but the surrounding fishponds and most of the associated settlement remains have been ploughed over and partly destroyed. Elsewhere paddocks and closes all surround or are connected to moated sites, as at Willoughton (2), while complexes of fishponds and even probably rabbit warrens have been recognized at Rand (1) and South Ingleby (Saxilby with Ingleby (3)).

Moated sites occur in a wide variety of situations, but for obvious reasons tend to be positioned on heavy land where local drainage or seepage filled the ditches, near streams, or close to spring-lines. The majority lie in or alongside existing or deserted villages and though a minority are now located in totally isolated positions, some of these appear to be on sites which were perhaps small settlements either during the period of the occupation of the moated site or shortly before as at Legsby (6) and perhaps Goltho (2).

Most of the moated sites recorded by the Commision seem to have had a manorial function, in that they mark the site of a principal residence of a manor, or in some cases a monastic holding or grange. Where the sites consist mainly of earthworks, they are usually surrounded by paddocks, closes and fishponds all of which formed part of the manorial appurtenances as at Buslingthorpe (1), Swallow (1) or Kettleby (Bigby (1)). Of the two isolated monastic granges at Saxilby with Ingleby (4, 5) one certainly and perhaps both had moated residences set within an array of outbuildings and closes. Where associated earthworks no longer survive, the topographical setting often within a rectangular arrangement of existing fields and closes indicates that they were part of a manorial *curia* as at Corringham (5) and Kettlethorpe (1).

A handful of moated sites lie within or are attached to medieval deer parks and appear to have originated as park-keepers' lodges, as at Glentworth (3, 4), Gainsborough (3, 4) and perhaps Bullington (3). That at Kettlethorpe (1) also seems to have been situated in a large late medieval park, though it clearly had a more important function as the residence of the Swynford family, lords of Kettlethorpe [**40**]. Three others seem to have had an even more specialized function. The moated bishop's palace at Stow (3) is one, though more curious is the site at Bardney (5) which had the well-documented purpose of a monastic centre for blood-

[37] *Linwood (1) from the SE, 28 March 1957. The two moated sites together with their associated enclosures which lay to the E of Linwood church are seen here before their destruction. The S (left-hand) moat was probably the site of the manor house of the S part of Linwood village which lay to the N, S and W of the church. The N moat was perhaps a garden. (Cambridge University Collection: copyright reserved)*

letting and recuperation. The small site at Tealby (3) certainly ended its life as a hermitage, though it may have had a different use earlier.

No certain dates for the origin of moated sites in West Lindsey have been found during the Commission's survey. The generally accepted date range for moated sites, from the 12th to the 15th century, has not been challenged, though most of the evidence is poor and circumstantial. Thus at Buslingthorpe (1) the moat can hardly have existed before its associated village was replanned, perhaps in the early 12th century. This, too, is an excellent example of the manorial residence of local mesne lords, the product of sub-infeudation, several of whom gave their name, as in this instance, to the place. Other obvious examples are at North Ingleby (Saxilby with Ingleby (2)) and at Rand (1). It is these people and their like who were evidently responsible for some of the 12th-century creation of planned settlements (see above). At Stow it is just possible that Giraldus Cambrensis saw the moat in 1186 while the one at Willoughton (2) is also likely to be of the same period. The moated site at Kingerby

(Osgodby (3)) is perhaps of the 13th century, remodelled from an earlier castle. The site at South Kelsey (4) may date from the early 14th century when its associated land, formerly belonging to the alien priory of Winghale (South Kelsey (1)), was being worked by Crown tenants. On the other hand it is perhaps more likely to be a 15th or even early 16th-century creation by the Hansards following marriage into the county families of Monson and Ayscough. The large moat at Kettleby (Bigby (1)) may be an early 15th-century creation, the work of the Tyrwhitts and associated with their clearance of the earlier village.

Three sites actually overlie earlier settlement remains, destroyed by the construction of the moat, or already abandoned. Bleasby (Legsby (2)) [27] may thus date from the 14th century, South Ingleby (Saxilby with Ingleby (3)) from the early 13th century and Coates (Stow (7)) from the late 12th century. The moated site at Bardney (5) is said to have been newly built in the early 15th century and the field evidence which indicates that it lies on earlier arable land might help to support this late date.

49

[38] *North Kelsey (2) from the NW, 21 January 1967. These fishponds, though now much altered, were once part of the appurtenances of the grange here which belonged to North Ormsby Priory. The earthworks just visible to the N (left) of the modern farm buildings are houses and garden plots probably laid out on pre-existing arable land in the early 13th century. (Cambridge University Collection: copyright reserved)*

Some moated sites retain buildings within them though many are now abandoned. The date of abandonment is usually unknown and indeed can often be seen as a long-drawn-out process. The site at Lea (2) lost its manorial function as early as the 14th century but it remained as an occupied site until the 17th century.

At least three moats are known to have been adapted to form parts of elaborate post-medieval gardens (see below) associated with 16th or 17th-century residences: Kettleby (Bigby (1)), Goltho (2) and South Kelsey (4). The site at Harpswell (2) if indeed it was originally a moat, was transformed into a garden feature, perhaps in the 16th or 17th century. A number of other alleged moats, almost all now either destroyed or severely damaged, also appear to have been the sites of post-medieval formal gardens. That at the deserted village of Reasby (Stainton by Langworth (2)) could either be the moated grange of a holding of Barlings Abbey, or a later post-medieval garden adapting older features. The moat-like remains at Snarford (2), also now destroyed but clearly overlying ridge-and-furrow, were probably entirely gardens as were those at Fulnetby (1) and Cammeringham (1).

Fishponds

Large numbers of fishponds are listed in the Inventory, and these well illustrate the wide variety of size, form and complexity that has been noted elsewhere. They range from large complexes of ponds at monastic sites such as Bardney (3), Sixhills (1), Heynings (Knaith (1)), Stainfield (1), Orford (Stainton le Vale (3)) and Winghale (South Kelsey (1)) to relatively simple ponds as at Willoughton (1). Many are merely adjuncts to manorial complexes as at Rand (1) and North Ingleby (Saxilby with Ingleby (2)) and are of fairly simple forms, presumably supplying little more than the manorial requirements. Others, including the large monastic fishponds, and also the smaller but equally complex sets of ponds at many monastic holdings such as Willoughton (2) and North Kelsey (2) [38] seem to imply fish-farming on a commercial scale, though those at Stow (3) are likely to have been necessary for the regular visits there by the bishops of Lincoln.

Most surviving arrangements of ponds still retain evidence of inlet, outlet and avoidance channels, though it is not always possible, following later alterations and destruction, to understand fully how they functioned. Certainly in some cases very elaborate systems of water control were constructed as at Cherry Willingham (2) and Welton (4). Occasionally the work involved the diversion of major streams as at Orford (Stainton le Vale (3)).

Many fishponds have evidence of multiple uses and indeed in some cases it is difficult to determine the primary function of ponds which also acted as reservoirs for water-mills. The line of undoubted fishponds at Firsby (West Firsby (1)) includes one which may have been a mill pond, while those at East Torrington (Legsby (5)) and Buslingthorpe (3) were also probably mill ponds. In other cases fishponds and mill ponds form part of the same complex of water management. The fishponds at West Rasen (1) can only have been operated when the leat to the manorial water-mill was functioning.

Islands within both fish and mill ponds, already noted elsewhere (RCHME 1979, lix) have been recognized in West Lindsey too, at Caistor (6), East Torrington (Legsby (5)), Stainfield (1), Welton (4) and West Firsby (1). Their purpose, for the breeding and protection of wild fowl, now seems certain, although no documentary proof has been forthcoming. Indeed little documentation has been found for fishponds in West Lindsey. Moated sites were also perhaps used as fishponds and at Osgodby (1) and Willoughton (1) ponds form part of the moated arrangements.

Water-mills and Windmills

The Commission has recorded a large number of sites of former wind and water-mills of probable medieval date. The former existence of more recent structures of this type can be ascertained from estate, Tithe, Enclosure and early OS maps. The Inventory contains only a small selection of the many sites.

Most of the water-mills recorded are associated with manorial sites, as at Firsby (West Firsby (1)) and East Torrington (Legsby (5)). This relationship reflects their importance in the manorial control of such sites. In physical terms most are relatively simple, consisting of rectangular or triangular ponds set across or to one side of streams with large dams to retain the water. As with fishponds, avoidance channels and leats survive, for example, at Buslingthorpe (3). Again, as with fishponds, evidence of other uses has been noted, including the island in the pond at East Torrington (Legsby (5)).

Only a handful of windmill mounds are listed. Most are simple circular mounds as at Brocklesby (7), Burton (4), West Rasen (2) [39] and Legsby (9). The latter two in particular are so large that they have been repeatedly misinterpreted as other categories of monument, even as mottes. Those at Scothern (2) and Brocklesby (7) overlie ridge-and-furrow.

[39] *West Rasen (2). A post-mill survived on this mound until the early 19th century, though it is likely that it was the site of a medieval windmill whose creation led to the alteration to the adjacent field system.*

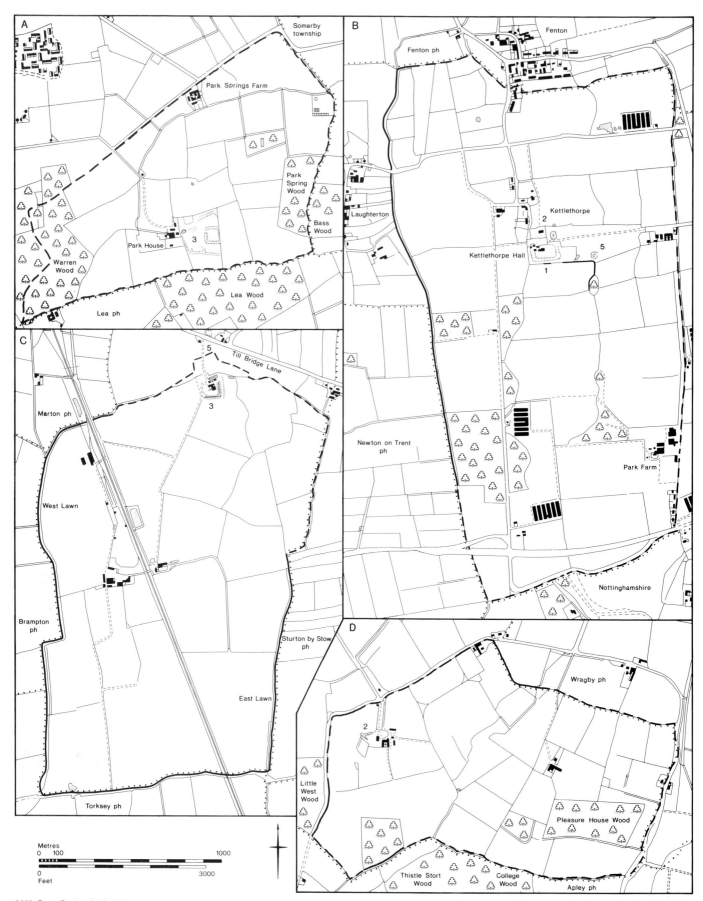

A

Somerby township

Park Springs Farm

Park Spring Wood

Bass Wood

Park House   3

Warren Wood

Lea Wood

Lea ph

B

Fenton

Fenton ph

Kettlethorpe

2

Laughterton

Kettlethorpe Hall   5

1

Newton on Trent ph

Park Farm

Nottinghamshire

C

5

Till Bridge Lane

Marton ph

3

West Lawn

Brampton ph

Sturton by Stow ph

East Lawn

Torksey ph

D

Wragby ph

2

Little West Wood

Pleasure House Wood

Thistle Stort Wood

College Wood

Apley ph

Metres
0   100   1000

0   3000
Feet

[40] *Deer Parks.* **A.** *Gainsborough (4).* **B.** *Kettlethorpe (4).* **C.** *Stow (4).* **D.** *Goltho (3).*

52

[41] *Gainsborough (4). The roughly wedge-shaped block of fields, lying in the SE corner of Gainsborough parish and shown on this estate map of 1795, is the medieval deer park perhaps referred to in the 13th century. (PRO)*

Deer Parks [40]

As elsewhere over much of England, medieval deer parks were common in West Lindsey, though most are located either on heavy clayland or generally poor soils which in medieval times were largely wooded. The low-lying western clay vale, parallel to the River Trent, is one such area in which a number of parks were situated.

The parks at Gainsborough (4) [41], Kettlethorpe (4), Stow (4), Goltho (3) and North Ingleby (Saxilby with Ingleby (2)) are described in the Inventory, but others whose exact location or precise bounds are not known have been omitted. These include Knaith (4), Thonock (2) and Kettleby (Bigby (2)). All these parks were probably once bounded by large banks, though later activities have in general reduced or destroyed them except for the massive E and W boundary banks of Stow park (4) and the similar NW boundary of

Kettlethorpe park (4) known as the Sallie Bank. Otherwise these park pales are now most frequently visible only as continuous boundaries associated with 'park' names.

The park at Stow (4) is notable not only for its size but also for its association with the moated bishop's palace there (Stow (3)). The parks at Glentworth (4) and Gainsborough (4) have moated lodges within them and the early park at Bullington (4) may also have done so. That at Kettlethorpe (4) is unusual in that it encompasses the supposed site of the village of Kettlethorpe and its moated manor. It may have been the hunting park attached to the residence of the Swynford family.

There are also a number of 16th or 17th-century deer parks, usually associated with county families resident in adjacent country houses, as at Knaith (3) and South Kelsey (6). Somerby in Corringham (10), Kettleby (Bigby (2)) and Glentworth (4) as documented are also in this post-medieval category.

[**42**] *Harpswell (2) from the SE. Though damaged by the modern farm buildings this prospect mound of late 16th or early 17th-century date still retains part of its spiral pathway leading to the summit. It originally lay in the corner of a formal garden. The mound was still used in the 18th century when it had a Gothick summer-house (see [**79**]).*

Garden Remains

The Commission's survey of West Lindsey has led to the discovery of a large number of abandoned gardens of various dates, now preserved as earthworks. These confirm the conclusion reached in Northamptonshire (RCHME 1979, lxiv) that such earthworks are extremely common, though perhaps still not fully understood. They are thus in serious danger of being destroyed without recognition.

The earliest noted, and certainly the most remarkable, are the gardens at the Bishop of Lincoln's palace at Nettleham (1). There not only does the layout of terraces and paths survive, but both historical and archaeological evidence suggest a mid 14th-century date for their construction. As such the site appears to be the earliest dated post-Roman garden yet known in England. No other medieval gardens have been found in the area and though the moated enclosure at Linwood (1) has been suggested as a possible garden there is no definite evidence for this theory. Though not perhaps strictly a garden the remarkable arrangement of fishponds associated with the moated bishop's palace at Stow (3) was certainly laid out for aesthetic reasons as well as for purely functional ones. It may be as early as the late 12th century in date. It is only one example of a growing number of medieval sites recently recognized all over England as being areas of land deliberately modified to enhance their visual appearance.

All the other gardens recorded in the Inventory are of post-medieval date, the majority of the 16th or 17th century. They all exhibit many of the features associated with gardens of that period such as terraced walks, canals and prospect mounds. They appear to have been laid out by prominent county families to go with new or rebuilt contemporary residences. Their survival as earthworks is either because the associated houses were abandoned by their owners, often after a very short period of time, or because they were incorporated into later landscaped parks.

The gardens on the site of Barlings Abbey (2) were laid out about 1623 by Sir Christopher Wray to go with his new house there and were abandoned soon after 1660, on the death of his widow, when the house was also left derelict. The same situation pertains at Nun Cotham (Brocklesby (2)), Orford (Stainton le Vale (4)) and probably Reasby (Stainton by Langworth (2)). At Somerby (2) the gardens of the Rossiter family, probably laid out in the late 16th or early 17th century were abandoned and incorporated into parkland in the 18th century as were the former gardens at Greetwell (2).

Sometimes the emparking itself led to the partial destruction of earlier garden remains with the result that it is extremely difficult to recognize them now. This is true at Somerby (2) and Knaith (3). At North Carlton (4) only fragments now remain.

In recent years a number of garden sites have been largely or totally destroyed by modern agriculture, including those at Scampton (2), Goltho (2), Glentworth (5) and Stainfield (3). The latter was a particularly tragic loss as the garden remains formed part of an almost unique piece of landscape development. Even so, occasionally this later destruction can produce information. The site at Knaith has revealed evidence that the former garden terraces were revetted in brick, a feature not visible in the surviving earthworks elsewhere.

Well-preserved layouts vary in elaboration from the cruciform plan at Claxby (2) to the simple arrangement of Stainton le Vale (4). The majority of the garden remains appear to be of one period and were abandoned before any major change in garden fashion led to their alteration. They thus give a valuable insight into the arrangement of gardens at various times. Those at Croxby (Thoresway (4)) are a particularly good example of this, for not only is the site extremely well preserved, but it also had a very short life, perhaps less than twenty years (1688–1702). The same applies to the gardens at Barlings (2) and Greetwell (2). Some sites show the development of garden design over a longer period with considerable alteration and adaptation. At Stainfield (3) the original gardens, probably of 1611, were replaced by a semi-formal emparking layout in a different position in 1707–11 so that both arrangements survived intact until recent destruction.

On the other hand the late 16th or early 17th-century gardens at Harpswell (2) [79, 80] were merely updated by the addition of a formal park around 1700 and then incorporated into a fully landscaped parkland, including a serpentine lake, in the mid 18th century.

Most of the gardens recorded appear to have been laid out on empty sites, though some show evidence of much earlier land-use. The Greetwell gardens overlie part of the deserted village there, while at Stainfield part of the early garden cuts through both ridge-and-furrow and a former hollow-way of the neighbouring deserted village. Three sites, however, appear to be medieval moats to which elaborate gardens were added in the 16th or 17th centuries: Goltho (2), Kettleby (Bigby (1)) [53] and South Kelsey (4). The latter also includes a contemporary brick 'summer-house' or gazebo. Some alleged moats are more likely to have been gardens but as they have been destroyed this cannot be demonstrated conclusively. Cammeringham (1) and Fulnetby (1) are examples of this.

All these 16th and 17th-century gardens included features typical of their date. Prospect mounds survive at Harpswell (2) [42], North Carlton (4), Claxby (2) and Burton (2), while elaborate terraces exist at Croxby (Thoresway (4)) and Stainfield (3), and a fine sunken garden is the main feature at Harpswell (2). Ponds and canals of various forms have been noted at Barlings (2) where they may be reused monastic fishponds, Croxby (Thoresway (4)), Grasby (3) and especially Claxby (2) and Kettleby (Bigby (1)). Architectural fragments remain at Scampton (2) and Harpswell (2).

The best post-medieval garden is at Croxby (Thoresway (4)), not only because of its fine state of preservation, but also because of the complexity of its layout with terraces, canals, moats and a cascade. In addition traces of the external leats have been recognized.

Post-medieval and Undated Earthworks

A selection of post-medieval earthworks of various types has been recorded by the Commission. They include two possible 17th-century Civil War fortifications at South Kelsey (5) and Kettlethorpe (5), as well as a tree ring (Legsby (10)) previously given a spurious antiquity. Two abandoned post-medieval farmsteads, Claxby (3) and Nettleton (5), are listed. Both illustrate the continuing transitory nature of settlement in West Lindsey. The abandoned Caistor Canal (Caistor (7)) has been noted and duck decoy ponds are recorded at Burton (5) and South Carlton (4) [43]

Amongst the still undated monuments recorded are the enclosure at Newball (3) and the site at Legsby (8), perhaps a medieval chapel. The gypsum quarries at Gainsborough (5) are documented as early as 1307 though the date of the present 'hills and holes' is perhaps much later. Many other landscape features of post-medieval and early modern date, intrinsically or cumulatively interesting, from the commonplace of numerous abandoned brickpits to the exotic of a hare park on the limestone upland of the Monsons' estate at South Carlton, have been noted in passing but not catalogued in detail.

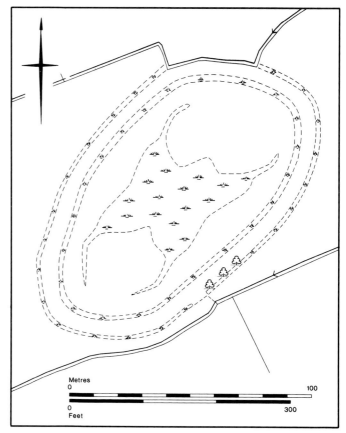

[43] South Carlton (4). Duck decoy as depicted on OS 25 in plan of 1885. The decoy was in existence by 1720, but was abandoned in the early 19th century. It was presumably constructed in the 17th century by the Monson family.

55

Conclusions

The Commission's work on the medieval and later earthworks of West Lindsey has, it is believed, shed new light on many aspects of settlement and land-use. Yet perhaps the most significant result is the importance of change in the landscape that has been revealed. Most of the sites described in the Inventory exhibit either in their physical form or from their documented history complex alterations of size, layout or function. The actual details may still be lost and some are perhaps irrecoverable, but the overall picture, of continuous and often profound change, is almost always apparent. This is nowhere better exhibited than at Stainfield (2) [24] where earthworks, crop and soil-marks, standing buildings and documents all combine to reveal a long history of landscape development from the 11th to the 20th centuries. The almost total destruction of the earthworks at Stainfield since the Commission's survey also illustrates the fragile nature of the material evidence and the continued threats to its existence.

Both the threat to and the fragility of the archaeological record is further illustrated by an analysis of the extent of damage and destruction noted over the last forty years or so, mainly as a result of the ploughing up of old pasture for arable or improved grassland. The Commission has recorded 260 sites in West Lindsey which are known to have comprised upstanding earthworks in 1946. Of these at least seventy-four have now been totally destroyed and a further fifty-nine have been extensively damaged or partly destroyed. Thus just over half of all the upstanding medieval and later archaeological sites in West Lindsey have been completely or partly lost in the last four decades. This is likely to be a conservative figure for it has not been possible to check the state of every site in recent years.

No one period during which most damage took place stands out. Only at 83 sites out of 133 is the date of mutilation or obliteration exactly or approximately known. At twenty of these the damage occurred between 1946 and 1960, though this may be a serious underestimate. Between 1961 and 1970 a further twenty-three sites were damaged or destroyed, between 1971 and 1980 fourteen sites and between 1981 and 1988 another twenty-seven.

The losses of the last seven years were ascertained by a rapid programme of site visits to check the state of the earthworks recorded by measured survey during the Commission's project; this was carried out in the last week of July 1988. The prime agency for destruction in the study area is agricultural land-use change, through ploughing up old pasture for arable or improved grassland [44, 45, 104]. This continues a trend evident since the last war. Of eighty-six sites revisited, six had suffered total or near total destruction, while a further twelve had been substantially damaged. All these were serious losses. Stainfield is a prime case, but in other instances too it is precisely that which made the remains distinctive that has been removed or degraded – the property block at the E end of Cabourne (1) here

[44] *Thorganby (1). The deserted village taken 21 September 1946 before its destruction. Almost every detail of the former earthworks is visible in this air photograph. (RAF)*

interpreted as a monastic demesne farm, the outer ring of closes at Kettleby moat (Bigby (1)), the separate settlement element in Riby park (1), the spread of settlement remains that linked the villages of North and South Ingleby (Saxilby with Ingleby (2, 3)) and the anomalous earthworks at the E end of Kingerby (Osgodby (4)). Elsewhere, at Croxby (Thoresway (3)), Stainton le Vale (1) and Swallow (1) the recent destruction of large areas of earthworks within very extensive villages remains has produced situations mirroring that at Thoresway (1), where any assessment of the development of the settlement is rendered difficult if not impossible because of similar earlier destruction. Only at Osgodby (2) and to a lesser extent Stainton le Vale is village infilling, directly or indirectly, the destructive force. It may be more commonplace as a threat than this selective fieldwork programme indicates, as the destruction noted in the list of sites investigated and in the archive, at Bardney (6) and Glentham (1), for example, illustrates. Finally, peripheral damage, in some instances marginal, though sufficient to cause concern had the sites been scheduled as Ancient Monuments, was noted in a further nine cases.

An additional potential threat noted but not quantified is that to standing buildings associated with or relevant to the archaeological sites. For example, Manor Farm at Firsby (West Firsby (1)) had been demolished without any check as to whether its 19th-century fabric contained any remains of its medieval manorial predecessor. Equally relevantly, NW Lincolnshire has a large number of already or potentially redundant rural churches, and the results of even small-scale excavations at Rand and Goltho churches show their special relevance to the understanding of associated settlement remains.

These losses to the heritage, which are probably representative of East Lindsey, Kesteven and South Humberside too, require direct and urgent action by agencies responsible for record and preservation. In simple terms, all but the most minor and insignificant surviving earthworks in West Lindsey warrant protection. Specifically, this should be extended at least to the following sites recommended by the Commissioners as most worthy of preservation:

[45] *Thorganby (1) from the S, 25 March 1966. The deserted village after destruction. Not only have the earthworks been utterly flattened but it is now difficult to interpret clearly the resulting soil-marks. (Cambridge University Collection: copyright reserved)*

Sites Most Worthy of Preservation

Apley
(1) Settlement Remains

Bardney
(2) Site of Benedictine Abbey
(3) Fishponds
(5) Moated Site at Southrey

Barlings
(1) Site of Premonstratensian Abbey
(2) Remains of post-medieval House and Gardens
(3) Enclosure

Bigby
(1) Moated Site, Garden Remains, Fishponds and Paddocks at Kettleby
(6) Site of Lime-kiln

Blyborough
(1) Settlement Remains
(3) Mill Dam

Brattleby
(1) Settlement Remains

Brocklesby
(1) Site of Premonstratensian Abbey of Newsham
(2) Site of Cistercian Priory of Nun Cotham with post-medieval House and Gardens

Broxholme
(1) Settlement Remains

Bullington
(3) Enclosure

Burton
(1) Settlement Remains
(2) Post-medieval Garden Remains and Park

Buslingthorpe
(1) Moated Site
(2) Deserted Village of Buslingthorpe
(3) Pond

Cabourne
(1) Settlement Remains

Caenby
(1) Settlement Remains, Moated Site and Ponds

Caistor
(4) Settlement Remains of Audleby
(6) Fishponds

Cammeringham
(1) Site of Alien Priory and post-medieval Garden Remains

Cherry Willingham
(2) Fishponds

Claxby
(1) Settlement Remains
(2) Garden Remains
(3) Deserted Farmstead

Cold Hanworth
(1) Deserted Village of Cold Hanworth

Friesthorpe
(1) Settlement Remains

Gainsborough
(5) Gypsum Quarries

Gate Burton
(1) Settlement Remains

Grange de Lings
(1) Monastic Grange

Great Limber
(1) House Site
(2) Settlement Remains

Greetwell
(1) Deserted Village of Greetwell
(2) Garden Remains

Hackthorn
(1) Site of Monastic Grange and Settlement Remains

Heapham
(1) Moated Site and Settlement Remains

Hemswell
(1) Site of Church

Kettlethorpe
(1) Moated Site
(4) Deer Park
(5) Enclosure

Knaith
(1) Site of Cistercian Priory of Heynings
(2) Settlement Remains

Lea
(2) Moated Site
(3) Moated Site

Legsby
(1) Moated Site at Bleasby
(2) Deserted Village of Bleasby
(3) Deserted Settlement of *Coldecotes*
(9) Windmill Mound

Linwood
(2) Settlement Remains

Nettleham
(1) Site of Bishop's Palace

Nettleton
(5) Deserted Farmstead

Newball
(3) Enclosure

Normanby le Wold
(1) Settlement Remains

North Carlton
(1) Settlement Remains
(3) Monastic Grange and Rabbit Warren
(4) Garden Remains

North Kelsey
(2) Fishponds and Settlement Remains

Northorpe
(1) Deserted Village of Southorpe

Osgodby
(1) Moated Site
(3) Moated Manor and Castle Site
(4) Deserted Village of Kingerby

Pilham
(2) Deserted Village of Gilby

Rand
(1) Moated Site
(2) Deserted Village of Rand

Riseholme
(1) Deserted Village of Riseholme
(2) Monastic Grange

Saxilby with Ingleby
(2) Moated Site and Deserted Village of North Ingleby
(3) Moated Site and Deserted Village of South Ingleby

Sixhills
(1) Site of Gilbertine Priory

Somerby
(1) Deserted Village of Somerby
(2) Garden Remains

South Carlton
(1) Monastic Grange
(2) Manorial Enclosure and Fishponds
(3) Settlement Remains

South Kelsey
(1) Site of Alien Priory
(4) Moated Site
(5) Enclosure and Platform

Spridlington
(1) Settlement Remains

Stainfield
(1) Site of Benedictine Priory

Stainton le Vale
(1) Settlement Remains

(2) Deserted Village of Orford
(3) Site of Premonstratensian Priory
(4) Garden Remains

Stow
(3) Moated Site of Bishop's Palace
(5) Deserted Settlement of Stow Park
(7) Deserted Village of Coates

Swallow
(1) Moated Site and Settlement Remains

Tealby
(3) Moated Site

Thonock
(1) Ring and Baileys

Thoresway
(1) Settlement Remains
(2) Monastic Grange
(3) Deserted Village of Croxby
(4) Garden Remains

Thorpe in the Fallows
(1) Deserted Village of Thorpe

Toft Newton
(3) Settlement Remains

Walesby
(1) Settlement Remains
(2) Deserted Settlement of Risby
(3) Deserted Settlement of Otby

Welton
(4) Fishponds

West Firsby
(1) Deserted Village of Firsby

West Rasen
(1) Settlement Remains
(2) Windmill Mound

Willoughton
(1) Moated Site
(2) Site of Preceptory of the Knights Templars and Hospitallers

A SELECT INVENTORY
OF MEDIEVAL AND LATER
ARCHAEOLOGICAL SITES IN WEST LINDSEY

‖‖‖‖‖‖	Surveyed earthworks		⬭	Water
⅃⅃⅃⅃⅃⅃⅃	Surveyed earthworks (OS recording)		⟫⟶	Stream + direction
▨▨	Archaeological detail transcribed from air photographs		⌐⌐	Drain + direction
▨	Building		○	Spring
⌐‑‑‑⌐	Site of former building		◉	Well
⹀ ⹀ ⹀ ⹀	Road/track/path			Marsh
‑ ‑ ‑ ‑ ‑	Course of former road/stream		♧ ♧	Woodland/tree planting
— —	Deer park boundary			Former woodland
· · · · · · ·	Parish/township boundary			Pottery scatter
	Ridge-and-furrow (centre of ridges)			Dumping
──	Walled garden			Slumping
‑ · ⌒	Contours in metres			Quarry

[46] *Key to the drawings in the Select Inventory.*

Metres
0   100   200

0   600
Feet

[47] *Apley (1) Settlement Remains.*

APLEY

(1) Settlement Remains (TF 108751) [47], formerly part of the village of Apley, lie on a low plateau of Boulder Clay between two streams at approximately 15 m above OD. The documentary history of this settlement is difficult to disentangle for, after being separately recorded in Domesday Book and the Lindsey Survey, it became part of the core of the estates of Stainfield Priory. This suggests that it may once have been a relatively small hamlet which was subsequently converted to or run as a monastic grange. Such a status would explain its continuing small size. It appears with Kingthorpe (2), a hamlet in the parish, as subsidiary to Stainfield in the *Nomina Villarum* and thereafter both evidently formed the un-named *membra* of Stainfield in the 14th and 15th-century subsidies. For a group of three settlements, they already in the early 14th century had numbers of taxpayers far below what might be expected of villages in this area, and reliefs in the 15th century are persistently high even on this low base level. The 63 persons over 14 years recorded in 1377 and the minimum of 10 households in 1428 must include Kingthorpe; the contribution of 5 persons to the Lindsey Musters in 1539 compares with Stainfield's 16; the 14 taxpayers in 1542–3, 9 households in the diocesan survey of 1563 and 8 and 9 families in 1703–23, continue a similar story.

An important factor behind Apley's continued small size may have been the early enclosure of the adjacent Stainfield, perhaps by the Tyrwhitts as successors to the priory, or even earlier by the priory in connection with their sheep flocks. A hint of the role of Apley may be contained in the term Apley Grange used in the grant of Stainfield Priory and its lands to Sir Robert Tyrwhitt in 1538, though no grange is listed in 1535. The marked population rise from the early 18th to early 19th centuries may owe as much to the removal of the Tyrwhitts' control through the failure of the direct line in 1760, and the opportunities for roadside squatter occupation, as to the general contemporary agricultural trend.[1]

No church is mentioned in Domesday Book, but institutions are recorded from the early 13th century onwards. The last institution of a priest recorded in the bishops' registers is in 1431, but in 1519 the visitation recorded 'omnia bene' and presumably there was no actual break before institutions were again regularly recorded from the Reformation onwards, with the important change that the living had become a curacy invariably held with Stainfield and presented to by the Tyrwhitt family.[2]

The church building, too, certainly survived the medieval period, being still fit for services at the start of the 18th century. By 1816 it had been replaced by a 'brick shed',[3] and this in turn was replaced in 1871 by the present St Andrew's church.[4]

Evidence for former settlement exists both as earthworks characteristic of a clayland village and as surface pottery scatters. This, combined with post-medieval and recent changes, makes overall interpretation of the plan uncertain. Nevertheless, a main hollow-way ('a'–'b') is flanked along its N side by rectangular closes. On its S side, a quite different pattern of large rectangular ditched closes extends E. The closes are full of ridge-and-furrow except at their N end where in a narrow rectangular block against the hollow-way ridges may overlie earlier occupation, with much modern disturbance to their E. The whole block of closes with their absence of obvious occupation resembles earthworks identified as monastic granges, demesne manors or farms within villages elsewhere in the area: it probably represents Stainfield Priory's documented grange or demesne manor here. The hollow-way is continued to the E by a farm track as far as the site of the medieval church. This is marked by an overgrown mound of irregular oval form ('d'), with many late 18th and 19th-century gravestones *in situ*.

The Tithe Map of 1849[5] confirms that in addition to the surviving N–S farm track ('b'–'c'), a further way ran up the E side of the churchyard ('d'–'e'). Since a spread of medieval and later pottery has been recorded around Apley High House along the N side of the present street, this may suggest an overall layout of two parallel streets linked by cross-lanes. This rectangular form may be an early feature and represent the hamlet of Apley to which the grange was later added.

The field E of the church, *Old Yard* on the Tithe Map, contains slight and irregular earthworks, mainly resulting from buildings and boundaries shown on that map and including a row of cottages. The sinuous ditch ('c'–'f') is shown as a hedge line on the Tithe Map, and the small triangle between it and the modern road to its N was then occupied by three closes with cottages. These, like similar surviving closes on the N side of the road to the W, and others formerly existing along the roads to the S and E, are probably late roadside encroachments.

1. PRO E179/242/113; *Book of Fees* I, 173; *Cal LPFD Hen VIII* XIII pt 1 (1867), 141; *VE* IV, 82.
2. Davis 1914b, 67; Lunt 1926, 240; Thompson 1940, 63; LAO typescript list of incumbents.
3. Foster 1926, 231; Cole 1913, 4; Marrat 1816, 71–2; Harding 1937, 27.
4. White 1872, 500; LAO Consec 279/2.
5. LAO B582.

BARDNEY

(5) Moated Site (TF 134691) [48] lies at approximately 7 m above OD on Boulder Clay on the NW edge of the small low island that gives Southrey its name, and outside the pattern of village properties lying to the SE.

The site is notable for its well-documented specialized function. It was created as a place of retreat for blood-letting and recuperation for the monks of Bardney Abbey – a use reflected in its name of Seney Place.[1] The 15th-century grave-slab of Prior Walter de Langton at Bardney Abbey records that he constructed the site from new 'cum clausura et ponti [bus]'. It was evidently normal for four monks to be in residence at any one time, but their behaviour was the cause of scandalous report in the episcopal visitations of 1437–40, one result of which was the removal of an unmarried woman and her replacement as warden by a man. The site was listed as the 'manerium voc' Seny Place' at the suppression of Bardney Abbey and valued at £4 13s 4d; as the 'grange called Seny Place or Sothery grange', it was granted to Robert Tyrwhitt in 1539. Bardney Glebe Terriers record 'the Hall Farm of Southrow... called Senox (or Seny) place' and the farm of 'Senex Place' in the early 18th century. In 1841, land associated with 'the Hall Farm in Southrey... formerly called Senex Place' extended to 178 acres (74 ha) in a block N and E of the site. Buildings still stood on the southern end of the island in the early to mid 19th century, although the farmhouse had been moved outside to the S; this was replaced later in the century by The Poplars.[2]

The site consists of a rectangular moat with a wet ditch generally 1 m–2 m deep, fed by a stream channel from the N; the S arm has been partly filled by post-Dissolution occupation and partly destroyed by a large pond. The ditch is shown interrupted on the N and on the E on the Enclosure and Tithe Maps of 1840 and

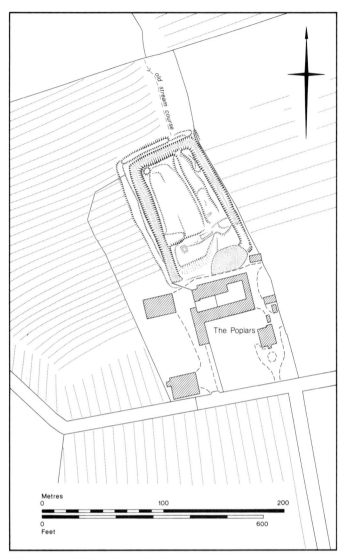

[48] *Bardney (5) Moated Site at Southrey.*

(7) Settlement Remains (TF 130726) [10, 49], formerly the hamlet and monastic grange of Osgodby, lie around the modern Lodge Farm, at about 14 m above OD on Boulder Clay. Osgodby appears to have been one of two hamlets in Bardney which were converted into monastic granges in the 12th century.

The site lies in the NE of the parish in an area which included much managed woodland until this century.[1] The farmland here was divided between the settlements of Osgodby and *Butyate*, both named in Domesday Book. The earthworks of *Butyate* were levelled in 1959 and all but a fragment of those of Osgodby in 1957.[2]

In 1086 Osgodby was sokeland of the manor of Bardney held by Gilbert de Gant. Before 1212 the family of de Gant granted their interest to Bardney Abbey.[3] The abbey subsequently held Osgodby and *Butyate* as part of its home demesne until the Dissolution, and this status resulted in there being little or no reference to them. The minimum recorded population of 16 sokemen at Osgodby in 1086 is the only figure available for this settlement.

The field remains are poor. Only W of the through road does a single pasture field preserve some fragments of earthworks, which comprise ditches defining roughly rectangular closes in part overlying ridge-and-furrow. There are no remains of identifiable buildings or yards, and the closes are not obviously served by a street, unless by the present road – a theory possibly supported by a scatter of medieval pottery along its E side ('a').

To the E of Lodge Farm, on the other side of the present street, evidence from aerial photographs and a scatter of medieval pottery shows that the settlement extended down the slope to a stream. A hollow-way ('b') appears to have entered this area from the S, probably providing a direct link with *Butyate* less than 1 km away. The crop and soil-marks fall into no readily analysable form but some appear to overlie earlier arable.[4]

Overall the remains most resemble those at Swinthorpe, or at Holtham in Legsby, both also monastic farms or granges which took over the sites of earlier settlement. Here, there may have been two nuclei served by separate roads which could perhaps have been only part of a dispersed 11th-century settlement pattern of sokemen, which in effect reasserted itself in the scattered farmsteads of the post-medieval period after a phase of nucleation under monastic influence.

1. OS 1st edn 1 in sheet 83.
2. *Lincs DB* 24/18, 38/10; NAR TF 17 SW 5 and 6.
3. *Book of Fees* I, 173; *Cal Chart R 1226–57* (1903), 147; *1327–41* (1912), 235ff, 238.
4. RAF VAP 3G/TUD/UK197/ptVI/5422-3; 541/445/3279-80, 4255, 4106; APs in NMR.

1841,[3] and the shallowness of the ditch and the shelving of its scarps at these points may reflect early features, perhaps the documented bridges. Much of the E side of the platform, however, is occupied by what appears to have been a long range of buildings, now represented by very substantial foundations up to 1 m high, with some signs of cross-divisions. A low bank survives along the inner scarp on the N and W with a circular mound 0.75 m high at the NW corner. The southern third of the platform is much disturbed, apparently by recent farm activity, including building foundations and a platform. These tally approximately with the positions of buildings shown on the mid 19th-century maps.

A broad low outer bank along the W side served as the headland for ridge-and-furrow to the W. Beyond the moat to the N the ridges of the furlong run on to a headland along the water channel. This suggests that the moat was a late intruder into former arable land, which continued to be ploughed to a shorter length, and corroborates the documentary evidence for the creation of the site.

1. *OED* seyny obs.; Thompson 1914–29 I, 237–8 'minutio'.
2. Brakespear 1922, 65–7; Thompson 1914–29 II, 14, 21, 23, 27–8; Dugdale 1817–30 I, 641; *Cal LPFD Hen VIII* XIV, pt 2 (1895), 299; LAO C187; Lindsey Award 152; OS 1st edn 1 in sheet 83.
3. LAO Lindsey Award 152; C187.

Lodge Farm

a

b

10

old stream course

Metres
0   100   200

0   600
Feet

[49] *Bardney (7) Settlement Remains of Osgodby.*

65

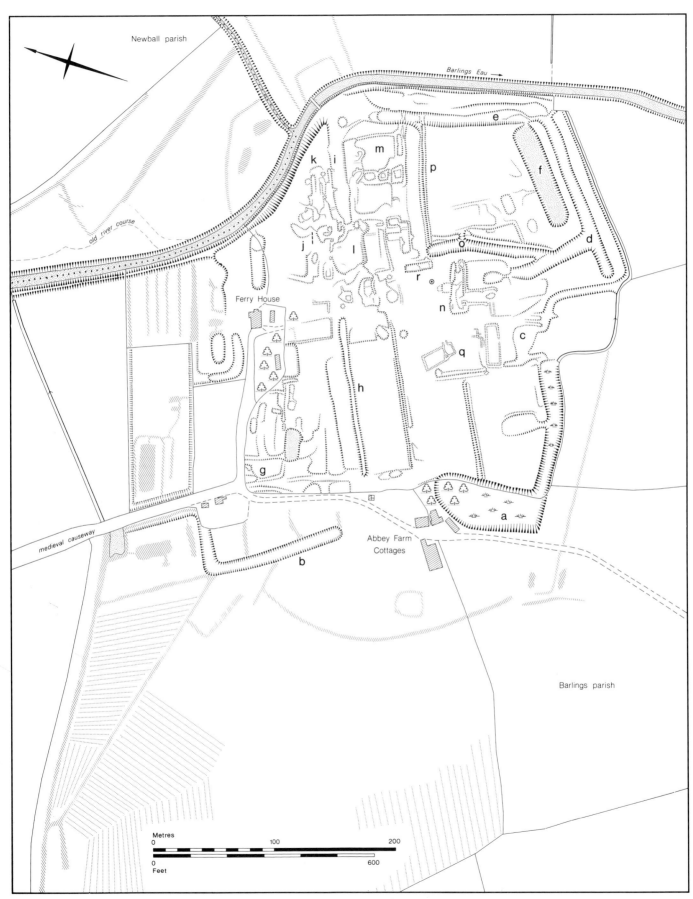

[50] *Barlings (1) Site of Premonstratensian Abbey, (2) Remains of post-medieval House and Gardens.*

Newball parish

Barlings Eau →

old river course

Ferry House

medieval causeway

Abbey Farm
Cottages

Barlings parish

Metres
0   100   200

Feet
0   600

[51] *Barlings (1). This view of Barlings Abbey by W. Millecent in about 1720–30 shows that only the crossing of the church survived, together with what are perhaps fragments of the cloisters. Sir John Tyrwhitt is said to have kept up the tower in the early 18th century, probably as a ready-made landscape feature in the distant view of his park at Stainfield (3) some 2 km to the E. The tower fell in about 1757. (Lincolnshire County Council)*

BARLINGS

(1) Site of Premonstratensian Abbey (TF 089734) [50, 51] is situated on a low island of Till at around 9 m above OD, set amongst peat fen lying at 4 m or less above OD. An earthen causeway, some 900 m long and followed by the modern road to the site, provided the only land link to the higher ground to the N. This causeway is apparently a monastic construction which gave rise to the field-name *Cowsey Garth* of 1538.[1] The name *Oxeney* for the site, frequently used to designate the abbey itself, accurately reflects the topography and perhaps its earlier land-use.

Though only a single field now lies in pasture and knowledge of peripheral features draws heavily on the evidence of air photographs,[2] the remains apparently offer a remarkably complete picture of a monastic establishment within a naturally circumscribed setting. Recognition of the post-medieval reoccupation of the site by a house and gardens (Barlings (2)), however, radically alters the perspective. Any of the earthworks that might previously have been given a monastic interpretation may be, and most probably are, features connected with the reoccupation, if only in adapting and reusing earlier features. Only the quadrant of large stone buildings in the NE corner of the precinct that marks the principal conventual buildings appears unaffected except by use as a quarry for stone and materials.

The abbey was founded in 1154 by Ralf de Haia.[3] It was a daughter house of Newsham, 13 of whose monks formed the initial community. The house was first established on the site described under (3) but was soon moved to Oxney itself.

Ralf de Haia's modest lead as benefactor was followed by a steady stream of others through the later 12th, 13th and 14th centuries, which ensured an unusually sustained growth for the abbey and

allowed the size of the community to be doubled. In 1376 the community numbered the abbot, prior, sub-prior, 25 monks, 5 *conversi* and 8 clerks. Further grants enabled the abbey to remain at this approximate size until the end of its life. It remained a relatively wealthy house and in 1300 was amongst the leading producers of wool for export. It was dissolved in 1537; reversions and rents of its demesne lands were granted to Charles Brandon in 1539.[4]

The remoteness of the location appears to have ensured the fabric of the church remained as a substantial shell for at least 150 years. By the early 18th century it was said that Sir John Tyrwhitt 'keeps up the tower', probably as a ready-made landscape feature in the distant view of his park at Stainfield Hall (Stainfield (3)). By the 1720s topographical drawings show only the crossing tower and abutting walls of the conventual church standing, together with fragments of part of the cloister [51]. The tower fell in about 1757 and by 1795 little more remained there than now.[5]

The island of Oxney is ringed by the line of a drain on the N, W and S and on the E by the Barlings Eau. The straight course of the latter, tight along the E flank of the island, may be in origin a monastic cut or canal. The precinct of the abbey occupied the NE part of the island: the present Abbey Farm lies in the SW part in a field called *Chapel House Close* in 1774.[6] It may occupy the site of, or even encapsulate, a monastic structure.

The precinct itself was bounded by a complex network of interlocked ponds, channels and leats, whose functions and relationships are now only partly intelligible since half lie in arable. The largest pond ('a') is a deep L-shaped water-holding feature set on the highest part of the island. Its function was probably that of a reservoir supplying the water to the S and SE side of the precinct. A second L-shaped feature ('b'), now in arable, may have served the same function from a slightly lower level for the former ponds to the N.

67

On the S a modern drain must perpetuate a by-pass leat from the SE corner of the large pond ('a') to the Barlings Eau. As an alternative water could be drawn through a system of channels via another shallow pond ('c') and probably into a long pond ('d') with a channel rejoining the by-pass leat at its SE corner. A comparable long pond on the E ('e'), shows signs of subdivision by low banks or dams at its N end and a narrowing at the S perhaps provided a point of control. A large rectangular water-filled pond ('f') may be part of this system for it has a sluice-channel at its E end. The whole arrangement ostensibly constitutes a set of monastic fishponds but the way in which the monastic drains must have discharged into them, their awkward arrangement and position adjacent to the post-medieval house mean that in their present form they are likely rather to be part of the post-medieval layout.

In the N the pond ('b') fed water via channels NW and N into the drain ringing the island and it also supplied at least one of the now destroyed rectangular ponds on both sides of the farm track and causeway. It also fed what appears to have been a series of embanked ponds E of the causeway via two parallel E–W channels. A large island, bounded on three sides by ditches, immediately N of Ferry House seems to have carried two pairs of small ponds, elsewhere identified as fish-breeding or sorting tanks. A pond E of the house may have had a similar function. The Barlings Eau generally marks the edge of the precinct on the E, though to its E, in Newball parish, air photographs show what may be a small adjunct to the precinct. Two small ponds are visible as well as traces of an earlier sinuous course of the river and a straight cut or leat. A bank, close to the existing hedge line there, is probably the boundary of the former medieval managed woodland of Newball Park Wood to the NE, which is now totally cleared.

The site was approached by land in medieval times, as now, along the artificial causeway from the N, to enter the precinct at the NW corner, presumably through a gatehouse. A mound of stone rubble with wall foundations ('g'), through which passes a hollowed way continuing the line of the causeway, probably marks part of the gatehouse complex. The hollow-way continues S and then perhaps turns E past an area divided by long low stone wall foundations ('h'). However, both the entrance gateway and the stone wall foundations may be part of the post-Dissolution layout.

There may also have been access from the E by ferry across the Barlings Eau and certainly water-borne traffic could reach the site along the river. Both must have needed a riverside landing place but the present broad depression ('i') apparently connected to the river, probably results at least in part from an E–W post-medieval track, shown on the estate map of 1774, that also cut across the adjacent claustral range.[7]

The conventual buildings occupied merely the NE quadrant of the precinct. The only surviving masonry fragment is the E bay of the N arcade of the nave of the church and part of the NW pier of the crossing ('j'). This, together with the evidence from early observers and from topographical drawings indicates that the very disturbed elongated range of earthworks running E–W at this point is the broad outline of the church. These earthworks suggest an exceptionally long narrow chancel ('k') matching the nave in length. Numerous moulded and decorated architectural fragments, probably from the conventual church, are to be found in buildings and gardens at Low Barlings and in Langworth. To the S of the presumed nave a roughly rectangular open area ('l') marks the cloister. Foundations on the S side indicate an E–W frater and irregularities at its W end might mark an attached kitchen or guest lodgings. Further S are the remains of another group of buildings

which may have included the reredorter at the S end of the dorter range. To the E of the cloister are two further former garths or gardens ('m') surrounded by traces of former buildings. These are perhaps the infirmary and, less likely, the abbot's lodgings.

1. *Cal LPFD Hen VIII* XIII pt 1 (1892), 326.
2. RAF VAP 541/185/4117-9; CUAC BAB 16, BKX 84; APs in NMR.
3. VCH *Lincs* II (1906), 202–5; Colvin 1951, 70–7; Knowles and Hadcock 1971, 185.
4. *Cal Pat R 1350–4* (1907), 214, 305; *1381–5* (1897), 242; Owen 1971, 66–7, 144; *Cal LPFD Hen VIII* XIII pt 1 (1892), 326; XIV pt 1 (1894), 260.
5. BL Add MS 5827, f209*v*; LCL Ross MSS XII, Lawress p 32; LCL Torrington MS notebooks; LCL Banks Collection I, 65; Andrews 1934–6 II, 350; Marrat 1816, 53; White 1842, 456; White 1979.
6. LAO PAD 2/25.
7. LAO PAD 2/25; 3 BNL 25.

(2) Remains of post-medieval House and Gardens (TF 089734) [50] lie within the precinct of Barlings Abbey and immediately S of the remains of the abbey buildings.

By the early 17th century, the site was acquired by the Wray family of Glentworth and Sir Christopher Wray created a residence there for his wife Albinia whom he married in 1623. After Sir Christopher's death in 1646 Lady Albinia continued to live at Barlings until her death in 1660. The house was probably abandoned soon afterwards and in 1672 Sir Christopher's son Edward sold 'the scite of the dissolved monastery of Barlings and capitall messuage there'. The land at Barlings passed through a number of hands before coming to the Tyrwhitts of Stainfield in the early 18th century.[1]

A drawing of the abbey in about 1730 by Millecent shows the Wray's house in a state of dereliction, but it is possible to establish that it was an L-shaped building of at least two storeys, with mullioned windows, an octagonal tower on the NW corner, and a canopied doorway in the centre of the N side.[2]

The surviving earthworks comprise the stone-foundationed walls of a large building of L-shaped plan ('n'). The details are obscured by mounds of stone rubble except that a low square projection in the N side may be the base of steps leading to the entrance.

Whether this house was newly built in 1623 or whether it was created out of an existing monastic structure, such as a guest house, is unknown. The octagonal turret shown on the 1730 drawing might suggest a date earlier than the early 17th century.

To the S and SE of the remains of the house, scarps and shallow ditches appear to form a complementary pattern of yards and closes and a broad deep channel or pond runs S to the peripheral chain of ponds ('d'). A second channel or pond ('o'), heavily banked on its E side and forming a branch to the other pond, appears to cut through a network of shallow ditches to its E but all may be merely part of an elaborate water garden contemporary with the house and whose N side may have been formed by a bank and ditch ('p').

To what extent the creation of this garden, which must have occupied most of the land within the former monastic precinct to the E of the house, also involved the modification of all or part of these ponds is unclear. The canal-like appearance of them all ('d', 'e', 'f') certainly suggests such a modification.

The foundation walls of two other very large buildings to the W of the site of the house have the dimensions of barns ('q'), and that to the N seems to have had a threshing porch at the S end of its E side. The whole group of earthworks, probably including a well ('r'), is spaced around a yard or forecourt entered from the NW.

To the W and NW of the house site and garden remains, the area within the monastic precinct is divided into a series of rectangular closes by stone rubble banks and shallow ditches ('h'). These may have been created in the early 17th century as part of the adjuncts to the house or they may be medieval in origin and adapted to the later arrangements.

1. Dalton 1880 I, 220–58, II, 83–4 and Appendix, 16, 21; Maddison 1902–6 IV, 1322–6; LAO FL Deeds 464, 914, 920, 958, 994; LCL Ross MSS XII, Lawress, 30–1; BL Add MS 5827, f209v.
2. White 1979.

(3) Enclosures (TF 080743) [52] on the site of the initial foundation of Barlings Abbey, a medieval monastic grange and a post-medieval house, lie immediately N of Barlings House. They are situated on Till, on land sloping gently S between 10 m and 5 m above OD at the N end of the artificial causeway leading to Barlings Abbey.

A note attached to a 13th-century Barlings charter records that 'the Abbey of Barlings is now situated in the said place of Oxeney, and the place where it was first founded is now called Barlings Grange'.[1] Abbot Matthew Mackerel's account of his part in the Lincolnshire Rising of 1536 recalls how he was met and coerced by horsemen 'in the way from Barlings Monastery to Barlings Grange' and forced to turn back[2] – a description that fits well with the causewayed access road, and suggests that this site was indeed that of Barlings Grange.

The grange continued as a secular residence after the Dissolution, at least until the second half of the 17th century. Indeed, since the will of 'John Wray of Barlings Grange' was proved in 1587–90, it seems likely that it survived as the Wrays' residence from their acquisition of the former monastic estate until the construction of their mansion on the abbey site itself, perhaps around 1623.[3] The farmhouse known as Barlings House, now a derelict 19th-century structure which overlies ridge-and-furrow, was certainly on the site S of the earthworks by 1824 and may be a direct replacement of the earlier house.[4]

The earthworks now survive in a small triangle of pasture and their former extent can only be ascertained by details recorded on early OS plans and on air photographs.[5] Additional difficulties of interpretation are caused by the continued occupation of the site, and by the trackway cutting across its NE side. This track may well have cut off the NE corner of an originally rectangular arrangement of closes and distorted the ditch system along the E side of the surviving earthworks, especially notable at the curiously clipped corner of enclosure ('a'). The track certainly existed on its present alignment in 1824 and may have been created when the site was still occupied for the ditches alongside it appear to have been adapted to continue functioning. The large pond ('b') is a recent drinking pond for cattle.

Despite these apparent later distortions and alterations, it seems likely that the medieval form of the site was of a large rectangular ditched enclosure, subdivided into closes and thus resembling the clayland monastic granges such as Collow (Legsby (4)). The S limit of the enclosure may have been a ditch ('c'), beyond which lay broad ridge-and-furrow. The large and well-defined inner close in the NW corner ('a'), may possibly have been the principal occupation area in this phase, but there is no surface trace of any major buildings within it and there seems to have been no provision for dams against the slope to hold standing water within its ditches. A quantity of medieval pottery, mainly from glazed jugs, was recovered from a limited area in the ploughed SW part of the closes during fieldwork. The water channel that dog-legs in three steps

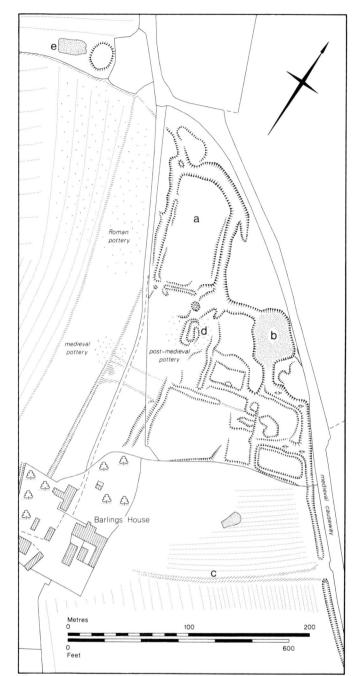

[52] *Barlings (3) Enclosures.*

around the E side of the earthwork may be part of the adaptation of the site in the late 16th century into a secular residence of substance. The channel was presumably fed by a spring at or near the rectangular pond ('e'), which is cut through ridge-and-furrow. The network of small rectangular blocks in the SE corner of the site, almost everywhere embanked as if enclosed by walls, may be part of a formal enclosed garden of the late 16th-century house. The rectangular structure ('d') is all that remains of a large building, around which a few pieces of post-medieval pottery were found during investigation. The layout of the walled blocks respects the position and orientation of this building, which thus may mark the site of the Wrays' residence.

The feature or way at 'c', though probably earlier the limit of the medieval complex, in 1824 was an access-way to Barlings House; it was evidently abandoned a few years later, perhaps with the reconstruction of the house.[6]

1. Dugdale 1817–30 VI pt 2, 917.
2. Cal LPFD Hen VIII XI (1888), 311–12.
3. Foster 1930, 29, 200, 16; LAO AD ACC 41.11.
4. OS 1st edn 1 in sheet 83.
5. RAF VAP 541/185/4117–8.
6. OS 1st edn 1 in sheet 83; LAO 2 PAD 2/53.

BIGBY

(1) Moated Site, Garden Remains, Fishponds and Paddocks (TA 033078) [1, 53] lie at 10 m above OD on deltaic sand and gravel deposits in a low-lying situation along the Skegger Beck. The site appears to be that of a medieval moat containing the garden remains associated with a 16th or 17th-century house there. The moat is surrounded by paddocks, some of which are of early 16th-century date. Another rectangular enclosure may be part of a 17th-century garden. The latter overlies the deserted village of Kettleby (3).

The Tyrwhitt family of Northumberland appears to have acquired the manor of Kettleby at the very end of the 14th century or at the beginning of the 15th century. With scarcely an exception the Tyrwhitt heirs throughout the 15th and 16th centuries were prominent as MPs or High Sheriffs for the county and in direct service of the Crown. Sir Robert (1482–1548) was notable as a Dissolution Commissioner and grantee of a large amount of monastic land. On some of these properties cadet branches of the family were established, as at Corringham and Stainfield. King Henry VIII stayed for two nights at Kettleby in October 1541 and a tradition states that Sir Robert hung the trees on the roadside from Kettleby to Brigg with sheep and oxen to show his ability to feast all comers.[1]

The decline of this branch of the Tyrwhitts, in contrast to those at Scotter, Stainfield and Corringham, may have stemmed from the fines and persecution of William Tyrwhitt (d 1591) and his wife for recusancy and harbouring Catholic priests. Nevertheless the family was resident at Kettleby until at least 1648, after which date the last male heir was forced by debts to sell up.[2]

The house at Kettleby was pulled down in 1696.[3] It is said to have been built to entertain James I, who came to Kettleby to hunt, presumably in the deer park (Bigby (2)); with its associated gardens it may therefore have been the work of Sir Robert Tyrwhitt (d 1617). Before the present farmhouse was built in the early 19th century, its site was described as 'scattered with ruins' of what 'seemed to have been a large pile of buildings' and it is marked as a ruin on Armstrong's county map of 1778. A 'long narrow archway once containing a drawbridge', destroyed in widening the entrance to this farmhouse, confirms that the earlier principal access was from the NW.[4]

The major surviving part of the earthworks consists of a sub-rectangular moated site, perhaps medieval in origin. The surrounding water-ditch is 2 m–3 m deep with traces of a much damaged outer bank only 0.4 m–0.7 m high on the S side. There are now two causeways giving access to the interior but the W one is probably relatively modern.

The farmhouse and its garden occupies the NW corner of the interior, but an elongated hollow ('a') 0.3 m deep may be the site of part of the post-medieval mansion or its predecessor. It extends into the modern garden, the surface of which is covered by quantities of early brick, building stone and mortar fragments. There are several substantial pieces of dressed or worked limestone around the farmstead, including a fragment of a cusped light. A carved stone head, possibly a 14th-century label stop, was found a few years ago, while cleaning out the ditch of the moat. It is now built into the farmhouse.

The SE part of the interior is occupied by the remains of a former garden, possibly of 16th or early 17th-century date. It is square, bounded by a 0.4 m high flat-topped bank or walkway with low prospect mounds at the NE and SE corners. The NE mound is steep-sided and 1.7 m high; its companion is only 0.9 m high and has been spread by subsequent ploughing. This ploughing has also damaged the interior of the garden but traces of slightly raised footpaths dividing it into four unequal parts are still visible. The NE quadrant of the interior may have been a matching orchard, as now.

To the E of the moat is a group of ponds between 0.75 m and 1.75 m deep. It is difficult to see how they functioned as a result of the dumping of refuse and truncation by a modern access road. However, the E side of the moat ditch is connected to the ponds by a channel ('b'), perhaps the point at which the water was led in or out of the pond. A series of narrow channels at their E end must represent sluices. The curious angular alignment of the ponds on the E might suggest a two-period development and the layout in its entirety may be a formally patterned water garden.

On the NW side of the moat are a series of enclosures, perhaps remains of former paddocks and orchards. Only part survive as earthworks; the rest are visible as crop-marks. Where they survive the enclosure boundaries consist of low banks 0.25 m–0.6 m high and shallow ditches 0.25 m–0.5 m deep. On the N these enclosures extend into ill-drained land which has no traces of medieval ploughing, whereas on the W they partly overlie ridge-and-furrow. These enclosures are divided into two parts by a broad access-way ('c') leading to the moated site. They are possibly to be associated with the early Sir Robert Tyrwhitt, perhaps even directly with the royal visit of 1541. The field-names *Willow Garth, Backside, Sand Croft, Old Orchard,* with the *Old Garden* and the *Ponds* recorded in 1674 appear to be attached to these closes.[5]

To the SW of the moat a large rectangular enclosure ('d') with rounded corners is anomalous in alignment and regularity within the concentric ring of the paddocks. Since 1975 it has been taken in with the arable to the S and survives only on the N and W as a deepened field drain, but it is shown as an earthwork on both recent and early OS plans, when its S and E sides were not field boundaries, and it already existed in this form by 1795. To judge from the OS plans its ditches were narrower and sharper than those of the paddocks.[6] It appears to have cut across the alignment of the paddocks to the N and certainly overlies N–S linear marks visible on air photographs ('d'), which are probably associated with the deserted village (3) to the S. It is likely to be a post-medieval garden similar to the slightly smaller and less rectangular garden at Goltho. It was perhaps associated with Sir Robert Tyrwhitt's early 17th-century house and gardens in contrast to the paddocks of his predecessors' residence.

1. Maddison 1902–6 III, 1018–21; LCL Ross MSS III, pedigree between pp 59–60; Cal Inq Misc VII (1968), 354, no 603; Feudal Aids III, 344 (1431); Hunter 1850, 145–56; Cal LPFD Hen VIII XVI (1898), 584; Moor 1901, 8.
2. Hodgett 1975, 182–3; LCL Ross MSS III pp 59–60; LAO ELWES 1/3, passim.
3. Jackson 1869, 90.

[53] *Bigby (1, 3) from the NE, taken 28 March 1957 before destruction in the late 1950s and 1980s. In the centre lies the site of Kettleby House, surrounded by the remains of its 16th-century formal gardens. Below, to the NE, are the fishponds. Beyond, to the W and NW, lie the closes and paddocks which surrounded the house and which in turn partly overlie the site of the deserted village of Kettleby. (RAF)*

4. *Gent's Mag* 69 (1799), 377; LCL Ross MSS III, 59.
5. LAO ELWES 1/3/20.
6. OS 1:2500 TA 0207–0307 (1970); OS 25 in Lincs 20.9 and 13; LAO LLHS 26.

(3) Deserted Village of Kettleby (TA 032076) [1, 53] lies at 11 m above OD on deltaic sands and gravels over Jurassic clays. The settlement was probably depopulated in the late 14th or early 15th century by the Tyrwhitt family.

Kettleby is first recorded in a will of about 1066.[1] In 1086 two manors there had a minimum population of 13, plus an unknown number of the 23 of the soke and berewick shared with Elsham. Thereafter and throughout the later Middle Ages Kettleby is subsumed with Kettleby Thorpe (Bigby (4)), also a deserted settlement, as an unnamed member of Bigby. By the mid 16th century it was totally deserted: for the Lindsey Musters in 1539 the village returned nil although Sir Robert Tyrwhitt was entered with 12 servants; Sir Robert was the sole taxpayer in 1542–3 and the single household in 1563 was clearly the Tyrwhitts'. The enclosure of Kettleby township and its conversion to pasture certainly pre-dated the mid 16th century since the manor in 1548 comprised 'a capital messuage, 1000 acres of pasture, 100 acres of meadow and 300 acres of marsh'. The enclosure may have taken place by the 15th century, perhaps as a direct result of the Tyrwhitts' acquisition of the manor.[2]

The earthworks of the village have been largely destroyed and only a few amorphous fragments remain at its E end. A hollowed platform ('e') has considerable quantities of pottery, animal bones, limestone blocks and gravel associated with it, while large amounts of pottery ranging in date from early Saxon to late medieval have been found on the site.

Air photographs[3] show that slight earthworks of the village formerly extended W into the next field, though these had already been reduced by ploughing by the 1950s. The remains then consisted of a hollow-way ('f'–'g') which was bounded on the S by ridge-and-furrow and on the N by ditched closes with house sites along their S sides. This suggests that the settlement was originally a single-row village. Field-walking in 1976 produced a range of post-Roman pottery similar to that found to the E, as well as a scatter of Roman material.[4]

1. Whitelock 1930, no xxxix.
2. LCL Ross MSS III, 58; Russell 1974, 5.
3. CUAC UB 10, 12; AQG 47.
4. Inf F. N. Field.

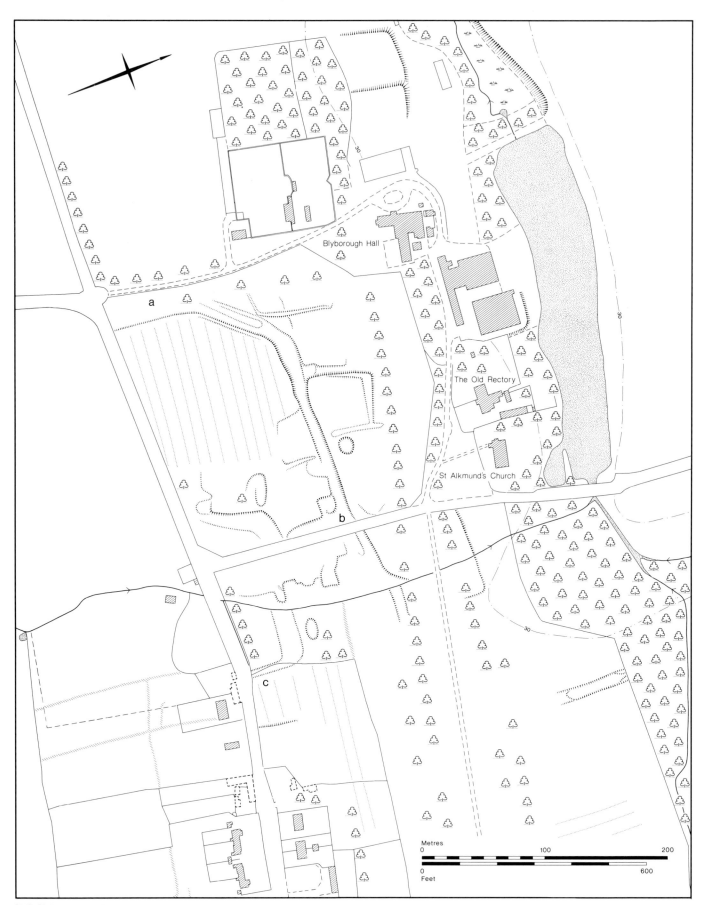

Blyborough Hall

The Old Rectory

St Alkmund's Church

a

b

c

Metres
0   100   200
0   600
Feet

[54] *Blyborough (1) Settlement Remains.*

(6) Site of Lime-kiln (TA 03210738) [1] lies S of the moated site at Kettleby House on the crest of slightly higher ground, at 14 m above OD ('h'). It has been reduced by ploughing to a height of less than 1 m and a former ramp on the N side has also been destroyed. The top is slightly hollowed. To the E, the 1970 OS 1:2500 plan shows a number of irregularities which cut through the ridge-and-furrow and probably represent surface quarrying.[1]

The late 18th-century field-name was *West Lime Kiln Close* and *Great Lyme Kilnes* and *Little Lyme Kiln* occur also in 1674.[2]

1. NAR; CUAC UB 12; RAF VAP CPE/UK2042, 3073–5.
2. LAO LLHS 26; ELWES 1/3/20.

BLYBOROUGH

---

(1) Settlement Remains (SK 933944) [54], formerly part of Blyborough, lie at 31 m above OD at the foot of the Jurassic Limestone scarp on Middle Lias Clay and shale. Though one of the 'greate depopulacions' reported in 1607[1] few traces of the early settlement exist in the parkland and those that do are poorly preserved.

The medieval manorial history of the settlement is complex and the detail unclear. All four manors, which were in separate lordships in 1086, can be traced into the 14th century, three of them with a succession of sub-tenants holding of the greater lords and presumably occupying minor manorial residences.[2] In the early 16th century the largest of the main manors came to Charles Brandon, Duke of Suffolk, along with other property in the parish. The manor then passed by marriage to a cadet branch of the Ayscough family who already had interests and a residence there and who held it until 1633. After two subsequent owners it passed by marriage in the late 18th century to the Luard family who remained the owners throughout the 19th century.[3]

The most clear-cut drop in population, in the late 16th century, is closely related to changes in ownership and direct lordly actions; so too, apparently, is a later recovery in the 18th century. There were also, however, earlier marked fluctuations. The minimum recorded population in 1086 at 43 heads of households is the highest documented until the mid 20th century. If it increased over the next two centuries, the number of taxpayers in the early 14th-century subsidies points to a decline at that period. Nevertheless at 29 in 1327–8 and 28 in 1332–3 the population was only just below the average for the wapentake. Relief of just below 50 per cent was allowed in 1352 following the Black Death and in 1389 the site of the principal manor was of no net value, 12 bovates of land lay 'long uncultivated', and an old windmill belonging to the manor stood in ruins and empty;[4] nevertheless 84 individuals paid the Poll Tax in 1377 and there were at least 10 households in 1428. Continuing reliefs at 26 per cent in the mid 15th century suggest less than complete recovery, but the settlement produced 16 persons for the Lindsey Musters in 1539 and 24 taxpayers in 1542–3.

In 1603 there were only 60 communicants, less than 50 per cent of the rural average for the archdeaconry. This decline was caused by Henry Ayscough. By 1580 the inhabitants of Blyborough had already complained to the Crown about his oppressions and encroachments, specifying enclosure of commons and other wrongs against which they sought redress. The survey of depopulation in 1607 reported that Ayscough as 'owner of the whole towne consistinge of xiii farme howses besides his Mannor howse hath inclosed the whole towne, decayed some of the howses, made the rest cottages and hath taken all the land from them'.[5]

In the early 18th century the population was still only 16, 19 or 17 families. By 1801, however, the population of Blyborough had jumped to 30 households. These were housed not, as presumably earlier, around the church, but in an estate village probably created by the Luard family on the E edge of the 18th-century landscaped park and in farmsteads around the parish.

The surviving earthworks scarcely begin to reflect the complexity suggested by the documents or the extent of what must have been a moderately large medieval settlement. Those that survive are poorly defined since they were ploughed during the Second World War.[6] They comprise the battered remains of a hollow-way continuing the line of the road from Willoughton N ('a') and then curving E. At the point ('b') where the hollow-way meets the road running N past the church it appears to divide: part continues E and part turned S and then E through a double bend to link (at 'c') with the existing road that climbs the scarp to the E. Indeterminate banks and ditches on either side of this hollow-way probably mark former streets and property plots as the 1838 field-name *Old House Close* (SW of 'b') suggests, though some of the earthworks E of the N–S road (SE of 'b'), may be the result of modern disturbance. The main hollow-way ('a'–'b'–'c') was a road in use until after 1855 although no structures lay along it even in the early 19th century. Both the E–W and the N–S arms of the modern road system were created by 1885, presumably by the Luards.[7]

The present estate village to the SE is a late 18th-century creation also of the Luards. All the plots there overlie ridge-and-furrow where it can be traced. On the other hand, on the S side of the village street, air photographs[8] seem to show traces of earthworks and the empty closes on the Tithe Map are named *House Close*.

1. BL Add MS 11574, f76.
2. *Lincs DB* 3/4; *LS* 2/5; Major 1960, 203–19; Moor 1902a, unpaginated; *Cal IPM* II (1906), 469; *VE* IV, 71; V, 305–6; Lees 1935, 101; *Cal LPFD Hen VIII* XVIII pt 1 (1901), 551; XX pt 2 (1907), 224, 330, 535–6.
3. Moor 1902a, unpaginated; Maddison 1902–6 I, 55–8; III, 913–14; LCL Ross MSS IV, pedigrees facing 121 and 122; Cole 1913, 153; monuments in Blyborough church.
4. *Cal Inq Misc* V (1962), 135–6.
5. *Acts of the Privy Council* XII (1896), 334; XIII (1896), 257–8, 336–7, 345; *Cal State Papers Dom 1581–90* (1865), 104; BL Add MS 11574, f76.
6. Local inf.
7. OS 1st edn 1 in sheet 83; LAO F35; STUBBS III/24; OS 1st edn 25 in sheet Lincs 36.13.
8. RAF VAP CPE/UK2563/4251–3.

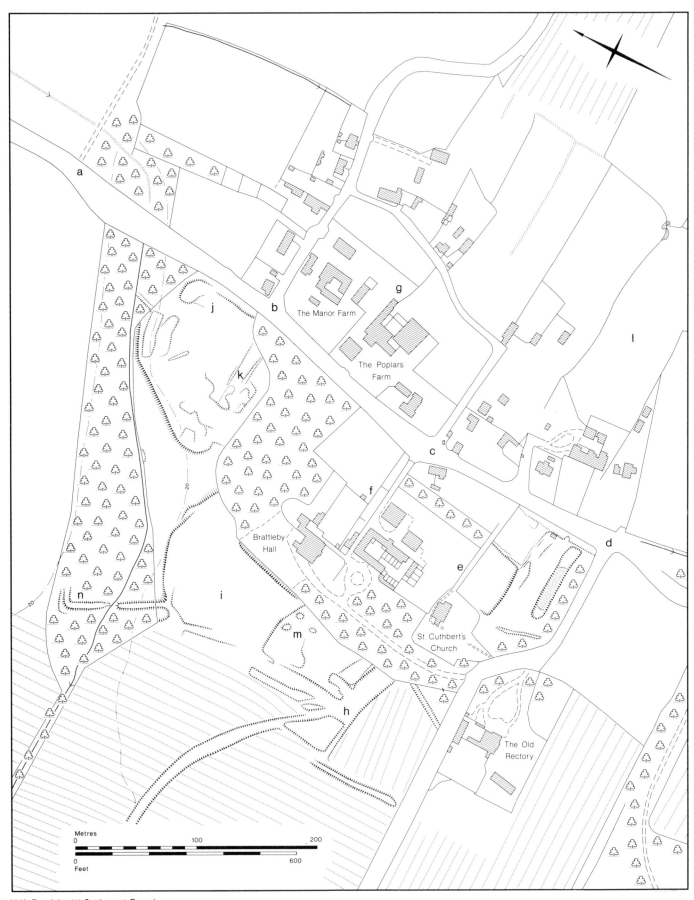

The Manor Farm

The Poplars
Farm

Brattleby
Hall

St Cuthbert's
Church

The Old
Rectory

Metres
0   100   200
0   600
Feet

[55] *Brattleby (1) Settlement Remains.*

(1) Settlement Remains (SK 947808) [55, 56], formerly part of Brattleby village, lie at about 24 m above OD at the foot of the scarp of the Jurassic Limestone ridge on Upper and Middle Lias Clay and shale. The village is notable for the major change to its presumed planned layout which took place in the early 19th century following modest alterations to the road system.

Though tenurially divided in 1086, by the early 12th century all the settlement was in a single lordship held by Robert de Haia. In the 13th century the consolidated manor of Brattleby had become part of the honour of the castle and county of Lincoln; in 1408 it was annexed to the Crown and became part of the Duchy of Lancaster.[1]

The population figures for Brattleby do not show any striking reversals, though in the early 14th century and again in the late 16th and 17th centuries the settlement was markedly smaller than others in the area. Since the 18th century the level of population has been remarkably stable.

Yet this apparent stability masks the most fundamental change in the physical layout of Brattleby. For in place of the present simple arrangement of a broad N–S through road with a few side turnings at right angles, an approximately parallel length of N–S lane to the E and the church tucked away to the W, the Enclosure Map of 1779[2] shows a very different pattern [56] where there were no direct through roads at all. This arrangement was altered in about 1815 by John Sexty and Edward Wright by the expedient of creating two new N–S sections of road ('a'–'b' and 'c'–'d'), through former closes in their possession, to create a continuous N–S road which retains its slight change in direction resulting from its piecemeal creation. Some of the abandoned former streets seem immediately to have been thrown into adjacent closes. Others were downgraded to paths, such as that to the church from the E ('e'), or absorbed, as in the drive to Brattleby Hall ('f'), or blocked off and built over ('g'). All these changes had certainly taken place by 1858, and probably already by 1824.[3]

A few field remains have survived this major change, but it was so profound that analysis of the earlier settlement arrangements is difficult. Nevertheless fragmentary earthworks in the park W of the Hall, taken with the Enclosure Map, may allow some planned elements to be picked out.

The most obvious feature of the village, as it is depicted on the Enclosure Map of 1779, is a roughly rectangular block bisected by a curving N–S lane, apparently the *Town Street* of 1721/2 and 1859,[4] and bounded on the N and S and part of the W side by lanes. In 1779 the E side of this block was divided into crofts running back from the main street and on the W the crofts were separated by two narrow lanes. The alignment of these lanes was carried on E of the main street by two property boundaries, producing an impression of what may have been a planned layout. Traces of some of these internal divisions are evidenced in part by existing boundaries and in part by former earthworks, visible on air photographs.[5] The possibility that this rectangular block was planned is given additional support by the fact that there were no direct roads emerging from it and that it thus bore no relationship to the surrounding communication pattern. It would seem likely that this block was laid out here, without regard to any existing adjacent roads. These may have been connected with the less regular but still roughly rectangular area to the W, as existing in 1779, which contained the church and Brattleby Hall, and which

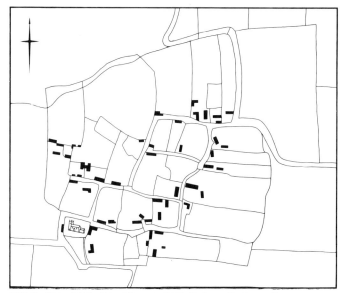

[56] *Brattleby (1) Brattleby Village in 1779. Redrawn Enclosure Map.*

was then partly surrounded and subdivided by a series of right-angled lanes. This area may have originated as a manorial *curia,* or an earlier centre of settlement, or both, and may also have been given its rectangular form by planning. The landscaping of the park and other alterations have left little evidence of this on the ground.

The principal surviving feature is a deep curving hollow-way between arable blocks that joins the W end of a very broad E–W hollow-way ('h'), the alignment of which is continued by the former street running E from the church ('e'). On the N side of this broad hollow-way is one earthwork close with traces of buildings at its S end facing the hollow-way; these seem to form the W end of an E–W settlement block, of which the church forms a part. The hollow-way may have only been abandoned when replaced by the new standard enclosure road to the S, and the line of the S and W sides of the closes is certainly shown as a boundary on the Enclosure Map. Earthworks in the close SE of the church, *Rectory Field,* include a fishpond, the sites of a dovecote and barns associated with a former rectory house – presumably the buildings shown on the Enclosure Map but not later. Four cottages called 'the poor houses' stood in this field too.[6]

To the N of the Hall and perhaps once part of the western block are other fragmentary earthworks. A group of buildings shown on the Enclosure Map (at approximately 'i') has left no detectable surface trace. Further NE (at 'j') several irregularities include the stone foundations of a building near the road. The linear hollow-way ('k') cutting through one irregular area is an early carriage drive to Brattleby Hall, re-routed by 1885 and subsequently abandoned.[7] Two other features of the old village plan which may be relevant to the history of the settlement are recognizable on the Enclosure Map. To the N of the *Town Street* block were three long closes extending N, two occupied by buildings, and a third empty. At the S end of the same block was a single close ('l') lying E–W with an open space at its E end. Both these areas of closes appear to be additions to the perhaps earlier regularly planned main block.

If the interpretation of the village plan proposed here is correct, then Brattleby may be the result of at least one and perhaps two phases of planning, together with later additions, which finally produced the form recorded in 1779. This ancient arrangement, of

Grange Farm

All Saints' Church

The Old Rectory

Carriers Farm

a

b

c

d

e

f

Manor Farm

Metres
0   100   200

0   600
Feet

[57] *Broxholme (1) Settlement Remains.*

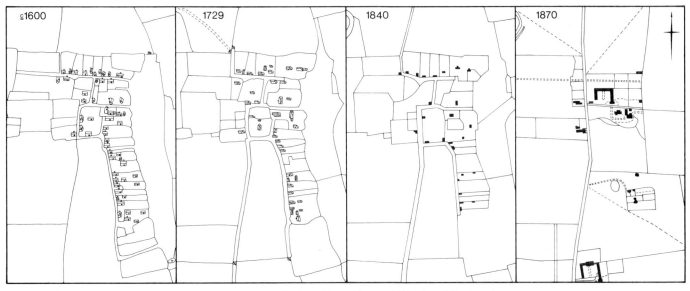

[**58**] *Broxholme (1) Broxholme Village c 1600, 1729, 1840, c 1870. Redrawn Estate Maps and Tithe Award Map (1840).*

whatever origin, was then finally destroyed in the early 19th century.

Other features in the area belong to the development of Brattleby Hall. This is a house of about 1780 with well-documented alterations of 1838–40 and additions of 1875–80.[8] The features include a ha-ha and tree mounds ('m') and a large earthen dam ('n') consisting of a straight embankment up to 3 m high. Though this dam once ponded back a lake associated with the landscaped park it may have been an adaptation of an earlier dam, perhaps of a water-mill.

1. *Lincs DB* 3/1, 24/6, 26/1; *LS* 3/4 and 19; *Book of Fees* I, 192; II, 1065, 1073, 1159; *Feudal Aids* III, 136, 176, 247, 271, 278; *Cal Pat R 1408–13* IV (1909), 79–80.
2. LAO LPC 1/14.
3. A deposition by William Auckland concerning the public roads in Brattleby, 1859, with maps of 1779 and 1858, in the possession of Rev Denzil Wright of Brattleby (copy in RCHME files); OS 1st edn 1 in sheet 83.
4. LAO TLE 15/2773; Auckland's deposition.
5. APs in NMR.
6. Letter (undated) in the possession of Rev D. Wright (copy in RCHME files).
7. Map of 1858; OS 25 in sheet Lincs 52.14.
8. LAO MISC DEP 118/1/2.

BROXHOLME

(1) Settlement Remains (SK 911781) [**57, 58**], formerly part of Broxholme village, lie approximately 10 m above OD on sandy Lias Clay. The settlement is of outstanding interest because of the excellent documentation of its post-medieval and early modern decline through a series of estate and printed maps from about 1600 onwards.[1] The morphology of the village itself points to considerable development and change in the medieval period.

The surviving medieval population records indicate that Broxholme was always a settlement of an average size in the area, and was little affected by the Black Death. The Monson map of about 1600 [**58**] shows and lists 25 tofts with buildings, of which one house is said to be empty, in addition to the church and parsonage,

and a written Monson survey of 1607–8 gives the same number, the same single empty house and all but three of the tenants have the same names. The map shows three closes or tofts W and NW of the church, and three more at the extreme S end of the village, empty. The survey of depopulations in 1607 found only one farmhouse decayed by William Dighton.[2] The map also shows that enclosure was well under way in all the former open fields, but not complete. The glebe was entirely enclosed in the period 1605–38, and an order of the Privy Council dated 1637 records that Sir John Monson had been returned by the Commission for Depopulations charged with 'depopulation and conversion of houses and lands in Cherry Burton, Owersby and Broxholme', fined £300, pardoned and discharged from his activities. The impact of this in the case of Broxholme was evidently slight for in 1676 there were 54 communicants compared with 62 in 1603, in 1662 21 people paid the Hearth Tax and in 1705–23 there were 21 and 22 households.[3]

John Dickinson's map of the manor of 1729 [**58**] shows the village to have been very similar in layout and occupation of the tofts to the situation of *c* 1600. In all within the village 21 tenants are listed and 20 properties shown with dwellings: the empty plots at the extreme S end had been thrown together into a single close.[4] There were 23 rising to 26 households in the early 19th century followed by a drop in 1851 to 19 households that held steady, albeit with a slightly falling population, until the end of the century.

However, the series of maps shows a far more dramatic change than these 19th-century population figures reveal. In 1824 the 1st edn OS 1 in map shows a largely unchanged form of settlement compared with a century earlier. This is confirmed by a sale map of 1838 and the Tithe Map of 1840 [**58**], both showing about 20 occupied plots within the old layout. By about 1870, however, a map of Captain George Robinson's estate reveals a total replanning, which includes the abandonment of most of the settlement's old internal streets with the consequent marooning of a group of three occupied properties 250 m S of the church in the middle of a field, where two cottages still stand [**58**]. A new through road had been driven straight N across the earlier layout and a few cottages located on its W side. Two large new farms had been planted at either end of the settlement – that now called The

Grange near the church with buildings dated 1847 and Manor Farm to the S.[5] Only the church and rectory were static, the latter rebuilt in 1831, the former in the 1850s.

This far-reaching modification of Broxholme followed the purchase of the manor in 1839 by Frederick Robinson, a successful Nottingham banker. It was presumably himself or his son – Stonehouse in 1845 refers to the father's 'great improvements on the estate' – whose application of up-to-date farming ideas, together with the necessary capital expenditure, transformed not only the settlement but the whole parish by re-enclosing it in a rigidly rectangular pattern of fields.[6]

The earthwork remains, both surviving and recorded on aerial photographs, can be matched with great accuracy with the cartographic evidence for the village layout over the period from around 1600 to the 1840s when Robinson reorganized the settlement. But it is also possible from those maps and the field remains to note some aspects of the layout that appear to reflect the early development of the settlement perhaps with a planned northern grid and including planned southern additions, one overlying ridge-and-furrow.

In the N, the alignment of the former principal E–W street ('a'–'b') is continued W by a hollow-way between blocks of ridge-and-furrow which already, by 1600, were within old hedged closes on the edge of the village. The way formerly gave access to Broxholme Bridge over the R Till, but had been enclosed by 1729; the E end of the street giving access to common moor along the E side of the settlement was also closed by that date. The remains of the closes on the N side of this street, shown as a block of rather regular plots on the estate maps, protrude N from Grange Farm. The street leading from the centre of its S side is shown in 1600 with two narrow properties along its E side that might have been encroachments on a wide street or small green.

Parallel to the N street, the surviving E–W street, though dating from the 19th century, follows approximately an earlier line, giving access to the former moor at its E end. Its predecessor is shown on all pre-1870 maps with a marked kink just W of the church: this was evidently caused by the street layout skirting a large rectangular property immediately W and SW of the church ('c') rather in the manner that a manorial focus or similar pre-eminent farm might be respected. Former closes or paddocks on its W side are represented by former earthworks, perhaps overlying the ends of arable ridges. Medieval pottery has been reported from the field W of Grange Farm.[7]

The most prominent earthwork feature on the site, a broad and deep hollow street with E–W ridge-and-furrow terminating on a headland along its W side, is aligned N–S. On the E lie the remains of the series of properties shown on the estate maps, separated by shallow ditches and with building sites and yards marked by platforms and hollows and by some wells. The tails of the properties run back to form the edge of the former area of common moor and this too must have helped to determine the layout of the S arm, which may to some extent be an encroachment on that moor. A deep E–W hollow-way ('d') represents the E–W cross-street giving access to the moor, shown on the map of c 1600, which also shows the main street making a small dog-leg at this point, smoothed out in the earthworks, as if the properties to the S represented a planned extension to the settlement. A second slight change of alignment ('e'), which is matched by a bulge at the end of the properties, may mark a further extension. The hollow-way is up to three times deeper at the N end than at the S and certainly the southernmost property, which lies beyond a further cross-street ('f') and is shown

on the map of c 1600 and identifiable on air photographs before levelling, overlies ridge-and-furrow.[8]

At the time of survey, an area of the settlement to the S of the surviving cottages was under plough. A thick clay spread marking the site of a cottage was associated with black occupation soil and a profusion of 19th-century pottery; to the S the soil was lighter, lacking long or recent occupation and produced only a thin scatter of medieval pottery and evidence of stone roof tiles for two buildings without occupation debris, probably barns.

1. Beresford and St Joseph 1979, 31–6.
2. LAO MONSON 17/1; Monson MSS VIII (at South Carlton); BL Add MS 11574 f78.
3. Johnson 1962, 141; LAO MONSON 19/7/1/8; PRO E179/140/806.
4. Monson MSS, map of Broxholme (at South Carlton).
5. OS 1st edn 1 in sheet 83; LAO MONSON 17/16/12, 17/31; H304; 7/NOTT/15.
6. LAO 7/NOTT/11–15; Harding 1940, 73.
7. *EMAB* 9 (1968), 21.
8. RAF VAP CPE/UK2012/4141–3; CUAC LI 24, 27, 29; APs in NMR.

BULLINGTON

(3) Enclosure (TF 106764) [59] lies in the SE of the parish on Till at 10 m above OD. The earthworks survive in dense, modern coniferous woodland, but until after 1946 lay in open pasture between Cocklode and Spring Woods in Bullington, and Great West Wood in Goltho.[1]

Documentary references, though inconclusive, indicate that the site may have been a hunting lodge or keeper's lodge in an early medieval deer park that included extensively managed woodlands. Domesday Book records 400 acres of underwood in Bullington and this probably included some or all of the later medieval managed woodlands of Cocklode, Spring and perhaps Short Wood and the cleared *Wlvedale* in Bullington and probably also at least West Wood in Goltho. An early 19th-century map shows all of Cocklode Wood and much of Short Wood still under a coppicing regime.[2]

In 1148 × 54 Simon de Kyme founded the Gilbertine priory of Bullington in his park at Bullington, but endowed it with only 'part of my park that they may dwell there, and part of my wood'. Philip de Kyme still referred to his park in about 1175.[3] Though the priory received such grants of woodland in both Bullington and Goltho, they were limited and the woods of Bullington were specifically excepted in William de Kyme's confirmation of the priory's grants in 1256.[4]

The manor of Bullington passed from the Kymes to the Tailbois in the 15th and 16th centuries. The description of James Hollingworthe of Old Bullington as 'keeper and servant to Sir Geo Tailboys' in 1533 may indicate continued use of the site.[5]

The site consists of a roughly polygonal area enclosed on the SW, NW and NE by a broad ditch 1 m deep and with a well-marked inner bank. This bank survives to a height of 1.5 m on the NW, but on the NE it is only 0.3 m high. Near the S corner it forms a 1 m high flat platform 15 m across. The entrance in the centre of the SW side is probably original although the ditch must have been bridged at this point. A gap on the NE is modern. The SE side of the site follows the course of an artificially deepened stream, here the parish boundary with Goltho. The broad flat-topped bank on the SE of this stream is the boundary bank of Great West Wood.

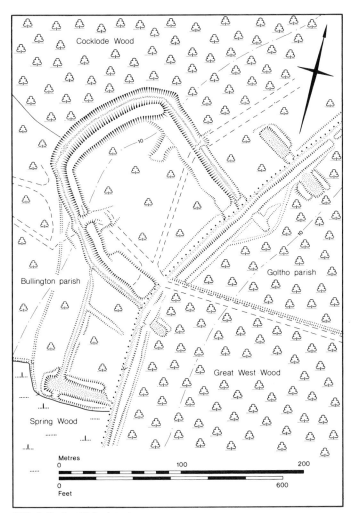

[59] *Bullington (3) Enclosure.*

BURTON

(1) Settlement Remains (SK 961744) [60, 61], formerly part of Burton village, lie at around 35 m above OD on Marlstone at the foot of the Jurassic Limestone escarpment.

Despite evidence for planned elements, Burton was a multi-manorial settlement throughout the Middle Ages and no holding was overwhelmingly predominant. When the village came into the hands of the Monson family in the later 16th century and was consolidated to single ownership in the 17th century, the change was considerable. It was marked by a protracted alteration in the nature and layout of the settlement, involving the contraction and simplification of the village under the influence and encroachment of the Hall and its parkland setting. This can be traced in the village morphology, and in the fragmentary earthworks, in combination with the evidence of estate maps.

As many as five entries in Domesday Book referred to holdings in Burton. Several of these can be traced through the later medieval period, but are not readily linked with development in the 15th and 16th centuries.[1] The Monson family had acquired a single manor in Burton sometime before 1593, but by 1607–8 Sir Thomas Monson was in possession of the greater part of the parish. Further direct and indirect purchases consolidated the estate which remained in the hands of the Monsons until 1945.[2]

Burton's recorded population remained at or above average for the neighbourhood throughout the medieval and modern periods, evidently little affected by the set-backs of the 14th and 15th centuries. Even the decay and conversion reported in 1607 and the prosecution and fining of Sir John Monson for 'depopulation and conversion of houses and lands in Cherry Burton, Owersby and Broxholme' in 1637 and the enclosure of much at least of the non-limestone part of the parish at this period have no catastrophic reflection in the population figures. In 1676 there were 95 communicants compared with 120 in 1603, and approximately 30, 42 and 37 households at the beginning of the 18th century.[3]

The siting of Burton may have been influenced by the presence of a Roman villa, at The Water House. The continuing importance of this location as a water source is indicated by the field-name *Fountain Garth* in 1848, *The Condyt* in *c* 1600 and perhaps by late 13th and early 14th-century personal names such as Robert 'ad pipe' and Gilbert 'Attepipe'.[4]

The morphology of Burton village is complex and without the surviving earthworks and series of estate maps, little understanding would be possible of the post-medieval development, and still less of the earlier medieval form of the village. Some element of at least the later medieval plan can be perceived from a combination of the earliest plan of about 1600 and the field evidence.

The village appears to have been articulated on two roughly parallel E–W streets extending up the limestone scarp. That to the S ran along the S side of the churchyard (approximately 'a'–'b') and has been destroyed by the later emparking. In *c* 1600 this was the principal entry into the village from Middle Street and led directly to the Hall, then perhaps newly rebuilt. The importance of this street may have been of long standing since it aligns with the E–W spine road of the parish to the W, the line of which is locally utilized by the Hall's impressive tree avenue. The old E–W street to the N is the present main street, which in *c* 1600 terminated half-way up the scarp. Between these two streets there was once a large open rectangular green, which by *c* 1600 had already been encroached upon, leaving only its E quarter open.

Attached to the SW side of the enclosure is a further small rectangular enclosure bounded on the SE by the stream, on the NW by a shallow ditch and on the S by an embanked pond. It is subdivided by a short cross-ditch. A narrow bank to the W is shown as a field boundary on the OS 1st edn 25 in plan.[6] Other small rectangular ponds exist in the surrounding area. They may be connected with wild-fowling.

The relationship of the enclosures both to the stream and to the surviving woodland is of interest. The use of the stream as one unimproved side of the enclosures suggests that the site was in no way defensive and unlikely to have been a manor house or lordly medieval residence.

The location of the enclosures on the parish boundary and their detailed form as well as their relationship to the woodland combine with the documentary indications to make a hunting lodge the most plausible explanation.[7]

1. RAF VAP CEP/UK1880, 3255–6.
2. *Lincs DB* 3/8, 13/26, 14/57; LAO PAD II/73.
3. Stenton 1922, 91; Stenton 1920, 8, no 10.
4. LCL Ross MSS X, 75; *Cal Pat R 1292–1301* (1895), 142; Stenton 1922, 91–2; Dugdale 1817–30 VII, 952.
5. LCL Ross MSS X, 79; Foster 1902, 185.
6. OS 25 in sheet Lincs 62.12.
7. Everson 1988.

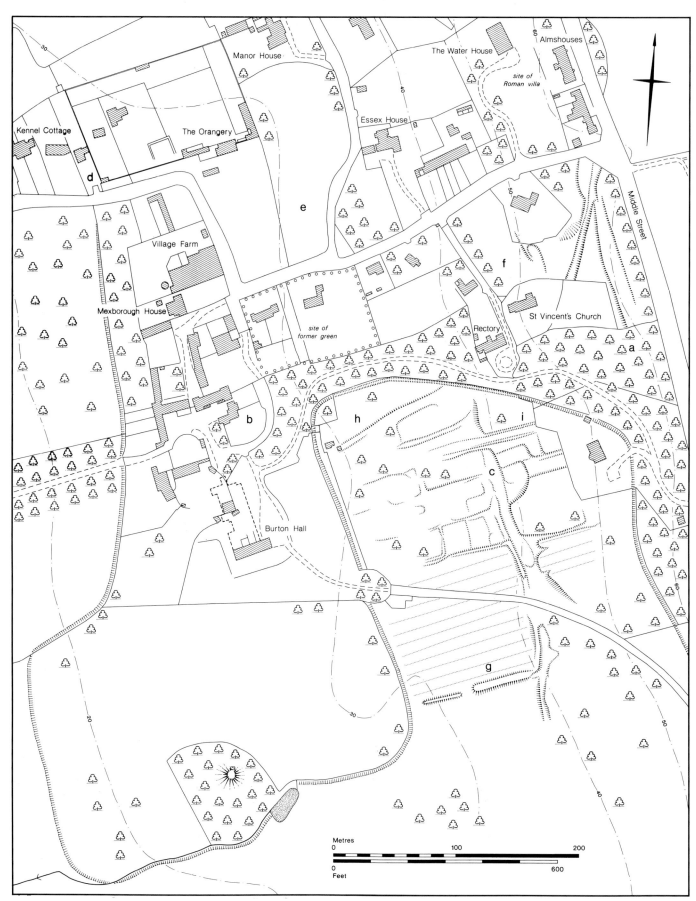

Manor House

The Water House

Almshouses

Kennel Cottage

The Orangery

Essex House

site of
Roman villa

d

e

f

Village Farm

Mexborough House

St Vincent's Church

Rectory

site of
former green

a

b

h

i

c

Burton Hall

Middle Street

g

Metres
0   100   200

0   600
Feet

[60] *Burton (1) Settlement Remains, (2) Garden Remains and Park.*

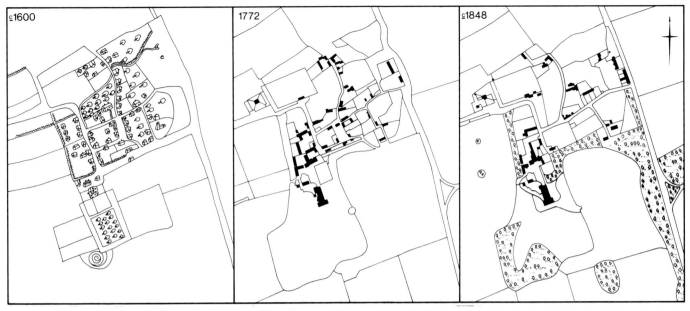

[**61**] *Burton (1) Burton Village c 1600, 1772, 1848. Redrawn Estate Maps and Tithe Award Map (1848).*

Streets once exited from all four corners of this green. That from the NE remains a curiously curved lane leading to the Manor House and a similar curved lane in the SE corner once joined what is now a hollow-way ('c'), lined on both sides by a series of rectangular closes with traces of former buildings at their street ends. The hollow-way and houses which once stood here had been abandoned by *c* 1600. The road from the NW corner of the green still exists, curving W around Mexborough House on the same line as in *c* 1600. No trace of the SW road can now be seen.

This presumed late medieval arrangement of green and streets has a regularity of layout that might suggest a planned origin. If this is so, an even earlier arrangement may be postulated of an originally N–S scarp-foot road, parallel to Middle Street, roughly on the line of the Manor House Lane and the hollow-way ('c') with the parish church on its E side. The diversion of this road into the E side of the later green would explain the curved nature of lanes entering the green on this side.

Further streets or former streets or roads complicate this apparently simple two-stage pattern and may represent either later development, or, more likely, part of the regularity imposed by the assumed replanning. The roughly N–S lane linking the church to the main N street is a realigned relic of a way which in *c* 1600 linked the two E–W streets. Likewise in the NW of the village a narrow property ('d') marks the S part of a lane which in *c* 1600 continued the line of the tails of the properties facing E on to the green. A former way descending the scarp diagonally to the E side of the churchyard is now marked only by a hollow-way.

In *c* 1600 this network of streets and boundaries defined the central core of the village and its green, as well as a series of large property blocks beyond, which were then, perhaps significantly, occupied by substantial farms or residences. Some, or all of these latter, may represent the sites of medieval manorial holdings, or their equivalent. The most obvious is that occupied by the Manor House ('Robert Beckett Junior his house' in *c* 1600) bounded on the W by the old lane ('d') and on the S by a former watercourse shown on the map of *c* 1600. To the E a property occupied by Beckett Senior extended up the scarp to Middle Street in a single block. To the S of the Manor House another block bounded on three sides by

streets contained the residence of the Rand family, shown as a large house in *c* 1600 ('e'). Another house, 'Bartholomew Chambers', stood immediately N of the church ('f') within a block also bounded by streets.

The form of the village as it was in *c* 1600 was thus perhaps the product of replanning around an E–W green of an earlier N–S linear settlement, with the contemporary or later addition of manorial or at least major tenurial property blocks, as well as other changes. This complex pattern was simplified and altered by a long process of encroachment and emparking by the Monson family which began in the late 16th century. Already by *c* 1600 properties SW of the church ('c') had been abandoned or cleared and the land incorporated into the garden layout of the Hall. In addition, the W end of the southern E–W street ('a'–'b') had been blocked, perhaps by the creation of the late 16th-century hall and gardens, and the present road, skirting via a series of right angles the enclosed grounds attached to the Hall, had been developed to provide the only route W out of the village.

By 1772 further major changes had occurred. All the independent 'manorial' blocks had either been vacated (as Chambers') or broken up (as Beckett's and Rand's). The newly landscaped park had taken over the southern E–W street, though a private drive still connected the Hall to the church overriding former village properties. If the rebuilding of the church tower in 1678 was for ornamental effect, this development may in part belong to the late 17th century. The buildings ancillary to the Hall had, by 1772, spread N to engulf the whole of the W side of the village. These included a complex series of stables and yards, a new detached walled garden (*The Orangery*) and kennels to the W. A new tree-planted walk had appeared along the W edge of the former village properties N of the Hall, and they themselves had been displaced by the present Mexborough House, built as a dower house in the later 18th century.

Though the village green and the village encroachments on its W side still existed in 1772, by 1824 the whole area had been cleared and turned into a paddock and later orchards. The effect of this, as shown on the Tithe Map of 1848 and on the early large-scale OS plans, was to push the village E on to the hill slope as far as Middle Street, around and alongside the Monson Almshouses, themselves endowed in the mid-17th century and rebuilt in 1875. Only since 1945 and the sale of the Monson estate has there been infilling by modern properties over the former green and within and to the W of *The Orangery*. This has blurred the former clear-cut segregation of the village from the Hall and its appurtenances which was promoted in the 18th century and pertained throughout the 19th and early 20th centuries.[5]

1. *Lincs DB* 7/9, 18/5, 24/3, 60/1, 68/1; *LS* 3/8, 3/19, 3/20.
2. Maddison 1902–6 II, 680–4; III, 810–12, 938–40; Monson MS VIII (at South Carlton); LCL Ross MSS XII Lawress, 58–9; LAO MONSON 19/7/3/2.
3. BL Add MS 11574 ff78, 82; LAO MONSON 19/7/1/8; MONSON 17/24; Johnson 1962, 144.
4. LM records; *EMAB* **9** (1968), 13; White 1882, 217; LAO H454; MONSON 17/2; EPNS records.
5. LAO MONSON 17/4, 17/24; H454; OS 1st edn 1 in sheet 83; OS 25 in sheet Lincs 61.14.

(2) Garden Remains and Park (SK 960743) [60, 61], of 16th-century and later date, lie around Burton Hall, at about 30 m above OD, on the SW side of Burton village.

In 1607–8 Sir Thomas Monson's principal residence was at Burton where he had 'orchards, gardines and scyte of the Hall or Mannor House' extending to over 6 acres. This house must have been recently created, perhaps on an earlier manorial site.

The plan of Sir Thomas's late 16th-century garden can be seen on an estate map of Burton of about 1600. It occupied a rectangle, aligned N–S along the level ground at the foot of the scarp and appended to the SW corner of the village. This area was divided in the ratio of 1:2:4 by cross-walls. The smallest block at the N end had three compartments with the house itself occupying the central one. The central block was divided unequally into a square and a rectangle, with the former filled with some unrecognizable central feature surrounded by parterres. The southernmost and largest block was tree-planted as an orchard or 'wilderness'. At the SW corner, and offset to the line of these compartments, was a large prospect mound with a spiral walk to its summit. This seems to have been approached by a walkway, perhaps terraced, along the W side of the gardens, which then turned E along the S of the gardens and returned N along the E as a broad walkway.[1] The only substantial remains of this garden is the prospect mound which still stands over 3 m high, incorporated into a later copse and with a 19th-century ice-house inserted into it.

To the E of the garden, the square enclosure, bounded by a stone-rubble bank ('g') and with traces of ridge-and-furrow within it, is that marked on the *c* 1600 plan and called 'The Hill Close in the Sheep Field next the stone wall' in 1607–8, confirming the gardens were enclosed by stone walls, as indeed is shown on a pre-1768 drawing of the house.[2] The land to the N and E of this enclosure was probably 'The Hill Close before the Hall Gates' and together these closes or paddocks formed an integral part of the Hall's setting, flanked on their W by the full length of the garden and on their N by the impressive broad way that descended the scarp and led to the house. The S edge of that way may be marked by the surviving scarp ('h'). The W side of the Hall and gardens was lined by a similar series of closes extending N to the modern road. By the end of the 17th century it appears from Glebe Terriers that this area was known as a park.[3]

The original garden layout seems to have remained largely intact until the second half of the 18th century. Then, in 1768, a new wing was added to the 16th-century hall and it was apparently at this time that the old gardens were swept away and replaced by a sinuously-edged large lawn S and SE of the house with a surrounding ha-ha

and beyond that a landscaped park. Thislewood's map of 1772 shows this park in the process of creation.[4] This remodelling of the Hall and its gardens also included the removal of former village properties N of the Hall and their replacement by Mexborough House as a dower house. A ditched embankment ('i') that overlies earlier earthworks may be a carriage-way or drive to the Hall, though it is not marked on any plans. The final extent of the emparking which, in the early 19th century, involved further encroachment on the village, the removal of houses and the incorporation of its former green into new paddocks and orchards, is shown on the Tithe Map and early large-scale OS plans.[5]

1. Monson MS VIII (at South Carlton); LAO MONSON 17/2.
2. LCL Ross MSS XII, Lawress, 77.
3. LAO Burton Glebe Terriers.
4. LAO MONSON 19/19, 26, 27; LCL Banks Collection, ff235–7; LAO MONSON 17/2, 28A/19/3/2.
5. LAO MONSON 28A/19/3/2; H454; OS 25 in 1st edn Lincs 61.14.

BUSLINGTHORPE

(1) Moated Site (TF 080852) [62, 63], formerly the site of the manor of Buslingthorpe, lies at 24 m above OD on Till in the centre of the deserted village.

The demesne of Robert de Todeni's manor in 1086 was tenanted by Berenger and Robert de Insula's estate in about 1115 by that *Buselinus* who apparently gave his name to the settlement. It may be that the creation of a substantial moated residence set within a clearly defined rectangular area, perhaps the foundation or rebuilding of the church, and the replanning of the settlement in a regulated manner were the reasons behind such a renaming. Documentary evidence for these events is totally absent, but the archaeological evidence at least gives the theory some substance.

By the later 13th century the manor was held by the family who gave their name to the settlement and the advowson of St Michael's church was also held in the manor. The family of de Buslingthorpe failed at the end of the 14th century and by 1431 the manor was in the hands of William Tyrwhitt. It remained with the Tyrwhitts at least until the end of the 16th century but once they had developed their principal residence at Kettleby their house here may have been abandoned, perhaps in the early 16th century. The present Manor Farm is a 19th-century building, and it is reported that the foundations of earlier structures have been dug up on its N side within the inner moat.[1]

The roughly rectangular area of a manorial block is defined in the earthworks by village streets to the N, W and S. In its centre an inner moated enclosure, sub-rectangular in plan, is partly occupied by the present farm. The moat is up to 2.5 m deep and water-filled on the N, W and E, and is shown in a similar condition on the Tithe Map of 1841.[2] Material from recent cleaning has been dumped on the adjacent village remains and contained part of a limestone window mullion and a little late medieval pottery. The SE section of the moat has been part-filled and landscaped into a lawn. Breaks in the moat to the W and E may be original, the latter giving access to an outer moated enclosure on that side, now only marked by an L-shaped pond to the N and NE which is shown on the Tithe Map as a broad ditch springing directly off the inner moat; any southward continuation had already been overlaid by a large crewyard. This outer enclosure is balanced on the W by the parish church which, despite total rebuilding of the nave and chancel in 1835, nevertheless retains a medieval W tower and 13th-century chancel arch from a larger earlier building.[3]

Manor Farm

St Michael's
Church

a

b

c

d

e

Metres
0   100   200

0   600
Feet

[**62**] *Buslingthorpe (1) Moated Site, (2) Deserted Village, (3) Pond.*

83

[**63**] *Buslingthorpe (1, 2) from the NE, 26 November 1980. The moated Manor Farm and the parish church are edged on three sides by the regular layout of the former village. All three perhaps result from a total reorganization of the settlement in the early 12th century. Downslope to the S, and surrounded by ridge-and-furrow, is a large embanked pond (3).*

The field to the E of the moat also contained earthworks before it was levelled for arable in 1969. Along the E boundary was a substantial linear ditched feature, 1.5 m–2 m deep, with slight banking on its W, and described on early OS maps as a 'moat' and shown as a broad water-filled feature turning W for a few metres at its S end on the Tithe Map. Two lines of banks or ditches running W at right angles to it at its N end were also recorded by the OS. In 1841 this field was named *Park Close*: it may indeed have been a small deer park or more probably a group of paddocks and orchards. Certainly the minimal find from field-walking there – a single medieval sherd – confirms the absence of occupation.[4]

1. *Cal IPM* VI (1910), 423; XIV (1952), 6; LCL Ross MSS XII, Lawress, 79–80, pedigree facing 87; Blair 1981; *Feudal Aids* III, 358; LM records; NAR TF 08 NE 6.
2. LAO F135.
3. Trollope 1861–2, 162; LAO DIXON 19/1/3 ff73–6.
4. RAF VAP CPE/UK2012/1065–7; CUAC LH 94–96, UA 57–62; LM records; *LHA* **5** (1970), 12; OS 25 in sheets Lincs 53.3 and 7.

(2) **Deserted Village of Buslingthorpe (TF 080851)** [62, 63] lies on Till at 18 m–23 m above OD on a S-facing slope above a small stream flowing W.

The village of Buslingthorpe changed its name in the 12th century during the tenancy of one *Buselinus*. In the late 11th and early 12th centuries it appears as *Esethorp* and *Esathorp,* the first element being either another personal name or a river name.[1]

The manor of *Esethorp* is recorded in 1086 with a minimum population of 14 heads of households. Buslingthorpe is listed separately in 1316 in the *Nomina Villarum* but in the subsidies of 1327–8 and 1332–3 only 13 and 12 taxpayers respectively amount to barely 15 per cent of the wapentake average. The impact of the Black Death brought 50 per cent relief in 1352, yet despite its small size the settlement had already by 1377 recovered to something like its early 14th-century size, with 63 persons listed in the Poll Tax and in 1428 it avoided exemption from the parish tax with a minimum of 10 households. Reliefs in the 15th century were only 7 to 8 per cent, albeit on a low base. Yet in 1539 Buslingthorpe found only 3 men for the Lindsey Musters, in the subsidies of 1542–3 and 1545–6 it was subsumed in the return for Faldingworth, and in 1603 there were only 10 communicants in total. A modest recovery is evident in the 17th century, with 18 communicants in 1676, and 5 households are recorded at the beginning of the 18th century, but this remained the level until the agricultural recovery of the late 19th century brought a rise to 16 in 1901. These households were not on the earlier settlement site but in farmsteads around the parish.

That conversion of arable for sheep was a factor in the decline of the settlement is perhaps suggested by the agreement recorded at the end of the 13th century by Sir Richard Buslingthorpe to deliver two sacks of good wool from his pastures in North Stainton (Stainton le Vale) and in Buslingthorpe to a merchant of Louth. The crude trends point, nevertheless, to a principal phase of conversion in the later 15th or 16th centuries, at that date the responsibility of the Tyrwhitt family. Already by 1447 William Tyrwhitt as patron of both Buslingthorpe and Firsby petitioned that the two livings be united because of their poverty, which had caused the churches to stand vacant for some years. At the beginning of the 17th century there is no record of depopulation, conversion or engrossment: it had happened long before. Successive diocesan surveys succinctly summarized the position: in 1602 'both church and chauncell are very ruinous...by reason there are no parishioners or very fewe there and of no abylitie'; in 1705–23 'nullus rector, nulla domus, nullus fundus'.[2]

The remains of the village are arranged on three sides of the manorial block and form three distinct groups. On the W, a N–S hollow-way, much disturbed in the close W of the church, perhaps formerly had a series of properties on its W side. Any regularity in this has been obscured both by the disturbance in the N and by a branch road running W and S ('a') to serve a group of four or five properties in the SW corner. On the N side is a block of perhaps five properties with traces of yards alongside a hollow-way at their S ends, and very regular dimensions. Its E end ('b') has been destroyed by modern arable and a cobbled area here has been recorded in a drainage trench.[3]

The E–W hollow-way along the S side of the manorial block also apparently has properties fronting its S side, and extending S to form a rectangular area. This hollow-way forms a T-junction ('c') with a deep hollow-way that serves at least two properties as it leads downslope, between ridge-and-furrow, to a triangular embanked pond (Buslingthorpe (3)).

A low bank and ditch ('d') running downslope is a hedge boundary, shown as such on the Tithe Map and 1st edn OS 25 in sheet, but removed before the 2nd edn of 1906.[4]

1. *Lincs DB* 18/3, *LS* 3/8; Fellows Jensen 1978, 88, 105, 290.
2. LCL Ross MSS XII, Lawress, 85; BL Add MS 11574; LAO Bishop's Register (Alnwick) 18 f70; Foster 1926, 234; Cole 1913, 155.
3. *LHA* 5 (1970), 12.
4. LAO F135; OS 25 in sheet Lincs 53.7.

---

(3) Pond (TF 081848) [62, 63] lies at 18 m above OD on Till in the bottom of a small W-draining valley.

The triangular embanked pond ('e') is created by an L-shaped dam with a W arm at right angles to the stream, at least 2 m high and with an S arm diminishing in height to 1 m at its E end. The ditch of an avoidance channel runs along its N side and over-spill backing up from the pond was channelled away along the S side. A water-mill probably stood over the gap in the dam, now utilized by the stream. Though undocumented this pond is probably a manorial appurtenance.

CABOURNE

---

(1) Settlement Remains (TA 143018) [64], formerly part of Cabourne village, lie at about 85 m above OD on either side of a narrow steep-sided Wolds valley, at the point where a series of dry minor valleys combine with the main one. The earthworks are of more than usual interest in that they may, in part, represent the sites of a series of medieval granges connected with sheep-farming.

Domesday Book records no less than seven holdings under Cabourne, but by the early 13th century these had been reduced to two principal secular holdings, which were for a time both held by Gilbert de Tours. There may be a hint of the topographical significance of this division in a reference to the fee of *Esthalle* in Cabourne, held by Gilbert around 1200.[1] More significant is a series of grants to local religious institutions, which perpetuated the 11th-century situation by creating a series of small demesne farms. The most important was Hugh de Baiocis's gift, before 1185, of 13 bovates and seven tofts to the Templars. Under their organization this became the *baillia* or economic and administrative centre for their lands and properties in NE Lindsey. The Hospitallers' later estate at Cabourne was far less important, with the status of a member of Willoughton Preceptory (Willoughton (2)), its centre reckoned only as 'unum croftum, absque domo'.[2] The Gilbertine priory of Alvingham also had a grange in Cabourne from at least the early 13th century. In 1535 the priory's temporality in the vill was worth 13s 4d, let. The same value was assigned to the former monastic possession in William Monson's hands in 1558, then detailed as '1 messuage, 1 toft, 40 acres land, 20 of pasture and 100 of warren and heath'.[3] In addition, Gilbert de Tours gave the

advowson of St Nicholas's church to the Augustinians of Wellow Abbey as part of their early endowment, and in the 14th century they held a manor at Cabourne, which is listed in 1372 among the dilapidations of the abbey's property that here involved a reduction from two ploughs to one. Around 1200 the same Gilbert gave the Dean and Chapter of Lincoln two tofts, a bovate of land and pasture for 180 sheep, as well as common pasture for their own sheep to the canons of Thornton Abbey as part of their early endowment. Hugh de Baiocis also gave Thornton Abbey a bovate, a messuage and common pasture in 1150–60 and Newsham Abbey held grazing for 200 sheep in Cabourne field, evidently a 13th-century grant.[4] The latter items indicate the early importance of grazing at Cabourne, no doubt heightened by the monastic interest: in 1251 × 1262 the Prior of the hospital of St John of Jerusalem in England granted in fee farm tofts, crofts, arable and meadow in Cabourne, and common pasture of the vill for a total of 700 sheep, part of the gift of Gilbert de Tours.[5]

The Dissolution naturally produced a multiplicity of secular ownerships in which the important Lindsey families of the St Pauls, the Tyrwhitts and the Monsons had a share, but between the mid 18th and the beginning of the 19th century the Pelhams of Brocklesby, Earls of Yarborough, had acquired practically the whole parish. At the parliamentary enclosure of Cabourne, in 1811–14, there were just two large farms within the village – the present Cabourne House and Church Farm – and a few cottages.[6]

Although the peak recorded population for Cabourne occurs in 1086 with a minimum of 39, two of the smaller holdings were already waste. The early 14th-century lists of 14 and 15 taxpayers represent barely more than half the average for the area – the impact presumably of monastic holdings and early conversion to pasture. Relief of 100 per cent in 1352 and exemption from the parish tax in 1428 with less than 10 households mark a further sharp decline, but reliefs in the 15th century were below 20 per cent and declining, albeit in relation to a low base level. Only 7 persons were available for the Lindsey Musters in 1539, there were 6 taxpayers in 1542–3, 12 households in 1563, 42 communicants in 1603 and 53 in 1676. At the beginning of the 18th century these levels had doubled, and the modern period has seen a characteristic late 19th-century peak of population.

A coherent chronological and morphological history for this settlement is made difficult by the complexity of the extant earthworks, the loss of upstanding detail in certain areas due to ploughing, and the positions of the surviving farmsteads and cottages. Generally the earthworks represent former close boundaries, low but well-defined banks and shallow ditches, associated with terraces and hollow-ways, marking the old village streets and lanes. The overall appearance of the earthworks is of a series of property blocks unlike conventional village plots. Occasionally the sites of former buildings are identifiable, but these are few, as evidence from the ploughed areas confirms. It is significant that on both sides of the valley ridge-and-furrow apparently underlies a number of the properties. Substantial sections of the earthworks must therefore represent later expansion or infilling for some activities not necessarily connected with normal village settlement.

The area around the church has particular claims as a location for early settlement. Since a number of valleys join here, it is topographically the most suitable site for settlement in the locality. Unfortunately this is the area where the earthworks are least well-preserved. To the NE of the church a well may mark the site of the early village spring. To the NW and N of the church are low

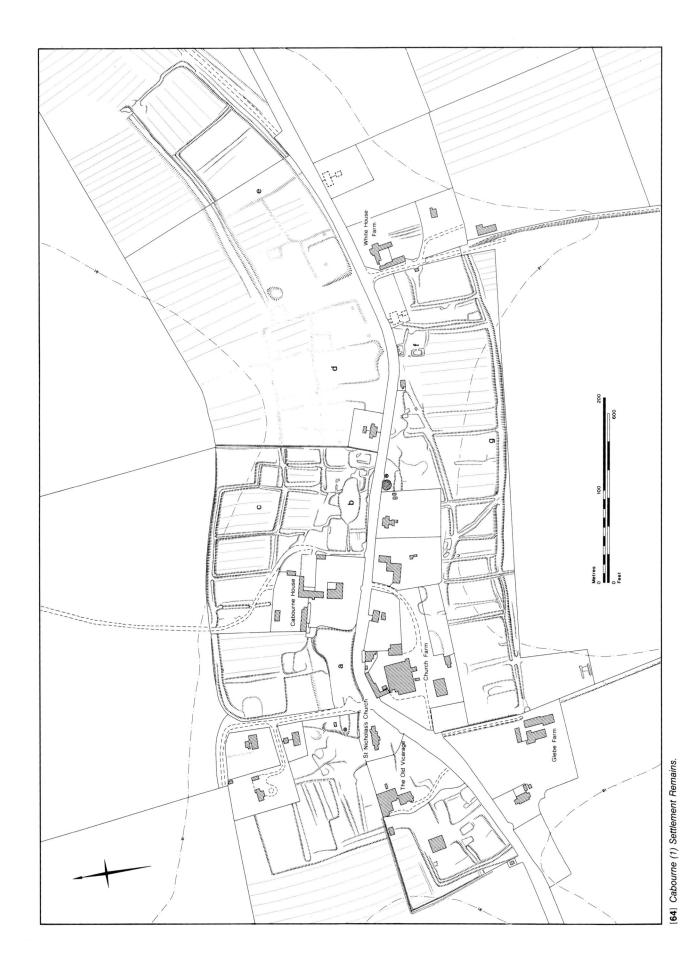

White House Farm

e

d

f

g

Cabourne House

c

b

a

r

St Nicholas's Church

The Old Vicarage

Church Farm

Glebe Farm

Metres
0   100   200
Feet
0   600

[64] *Cabourne (1) Settlement Remains.*

86

earthworks rendered indeterminate by levelling and ploughing in 1965. Air photographs show that prior to this they were associated with the sites of former rectangular buildings. Field-walking produced 13th to 15th-century pottery and slag.[7] The Old Vicarage and its gardens have removed any remains immediately W of the church. In the paddock SW of the vicarage, fragmentary earthworks representing buildings and small plots are cut by a bank and ditched boundary feature that nevertheless lies within the limits of the old enclosures mapped in 1814, which follow the field boundary and include the block of ridge-and-furrow to the N. Both this close and that NW of the church had the field-name *Coney Close* in 1814 and contained no buildings.[8]

To the E of the church, the valley floor has been obscured by a former pond ('a') shown as water-filled in 1814, and by Cabourne House and Church Farm, which have perhaps overlain early settlement. Another pond ('b') cuts through earthworks which comprise tofts with foundations of stone buildings and boundaries which pick up the close divisions rising up the valley side. The pattern possibly continued westwards as it does to the E; alternatively, the pond ('a') and farms may represent the infilling of a former green in front of the church with the well or spring at one end.

The closes N and NE of Cabourne House ('c') are much longer than those to the immediate E but are divided half-way up the slope by a terrace-way that continues through as the back boundary of the block of closes to the E ('d'). Both overlie ridge-and-furrow. The earthworks of the eastern block ('d') were levelled and ploughed in 1968 exposing the course of a road and close boundaries. The latter contained only two clear occupation areas, one comprising the chalk foundations of a building of about 25 m × 10 m, the other sherds of medieval pottery.[9]

A very well-defined block lies further E ('e'). Although different in consisting of a ladder pattern of fairly broad closes, it too overlies former arable. Whether all of its enclosures contained structures is uncertain but there were rectangular buildings in the westernmost.

On the S side of the valley, the pattern of closes is confused by late additions. It may have consisted of perhaps five large closes similar to those to the N, with later subdivisions. On the other hand, it could have been an abandoned section of the village which had later properties superimposed on it whose boundaries did not coincide with the earlier patterns. Chalk rubble foundations ('f') mark the position of a farm complex set on top of earlier arable.

The former village street system also raises problems and reinforces the impression that the settlement remains and other earthworks are not all contemporary. An old track (SE of 'e') following the main valley merges with the modern road at its SW end. As the latter road veers to follow the valley bottom, a hollow-way (W of 'f'), appears running up on to the S side of the valley. Its relationship to the close boundaries is interesting. In some instances it seems to cut across them obliquely while in others it is crossed by them. This hollow-way perhaps once skirted a large former green to the N, although the apparent lack of buildings on its S side argues against this and its origin may lie in a division between the front area of properties and appendant closes. Following the S lip of the valley and at right angles to the boundaries of the closes is a terrace-way ('g') partly defined by a well-marked lynchet. At its W end it probably turned N by Glebe Farm to join the main road. On the N slope of the main valley a former way, part terraced and part hollowed and fronting an old headland, bounds the main block around Cabourne House ('c'). It then turns sharply three times to form the rear of the next block ('d') where at least one building was built against it. Further E again the street meets the adjacent block ('e') and becomes a terrace-way. The form and situation of this way is directly comparable with that on the opposite side of the valley.

Despite the difficulties of interpretation, the settlement remains at Cabourne do seem to fall into distinct blocks that are not necessarily all contemporary. At the same time, they may also have a tenurial significance and be grange farms connected specifically with the documentary evidence for sheep grazing: what appears as a single farm and paddocks that make up the north-eastern block ('e') might readily be a grange with home closes for breeding, while the block of closes around White House Farm, separated it seems from the village remains to the W, could be similar or even an eastern manor in named contrast with one near the church.

1. *Lincs DB* 14/38, 22/8, 25/4, 25/9, 27/13, 27/18, 44/18; *LS* 8/5, 6, 8, 9; *Book of Fees* I, 155, 156; II, 1077, 1086, 1472; Foster and Major 1931–73 IV, 262–3.
2. Lees 1935, 104–6; Larking 1857, 146.
3. VCH *Lincs* II (1906), 193; *VE* IV, 58; LCL Ross MSS V, 63.
4. VCH *Lincs* II (1906), 163; Gibbons 1888, 96; LAO typescript list of incumbents and patrons; *Cal Inq Misc* III (1937), 323; Dugdale 1817–30 VI, 326–7; Foster and Major 1931–73 IV, 262–3, 266; *Cal LPFD Hen VIII* XXI, pt 1 (1908), 378; XIV pt 1 (1894), 259; *Cal Chart R* III (1908), 386; LAO MCD 105.
5. LAO FL Deeds 3004.
6. LAO LCS 1/7, 14/6; MONSON 28B/13/7–8; PT 1/1–4; BRAD 1/8/1; YARB 4/5/1.
7. RAF VAP CPE/UK1746/2052; *LHA* **4** (1969), 111.
8. LAO YARB 4/5/1.
9. *LHA* **4** (1969), 111.

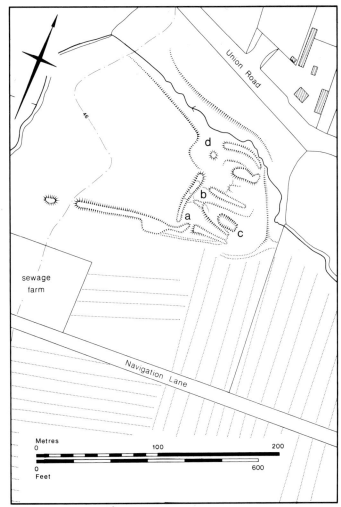

[**65**] *Caistor (6) Fishponds.*

CAISTOR

(6) **Fishponds (TA 108012)** [65] lie at about 46 m above OD, 1 km W of Caistor church alongside a small W-flowing stream fed by springs emerging from the base of the small promontory on which the town of Caistor stands. The stream now runs in a channel in places over 2 m deep but it is cut through the Cover Sands to the underlying clay. The site has been somewhat damaged but consists of two roughly triangular ponds ('a' and 'b') up to 0.5 m deep at their W ends becoming shallower to the E. Each has a dam 1 m in height on the W, which together form a continuous bank. Another pond ('c'), approximately 0.75 m deep, is set into the lower E end of the broad bank dividing the two main ponds. It is probably a fish-breeding or sorting tank. A fourth, more irregular, pond ('d') does not have a dam: it slopes gently N towards the stream and has a small island within it. Slight traces of a hollow on the SE may indicate a leat bringing water from upstream to feed the ponds through the surviving gap in the S bank. Sluices here, and at the other narrow gaps in the banks, would have allowed close control of water flow, and discharge either across the meadow to the W or back into the stream.

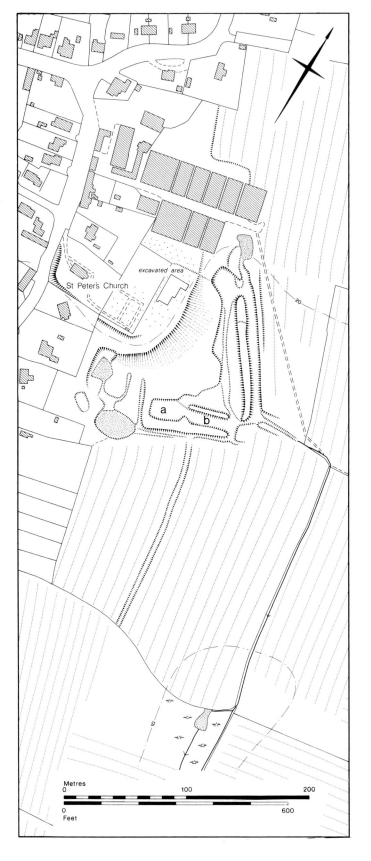

[**66**] *Cherry Willingham (2) Fishponds.*

CHERRY WILLINGHAM

(2) Fishponds (TF 033724) [66] lie on the edge of Cherry Willingham village at about 20 m above OD on Blisworth Clay. No direct contemporary reference has been found to the fishponds, but they were probably appurtenances of the manor held from the 12th to the early 15th century by the Marmion family of the fee of Gant.

Two ponds are shown on the Tithe Map, with the field-name *Cross Homestead*.[1] The earthworks fill the shallow valley to the E of the church and they provide in a simple manner complex options in water management. Two approximately parallel leats separated by a bank 1 m high served to channel water from a spring (now a small pond) at the junction of the Blisworth Clay and the overlying Cornbrash. The W channel, apparently the original stream bed, feeds a pair of ponds ('a' and 'b') with a common downslope dam 1 m–1.5 m high. A second dam-like bank 1 m high at right angles to the channel, along the N side of the E pond ('b'), may have allowed water to be ponded in the W channel to form an irregular and shallow elongated pond, as well as forcing water into the W pond ('a'). A gap, and presumably sluice, at the E end of the main dam allowed the ponds to discharge. A straight E leat branched at its S end to provide an avoidance channel into what is now a hedge-line dyke, as well as access to the main E pond ('b'). Irregular ponds and hollows to the W of the earthworks perhaps result from small-scale extraction of sand and clay, but the oval cattle pond seems to have obliterated a small rectangular pond shown on the Tithe Map. It was perhaps linked with and fed by surviving ditches, and may have been part of the fishpond complex. Field-walking of the ploughed top of the knoll to the W has produced pottery of early Saxon to early medieval date. Excavations in 1980 located evidence of occupation of the 5th to the 12th centuries including a sunken hut, drainage gullies, fences and an iron-smelting furnace.[2]

1. RAF VAP 3G/TUD/UK197/5409–10; *LS* 3/15; *Book of Fees* I, 190; *Cal IPM* I (1904), 312; III (1912), 21; V (1908), 272; LCL Ross MSS XII, 343–4; LAO A600.
2. Everson 1979, 79–80; Field 1981, 70.

CLAXBY

(1) Settlement Remains (TF 112946) [67], formerly part of Claxby village, lie at about 50 m above OD at the foot of the Wolds scarp on Cover Sands and Kimmeridge Clay. The village is a good example of a complex development which is almost impossible to explain in detail. Certainly its present form bears little relation to the earlier layout.

Both in tenure and in returns on which an assessment of population might be based, Claxby is bound up with Normanby le Wold throughout the medieval period, so that little can usefully be detailed. There were, however, a multiplicity of tenurial interests in the parish at least until the Dissolution. By the mid 16th century it appears to be similar in size to Normanby, and thereafter it began to fare rather better. There is nothing in the post-medieval documentation that implies any depopulation.[1]

Most of the surviving earthworks within the village relate to the former post-medieval gardens and park of Claxby House and the development and changes which produced these features as well as a lack of early plans make any analysis of the development of the medieval village more than usually conjectural. Nevertheless its principal focus and orientation seems likely to have been a N–S street now represented by St Mary's Lane and its continuation S as a broad hollow-way ('a'). Perhaps significantly this links neatly at both ends with roads outside the settlement that form sections of a way, now largely footpaths and bridle roads, that runs along the foot of the scarp to both N and S. No village remains relating to this street have survived later changes, unless the empty closes at the N end ('b' – field-name *Town End Close* in 1847) were village properties.

A second village focus may be indicated by scatters of medieval pottery together with a bronze annular brooch, found in a ploughed close at the E end of Boggle Lane ('c'). This area lies on rising ground at the foot of the scarp and just below a spring; the large close to the NE was *Elvin Garth* in 1847. Some ill-defined scarps, banks and terraces to the N of the stream ('d') may mark abandoned properties, and a triangular open area immediately to the W and also N of the stream ('e'), shown on all 19th-century plans, may have been an associated green.[2]

Boggle Lane provides a link between the N end of St Mary's Lane, and the presumed second nucleus. The existing closes on the N side of this lane have a remarkably regular aspect, and in 1847 comprised considerably more than now survive. Though they enclosed poor waterlogged land at the foot of the scarp, they were formerly under arable cultivation. The pattern of closes to the S of the lane has been almost completely obliterated, but the Tithe Map of 1847, as well as some ditches faintly visible on air photographs ('f'), give slight indications of a set of closes similar to but shorter than that on the N. This regularity of form might suggest that the lane and its closes were a late, planned, development, perhaps removing or relocating the principal village focus from St Mary's Lane as that area was engulfed by Claxby House and its gardens, perhaps therefore as late as the 17th century.

The only surviving N–S through-way is the present Mulberry Road along which a major part of the village is now located. This was certainly in existence by the early 19th century, but the fact that its adjacent properties are characteristically shallow and, more importantly, that it overrides the remains of the 17th-century garden indicates that it is a later element in the village plan.[3]

1. *LS* 7/1–4; *Book of Fees* I, 153; II, 1018, 1083, 1088; *Feudal Aids* III, 152, 161, 220, 229, 268, 290, 299, 356.
2. RAF VAP 541/185/3052–3, 4078–9; air photographs in NMR; LM records; local inf; LAO D479.
3. LAO DIXON 19/2/1/4.

(2) Garden Remains (TF 112946) [67] lie on the W side of Claxby village at 50 m above OD. They represent the site of an elaborate formal garden, probably of 17th-century date, together with the results of later landscaping.

By the early 16th century, the major landowner at Claxby, the Witherwicke family, appears to have been resident at Claxby House. Marriage of a daughter and sole heiress in the early 17th century took the estate to the Catholic George Markham of Ollerton (Notts), but the resident successors were another Catholic family, the Fitzwilliams. Subsequently the estate passed through several hands before it was acquired by the Yarborough Estate which, in the 19th century, owned almost the whole parish.[1]

The present Claxby House is an early 19th-century structure, said to have been built in 1809–10, replacing an earlier house. This

Normanby le Wold parish

Woodland View

Boggle Lane

Mulberry Road

Normanby Rise

St Mary's Lane

Claxby House

St Mary's Church

Rectory

a b c d e f g h i j k

Metres
0   100   200

0
Feet   600

[**67**] *Claxby (1) Settlement Remains, (2) Garden Remains.*

latter is shown on Nattes's drawing of 1795 as a very undistinguished structure of probably 18th-century date, and it appears to have been little more than a farmhouse.[2] It may, however, have incorporated an earlier building of higher status. A date-stone of 1662, reset in a garden wall, may indicate some work at that time.

Immediately E of Claxby House is a group of earthworks which is the remains of a garden, formerly associated with the house. The most prominent feature is a series of broad marshy ditches known as *Claxby Stew Ponds*, and which has been interpreted as a moated site, the ditches forming the three sides of a broad platform ('g').[3] However, although the site may have originated as a medieval moat, its present form is that of the centre-piece of a formal garden, though much altered. The apparent northern E–W ditch is relatively narrow and was probably once only the inlet and outlet channel to a T-shaped pond before the adjacent stream was straightened. The feature is indeed depicted as an equal-armed T-shaped pond on an early 19th-century estate map and on the Tithe Map of 1847. These also show the arms with rounded ends, an echo of which survives only in the curving bank beyond the stream at the N end of the N–S arm. The terminations of the other arms have been modified by the house to the W and the construction of Mulberry Road to the E. The S arm to complete an equal-armed cruciform arrangement is supplied by a broad embanked area leading to a mound ('h'). This mound is 3.5 m–4 m high and though no doubt altered by the intrusion of an ice-house, it certainly existed at the beginning of the 19th century when it was described as 'an ancient tumulus'.[4] This cruciform arrangement forms the focus of a garden layout of rectangular enclosures, marked in part by scarps and ditches on air photographs, that extended E of Mulberry Road to the ditched boundary ('i') and S to the well-preserved straight ditch ('j'). Two ancient mulberry trees to the S of the house may be relics of the formal planting here.

These gardens are likely to be of late 16th or early 17th-century date and therefore associated with the residence of the Witherwickes or the Fitzwilliams at Claxby. By the end of the 18th century, at least, the house had declined in status if Nattes's view is correct and certainly the gardens themselves had been abandoned and cut across by Mulberry Road by the early 19th century. The rebuilding of the house in 1809–10 led later to the creation of a small landscaped park, which extended S from the old garden and incorporated an earlier oval enclosure ('k') bounded by a shallow ditch that itself is cut through ridge-and-furrow. This enclosure is shown as a hedged field on the early 19th-century estate map but by 1847 it was within the new park. Its boundary was marked by mature trees by the late 19th century.[5]

Some of the earthworks W and SW of the Rectory and the church are marked on the Tithe Map of 1847 as existing field boundaries though others seem to relate to an earlier field pattern. Most of these were removed in the second half of the 19th century as part of the creation of Claxby Park.

This emparking was probably carried out by the Yarborough's tenants at Claxby throughout the 19th century, John Joseph Young and his sons. The Youngs, members of the Catholic family of the same name at Kingerby Hall, farmed a large area of land occupying almost all the S part of the parish and were by far the largest tenants in Claxby.[6]

1. Maddison 1902–6 III, 1096–7; Cole 1911, 99–100; LCL Ross MSS IV, Walshcroft, 17, 20, 21; Cole 1913, 32; White 1856, 474–5.
2. LCL Banks Collection I, 295; Weir 1828, 248; local inf.
3. NAR TF 19 SW 15.

4. Weir 1828, 248.
5. LAO DIXON 19/2/1/4; D479; OS 1st edn 25 in sheets Lincs 37.16, 38.13.
6. LAO D479; White's, Kelly's and Post Office County Directories.

(3) Deserted Farmstead (TF 11039664) [2, 68, 69] is situated on an exposed ledge which interrupts the main W-facing scarp of the Wolds at 125 m above OD, some 300 m W of Acre House. The site represents a post-medieval farmstead abandoned in the 19th century.

Acrehouse was an important holding of Newsham Abbey and the surveyed earthworks have been identified as the site of the associated grange farm.[1] However, it is much more likely that the grange itself lay at the foot of the scarp in the centre of a block of land attributable to Newsham Abbey's holding where there are a concentration of field-names containing *Acrehouse* (TA 104966) [2].

Seventeenth-century inventories show 'Acrehouse' as a residence, perhaps a successor to the medieval grange, occupied by the family of Green, probably as tenants of the Pelhams, later Earls of Yarborough.[2]

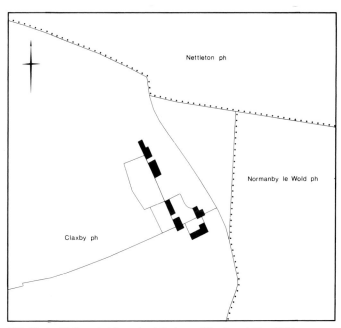

[68] *Claxby (3) Deserted Farmstead. Redrawn Tithe Award Map 1847.*

Acrehouse was rebuilt in 1778–9; on Armstrong's map of 1778, it is shown high on the Wolds scarp on the site of the surviving earthworks, which thus may represent a post-Dissolution move though still within the land formerly belonging to Newsham. In 1842 George Whitworth 'gent.' lived at Acre House; in 1856 the occupier was Robert Gooseman as it had been at the time of the Tithe Award in 1847.[3] In addition to 216 acres in Claxby, Gooseman occupied an adjacent 109 acres in Normanby owned similarly by the Earl of Yarborough, and this allowed the earlier farmhouse on the Wolds scarp to be abandoned in the early 1850s in favour of the new site 300 m to the E in Normanby parish. Thereafter George Brooks and his successors at Acre House appear in directories under Normanby le Wold.[4]

The site lies chiefly on the NW side of the track which drops down on to the ledge near the S end of the settlement with branches into

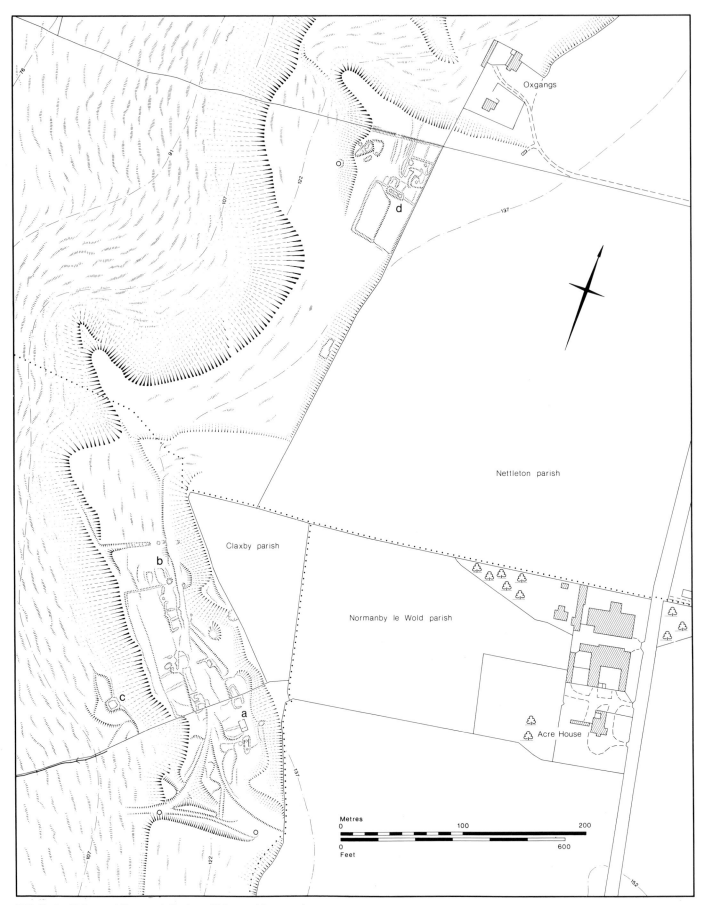

Oxgangs

Nettleton parish

Claxby parish

Normanby le Wold parish

Acre House

Metres
0   100   200

0   600
Feet

[**69**] *Claxby (3) Deserted Farmstead, Nettleton (5) Deserted Farmstead.*

the settlement itself. Low banks representing the remains of walls, scarps and hollows define a series of rectangular buildings and short paddocks, the form and arrangement of which suggest no more than a post-medieval upland farmstead whose linear plan is reflected by the topographical constraints. Practically every element can be reconciled with the farmstead shown on the Tithe Award Map of 1847 [68], whose buildings were arranged in two main groups. The main building ('a') is particularly well marked and wall remnants show that brick and Tealby Limestone were used in its construction. A number of holes ('b') probably reflect mining subsidence, while a square building, not shown on the Tithe Map, below the farmstead ('c') and on the edge of stabilized mud flows, may represent an isolated barn or a shepherd's cottage.

1. Foster and Longley 1924, xlviii; Stenton 1920, 171, no 238, 193, no 258; *Feudal Aids* III, 161 (1303), 220 (1346); *VE* IV, 74; *Cal LPFD Hen VIII* XIV pt 1 (1894), 260.
2. LAO INV 154/522 (1647/8); INV 194/162 (1699/1700).
3. LAO YARB 5/2/17/1; Gibbons 1975, 73; White 1842, 407, 1856, 475; LAO D479.
4. LAO D483; YARB 4/8/8, 5/2/17/5; White 1872, 489.

COLD HANWORTH

(1) **Deserted Village of Cold Hanworth (TF 035831)** [70] lies on Till at 13 m above OD, between the confluence of the Barlings Eau and one of its tributaries, on rising ground slightly above their floodplains. Cold Hanworth parish occupies the lower, E, end of a land block spanning the limestone dipslope which it shares with Hackthorn.

Cold Hanworth was clearly always a smaller than average settlement and seems never to have recovered from a late 14th-century decline and perhaps subsequent enclosure.

Though two shared entries with Hackthorn prevent a precise calculation of minimum recorded population in 1086, it was almost certainly at least as high as the level of the early 14th-century subsidies, when 15 and 17 taxpayers represent almost exactly half the average for the wapentake. It had nevertheless been listed separately rather than as a dependency in 1316. There was relief of only 16.3 per cent in 1352, immediately after the Black Death, but the Poll Tax in 1377 returned only 19 persons over the age of 14 years and there were less than 10 households in 1428. The 15th century, with reliefs persistently over 30 per cent, apparently saw little recovery, though the settlement produced 8 men for the Lindsey Musters in 1539 and 5 taxpayers in 1542–3. There were only 24 communicants in 1603, less than 20 per cent of the rural average for the archdeaconry, and 17 in 1676.

From at least 1389 until about 1600 the lordship of Cold Hanworth was in the hands of Robert Sutton and his descendants 'one of the greatest Lincolnshire families of the 14th and 15th centuries', and certainly non-residents. It was perhaps the Suttons who contributed to the decline of the village. In 1558 the manor comprised four messuages, five cottages and 250 acres of land.[1] The survey of depopulations in 1607 recorded that Robert Grantham had enclosed 26 acres for pasture, but slightly earlier Glebe Terriers appear to show much of the parish in closes already. By the late 18th century Cold Hanworth was reckoned to be 'old enclosed'.[2] There were only 4 households in 1705–23, but the growth from 7 rising to 13 in the first half of the 19th century established a pattern for the parish described in 1842 as 'divided into six farms... the houses scattered' that persists to the present.[3]

The W half of the site was levelled by ploughing before the Commission's survey, but the pattern of the former earthworks here can be reconstructed from aerial photographs and scarps plotted by the OS before destruction.[4] The axis of the village seems to have been an apparently meandering W–E hollow-way ('a'–'b'–'c'). Settlement closes defined by ditches occur on either side. The irregular line of this hollow-way may suggest a disjunction between the E and W parts of the remains (perhaps on the line 'b'–'d') and the possibility that the W part marks an expansion, probably planned, from a core focused on the church.

Two dwellings in small closes lying outside the main area of earthworks ('e') are marked on the Tithe and Drainage Maps of 1842 and 1848, but not on the early OS 25 in sheets of 1883–8. These early maps also suggest an E–W way along the N side of the churchyard, perhaps a back lane similar to that on the S. To the SW of Church Farm ('f') the ridge-and-furrow has been damaged by later earthworks. These together with Church Farm are away from the main core of the old village and possibly represent relatively late activity.

1. Hill 1965, 166; LCL Ross MSS IV, Aslacoe (East) 48; Maddison 1902–6 III, 938–40.
2. BL Add MS 11574 f81; LAO Cold Hanworth Terrier Bundle; Russell 1975, map 10.
3. White 1842, 482–3.
4. CUAC LI 9; RAF VAP 541/185/4163–4; OS 1:2500 sheet TF 0283–0383.
5. LAO 3BNL 25; H538; OS 25 in sheet Lincs 53.9.

Metres
0   100   200
0   600
Feet

[70] *Cold Hanworth (1) Deserted Village of Cold Hanworth.*

[71] *Fulnetby (3) Deserted Settlement of* Helethorpe.

FULNETBY

(3) Deserted Settlement of *Helethorpe* **(TF 086787)** [71] has hitherto been unlocated.[1] It is situated in the south-western corner of the parish on Till at around 20 m above OD.

Helethorpe is documented by name from 1212 but never in taxation returns and in 1563 only one household is still ascribed to it, though not necessarily on this site. The name survives as late as 1711 and to about 1800 for the township area belonging to the settlement.[2] Earthworks on the site are recorded on early aerial photographs but were subsequently destroyed. In plan they form a rectangular block that might be either a single large demesne farm or a small settlement. The ditched and embanked arrangement of the whole may argue for the former. The site appears to have been inserted into an arable field system at the junction of several furlongs. Field-walking in 1977 produced pottery of the 12th to early 15th century, but no later. In one area was a very large and dense scatter of tile of shelly fabric which could indicate manufacture on the site.[3]

1. Foster and Longley 1924, lxxxvi.
2. *Book of Fees* I, 172; LAO MISC DEP 65/2/1, 3 BNL 10.
3. RAF VAP CPE/UK1880/2257, 5258; 541/185/3045–6; air photographs in NMR.

GAINSBOROUGH

(4) Deer Park (centred SK 835885) [40, 41] occupied about 144 ha in the SE corner of the parish. It is identifiable only as a coherent block of fields on early estate maps, the majority with *Park* names.[1] Its existence may be indicated by the grant of free warren in the 13th century and Leland certainly reports 'a parke by Gainesborow longging to the Lord Borrow'. By 1601 it was disparked and divided into closes. Extensive areas of ridge-and-furrow are visible within it.[2] A moated site at SK 836881 (Gainsborough (3)) was presumably the park-keeper's lodge, with surrounding paddocks, orchards or gardens. Its earthworks were destroyed between 1963 and 1967.

1. LAO BRACE 17/18; BACON PLANS 39; Gainsborough parish plans.
2. Beckwith 1972, 11–12; Toulmin-Smith 1964 I, 33.

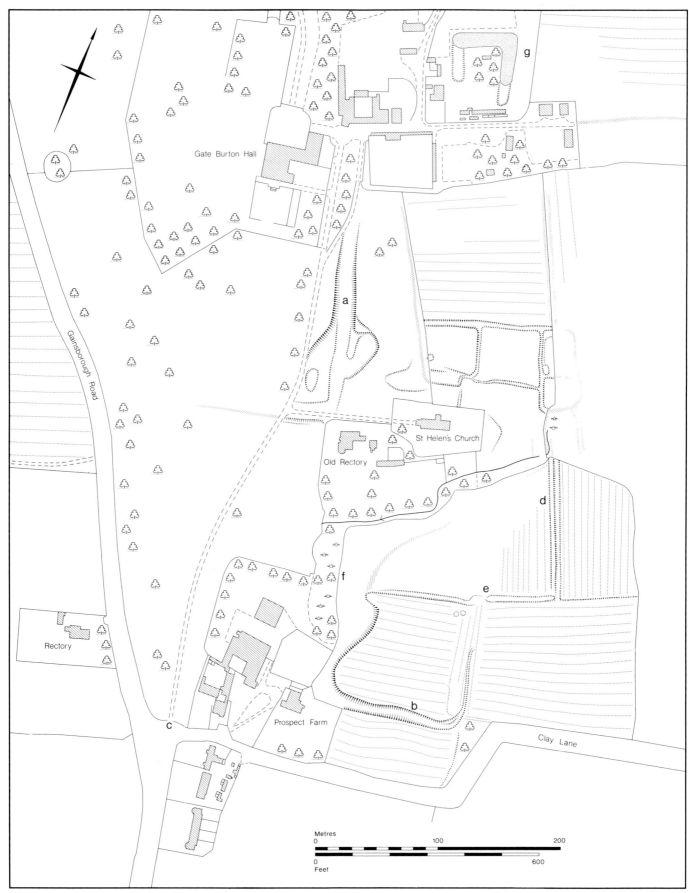

[72] *Gate Burton (1) Settlement Remains.*

(1) Settlement Remains (SK 838829) [72], formerly part of Gate Burton, lie at 20 m above OD on Cover Sands, just over 1 km E of the R Trent. They are a classic instance of settlement shift and dispersal caused by emparking in the 18th century.

In the 17th and early 18th century the lordship of Gate Burton formed part of the Knaith estate of the Lords Willoughby of Parham; it was sold, perhaps as early as 1739, to the Hutton family, formerly of Treswell (Notts) who were presumably responsible for the removal of the village from its ancient site. William Hutton's house of 1774–80 forms the core of the present Gate Burton Hall but the surrounding landscaped parkland may be older, since the ornamental temple to the NW was allegedly erected in 1747 when perhaps the village was also cleared.[1]

There is little sign in the tax and other survey returns of any marked or permanent decline in population until the 18th century. In 1086 a minimum population of 10 heads of households is recorded; in the early 14th century 24 and 25 taxpayers in 1327–8 and 1332–3 respectively are slightly over the average for the wapentake. Relief of 21.3 per cent was allowed in 1352; no Poll Tax returns survive, but the impact of the Black Death cannot have been great since Gate Burton was not exempt from the parish tax in 1428 and therefore must have retained at least 10 households. Nevertheless continuing reliefs of 20–25 per cent in the mid 15th century may indicate some long-term retreat. In 1539 14 men were produced for the Lindsey Musters; there were 12 taxpayers in 1542–3 and the 81 communicants in 1603 represent about 65 per cent of the rural average for the archdeaconry. There were 69 communicants plus 5 nonconformists in 1676. No depopulation, enclosure or engrossment was reported in 1607. Rentals of the Willoughby lands in 1654 and 1660 mention 7 farms and 2 cottage houses, and 8 farms and 2 cottage houses and a cottage respectively. In the early 18th century 21 and 20 families were returned.[2]

Emparking by the Huttons evidently had a marked effect, and was perhaps linked with enclosure. Glebe land in 1724 still lay in strips in the open fields but by 1788 it was in closes. A petition of 1784 to rebuild the church claimed that the parishioners consisted only of 'four farmers... a small number of cottages and another householder' besides the rector and the lord of the manor.[3] The population of 13 households in 1801 may by then have been recovering: it rose to 20 households by mid-century and 25 a century later. It was, however, no longer housed on the earlier village site but in cottages around the park, in a small estate nucleus at the park gates and in scattered farmsteads elsewhere in the parish.

The field remains are characteristically poor as is often the case at villages removed for late emparking. The most prominent are two hollow-ways: one, ('a') runs approximately N–S and, though its very broad and smooth profile may result from continued use as a carriage road within the park, it perhaps marks the former line of the Gainsborough road before the creation of the parkland. It is named in the Glebe Terriers as *Town Street* upon which the parsonage abutted. The second hollow-way ('b') continues the direct line of Clay Lane downhill off the higher land to the E. Both hollow-ways therefore indicate fundamental alteration to the road system in the 18th century: indeed the W diversion of the Gainsborough road is shown on earlier maps to have been even more marked than now appears, amounting practically to a right-angled turn at the park gates ('c') before modern roadworks smoothed the alignment.[4] To the N and E of the church is a series of ditched earthwork closes that clearly once continued into the ploughland to the E, where traces of their extent are visible as soil-marks on air photographs.[5] No properties are shown here on the Tithe Map of 1848 apart from the church, the Old Rectory and its outbuildings. The closes may mark former village remains. However a prominent bank and ditch ('d'–'e') on the hill-slope to the S that forms two sides of a large rectangular block on the same alignment as the closes, raises the possibility of an early manorial *curia*. This might have encompassed both the church and the Old Rectory and have been split by a diagonal chain of ponds fed by a spring E of the church, if these are not solely 18th-century features. Only the largest of these ponds is now obvious as a reedy hollow ('f'), but at least two more are shown on early OS plans along the S boundary of the Old Rectory garden and all are named as 'fishponds' in the Tithe Award.[6]

The former limit of the village to the NE is presumably indicated by the Tithe Award field-name *Town End Close* immediately E of the kitchen garden of the Hall: the Hall, outbuildings and garden may have occupied much of the earlier village site. In the kitchen garden a three-sided 'moat' ('g'), shown on 19th-century maps in the same form, is aligned with the garden boundaries and is probably an ornamental and recreational feature.[7]

1. LCL Ross MSS I, Well, 1–2 and Hutton Pedigree facing 10; Pevsner and Harris 1964, 246.
2. BL Add MS 11574; John Rylands Library MS 2587, ff1–2.
3. LAO Gate Burton Glebe Terriers; FB1/25, FAC/4/10.
4. OS 1st edn 1 in sheet 83.
5. CUAC AUE 18; RAF VAP CPE/UK2009/1065–6, CPE/UK2012/1130–1, 3122–3; air photographs in NMR.
6. LAO F580.
7. LAO F580, 3 BNL 17; NAR SK 88 SW 10.

GOLTHO

(2) Moated Site and Garden Remains (TF 117766) [40, 73] lie around Goltho Hall on Till at 20 m above OD, in the NW corner of the medieval deer park (3) and just under 1 km S of the deserted village of Goltho (1).

Though Goltho Hall is probably the site of a late medieval moated park lodge and perhaps of an earlier medieval settlement, the features recoverable from field investigation and air photographs are most likely to be all post-medieval formal garden remains associated with the house of the Grantham family and their successors the Mainwarings, although earlier details may have been adapted.

The manor of Goltho was held in the 12th, 13th and early 14th centuries by the family of Kyme and passed by marriage to the de Umfravilles and before the end of the 14th century to the Tailbois family. Both Kymes and Tailbois seemed to have regarded Goltho as their principal residence. Excavations at the village of Goltho (1) have shown that the manorial residence there was abandoned by the end of the 12th century. Though the earthwork at Cocklode Wood in Bullington parish (Bullington (3)) has been suggested as its replacement a more likely alternative is that a residence within the extensive deer park, on the site later continuously occupied by grand houses, served for the late medieval manorial lords too.[1]

The Tailbois line failed in the early 16th century and Goltho was bought by the family of Grantham, successful Lincoln merchants, who put their money into land and established themselves as county notables. Goltho was evidently turned into a suitable country seat for the successive generations of active public figures. It passed by the marriage of Elizabeth Grantham (d 1692) to Lieut Col

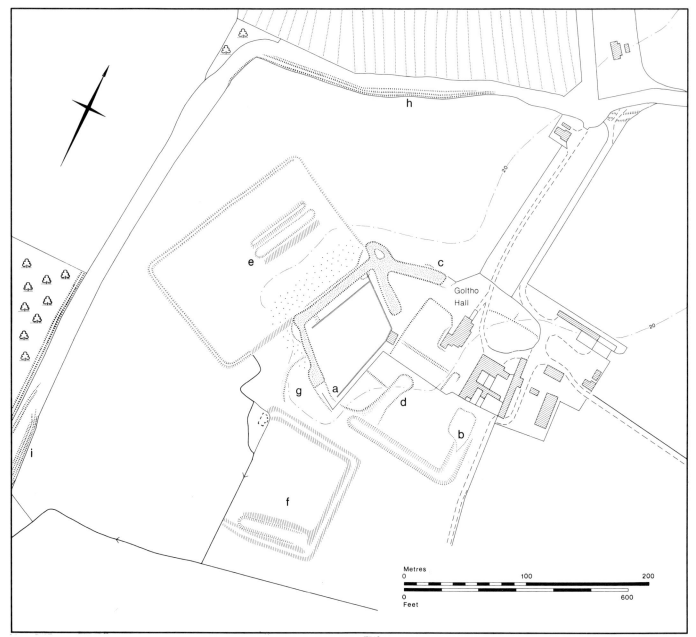

[73] *Goltho (2) Moated Site and Garden Remains, (3) Deer Park.*

Charles Mainwaring of Martinsand (Cheshire) and was used as a principal residence at least until the death of Thomas Mainwaring in 1789.[2] A drawing, probably by Nattes around 1790, of a red-brick mansion of about 1700 is preserved in the Banks Collection. This house perhaps stood on the site now occupied by the 19th-century Goltho Hall. An earlier and grander mansion is described in the probate inventory of Sir Thomas Grantham (d 1630) and included some additions to an earlier building. He represented the county in parliament over the period 1604–29 and was renowned for the style and scale of his hospitality. His son, Thomas Grantham, who died in the 1650s, repaired or rebuilt Goltho church while High Sheriff in 1638–9.[3]

The garden layout is of a form generally datable to the late 16th or early 17th century. It could have been the work of either of the Thomas Granthams or both successively. To the W of Goltho Hall the only unploughed feature is a four-armed water-filled moat. The

S arm now terminates in recently dumped fill ('a'). Its former E continuation is recorded on OS 1:2500 plans, with a right-angled turn N to the site of a large pond ('b') recorded on earlier OS sheets.[4] This obliterated section strongly suggests itself as part of an outer moated circuit linked to the surviving N arm ('c'), whose NE corner has been infilled by farm buildings and gardens. The present S, W and central arms probably formed an inner rectangular enclosure, perhaps originally the principal building platform whose return on the E can be traced with difficulty in levelled but uncultivated land as a broad scarp and depression ('d').

The limited survival of this inner moat was clearly determined by the construction within it of a brick wall around three sides of a 19th-century garden; this did not occupy its whole platform. The N wall includes an earlier section with diaper work in vitrified brick, presumably part of the Granthams' complex.

Attached to the NW of the moat lay a large rectangular embanked

98

close ('e'), probably a garden. Its clay bank is readily visible as a soil-mark in the ploughed land and the interior has darker more organic soil than the surrounding area. The internal pond was probably ornamental. To the S, a second ditched and banked enclosure ('f'), now also ploughed out, was trapezoidal in shape. A pond, perhaps later in date, lay along the full length of its S, downslope boundary, with an outlet to the E. A suggestion[5] that this was an original medieval moat is rendered unlikely by the scale of its ditch, its downslope location, and the lack of associated surface finds, save for a scatter of post-medieval pottery. It is therefore more likely to be a garden feature.

Within the triangle formed by these two enclosures and the S moat arm, a platform ('g'), perhaps for a building, is distinguished also by black soil, building debris and much post-medieval pottery. Similar pottery was recovered along the W arm of the moat and there was a thin scatter of medieval pottery throughout the whole area. The early OS 25 in plan shows a scarp S of the Hall, probably a ha-ha which has been obliterated by the S extension of the garden in recent times.

1. Beresford 1975, 3–5; 1977, 47–68; 1982, 13–36.
2. Maddison 1902–6 II, 421–4, 745; III, 945–7; Hill 1956, 22, 114–15, 127; tombs in Goltho Chapel.
3. LCL Banks Collection II, 141; Pevsner and Harris 1964, 250; Hill 1956, 114–15, 211n; LAO Probate Inventory 136/334; ANDR 1.
4. OS 1:2500 sheet TF 1076–1176; OS 1st edn 25 in sheet Lincs 63.9.
5. NAR TF 17 NW 10.

(3) **Deer Park (centred TF 123765)** [40, 73] lies on undulating Till between 15 m and 20 m above OD. The park is not directly documented until the early 17th century, but a reference to a wood with herbage called *Les Laundes* appurtenant to Gilbert de Umfraville's manor of Goltho in 1381 probably indicates its existence at that date. Its size and integration both with the parish boundary and with areas of medieval managed woodland to its W and S also argue its medieval origin. Sir Thomas Grantham's probate inventory of 1630 refers to livestock – sheep, cattle and horses – 'in the parke hill and park'.[1]

A substantial bank up to 1.5 m high with an overall width of 10 m complete with flanking ditches formerly surrounded an area of 174 ha (417 acres) in the SE of the parish. The recent widespread conversion to arable has removed the earthwork for much of its length except as a residual rise along the edges of ploughed fields. This park pale now only survives in a few places, notably in pasture on either side of Shepherd's Farm (TF 123771), along the S edge of Black Plantation (TF 11867605–11567587) and SW of the entrance lodge of Goltho Hall for lengths of 210 m and 180 m in the roadside verge ('h', 'i') [73].

1. *Cal IPM* XV (1970), 180; LAO Probate Inventory 136/334.

GREAT LIMBER

(1) **House Site (TA 138085)** [74] lies at the extreme E end of the village, on glacial sands and gravels overlying chalk at 43 m above OD. The prominent earthworks have long been identified as the remains of an alien priory or grange belonging to the Cistercian abbey of Aunay-sur-Odon (Calvados) and scheduled as such.[1] It is doubtful whether the documents justify this identification.

The original grant to the abbey by Sir Richard de Humet, then lord of the largest manor in Great Limber, in or before 1157, and its confirmation about 1178, makes it clear that only the advowson

of Limber church was involved and not the secular estate that amounted to half the vill, which remained in de Humet's hands.[2] In 1392 the Carthusian priory of St Anne of Coventry was licensed to acquire the 'alien priory' of Limber with other possessions, including the advowson of Limber. In 1535 Coventry Priory still held the church, but no lands or tenements in Lincolnshire. The Limber possessions were granted in 1544 to John Bellowe and were then described as 'the rectory of Moungath in Lymber Magna *alias* the rectory of Magna Lymber and Parva Lymber'.[3]

The most likely origin of the site is in the holding of the Templars and the Hospitallers in succession to them. In 1185 the Templars held 30 bovates and 2 tofts in Limber. This estate formed part of their *baillia* of Cabourne, and was let into secular hands.[4] The Hospitallers succeeded to the property in the early 14th century, and evidently organized it as a *camera* or manor of their preceptory at Willoughton (Willoughton (2)). In 1338 the capital messuage was in disrepair but had a dovecote and garden attached and the whole estate was run by a steward. In 1535 the land was still run by a bailiff or steward.[5] After the Dissolution the chief messuage remained in the occupation and tenure of Thomas Smyth but soon afterwards passed into the hands of Sir William Pelham.[6]

The subsequent history is unclear, which, because of the nature of the earthworks, is unfortunate. Sir William Pelham had no residence in Limber on his death in 1587 and his son subsequently made his home in a new house at Brocklesby, built in 1603.[7] None of Sir William's tenants in a 1587 survey was specifically notable except for John Gaulton or Galton, gent, who certainly held one of the medieval manors, and perhaps that of the Hospitallers. His tenement had a 'stoare house for husbandrie, a barne, a stable and a dove coate and orchard, a foregarth and certain cloases about the house by estimacon vii acres'. No further record that might refer to the site has been noted. The estate map of 1676 marks the main enclosure, but there are no buildings within it [75]. Capability Brown's plan of 1770 shows nothing in the area.[8] By 1812 Limber House, an enclosure farmstead, had been erected, its yard laid askew across the NE corner of the main enclosure.[9] This house was demolished after the Second World War, though the farm buildings remain.

The extremely well-preserved earthworks lie immediately W and SW of the former Limber House farmyard, surviving in places to 1.5 m high. The earliest feature of the site is ridge-and-furrow, principally orientated N–S within the settlement closes to the W of the site, but in broad ridges running E–W inside the closes ('a'). The settlement closes overlie the ridge-and-furrow to the W and the site here described is actually the E section of these closes, perhaps originating at the same time, but having a quite different and more complex history.

At the N end of the area are two rectangular closes ('a') defined by low banks bounded on the N by the modern farm track. Rather irregular slight banks and platforms at the E end of the two closes, now much disturbed, may be the foundations of former buildings which faced on to a former N–S road whose line lay across the farm buildings. That a road once existed here is clear from the fragmentary and one-sided hollow-way that still exists further S ('b') and which met the main E–W hollow-way ('c'). There were probably once four equal-sized closes between the farm track and the hollow-way, perhaps pointing to an element of planning.

To the S of the two N closes, overlying the S two and quite distinct in scale, is a large rectangular embanked enclosure whose NW corner overlies the low close bank to the N and on its S side diverges slightly from the hollow-way ('c'). The surrounding bank

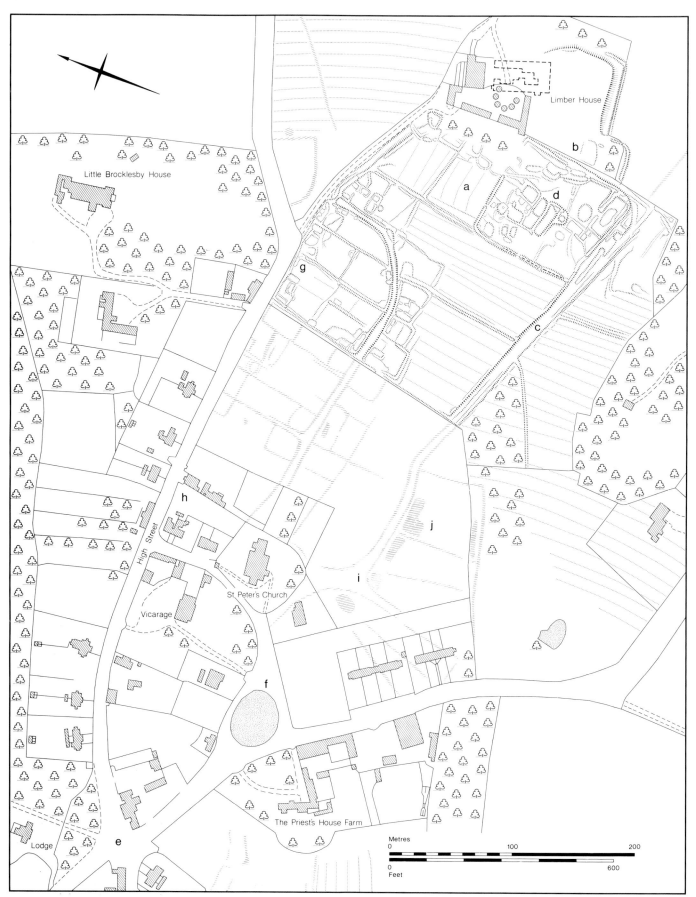

Little Brocklesby House

Limber House

St Peter's Church

Vicarage

High Street

The Priest's House Farm

Lodge

a

b

c

d

e

f

g

h

i

j

Metres
0   100   200
0   600
Feet

[74] *Great Limber (1) House Site, (2) Settlement Remains.*

100

of this enclosure is over 1 m high rising to almost 2 m high in the SE corner. Along much of the W side a narrower wall foundation is visible on the bank top, apparently constructed of brick and flint. Narrower sections of additional height along parts of the SE side make it likely that such a wall surrounded the whole enclosure. There are now three narrow gaps in the enclosure bank, two on the W and the other on the N, but the principal entrance is likely to have been on the E part of the N side, though here the gap may be the result of later disturbance. Apart from a large barn-like structure in the SE corner, the principal internal features are a series of large wall foundations forming a compact rectangle of former rooms ('d') that must be the ground or basement plan of a house of considerable size. Where these foundations have been disturbed there is evidence of brick and flint fabric. A roughly square projection at the SE corner with even more massive foundations may be the base of a tower. Slighter walls, scarps and building platforms divide the remainder of the enclosure into five closes, arranged symmetrically around the house site, presumably as gardens, courts or yards.

The field remains thus indicate that the site was once arable land, which was later occupied by closes. Some of these closes contained buildings, laid out as part of the settlement remains to the W. Later the large S enclosure was constructed and this in turn was subsequently remodelled by the addition of a wall and the insertion of a large house with associated gardens or yards. The last three phases might be connected with the occupation of the Templars, Hospitallers, and then John Galton's house of the late 16th century, the whole being finally abandoned in the 17th century.

1. Weir 1828, 209; VCH *Lincs* II (1906), 242; Knowles and Hadcock 1971, 129–30; Owen 1971, 150; OS 1st edn 25 in sheet, Lincs 21.10; NAR TA 10 NW 3; DOE 1978, 61 (222).
2. *LS* 11/10; *Cal Docs Preserved in France 918–1206* (1899), 185, 187; *Book of Fees* I, 175; II, 1476.
3. *Cal Pat R 1391–6* (1905), 242; *VE* III, 53; Dugdale 1817–30 VI, 15–17; VCH *Lincs* II (1906), 242; VCH *Warwicks* II (1965), 83–6; *Cal LPFD Hen VIII* XIX pt 2 (1905), 81.
4. Lees 1935, 104; *Book of Fees* I, 156; II, 1476; *Cal Chart R 1257–1300* (1906), 21; *Cal Inq Misc* I (1916), 289.
5. Larking 1857, 146, 150; *VE* IV, 137.
6. *Cal LPFD Hen VIII* XX, pt 1 (1905), 212, 672; *Cal Pat R 1563–6* (1960), 6; Maddison 1902–6 II, 477; LCL Ross MSS III, Yarborough, 249; LAO YARB 5/1/1, f9r, v.
7. LAO YARB 5/1/1, ff9v–11r; Pevsner and Harris 1964, 200.
8. LAO YARB 4/18/1; map in Estate Office Brocklesby Park, printed in Fuller 1976, fig 7.
9. PRO C54/9575; OS 1st edn 1 in sheet 86.

(2) Settlement Remains (TA 137086) [74, 75], formerly part of Great Limber, lie around the existing village, on glacial sands and gravels overlying chalk, at around 43 m above OD.

The complexity and extent of the field remains, most of which have been destroyed and are only visible on air photographs, together with the equally complex documented manorial history and population records of Great Limber, make any overall interpretation virtually impossible. Together they only dimly illustrate the considerable physical and tenurial changes that have taken place in the village.

The late 11th and early 12th centuries seem to have been a time of consolidation of tenure in Great Limber, which was followed by the breakup of estates through monastic grants in the later 12th century. Of the six entries in Domesday Book, two were sokeland, and three of the manorial holdings contained a total of five pre-Conquest manors, while the fourth was waste. In about 1115 only two holdings were returned.[1] Of these, the descent of only the larger principal manor can be fully traced through to the 16th century when the Pelham family acquired it. The 12th and early 13th-century holders of this manor made a number of grants to monastic houses and other land in Limber was acquired by further houses. The second largest manor by the late 11th century was held by the Templars who were succeeded by the Hospitallers in the early 14th century. All these ecclesiastical lands were finally acquired in the later 16th century by the Pelhams and thus the whole parish came into their hands. It has remained part of the Yarborough Estate ever since.[2] In crude population terms Great Limber appears always as a large village, though it certainly varied in size over the centuries. In general, the recorded population of 88 in 1086 was not matched again until the end of the 19th century and certainly had fallen dramatically by the early 14th century when 40 and 38 taxpayers are listed in 1327–8 and 1332–3 respectively. No relief is recorded in 1352, and since the Poll Tax returns do not survive it is not possible to assess the impact of the Black Death. There were more than 10 households in 1428, no relief in 1458 and only 7.3 per cent in 1463. In 1524, 42 people paid tax. Only 15 names are listed in the Lindsey Musters, but there were 66 taxpayers in 1542–3, 60 households in 1563 and 180 communicants in 1603. An estate survey of 1587 lists 20 substantial indentured tenants, 25 cottages tenanted at will, as well as approximately 9 other messuages and tenements and 10 more cottages, all in the hands of Sir William Pelham.[3] Much piecemeal depopulation was recorded in 1607: Sir William Pelham had 'ii houses of husbandrie burnt down which are not reedified' and had converted one farm to a cottage. Seven of his tenants had between them 'wasted' one house and converted eight other farms to cottages and engrossed land. In addition, Pelham and John Terry had each 'stopped a high waye by inclosure'.[4] In 1662, 53 people paid the Hearth Tax, there were 148 communicants in 1676 and over the period 1705–1723, 50, 40 and 44 households were returned in the diocesan survey, a clear drop of one third from 150 years earlier. A massive alteration to the village plan took place apparently in the late 17th or 18th centuries, perhaps as part of an estate re-organization, though this is not reflected in the recorded population. The population rose steadily from 52 households in 1801 to 88 in mid-century, much of it in new development by the Yarborough Estate, and has levelled out and remained at just over 100 in this century.[5]

The settlement remains fall into two parts on either side of the present village. In the W half, there were formerly large areas of earthworks preserved in pasture, but these were totally destroyed in 1976 and are now only visible on air photographs. They include hollow-ways, closes and sites of buildings, almost all shown in occupation and use on an estate map of 1676 [75]. By 1812 and 1824 many of the streets were apparently still in existence, but only a handful of the buildings and closes remained. In addition, a new road running NW past Pimlico Farm from the village centre towards Kirmington (the modern A18) had been created, one of the results of the creation of Brocklesby Park and of the enclosure of Great Limber parish in 1812. By the end of the 19th century, all the old streets with one exception had been abandoned.[6] Field-walking of this area has produced medieval pottery of 13th and 14th-century types.[7]

The existing village centre is marked by two triangular open spaces. The W one ('e') is now obscured, but on the 1676 map contains what may represent a market cross. The E space ('f') is still open and contains a large pond. The two are linked by a broad street and together probably form the site of the weekly market and annual fair granted in 1256–7 to Robert de Beaumeys and

Limber House

Great Limber 1676

St Peter's Church

Vicarage

The Priest's House Farm

Mausoleum

Pimlico Farm

Boundary Farm

Metres
0   100   200

0   600
Feet

[75] *Great Limber (2) Settlement Remains. (Inset) Great Limber Village 1676. Redrawn Estate Map.*

confirmed to Philip le Despenser in 1391. It was still referred to as a market place in 1587.[8]

To the E of the church was also once an extensive area of earthworks. Half of these were levelled and ploughed up in 1967, leaving only the E section protected by scheduling as part of the alleged monastic site (1). Despite the destruction, the overall layout is recoverable from air photographs as well as some earthwork details in the unploughed section.

A series of at least seven long closes set at right angles to the High Street extended S. In the preserved part these closes contain the stone foundations of former buildings set around hollowed yards. In 1676 only two dwellings stood on this frontage (approximately at 'g'), and in very small closes of limited depth. By 1812 these had disappeared. Further S, parallel to High Street, a broad, deep hollow-way extends to the E end of the church. At its E end it turns sharply to pass between the line of building remains and this may indicate its secondary adjustment to existing features, or that the creation of the easternmost frontage plots caused its diversion. Sites of former buildings also exist in places along this hollow-way; those on the S side are in very short closes that overlie ridge-and-furrow. This hollow-way may have functioned as a back lane and later developed into a street.

Neither this street nor its associated buildings survived in 1676 except for three structures, perhaps all barns, immediately SE of the church, where one building was still shown in 1812. After ploughing of this area in 1967, field-walking recovered a general scatter of Roman pottery. It also led to the identification of building sites along the hollow-way and on the High Street frontages where spreads of medieval shelly and gritty pottery, Humber Ware and some post-medieval pottery were noted.[9]

The closes on the S side of the hollow-way or street extend as far as a further, straight hollow-way ('c'). Spanning the whole area from the High Street to this hollow-way are a series of three or four narrow, very straight, N–S banks which perhaps mark out closes or fields that post-date the abandonment of the closes and hollow-ways; they did not exist in 1676 but one boundary is mapped in 1812. This whole complex indicates considerable changes of layout and function over a long period of time even if the details are irrecoverable. The hollow-way ('c') extended W to form a junction, shown on the 1676 map, with a street running N–S just E of the church ('h'–'i'). In their SE angle a further loop road, now visible as a ditch, enclosed a large property, including a house and outbuildings, in 1676 ('j'). While this loop road, as well as the hollow-way ('c'), had been abandoned by 1812, the N part of the street ('h'–'i') survived as a cul-de-sac until engulfed in the gardens of modern properties N of the church.

1. *Lincs DB* 1/67, 2/24, 14/31, 25/3, 30/8, 40/1; *LS* 11/1, 3, 10.
2. *Book of Fees* I, 157; II, 1476; *Cal IPM* IV (1913), 184; XV (1970), 195; *Feudal Aids* III, 243, 343; LCL Ross MSS III, Yarborough, 248–9; *VE* IV, 73, 74, 75, 175; VCH *Leics* II (1954), 27–8; VCH *Lincs* II (1906), 153, 165–6, 201; *Cal Pat R 1563–6* (1960), 6.
3. LAO YARB 5/1/1, ff9r–11r, 18v.
4. BL Add MS 11574 ff77, 85, 89, 93; LAO YARB 5/1/1.
5. PRO E179/140/806; Fuller 1974, esp chs 6 and 7; 1976, 14–24.
6. RAF VAP CPE/UK1880, 3194–8; CUAC AUI 26–8; HSL UK 71.207, 13.3725–6; air photographs in NMR; LAO YARB 4/18/1; 'A plan for Disposing of the Plantations in the estates of Great Limber and Audleby' by Lancelot Brown, c 1770 in the Estate Office, Brocklesby Park; PRO C54/9575; OS 1st edn 1 in sheet 86; OS 1st and 2nd edn 25 in sheet, Lincs 21.9.
7. LM records; *LHA* 11 (1876), 56.
8. *Cal Pat R 1388–92* (1902), 497; *Rot Hund* I (1812), 266, 399; *Placita de Quo Warranto* (1818), 415; LAO YARB 5/1/1, f9v.
9. *LHA* 4 (1969), 105, 111–12.

GREETWELL

(1) Deserted Village of Greetwell (TF 014716) [25, 76] lies on the S-facing slope of the Witham valley on Great Oolite Limestone and Upper Estuarine Clays, at 10 m above OD. The village has a long history of depopulation and decline from at least the early 15th century. Enclosure in the early 17th century may have further reduced the settlement, but the virtual abandonment of Greetwell finally took place in the first half of the 18th century, perhaps the result of estate reorganization.

The minimum recorded population of 21 for Greetwell in 1086 shows no decline by the early 14th century when 27 and 19 taxpayers are listed in 1327–8 and 1332–3 respectively, the former somewhat above the average for the wapentake. The relief in 1352 at 24.1 per cent is not large, yet in 1428 the parish was exempt from tax with less than 10 households. Reliefs at 15 per cent and 20 per cent during the 15th century show some, although not total, recovery. There were 8 people listed in the Lindsey Musters of 1539, 12 taxpayers recorded in 1542–3 and 88 communicants in 1603, over 70 per cent of the rural average for the archdeaconry.

No recent enclosure or destruction of property was recorded by the survey of depopulations in 1607, only that 'Sir Thomas Dallison hath stopped a high way ther'. Yet more than half the parish was enclosed in pasture and meadow before 1650 and therefore probably while the Royalist Dallisons were tenants of the Dean and Chapter of Lincoln's manor. It is possible that some of the village may have been cleared at this time when the formal gardens (2) S of the Hall could also have been laid out. The same 1607 survey lists 10 cottages, 6 occupied messuages and 1 without a tenant; in 1676 there were only 18 communicants plus 2 papists and 2 non-conformists.[1] At the beginning of the 18th century there were 8 or 9 households here, but by 1752 it was said that there were 'only three families in the town and they in harmony'. The census in the early 19th century shows a rise from 4 to 7 households, falling back to 4 again in 1851. Looking back from the beginning of the 19th century William Marrat moralized on 'the melancholy solitude of this once populous little village contrasted with what it was half a century back . . . the robust honest peasant banished to the memphitic atmosphere of the crowded manufacturing town while his healthy labours are imperfectly supplied by the powers of machinery . . . sacrificed to the enriching of a few overgrown tenants and some griping steward'. By this time the whole parish was farmed by two tenants of the Dean and Chapter, one occupying the old manor house, the other the large farmhouse to its N (now Greetwell Hall Farm).[2] In the first half of the 19th century the former was altered and enlarged, and in 1856 the occupier, Mr Straw, was said to be converting the surrounding field into a park and excavating the old village foundations to secure building materials.[3]

The post-medieval tenure of the manor of Greetwell clearly had a crucial bearing on the later decline of the settlement. In 1475 Bishop Thomas Scot (or Rotherham) and others were licensed to grant the manor to the Dean and Chapter of Lincoln.[4] At the end of the 16th century Greetwell became the residence of the Lincoln branch of the Dallison family, who were responsible for the early core of Greetwell Hall. The Civil War evidently saw the end of their tenure: Sir Charles Dallison, Royalist Recorder of Lincoln, claimed in 1661 to have lost £1000 in money and £400 a year in land, and compounded for his estate at half its value, in the Royalist cause.[5] The effect of the Dallison tenure may well have been the

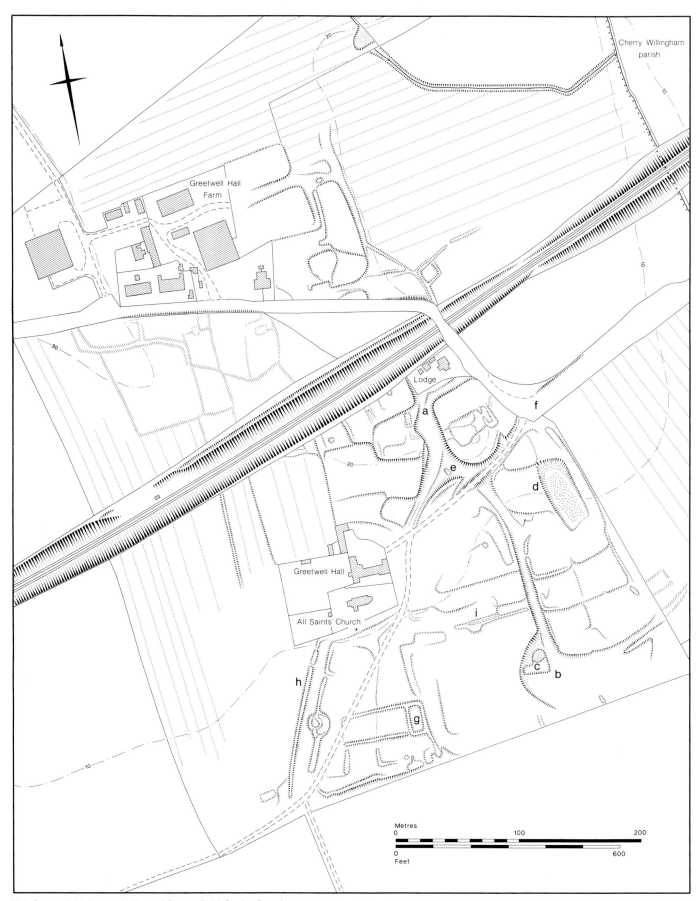

[**76**] *Greetwell (1) Deserted Village of Greetwell, (2) Garden Remains.*

abandonment of that part of the village around the church and Hall and the focusing of what remained along the E–W through road to the N at the top of the hill. It was, however, the Dean and Chapter's own deliberate policy of estate management a century later, if Marrat is to be believed, that finally reduced the settlement to its latter-day state.

The surviving earthworks form two groups: one lies near the 11th-century church and Greetwell Hall with its late 16th or 17th-century core and the other to the N around Greetwell Hall Farm along the E–W through road. Ploughing and construction of the railway in 1848 have destroyed the link between these groups.

To the E of the church and Hall, a well-marked hollow-way ('a'–'b') runs across the slope, with terraced and embanked closes on either side. Clear building foundations are visible within some of these closes though a depression ('c'), a large quarry ('d') and irregularities elsewhere where buildings might be anticipated, probably mark Mr Straw's mid 19th-century stone-gettings. On Armstrong's map of 1778 the hollow-way is shown as a track leading S down to a ferry which provided a river-crossing to Washingborough.

This hollow-way has been altered by three phases of driveway to the Hall since the mid 19th century. The modern drive crosses the hollow-way on a prominent embankment. The Tithe Map of 1848[6] shows it taking a more sinuous route which must have been abandoned during the next decade when Straw's Lodge, dated 1856, and gateway were built. From here the drive entered the hollow-way and then branched SW ('e'). In fact, this branch is probably a medieval street, in all likelihood that stopped by Sir Thomas Dallison in the early 17th century to create a drive to the Hall, which survived until at least 1824 since it gives access to the church and properties on its NW follow its line. The Tithe Map shows that there were buildings N and S of the road ('f '); that on the S side was perhaps a lodge.

To the N of the railway surviving earthworks consist of closes, some of which are lined on the W side of a N–S ditch, perhaps a continuation of the hollow-way ('a'–'b'). Others, particularly those ploughed out but visible on air photographs, may have been orientated on the E–W through road to Cherry Willingham, though the alignment of this was clearly altered to accommodate the railway bridge.[7] The E fringe of the surviving earthworks apparently overlies abandoned arable: this may support the idea of a shift of properties from the lower part of the village, sometime in the 17th century.

1. BL Add MS 11574, f93; Johnson 1962, 141 citing the parliamentary survey of 1650, LAO CC 16/152799.
2. Varley 1945–7, 167; Marrat 1816, 1–4; Allen 1834, 48.
3. MHLG List; newspaper report, 29.2.1856, in LCL Ross MSS XII, 184.
4. *Cal Pat R 1476–85* (1901), 176; *VE* IV, 11, 12.
5. Maddison 1902–6 I, 286–7; Holmes 1980, 149; *Cal State Papers Dom 1661–2* (1861), 185.
6. LAO E492.
7. RAF VAP 3G/TUD/UK197/pt VI/5466–8; CUAC PG 67–73, 75–81; OS 1st edn 1 in sheet 83.

(2) Garden Remains (TF 014715) [25, 76], probably of late 16th or early 17th-century date, lie immediately S of Greetwell Hall and church and adjacent to the site of the former village of Greetwell, on Upper Estuarine Clays at 10 m above OD.

The earthworks are the remains of a formal garden associated with the Hall and presumably laid out by the Dallison family soon after they took over the estate as tenants of the Dean and Chapter of Lincoln in the late 16th century, when they rebuilt the Hall. The construction of this garden may also have included the clearance of at least part of Greetwell village. The garden appears to have had a relatively short life for the Dallisons left Greetwell during the Civil War and the estate was leased to tenant farmers.[1]

In a parliamentary survey of 1650[2] the area was a close of pasture called the *Hall Garth* with foundations within it that were said to be those of the manor house. It then contained two barns, one of five and another of three bays, an orchard, a garden and the parsonage house, actually the principal residence occupied by the Dallisons. The area was finally emparked in the mid 19th century.[3]

The site forms a roughly rectangular area bounded on the E by the main hollow-way of the former village and with the Hall and church in the NW corner. To the S of the church a large building platform ('g') lies at the E end of a former walled plot, while to the S further fragmentary foundations appear to be grouped into a walled yard. These foundations may well be the barns recorded in 1650. Access to the latter is provided by a walled way or track ('h') leading SW from the Hall and which also evidently opened on to the surrounding fields. Half-way along this track, the E wall contains a large hollow-topped mound, certainly the remains of a substantial building and possibly a tower-like summer-house set in the SW corner of a sub-rectangular area which is subdivided by a N–S terrace or scarp. To the E is a larger rectangular area bounded on the NW and N by a broad terrace ('i'). Other scarps and terraces lie to the N again, though it is not clear whether these are part of the gardens or of the earlier village here.

1. Maddison 1902–6 I, 286–7; Holmes 1980, 149; *Cal State Papers Dom 1661–2* (1861), 185.
2. LAO CC 16/152799.
3. Newspaper report, 29.2.1856, in the LCL Ross MSS XII, 184.

HACKTHORN

(1) Site of Monastic Grange and Settlement Remains (SK 995824) [77], formerly part of Hackthorn, lie within and around the existing village at 25 m above OD. The village and its earthworks extend for 1.4 km along both sides of a shallow valley running E–W across the lower dipslope of the Jurassic Limestone ridge and occupy a location similar to Firsby (West Firsby (1)) and Riseholme (Riseholme (1)), made viable by reliable water supplies.

Although a precise figure cannot be arrived at because of two shared returns in Domesday Book, no recorded population for Hackthorn matched that of 1086 until the latter part of the 19th century. The 25 taxpayers listed in both early 14th-century subsidies is certainly no increase on the 1086 level and represents only about 80 per cent of the wapentake average, although alienation of land to monastic interests is clearly a factor. Post-Black Death relief in 1352 of 21.9 per cent and only 50 persons recorded in the Poll Tax of 1377 mark a further fall, but there were at least 10 households in 1428. Low reliefs in the 15th century apparently reflect the recovery, confirmed by the figures of 19 or 26 taxpayers in 1542–3 and 90 communicants in 1603, although this was still only three-quarters of the rural average for the archdeaconry. The return of only 42 communicants in 1676 marks a sharp decline before a return to a similar level of 26–30 households at the beginning of the 18th century, and the same number in the early 19th century provided the basis for growth in the later 19th century.

The tenurial network lying behind these trends is as complex as neighbouring Firsby's is simple and may throw some doubt on any attempt to identify a single lordly hand as responsible for the similarities in plan between the two settlements. There are eight entries and six lords in Domesday Book including three principal manors. The same main holdings existed in the early 12th century together with three smaller estates.[1] Monastic grants in the late 12th and 13th centuries and the consolidation of other holdings simplified the secular tenure so that from the mid 13th century only two estates dominated and they were united in the later Middle Ages.[2] In the late 17th century the Cracroft family of Whisby acquired Hackthorn and became resident before 1677. It was the Cracrofts who, after enclosure of the parish in 1779, rebuilt the Hall in 1792 to the W of St Michael's church in the existing landscaped park. This replaced the earlier hall which stood NE of the church.[3]

Several religious foundations had small interests in Hackthorn in the medieval period. These included the Dean and Chapter of Lincoln, the Prior of Thornholme, the Knights Templars and Barlings Abbey.[4] However, the principal religious holding was a grange belonging to Bullington Priory, which eventually grew to a considerable size.[5] The grange was still being referred to in the late 17th century and presumably the present farm of that name, shown on the 1st edn 1 in OS map of 1824, indicates its location at the E end of the village.[6]

The morphology of the settlement shows marked similarities to the plan of the deserted village of Firsby (West Firsby (1)), situated 3 km to the N, where a manorial block containing a church occupies the W end of the earthworks. At Hackthorn a similar topographical position is occupied at least by the later Middle Ages by a manorial block encompassing St Michael's church which is recorded in Domesday Book and has produced pre-Conquest grave-slabs. The surviving Hall was built on the W edge of this block in order to give unrestricted room outside the village for the creation of the park and ornamental lake, though whether this landscaping destroyed earlier remains is uncertain.

At Firsby an axial way led along the S side of the Ancholme valley with a well-defined and regular series of properties on its N side running down to the river and with cross-tracks leading across the river to serve farmsteads on its N bank. At Hackthorn too, a through street lies on the S side of a valley. All the housing of before the middle of the 19th century lies on the NW side of the street and there is ridge-and-furrow on its S. To the S of Popples Cottage, the modern road leaves this line to skirt the perimeter of the park but the street formerly continued SW, where it is represented in the park by a hollow-way continuing its line. On the N side of this hollow-way ('a'), walls of limestone rubble standing up to 1 m high mark the position of at least six former properties, some containing the remains of rectangular stone buildings. It is possible that these were cleared when the Hall and park were laid out at the end of the 18th century in order to create an uncluttered view, and replaced by the estate cottages which form the core of the present village in a block on the N side of the axial street. Since no map survives accompanying the Enclosure Award of 1779 this is a conjecture only.

Mounds and depressions cutting through ridge-and-furrow on the S side of this hollow-way are old quarries and are probably the 'Hackthorn quarry' which supplied the stone for All Saints at Cold Hanworth, dedicated in 1863.[7]

Farms and dwellings scattered along the N side of the valley – Long Acres, Yew Tree Farm and Washdyke Cottages – are all surrounded by fragmentary earthworks forming closes and groups of buildings or, in the last case, by ploughed settlement remains that have produced much medieval pottery. The arrangement probably reflects what had gone before with earlier farmsteads served, like their surviving counterparts, by cross-lanes emanating from the axial street on the S side of the valley. A good example occurs E of Yew Tree Farm ('b') where earthworks of former farmsteads are approached by a hollow-way. The settlement remains at the E end of the village, although largely destroyed by ploughing and only recoverable from soil-marks recorded on aerial photographs,[8] form a large group of closes with a stepped-in rear boundary, similar to the arrangements at, for example, Cabourne. This block, on both sides of the stream, appears as a Dean and Chapter leasehold property on a 19th-century estate map and may represent part of the early 13th-century gifts to St Mary of Lincoln that included 'two tofts, between the toft of Adam Woodcock and the *stagnum* of the canons of Bullington'.[9] Bullington's grange presumably lay further E again.

The same estate map seems to mark a track following the stream in the centre of the village which survives partly as a hollow-way ('c'–'d') and partly as a lane. Initially this may have been no more than the former course of the stream that was later utilized after the latter had been realigned along the more direct route. The stream has certainly been straightened further E where the marshy trough ('e') represents a former bend. The occurrence of ridge-and-furrow on the valley side to the W of Long Acres indicates that the village remains to the E were earlier separated from the church and manorial complex to the W, as at Firsby.

1. *Lincs DB* 2/17, 16/21, 26/14, 26/15, 28/12, 28/13, 45/3, 47/2; *LS* 2/4, 9, 11, 12, 13, 16.
2. *Book of Fees* II, 1082, 1096; *Feudal Aids* III, 151, 228, 238, 290, 309; LCL Ross MSS IV Aslacoe (East), 36; Maddison 1902–6 III, 914–16.
3. Maddison 1902–6 I, 271–83; LAO Lindsey Awards 39; Pevsner and Harris 1964, 261; LCL Banks Collection.

Washdyke Cottages

20

The Grange

4. Foster and Major 1931–73 IV, 42–76; *VE* IV, 9; *Book of Fees* I, 189; *Feudal Aids* III, 228; *Cal IPM* XV (1970), 179; *Cal IPM* 2nd ser Henry VII, I (1898), 446; *VE* IV, 130; *Cal Pat R 1388–92* (1902), 187; *VE* IV, 32.
5. Stenton 1922, 91–2, 100; Stenton 1920, 16, 21–32, 62–3; Foster and Major 1931–73 II, 24–5; BL Harleian Charters 45B21, 45B26, 57C22; *VE* IV, 84.
6. *Cal LPFD Hen VIII* XIV pt 1 (1894), 259; *Cal Pat R 1566–9* (1964), 330; *1569–72* (1966), 160; LAO FL Deeds 1603; LCS 14/17; ANDR 2 (survey book of 1745); OS 1st edn 1 in map sheet 83.
7. LCL Ross MSS IV Aslacoe (East), 50.
8. RAF VAP 541/185/4159–62; air photographs in NMR.
9. LAO 2CC 58/12663; Foster and Major 1931–73 IV, 43.

HARPSWELL

(1) Settlement Remains (SK 933899) [78], formerly part of Harpswell village, lie at the foot of a W-facing scarp of the Jurassic Limestone ridge at 40 m above OD, on Middle and Upper Lias Clays and shales. Little remains on the site of the village as later gardens, themselves abandoned, overlie it. Harpswell is notable as one of the great depopulations of the early 17th century in Lindsey.

In 1086 Harpswell was divided between two manors, together with the soke belonging to Kirton. Although the descent is difficult to trace it seems probable that these two manors persisted until amalgamated in the 16th century by the Whichcote family. The latter had already acquired one of the manors in the 15th century and remained resident at Harpswell until 1776.[1]

A total minimum population of 25 is recorded in 1086 and this had risen by the early 14th century to 54 listed taxpayers in 1327–8 and 43 in 1332–3, in the earlier case nearly twice the average for the wapentake making it one of the most populous settlements within West Lindsey. In 1352 relief of 50 per cent was allowed after the Black Death and only 85 persons over 14 years of age were returned in the 1377 Poll Tax; there were at least 10 households in 1428. Reliefs were about 15 per cent in the 15th century. Only 10 men were listed for the Lindsey Musters of 1539, yet 31 taxpayers are recorded in 1542–3 and 80 communicants in 1603. The survey of depopulations of 1607 reports among the great depopulations in Lindsey 'Sir Hamond Whitchcot, owner of the whole towne consistinge of 11 farms besides his mannor howse hath inclosed most of the saide howses and of the rest made cottages, and hath converted 500 acres of arrable land into pasture'. A Duchy of Cornwall survey in 1616 confirms the result of 'the tenements nowe ruyned and the landes enclosed'.[2] In 1676 64 communicants were returned: at the beginning of the 18th century there were 16 or 17 households in Harpswell, a level more or less maintained until recently.

Very little of the field remains can be associated with the medieval settlement of Harpswell, apparently so effectively removed by the Whichcotes. The wooded close E of the church, named *Hallowed Lands* (not on plan), contains a broad linear hollow cut deeply into the scarp.

The continuation of its alignment is perhaps marked by the irregular hollow-way ('a'–'b') which is blocked at either end by the earthworks of the later formal garden. Slight scarps at right angles on either side may indicate former village property divisions. On the W edge of the earthworks, two fragmentary rectangular closes ('c'), apparently not part of the adjacent garden, lie on the same alignment. Where they now lie partly in arable cultivation a scatter of medieval pottery was recovered during the Commission's survey. The moat ('d'), though in its present form an ornamental feature,

may possibly reuse or adapt an earlier manorial site. A broad ditch or hollow-way with fragmentary remains of a bank on its S side, parallel to the main road in the N ('e'), might be an alternative road line disturbed by tree-planting or mark the boundary of the later park.

1. *Lincs DB* 1/42, 2/27, 28/11; *LS* 2/9, 16; *Cal IPM* IV (1913), 284; *Cal Inq Misc* V (1962), 88, 91, 135–6; *Feudal Aids* III, 356; Maddison 1902–6 III, 1069–73; Lloyd 1973, 1.
2. BL Add MS 11574, f76; CUL MS Ff 4.30(c), f27.

(2) Garden Remains (SK 933899) [42, 78, 79, 80] overlie the remains of Harpswell village, at the foot of the W-facing Jurassic Limestone ridge at 40 m above OD. These gardens are almost certainly the creation of successive generations of the Whichcote family perhaps prior to and following their removal of the village of Harpswell in the early 17th century.

The clearance of the village either gave way to Harpswell Hall and its gardens standing within an emparked setting or led to the construction of the park alongside an existing garden of 16th-century date. As a result of this emparking the by-road to Upton was diverted to the S. The Hall stood on the S side of the site ('f') and its brick foundations were encountered in recent drain-laying. As shown in Nattes's drawings of 1793 [79], it was an early 17th-century H-shaped house at the core with substantial 18th-century extensions. To its NW a prospect mound ('g'), 3.5 m high, stands at one corner of the formal garden [42]. Despite damage by the adjacent modern barn, a hollowed spiral pathway can be traced giving access to the summit, where stood a gazebo shown as an 18th-century Gothick building by Nattes. To the E of this the slightly higher ground, now occupied by Hall Farm and its outbuildings, has on its S-facing slope a terraced garden retained on three sides by a substantially buttressed brick wall, its former internal terraces smoothed by later use as an orchard ('h'). Here, too, the archways and ornaments shown by Nattes have a classical, probably 18th-century appearance. Between this terraced element and the site of the Hall, is a sunken garden ('i') up to 1 m deep. It comprises a square W part with a central circular feature, perhaps formerly with flower-beds, only a few centimetres in elevation, and a rectangular E extension with opposed square niches or bays, perhaps for stairs or statuary. This forms the SW end-point for a broad sunken drive with a slightly raised central agger and wide flat-topped banks to the N and S, which seems to take the tower of the parish church as its focus. This drive is mapped as a way in use in 1824 with a screen of trees along its S side, of which only three decayed walnuts survive; elsewhere in the parkland a few ancient elms, chestnuts and oaks still stand. To the S of the drive the natural watercourse has been widened into a *Serpentine* water feature, shown on Armstrong's county map of 1778 and so named on early OS 25 in sheets, which also identify the area to its S and SW as *The Wilderness*. To the W of the site of the Hall ('f'), the large water-filled three-sided moat ('d') forms another ornamental element in this elaborate garden: its broad expanse of water gives an impression of an angled canal. The broad causeway on the E is closed by a tall brick screen wall with central openings, pilaster buttresses and stone cappings, identical in materials and style to those surrounding the terraced garden and screen wall ('h') of the Hall. Crop-marks recorded on the sloping ground S of the stream are largely old field boundaries.[1]

These garden and landscape features are clearly the sum of several phases of activity or prolonged change. At their heart is a neatly squared garden of late 16th or early 17th-century type with a prospect mound in its NW corner and with the house in the centre

Hemswell parish

St Chad's Church

Church Farm

a

e

Hall Farm Cottages

The Serpentine

b

Moat Cottage

Hall Farm

h

i

The Wilderness

f

g

c

d

Metres
0   100   200

0   600
Feet

[78] *Harpswell (1) Settlement Remains, (2) Garden Remains.*

[**79**] *Harpswell (2). This view of Harpswell Hall from the W in 1793 also shows the walled terraced garden and the prospect mound, both of which survive as earthworks [**42, 80**]. The avenue beyond the house has long since disappeared though its position is marked by linear banks and scarps across the park. (Lincolnshire Library Service)*

of the S side. It can be associated with depopulation by Sir Hamond Whichcote (d 1651) or even with his father Robert (d 1578) and overlay the abandoned W end of the medieval village. The well-documented depopulation may have led principally to the creation of a park. Other features belong stylistically to the end of the 17th or 18th centuries. The most plausible context for the creation of most of them is the marriage in 1700 of Colonel George Whichcote, after his return from the wars in Flanders and a period when Harpswell appears to have been neglected, to Frances, sister of Sir John Meres. Certainly the correspondence of the steward, John Wallace, with Colonel Whichcote's widow in the period 1772–7 is full of references to the park and the gardens, and continuing work on them despite straitened finances, indicating not only the existence of many of the features but also Madam Whichcote's keen

interest. This may have continued in the later life of the son Thomas, when his fortunes were eased by bequests from his uncle (d 1735). Thomas was MP for the county from 1741 to 1768.[2] It is possible that the serpentine lake is Thomas Whichcote's work and was an attempt to make the existing gardens and park less formal and more in keeping with the landscaping ideas of the mid 18th century. Harpswell Hall survived into the 19th century, to be demolished about 1836, though the Whichcotes did not sell the estate itself until 1918.[3]

1. Lloyd 1973, frontispiece, reproduced from LCL Banks Collection II, 233; OS 1st edn 1 in map sheet 83; OS 25 in map Lincs 44.5 and 9; air photographs in NMR.
2. Maddison 1902–6 III, 1069–73; Lloyd 1973, *passim.*
3. OS 1st edn 1 in map sheet 83; local inf.

[**80**] *Harpswell (2) from the W. The remains of the 18th-century terraced gardens lie on the left. Harpswell Hall stood on the right and the 16th or 17th-century formal garden earthworks are visible in the centre with the alignment of the formal avenue detectable as a long hollow extending towards the parish church in the distance.*

Springthorpe
parish

b

c

Elm Tree Farm

a

d

All Saints' Church

Chestnut Farm

Metres
0   100   200

0   600
Feet

[**81**] *Heapham (1) Moated Site and Settlement Remains.*

110

(1) Moated Site and Settlement Remains (SK 881887) [18, 34, 81], formerly part of the village of Heapham, lie on Boulder Clay on a very slight N–S ridge at 20 m above OD.

The site represents one part of a regular and possibly planned polyfocal settlement, perhaps overlying earlier fields. The relationship of the parish church to both nuclei is noteworthy.

Two modern farms and their associated earthworks lie quite topographically distinct and to the E of a second nucleus (Heapham (2)). This latter nucleus comprises village properties laid out on either side of an E–W street and is the focus of modern Heapham. The two elements are separated by a low-lying basin where water springs and collects, feeding a stream flowing S. On the N side of this basin stands the parish church, itself isolated from both settlement nuclei by ridge-and-furrow. Both nuclei are shown as blocks of old enclosures on the Enclosure Map of 1776, which also emphasizes the long, narrow and slightly curving form of several of the properties in the S part of the E nucleus and much of the S row of the W nucleus, which points to both parts of the settlement being developed over former arable strips. Many of the roads surrounding the church have been mistakenly taken to be former village streets but are late 18th-century enclosure roads, albeit following earlier arable headlands.[1]

Two tenurial elements do appear and persist in the documentation for Heapham but it is not clear how they relate to the topographical division: nor is it certain when either was manorialized in a way that might have given rise to a moated residence. In 1086 the larger holding at Heapham was sokeland of the royal estate at Kirton in Lindsey; the smaller, held by Count Alan, was berewick and soke of his manor of Lea.[2] This latter was presumably 'the manor of Heapham' which in the mid 15th century and for at least the next 100 years was linked with the manor of North Ingleby. If a moated residence had been created on this, the smaller holding, it may have been occupied by the sole taxpayer not on the Kirton sokeland in 1332–3. Indeed the greater part of the site may be merely the remains of a manorial *curia*.[3] By contrast the 11th-century royal sokeland passed down with the manor of Kirton from the 12th century from the hands of the Earls of Cornwall and latterly of the Duchy estates, until it was sold off in the 19th century.[4]

Population figures for Heapham show no strong trends, but there are troughs notably in the 14th to 15th centuries and the late 16th to 17th centuries. There were 16 sokemen on the royal holding in 1086 and 4 on Count Alan's. In the early 14th century, 22 taxpayers in 1327–8 and 27 in 1332–3 represent just over the average for the wapentake. In the latter case, however, where a differentiation is made, all but one were on the royal sokeland. Although the immediate post-Black Death relief in 1352 was only 7 per cent, in 1377 as few as 38 people over 14 years of age were listed for the Poll Tax, and while there were at least 10 households in 1428, reliefs of 20 per cent and 15 per cent were still allowed in 1448 and 1463 on the assessment of the royal sokeland which was again differentiated. The figure of 24 taxpayers in 1542–3 appears to represent a return to earlier levels, but in 1603 there were 60 communicants, less than half the rural average for the archdeaconry, and the survey of Kirton Soke names only 11 tenants' messuages here.[5] In 1676 71 communicants were returned; by the early 18th century there were again 25 and 30 households and similar levels have been maintained since, with but limited movement away from the older nuclei to roadside properties along Common Lane leading to Harpswell.

At the N end of the E nucleus lies a small moated site ('a'). A very slight external bank on the W may have originally served to dam water that could be led in by a ditch in the NE corner and allowed out in the centre of the W side. A pond ('b'), shown more nearly rectangular on early large-scale OS plans, perhaps formed the N side of a trapezoidal block of manorial closes surrounding the moat. The property block could have been larger still, and may have included two other closes to the N and E, thus forming a square block within the old enclosures of 1776. Both these closes contain ridge-and-furrow. This block, made up of *Moat Close, Great Close* and *Ner Gars* in 1776, had a building standing in its SE corner ('c'). Then, the pre-enclosure open field to its E was called *Hall Field*.[6]

To the S is a ladder-pattern of regularly spaced ditched closes aligned E–W, with dwellings at their ends. Those around Chestnut Farm overlie ridge-and-furrow and their boundaries reflect the curving strips; along the E side of the street the map of 1776 shows dwellings in a series of similar narrow closes lying within the old enclosures, the northernmost of which is marked by earthworks ('d'). This, coupled with the curious misalignment of the S part of the N–S street suggests a distinct addition to the earlier layout N of the E–W cross-street, perhaps totally of post-medieval date.

1. LAO LINDSEY ENCL 222.
2. *Lincs DB* 1/39, 48, 12/5; *LS* 4/2; *Book of Fees* I, 191; *Cal IPM* II (1906), 216–17.
3. Foster 1927, 101–3; PRO E179/135/16.
4. Davis *et al* 1913–69 III, 184, no 494; *Feudal Aids* III, 248; *Cal IPM* III (1912), 471, 474; XV (1970), 72; *Cal Inq Misc* IV (1957), 118; Moor 1905, 6–8.
5. CUL MS Ff 4.30(c), ff50–1.
6. OS 25 in map, Lincs 43.11; LAO LINDSEY ENCL 222.

KETTLETHORPE

(4) Deer Park (centred SK 850753) [40], covering some 340 ha (850 acres), occupied the whole of the E part of the parish and encompassed both what remains of the medieval settlement of Kettlethorpe (2) and its associated manor house (1), now Kettlethorpe Hall. This unusual situation suggests that, in the later medieval period at least, Kettlethorpe was little more than a palatial residence belonging to the Swynford family set within a hunting park and perhaps comparable to the Bishop of Lincoln's residence at Stow Park (Stow (3)). It was probably supported by the two villages of Laughterton and Fenton, which lie immediately outside the park.

In 1383 Katherine Swynford was licensed to enclose and make a park of 300 acres.[1] This may have been part of the existing park or an extension of an older one.

The W boundary of this park extends from the NE corner of Laughterton village, southwards along the edge of Newton on Trent parish. Here a feature known as Sallie Bank comprises a ditch or stream on either side of a bank up to 10 m across and 3 m high and extends for some 1.7 km. A further stretch of approximately 500 m survives to the N forming the park's NW corner. The E boundary was probably the line of a stream called Border Drain, parallel to this bank, E of Kettlethorpe and immediately E of Park Farm. To the S its limit was presumably the parish boundary of Thorney (Notts) while on the N the modern parish, formerly the township, boundary with Fenton marked its line. A second length of bank perhaps part of an earlier park pale, up to 10 m wide and 1 m high with an external ditch, runs E and then S from Kettlethorpe Hall. It marks the limit here of a small park which, in the early 19th century, covered less than 40 ha.

1. Cole 1911a, 422.

(5) Enclosure (SK 851756) [40, 82] is situated at approximately 15 m above OD on the crest of a steep rise overlooking Kettlethorpe Hall and village.

The site lacks any direct documentation. It comprises an almost square enclosure, bounded by a broad rounded bank and wide external ditch on the N, W and part of the S sides, those fronting the falling ground. Along the S end of the E side are the foundations of a two-celled building. To the E a shallow gulley leads into a circular hollow. This hollow cuts through a linear boundary or former hedge line marked by a scarp and a shallow ditch. The whole lies over and askew to ridge-and-furrow. The earthwork is similar in form to that at South Kelsey (5). Like that, it may be a Civil War fortification or gun position. Kettlethorpe Hall was held in the 17th century by the Hall family, who were of Parliamentary leaning. In 1644–5 the Torksey area was the scene of skirmishing between Royalist parties from Newark and patrols of Parliamentarians holding the county, with crossing places of the lower Trent amongst the targets.[1]

1. Maddison 1902–6 II, 441; Holmes 1980, 174, 176–7.

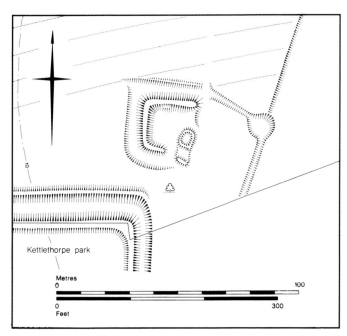

[82] *Kettlethorpe (5) Enclosure.*

KIRMOND LE MIRE

(1) Settlement Remains (TF 188925) [83], formerly part of Kirmond, were destroyed in 1975 without prior record, but air photographs allow reasonable detail of the layout of the settlement to be mapped.[1]

The arrangement of the former earthworks suggests a dichotomy between the existing properties and their associated earthworks grouped irregularly around the church on the valley side and to its E, and a very regular two-row street village along the valley bottom. Pottery from the destruction of the latter included Saxo-Norman wares, principally near the through road, medieval shelly and local sandy wares and post-medieval wares from one area.[2] A distinct group of earthworks with large buildings to the SE between the streams may well be one of the two otherwise unlocated monastic granges held in Kirmond by Stainfield and Sixhills Priories. The grouping of modern properties on the hill may be the effect of the modest regrowth of the settlement in the 19th and 20th centuries along the through road. Persistently high reliefs suggest a substantial decline in the 15th century, perhaps with conversion to sheep. There was a further and decisive drop in the 17th century to a level which might easily have caused the complete disappearance of the settlement.

The former earthworks E of the main stream, in Binbrook parish, are the remains of the settlement of Beckfield, also destroyed in 1975.

1. RAF VAP CPE/UK1880/2492–3; CPE/UK2012/4046–7; 541/185/4040; CUAC AFP 61–2; HSL UK 71.210, Run 19, 4034–5.
2. Inf R.C. Russell.

KNAITH

(1) Site of Cistercian Priory (SK 846853) [84] lies at 19 m above OD on a low knoll of Cover Sands over Till.

The Cistercian nunnery of Heynings has hitherto been identified with the earthworks at Hermit Dam in Lea (Lea (2)) or alongside the parish church at Knaith (Knaith (3)). The present identification with the remains at Park Farm South rests partly on the nature of the earthworks and associated finds at all these places and partly on documentary and other considerations which render the alternatives untenable.

The nunnery was founded for brethren and sisters after 1135, probably in the reign of Stephen or early in the reign of Henry II. There were a prioress, sub-prioress, 13 nuns and 2 lay sisters in 1376, and a prioress and 11 nuns at its dissolution in 1539. The nunnery site was then granted to Sir Thomas Heneage. At his death in 1553 it passed by marriage to Lord Willoughby of Parham, along with the manor of Knaith. Reference to a 'messuage in Heynings' in 1553 hints at the possibility of some secular settlement at the priory gates and some occupation seems to have persisted here under the name of Knaith Park. It is by this name that Park Farm South is noted on the 1st edn OS 1 in map, though only the two farms are shown. By the time antiquarian interest revived in the early 19th century, knowledge of the location of the priory was completely lost.[1]

The varied state of preservation of the earthworks, from good to over-ploughed and selectively infilled, makes overall interpretation difficult, and dumping and extension of farm buildings has continued to erode the remains. On the S, an interlinked series of

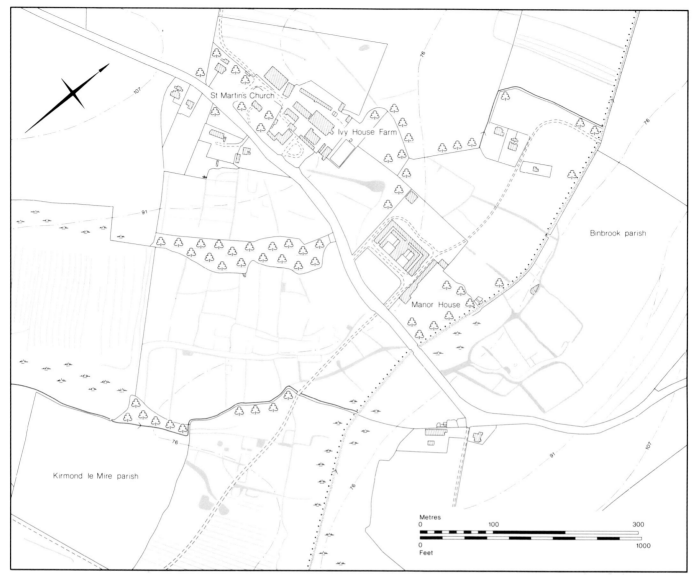

[**83**] *Kirmond le Mire (1) Settlement Remains.*

leats, generally less than 0.5 m deep but in places embanked for greater depth, of which the present N-flowing stream must have once formed part, are a remarkable survival. One branch feeds through shallow ponds ('a'); one contains two low islands and has a small elongated pond or 'tank' alongside. The leats feed into a moat-like feature ('b') that is in places up to 1.5 m deep and forms the S and SE sections of a precinct enclosure. On the W the stream changes direction significantly to accommodate itself to this feature and presumably forms the W boundary. Where it changes direction again ('c'), a broad deep ditch, though partly filled, strikes NE and may indicate the N side of the enclosure, whose circuit on the NE has been obscured by later farm buildings.

Much of the enclosure so formed is occupied by the 18th-century farmhouse, its yards, buildings and garden. Levelling for a lawn S of the house revealed extensive occupation debris, while excavations close by uncovered at least two inhumations. Digging for foundations of new farm buildings has revealed at least five and perhaps as many as twelve further burials. It seems likely that this is the area of conventual buildings with the cemetery to their E.

Medieval glazed roof tiles, a stone roof slate, a few fragments of later medieval pottery and other finds have been discovered in casual diggings.[2] In the SW corner of this presumed precinct is a group of four fishponds.

On the N, an outer precinct is clearly defined on the N and W by a ditch, in places 1 m–1.5 m deep. Within it the area may formerly have been divided by ditches into smaller compartments: extensive hollows and banks, although difficult to interpret in detail, may indicate the location of buildings or their later robbing for stone, although there are the clear foundations of one large barn-like building, some 16 m by 8 m ('d'). To the E, the limits of the precinct are most clearly marked by a massive headland ('e') with ridge-and-furrow beyond to the E. This headland and another to the S were over-ploughed after the abandonment of the priory by extending the earlier ridge-and-furrow to the W. The over-ploughing cut at right angles three earlier broad ridges ('f') and reduced the presumed sites of earlier features to smooth mounds and banks. The end of a massive building ('g') apparently approximately 15 m wide, standing on a marked platform, is

Park Farm
North

Park Farm
South

h

f

g

e

d

c

b

a

Metres
0   100   200

0   600
Feet

[**84**] *Knaith (1) Site of Heynings Priory.*

overlain by 20th-century farm cottages and gardens, but two degraded wall foundations protruding E from them may indicate its length. It lies approximately in the middle of the N side of the monastic complex where it is approached by a hollow-way from the NW. Scarps and irregularities alongside this hollow-way ('h') and others apparently outside the precinct further NW may represent secular settlement at the priory gate.

Crop-marks of ditches and ponds in the ploughland W of the earthworks raise the possibility of further features ancillary to the monastic site. These lay, however, within the late medieval deer park of Knaith Park (4), and may, in part at least, be former woodland features similar to the ponds recorded in Cocklode Wood at Bullington (Bullington (4)) and Great West Wood at Goltho, for example.[3]

1. VCH *Lincs* II (1906), 149–51; Owen 1971, 144; *Cal LPFD Hen VIII* XIV pt 1 (1894), 377; XV (1896), 289; Maddison 1902–6 III, 1088; Knowles and Hadcock 1971, 271, 274; OS 1st edn 1 in sheet 83.
2. LM records; local inf.
3. RAF VAP CPE/UK2012/1103–4; CUAC AWR 85; air photographs in NMR.

(2) Settlement Remains (SK 829847) [26, 85], formerly part of the village of Knaith, lie between 5 m and 20 m above OD on the lower and upper terraces of the E bank of the R Trent, at a prominent bend in the river.

The documentary evidence for Knaith from 1086 onwards indicates a settlement which, while always small, nevertheless underwent considerable fluctuations in its size and prosperity. This may be as much the result of the fortunes of its lords as of the poor sandy soils of its land.

The low minimum recorded population of 3 in Domesday Book is in line with later evidence. Walter de Billinghay's manor in 1305–6 had 8 free and 2 bond tenants, while the early 14th-century subsidies list 12 and 13 taxpayers which is only just over half the average for the wapentake. The impact of the Black Death in 1349 is difficult to assess. Relief allowed in 1352 was only just over 12 per cent but when the manor of Knaith came into the hands of the Crown in 1356–7, on the minority of the Darcy heir, it could not be let 'because it is ruinous and the land sandy'.[1] Certainly there was a rapid recovery soon afterwards, perhaps because of the affluent resident Darcy lords. Thirty-six people over the age of 14 paid the Poll Tax in 1377 and there must have been at least 10 households there in 1428. The mid 15th-century reliefs are higher and this may be because during that century the manor passed in and out of royal hands.

By the early 16th century there was again a resident Darcy lord at Knaith and in 1553 the whole estate passed to William, 1st Lord Willoughby of Parham, and his family made Knaith its principal residence.[2]

It was, perhaps, the arrival of the Willoughbys that led to the removal of the ancient village of Knaith and its replacement by landscape gardens and park (Knaith (3)). If so, this desertion did not result in any fall in population. Indeed, though only 9 persons are listed for the Lindsey Musters of 1539, the 16 taxpayers in 1542–3 and the 73 communicants in 1603 appear to represent a rise in population at this period. No desertion was officially revealed in the 1607 survey. Both the displaced inhabitants and the increased numbers may have been accommodated in two locations, one SE of the old village along the Gainsborough road and the other at Knaith Park in the NE of the parish. The settlement on the Gainsborough road appears to date from the first half of the 17th century, while Knaith Park was a recognizably separate place by the same time. However, it may have had earlier origins as the secular settlement adjacent to Heynings Priory.[3]

By 1676 the number of communicants had plummeted to 30 and at the beginning of the 18th century the population of the parish was reduced to two or three households. Whether this decline was connected with emparking or simply with the difficulties of the Willoughbys is not known but certainly Francis, 5th Baron Willoughby of Parham, suffered severely during the Civil War and the Knaith estate no doubt suffered also through his active role in the war and resulting long exile. It may be that during this period the newly established area of settlement on the Gainsborough road declined. It had certainly reached its present form when the Tithe Map was made in 1850 and probably by 1824.

The remaining earthworks fall into two clearly defined groups. The first NE of the church must represent, at least in part, the site of medieval Knaith. These earthworks seem to illustrate the part played by the river and its utilization in not only affecting the form of the settlement along its bank, but also perhaps in helping to sustain occupation. Two former streets ('a' and 'b'), which survive largely as hollow-ways, leave the Trent at right angles to run E to the edge of the upper terrace. A modern drain in between and parallel continues the line of the present Knaith Hill road riverwards and may thus follow the line of another former street. Slight scarps, banks and depressions, presumably representing former close boundaries and house sites, are associated with these lanes. Medieval pottery fragments were observed in this area during the Commission's survey. The S limits of this settlement are uncertain as the development of the Hall and its gardens has obliterated any ground evidence for settlement E and S of the church. The plan thus emerges as a small rectangular block with streets so arranged that direct access to the river is afforded. Some other Trent-side settlements in the region, notably Marton, still retain a similar pattern of dwellings arranged along parallel roads leading from the river.

At the N end of the site is a terrace-way and hollow-way ('c') which represents an earlier course of the present road to Gainsborough prior to its realignment in this century, though the sharp bends in its course and the fact that it appears to have cut through ridge-and-furrow suggest that it is not an original road line. It could be either the result of a medieval alteration to the through road thus avoiding the village centre or, and perhaps more likely, a post-medieval realignment of an older more direct route through the village, carried out as part of garden and park landscaping.

The second group of earthworks lies S of Terrace House Farm, on the E side of the Gainsborough road. The ground between Dutch Cottage and Terrace House Farm apparently once contained properties as it is divided into large enclosures with, on their E sides, a hollowed track which preserves earlier ridge-and-furrow in its bottom. Inside the enclosures is a series of scarps and hollows adjacent to the existing road. A boggy linear hollow ('d') is perhaps an earlier course of the modern road.

It is probable that these are the remains of a new village laid out along the road on the upper terrace away from the church. That the settlement, whatever its date, is a secondary part of Knaith is clear from the fact that it lies on top of ridge-and-furrow. This settlement, in part still perpetuated by the extant farm and cottages, may have been a deliberate foundation in order to rehouse the inhabitants of the original village cleared to produce an open area for the expansion of the Hall, its gardens and approaches. Dutch Cottage in the centre of the earthworks could be a survivor of this

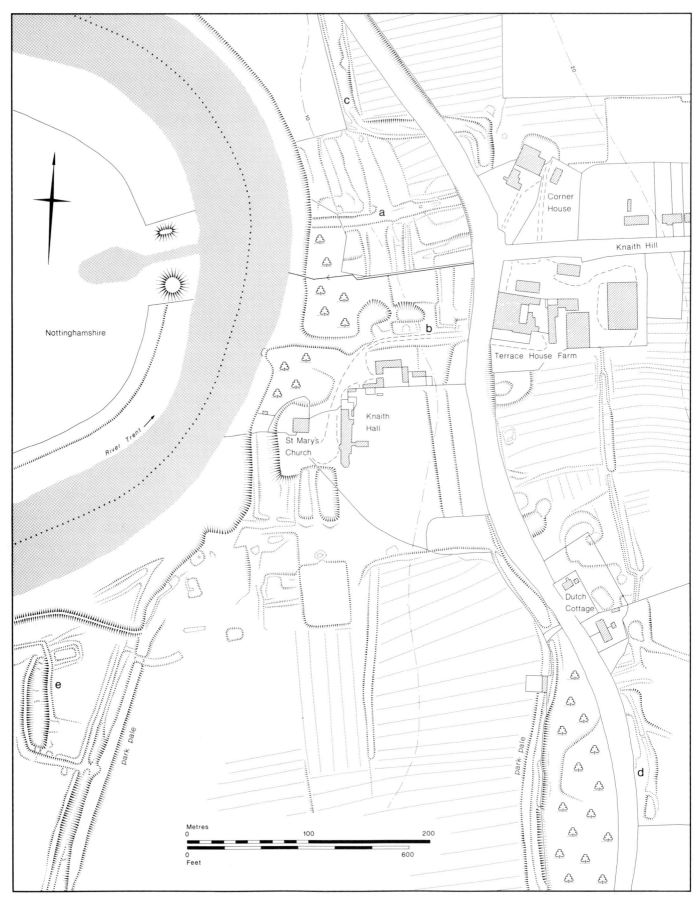

Nottinghamshire

River Trent

Corner
House

Knaith Hill

Terrace House Farm

Knaith
Hall

St Mary's
Church

Dutch
Cottage

park pale

park pale

a

b

c

d

e

20

10

Metres
0   100   200

0   600
Feet

[**85**] *Knaith (2) Settlement Remains, (3) Garden and Park Remains.*

development. The cottage, with a brick Dutch gable at its W end, appears to be no earlier than 1600, yet seems to be part of the layout of the new settlement. If this is correct, then the new village was perhaps laid out around 1630 when work on the Hall, church, gardens and park was being undertaken.

1. *Cal IPM* IV (1913), 240; X (1921), 258.
2. Toulmin Smith 1964 I, 32; *Cal LPFD Hen VIII* XIV pt 1 (1894), 377 no 790; Maddison 1902–6 III, 1038–9.
3. BL Add MS 11574; Foster 1930, 20, 121; Armstrong 1778; Cary 1787.
4. *Cal State Papers Dom 1660–61* (1860), 502; Holmes 1980, 203–17; OS 1st edn 1 in sheet 83; LAO H596.

(3) Garden and Park Remains (SK 828845) [26, 85] lie immediately S of Knaith Hall and church in grassland close to the R Trent.

The earthworks, previously identified as the site of Heynings Priory (Knaith (1)), appear to be the fragmentary remains of a garden and associated park whose form would suggest a late 16th or early 17th-century date for their construction. Their partial destruction is likely to have been the result of 18th-century landscaping. The documentary record as well as the architectural history of the church and Hall suggest a long period of landscape improvements.

In 1553 the Knaith estate passed to William, 1st Lord Willoughby of Parham, and the house became the family's principal residence. If they did not build the present hall then, the Willoughbys substantially refurbished an earlier house, from which 15th-century brickwork is said to survive in the present cellars. They also created a new park extending S from the Hall which is shown on Saxton's map of about 1576 as reproduced a century later by John Speed. They appear, too, to have removed the old village of Knaith to a new site further SE (Knaith (2)) as well as diverting the Gainsborough road away from the Hall. Whether it was Lord Willoughby or his successors who created the gardens S of the Hall is not known.[1]

About 1630 the medieval parish church was reduced, reroofed and refurnished and turned effectively into a private chapel.[2] The alterations seem to have also been intended to make the church a feature of a garden design. From the garden side to the S it appears to be the E end of a church with a chancel and N chapel. This relationship between the church and gardens implies that the latter were also laid out in the early 17th century and this, together with the alterations to the house, suggests that a major estate reorganization took place at this time. If this is so, the removal of Knaith village to the new site as well as the diversion of the Gainsborough road might have been part of the same programme.

At the end of the 17th century Knaith passed by marriage to the Berties, Earls of Abingdon; it was sold to Richard Dalton in 1761. He and his son Henry were certainly responsible for the late 18th-century alterations to the Hall which made it again a place of note. It was probably one of the Daltons who destroyed the formal gardens and opened out the view to the landscape parkland and to the R Trent which afforded to John Byng 'a constant scenery of traffic' on his visit there in 1791. In 1826 Knaith was sold to the Huttons and became part of their Gate Burton estate.[3]

At least part of the extent of the early post-medieval park is marked on the ground by massive N–S banks lying on either side of the present parkland. Broad ridge-and-furrow within this pale demonstrates that the emparked area had formerly lain in open-field arable. Immediately S of the church rectangular depressions, terraces, low banks and broad scarped enclosures, apparently in part overlying ridge-and-furrow, are the remains of late 16th or early 17th-century formal gardens. These earthworks are now much degraded and incomplete as a result of later landscaping, but large quantities of broken brick and mortar, visible in mole upcasts, indicate that these gardens were at least in part walled while the terraces may have had brick revetments. They incorporate the S part of the early churchyard, whose W boundary is marked by a scarp continuing the line of the present limit of the churchyard. To the SW an irregularly arranged group of hollows and platforms, some with masonry *in situ*, marks the positions of former buildings. In some instances they may have been related to the gardens, although an L-shaped building in a narrow close is shown here on the 1850 Tithe Map.[4]

To the SW of the gardens, on the W side of the park boundary bank, is a 2 m deep outer ditch which may have led water into a deep oval pond ('e') bounded by banks 0.7 m high. Attached to the pond on the NE is a small rectangular enclosure defined by a shallow ditch and slight outer banks. These earthworks might have been an ornamental water feature, although their location outside the park pale makes this doubtful. A more likely interpretation is that they represent the site of a water-mill. They are bounded on the N by a modern flood bank.

1. Camden 1695, 472; Maddison 1902–6 III, 1038–9; Pevsner and Harris 1964, 290–1; Speed 1676, between 63 and 64.
2. Micklethwaite 1891–2, 206–7.
3. Newcomb 1972, 13; Andrews 1936 II, 399; drawing of 1793 by Nattes, in LCL Banks Collection II, 355, 357.
4. LAO H596.

LEA

(2) Moated Site (SK 843872) [86] lies in the formerly wooded E end of the parish at 17 m above OD in the bottom of a broad natural basin NE of a wood called Hermit Dam. It was at one time assumed to be the site of the Cistercian nunnery of Heynings but subsequently it was identified as the manorial residence of the Trehampton and de Braose lords of Lea.[1]

The family of Trehampton held the manor of Lea from the 12th to the 14th centuries and perhaps from the Conquest. In 1322 John de Trehampton forfeited the manor and it was granted to William de Aune, the King's Constable of Tickhill Castle. When it was returned to the family by Edward III it was evidently not John de Trehampton who lived there, for in 1330 John de Braose, husband of John's sister, received licence to crenelate the manor. It is unlikely that it was used as a principal residence much beyond the 14th century.[2]

The date of the creation of this isolated moated site and its relation to the manor of Lea is uncertain. It must have been in existence before 1235 when Ralph de Trehampton obtained grant of a chantry in his chapel in his manor house at Lea.[3] It may be that the earlier grant of free warren over the demesne of Lea, obtained by Roger de Trehampton in the time of Henry II, marked a move of the manor away from the village.[4]

What is probably a distinct block of land, perhaps in origin a park (Lea (4)), associated with the moat, is described in an indenture of 1585. It lay outside the open fields of Lea and stands out as a clearly defined unit on an estate map of 1826. Writing in the early 19th century Stark reports a 'sort of hamlet (called Lea Wood) consisting

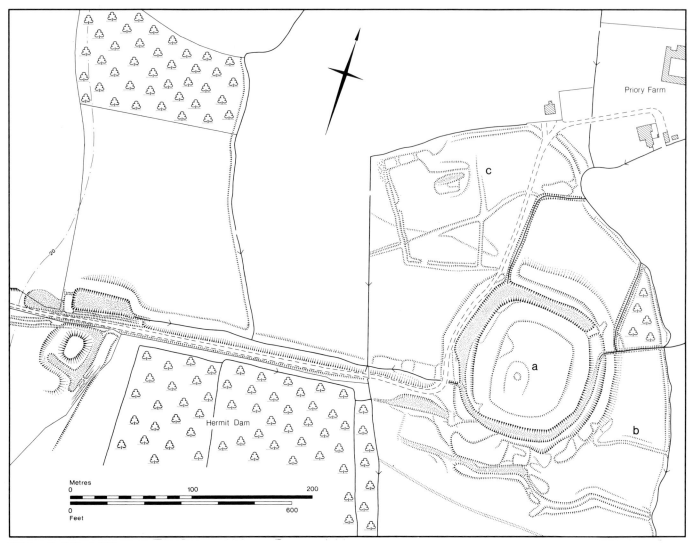

[86] *Lea (2, 3) Moated Sites.*

of a few cottages which stood near the site ... but of which there is no remains'. The existence of this settlement is confirmed by references to its inhabitants in the late 16th and 17th centuries. No settlement is shown on Armstrong's map of 1778 nor on the OS 1st edn 1 in map of 1824.[5] The interior of the moat and its N annexe have been repeatedly ploughed. Stark records a hearsay account of walls standing a yard high in the mid 18th century and by the 1840s carved stones, roofing slates, glazed bricks and other finds had been turned up by the plough.[6]

The moat, which is called *Lacy Hill Close* in the early 19th century, although roughly square in plan, has markedly curved E and W sides. Despite plough damage surviving scarps show that the interior was slightly raised and that former buildings may once have stood on what is now a low mound with a central hollow ('a'). This comprises dark earth containing fragments of brick and limestone. The perimeter bank and ditch are in a variable state of preservation. On the NW the ditch is 1.75 m deep and filled with water, whereas on the SE a drain has been cut through its bottom. The external bank is best preserved on the E where it still stands to a height of 1.5 m. To the S it has been severely mutilated, while on the W it forms a causeway for the track leading to Priory Farm. On the N

the bank has been set back slightly from the edge of the ditch and is only just visible as a broad spread 0.25 m high. Attached to the N side is an outer enclosure, called *Orchard Piece* in the early 19th century, defined by well-marked water-filled ditches up to 1 m deep which are linked to a small stream which forms the NE boundary.

To the E and S of the moat other shallow ditches with intermittent banks run W from the stream. These are presumably watercourses, perhaps bounding additional enclosures or serving merely as drains of relatively late date. The northernmost ('b') extends as far as, but not through, the bank of the moat. This makes the function of the ditch as a probable watercourse difficult to envisage, unless it pre-dates the moat whose construction would have blocked and destroyed any earlier continuation to the W. Sinuous ditches such as these are not unknown in wooded areas and if these are earlier than the moat then it is possible that the latter was built in what had been woodland in the early Middle Ages.

The boggy grassland NW of the moat ('c') is occupied by a group of slight earthworks of at least two phases, including an L-shaped low bank and shallow ditch which cuts across an earlier cross-shaped ditch system connected to the N enclosure. The bank could have enclosed a post-medieval farm or cottages whose remains may be

118

represented by the hollow and scarped areas in the NW quadrant. This may equate with the 'sort of hamlet' near the moat mentioned by Stark.

1. Stark 1817, 314–15; 1841, 44–5; Anderson 1880, 74.
2. LS 4/2; *Book of Fees* I, 191; II, 1072; *Feudal Aids* III, 134, 259, 277, 365; Moor 1902b; LCL Ross MSS I, Corringham, 115–17; *Cal Pat R 1321–4* (1904), 108; *1330–4* (1894), 17.
3. Moor 1902b.
4. *Placita de Quo Warranto* (1818), 427a; *Cal Pat R 1281–92* (1893), 124.
5. LAO 2 AND 1/1/27; MISC DON 196; Stark 1841, 48–9; *Cal Pat R 1563–6* (1961), 48; LAO AND 1/2/1/4/1/8; Foster 1930, 109, 156; Brace 1948, 85; OS 1st edn 1 in sheet 83.
6. Stark 1841, 44; MS note dated 1877 on LAO MISC DON 196; *Catalogue of Antiquities* 1848, 13.

(3) Moated Site (SK 839871) [86] lies 300 m WSW of the moated site (2) and 17 m above OD, on the W side of the same natural basin. The site has not apparently been noted before.

It consists of a small sub-rectangular mounded platform of unknown function and date which has been damaged by ploughing. Its perimeter is delineated by a ditch, wet in places, but which has been encroached upon by the track to Priory Farm. This track is shown on an estate map of 1826, narrowing at this point, and thus the moat is likely to pre-date it. The large rectangular embanked pond lying N of the track is also depicted in 1826.[1]

1. LAO MISC DON 196.

LEGSBY

(1) Moated Site (TF 131848) [27, 87], probably a manorial complex associated with the deserted village of Bleasby but clearly later than parts of it, lies at 34 m above OD on a low narrow ridge of Till.

Two manors in Bleasby are recorded in 1086, but by the late 13th century both appear to have been in the hands of the Bleasby family who took their name from the village and who appear to have been in residence there from the mid 12th century. By the middle of the 14th century they had become tenants of both the abbots of Louth Park and the priors of Sixhills, whose houses had been granted land there in 1154–61 and in the 13th century respectively.[1] The family remained resident throughout the 14th century and in the 15th and early 16th centuries they took a prominent role in county affairs. The direct family line was broken at the end of the 16th century but the residence appears to have continued in use until the mid 17th century.[2]

The square or slightly trapezoidal moat ('a') which must have contained the residence of the Bleasby family is the most prominent feature within the village earthworks. Its broad ditch is up to 2 m deep and intended to hold water which would have been retained by outer banks on its S and E sides; an outlet channel leaves the SE corner. A low causeway in the centre of the N side may mark an original access to the platform, on which traces of stone or brick building foundations occupy the N half. The S arm of the moat overlies and blocks an earlier hollowed street ('b'–'c'). The full extent of the associated manorial complex may be roughly defined to the S and E by a series of ponds ('d', 'e', 'f' and 'g') created by contour dams. To the S ridge-and-furrow has been overlaid by long narrow ditched enclosures which are bounded on the SE by the course of the stream whose earlier alignment is shown on the Tithe Map of 1846. This presumed manorial area has been subdivided

into enclosures by banks and ditches of various strengths. Some may be contemporary with the moated site; others could represent earlier village properties swept away when the moated site was constructed. Scarps and depressions ('h') relate directly to the farm, outbuildings and surrounding closes shown on the Tithe Map.

Alternatively, two of the ponds ('f' and 'g'), though designated 'moat' since the earliest large-scale OS maps, may be post-medieval features. If they are not medieval, the limit of the manorial complex may have been the well-defined ditch running NW–SE (from 'k') that bounds a series of closes clearly associated with the moated residence and which was still in 1846 a curving field boundary.[3]

Whichever interpretation is correct, one feature stands out. The moat and its associated complex are clearly laid out over an earlier road system and perhaps part of an earlier village. It may be that this reorganization took place in the later 14th century and was therefore carried out by the Bleasby family when the village had suffered depopulation. However, in the absence of any evidence for the period of depopulation of the village, such an interpretation must remain speculative. More certain is the fact that following the abandonment of the site, the main through road was diverted across the manorial area.

1. *Lincs DB* 28/29, 48/11; *LS* 16/11, 16/17; *Book of Fees* I, 171; II, 1003; Dugdale 1817–30 V, 414; Stenton 1920, 67, 352; Stenton 1922, nos 8, 11, 12, 19, 21, 25, 32, 36, 38, 62; Foster and Major 1931–73 IV, 73–4; *Cal IPM* VIII (1913), 351; XI (1935), 18; XV (1970), 126; *Cal Fine R 1377–83* (1927), 184.
2. *Cal Fine R 1399–1405* (1931), 89; *1413–22* (1934), 87, 122, 301; *Cal Pat R 1429–36* (1907), 382; *Cal Close R 1500–1509* (1963), 355; Maddison 1902–6 I, 143–4; Gibbons 1898, 42; PRO E317/3.
3. LAO D433; OS 1st edn 25 in plan, Lincs 54.5.

(2) Deserted Village of Bleasby (TF 130848) [27, 87, 88] lies around the moated manor site (1) at 34 m above OD on a narrow low ridge of Till.

No period or reason for the abandonment of Bleasby can be postulated, nor is any continuous assessment of its population possible. For national taxation purposes Bleasby was regularly reckoned as one of Legsby's unnamed members and only exceptionally appears in ecclesiastical surveys because it never acquired a church or chapel, but looked again to Legsby. A minimum population of 10 is recorded between the two manors in 1086 and there were 7 households there in 1563. Only 3 dwelling-houses are shown on the site of the village on the Tithe Map of 1846 [88] and they seem to lie in the same two groups of buildings indicated on the OS 1st edn 1 in map of 1824.[1]

The village remains have been made particularly difficult to understand because of changes in the road system, the late survival of the two groups of properties within the earthworks and by the creation of Bleasby House and its farmyard which has obscured the earlier pattern and divorced one section of the village remains from another. Even so it is possible to suggest that the manor complex, at least in its later form, was an intrusive element and that the original settlement had a regular plan.

The OS 1st edn 1 in map of 1824 shows the road serving Bleasby following the irregular alignment represented in the earthworks by a broad hollow-way ('i'–'j'–'k'–'l'). This has been ploughed out as it diverges from the modern road ('i') but can be seen as a soil-mark on air photographs. To the E ('k') the hollow-way cuts across the corner of a rectangular close, part of the manorial complex, and presumes the abandonment of the latter. The terrace ('l') alongside the W side of the moat and the curve further SW ('j'–'k') may

[**87**] *Legsby (1) Moated Site at Bleasby, (2) Deserted Village of Bleasby.*

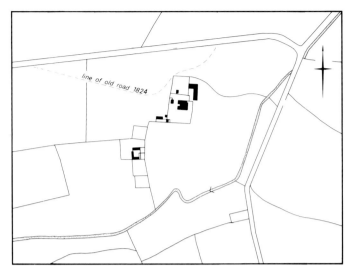

[88] *Legsby (2) Bleasby Village, 1846. Redrawn Tithe Award Map.*

(3) Settlement Remains (TF 159848) [89], perhaps the site of the deserted village of *Coldecotes* and a later monastic grange, lie on a S-facing slope at the E end of a low clay ridge 60 m above OD.

The site of *Coldecotes* has not previously been identified and it has usually been associated with the adjacent settlement of Collow (4).[1] Its existence was first noted in 1086 when it was listed in Domesday Book as part of the soke of the manor of Wragby with a recorded population of seven. Thereafter its size and fortunes are poorly documented and difficult to detail. By the early 12th century it had become separated from Wragby and was held as an independent manor directly of the crown. In 1307 *Coldecotes* passed from the Grelle or Grellys family to the de la Warres when it was part of the adjacent manor of Sixhills. Its previous prosperity, when the manor had dwelling-houses, gardens, orchards and a dovecote, was recalled in 1322, but by then the houses were in ruins. In 1407 Thomas de la Warre granted *Coldecotes* to the Gilbertine priory of Sixhills. It then comprised nothing but 50 acres (20.8 ha) of meadow and 300 acres (125 ha) of pasture. Following the acquisition of the estates of the priory by the Heneages of Hainton at the Dissolution, *Coldecotes* survived into the early 17th century as a group of now unlocatable fields in Legsby to which three messuages seem to have been attached, and as a place recognizable to the Consistory Court of Lincoln in 1615. Thereafter all knowledge of the place is lost.[2]

The earthworks recorded here lie centrally within an area of land which can plausibly be defined as the township of *Coldecotes*; as no other site has yet been identified within the area it seems likely that the earthworks mark the position of the former village.[3]

The poor and incomplete remains appear to be parts of the N and W sides of a rectangular enclosure defined by shallow ditches and low scarps, nowhere more than 1 m in elevation. A probable line of the E side is visible as crop-marks on aerial photographs.[4] Similar low banks and scarps mark out two rectangular inner divisions.

These remains are cut through, not only by a 19th-century hedge line ('a') and a track ('b'), but by an earlier system of enclosure hedges, now earthwork features ('c'), which had already been abandoned by 1814.[5] This system, perhaps part of the 16th or early 17th-century enclosures of the township, in part roughly follows an E–W division between blocks of ridge-and-furrow though it also clearly overlies the ridges. In form, size and siting the remains more closely resemble those of a monastic grange than of a village. It is possible that the site of the original settlement, already deserted in 1322, was reoccupied as a grange from which the adjacent pastures were run after the acquisition by Sixhills Priory in 1407.

1. Foster and Longley 1924, lxxxv
2. *Lincs DB* 34/14; *LS* 16/8; *Rot Hund* 1/364a; *Cal Close R 1279–88* (1902), 156; *Feudal Aids* III, 246, 367; LAO HEN 7/35/2; Hill 1939, 68–9; *Cal Pat R 1405–8* (1907), 334; LAO HEN 3/2, 3/3.
3. LAO D433; D563; HEN 8/1/9.
4. Air photographs in NMR; HSL UK 71.207 Run 15, 3788–9; UK 71.52 Run 17, 0142.
5. LAO HEN 8/1/9.

similarly mark a new alignment, possible only after the properties had been abandoned. The road in 1824 served two groups of properties on its S side, now represented only by earthworks ('h' and 'm'). By 1846 the Tithe Map shows the road on its present alignment, but the properties remained in the field and were described as a house and garden with two cottages, outbuildings and closes. This farm was replaced by the new Bleasby House to the N around 1850.

The foundations of a large building ('m'), probably a farmhouse, are obvious in the earthworks, and to its SW a derelict group of brick outbuildings stands in a network of small rectangular ditched and formerly hedged closes, that overlie ridge-and-furrow. Indeed the pair of long ponds ('f' and 'g'), rather than marking the limit of the manorial block, may have been associated with the post-medieval farm. Their contour dams appear to overlie ridge-and-furrow, and their overflow and outlet channels cut through it.

With allowances made for these later features, the main part of the early settlement may perhaps be seen as structured around three parallel NW–SE roads linked by at least one cross-lane. Thus one early hollowed street ('b'–'c') is blocked by the moated site ('a'). To the SW the hollow-way ('i'–'j') from the W has a similar alignment with village properties on its N side both E and W of the modern hedge and drainage ditch, while on its S side the plot on the W of the hedge clearly developed over the ends of earlier arable ridges. The right-angled turn ('j') may have been an original cross-lane. It has traces of buildings and yards in plots on its W side, which appear from faint traces in a grass paddock formerly to have continued to the N of the modern road, presumably served by the street continuing in that direction. The position and alignment of the E end of the modern road may also be a relict of another NW–SE lane defining the NE side of the manor.

To the NE of Bleasby House, a hollow-way ('n') following the spine of the ridge may pick up the diversion from around the moated site. The fragmentary closes wedged between and possibly overlying blocks of ridge-and-furrow on either side of it may originate either as properties relocated by the creation of the moated site and manorial complex, or possibly as the nucleus of the second manor recorded in Domesday Book although perhaps later replanned.

1. LAO D433; OS 1st edn 1 in sheet 83.

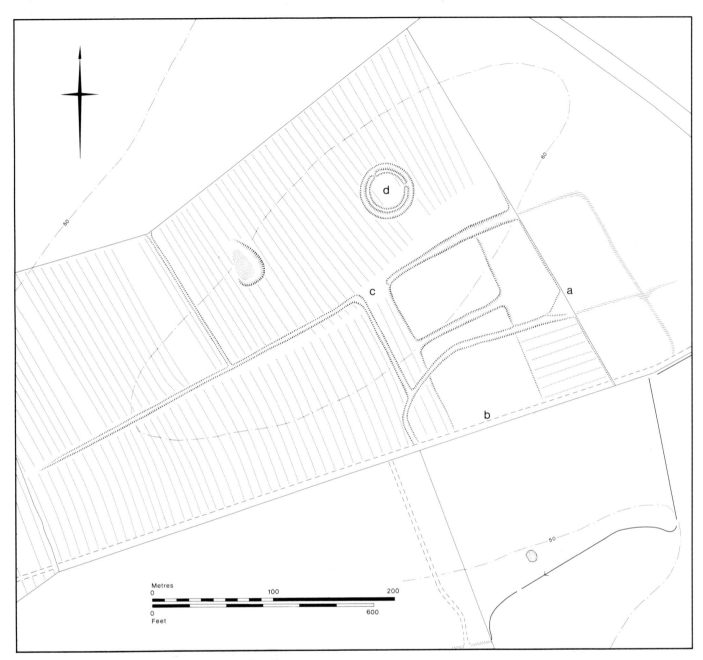

[89] *Legsby (3) Settlement Remains of* Coldecotes, *(10) Tree Ring.*

(4) Site of Monastic Grange (TF 140837) [90] at Collow lies at the N end of a low spur of Till at about 35 m above OD, and extends S to a small W-flowing stream, once the N boundary of East Torrington parish and township.

Its documented existence as a settlement in 1086 relies on an incorrect identification with *Coldecotes*, which was evidently a separate settlement (3). It does not occur in lists of vills or early tax returns. It is first certainly recorded in 1199/1200 or earlier as a holding of the Cistercian abbey of Louth Park, founded in 1139, and thereafter from the mid 13th century as a grange of that abbey.[1] Though perhaps not included in the abbey's original limited endowment, it may have formed part of the flow of benefactions soon afterwards which are listed in a charter of Henry II of 1154 × 1161. Among the gifts was land 'tam in boco quam in plano' in the fields of Bleasby given by five benefactors principally the family of Joscelin of Bleasby. With gifts also in the fields of Torrington and Lissington nearby, this may have perhaps created the land unit which survives to be traceable as the small township of Collow on the Legsby Tithe Map of 1846.[2]

Probably by the later 15th century and certainly by the early 16th the grange was leased into secular hands.[3] At the Dissolution it was granted first in 1537 to Thomas Burgh, Lord Burgh, and then in 1539 to the Duke of Suffolk, from whom it passed later in the century to local hands. In 1563 two households are listed and administrations of probate are recorded for residents at Collow in 1575 and 1592.[4] The present Collow Abbey Farm is probably 17th-century in origin.

The earthworks are bounded on the W and E by broad ditches now partly destroyed or altered. The exact position of the N boundary is uncertain though the course of the N drain may be

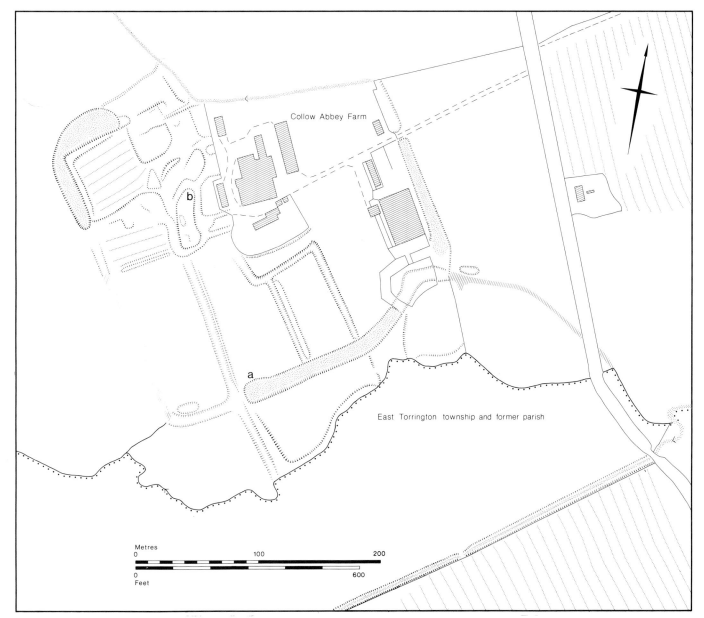

[**90**] *Legsby (4) Site of Monastic Grange at Collow.*

Collow Abbey Farm

East Torrington township and former parish

Metres
0   100   200

0   600
Feet

relevant. The S boundary is also problematical. It could have been the stream, though a broad ditch N of the latter is more likely. Wood, said to be parts of a mill, has been found at its W end ('a'),[5] and the ditch may have been primarily designed or at least utilized at some period to lead water from a point up the stream down to a water-mill.

A series of low platforms emerges from under the W end of Collow Abbey Farm and may represent the sites of former buildings served by a branch hollow-way ('b') to the SW. The platforms and hollow-way are bounded by small blocks of ridge-and-furrow and the fact that one ridge in the N block turns to avoid one of the platforms may indicate that the ridge-and-furrow is contemporary with the platform. To the S, low banks and ditches divide the side of the spur into rectangular enclosures or paddocks and extend to the possible mill leat. Slight earthworks continue the line of two of the divisions to the stream, but are different in character to their counterparts N of the leat.

1. PRO E179/242/113; LAO Vicars Choral 2/1/80; *Rot Hund* 1/364b.
2. VCH *Lincs* II (1906), 140; *Cal Chart R 1300–26* (1908), 247–8; Dugdale 1817–30 V, 414; LAO D433.
3. Venables 1873, 55; Dugdale 1817–30 V, 415; *VE* IV, 57a.
4. *Cal LPFD Hen VIII* XIV, pt 1 (1894) 260a; LAO TYR 7/27; Foster 1921, 19, 125.
5. LM records.

(5) Deserted Village of East Torrington (TF 147835) [**91**] lies at about 43 m above OD on the N side of a low ridge of Till, between two streams flowing W.

The documentation of the two adjacent settlements named Torrington, latterly distinguished as East and West (or less commonly Little and Great), is characteristically difficult to disentangle.

Surviving earthworks indicate that the settlement once had a regular plan but it is unclear when it was deserted. Its later history

123

Collow township

old river course

h

g

Roman pottery

a

b

St Michael's
Church

Ivy House

f

c

e

d

Metres
0   100   200
0   600
Feet

[91] *Legsby (5) Deserted Village of East Torrington.*

illustrates in part a radical 19th-century change in layout associated, as at Bleasby in the same parish (2), with mid-century prosperity and confidence in tenant farming and innovation in farm buildings and practices. The settlement was part of the pre-Conquest soke of Wragby. The Domesday Book record of demesne on this sokeland and the comment that 12 sokemen had nothing may suggest the manorialization was under way although a recent development.[1]

From the minimum recorded population of 12 in 1086, East Torrington shows no marked growth by the early 14th century, when it appears linked to West Torrington in the *Nomina Villarum* in 1316, and its 14 taxpayers in 1327–8 and 1332–3 represent only just half the average for the area. Yet it appears relatively little affected by the Black Death; no relief is recorded in 1352, 54 persons are listed for the Poll Tax of 1377 and there were at least 10 households in 1428. The reliefs of the 15th century, too, were no more than 10 per cent. In 1524 13 persons paid tax; the settlement produced 7 men for the Lindsey Musters of 1539, 9 taxpayers in 1542–3, 18 households in 1563 and 70 communicants in 1603.

The survey of depopulations in 1607 recorded only engrossing by the rector, to the extent of occupying the land of a farm and letting the house stand empty. In 1662 14 persons paid the Hearth Tax and in 1676 only 41 communicants were returned; this, together with the figures of 11 and 13 families in the period 1705–23, perhaps shows some drop in population in the 17th century that may have been associated with the enclosure of the parish about 1670. The 19th-century figures, fluctuating between 15 and 21 houses, included at least two farms away from the village nucleus.[2]

The earthworks lie within a roughly square block, crossed obliquely by an E–W hollow-way ('a'–'b') with property plots containing typical clayland crewyards aligned on its N side. This main street is still shown in use in 1824 and is depicted as two straight sections with a marked dog-leg in the middle. At its E end ('b') it turned S to link with the present road where the latter still bends slightly ('c'). The street's alignment had earlier evidently continued as field ways between open field furlongs both to E and W. In 1824 there was only a single surviving property on the S side of the main street, approximately on the site of the present Ivy House. By 1849 the street had been closed off and the return S ('b'–'c') was similarly closed and later obliterated by the extended farmyard. These changes may have been the direct consequence of the construction of Ivy House and its farm buildings, while William Wilkinson was tenant. The rebuilding of the church in 1848–50 probably formed part of the same phase of improvement.

The road round the SE and SW sides of the settlement, though perhaps originating as a back lane such as marks the NW edge of the earthworks, was well developed by the early 19th century as a broad way, perhaps almost amounting to a long narrow green, along the N side of which in particular properties fronted or had encroached. Buildings now destroyed as shown on the Tithe Map[3] ('d', 'e', 'f') and the property plots of others further E, indicated on the OS 1st edn 1 in map, may be represented by the slight earthworks SE of Ivy House. The development of a road fringing the earlier settlement as the main access of the early modern layout is closely paralleled at Linwood (2).

The medieval settlement may have had a planned regularity of form; the dog-leg in the main street could have resulted from its skirting a manorial block, perhaps occupying the SW quadrant which included the church. Two groups of closes which created marked bulges ('a' and 'g') may be later additions: both apparently disrupt ridge-and-furrow furlongs. The N one ('g') has a hollow-way on its W side which runs down the slope through ridge-and-furrow to the somewhat disturbed earthworks of an embanked pond

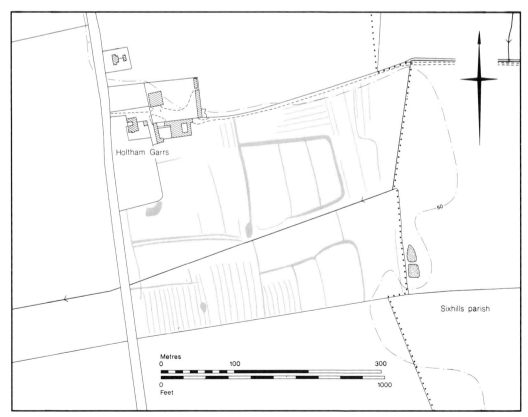

[92] *Legsby (6) Deserted Settlement of Holtham.*

125

('h'), probably the site of a water-mill. These are similar in form and function to the earthworks at Buslingthorpe (3) except that instead of constructing a dam across the stream which is here the parish/township boundary, a pond was created alongside the stream and thus totally within East Torrington. The pond was presumably fed by a leat to its SE corner, now ploughed out, taken off the stream to the E. Water was retained against the slope by dams to the W and N and a gap in the SW corner may have allowed overspill. A raised area in the E half may have been an island within the pond.

A few sherds of Roman pottery were picked up on the earthworks during survey.

1. *Lincs DB* 27/20, 21, 34/18; *LS* 16/6; *Book of Fees* I, 172; Davis 1914b III, 197.
2. BL Add MS 11754, f88; PRO E179/140/806; Wheeler 1909–10, 30.
3. LAO D563.

(6) Deserted Settlement Remains (TF 153863) [92] of a village or manor and monastic grange at Holtham.

Two sokeland holdings are recorded in 1086, one of them then waste: thereafter Holtham does not appear in national tax returns, perhaps being subsumed as a member of Legsby, perhaps because it amounted to no more than a demesne farm. The manor of Holtham was granted to Sixhills Priory in 1389 and then run as a grange until the Dissolution. In 1563 four families were recorded there.[1] The earthworks, which occupied a field named *Home Close and Moat* in 1846, were destroyed between 1963 and 1971 but they appear to have been inserted between pre-existing arable furlongs. They were dominated by a large moat-like ditched enclosure subdivided into three internal paddocks. External features appear to include channels feeding and draining the ditch and other possible enclosures and a trackway. Traces of ridge-and-furrow surround the site. There are no obvious village remains.

1. *Lincs DB* 22/36, 22/37, 40/13; *LS* 16/3; *Cal Pat R 1388–92* (1902), 34; Dugdale 1817–30 VI, 964.

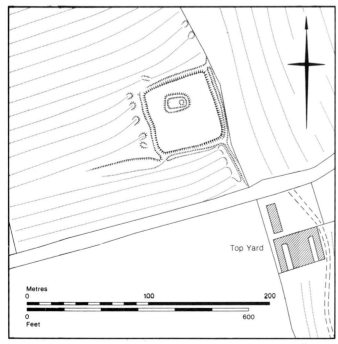

[**93**] *Legsby (8) Site of Chapel(?).*

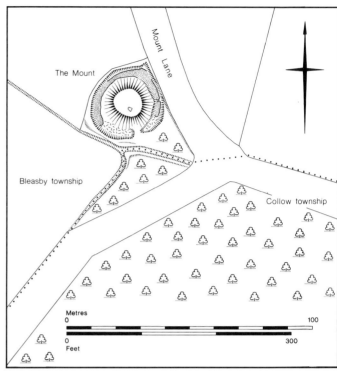

[**94**] *Legsby (9) Windmill Mound.*

(8) Site of Chapel(?) (TF 15778392) [93] lies in the former parish of East Torrington, just over 1 km E of East Torrington village, adjacent to Top Yard Farm at about 60 m above OD.

The field-name in 1849 was *Chapel Hill* and it was then glebe land. Local tradition asserts that this is the site of the former church of East Torrington, but this is unlikely in view of the distance from the village and because St Michael's church within East Torrington had a medieval predecessor on or near its present site. Whether it can be identified with a chapel erected, evidently in the 13th century, to service the settlement of *Coldecotes* because of the distance to Torrington is unclear.[1] A suggested site for *Coldecotes* lies 900 m away to the N (3).

The earthwork lies within an area of well-marked ridge-and-furrow. It consists of an almost square enclosure with a broad ditch up to 1 m deep. In the centre of the N half are the stone foundations of a rectangular building orientated E–W. The stones include pieces of dressed Spilsby Sandstone.

The enclosure was clearly laid out on land previously under cultivation and so truncated five ridges which were thereafter ploughed to a shorter length. One was subsequently cut away by what may be a hollow-way from East Torrington.

1. LAO D563; Harding 1937, 35; Hill 1939, 69.

(9) Windmill Mound (TF 13258397) [94], known as The Mount, lies at 35 m above OD on Till. It is mapped in 1824 as a 'Tumulus', and more recently assessed as an ornamental feature of probable 18th-century date and as a small motte.[1] It is situated in a small copse called *Holt* on the 1846 Tithe Map of Legsby which also shows that the wooded area represents a piece cut out of a triangular field called *Mill Hill*.[2] The mound occurs on the Bleasby side of the former township boundary with Collow at a point where the boundary, represented by a partially embanked drain, changes direction sharply. No date can be assigned to the site though in 1256

Richard Crane of Bleasby was convicted of theft of goods at Bleasby mill.[3]

The mound is 20 m in diameter and 2.4 m high with a flat top 11 m across. The surrounding ditch is 5 m wide, partly water-filled and 0.5–1.5 m deep. A ramped causeway on the S appears original. A small crater on the S side of the summit is a recent disturbance.

1. OS 1st edn 1 in sheet 83; NAR TF 18 SW 11; King 1983 I, 261.
2. LAO D433.
3. Foster and Major 1931–73 II, 197.

(10) Tree Ring (TF 15838498) [89] lies in a prominent position on a narrow E–W ridge of Till at about 60 m above OD.

The slight earthwork ('d') consists of a low circular earthen bank only 20 cm high with a shallow external ditch. The gap through the bank on the N side may be original though a second gap on the E is perhaps the result of cattle trampling.

In the past the site has been variously identified as a Bronze Age ritual site or a Roman signal station. It is however a tree ring, probably associated with 18th-century landscaping. It overlies ridge-and-furrow and is depicted, complete with its stand of mature trees, on an estate map of 1814.[1]

1. LAO HEN 8/1/9; Everson 1979, 69–70.

LINWOOD

(1) Moated Sites and Deserted Settlement (TF 115857) [37, 95] lie at 35 m above OD on a low E–W ridge of Till and form the S part of the polyfocal village of Linwood.

Assessment of the population trends of Linwood cannot distinguish the two parts of the settlement after 1086: they show remarkable and largely unexplained changes of fortune. The larger of the two Domesday Book manors had a minimum recorded population of 25, the smaller of 8. The number of taxpayers in the early 14th-century subsidies, at 14 in 1327–8 and 16 in 1332–3, represent only 50 per cent and 55 per cent of the average for the wapentake and an obvious crude fall from Domesday Book levels. Since there was little monastic interest in the settlement, this must mark a genuine pre-Black Death decline. Relief of over 50 per cent was allowed even on this low level in 1352; the Poll Tax does not survive but there were at least 10 households in 1428. Reliefs of over 20 per cent were allowed in the mid 15th century indicating modest recovery, yet a century later the settlement could produce 31 and 37 taxpayers for the lay subsidies of 1524 and 1525, 28 persons for the Lindsey Musters of 1539, 37 taxpayers in 1542–3, 43 households in 1563 and 150 communicants in 1603. Factors in this growth may have been the release from the Beaumont Fee (see below) and the continuing emergence of nearby Market Rasen as a local centre. The 17th century saw a sharp decline, by nearly a half, in which enclosure and engrossment were probable factors. The survey of depopulations in 1607 reported that, in addition to decaying the manor house, Robert Tyrwhitt had converted two farms to cottages and let the land; John Robinson had dealt similarly with another farm. The enclosure of the parish took place in the period between 1600 and 1668.[1] By 1676 the number of communicants had fallen to 69; in the early 18th century there were 25 and 22 families remaining. There was a similar level in the first decades of the 19th century and the population rose in the 1830s to 39 households and has maintained that level since.

Of the two manorial holdings recorded in Domesday Book under Linwood, the larger was held by Alfred of Lincoln and the smaller by Durand Malet. It is likely that the larger 11th-century manor was centred on the earthworks here described and that the smaller manor was associated with the northern group of earthworks (2). Alfred's holding remained the residential demesne manor and a unit in an estate or barony of moderate size until the 15th century. It had passed by marriage by the mid 12th century to Ralph de Bayeux and then about 1250 to the Rabayns by inheritance.[2] Dispute over the inheritance gave rise to an unusually detailed survey incorporated in an *inquisition post mortem* in 1288. All aspects of the manor were detailed and valued. They included 'the fruit and herbage of the garden' and 'the dykes surrounding the *curia*'.[3]

This manor of Linwood was granted to Henry Beaumont in 1318 and thereby became part of a similar moderately extensive estate whose principal residence was at Folkingham in Kesteven. Management of the Beaumont's Lindsey demesnes came to be entrusted to substantial local men including Sir William Tyrwhitt, appointed in 1441.[4] The manor was forfeit with William Viscount Beaumont's other estates in 1461–2; its granting by the Crown to a succession of people suggests its decline as a residence or possible abandonment.[5] In 1607 Robert Tyrwhitt was said to have decayed the manor house at Linwood, presumably marking the final end of any use of the residence.[6]

The moated earthworks no longer fully survive. Before 1962 they were well preserved in ancient pasture but were then filled in and deemed to have been destroyed. The principal features nevertheless remained traceable in plan and slight elevation until 1980 when the site was converted to arable.

As shown on early OS maps and plans and on aerial photographs, the site focused on an almost square moated enclosure ('a') with its N arm slightly curved. The moat held standing water, and at the SE corner was an outlet via an arrangement of ditches surrounding an islet into the outer enclosure ditch. Descriptions of the monument before destruction referred to mounds of buildings visible within the moat and after recent ploughing part of a late medieval stone corbel with a carved figure was picked up and deposited in the church.[7]

An outer enclosure boundary, consisting of a water-holding ditch and presumably forming part of the documented dykes surrounding the *curia*, curved round the E and along the S side of the main moat. At its W end the existing hedge line truncated it sharply, suggesting that it formerly continued W as it is apparently shown doing on the OS 1st edn 1 in map to a point SW of The Old Rectory ('c').[8] If this is so, the space enclosed almost certainly included the church. The area to the E of the moat ('a') may have formed a garden, with the islet as an associated feature.

On the NE was a second, rectangular, moated enclosure ('b'). This had an entrance causeway at the W end of the S side. It has been suggested that this enclosure might have been a garden but the description of the site before destruction refers to clear traces of buildings within this moat, which can also be faintly seen on air photographs. Alternatives may therefore be that this moated site was not contemporary with that to the S but its predecessor or successor, or that its contemporary function was to contain the agricultural buildings.

To the N and W of the church, the E of two existing paddocks contains some traces of ditched divisions visible on air photographs. These divisions together with the paddocks may be the remains of former village properties.

1. BL Add MS 11574, ff79, 86; Johnson 1962, 140.
2. *Lincs DB* 27/7, 44/10; *LS* 7/16; Massingberd 1904–5, 46–50.
3. Massingberd 1904–5, 57–8; PRO C133/51/9; *Cal IPM* II (1906), 422–3, 425.

[95] *Linwood (1) Moated Sites and Settlement Remains, (2) Settlement Remains.*

128

4. *Cal Pat R 1317–21* (1903), 71; *Cal Fine R 1422–30* (1935), 174, 208; Lloyd and Stenton 1950, 37.
5. *Cal Pat R 1461–7* (1897), 179, 195, 227, 345; *1467–77* (1900), 19, 310, 518, 523; *Cal LPFD Hen VIII* I pt 1 (1920), 160; pt 2 (1920), 729; LAO CRAGG 5/1/54; *Cal Pat R 1547–8* (1924), 222, 254.
6. BL Add MS 11574, f79.
7. OS 25 in plan Lincs 54.1; CUAC JZ 76–82, LH 88–9, UA 63, 65–7, UZ 72; LM records.
8. OS 1st edn 1 in sheet 83.

(2) Settlement Remains (TF 112865) [95], formerly part of the village of Linwood, lie at 35 m above OD on a low E–W ridge of Till. They form the N part of the polyfocal village of Linwood and were probably replanned in the 12th century. For details of population see (1) above.

It is likely that the smaller of the two manors listed in Domesday Book was associated with this nucleus. The manor is recorded as being held by William Meschin in the early 12th century and by William de Curci in 1212,[1] but was perhaps already held of them by the Malet family who remained there until at least the mid 13th century. Its later history is obscure. The purchase of half a knight's fee by Elias de Rabayn in about 1250 may mark the effective absorption of the smaller into the larger manor, even though they continued to be distinguished.[2]

The SE part of the earthworks was ploughed up for arable between 1966 and 1969, but good air photographs of the earthworks before ploughing and of soil-marks after allow a reasonable transcription of detail.[3] Elsewhere the earthworks are well preserved and impressively extensive, although in detail rather indeterminate as is usual where properties are abandoned piecemeal.

A number of straight and narrow ditches coincide with field boundaries shown on the Tithe Map (eg 'e', 'f', 'g' and 'h') although perpetuating older divisions, and the rectangular network ('i') matches a compact block of small garden plots on the same map.

Before the increase of population in the 1830s, linked presumably to the agricultural up-turn of the period, the settlement's street system was far more complex and can be traced within the earthworks. Ways still shown in use in 1824 include the axial E–W street ('j'–'k') along the ridge; the well-developed hollow-way ('l'–'m') that served as a back lane for a regular row of properties to its N; and the way ('n'–'o') that ran down the slope and continued S across to the church. By 1842 this network had been reduced to the present road system.[4]

The earthworks also contain the fragmented line of a further curving hollow-way ('p'–'i' and beyond). This formed a back lane to the row of properties facing the E–W axial street ('p'–'k'), and also provided access to properties to the N backing on to the modern road. The properties both in the row on the N side of the axial street and on the S have hollow yards typical of clayland villages. The start of the back lane ('p') and the southward curve of the axial street S of the manor house, as well as the course of the modern through road, together suggest that the block in the NW, around the 19th-century manor house, was an early manorial unit.

A possible sequence of development may be suggested as follows. The earliest road alignment may be that of the N–S street ('n'–'o'), which is on the line of the road running N to Market Rasen and provides the direct way across the valley to the church. Pottery from the ploughed earthworks in this area includes not only medieval and post-medieval types but also Middle Saxon and Roman sherds attesting an early settlement focus. The development or establishment of the E–W access-way ('j'–'k') apparently cut the N–S through-way. The arrival of this E–W alignment and its associated properties may not have been fortuitous. Not only does it block the presumed N–S route but the whole settlement has a marked degree of regularity including plot widths and lengths. The position of the manorial *curia* in the NW corner of the resulting block is also noteworthy. If these remains are the result of conscious planning they may well be associated with the Malet family in the 12th century or the Rabayns when they perhaps reorganized the manor after 1250. The properties N of the back lane ('p'–'i') may represent later infilling resulting from the re-routing of the old direct way to the W of the main settlement. With the decline of the internal street network and of the S settlement block, recent properties have turned outwards to face the later through road.

1. *Lincs DB* 44/10; *LS* 7/7; *Book of Fees* I, 154.
2. Foster and Major 1931–73 IV, 220–2; Stenton 1922, 18; *Rot Hund* I, 361, 370; *Feudal Aids* III, 158, 233, 268, 296; *Cal IPM* II (1906), 257, 423.
3. RAF VAP CPE/UK2012/1060–1, 1297–8; CUAC UA 68, UZ 73, AHD 9, 12, 14; air photographs in NMR.
4. OS 1st edn 1 in sheet 83; LAO F309.

NETTLEHAM

(1) Site of Bishop's Palace (TF 006752) [18, 96], one of the palaces of the medieval bishops of Lincoln, lies on the S side of the village High Street on Lincolnshire Limestone at 25 m above OD. The earthworks include the remains of the only enclosed medieval garden arrangement known in England.

The history of the site is extremely well documented. In the later 11th century Nettleham was a royal manor which was granted in 1101 to Robert Bloet, Bishop of Lincoln.[1] Thenceforth Nettleham not only served as a manorial holding but also as an administrative and residential base where visiting dignitaries could be accommodated at a minimum distance from Lincoln. Edward I stayed there in 1284 for nearly a fortnight and again in 1301 when he held parliament in Lincoln, and probably again in 1303 and 1304. The palace appears to have played a complementary role to Stow Park (Stow (3)) and was favoured by many of the bishops throughout the later Middle Ages.[2] In 1336 Bishop Henry Burghersh was licensed to crenelate the manor and surround it with a stone wall and in 1432 the garden within the manor was the scene of a consultation between Bishop Grey and the Dean and dignitaries of Lincoln Cathedral.[3]

In 1536 the host of the Pilgrimage of Grace attacked and damaged the manor house, but it remained in use for another 50 years. It may have been the personal tragedy of the death of Bishop Wickham's daughter at Nettleham in 1585 that effectively ended its use as an episcopal residence, for when in 1630 Bishop Williams obtained royal licence for its demolition it was claimed that the site had been deserted for 60 years and more.[4]

In consequence, in 1633 and 1634 building material was taken from Nettleham to the Palace at Lincoln for work there. Parliamentary Commissioners in 1647 accordingly found the residence 'hath been of very large buildings, and convenient and necessary, having had a fair chapel which is demolished, and great parts of other buildings also demolished', but they described in detail what remained. This included a range containing the King's chamber and two other chambers, a second range containing the

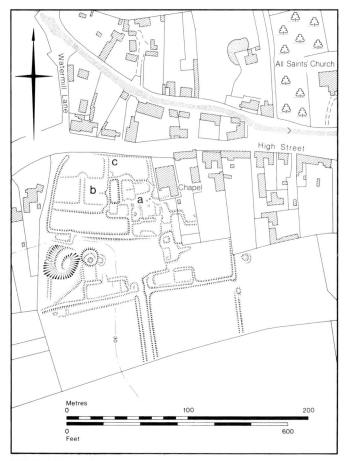

[96] *Nettleham (1) Site of Bishop's Palace.*

long chamber, the little stable, the little kitchen and adjoining little brewhouse, and a third long range called 'the officer's lodgings'. Other ruined buildings and walls were a potential source of stone as were other materials such as the '21 pieces of timber from an old barn fallen down'.[5] The manor was sold in 1648 but was restored to the Bishop in 1660, and thereafter leased out. There were no buildings on the site in 1777.[6]

The remains fall into three parts. In the NE, set around the 19th-century nonconformist chapel, there is a large area occupied by massive earthworks of generally rectangular form up to 2 m high ('a'). These earthworks are the palace buildings which clearly extended further E into the area now occupied by the first two properties E of the chapel. Though individual structures or perhaps rooms can be recognized, no overall plan is identifiable. It may, however, be suggested that the large rectangular platform on the W might have been the private section of the buildings as it lies adjacent to the second main section of the site to the N and W which is the garden.

This area ('b') is bounded by a low bank, once a stone wall, on the S and W, and traces of the same wall underlie the modern boundary wall on the N. There is also a short length of walling extending from the NE corner to the main block of buildings. This suggests that the area was perhaps enclosed by a high stone wall, thus making it a private garden. Its identification as a garden is supported by the interior features which survive. On the S is a long flat terrace cut into the rising ground which at its E end extends beyond the W end of the palace buildings. The N side of the terrace is marked by a low scarp 0.5 m–1 m high. Below this is a group of

much lower scarps, nowhere more than 0.3 m high, which divide the area into rectangular blocks. These are presumably the remains of paths and flower-beds. A large projection on the W side of the main building which overlooks this area may be either the site of steps giving access to the garden or the base of an oriel window or tower allowing views from the palace across the garden. In the NE corner of this area is another open rectangular space which is also perhaps part of the garden.

The third part of the site, to the S, is of a very different character to the foregoing and is laid out on a different alignment. It consists of an embanked trackway which emerges from the modern arable in the S and runs straight dividing two perhaps outer enclosures until it meets a narrow gap through long E–W banks. On either side of this gap are projecting platforms 1 m high largely composed of fallen masonry. The W platform is still markedly rectangular. It is likely that these projections are the bases of a formal gatehouse to the palace, and thus the trackway was the main approach road. This idea is supported by the fact that on either side of the projections are the stone footings of two, almost identical, very large buildings, each with an original entrance in the centre of their N sides. These are likely to be two massive barns, symmetrically arranged on each side of the gatehouse. Beyond this presumed gatehouse and barns is an open space which is perhaps a courtyard, now divided into two parts by an area of tumbled masonry and at least two building platforms which extend S from the main palace block almost to the N side of the E barn.

The W side of this courtyard is occupied by a large quarry dug some 5 m deep into the underlying limestone rock. From its base a terrace-way or ramp curves upwards to meet a circular mound set on the lip of the quarry 1.5 m high and with a well-marked depression in its summit. Attached to this mound on its E side are the foundations of a small rectangular building. The mound is presumably a lime-kiln, the attached buildings being the stokehole with the quarry supplying the limestone. Immediately N of the quarry are the foundations of another stone building which appears to have encroached upon the boundary wall of the garden.

Limited excavations were carried out on the site in 1959.[7] Little of intrinsic value was discovered although the findings agree with the analysis of the earthworks offered above. The principal layer encountered in trenching the NW corner of the site was one of dark brown soil with no old turf line and a mixture of sherds suggesting cultivated ground. In the NE corner of the garden a stone-lined well or cistern ('c') had been deliberately filled-in in the early to mid 14th century; the foundation of the garden's E boundary wall lay within a few millimetres of the well, yet no assessment of their relationship is recorded nor is the relevant excavated section published. If, however, the wall was later, the filling of the well may have been preparation for it and give the date of the creation of the garden. It is tempting to associate this with a major refurbishment connected with Bishop Burghersh's licence to crenelate. Before the garden there had apparently been major structures of timber and stone here, perhaps dated by Saxo-Norman pottery. Middle Saxon sherds and loom weights were also collected as well as a thin scatter of later Roman pottery. From the palace itself medieval green-glazed pottery and an inscribed ring are recorded. Carved stones found in constructing the Methodist Chapel in 1899 were built into its kitchen wall; the N boundary wall contains a window head and other reused masonry; stone heads from label stops are built into 30 and 62 High Street. There is some suggestion that the stone cottages fronting High Street E of the chapel may have originated as part of the stables.[8]

The remarkable preservation of the earthworks on this site allows some tentative interpretation. The palace building and its presumed garden appear to be a coherent unit. If this is so the garden is likely to be a medieval one, of the mid 14th century and thus the earliest known survival of this type of site in England. The fact that the approach road, gatehouse and barns lie on a different alignment may be the result of a later, late medieval, replanning of the site to give a formal entrance with semi-defensive proportions.

1. *Lincs DB* 1/35; Foster and Major 1931–73 I 18, 41–2.
2. Baker 1957, 12–16, 23–4 and *passim*; Davis, F. N. *et al* 1925, 353–8; Hill 1954, 207–14; LAO Registers of Bishop Dalderby.
3. *Cal Pat R 1334–8* (1895), 330; Archer 1963–82 I, 161; Thompson 1914–29 I, 132; Foster 1912, 91, 92, 97; Baker 1957, 23–4.
4. Baker 1957, 25ff; Cole 1917 II, 134; III, 166; *Cal State Papers Dom 1629–31* (1860), 166, 190.
5. LAO Bishops' Accounts 23/B; 2CC8/152867, partly transcribed in Baker 1957, 41–2.
6. Baker 1957, 44–5; LAO Nettleham Parish Plans.
7. *Med Archaeol* 4 (1960), 153; Russell and Moorhouse 1971, 19–27.
8. LM records; LM Jarvis MS, 179; Baker 1957, 52–3, 90.

NETTLETON

(5) Deserted Farmstead (TF 11189710) [69] lies on an exposed ledge below the crest of the main W-facing scarp of the Wolds at 130 m above OD.

The open fields of Nettleton were enclosed in 1791–5 and there appears to have been no immediate spread of farmsteads on to the former open fields. By 1824, however, a farmstead on this site is shown on the OS 1st edn 1 in map.[1] The buildings of this farm were still depicted on the OS 1:10560 plan Provisional Edition of 1956, though based on pre-1930 revision.

The earthworks seem to represent a farmhouse ('d') with a yard and outbuildings to the N. A small paddock S of the house is subdivided by a slight scarp and may have been an orchard and garden. To the W of the remains there is a stone-revetted spring and a deep hollow. The latter may have been dug by the army who are known to have used the site during the Second World War.[2]

1. LAO Lindsey Enclosure 61; OS 1st edn 1 in sheet 86.
2. Local inf.

NEWBALL

(1) Settlement Remains (TF 073764) [97], formerly part of the village of Newball, surround the two farms making up the modern hamlet and lie at 14 m above OD on a low hill of Till on the E side of the Barlings Eau. The early development of the village is obscure, but the late abandonment of part of it is well documented.

The modern civil parish was only a township within Stainton by Langworth parish in the medieval period and the settlement never acquired a parish church. A manorial chapel was licensed in 1313 for the manor of John de Bayeux here. As a result of sub-infeudation of the Earl of Chester's 11th and 12th-century manor, the Bayeux family held land in Newball in the later 13th and 14th centuries, which by 1428 had passed into the hands of the Abbot of Barlings. A second manor at this time was held by the family of Gumbald.[1]

For most administrative purposes, Newball was returned with Reasby as a member, commonly unnamed, of Stainton and little idea of its population level can be ascertained. The only figures available are a minimum recorded population of 15 in 1086, 10

households in 1563 and 17 in 1841. Yet 18th and early 19th-century estate maps and later OS plans actually show the gradual abandonment of dwellings on the village site at this time and its reduction to the present two farms. To what extent the settlement shared in the 'great depopulations' and enclosure documented for Stainton by the 1607 survey is unclear. Enclosure of all but the commons had taken place by 1735.[2]

The earthworks fall into two distinct groups, with those W of Manor Farm probably representing the earlier part. These are associated with an abandoned street now surviving as a hollow-way in places more than 1 m deep. At its S end, this hollow-way takes up the line of the modern road from the SE, before turning N and curving along the W side of Manor Farm. Its line is continued by a farm track, formerly with cottages on its W side, which swings sharply back to the modern road, though the earlier alignment may have continued a little further N before turning E, as the estate maps of 1735 and 1824 appear to show. This was a road in use until at least 1735 but marked only by a hedge line in 1824. The remarkable loop that it makes may have been taking account of a demesne manor house on the site of Manor Farm.

Slighter hollow-ways spring at right angles off the W side of the main hollow-way, serving a group of rectangular property plots and, at the NW, giving access to the river down the steep natural slope. Several of the plots show slight irregularities, presumably marking the sites of former buildings, but the most well marked are the rectangular stone foundations of a large building set alongside a deeply hollowed yard ('a'). On a clay site this is presumably a post-medieval feature, yet it is not depicted on the map of 1735 nor on any later maps. A building is shown immediately to the SE ('b') in 1735 but that had gone by 1824.[3]

This part of the settlement was almost certainly more extensive than the existing earthworks. The field-name *Town Close* is applied about 1750 both to these earthworks and to the ploughed land immediately to their S.[4] Field-walking here has produced a scatter of both medieval and post-medieval pottery, including a group of 17th-century wares. Two Roman sherds have also been found.

A picture of gradual, probably largely post-medieval, abandonment of these parts of the settlement may be balanced by the evidence of the second group of earthworks situated NW of Walk Farm. These form a series of long enclosures separated by narrow ditches and which formerly had buildings at their S ends. Structures are shown on the estate maps of 1735 and 1824 on the site of Walk Farm and within the south-westernmost close ('c'). The earthworks of former buildings and a yard occupy the next close ('d'). In addition the 1735 map depicts a house N of Walk Farm ('e'). This part of Newball appears to have been laid out on top of old arable represented by ridge-and-furrow visible in the backs of the enclosures. Both maps also mark buildings at Manor Farm and at The Cottage and the later map has additional structures nearby ('f' and 'g'). This occupation in the area of The Cottage may similarly overlie earlier arable and be contemporary with the Walk Farm remains. The ploughed land E of Manor Farm too has hollows with stone and tile scatters, perhaps indicating house sites associated with 13th-century and later medieval pottery as well as 17th-century sherds. This area of settlement may also have overlain ridge-and-furrow.[5]

Perhaps contemporary with the second group of earthworks is the modern road which runs through the village parallel to the enclosure ditches to the NE. It is probably of no great age as it is level with the surrounding fields. The same is true of the track to Walk Farm which may once have served the former buildings ('c' and 'd').

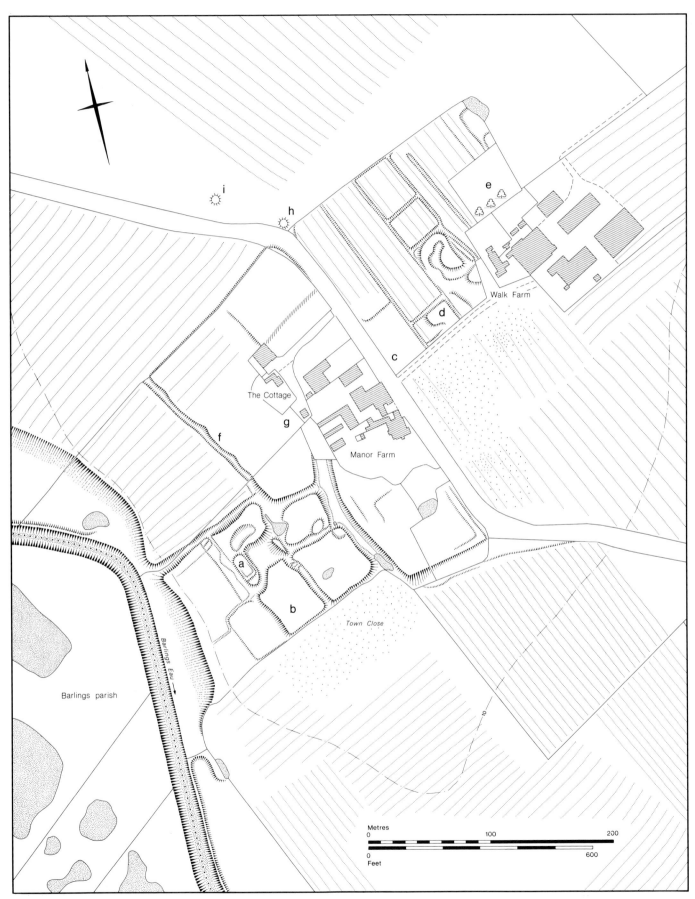

i

h

e

Walk Farm

d

c

The Cottage

g

f

Manor Farm

a

b

Town Close

Barlings Eau

Barlings parish

10

Metres
0   100   200

0   600
Feet

[**97**] *Newball (1) Settlement Remains.*

Two 'tumuli' ('h' and 'i') marked on the 1824 map, and later,[6] lay on the N edge of the settlement. It is possible that both were windmill mounds.

1. Owen 1975, 21; *Lincs DB* 13/45; *LS* 16/1; *Book of Fees* I, 172; II, 1002, 1062, 1091; *Feudal Aids* III, 165, 222, 302; *Cal IPM* III (1912), 317–18; 2nd ser II (1915), 377–8; *Cal Inq Misc* I (1916), 245.
2. Nottingham University MA 2P/297, 311; LAO E385; BL Add MS 11574, ff76, 83, 87.
3. Nottingham University MA 2P/297, 311.
4. Nottingham University MA 2P/298.
5. RAF VAP 541/185/4092–3.
6. LAO PADLEY 2/26 and E 385.

(3) Enclosure (TF 084760) [98] lies on clay at about 13 m above OD in an area of closely planted coniferous woodland. Its date and function are uncertain.

In Domesday Book, 500 acres of woodland for pannage is recorded in Newball, which presumably represents the later documented medieval managed woodlands which all lay within the parish and occupied more than half its area.[1]

Estate maps show that practically the full extent of these woods still existed in 1735, and, though clearance had started, in the early 19th century the main part of Newball Wood remained under a coppice regime.[2] Clearings and rides are marked on the earlier map but the site of the earthwork lay within the sinuous and unbroken woodland boundary and is shown completely tree-covered. This boundary survives to the W of the enclosure as a hedged bank 0.5 m high marking the W edge of the wood, beyond which lies ridge-and-furrow. On the map of 1824 the earthwork is accurately depicted with bank and external ditch and named *Castle Hill*. No entrances are indicated and it is shown covered by trees. The deciduous trees were cleared during the Second World War and the earthwork has since been bulldozed and replanted.

The enclosure has an internal area of 2 ha, bounded by a bank and outer ditch which are especially well marked on the E, where the bank is up to 1 m high and the ditch 1.4 m deep. Elsewhere the earthwork is less well preserved, especially on the W and N, where the bank just survives as a spread platform. The ditch has also been mutilated close to Newball Wood House, where it has been enlarged to provide drinking water for animals. Elsewhere the bottom of the ditch is followed by a drainage gully made relatively recently and which has been cut across the fronts of the two opposed entrances which interrupt the E and W banks. The strength of the original earthwork, evident even from its present degraded state, its size and plan have led to its interpretation as a 'medieval refuge', presumably a defensive work of some kind.[3] This seems unlikely not least because of the complete lack of documentation, though its topographical location, on the edge of dry land close to the Barlings Eau, may be significant.

The idea that the enclosure is a medieval hunting lodge is equally implausible. It lies both within and under managed woodland which itself is presumably of medieval origin and again there is no

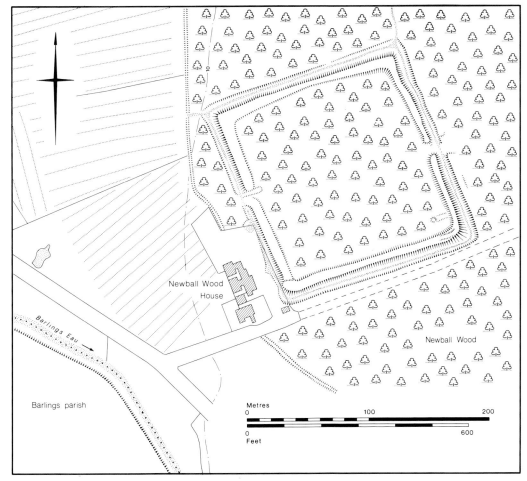

[**98**] *Newball (3) Enclosure.*

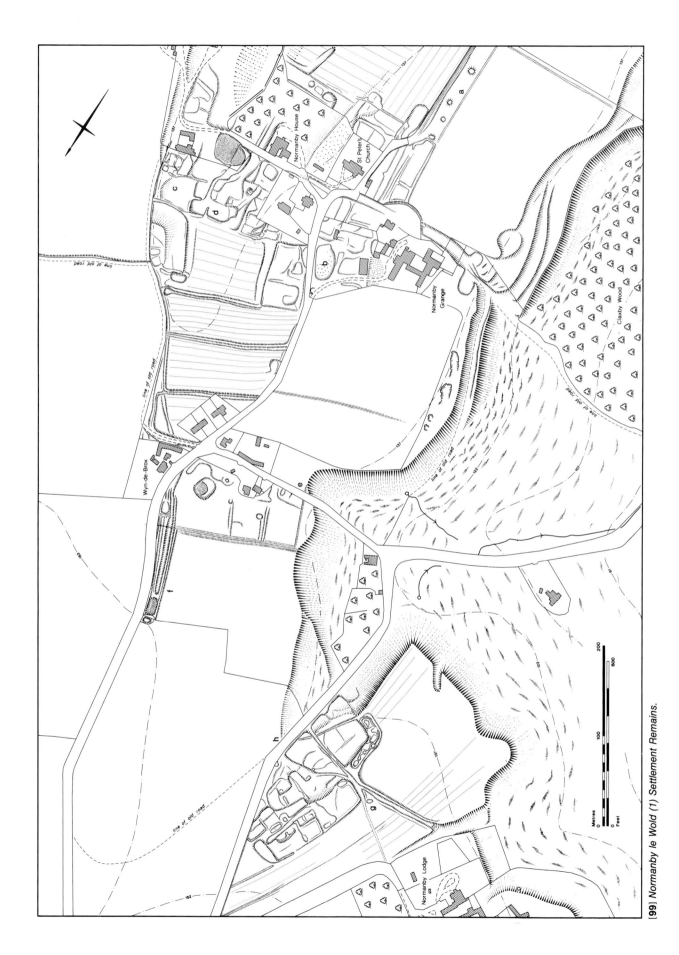

St Peter's Church

Normanby House

Normanby Grange

Claxby Wood

Wyn-de-Brox

line of old road

line of old road

line of old road

line of old road

line of old road

Normanby Lodge

a

b

c

d

e

f

g

h

Metres
0   100   200
Feet
0   600

[99] *Normanby le Wold (1) Settlement Remains.*

134

evidence of an associated park either in the documentary record or on the ground.

The relationship of the site to the woodland perhaps speaks both against a medieval date for the enclosure and provides a mechanism for its survival from an earlier period.

1. *Lincs DB* 13/45; *Curia Regis Rolls* III (1926), 172, 233, 317; Walker 1954, 98–9; *Cal Chart R 1300–26* (1908), 251.
2. Nottingham University MA 2P/297 and 311.
3. NAR TF 07 NE 14.

NORMANBY LE WOLD

---

(1) Settlement Remains (TF 122951) [99], formerly part of Normanby village, lie on the limestone plateau between the High Wolds and the main W-facing escarpment at about 140 m above OD. This position is untypical of the area and is the most elevated in the county. The surviving earthworks, together with the extant buildings of the village, indicate that Normanby once had three or four separate nuclei linked to and arranged around a complex road system now largely abandoned. In addition, a settlement site associated with a spring 750 m SSE of Normanby church (TF 126941) was partly excavated in 1968–9 and produced pottery of Middle Saxon types.[1]

The early history of Normanby was closely connected with Claxby to the W and Walesby to the S. The parish boundaries which Normanby shares with these places are highly irregular in contrast to those which delimit the three parishes combined. In addition, the topographical relationship between the scarp-top settlements which make up Normanby and the low-lying Claxby (Claxby (1)) is similar to that between Upper Walesby, Otby and Risby and the lower village of Walesby (Walesby (1, 2, 3)). This assumed association is reflected in documents, for during the whole of the medieval period Normanby and Claxby are returned together in most national tax returns. Together they have a minimum recorded total population of 79 in 1086, although in the early 14th-century subsidies only 27 and 30 taxpayers are named. The post-Black Death relief in 1352 was less than 40 per cent and both parishes could number more than 10 households in 1428. With very low reliefs in the 15th century, the settlements emerge from the medieval period with each finding 15 persons for the Lindsey Musters in 1539 and with 20 taxpayers at Normanby in 1542–3 and 24 households in 1563 and 90 communicants in 1603. The figures for Claxby at those dates were 28, 40 and 102 respectively. In 1676 only 43 communicants were returned, and by 1705–23 there were only 10–12 households at Normanby. Whether this was caused by the conversion to pasture as elsewhere is not known and certainly no depopulation or conversion was noted here in the 1607 survey. The date of enclosure is also unknown but it had apparently taken place well before the late 18th century.[2]

The medieval tenurial position in Normanby is not entirely clear, but it is possible that it relates to the physical division of the settlement remains. Four secular holdings are recorded in Domesday Book and in the Lindsey Survey. Three of these continued to be recorded at least until the 15th century despite small grants to a number of religious houses.[3] The largest of the 1086 manors evidently went to enlarge the holding of the Knights Templars in Normanby which was given to them in 1185.[4]

The southern nucleus (TF 123948) is the largest and contains the parish church but was perhaps once two separate parts. The major settlement lies around the church but extends E across a steep-sided valley on either side of an E–W road. Though it is no longer a through route, the OS 1st edn 1 in map of 1824[5] shows this road as part of a track running from Claxby up the scarp face and across an area of mud flows, landslips and former quarries which are a characteristic feature of the scarp edge in this region. This track is visible as a hollow-way SW of Normanby Grange but has been destroyed by a modern garden further E. It reappears as a private drive until it meets the N–S road through the settlement and its line is traceable as slight scarps and a footpath NE of the church. It continues past Normanby House and its terraced garden as a modern road into the valley bottom. Another N–S track crosses the one described above near the church. To the S of the church this is traceable as a slight hollow-way cut into by a later quarry. On its W side ('a') four mounds, only 0.25 m high, may represent a Bronze Age linear barrow cemetery; the northernmost has been cut into by the village earthworks. A fifth, larger mound lies some way S (at TF 12159435, not on plan). The N–S track which passes the church, forms a crossroad with the E–W route. It is possible that this junction lay at the centre of the original nucleus here and that subsequent movement took place along the E–W track. However, the curve in the road N of the crossroads may be the result of later realignment; it crosses a large hollow ('b') containing medieval pottery which may once have been a yard.

Traces of a third road are visible on the E side of the valley where there are fragments of a hollow-way. The OS 1st edn 1 in map and the Tithe Map of 1848[6] both show a road which then continued the main E–W road in a broad curve up to the E side of the valley and NW along the valley edge to the middle nucleus of Normanby. This road may have served a separate nucleus now comprising two former farmsteads, represented by the earthworks of buildings grouped around a central yard ('c') and the remains of another building further N. Immediately E of the latter the modern hedge running ENE on to the Wold top overlies a prominent lynchet, probably an earlier boundary. According to both the OS 1st edn 1 in map and the Tithe Map this hedge was followed on its N by a road which met the Caistor High Street 1.9 km to the E.

Some of the earthworks in this settlement area warrant individual mention. Near the head of the valley a pair of ponds ('d') have probably been replaced by the extant pond to the S. It is of interest that the latter is divided by a stone wall, each half managed by a separate farm. This arrangement may explain the earlier need for two ponds. Scarps and depressions W and SW of these ponds represent the sites of former buildings and associated enclosures extending up the valley side. All are not necessarily of great antiquity and the Tithe Map marks a building in this area. The map also shows enclosures W and S of the church whose boundaries survive as low banks. The enclosure S of the church, perhaps once part of the churchyard and possibly of two phases, appears to overlie ridge-and-furrow. Old quarry pits flank the SW and SE corners of this enclosure and further quarries lie to the E. To the E of the church medieval pottery found in a garden may indicate former occupation.

The southern nucleus is separated from the middle nucleus by blocks of ridge-and-furrow divided by low banks and ditches. All but the southernmost of these are shown as field boundaries on the Tithe Map. It is possible that these blocks, together with an area of settlement remains in their SW corner (NE of 'b'), might be the site of a monastic demesne farm. The arrangement of the earthworks is very similar to those at Cabourne (1).

The middle nucleus (TF 122951) is shown on the 19th-century maps as a small settlement lying along another E–W road from Claxby on to the Wolds. This road, which still exists as far E as its crossing point with the N–S road, continued on for a short distance and then turned S to form the valley-edge track to the southern nucleus. Only the W part survives as a raised causeway.

The present settlement is still broadly similar to the 19th-century one, although buildings marked on the Tithe Map on the edge of the main group ('e') have disappeared. Earthworks consisting of slight banks and scarps and a pond lie on the N side of the settlement. A prominent dyke-like feature in the same area ('f') is probably the result of quarrying.

The northern nucleus (TF 119953), now completely deserted, is situated on the NW side of a small valley running back from the edge of the main scarp. The bottom of this valley is occupied by a road running N from the road from Claxby and the middle nucleus. According to the OS 1st edn 1 in map the former road once continued S across the Claxby road and ran along the mud flows at the edge of the settlement remains. Another track is marked on the OS map extending from the bottom of the valley across the settlement remains where it may survive as one of the two hollow-ways ('g') which overlie ridge-and-furrow to the W. This may have met yet another road from the NE end of Claxby to the Wolds, part of whose line is preserved as the present drive to Normanby Lodge.

It is not clear whether this northern nucleus extended across the valley to the E. The land is now cultivated and no earthworks survive, though the Tithe Map marks buildings further S, immediately NW of the surviving houses near the road junction, and the OS 1st edn 1 in map shows a building to the N ('h').

The surviving earthworks fall into two parts. At the S end, S of the hollow-way ('g'), an L-shaped scarped block up to 1 m high has a hollowed top and contains fragments of building stone and tiles. It probably represents a former range of buildings set along two sides of a large yard. This may be the site of a farmstead, later replaced by Normanby Lodge which certainly existed by the early 19th century. To the N of the hollow-way the earthworks appear to be the remains of a small hamlet consisting of several rectangular stone buildings within small plots, arranged on either side of a terrace-way ('i'). The date of this farmstead and hamlet is uncertain although the documentary and field-name evidence suggests that it may be correct to equate it with the holding of the Templars and the Hospitallers, perhaps with a small attendant planned settlement.

1. *LHA 5* (1969), 11; Addyman and Whitwell 1970, 96–102.
2. BL Add MS 11574; Young 1799, 336, 414, 425.
3. *Lincs DB* 14/8, 28/23, 30/36; *LS* 7/3, 4, 7, 14; *Book of Fees* I, 154, 158; II, 1018; *Feudal Aids* III, 152, 158, 161, 220, 229, 233, 268, 291, 296, 299; Foster and Major 1931–73 III, 189–201; Dugdale 1817–30 VII, 960; VI, 327; IV, 58; *Cal LPFD Hen VIII* XIV pt 1 (1894), 260.
4. Lees 1935, 106; Larking 1857, 148.
5. OS 1st edn 1 in sheet 83.
6. LAO D483.

NORTH CARLTON

(1) Settlement Remains (SK 944776) [26, 100], formerly part of North Carlton village, lie between 17 m and 30 m above OD at the foot of the Jurassic Limestone escarpment on Middle Lias Clay and shales, between two streams draining W. The development of North Carlton is not easy to explain, but there appears to have been a planned two-row extension to a pre-existing settlement. Clearance

of properties in the early 17th century, perhaps for gardens, was continued by 18th-century emparking which also involved the reorientation of the village.

North Carlton is distinctively identified thus in one Domesday Book entry. It is unclear which other entries listed as Carlton relate to this one but it is possible that at least two of them may.[1] By 1303 the principal manor had been granted to Barlings Abbey, and it was augmented by many smaller gifts in both North and Middle Carlton. It remained in the hands of Barlings until the Dissolution when it was granted to Charles Brandon, Duke of Suffolk, in 1538.[2] Two decades later it had passed by marriage to the Ayscoughs of Blyborough and thereafter again to the Monsons of South Carlton by purchase.[3]

The single Domesday Book entry records a minimum population of 6. If the other two holdings were involved this would be 23. In 1327–8 North and Middle Carlton shared 13 taxpayers, about 51 per cent of the wapentake average, and in 1332–3 North Carlton alone had only 7, about 28 per cent of the average. Much, if not all, of the reason for this low figure must lie in the dominant holding of Barlings Abbey, which was exempt from the subsidy. Relief of 50 per cent was allowed in 1352 and 49 persons paid the Poll Tax in 1377. Reliefs in the mid 15th century were nil, albeit on a very low base figure. The parish produced 15 men for the Lindsey Musters in 1539, 16 taxpayers in 1542–3, and 92 communicants in 1603. No depopulation, conversion or engrossment, was reported in 1607, although about 144 acres of Lady Monson's land in hand at that date already consisted of enclosed grounds.[4] She received rent from 11 tenants with recorded houses and land, and a further 10 with houses. In 1636 Sir Robert Monson was accused of depopulation and conversion of arable to pasture extending to six farms and 600 acres.[5] Certainly there were only 52 communicants in 1676 and the population had fallen to 14, rising to 19 households in the early 18th century. In 1771 when the medieval church was taken down and rebuilt the faculty application claimed that the parish was 'very small, consisting of only five farms besides cottages'.[6] Nevertheless a total of 20 houses appears in the 1801 census and this rose sharply to 35 in 1841.

The field remains surviving as earthworks link and extend the two elements of the present village layout. These comprise a group of village properties around the parish church in the E and the principal manorial residence, the Old Hall, with its farms and dependent cottages, in the W.

The short length of an E–W road along the N side of the churchyard is continued W by a deep hollow-way, which turns S at right angles, and then again at right angles W on to the line of the modern road ('a'). One surviving property, the late 18th-century Old Smithy, fronting the N side of this hollow-way, is marked on the earliest estate map of 1805. A further plot to the W is marked by earthworks and others to the E are now overlain by new housing. Three further plots, all vacant by 1805, front the S side of the hollow-way.[7] This E–W street may formerly have continued due E, and in doing so it might have served as an axial street to what is now a double depth of properties by the modern road. Further support for this idea is seen in the surviving structure of Cheyne House, since of its two parallel ranges, that on the N fronts on to the supposed lost street while the late 18th or early 19th-century S range reverses the range to face S. Irregularities in the property boundaries to the E ('b') may add weight to this suggestion of an absorbed former street. If this is correct, the modern road has developed from the back lane of an earlier two-row village street. The only developments on the S side of this street are two closes (S of 'a') where a dwelling is mapped in 1805 and 1844 but which had gone by 1889. What could be part of a further back lane on the N is shown on early maps extending E (from 'c').[8] This presumed regular two-row settlement block is perhaps, in part, an addition to an earlier settlement area to the W.

The block of properties on the N–S street N of the church is a late intrusion into this earlier plan, partly reorientating the settlement. Two distinct phases of building are evident here. On the E side of the street are late 18th and early 19th-century dwellings, some shown on the estate map of 1805 and perhaps originating as pairs of estate cottages, and on the W are 20th-century houses built into vacant paddocks.

At first sight, the occasion for the abandonment of the properties W and NW of the church appears likely to have been the depopulation by Sir Robert Monson and his family over a period of years before 1636, the reason being the desire to create a more secluded emparked setting for his residence by pushing the village E. Even the number of farms reported demolished fits the field evidence well.

However, a more convincing sequence of change is that the documented 17th-century depopulation related to properties cleared from the site of the present Old Hall and its gardens and that the establishment of this block across the earlier W end of the village caused a diversion of the hollow-way. Only in the later 18th century, perhaps, was the E side of the formal gardens opened out on to a landscaped park in the contemporary fashion, with the properties up to the line of the N–S street cleared and emparked, with the exception of the Old Smithy and the church. Refurbishment of the latter was part of the scheme. The effects were the creation of the N–S street with a one-sided aspect of what may originally have been estate cottages, the street dog-legging W and S around the churchyard, the closure of the axial street W of the church, and the development of the existing E–W road along the former back of the properties. This move will also explain the reversal of the main elevation of Cheyne House.

In addition, where the road along the S of Old Hall Farm forks, a small triangular green is probably only the tip of an earlier large open area. The 19th-century maps make it clear that the road here opened out W in a funnel on to an area N of the stream, now occupied by Newport Farm, with the field-name *Greens*. Early air photographs show the area devoid of ridge-and-furrow and laced with sinuous drainage ditches. Buildings shown in 1805, as now, on either side of the road running S are clearly late encroachments and they may have originated as an estate hamlet replacing properties cleared in the late 18th-century emparking.

1. *Lincs DB* 24/4, 33/1, 68/3; *LS* 3/19; Foster 1927, 88.
2. *Book of Fees* II, 1065, 1092; *Feudal Aids* III, 167, 223, 302; *Cal Pat R 1281–92* (1893), 392, 429; *1343–5* (1902), 439; *1348–50* (1905), 92; *1388–92* (1902), 193; *Cal Chart R 1327–41* (1912), 7; *VE* IV, 130; *Cal LPFD Hen VIII* XIII pt 2 (1893), 494.
3. *Cal LPFD Hen VIII* XVI (1898), 647; Cole 1920, 33; LCL Ross MSS XII, Lawress, 93-4; *Cal Pat R 1575–8* (1982), 132; Maddison 1902–6 I, 57; II, 683.
4. BL Add MS 11574; Monson MS VIII (at South Carlton).
5. BL Cott Ch ii 25 (1).
6. LAO FAC/3/29.
7. LAO MONSON 17/16/6.
8. LAO MONSON 17/31; A572; TLE 43/15.

(2) Deserted Village of Middle Carlton (SK 948773) [100] lies at 30 m above OD on a slight rise at the foot of the Jurassic Limestone escarpment on Middle Lias Clay and shale.

Three principal factors make a coherent account of the tenurial history of Middle Carlton impossible without further research: first the multiplicity of Carltons lying together almost contiguous in Lawress wapentake plus the existence of at least five other settlements of that name elsewhere in Lincolnshire; secondly, several levels of sub-infeudation and gifts to religious institutions in the Lawress Carltons which themselves generated variant names for these settlements; thirdly, variant names evidently applied to Middle Carlton itself, including Little Carlton, Carlton Mackerel, Barton, Barton by Northcarlton, Barthon by South Carlton, Carlton Barton, Barketon and Barkeston.[1]

The same factors together with the small size of the settlement which gave rise to the commonest of these aliases make it extremely difficult to discern population trends. Which Domesday Book entry or entries apply to it are uncertain, although the existence of the settlement is confirmed by Saxo-Norman and earlier Saxon pottery found on the site while field-walking.[2] In 1327–8 it is returned with North Carlton with only 13 taxpayers together, and in 1332–3 it is returned with South Carlton with 33 taxpayers. In both cases Middle Carlton probably contributed 6 or 7 taxpayers and was as large (on this index) as North Carlton. In 1377 its adults over 14 years of age were numbered with South Carlton for the Poll Tax and this direct reference may suggest that the report in 1398 and 1399 of the church of Middle Carlton having been destitute of parishioners for 40 years was an over-statement or over-simplification of the effects of the Black Death.[3] The parish was indeed exempt from tax in 1428 with less than 10 households, but Little Carlton was named and coupled with South Carlton in relief allowed in the subsidies of 1448 and 1463. That this might actually imply some continuing occupation of the settlement is confirmed by surface finds from the ploughed site which included pottery extending in range until the early 16th century. Architectural fragments, perhaps from the documented church, have also been reported and either one or two medieval grave-slabs. The church was not returned in the subsidy of 1526.[4]

While the nature of the last surviving occupation is uncertain, the timing and picture of protracted decay corresponds well with the field evidence and undermines earlier assessments of a notable and clear-cut Black Death desertion.

The site of the village lay 400 m SE of North Carlton village in a group of closes with the field-name *Barton*. The boundary of the rectory lands of Middle Carlton, shown on the Tithe Map, depicts the N and S edges of the settlement and presumably preserves the demarcation between North and Middle Carlton. Until 1953 the latter was extremely well preserved as earthworks with the sites of houses with limestone walls readily identifiable and the site of the church allegedly traceable. Ploughing that year, extended in 1959 and again in several stages since, has brought the whole site into arable cultivation.[5]

Air photographs taken before destruction indicate that the village was arranged around the junction of three hollow-ways, each lined by closes. A major two-cell structure, perhaps the church, orientated E–W and set within a small sub-rectangular close, lay immediately W of the road junction.[6]

1. Foster 1920, lvii–lviii.
2. Everson 1979, 79.
3. *Cal Papal Letters 1396–1404* (1904), 168; LAO Bishops' Registers 13 (Beaufort) ff121*v*–122.
4. LM records; Salter 1909, 37–40.
5. LAO MONSON 17/17/6; NAR SK 97 NW 6.
6. RAF VAP CPE/UK2012/4144-7; CUAC UB 49, 51; APs in NMR.

[100] *North Carlton (1) Settlement Remains, formerly part of North Carlton, (2) Deserted Village of Middle Carlton, (3) Site of Monastic Grange and Rabbit Warren, (4) Garden Remains.*

138

(3) Site of Monastic Grange and Rabbit Warren (SK 943774) [100], perhaps the possession of the Premonstratensian abbey of Barlings, lie E and SE of Newport Farm at 17 m above OD on Middle Lias Clay and shale.

The manor at North Carlton held by William Wildeker in the 13th century was transferred to Barlings Abbey before 1303. The manor or grange remained in the hands of the abbey until the Dissolution.[1]

A distinct group of earthworks, clearly not village remains and not in origin part of the post-medieval garden and park layout, lies E of the N–S farm road that leads to South Carlton. They are bounded on the E by a surviving hedge line and on the S either by the stream or more probably a boundary just S of it that continues the hedge line. The latter formed the boundary of the rectory lands of Middle Carlton lying to the E and S. The remains consist of a series of large closes or ditched paddocks overlying earlier arable: only in the SW and SE are there signs of occupation that has levelled or lowered the arable traces. This is similar to monastic properties, especially granges, identified elsewhere in this study, and may represent the demesne farm of Barlings Abbey.

In the southernmost of the closes ('d') are at least eleven mounds of various plan form from circular to elongated oval and with heights of up to 1.5 m, some clearly ditched, which appear to post-date the close itself. Their date is unknown and their function uncertain, but they may be forms of pillow mound making a compact rabbit warren.

1. See North Carlton (1) above for references.

(4) Garden Remains (SK 943777) [100], of late 16th or early 17th-century date, lie around North Carlton Old Hall at 19 m above OD on Middle Lias Clay and shale.

The Monsons, already established at adjacent South Carlton, acquired the manor of North Carlton in the late 16th century, perhaps in 1568. The Old Hall, of late 16th-century date, was presumably of their building as was the garden.[1] In 1607–8 the manor was in the occupation of Lady Monson and included 'the scyte of the hall or mannor house', 'the great parke' and 'the little parke'. 'Dame' Monson was included with Sir Thomas and Sir Robert Monson in the allegation laid in 1636 of engrossment and depopulation of land and properties in North Carlton that extended to six farms and 600 acres, though the thrust of the accusation fell on Sir Robert, by then certainly resident.[2]

Although the house and gardens were laid across earlier cleared properties and caused the diversion of the village street, all the field remains around the Old Hall can be interpreted in the context of an elaborate formal garden of late 16th or early 17th-century type. It occupied the whole area between the stream on the N and the road on the S, was as near square in overall plan as the topography allowed, and was divided into a series of rectangular compartments. At its centre stood the Old Hall. The house was surrounded on the N, W and E by a broad water-filled moat; the principal S front may always have been open. Only the L-shaped E and NE arm survive as a water-filled feature and the W and NW sections are now dry ditches, the latter up to 1.2 m deep with a bank along its N side acting as a dam against a slope of sufficient dimension to have maintained water in the W arm. A solid causeway ('e') performed the same function for the E arm, and gave access to the N close (*Little Garth* in 1805)[3] symmetrically formed by the elongated N arm of the moat, by an inlet channel on the E, now filled and

levelled, bringing water into the moat from the stream and by an outlet on the W. This may have been the *Little Parke* of 1607–8, extending to under 2 acres. The L-shaped tree-planted area W of this close, called *Pleasure Ground* in 1805, and the rectangular area S of it, recently an orchard, were balanced on the E by an area defined by stony banks ('f' and 'g'), presumably former limestone walls. Of the three compartments across the S front of the Hall, that on the SW, now occupied by the Old Hall Farm, may always have contained stabling. The centre one is defined on the E by a slightly curving scarp ('h') and the large pond within it, shown on the earliest estate map, may have originated as an axial ornamental feature. The SE compartment, bounded on the E by the village hollow-way ('a'), is now almost featureless. The *Greate Parke* of just over 23 acres lay to the W of the house, where the field-name *Park* was recorded in 1805.

This enclosed garden layout was probably opened out on its E side in the later 18th century following contemporary fashion. The reconstruction of the body of the church with classical details in 1771–3, substantially financed by Lord Monson, may owe as much to this as to parochial needs.[4] The stream ('i') E of the inlet to the moat is mapped as notably sinuous and rather broad before its recent straightening. This may have been a deliberate artificial effect to create a serpentine feature similar to that at Harpswell (2).

1. LAC 3 (1951–2), 7; Pevsner and Harris 1964, 325.
2. Monson MS VIII (at South Carlton); BL Cott Ch ii 25 (1).
3. LAO MONSON 17/16/6.
4. LAO FAC/3/29; TLE43/15.

NORTH KELSEY

(2) Fishponds and Settlement Remains (TA 043010) [38, 101] at North Kelsey Grange, probably the site of a monastic grange, lie on the floor of a shallow valley cut through Till over Oxford Clay and draining W to the R Ancholme, at 17 m above OD.

By the early 13th century the Gilbertine priory of North Ormsby, founded 1148–54, held land here, including a court or grange. Gifts in that period included 2 bovates of land as well as land alongside the court to allow its extension and the creation of attendant tofts. The text of the grant of the latter is of particular interest in view of the field evidence: 'and for the tofts which belonged to those bovates I have given them two selions which lie on the north of their court that they may make tofts of them or sow them'. In addition the heads of 3 selions were also given 'next their court on the west that they may surround them with a hedge or ditch'.[1] The grange and its associated estates remained with North Ormsby until the Dissolution.[2]

The earthworks of the fishponds are sliced through by the modern Creek Drain and several former field boundaries have been removed, but it is their unusual and complex form of water management rather than this disturbance that makes them difficult to understand. The system was fed by an old stream cut ('a'–'b'–'c'–'d'), itself artificial, and which is partly shown as the stream course in 1776.[3] At the W end is a trapezoidal pond ('e') with a symmetrical low central island on which a rectangular hollow with an outlet to the N may have been a fish-breeding or sorting tank, and slight scarps and a mound at its W end perhaps the remains of a building. Water was retained by banks up to 1.5 m high forming an L-shaped dam on the N and W fading out S against the slope

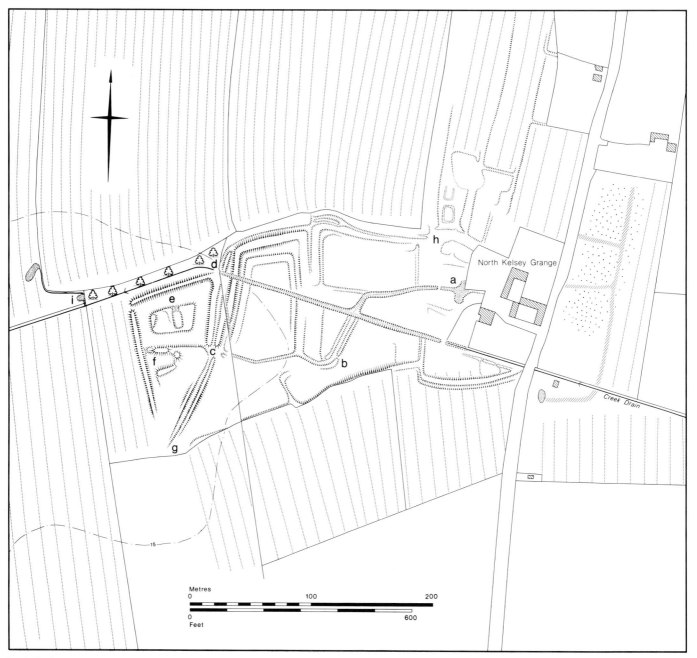

[101] *North Kelsey (2) Fishponds and Settlement Remains.*

with an outlet in the NW corner and an inlet in the SE ('c') from the feeder stream. Against the SW side of this pond is a further rectangular embanked tank ('f') which has an inlet to the SW and an outlet at the NW, narrowed for a sluice. An embanked ditch ('g'–'c') appears designed to drain water from a low-lying area S of the hedge line and may be a late addition to the complex, and irrelevant to its function.

Further E a rectangular pond is bounded on the W and N by broad banks 0.5 m–1.5 m high acting as dams and on the S by the feeder stream. Water could be let from it along a shallow channel to the foot of the banks and might have stood against them in a shallow shelving sheet. A second similar pond lies to the E again with embanking along its N and W sides. A channel along the N side of the N bank may have provided an avoidance channel for the system.

North Kelsey Grange Farm lies E of these ponds and may lie within the court of the medieval grange. The presumed boundary of this court is most clearly marked on the S and SW by a low bank and ditch that cuts off the heads of a number of arable ridges. It was formerly bounded on the N by a through-way ('h'–'i') running along the N side of the earthworks and still called *Grainge Lane* in 1813. The W end of the lane is shown on maps of 1776 and 1813. Only the E end is shown in 1824, as a cul-de-sac, and by the 1840s after enclosure and when the present farm had been built it had been abandoned completely.[4] Closes and building foundations N of ('h') overlie ridge-and-furrow. They are probably tofts created from the arable land granted in the 13th century.

To the E of the modern road the three former closes, visible on air photographs, are now levelled.[5] Pottery, all generally of 13th or early 14th-century date, was found during survey. These

140

earthworks may also be tofts laid out over the selions granted to North Ormsby in the 13th century.

1. Stenton 1922, 59–60, nos 44–47.
2. *VE* IV, 59.
3. LAO NEL 3/5.
4. LAO NEL 3/5; STUBBS 1/23/1, 3/42; 2 NEL 7/8 and 10; OS 1st edn 1 in sheet 86.
5. RAF VAP CPE/UK1746/3068–9.

NORTHORPE

(1) Deserted Village of Southorpe (SK 896952) [102] lies on Till at just above 15 m above OD on either side of a small E–W valley. Southorpe is an excellent example of a small polyfocal settlement. It seems to have been finally abandoned in the 15th century after its land was converted to pasture.

Because they are referred to by the simplex form of the place-name, the early documentary history of Southorpe is difficult to disentangle from that of Northorpe. The reference in Domesday Book to land 'in the other Torp' that was inland of the manor of Torp, ie Northorpe, may however suggest that Southorpe was meant.[1] Southorpe is first clearly recorded by this distinguishing name towards the end of the 12th century when its church already existed.[2] In the early 14th-century subsidies only 10 taxpayers are named, scarcely over 50 per cent of the average for Corringham wapentake. The relief in 1352 was little over 10 per cent, yet still only 30 individuals appear in the Poll Tax in 1377 and the settlement was exempt from the parish subsidy of 1428 with less than 10 households. Reliefs were twice as high in the mid 15th century as they had been 100 years earlier, and the record in rentals of 1428 and 1445 of lands that were then enclosed and increased in value may indicate a general trend of conversion to sheep pasture.[3] The settlement does not appear in later sources indicating depopulation or population levels until the 19th-century census returns which record the existence of outlying farms.

The church at Southorpe, dedicated to St Martin, survived into the early 16th century. There continued to be inhabitants of Southorpe parish, who in 1640 made formal arrangements to use and support Northorpe church. These may have included occupiers of the old village site, and particularly of the moated manor, referred to in 1347–8. On early printed maps buildings are shown within the moated enclosure, the remains of which survived until it was levelled and ploughed in 1966.[4]

The earthworks of the settlement are well preserved in pasture except for two closes on the N now in arable and the levelled and re-grassed field containing the moated manor. They fall into two distinct parts on either side of the valley, separated by blocks of ridge-and-furrow but linked by a N–S hollow-way that crosses the stream at right angles.

On the S-facing slope lies an extensive manorial complex, centred on an almost square moat ('a') whose ditch was formerly up to 2 m deep. Although now very much smoothed by levelling, it remains a substantial earthwork. There may have been a causewayed entrance at the NW corner. Medieval and later pottery was collected after levelling. A slighter outer enclosure to its W contains a chain of fishponds ('b') comprising two rectangular ponds up to 1 m deep divided by a dam, with a tank at their S end. To the W again, an irregular and disturbed platform ('c') contains what may be the foundations of a stone building orientated approximately E–W which is said to be the site of the church and graveyard.[5] Together these appear to form a manorial block that may have extended to the rectangular close lying alongside the hollow-way on the slope down to the stream, since this is enclosed on the N and W by a stony bank up to 1 m high and contains only very slight ridges.

Along the N side of this complex, part or all of an irregular E–W hollow area may have been the green apparently implied by the personal name 'Robert on the Grene' in the 1327 subsidy return. Beyond lie perhaps seven or eight platforms, some with irregular hollows probably marking former yards and buildings, arranged in a layout with a roughly rectangular core, whose less regular periphery may indicate expansion. The two platforms which lay N of the 19th-century boundary between Southorpe and Northorpe and are now destroyed are specifically said in the Northorpe Tithe Award in 1839 to be 'part of Chapel Garth'.[6] Alternatively the rectangular core may be the remains of an infilled green with the closes N of the present parish boundary and W of the N–S hollow-way representing former properties around its edge. The presence of a large formal green might explain the forked hollow-way at the E end and the small open areas between the central platforms.

The N–S hollow-way crossing the stream forms a junction at right angles with the main street in the S part of the settlement. Perhaps five properties fill the land between the street and the stream. The three, rather better defined, properties S of the street may actually disrupt and reorganize earlier arable and therefore represent expansion and change.

The age and function of ditches and hollows E of the moat, plotted from soil-marks visible on air photographs, is uncertain.[7]

1. *Lincs DB* 16/25.
2. PRO E242/113.
3. Maddison 1907–8, 34, 41.
4. Moor 1904, 15, 17; *Cal IPM* IX (1916), 34; LAO LCS 12/6; OS 1st edn 1 in sheet 86.
5. *EMAB* **9** (1966), 26; NAR SK 89 NE 4; Moor 1904, 19.
6. LAO A168.
7. CUAC RZ 63; RAF VAP 58/RAF/5853/F21/0004–5.

(2) Settlement Remains (SK 895971) [103, 104], formerly part of Northorpe, lie in and around the existing village at about 15 m above OD on Till.

Northorpe shows a notable topographical similarity to Southorpe (1). Its siting is almost identical, on the N and S slopes of a small E–W valley. The present village lies on a dominant E–W axis of the S-facing slope. A road from it crosses the stream at right angles to service two large closes on the N-facing slope. That W of the road, named *Castle Dyke* in 1839, shows traces on air photographs of ploughed-out settlement remains; that E of the road contains the site of the Old Hall. The present Northorpe Hall and park are a 19th-century creation.[1]

Ploughed earthworks of ponds and other features at the W end of the E–W street produced no pottery during field-walking: they may have been garden remains associated with the manor house.

1. RAF VAP CPE/UK2563/3209–11, 4209–11; CUAC RZ 64, AWS 5 and 7; LAO A168.

(3) Deserted Settlement (SK 893973) [103, 104], 600 m NW of Northorpe church, lies on Till in a field named *Collin Croft* in 1839 and is completely undocumented. Its earthworks were destroyed between 1956 and 1969.[1] Field-walking in 1977 located scatters of stone perhaps indicating house sites or yards, iron slag and much

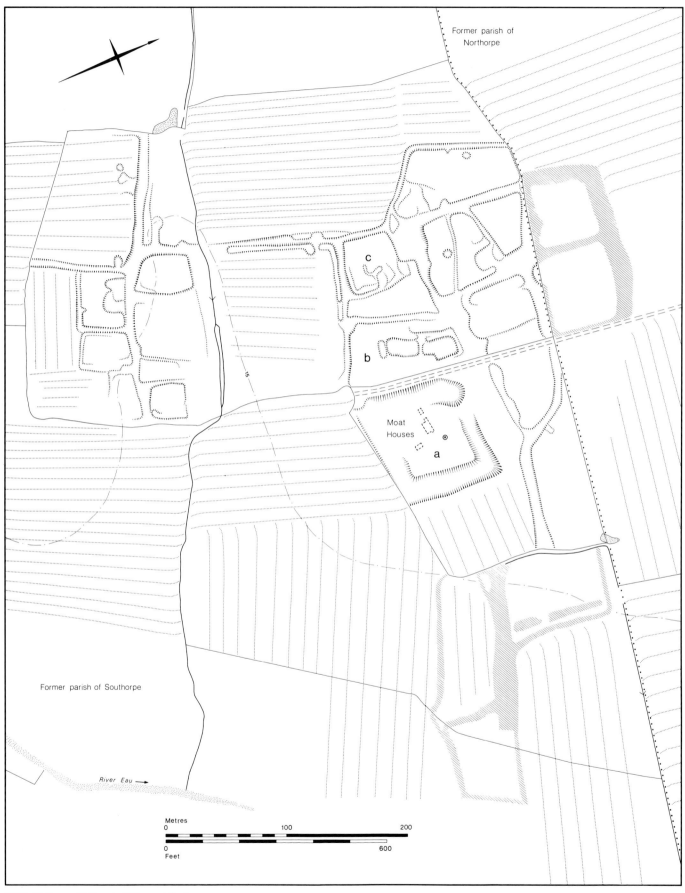

Former parish of
Northorpe

c

b

Moat
Houses

a

15

Former parish of Southorpe

River Eau ➝

Metres
0   100   200

0
Feet   600

[**102**] *Northorpe (1) Deserted Village of Southorpe.*

Scotton parish

Kingscliffe
Farm

The Old
Vicarage

Manor House

Church

line of old road

Old Hall

Northorpe Hall

Metres
0   100   300

0   1000
Feet

[103] *Northorpe (2) Settlement Remains, formerly part of Northorpe, (3) Deserted Settlement.*

[104] *Northorpe (2, 3) from the S, 31 January 1969. Modern agriculture has almost entirely destroyed all the former settlement earthworks here. In the centre and right foreground traces of part of Northorpe village can just be seen. In the far distance left, the outlines of a separate unnamed and undocumented hamlet are visible. (Cambridge University Collection: copyright reserved)*

medieval pottery including Saxo-Norman or earlier types and later medieval wares. The latter perhaps indicates desertion in the later 15th century. The site comprises a series of ditched closes lying on the E side of a hollowed street.

1. LAO A168; CUAC RZ 64–66, AWR 97, AWS 4–7.

OSGODBY

---

(1) Moated Site (TF 068928) [105] lies separate from and to the NW of the village in a shallow clay valley at 15 m above OD. The surviving earthworks are partly obscured by the existing Manor Farm and are cut through by a modern stream channel. They may mark the site of the Tournay manor which seems to have been established sometime in the early part of the 14th century (see (2) below).

The remains consist of a broad straight moat or fishpond ('a') with a bay or return about half-way along that extends E into what was perhaps the platform of the moated site. There are also the traces of a filled-in return E at the N end. Along its W edge is a bank acting as a dam with a gap near its S end.

This moated site, if such it was, must have been positioned more or less on the line of the natural course of the stream which would have fed it from the S; a narrow outlet at the N end was controlled by a sluice. Parallel to its W side is a narrow channel which may have functioned as an avoidance leat. This seems to have cut through ridge-and-furrow which was then reformed by continuous ploughing, so producing a headland against the W side of the leat. This would indicate that the monument is a later medieval innovation in the landscape.

(2) Settlement Remains (TF 074927) [105, 106], formerly part of Osgodby, lie about 21 m above OD on Cover Sands overlying Till. Osgodby was one of a group of four settlements, now all within Osgodby parish. In the medieval period Kingerby was a separate parish while Osgodby and Usselby were dependent settlements of Kirkby within the latter's parish.

The early medieval tenurial history of Osgodby is extremely complex and concerns relatively small holdings.[1] Only in the later Middle Ages does a consolidated estate seem to have been put together by the Tournay family. They held lands and tenements in Osgodby by the early 14th century and the estate was termed a

144

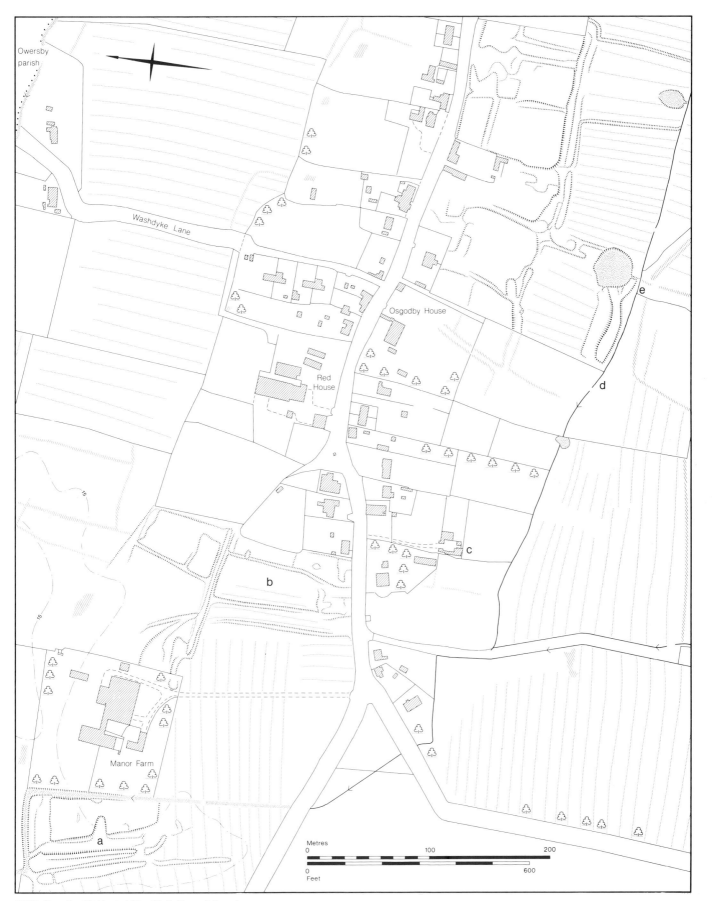

Owersby parish

Washdyke Lane

Osgodby House

Red House

e

d

c

b

a

Manor Farm

Metres
0   100   200

0
Feet   600

[105] *Osgodby (1) Moated Site, (2) Settlement Remains.*

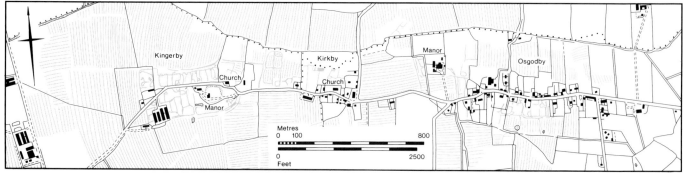

[**106**] *Osgodby Parish. Topographical relationship of Kingerby, Kirkby and Osgodby.*

manor in 1362. The licences for divine services 'in capella sive oratoria de Osgotby' in 1406–7 must refer to a manorial chapel and therefore manorial residence.[2] But with their principal residence at Caenby not far distant, the Tournays are unlikely to have had much use for a major residence at Osgodby and the land seems to have been leased throughout the later medieval period. This pattern may have secured the continuing occupation of the manorial site (1) as a tenanted farm to the present.[3]

Any assessment of population trends is almost equally difficult since Osgodby is regularly recorded in combination with Kirkby and Usselby, both settlements in the same parish. As a result no precise figures are ascertainable. In general terms Osgodby seems to have been an above average sized settlement by the early 14th century, suffered considerably under the impact of the Black Death and then recovered rapidly.

At first sight Osgodby is morphologically a simple double-row village based on a slightly meandering E–W road. The N row is almost completely built up: gaps on the S side contain earthworks of former properties which complete the pattern. To the E of Osgodby House, especially, perhaps six closes with platforms and hollows representing former buildings and yards fronting the street run back from the street to a ditch or back lane along their S side, with a bank beyond which perhaps served as a headland. The ridge-and-furrow between this and the stream was subsequently divided by ditched boundaries into small rectangular fields or paddocks. Several of these boundaries, though in existence in 1806, are still shown on recent OS plans; by contrast the former village closes are shown vacant in 1806 and subsequently.[4] At the W end of the settlement and N of the road, too, are at least two narrow plots ('b') bounded on the W by what appears to be a N–S way with flanking ditches, perhaps formerly giving access to Manor Farm but later blocked by a tree-planting bank. These plots were not mapped in 1806 or later.

A more complex pattern may lie behind this relative simplicity, however. The original core of the settlement may have been to the W of Osgodby House. Here, the 1806 map indicates the remnants of a regular plan now only partly recoverable on the ground. It is possible that this may have been a planned creation and perhaps incorporated a triangular green or outgang, a fragment of which survives W of the Red House. Personal names referring to a green are found in 14th-century documents.[5] The green may have been infilled by properties along the street running WSW, that may represent subsequent expansion of the village in this direction. The plots and house sites on the N side of this street ('b') overlie ridge-and-furrow and the property boundary ('c') may fossilize an arable reversed-S. The N–S track or hollow-way (W of 'b') and the corresponding existing lane to the S evidently therefore formed a

termination for this stage of the settlement's development in this direction.

On the S side of the village the site of a building marked in an old enclosure in 1806 ('d') has produced post-medieval pottery.[6] Pre-enclosure hollow-ways passing it and branching S to Middle or West Rasen and SE to Market Rasen ('e') perhaps significantly seem, like Washdyke Lane from the N, to focus on the suggested early core of the settlement.

To the E of Osgodby House, the surviving earthworks appear quite regular in plot width; they are almost identical to the corresponding properties N of the road. Although the ridge-and-furrow to their S may just possibly have been ploughed or dug to the short length between the back lane and the stream, it is unlikely that it was laid out so. This block N and S of the street then could be a planned settlement addition over earlier arable.

Further E again [**106**, not on **105**] the properties on the N of the village street become shorter; a corresponding shortening on the S may be seen on the Enclosure Map, and the whole may represent a further expansion. To the E again there is further, 19th-century expansion beyond the old enclosures, corresponding with a doubling of population in the first half of the century.

This series of developments, as analysed, might give some explanation of the sinuous line of the main street as originating in cumulative sections added on slightly different alignments to an early planned core. The dating of the establishment of the presumed early part and of these expansions is uncertain. They may belong to either the pre-14th-century growth in population, or to late medieval recovery from the set-backs of the Black Death or to both. On the other hand it is more likely that the unity of tenure achieved by the Tournays by the early 14th century led to the series of planned developments.

1. *Lincs DB* 4/19, 14/10, 16/9, 11, 28/22, 24, 35/10, 68/43, 46; *LS* 7/9, 13–15, 18.
2. LAO FL Deeds 3172, *etc*; Maddison 1907–8, 1–42, esp 12; Archer 1963–82 I, 89, 156.
3. Maddison 1907–8, 23, 36.
4. LAO 4 BM 15; OS 1st edn 25 in plan Lincs 45.3.
5. LAO FL Deeds 3026–7; PRO E179/135/11 and 16.
6. LM records; LAO 4 BM 15.

(3) Moated Manor and Site of Former Castle (TF 056928) [**107**, **108**] lies in the centre of the former village of Kingerby at 20 m above OD on a low ridge of Till. The earthworks appear to reflect a documented change between a 12th-century site of military pretensions and a later manorial residence.

In 1086, the manor of Kingerby was held by the Bishop of Lincoln who remained tenant-in-chief until the late Middle Ages.[1] In the 12th century the family of Amundeville were the tenants, with

146

a substantial residence at Kingerby, and before 1166 Lady Beatrice de Amundeville gave the advowson of Kingerby church to the Augustinian priory at Elsham.[2]

In the early 13th century Peter de Amundeville was amongst those who opposed King John and only by payment of a fine recovered his *domus* at Kingerby in 1216. That it was then a military stronghold is indicated by Henry III's recalling in 1218 that the *castrum* of Kingerby had been burnt and captured in John's reign but not razed and ordering it to be completely destroyed forthwith.[3] In the later 13th century the manor was held successively by William and John de Dyve, who were evidently resident. In the 14th century the manor was held jointly by the Bussy family and the Disneys with the latter apparently succeeding the former as resident lords. Their 14th-century monuments are in the church and memorial glass formerly existed in its windows.[4] The Disneys had Kingerby until almost the end of the 16th century, when it was sold to Sir Thomas Pickering; the manor passed through various hands until bought in about 1780 by the Young family.

A drawing of Kingerby Hall in 1795 [**107**] shows a late medieval, perhaps 14th or 15th-century, two-storey wing at right angles to a post-medieval house which may have incorporated or remodelled a medieval hall range. This was replaced by the present hall and stables in about 1812.[5]

Kingerby Hall stands within a broad-ditched roughly square inner enclosure of hardly more than moated proportions. On the S side the ditch has been partly filled and smoothed by landscaping for the early 19th-century house, which nevertheless stands prominently on the elevated interior. On the N the ditch is still water-filled and the interior platform stands at least 2 m above it and 1.5 m above the outside ground level. This exceptional elevation of a large platform may have its origin in the levelling of a castle motte or more plausibly in a ringwork on the site. On the E lies an outer enclosure delineated on the N and E by a broad curved ditch and inner bank up to 2.5 m high. This defensive aspect

suggests that it is a surviving early bailey. The modern road from Kirkby turns sharply NW to follow the outside of the defences, and a broad flattened or hollowed strip, evidently trimming the ends of ridge-and-furrow, must mark a similar road skirting the S and linking with the network of village roads further W. At the NW corner of the moat a ditch of similar proportions to the E bailey runs W with a fragment of inner bank surviving destruction by the stables. Its turn S and further alignment may be indicated by a low scarp ('a'). This scarp then turns E and defines the N side of the hollowed through-way. The enclosure so formed may have comprised a second bailey that has been subsequently almost totally obliterated and landscaped.

1. *Lincs DB* 7/58; *LS* 7/2; *Book of Fees* II, 1018, 1075; *Feudal Aids* III, 140, 243, 281.
2. Clay 1939–47, 109–37; Davis *et al* 1913–69, III 148; *VCH Lincs* II (1906), 171; *Pipe Roll Soc* NS 6 (1929), 162.
3. *Rot Obl et Fin* (1835), 595–6; *Cal Pat R 1216–25* (1901), 182; Renn 1973, 218.
4. *Book of Fees* II, 1018, 1075; *Placita de Quo Warranto* (1818), 412; *Cal IPM* III (1912), 73; *Feudal Aids* III, 140, 216, 281, 357; Pevsner and Harris 1964, 286; Cole 1911, 68–9.
5. Trollope 1861–2, 145–6; Maddison 1902–6 III, 1128–9; LCL Banks Collection II, 309.

(4) Deserted Village of Kingerby (TF 055928) [**28, 106, 108**] lies at 20 m above OD on a low ridge of Till. The village had an extremely regular layout indicating a planned origin, perhaps by the Amundeville family in the 12th century. Its abandonment was probably the result of conversion to pasture in the 17th century.

Although now part of the civil parish of Osgodby, until recently Kingerby was a separate ecclesiastical parish and the settlement is recorded in all medieval and later returns. Its highest recorded population occurs in Domesday Book with a minimum of 33 heads of households returned. The next available figures, 28 and 27 taxpayers in the early 14th-century subsidies, almost precisely the average for the wapentake, must presumably represent a drop from an intervening maximum. The effects of the Black Death brought

[**107**] *Osgodby (3), Kingerby Hall, drawn by C. Nattes in 1795. This late medieval and later building stood within the moated site at Kingerby. The Hall was pulled down in the early 19th century. (Lincolnshire Library Service)*

147

[108] Osgodby (3) Moated Manor and Site of Former Castle, (4) Settlement Remains of Deserted Village of Kingerby.

148

just over 50 per cent relief in 1352 and reliefs of 20 per cent and 10 per cent were allowed successively in the 15th century, perhaps hinting at some recovery. In 1539 Kingerby produced 7 men for the Lindsey Musters, but 15 taxpayers are listed in 1542–3, 16 households in 1563 and 50 communicants in 1603. By 1676 there were only 27 communicants and at the beginning of the 18th century only 4 households. The principal cause of this 17th-century depopulation was apparently conversion of arable to pasture, already partly documented in the survey of depopulations of 1607 which reported 4 individuals as each having converted 20 acres to pasture and having taken land from 'a severall farme and made the howses cottages'.[1] An important factor in the physical development of Kingerby was the endowment of the Augustinian hospital and later priory at Elsham by its founder Beatrice de Amundeville and her sons of both land in and the advowson of Kingerby. In 1270 the newly constituted vicarage of Kingerby shared a substantial manse and court with the priory which included a principal residence with hall, solar and offices, and a great gate and the priory's tithe barn on their western half of the site.[2]

The village earthworks partly reflect some elements hinted at by the documentation but principally reveal otherwise undocumented and complex changes. Until the late 19th century, when a diagonal section of new road cut the SW corner, the through road followed a dog-legged course at the W end of the settlement ('b'–'c'–'d'). This was dictated by two strikingly regular blocks of village properties, one aligned E–W along the N side of the modern road ('d'–'e') and the other N–S along the W end of the settlement (W of 'c'–'d'). The former block is limited at its E end by a deep hollow-way running N (from 'e') across the valley towards Owersby. The rear of this block is marked by a deep and narrow back lane, that opens in the W to a roughly triangular area within which a pond is shown on early OS plans, perhaps a small peripheral green.[3]

The two blocks are of a similar depth at 60 m–70 m and in each the properties are separated by shallow ditches. Areas of former buildings at the street ends of the properties are marked principally by shallow scoops representing crewyards. The N–S block forms a neat and deliberate closure to the settlement layout. If the creation of both blocks was not a unitary scheme, the W one could represent an addition to an earlier N block, in either case presumably under lordly direction and probably laid out as appendages to the 12th-century castle of the Amundevilles.[3]

To the S and E of the dog-leg street are the earthworks of a number of irregular detached properties some containing shallow depressions ('f'). Their southern limit is marked by a hollow-way continuing E from 'c' and perhaps formerly linking with a way around the S fringe of the manorial earthworks to join the road to Kirkby. Although presumably in occupation through the later medieval period, these earthworks may be part of a settlement that pre-dates the planned development to the N and W. The W planned block encompasses them and the main E–W hollow-way ('f') may be, significantly, on line with the road to Kirkby, E of the Hall.

The church of St Peter and the former vicarage, now Beech House, lie within a further well-defined block between the hollow-way running towards Owersby ('e') and a similar feature to the E ('g'). These two hollow-ways are linked by a prominent back lane or boundary ditch. The block, so defined, overlies earlier arable, and contains a rectangular scarped platform on which the church stands and which may be a former churchyard. Ironstone building foundations, a well and deep hollows NW of the church reflect a dwelling and attendant closes still shown on early OS plans. An

archaeological excavation in 1965 revealed building remains, and medieval and Roman levels with associated pottery.[4] This block must be the manse of Kingerby vicarage, as described at the end of the 13th century, which it shared with Elsham Priory, and it generally resembles earthwork groups at, for example, Cabourne and Swallow, identified as monastic holdings.

Yet another block of settlement earthworks lay to the E again extending as far as the former parish boundary, until levelled in 1980. It comprised a series of closes with building platforms lining the street and an embanked pond beside the stream, all overlying ridge-and-furrow. These earthworks might also mark the site of a monastic grange, but since no holdings are documented apart from that of Elsham they probably represent a shift of village properties. Field-walking has produced a quantity of late medieval pottery here as well as some of early Saxon date.[5]

1. BL Add MS 11574, ff82, 86; LAO MISC DEP 332.
2. VCH *Lincs* II (1906), 171; Dugdale 1817–30 VI, 559; *VE* IV, 72; *Cal LPFD Hen VIII* XIV pt 1, (1894), 260; Davis, F.N. *et al* 1925, 39.
3. LAO PADLEY 2/57; PRO IR 30/20/197; OS 1st edn 1 in sheet 83; OS 25 in sheet Lincs 45.2.
4. OS 25 in sheet Lincs 45.2; *EMAB* 8 (1965), 16, 24.
5. Pers inf R.C. Russell.

OWERSBY

(1) Settlement Remains (TF 058956–064935) [109, 110], formerly parts of Owersby, were once the S section of a long line of medieval settlements extending for almost 4 km across undulating clayland at 10 m–20 m above OD. The N section comprised the former village of Thornton le Moor (2), now almost deserted, and the hamlets of Beasthorpe (3) and *Cauthorpe* (4), both now deserted. These last three places lay within the former parish of Thornton le Moor. The understanding of these settlements is particularly difficult since they appear in documents in different combinations at different dates, and there are, in addition, a number of special problems of interpretation.

Including the three separately named places in Thornton, there appear to have once been at least nine separate settlement nuclei extending in a N–S line each perhaps arranged around E–W streets. The individual nuclei are still separated by ridge-and-furrow which also underlay some of the settlement earthworks. Until the 1960s the existing villages and hamlets were all associated with areas of earthworks of former occupation and at least four of them were completely deserted sites. Most of the earthworks have been destroyed and in 1981 the Royal Commission surveyed the only large area that survived in Owersby [110]. These have now been largely obliterated.

Owersby and Thornton le Moor were separate parishes, but Owersby had much the larger size and population. Six separate manors are listed in Domesday Book containing in total a minimum recorded population of 90. There were 55 and at least 60 taxpayers in the early 14th-century subsidies, twice the wapentake average, and the assessment of the settlement in 1334 puts it in the same category as many local market centres. The impact of the Black Death brought 82.5 per cent relief in 1352 but low reliefs in the 15th century indicate an almost complete recovery that led to 30 and 28 taxpayers being recorded in 1524 and 1525 and no less than 80 in 1542–3.

From the later 16th century, documentary sources often divide Owersby into two parts, one of which is usually returned with

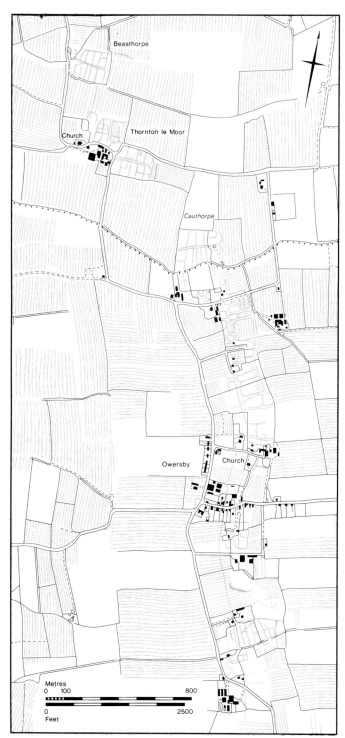

[109] *Owersby (1, 2, 3, 4) Settlement Remains of Owersby, Beasthorpe, Cauthorpe and Thornton le Moor.*

nuclei marked on an estate map of 1805,[2] when taken together with the evidence for a possible township at the S end of Owersby, may not be mere coincidence but may point to a polyfocal layout of tenurially based origin.

The second important aspect is that the major period of depopulation of Owersby, from which it did not recover, was in the 17th century, probably connected with the conversion to pasture. Between 1532 and 1602 the Monson family acquired the two main manors there. In 1607 it was recorded that one dwelling-house and a barn had been allowed to fall down by a tenant of Sir Thomas Monson who himself had taken 320 acres from four farms and turned them into cottages, and that Sir Edward, William and Francis Ayscough had between them taken the land from three farms and let the houses stand empty or be occupied by cottages. A survey of the Monson manor in 1607–8 shows the former *West Field* of 2532 acres (1055 ha) enclosed and the whole parish may have been completely enclosed by 1625. Monson was certainly prosecuted in the Star Chamber although the direct effect on population is unknown.[3]

The earthworks near Tattershall House (TF 060954) [110] represent two of the former nuclei of Owersby lying at the N end of the settlement. That to the N is laid out on either side of an E–W street now a boggy hollow-way ('a'–'b') which continues the line of the modern road approaching Tattershall House from the W. The present road E of the house cuts across the village remains. The main hollow-way had certainly been abandoned by 1805 when a map of Owersby shows the road then running on a more northerly line, now another hollow-way ('c'–'d').[2]

A number of rectangular ditched closes, probably once containing houses, lie on either side of the main hollow-way, with behind them, long paddocks bounded by narrow ditches and all overlying ridge-and-furrow. The 1805 map marks at least two standing buildings in this area while a structure marked on the 1976 OS 1:2500 plan ('e') was demolished shortly before the Royal Commission's survey. Further slight earthworks lie to the N of the northern hollow-way ('c'–'d').

The southern nucleus lies on both sides of another road ('f'–'g') which is also marked on the 1805 map, and which is similarly flanked by ditched and embanked closes containing hollows and platforms, probably the sites of former houses. Some of these again overlie ridge-and-furrow. A standing structure marked on the 1976 OS plans ('h') has been subsequently removed, while the 1805 map shows other buildings to the SE ('i'). On the E an irregular linear hollow may represent a former N–S road.

Former settlement remains to the S of this road can now only be recovered by transcription of former earthworks and soil-marks from aerial photographs [109].[4] Both in their organization in a series of groups or nuclei around E–W streets and in their detail of ditched closes, in places overlying ridge-and-furrow, they resemble the remains investigated in detail at the N end.

Prolific finds of Saxon, Saxo-Norman, medieval and post-medieval date have been reported from the various areas of ploughed-out village remains in Owersby as well as evidence for Roman settlement in the same locations.[5]

1. LAO MONSON 8/3; 19th-century Census Returns.
2. LAO MONSON 8/4.
3. LAO MONSON 2/2, 4; BL Add MS 11574, ff79, 86; Survey Book in Monson Library at South Carlton; Johnson 1962, 136, 140; PRO Star Chamber 8/18/9.
4. RAF VAP CPE/UK1746/1064–5; 1880/1465–6, 3466–7, CUAC AQR 14–16, 18–20.
5. LM records; *LHA* **4** (1969), 117; **5** (1970), 11.

Osgodby. This makes it impossible to ascertain accurate population levels although there is an implication arising from this situation that the extreme S end of Owersby was once a separate township.[1] The overall population trends for Owersby clearly conceal two important aspects of its history. First is the former existence of at least six separate nuclei which together made up the medieval village and which may even have been separate townships or economic units. The six manors of Domesday Book and the fragments of six

North End Farm

Former parish of
Thornton le Moor

Tattershall House

Tattershall
Farm

a

c

d

e

b

East Manor
Farm

h

f

g

i

Metres
0   100   200

0   600
Feet

[**110**] *Owersby (1) Settlement Remains of Owersby.*

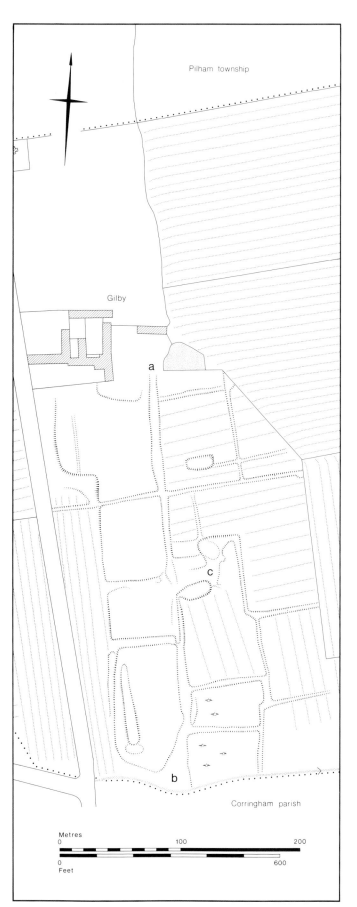

[**111**] *Pilham (2) Deserted Village of Gilby.*

PILHAM

(2) Deserted Village of Gilby (SK 864932) [**111**] lies on Till at 20 m above OD on ground sloping S. The earthworks may represent only the southern fringe of a settlement whose place-name, interestingly, contains a Scandinavian personal name of Irish origin, which may be relevant to the Norwegian settlement of this area.[1]

The first reference to Gilby is in 1138–9. The settlement is named as a junior partner to Pilham in the *Nomina Villarum* and returned with Pilham in the lay subsidies of the early 14th century.[2] Thereafter it is not separately recorded in taxation lists or population statistics. In the first half of the 15th century the Tournays of Caenby rented land at Gilby but held no dwellings there. That there was a least one resident is suggested by the name of 'Ricardus Warton de Gylbe' recorded in 1431.[3] In 1616 four holders of messuages are listed, two of whom also held messuages in Pilham; in addition there were seven tofts untenanted or without cottages and one called 'The Town House'. Continued occupation is evidenced by wills and inventories of the 17th and early 18th centuries. Gilby is shown as a settlement on Armstrong's map of 1776–8 and an early 19th-century estate map depicts two groups of buildings, one the present farm. White's *Directory* in 1842 notes that 'the parish [of Pilham] includes the hamlet of Gilby (now only one farm)', the situation as it remains today.[4]

The survey of 1616 says of Pilham and Gilby that 'these two townships lye together, their lande intermixte'. The early 19th-century estate plan, after enclosure, marks a township boundary between the two that may therefore be of recent creation.

The former settlement is now represented in part by earthworks and in part by a surviving farm, its yard and cottages. Any early features are difficult to disentangle from post-medieval and modern buildings and boundaries, but they seem to comprise a N–S hollow-way ('a'–'b') and a series of perhaps four sub-rectangular plots along its W side, making a single-row arrangement. The existing farmhouse may have occupied the next plot to the N. The marked narrowing of the southernmost plot, together with its awkward relationship to the ridge-and-furrow on the W, may indicate that the whole group formed an extension to the main core of a settlement which lay N of the farm.

All the earthworks to the E of the hollow-way overlie ridge-and-furrow and are late features. A building and yard ('c') are shown on the early 19th-century estate map though they are not marked on the OS 1st edn 25 in plan; the narrow ditches precisely match hedge lines on that map.[5]

1. Fellows-Jensen 1978, 48, 265.
2. Foster and Major 1931–73 I, 59, 191.
3. Maddison 1907–8, 33, 40; *Feudal Aids* III, 365.
4. CUL MS Ff.4.30(c), ff37–8; LAO AD ACC 40/6; INV 189/139, 220/B/28, 181/204, 184/46, 196/52; WILLS O.943; BACON PLANS 24; White 1842, 497.
5. LAO BACON PLANS 24; OS 25 in plan Lincs 35.14.

(1) Moated Site (TF 106791) [25, 33, 112] lies at 20 m above OD on Till and occupies the W part of the deserted village of Rand (2). The relationship of this site to the deserted village is complex and can only be ascertained by analysis of the tenurial history of Rand, excavation and fieldwork.

In the late 11th century Rand formed part of the compact soke of the manor of Wragby, held by Erneis de Burun and in about 1115 by Geoffrey, son of Payne.[1] Not until after 1153 when William Trussebut made good his claims to the de Burun lands is a process of sub-infeudation and manorialization recognizable. Trussebut created several new fees from the soke, particularly at settlements near Rand, and his second son, Robert, continued the process by creating further fees at *Helethorpe* (Fulnetby (3)) and Rand between 1190 and 1193 for John and Stephen Burdet respectively. The Burdets were already resident and prominent in Rand by 1165 but it is possible that the establishment of the manorial complex together with the replanning of the village did not take place until the Burdets took full possession in the late 12th century. The manor then descended to the Burdet heirs until after 1346.[2]

Excavation at the church in 1982 established at least two phases of construction, together with earlier burials, pre-dating an enlargement of the nave that included a mid 12th-century arcade for a N aisle.[3] Analysis of Domesday Book and related documentation has suggested that Rand was a daughter church in the *parochia* of a minster at Wragby. It is not until the 13th century that there is evidence that the church had become a manorial appurtenance. It is possible that the transfer of the advowson of the church to the manor of Rand, perhaps in the 13th century, also marked the extension of the *curia* to encompass the church and part of the village. It may also be significant for the end of the use of the site as a residential manor that in 1461 William Willoughby of Lincoln, son and heir of Richard Willoughby, lately lord of the manor of Rand, granted the advowson to Bullington Priory.[4]

The manorial complex focuses on a square moated site with a broad surrounding ditch up to 2 m deep, lying in a field called *Hall Close* in 1842.[5] This ditch formerly held water which was led in at the SE corner by a leat from the NW corner of the modern churchyard, and retained by banks on the N, E, and W. Breaks at the NW corner and at the centre of the N side, presumably controlled by wooden sluices, allowed water to be released. On the central platform slight earthworks indicate the position of former buildings. Access must have been in the centre of the S side, although the present causeway may be a modern creation.

To the S of the moat lies a group of four small irregular fishponds ('a') that are carefully graded into the slope, with the highest to the E and outlet on the NW. To the NE of the moat a long bank ('b'), approximately 1 m high, with an additional long mound at its S end and protected by a double hedgerow, is perhaps a former rabbit warren. A linear ditch ('c') parallel with the stream may have been a mill leat: the close between the present stream channel and the parish boundary was named *Mill Croft* in 1842.

This well-preserved manorial site clearly lies on top of earlier ridge-and-furrow, but also, and more importantly, lies neatly at the NW corner of the deserted village. However, what may well be an enlargement of this complex is also visible. It forms an approximately square enclosure or *curia*, bounded on the E by a deep hollow-way running N (from 'd'), whose line is taken up by a hedge with a marked ditch on its E side, and on the S by a broad hollow-way running W along the N side of Church Farm. To the N of the church this enclosure took in former arable and the NW corner of the village. It was subdivided by a shallow ditch which cuts across the ridge-and-furrow. On the S of the church, village plots may also have been taken in, although the principal surface feature in one of the two large earthwork closes is a circular embanked site with stone foundations ('e'), perhaps a former dovecote. The *curia* thus encompasses the church of St Oswald in a way that might at first sight suggest that it was a lordly foundation or *Eigenkirche*. Instead, both the tenurial history and the configuration of the earthworks perhaps rather suggest a period during which both the first stage of the manorial site and the adjacent village could have been laid out, and that only later the *curia* was expanded to take in the church and part of the village within its boundaries.

1. *Lincs DB* 34/21; *LS* 16/6.
2. Clay 1955, 1–106; *Book of Fees* I, 172, II, 1061, 1063; Stenton 1920, no 101; *LNQ* **9** (1907), 144; *Placita de Quo Warranto* (1818), 415a; *Placitorum Abbreviatio* (1811), 206b; *Feudal Aids* III, 171, 224, 270, 304, 360; *Cal Inq Misc* II (1916), 317; *Cal Close R 1413–19* (1929), 19, 208.
3. Field 1983, 101–3.
4. Inf D.L. Roffe; Stenton 1920, nos 22, 56, 101, 114; Stenton 1922, 94, 97; Davis 1914a, 53; Hill 1948, 40; BL Harl Ch 58 B 22.
5. PRO IR 29 and 30/20/257.

(2) Deserted Village of Rand (TF 108791) [25, 33, 112] lies at 20 m above OD on Till.

The population trends of the settlement are difficult to form into a coherent picture since it was always returned for medieval taxation purposes as one with its members, Fulnetby and *Helethorpe* (Fulnetby (2), (3)), or in the 16th century and after usually with Fulnetby. None of the documentation, anyway, hints at the planned origin apparent in the earthworks or at the relationship of the settlement to the creation of a large manorial complex (1) perhaps in the later 12th century. It is also only in the earthworks that the evidence for the reorientation of the settlement and the subsequent expansion of the manorial complex in the 13th century is visible.

The minimum recorded population in Rand in 1086 is 13. As far as can be ascertained the settlement had increased in size by the mid 14th century and either suffered little or recovered swiftly from the effects of the Black Death. Yet by the mid 16th century Rand was relatively small and the 7 households there in 1563 contrasts with the 15 households at its formerly dependent settlement of Fulnetby. In 1783 the ruinous N aisle of the church was removed when the whole building was described as 'much larger than necessary'; by the early 19th century only the present Church Farm stood on the site.[1]

The principal period of desertion therefore probably lies in the later 15th or early 16th century, when conversion to pasture is likely to be the main cause.

The village earthworks are complex and point to an otherwise undocumented planned origin and a radical later change in the arrangement of the settlement. The earliest recognizable element is a highly regular layout based on a broad hollow-way running almost due E from the church. On its N side lie a series of properties that appear to be rather regular square plots except for the one at the E end. Similar properties fronted the S side of the street, although they have been much disturbed here by later development. The church stood at the E end of this simple layout apparently integral with or an earlier focus for it. What may be the earliest part of the manorial complex lay to the NW. This regular planned appearance may be the result of sub-infeudation of the manor of Rand to the Burdet family in the late 12th century, perhaps in part on a previous area of settlement.

Fulnetby parish

old river course

c

b

a

St Oswald's Church

Rectory

Church Farm

e

d

f

i

g

j

h

Metres
0   100   200

0   600
Feet

[**112**] *Rand (1) Moated Site, (2) Deserted Village of Rand.*

154

Properties at the W end and around the church were probably subsequently taken into a newly created manorial enclosure bounded on the N and W by straight hollow-ways and ditches, a process which may have taken place in the 13th century. Perhaps as a direct result of this and especially of the blocking of the W end of the main street that it implies, a branch hollow-way seems to have developed ('f'–'g'–'d') cutting diagonally across earlier properties in order to pass round the manorial block. Farm groups, marked by shallow hollow yards and in some instances recognizable building sites, developed along it and along another hollow-way running E ('g'–'h'). Very irregular remains along the S fringe of the earthworks and cut through by the farm track may be further properties fronting on to a narrow but continous hollow-way more like a back lane than a main street. Rectangular building foundations survive in two places ('i' and 'j') which on this clayland site are likely to be post-medieval rather than earlier structures.

1. LAO FAC/4/8; OS 1st edn 1 in sheet 83; PRO IR 30/20/257.

RIBY

(1) Settlement Remains (TA 184073) [31, 113], formerly part of the village of Riby, lie at 30 m above OD on chalk at the E foot of the Wolds. The surviving earthworks have been disturbed by intensive parkland tree-planting and their relationships are obscure. They nevertheless indicate that formerly the settlement was probably made up of two distinct nuclei which may relate to the medieval tenurial situation.

In 1086 Riby was divided between two holdings. One was sokeland of the Earl of Chester, already then sub-infeudated, and the remainder a manor belonging to Roger of Poitou. Although by about 1115 the holdings were held together by Geoffrey Fitzpayne, a century later the two manors were again separate and remained so until the end of the 17th century when the unified estate passed to the Tomline family. It was the latter who created the parkland that still survives today.[1]

Another manor in Riby, together with the advowson of the church, was held by the Augustinian abbey of Wellow, perhaps from its foundation in the reign of Henry II. This was apparently usually leased.[2]

The overall population figures give the impression of a large, or at least larger than average, settlement throughout the medieval period and on which the Black Death had remarkably little long-term effect. It was almost halved in size between the mid 16th and early 18th centuries, probably through enclosure and the creation of the landscaped park. No precise minimum figure for 1086 is possible, but approximately 40 heads of households is likely. In the early 14th century 29 and 33 taxpayers are listed and this is probably a fall from earlier population levels. A relief of 35.7 per cent was allowed after the Black Death in 1352 but no less than 157 persons paid the Poll Tax in 1377. Reliefs of 16.8 per cent were being allowed in the mid 15th century, but in 1524 and 1525, 27 and 24 taxpayers were returned and in 1539, 13 men were produced for the Lindsey Musters. In 1542–3, 20 or 37 people paid tax and in 1563 there were 44 households. In 1603 there were only 95 communicants returned and in 1676, 117, but there is no hint at all in the survey of 1607 of any form of depopulation. By the early 18th century the population was reduced to 30 and 23 households, a level which was maintained for a century.

Of the two nuclei, one is associated with St Edmund's church.

Surviving earthworks to its SW comprise a hollow-way ('a') with rectangular property plots and stone-walled foundations at least on its NE side. To their NW the OS 1st edn 1 in map shows that, in 1824, a series of houses extended to the modern through road and SW along a street approximately continuing the alignment of the present street past Church Farm. These were all removed and replaced by later 19th-century tree plantations.[3] There were perhaps also earlier village properties in the area around Church Farm which is now under permanent arable. This destruction, the masking effect of the tree plantations, the detached walled gardens SE of the church and the absence of any plan earlier than OS maps make understanding of the layout of this settlement block impossible.

A second focus lies to the S in Riby Park occupying the sides of a dry valley. Although contiguous with the church nucleus, it nevertheless has its own inner coherence based principally on a deep hollow-way ('b'–'c'), running SW down the slope, suggesting a distinct and separate settlement. At its core it has a loosely enclosed area ('d') containing ridge-and-furrow which may be earlier in date. The enclosure resembles those suggested monastic grange farms identified in nearby villages such as Cabourne (1) and Swallow (1). If this identification is correct it is just possible that this area might represent the medieval holding of Wellow Abbey. On the SE side of the hollow-way a set of closes contains many stone-built banks, in places overlapping but not obviously forming groups of buildings. At the SW end of the main hollow-way ('c') a second hollow-way runs at right angles along the bottom of the slope broadening out in front of the site of the former mansion house. A number of properties lie on its NE side and part of its SW.

If not related to one of the two medieval manors, the whole nucleus could be a secondary development, and since many of its peripheral closes overlie ridge-and-furrow it must have at least experienced enlargement. It may, at latest, have been swept away by the early 18th century for the creation of the Tomline's mansion and park. A linear feature ('e'), part bank and part hollow, which cuts across the settlement remains is probably a carriage drive along the avenue of trees. Some of the other unexplained disturbances in the area may have resulted from military activities carried out here in 1915–16.

1. *Lincs DB* 13/19, 20, 16/1; *LS* 11/15, 17; *Book of Fees* I, 155, 222, 226; *Placita de Quo Warranto* (1818), 401; *Cal Close R 1429–35* (1933), 207; Maddison 1902–6 I, 361–3; III, 996–7; *Cal IPM* XVI (1974), 333–4; 2nd ser I (1898), 261; LCL Ross MSS III Yarborough wapentake, 307–8; LAO 2PT *passim*; Hill 1966, 269; LCL Banks Collection III, 213; Strong *et al* 1974, 189; Binney and Hills 1979, 38.
2. VCH *Lincs* II (1906), 161–2; Massingberd 1896, pt 1, 24–5; Davis 1914b, 59; *Cal Inq Misc* III (1937), 323.
3. OS 1st edn 1 in sheet 86; OS 1st edn 25 in Lincs 21.15 and 16.

RISEHOLME

(1) Deserted Village of Riseholme (SK 982753) [114] lies on the S side of the park of Riseholme Hall at approximately 40 m above OD on Jurassic Limestone. Before the large artificial lake was created in the 18th century the village earthworks lay on the N-facing side of a broad E-draining valley.

The surviving earthworks fall into two parts, the larger of which appears to comprise the remains of that part of the village of Riseholme which was replanned over former arable land, almost certainly in the 12th century and perhaps by Hugh Bardolf, then the major tenant at Riseholme. The other earthworks may be an

Church Farm

St Edmund's Church

a

Riby Grove

e

d

b

c

Metres
0   100   200
0   600
Feet

[113] *Riby (1) Settlement Remains.*

associated manorial complex, but are more likely to be the remains of a later monastic grange (2). There is also evidence that the village extended across the valley, perhaps as a separate centre in the area now occupied by the Hall.

Domesday Book records five holdings in Riseholme but by the beginning of the 12th century this had been reduced to three. By 1166 one of these was tenanted by Hugh Bardolf I, father of the King's Justiciar, Hugh Bardolf II. It is possible that Bardolf, who in this same period laid out a new castle and its associated village and church at Castle Carlton on the Lindsey Marshland, was also responsible for the replanning of at least part of Riseholme.[1]

Bardolf also granted considerable land in the parish to the abbeys of Kirkstead and Barlings in 1166 and 1168 which became the basis of extensive sheep-farms. These were enlarged in the 13th and 14th centuries by grants by Edmund Foliot whose family succeeded to the manor. In the mid 16th century the family of St Paul of Snarford acquired both the former monastic holdings and in 1610 purchased the lay manor, so consolidating the parish into single ownership.[2] In 1721 the estate passed to the Chaplin family who created the substantial residence as well as the ornamental lake and parkland setting. In 1839 the property was bought as a residence for the Bishop of Lincoln and the house was then extended and a new church built.[3]

The population records for Riseholme reflect these tenurial changes and particularly the conversion to sheep which the monastic interests introduced in the late medieval period and which was evidently intensified after the Dissolution. In 1086 the recorded population of Riseholme was 10. The number of taxpayers, 17 and 18 in the early 14th-century subsidies, at two-thirds of the average for the wapentake, is hardly surprising for a small parish which already had extensive sheep pastures and might suggest a fall from an earlier high point. Relief of 40 per cent in 1352 and exemption from the parish tax in 1428 with less than 10 households shows the impact of the Black Death, which itself may have encouraged the additional monastic grants at the end of the 14th century. Nevertheless, 15th-century reliefs were not high, and, although only 2 persons were found for the Lindsey Musters in 1539, 7 taxpayers were listed in 1542–3.

There was a marked change by the end of the century: the 12 communicants of 1603 are matched by the reports of 1602 that 'the whole towne savinge one howse is ruinated and down' and that the medieval church was 'utterly ruinated'. As late as the 1550s the church was the object of bequests and a place of burial: yet a Glebe Terrier of 1601 records 'only the churchyard and no church'. Twenty years later Nettleham parish registers record the burial there of Riseholme inhabitants and the diocesan survey at the beginning of the 18th century confirms that the living was a sinecure with no church.[4]

The decline of Riseholme is likely to be the result of a combination of medieval sheep-farming and disease. Its final abandonment could have been the result of under-exploitation by the St Paul family following the removal of the monastic interests, although it is perhaps significant that the 1607 survey of depopulations only records the decay of the church. The glebe lands still lay in common fields at the beginning of the 17th century, but when mapped in 1791 the whole parish was enclosed.[5]

The village earthworks are in good condition, but the overall plan is partly obscured by large amounts of spoil from the adjacent lake which has been dumped over the N edge, while the lake itself may cover part of it. More importantly a fuller understanding of the settlement is impossible because of the loss of features which undoubtedly existed N of the stream in what would appear to have been the prime settlement location. These are shown by the 1601 Terrier to have included the site of the medieval church which probably lay just W of the present one. In 1601 an E–W way evidently ran along the S side of the church, probably on the line of the present E drive, but the 'hygheway through the towne' ran N–S; at least two farms survived in this area, together with village closes.[6]

In the surviving earthworks, this principal N–S alignment may be picked up by a hollow-way which emerges from the S side of the lake dam, runs straight for 90 m and then curves SW. It is here adopting the alignment of an evidently older hollow-way that formed the N side of a furlong block of arable and itself appears to ride over the tails of the village properties. Furthermore, S of the crossroads with the main NE–SW street the N–S way may represent a cut through properties. Beside the modern road it is blocked by a low earth bank which stops within the hollow-way. This bank continues E cutting ridge-and-furrow along the roadside with standing mature trees or stumps evenly spaced.

The rest of the village earthworks depend on an alignment running NE–SW. An almost exactly straight length of hollow-way, clearly once the main street, is lined on both sides by well-preserved rectangular building sites with stone walls up to 1 m high. On the S side these buildings are associated with ten small closes or crofts, bounded by low stone walls. On the N side there were once perhaps between nine and eleven similar closes although these have now been covered by spoil from the lake. The central section of the main hollow-way or street has a later subsidiary hollow-way within it and the building sites on the S appear to have encroached across the original hollow-way by up to 4 m–5 m. A well-marked rubble-filled bank is set just outside the rear banks of the closes on the S. It turns S, crossing over earlier ridge-and-furrow, until it reaches the modern road and the edge of the N–S hollow-way noted above. A N–S bank ('a') goes with this feature to form a series of formerly walled paddocks beyond the village crofts. A low oval mound and an adjacent circular one with a depressed centre ('a'), both of which lie over a headland, are sited in the corners of two of these paddocks. The suggestion that the latter mound may be the base of a dovecote, is less convincing than that it had some function for stock, probably sheep, management.

Other notable features of the village remains include the ill-defined ridge-and-furrow overlain by the closes of the village in two places ('b' and 'c'), and at least two building sites and associated closes at the W end of the main hollow-way which appear to be outside the rectangular arrangement of the main village.

Limited excavations were carried out on the site in 1954–5.[7] A building platform near the centre of the village on the N side of the main hollow-way was excavated and found to contain the foundations of a single two-roomed house. The building appeared to have been constructed in the first half of the 13th century and had been abandoned by the middle of the 14th century. There was evidence of earlier, 12th-century occupation beneath the building, perhaps including wooden structures. A well, in a yard on the S side of the street, was also partly excavated. Its upper fill contained nothing later than 14th-century material.

A tentative interpretation combining both archaeological and documentary evidence of the site is possible. The form of the settlement recorded in Domesday Book is totally unknown, but an early focus clearly existed N of the stream, where the church was already present at the beginning of the 12th century. In view of the link it probably represents across the valley and its definition by

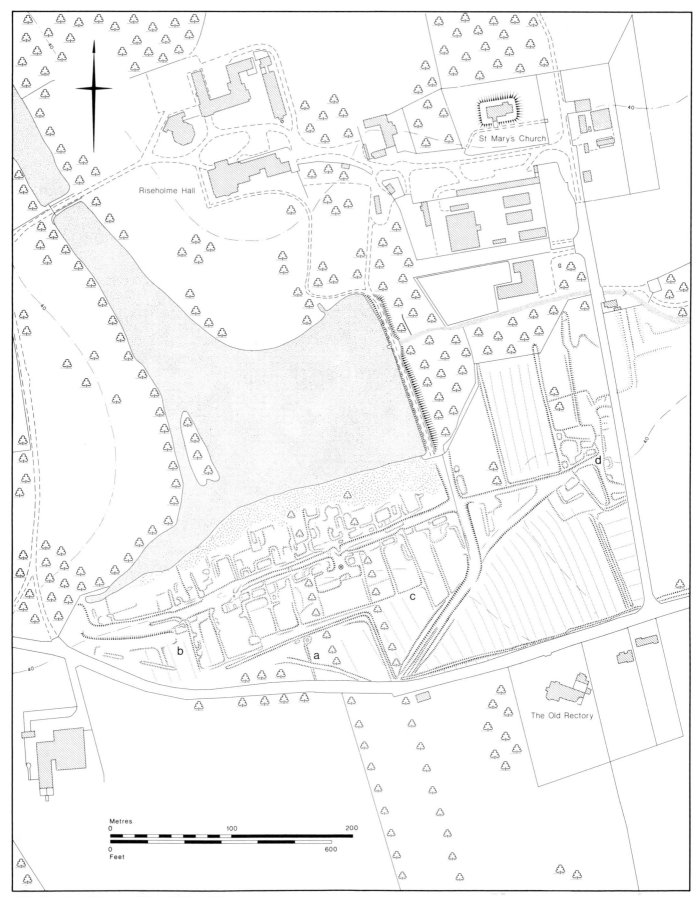

[114] *Riseholme (1) Deserted Village, (2) Site of Monastic Grange.*

158

arable blocks, the earliest of the extant earthworks is presumably the hollow-way running N towards the modern dam. Earthworks at the junction S of the dam may mark an early focus comparable to that N of the stream. The next clear stage is the laying out of the village to produce a neat rectangular plan. This was created, at least in part, on land previously under cultivation. If the limited excavation results are valid for the whole site then the village may have been planned and laid out in the late 12th century, perhaps by Hugh Bardolf, with wooden buildings subsequently replaced by stone ones, and with perhaps some extension to the W at a later stage. The occupation of this new village was apparently short-lived as the excavations indicate abandonment during or after the 14th century, perhaps as the monastic sheep regime developed. The creation of walled paddocks with associated buildings over the headland and ridges to the S of the village may imply further abandonment of arable land in favour of pasture at that time, if not earlier. It is possible that the encroachment of a few properties on the village street is related to these changes and in itself this speaks anyway of a low population.

1. *Lincs DB* 8/13, 24/2, 26/2, 19, 68/47; *LS* 3/1, 3/4, 3/19; Clay 1966, 4–28; Everson 1986, fig 1.
2. See Riseholme (2).
3. Baker 1956, 20–37, 39, 41.
4. Foster 1926, 235, 243; *VE* IV, 129; Baker 1956, 25–8; Cole 1913, 168.
5. BL Add MS 11574, f94; Baker 1956, 45; LAO 2 CRA 2/2/62.
6. Baker 1956 34, 44–5.
7. Thompson 1960, 95–108.

(2) Site of Monastic Grange (SK 984754) [114] lies immediately E of the deserted village of Riseholme on Jurassic Limestone at about 40 m above OD. The earthworks are probably the site of a monastic sheep grange, perhaps held by Kirkstead Abbey during part of the medieval period but by Barlings Abbey at the Dissolution.

In 1154 Ralf de Haia granted a property in Riseholme to Barlings Abbey as part of its foundation endowment. In 1166 Hugh Bardolf, holding from the de Haias, granted half a carucate of land with pasture for 500 or 600 sheep in Riseholme to Kirkstead Abbey. Two years later he gave a carucate of pasture for a similar number of sheep to Barlings Abbey.[1] Both gifts were subsequently confirmed and extended, most notably by Edmund Foliot's grant of pasture for 700 sheep to Kirkstead in the 13th century and by the gift to Barlings in 1398 of the manor of Riseholme formerly of the de Haia fee.[2] It is likely that these grants led to the establishment of at least two monastic grange farms. By 1325 Barlings Abbey held the 'Grangeam Super le Lynges' which gave its name to the present civil parish N of Riseholme and was formerly an extra-parochial part of it.[3] Some arrangement appears to have transferred Kirkstead's interests to Barlings, for a second grange recorded in the 16th century and known as Riseholme Grange also belonged to Barlings.[4] It is the latter that may be represented by the earthworks to the E of the village site.

In 1538 Charles Brandon, Duke of Suffolk, was granted the property of Barlings and Kirkstead Abbeys including the granges in Riseholme, which he leased out. By two purchases of 1544 and 1560 the family of St Paul acquired large parts of the Duke's interest in the parish and consolidated them by the purchase of the manor of Riseholme and Riseholme Grange in 1610.[5]

At the E end of the site of the deserted village of Riseholme the main street forms a crossroads. Its line is continued as a slighter hollow-way into a compact area of massive earthworks ('d') which might be interpreted as a manorial complex, although in view of the documentary evidence cited above it is more likely to be a monastic grange. Just before it reaches this complex, the road is joined from the SW by another hollow-way which itself leaves the main hollow-way to the SW, though its junction with the latter is now blocked by a scarp. The combined hollow-way continues E and is also blocked by a scarp which has the appearance of a recent disturbance. Beyond, the hollow-way forms a T-junction where the S arm extends S and then SE before being cut by the modern drive to the Hall, and the N arm runs into a small rectangular open space. Around this junction is a series of rectangular building platforms edged by stone-rubble walls ranging from 0.25 m to 1.5 m in height, presumably the site of a principal residence and its outbuildings. To the N and NW are at least three long rectangular closes extending downslope towards the stream. The largest has slight ridge-and-furrow within it, while the two small E ones are subdivided by a later E–W scarp. Further W, immediately E of the crossroads and on either side of the approach hollow-way, are other building platforms. This complex probably extended further E across the modern drive where some low, spread scarps still remain after modern ploughing. A narrow approach-way from the S, flanked by low banks, occupies the headland of a block of ridge-and-furrow and is cut by the tree bank along the modern road.

1. VCH *Lincs* II (1906), 204; Clay 1966, 4–28.
2. *Cal Inq Misc* II (1916), 58; *Cal Inq Ad Quod Damnum* (1803), 428a; *Cal IPM* III (1821), 159; *Cal Pat R 1396–9* (1909), 340; Baker 1956, 18–19.
3. *Feudal Aids* VI (1920), 617; Grange de Lings (1).
4. *VE* IV, 130; Dugdale 1817–30 VI pt 2, 918.
5. *Cal LPFD Hen VIII* XIII, pt 1 (1892), 326; pt 2 (1893), 494; XIV pt 1 (1894), 260–1; XIX pt 1 (1903), 507; Baker 1956, 20–4.

SAXILBY WITH INGLEBY

(2) Moated Site and Deserted Village of North Ingleby (SK 893778) [26, 115] lies at 12 m above OD on Lower Lias Clay. It occupies the S-facing slope of a shallow valley draining E and forms an almost continuous spread of earthworks with South Ingleby (3). The earthworks indicate a major reorientation of the settlement which may have been connected with its management as one with South Ingleby in the 14th and 15th centuries.

Although the two settlements of Ingleby are commonly distinguished as North and South in documents from the early 14th century onwards, their history is difficult to disentangle with confidence because of confusion with the name and Ingoldsby in Kesteven. Practically nothing can be gathered from the national and diocesan returns about the settlement's size and fluctuations of population since they are commonly returned either implicitly or explicitly as members of Saxilby, which was itself a flourishing settlement. North Ingleby was in closes by the later 16th century and contemporary references to 'shepecot garthes' suggests conversion to sheep; a survey of Monson property in Ingleby around 1600 shows almost all the land then enclosed.[1]

It is possible to identify one of the two manors held in 1086 by the Bishop of Bayeux and held subsequently by Robert de Haia as North Ingleby.[2] This manor can be traced through the hands of various chief lords and resident tenants until at least the early 14th century. Locally the most important were Robert of Ingleby and his descendants, mesne lords and evidently resident in the 12th and for much of the 13th centuries: they presumably created the moated residence and perhaps imposed regular planning on the settlement.

[115] *Saxilby with Ingleby (2) Moated Site and Deserted Village of North Ingleby, (3) Moated Site and Deserted Village of South Ingleby.*

From the early 14th until the early 15th century there are indications that North Ingleby was sublet and held with South Ingleby by the Daubney family.[3] It is possible that the massive alterations to both the settlements of North and South Ingleby, visible on the ground, relate to this period.

Even so the capital messuage of North Ingleby appears to have been occupied from the 15th century onwards and surviving documents suggest the site was never abandoned.[4] A manorial or free chapel first mentioned in 1232 was clearly not new at that date for a chaplain was named in the later 12th century. Its continuing existence is well documented in 13th, 14th and 15th-century records. White's *Directory* reports that 'several stone coffins and other antiquities' were dug up before 1872, and it is said that a holy water stoup excavated from the chapel site is set in a wall within the farmhouse.[5]

The earthworks of North Ingleby can be divided into two groups, namely the village remains and the site of the moated manor and its appurtenances which occupy the whole area E of the N–S through road and N of the straight-ditched boundary ('a'–'b') which appears to have been strongly embanked in places on its N side.

The manorial complex is centred on a moated enclosure still occupied by Ingleby Hall, its ditch on the surviving S side up to 2.5 m deep. Its overall shape is now lost because of infilling on the N, but the extant portion is polygonal or curving in form although rather mutilated. On its W side lies a chain of fishponds ('c'–'d'–'e'). Although the links have been obscured by the driveway to the farm, they appear to have been interconnected and joined to the moat. To the E of the moat another pond ('f') may have also served as a long shallow fishpond, with a dam at its E end. It divides three large paddocks on its S side, which contain traces of ridge-and-furrow but no signs of buildings or yards of a village type, from a small park on its N side. This park is bounded by a bank or pale that runs N along the modern road and then turns E and S to encompass a field of 4.69 ha before returning along the N side of the long pond ('f'). 'A close called the park' is recorded in 1454, in 1569–70 'the deer parke', and in 1649–50 a close of 9 acres (3.75 ha) called 'The Park or the Deer Park' are also referred to.[6] This park contains a block of ridge-and-furrow.

In the village remains, the street system is complex and may reflect fundamental changes in the layout of the settlement. There is, as at South Ingleby, an E–W hollow-way ('g'–'h'), parallel to the S edge of the manorial complex. It is possible to recognize, beneath later changes, and most obvious at the W end, regular settlement closes lying between the two. Closes and village properties on the S side of this S hollow-way are small, more irregular, and apparently overlie the ends of ridge-and-furrow. A partly hollowed N–S road skirts the W edge of the manorial park on the line of the modern road with a group of properties on its W side in a rectangular block that also appears to be a development over earlier arable land. At the SW corner of the manorial block ('a') this road skews diagonally SE as a deep hollow-way until it crosses the E–W hollow-way ('g'–'h') and resumes a direct course S downslope between ditches to the stream. A raised elongated triangular close ('i') is occupied by a two-celled building with stone foundations orientated E–W and measuring approximately 25 m by 12 m overall, which must be the remains of the documented chapel. To its E, two or three properties with hollow yards and slight traces of buildings front the diagonal hollow-way with ditched paddocks to the E containing ridge-and-furrow.

The effects of the apparent alteration to the settlement involving the development of this diagonal hollow-way appear also to have included a dispersal of properties. Several lie downslope in ditched closes overlying earlier arable, notably those E of the modern road and alongside the stream. From the SW corner of the manorial complex ('a') the modern road S, too, cuts across the regular layout, yet must follow an old way, since it serves these properties either itself or by access-ways from its E side; it is the *Ingleby Lane* of a 17th-century survey and it proceeds S past South Ingleby directly to form the *South Green Lane* of 1648 leading to the settlement around Saxilby church.

When field drains were laid through the village earthworks in January 1976 finds included medieval pottery dating from the 12th century onwards and some 16th-century wares, stone and tiles.[7]

1. PRO E164/38 ff94–5; LAO MONSON MSS VIII; LAC 8 (1956–7), 17.
2. *Lincs DB* 4/2, 18/1, 22/30; *LS* 3/3, 4, 16, 17; Whitwell 1969, 132; Foster 1927, 93.
3. *Book of Fees* I, 192; II, 1064; *Feudal Aids* III, 136, 247, 278, 358; *Cal IPM* IV (1913), 222; VI (1910), 89; VII (1909), 234; X (1921), 55; XIII (1955), 91; *Cal Inq Misc* VII (1969), 37; Foster 1927, 94–101.
4. *Cal Pat R 1446–52* (1909), 457–60; PRO E164/38 ff94–5; E317/22 (Lincs).
5. Gibbons 1888, 68; Stenton 1920, 143; BL Harl Ch 44 G 34 and 40, 44 H 4, 43 H 27 and 34; Owen 1975, 20; Turner 1878, 648; *Cal Pat R 1446–52* (1909), 457; Foster 1927, 98, 101–2; White 1872, 381; NAR SK 87 NE 3.
6. Turner 1878, 146–7; PRO E164/38 ff94–95; E317/22 (Lincs).
7. Finds in LM.

(3) Moated Site and Deserted Village of South Ingleby (SK 893771) [26, 115] lies at 12 m above OD on Lower Lias Clay, on flat ground S of a shallow valley which separates it from North Ingleby. The present survey shows evidence of a complete rearrangement of the settlement before its desertion, with direct links to developments at North Ingleby.

The difficulties of documentation of this settlement have been noted under North Ingleby. Its manor, held by Robert de Todeni in 1086, was in the hands of Wigot of Lincoln around 1115 and then passed to the family of Daubney (d'Albini or de Albiniaco) who remained tenants until deprived by forfeit in 1483. They are said to have been often resident although their principal holdings lay elsewhere.[1]

A manor house at South Ingleby is recorded in 1304-5 with a dovecote and a windmill: the site of the latter may be that formerly marked by a mound (SK 89487686) known as *Mill Hill*, levelled in 1950. In the early 14th century the Daubneys had begun to hold demesne land in North Ingleby together with their manor of South Ingleby in an arrangement which is referred to periodically at least until the first quarter of the 15th century and this situation may have caused the alterations in the road network and settlement layout at both places.[2]

After its forfeiture Sir Thomas Burgh had custody of South Ingleby manor and before 1539–40 it had passed to the Monsons of South Carlton. A house and farm buildings stood in the SW quadrant of the moated enclosure around 1800 and were not demolished until after 1945.[3]

National and diocesan returns give no indication of population size and change after the minimum of 30 recorded in 1086. In 1304-5 two free tenants and 15 villeins were recorded in a manorial extent. A Monson survey of 1607–8 shows the townships in closes at that time, having presumably been converted to pasture for sheep at an unknown date. There were no houses outside the moated enclosure in 1800.[4]

As at North Ingleby the earthworks indicate a complex series of changes which the documents do not begin to hint at. Dominating them, and hitherto the only settlement feature recognized, is a moated enclosure with its long sides slightly splayed out in a symmetrical double-rhomboid shape. Its S half is apparently subdivided, but closer examination shows that the ditch surrounding the SW platform or enclosure ('j') is more deeply and broadly dug and protrudes significantly at its NW and NE corners beyond the adjacent ditch alignment. This is likely to have been the principal manorial moat containing residential buildings just as it did the later farm. A raised platform along the E side of this enclosure and stone scatters mark these sites. The causeway access in the middle of the N side may be original though the gap itself is of recent creation formed by pushing material from the platform into the ditch. The whole N half of the overall moated complex and the L-shaped portion S and E of the main platform, now obliterated by the present farmyard, can be seen as ancillary closes to the smaller core. Indeed the marked kink on its W may suggest that the greater part of the N half is likely to be an extension to an earlier complex.

A prominent bank ('k'), along the N outside edge of the enclosure and separate from the headland to its N, at 0.75 m overtops the inside of the moated enclosure and its slight inner banking. While perhaps simply an exaggerated counterscarp, it may rather have been a rabbit warren similar to the feature in the manorial complex at Rand (1). Much slighter banking along the W outside of the enclosure seems to be a headland for the adjacent ridge-and-furrow.

To the W of the principal moat lies a battered E–W hollow-way ('l'–'m'), its E end blocked completely and thus put out of use by the moat. At the E end a deeper area, still up to 0.75 m deep, despite modern dumping, might possibly later have operated as a fishpond. On its S side are the remains of property platforms encroached upon from the S by ridge-and-furrow and cut through by the modern road to Saxilby. This hollow-way and its associated closes may represent the site of the early village.

Similar traces of further property plots on the N of the hollow-way have been more completely overploughed by ridge-and-furrow. The field is divided into small closes by narrow ditches, presumably formerly hedged, and contains a deep pond ('n'). Occupation plots with hollowed yards and perhaps traces of buildings are most obvious in the field to the N ('o', 'p' and 'q'), clearly overlying earlier arable and served by the modern road and an E–W hollowed access-way. Irregularities, perhaps representing former buildings, all along the E side of the modern road to the N and S of the long pond ('n') are probably similar. All these may mark the dispersal or rearrangement of the settlement, also apparent in the earthworks of North Ingleby.

The evident similarity of development in the two settlements, together with the fact that these seem to ignore the ancient township boundary dividing the two, encourages the suggestion that the major changes occurred when they were in the same tenure under the Daubneys in the 14th century and that the demographic and economic changes of that period were both a cause of and provided the scope for these physical changes.

During the survey a scatter of Roman pottery was recovered in the ploughland along the E side of the moated enclosure.

1. *Lincs DB* 18/1; *LS* 3/16; *Book of Fees* II, 1064; *Feudal Aids* III, 358; Whitwell 1969, 132; Cockayne 1910–59 IV, 93–105.
2. PRO C133/120/2; *Cal IPM* IV (1913), 222.

3. LCL Ross MSS XII Lawress wapentake, 242–3; LAO MONSON VIII, Survey of Ingleby; MISC DON 294/5-6.
4. *Lincs DB* 18/1; PRO C133/120/2; LAO MONSON VIII; MISC DON 294/5-6.

SIXHILLS

(1) Site of Gilbertine Priory and Later Settlement (TF 163872)
[116] lies at around 70–75 m above OD on Till at the foot of the W-facing scarp of the Wolds.

The priory, dedicated to St Mary, was founded in 1148–54 as a double house of canons and nuns of the Gilbertine order perhaps by Robert de Gresley, or his son. Its secular endowment was concentrated locally and its spiritualities were only a little more scattered. Substantial gifts continued throughout the 13th century with the result that the priory was relatively prosperous. As with other houses of the same order, Sixhills was much engaged in the production of wool, of which it was a leading exporter in the 14th century, organizing its activities at granges such as those at *Coldecotes* and *Holtham* (Legsby (3, 6)). The later 14th and 15th centuries saw a considerable decline in the wealth of the priory.[1]

The priory was dissolved in 1538 and in 1539 its site and lands were granted to Sir Thomas Heneage. A substantial post-Dissolution house must have existed on the site, since the third and fourth sons of Sir Thomas Heneage were born at Sixhills Grange in 1594 and 1599 and the place figures in late 17th and early 18th-century Heneage settlements and leases. In addition, there seems to have been a small hamlet there in the late 16th and 17th centuries; in 1563 the diocesan survey records two households on the site and inventories and other casual references provide confirmation.[2] The present house, The Grange, though said to be of 16th or 17th-century date possibly incorporating part of a medieval structure, carries two date-stones of 1747.

The remains of the priory are poor, consisting of only a single field of earthworks around the existing farm and traces of former earthworks visible on air photographs in the arable fields to the E, SW and S. Throughout, there is a complex pattern of banks, ditches and scarps, many of them clearly not contemporary and some directly identifiable with field and close boundaries on 19th-century estate maps. Most defy detailed interpretation and at the same time confuse the overall picture.

Not even the area of the monastic precinct is known. It appears to have been bounded on the N by a water channel fed by a spring on the hillside to the E. The central section, however, is a broad ditch with a large outer bank on its N ('a'), perhaps functioning as a linear fishpond. At right angles to its E end a similar broad linear depression ('b') is more clearly a fishpond, though the narrowing and arrangement of channels at its S end may mark the site of the water-mill listed among the priory's possessions at the Dissolution and reported as 'long since decayed' in 1625.[3] Further rectangular depressions ('c' and 'd'), may also have been components in a fishpond complex.

Despite present appearances, the long fishpond ('b') was not the E side of the precinct. The modern road N to North Willingham was realigned in the 1830s, parallel to, but downslope of an earlier road, thus cutting through the precinct. The former road ran along the outside of the precinct wall, which is visible on air photographs and of which just a stub survives as an earthwork ('e'), with ridge-and-furrow to its E. The course of this old road has been observed during field-walking as a strip of cobbles associated with bone and pottery of the 13th to the 18th centuries. The W and S boundaries

North Willingham
parish

line of old road

a

c

b

e

d

i

The Grange

h

f

g

Metres
0   100   200

0
Feet   600

[**116**] *Sixhills (1) Site of Gilbertine Priory and later Settlement.*

163

of the precinct are not known and a broad bank ('f') may only mark a division between courts. Elsewhere are many extant and ploughed-out features, few of which are intelligible. Field-walking in the area of a large round mound ('g') has recovered medieval pottery associated with cobbled surfaces, broken tiles, wasters and kiln furniture, suggesting a medieval tile kiln.[5] Of the earthworks around The Grange, a right-angled scarp W of the house ('h') seems to relate to the existing building, perhaps a building platform or the edge of a former garden. A stony bank running N from this platform turns NE overriding earlier features and then returns S on top of the dam of the fishpond ('b'). It may have continued SW towards the house again, where it terminates on the edge of a recent pond. It thus seems to form the boundary of a walled close or paddock associated with the house, but if so, it had been abandoned by 1814. A scarped platform ('i') and associated stone banks may mark the position of late roadside properties, as two buildings are mapped E and NE of The Grange in 1814.

1. VCH *Lincs* II (1906), 194–5; Knowles and Hadcock 1971, 194, 196; PRO 242/113; Stenton 1922, 1–38; Owen 1971, 66–8.
2. Maddison 1902–6 II, 483–4; LAO NW I/6/6, I/8A/3B and 11, I/9/1; *LNQ* **5** (1896-8), 115; LAO LCC ADMON 1590: 133, INV 33/28 and 200, INV 179/369; TdE C13/MISC IV; Hill 1939, 69–70.
3. Hill 1939, 70.
4. OS 1st edn 1 in sheet 83 (1824); LAO HEN 8/1/9, 3 HEN 3/13, 16; *LHA* **5** (1970), 13.
5. *LHA* **5** (1970), 13.

SNELLAND

(2) Deserted Settlement (TF 063805) [117], formerly the village and monastic grange of Swinthorpe, lies at 21 m above OD on a low ridge of Till.

The three holdings recorded in Swinthorpe in 1086 had been reduced to two by 1115. In the mid 12th century substantial grants were made to Kirkstead Abbey by tenants of both estates and confirmed by their lords; one included arable, a plot or tenement to erect their buildings in Swinthorpe, and pasture for 600 sheep and 40 cattle in Snelland and Swinthorpe. There were other gifts to Kirkstead in Snelland, which gave rise to exchanges that tended to consolidate the monks' holding in the parish. A grange was certainly created there by the late 12th century, and although some kind of residence was apparently maintained at Swinthorpe, it was perhaps only after the Dissolution that the term grange came to be applied to it. Barlings Abbey also held a messuage at Snelland at the Dissolution and a house and gardens in Swinthorpe.[1]

Since Swinthorpe was so rarely recorded separately from Snelland, no population trends are recoverable. In 1086 the minimum recorded population is three. While the seven households listed in 1563 might suggest it was deserted in medieval times, of the five dwellings in the 1841 census, only two according to the near-contemporary Tithe Map were, as now, adjacent to but not on the earthwork remains.[2]

Slightly less than half of the settlement remains visible on early air photographs remained for investigation as earthworks by the Commission. The E part had been converted to arable at some date after 1946. In overall plan the W half forms a compact and regularly laid out group of earthworks apparently consisting of two contiguous tiers of small enclosures or property plots, with remains of at least two or three former building platforms and hollow areas within them. A deep linear hollow-way ('a'–'b') which dog-legs through the settlement and which continues the alignment of an established footpath and former way due S to Reasby possibly marks the principal internal street. Another narrow hollow-way ('c') that diverges from the modern road along the N side of the ploughed remains may mark a way leading in from Snelland to the E. In any case it forms the N side of a coherent rectangular block, otherwise fossilized in existing hedge lines, whose overall alignment is slightly at an angle to the W part of the remains. Within this block the most clearly marked feature appears to be a close ('d') which may cause the dog-leg in the main hollow-way and have been residential. To its E are perhaps two slightly defined closes or paddocks overlying ridge-and-furrow. This type of configuration has been interpreted elsewhere as monastic granges or farms, and may be so here.

Immediately W of the settlement remains, a rectangular area of ridge-and-furrow is contained within hollow-ways or broad ditches. The SW corner of the settlement area has apparently cut into the NE edge of an arable furlong: this happened sufficiently early in the medieval period for ploughing to continue to a shorter length and for a headland to form against the settlement boundary.

Interpretation is necessarily tentative because of the fragmentary survival of the field remains. However the remains suggest either the expansion of an early nucleus over former arable or the new creation of a settlement within a network of arable furlongs, in either case involving one, or perhaps two, monastic farms. The grants to Kirkstead Abbey and resultant reorganization provide a 12th-century context for the initial development, though the existence of a grange of Barlings Abbey in the parish might also be significant.

1. *Lincs DB* 1/37, 2/12, 28/27; *LS* 16/11, 13; Stenton 1920, 150–63; *VE* IV, 35, 130; *Cal LPFD Hen VIII* XIII pt 2 (1893), 494; LAO 2 ANC 3/B/25; LAO PADLEY III/280; PRO SC6/Hy VIII/2050; Dugdale 1817–30 VI, 918.
2. PRO IR 29 and 30/20/293.

SOMERBY

(1) Deserted Village of Somerby (TA 062063) [118] extends from the lower slope of the main W scarp of the Wolds into an area of ill-drained clay between 40 m and 20 m above OD. The village is an example of late medieval desertion for sheep. Its earlier history is less well understood and the earthworks may present either one part of a polyfocal settlement or be the result of village migration.

Documentary evidence shows Somerby tenurially split into two principal holdings for much of the medieval period and also persistently below the average of the expected size from at least the beginning of the 14th century. The larger of the 1086 holdings, that of William de Percy, was held of the Percy fee from the mid 12th century by Gilbert de Arches and his descendants, in the 14th century by William de Cantilupe and William Ergun and for the first half of the 15th century by Robert de Cumberworth and his son Sir Thomas de Cumberworth.[1]

The other 1086 holding was Earl Hugh's and subsequently came under the fee of Thomas de Grelley and was still recorded as such in 1428, although then without a named tenant.[2]

No precise population figure is possible for 1086 but a likely minimum is 18–19. The early 14th-century subsidies record only 18 taxpayers, just two-thirds of the average for the wapentake. Relief was 38.5 per cent in 1352 but 63 persons paid the Poll Tax in 1377 and at least 10 households existed in 1428, perhaps marking some recovery. Reliefs more than doubled between 1448 and 1463, against a wider trend. The 7 taxpayers of 1542–3 and the 5 households of the diocesan survey of 1563 mark a reduced level of

The Poplars

Grange Farm

b

c

d

a

Metres
0   100   200

0
Feet   600

[**117**] *Snelland (2) Deserted Settlement of Swinthorpe.*

population that showed no up-turn until the later 18th century brought the number of households in the parish up to between 11 and 13 throughout the 19th century.

Conversion for sheep was evidently a prime factor in these population changes in both the 15th and 16th centuries. Sir Thomas Cumberworth's will of 1450/1 includes gifts of sheep by the score, totalling some six hundred, from his estates at Stain, Limber and Bonby, but especially from Somerby and refers to 'my sheperd...and...my swynnard' there. In the 1607 survey of depopulations, Richard Rossiter, whose father of the same name had acquired Somerby in the early 16th century, was accused of great depopulations in his neighbouring estates at Searby and Little Limber but Somerby is not mentioned since the process had already taken place.[3] Nevertheless its effect was current, since in 1603 the three inhabitants, including Rossiter and the incumbent, petitioned to take down the existing chancel of the church and reduce the crossing tower into a chancel. The archdeaconry survey of the same year also reported that 'the church ys in great decay for that there ys parishioners but only the lord Mister Rosseter...in whose hands are all the tenaments'.[4]

Analysis of the surviving settlement earthworks is complicated by the superimposition in part of post-medieval garden earthworks, themselves subsequently slighted, and by the location of the earthworks on wet land on the spring-line which has preserved the field in pasture, but caused broad, rough, surface drainage channels to be dug even within living memory. In addition the situation of the earthworks away from the church presents problems of interpretation. The documentary evidence makes it doubtful that the village was ever large enough, certainly not in the later medieval period or later, to have extended N to and beyond the church. It does nevertheless point to two factors, early tenurial duality and the scale and pretensions of the manor at least by the 15th century under the Cumberworths, both of which might provide a background to the remains. Earlier village properties in close proximity to the church need not have been a continuation of the settlement represented by the extant earthworks. They could have formed a separate nucleus related to the second manor. On the other hand the space between the church and the present Somerby House may have been created by the expansion of the manorial *curia* during the later Middle Ages which may have been sufficient to push the

Home Farm

St Margaret's
Church

Somerby
House

k

f

b

e

g

h

d

c

a

i

j

l

m

Metres
0   100   200

0   600
Feet

[**118**] *Somerby (1) Deserted Village, (2) Garden Remains.*

[119] *Somerby (2), Somerby House from the S, drawn by C. Nattes in 1795. This unusual house was built by Sir Edward Rossiter in 1660. The style of the elevations link it with the Artisan Mannerist houses of the South-East and East Anglia but the proportions of the façade suggest connections with the more sophisticated architecture of Pratt and Webb. The curious double-pitched roofs are more characteristic of N Germany and the Netherlands than of England. The house was demolished in the early 19th century. (Lincolnshire Library Service)*

attendant village on to the more unfavourable land now occupied by the earthworks.

The settlement remains take the form of a prominent meandering hollow-way ('a'–'b') serving former individual farmsteads ('c', 'd', 'e' and 'f'). These are represented by the remains of rectangular buildings grouped around yards and situated within small plots. They are probably late medieval in date. In the central part of the settlement the plots are irregular in shape and arrangement. Lesser hollow-ways leave the main street and on the E, where they may have been deepened by spring erosion, they serve further farmsteads ('g', 'h'). Other dwellings or perhaps barns are also recognizable elsewhere ('i', 'j' and 'k'). The properties at the S and E limits of the village were laid out on top of broad ridge-and-furrow. The ridge-and-furrow underlying the S part of the settlement (area of 'a'–'i') and running NW–SE appears to have been truncated on the SE by later ridge-and-furrow aligned in the opposite direction.

At its NE end ('b') the main hollow-way has been blocked by material belonging to a group of amorphous earthworks which lie SE of Somerby House. These may represent the remains of dismantled formal terrace gardens of the 17th century (2). Their relationship to the village must mean that the latter had been deserted for some time before they appeared. On the NE the earthworks are bounded by a terrace-way running along the hillside, which N of Somerby House bifurcates ('l'), with one arm extending towards the church and the other linking up with the modern road. Two depressions SW of the church are probably former quarries.

1. *Lincs DB* 22/38; *LS* 11/6; Clay 1963, 146–8; *Book of Fees II*, 1013, 1093, 1478; *Feudal Aids* III, 169, 224, 303, 344.
2. *Lincs DB* 13/18; *LS* 11/17; *Book of Fees* I, 157; *Feudal Aids* III, 158, 232, 295.
3. LCL Ross MSS III, 344–6; BL Add MS 11574, f76; Holmes, 1980, 21.
4. LAO Court Papers 69/1/43; Foster 1926, 232, 317.

(2) Garden Remains (TA 062063) [118] of perhaps 16th-century and later date, lie around and to the W of Somerby House between 40 m and 20 m above OD.

During the tenure of the Cumberworth family in the early 15th century the manor house at Somerby was a major residence, and certainly in keeping with Sir Thomas Cumberworth's position as High Sheriff and Member of Parliament.[1] This house was presumably located close to the site of the later Somerby House or possibly nearer the church. No trace survives.

The manor was acquired by the Rossiters in the early 16th century and the family was resident at Somerby from before 1550. The house became the centre of an extensive local estate. In 1660 Sir Edward Rossiter built a new house of classical design on the site of the present one [119]. Both this house and its predecessor were presumably surrounded by formal gardens which may, in part, survive as the area of amorphous earthworks SE of Somerby House and which overlie and block the main hollow-way of the medieval village ('b'), and which include at least one elongated terrace feature.

The Weston family purchased the manor in 1750 and it was Edward Weston who was probably responsible for the large brick-walled garden and lake to the W of the house. They appear on Armstrong's county map of 1776–8 and are probably contemporary with the late 18th-century Home Farm and the Doric column N of the church.[2]

Former terraces are still visible in the grassed interior of the walled garden. A narrow ridge ('m') apparently on top of ridge-and-furrow continues the line of a medieval terrace-way SE from Somerby House. It is probably an ornamental walk, also of the 18th century.

The 17th-century house was rebuilt in the early 19th century and the formal gardens replaced by open parkland to the S.[3] This house was in turn demolished around 1960. Its replacement is completely modern.

1. LCL Ross MSS III, 341; *Names of Members returned to serve in Parliament* pt 1 1213–1702 (1878), 281, 295, 300, 308, 330.
2. Maddison 1902–6 III, 833–4; Holmes 1980, 174–6, 200–3, 217–18; monuments in Somerby church; LCL Banks Collection III, f303; HMC *10th Report* (1885), 9–13 and App I 199–520; Schweizer 1977.
3. Pevsner and Harris 1964, 365.

SOUTH CARLTON

(1) Site of Monastic Grange (SK 948764) [120] lies at approximately 20 m above OD on Middle Lias Clay, adjacent to but W of the village of South Carlton.

Before about 1220, Robert Bardolf granted half his holding in South Carlton to Barlings Abbey. The abbey retained this estate until the Dissolution when it was granted to Charles Brandon, Duke of Suffolk. In 1544 it was sold to William Monson, thus uniting it to the secular manor of South Carlton.[1]

The effect of Bardolf's grant to the abbey may have been to reorientate the secular settlement in the E of the village, leaving room to the W for the monastic manor. The earthworks ('a') here comprise scarps forming large paddocks with associated foundations of stone buildings. They do not form a clearly diagnostic layout but probably represent the manor or grange of Barlings Abbey. The site is bounded on the W and S by a ditched watercourse and probably included part of the former arable area to the E.

1. LCL Ross MSS XII, Lawress wapentake, 112, 132; *Feudal Aids* III, 136, 140, 216, 278, 281; *VE* IV, 130; *Cal LPFD Hen VIII* XIV pt 1 (1894), 261; XIX pt 2 (1905), 74.

(2) Manorial Enclosure and Fishponds (SK 951766) [120] lies at the N end of South Carlton village at 20–30 m above OD on Marlstone.

The tenurial history of South Carlton is complex and requires further clarification, but the main outlines seem clear. There were, by the 12th century, two principal manors and these probably continued an earlier pattern of tenure recorded in Domesday Book.[1] By the early 13th century both manors were held as one by the Bardolfs. Shortly before 1220, Robert Bardolf granted much of his holding to Barlings Abbey and this is the tenurial pattern documented through the later medieval period. Barlings Abbey held one manor and the other remained in secular hands, principally those of the Paynel family.[2] In 1506–7 the latter was sold to John Monson of South Kelsey, who made South Carlton his main residence. After the Dissolution, the manor of Barlings Abbey was acquired by the Monsons who thus held the whole parish.[3] In the late 16th century, however, the family's alternative and frequently preferred principal residence became Burton Hall, and certainly throughout the 18th and 19th centuries the old manor house here was occupied by tenant farmers.

The principal late medieval secular manor house probably stood alongside the church, which may have been encompassed within the *curia*. The surviving field remains, however, appear to belong to the extended manorial complex created by the Monsons in the 16th century, which at least in part involved the diversion of a former village street. The complex is described in a survey of 1607–8 as 'the scyte of the Hall or Mannor House with all the foreyards, orchards, gardins, ponds and hopyards about the same'.[4] It occupied a roughly square block 200 m across with the manor house in the centre, bounded on the S by the hollow-way of the diverted street ('b') and a strong bank ('c') continuing that line E before turning N on the rising scarp. On the W the boundary was probably the N–S line of an ancient way linking the villages along the foot of the limestone scarp, now marked by the modern street and part of a hollow-way W of the church ('d'). The N and E boundaries were the outer limits of the existing patchwork of the stone-walled paddocks and gardens.

Within the S boundary of this area is an E–W chain of ponds draining W. Only the two easternmost remain water-filled. The larger forms an ornamental feature which is shown on maps of 1805 and 1845, while the other in 1845 appears as a long narrow N–S pond which may once have extended further N.[5] Below and to the W, and separated by earthen banks forming dams, are the remains of three further ponds, now partly destroyed in later gardens.

1. *Lincs DB* 4/1, 68/2; *LS* 3/2; Foster and Major 1931–73 IV, 253–4; *Book of Fees* II, 1065, 1073, 1076.
2. LCL Ross MSS XII, Lawress wapentake, 132; *Feudal Aids* III, 136, 140, 216, 264, 278, 281, 358, 368.
3. LCL Ross MSS XII, 108; LAC 3 1951–2, 7; Maddison 1902–6 II, 680–4; *Cal LPFD Hen VIII* XIV pt 1 (1894), 261; XIX pt 2 (1905), 74.
4. Monson MS VIII (at South Carlton).
5. LAO MONSON 17/16/4; B 354.

(3) Settlement Remains (SK 951765) [120], formerly part of South Carlton, lie at 20–30 m above OD on Marlstone and Middle Lias Clay. The complex appearance of the village may reflect an original duality of settlement later joined together and considerably altered as a result of changes in tenure and population.

No secure figure for the minimum recorded population in 1086 is possible. Nevertheless for the two manors which probably made up South Carlton 22 persons are listed. Despite the grant to Barlings Abbey, 27 taxpayers paid the subsidy in 1327–8. From 1332 the returns include Middle Carlton. Relief of 44.4 per cent was allowed in 1352 after the Black Death but the figure of 111 paying the Poll Tax in 1377 suggests a strong recovery. Continuing reliefs of 17 per cent in the mid 15th century may relate principally to the decline of Middle Carlton, for in 1542–3 the settlement had 21 taxpayers. The later 16th century may have been a period of contraction for only 16 households were recorded in 1563 and 68 communicants in 1603 and 63 in 1676. By the early 18th century about 22 households are recorded. This had risen to 27 by the beginning of the 19th century and to 37 by its close. The surviving maps and plans indicate that South Carlton saw little morphological change over this latter period.

The plan of South Carlton is full of anomalies. Without the knowledge of the earthworks of abandoned properties it would appear to be a village based on an almost square green with properties fronting on all but the E side and which have encroached on the S. With the earthworks, the superficial impression is that of what has been termed a loop village of complex form – an impression strengthened by the manner in which the main N–S hollow-way apparently bifurcates ('e').

What is more fundamentally anomalous, however, is that most of the neighbouring settlements along the scarp edge of the limestone ridge now have, or formerly had, a layout based on E–W streets which reflect both the topography and the strip form of their parishes. This, too, may lie behind the plan of South Carlton, which on close examination seems to be the result of complex changes resulting largely from the tenurial history summarized in the previous monument (2).

St John the Baptist's Church

The Manor House

Chartfield House

Hawthorn Farm

Cedar Farm

old stream course

a

d

i

b

h

c

e

f

g

Metres
0   100   200

0   600
Feet

[**120**] *South Carlton (1) Site of Monastic Grange, (2) Manorial Enclosure and Fishponds, (3) Settlement Remains.*

The early medieval form of the village may have been two separate nuclei following the two Domesday Book and later manors, each based on an E–W street (cf North and Middle Carlton and North and South Ingleby). The S nucleus may have lain on or near the alignment of the present S street ('f'–'g'). Some traces of properties survive as earthworks on both sides of this street. Their depth N and S of the street is very similar and might suggest a planned origin. In the N the former nucleus may also coincide with the present E–W street.

These two possible nuclei are connected by the principal earthwork remains of the site. These focus on an N–S hollow-way ('e') and indeed cut through a fragment of ridge-and-furrow ('h'), perhaps once arable land which separated the two nuclei. The hollow-way is bounded on its E by three very regularly sized properties with traces of stone buildings at the street end and in two cases by long back tofts whose E ends are cut through by the existing road. This may be a planned development filling in and bringing together the E ends of the two earlier foci. It is tempting to associate this with the tenure of the Bardolfs, not only because of their work on village planning elsewhere (see Riseholme (1)) but because of Robert Bardolf's gift to Barlings Abbey in the early 13th century, whereby he kept half of each of the older manors in his own hands. This may have led to a reconstituted and certainly reoriented settlement.

On the W side of the main hollow-way the foundations of further stone buildings lie along the modern street, with plots behind, but without the same clear regularity of plan as that to the E. These may therefore be the result of a secondary development along the hollow-way. Other features which may also relate to later changes include the hollow-way to the N ('b'). This may have been developed as late as the 16th century as the extended manorial complex (2) to the N led to the replacement of the earlier E–W road. Both the hollow-way running W (from 'e') and the presumed way curving SE from the same point may also be later developments. The former hollow-way may also be connected with the existence of a further rectangular block of properties ('i') whose crofts appear as earthworks, albeit slight and much disturbed, behind the farmstead still standing on the N–S street frontage. These remains may be of any date, though they had certainly been abandoned by 1720. The position here is complicated by the modern street. Though certainly in existence by 1720, its perfectly straight alignment and sharp angles where it continues N and S appear to be a recent development, as does the street along the E side of the village for the same reason. Both may have appeared following the abandonment of the main N–S hollow-way and its associated houses which had also taken place by 1720.[1] It is possible that this abandonment occurred during the 17th-century slump in population. Such a hypothesis would then indicate a further remodelling of the village in the late 17th or early 18th centuries.

1. Monson MS map of South Carlton (at South Carlton).

SOUTH KELSEY

(1) Site of Alien Priory of Winghale (TF 030970) [121] lies in the SW corner of the parish at about 7.5 m above OD on gravel locally overlying Jurassic clays. Large quantities of Middle Saxon pottery together with Roman and Iron Age material have been turned up in shallow gravel quarries near the farmstead and confirm the antiquity of the site.[1]

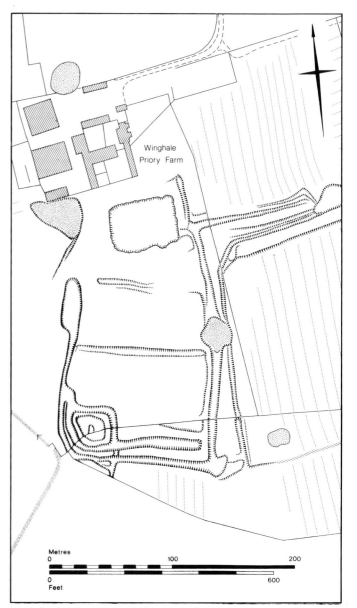

[121] *South Kelsey (1) Site of Alien Priory of Winghale.*

The origin of the monastic community here is obscure, but presumably lies in an endowment very soon after the Conquest. As a collegiate foundation and not the interest of any tenant-in-chief it is not directly recorded in Domesday Book, but is referred to obliquely through the 1½ carucates in Owersby belonging to Roger of Poitou that were held by the 'ecclesia of Wingeham'. In the early 12th century the monks of Winghale held similarly in Owersby of the Count of Mortain. By then, William, Count of Mortain, had in 1103–4 formally granted to the abbey of St Martin of Marmoutier at Tours his manor of Winghale on condition of the establishment there of a community of twenty monks.[2]

Whatever the original intention, Winghale in the 13th century appears as a cell of the abbey of St Martin at Sées in Normandy. It was dedicated to St John and its endowment was apparently of little more than 1 carucate in South Kelsey, the advowson of the church there, and pensions of other local churches.[3]

After the priory was taken into the king's hands in the 14th century, its fortunes can be followed through the Exchequer accounts of rents raised for its custody.[4] In 1441 Henry VI gave the reversion to King's College, Cambridge; it was exchanged for tenements with Trinity College in 1443 and finally confirmed to them in 1461.[5]

A large area of old enclosures along the W end of the S parish boundary of South Kelsey at the time of the parish's parliamentary enclosure in 1794–8, including the priory site, probably represents the priory's lands. One household is recorded at Winghale in the diocesan survey of 1563 and buildings are shown on the site on maps of 1794 and 1847, at approximately the position of the present farmstead.

The earthworks are extremely poor except for a fishpond complex at the S end of the site. The principal monastic buildings presumably lay beneath and immediately around the existing farm though its structure shows no obvious sign of early fabric. Inhumations without grave goods, first noted in 1847, have been found over many years in digging for gravel S of the farm, and more recently six or seven skulls are reported from N of the buildings.[6] To the S, down the slope, a group of three closes or paddocks is defined by broad well-marked ditches on the E and W and scarps and slight ditches across the slope. On its S this rectangular layout is closed by a fishpond complex that includes, at its W end, a roughly square, ditched arrangement whose central island is hollowed to form a shallow pond.

Blocks of ridge-and-furrow with well-developed headlands on the E side of the site have been overlain and much cut about by later hedge lines that can be identified with boundaries on early maps.

1. *LHA* **8** (1973), 38–9; finds in Scunthorpe Museum.
2. *Lincs DB* 16/8, 70/15; *LS* 7/15; *Cal Docs Preserved in France* (1899), 436–7; Davis *et al* 1913-69 II, no 680.
3. Davis 1914 b, 132–3; Davis 1914a, 62; Davis, F.N. *et al* 1925, 71; *Placita de Quo Warranto* (1818), 398; *Rot Hund* I (1812), 328, 370, 399; *Cal IPM* VI (1910), 241; Lunt 1926, 240; *Taxatio Ecclesiastica* (1802), 57; *VCH Lincs* II (1906), 241–2.
4. *Cal Close R 1337–9* (1900), 164; *Cal Fine R 1337–47* (1915), 421–33; *1347–56* (1922), 67, 319; *1356–69* (1923), 81; *1369–77* (1924), 159; *1377–83* (1927), 71; *1383–91* (1929), 38, 245; *1391–9* (1929), 250, 288; *1413–22* (1934), 81; *1422–30* (1935), 65; *Cal Pat R 1343–5* (1902), 539; *1399-1401* (1903), 501; *1405-1408* (1907), 383–4; *1429–36* (1907), 461; *1436–41* (1907), 557; *1441–6* (1908), 160; *1461–7* (1897), 73; *Cal Inq Misc* IV (1957), 105.
5. LAO South Kelsey Parish Deposit; A530.
6. OS 2nd edn 25 in (1906), sheet Lincs 37.5; local inf; LM records; Russell and Moorhouse 1971, 14.

(4) Moated Site (TF 045976) [16, 122] lies at the extreme S end of South Kelsey village on a slight rise of Boulder Clay at 22 m above OD. The site appears to have been associated with and lay on the N edge of a large block of land lying along the S parish boundary of South Kelsey and most clearly shown on the Enclosure Map of 1794 as a block of old enclosures. This land was almost the sole possession of the small alien priory of Winghale (1) which lay at its W end. From the early 14th century onwards when the priory was taken into the hands of the Crown, the land was usually rented out and it is likely that the moated site was constructed during this period as a more convenient place for the demesne farm than the relatively isolated priory site.

The land was finally granted to King's College Cambridge by Henry VI in 1441 and passed to Trinity College by exchange in 1443. The College still held this land in 1461, but sometime later it came into the hands of the Hansard family. In or soon after 1521 the land passed by marriage to the Ayscoughs of Stallingborough.[1]

It seems likely that about this time the moated site was altered and a new hall and gardens constructed within it. This house then served as the principal residence of the Ayscoughs, in parallel with that at Stallingborough, up until the end of the 17th century when the male line failed. It passed by marriage to the Thornhagh family who resided there until *c*1790. The Hall was then demolished and replaced in about 1810 by the present farmhouse.

The site, together with its park, was described in detail in 1591 in a survey of the demesne of Sir Edward Ayscough. At that time it comprised the manor house, garden, orchard and court, all encompassed by a moat, with, to its E, an outer court also moated. On its W side was an N–S road called *Park Lane* and on the S an E–W way leading to the entrance. On its N and E were closes. All this is shown on the Enclosure Map of 1794 [**16**].

By 1824 the road to the W had been straightened and moved W to its present alignment, access to the new farmhouse had been changed to the N side of the moat, and new farm buildings had been erected over the NE corner of the main moat. The N and much of the E side of the moated outer court had been drained and partly filled by this date, while beyond to the N and S emparked and tree-planted vistas had been created.[2] This latter situation still very largely pertains.

Most of the N and all the W and S sides of the main moated site survive intact and water-filled. The S, at 20 m across, is twice the width of the other arms, a proportion which is similarly recorded on all early maps and is probably a 16th-century modification. It was undoubtedly designed to present an impressive sheet of water to the visitor approaching the house along the main S entrance way. At its E end this arm ended abruptly on a causeway which still survives, separating it from the S arm of the outer enclosure. The ditch of the main moat once turned N at this causeway to form its E side. This side has been filled in except for the extreme S end. Originally this arm had another roughly central causeway that carried the approach-way into the main courtyard of the house. This situation, and the house itself, is shown on a drawing made between 1756 and 1787.[3] This shows the E arm of the moat broken by the causeway with, beyond, a brick-walled forecourt. The wall is shown pierced by a double gate, set in a stone surround and surmounted by a pediment-like feature. The gateway still survives but without its pediment, reset in a later farm building on the site. At the SE corner of the outer court, the drawing shows an octagonal tower, probably a garden feature. This also survives, and though much altered, is constructed of 16th-century bricks with stone dressings. From the gate, an axial path crossed the court to the two-storey entrance porch of the main E front of the house. The house was also of two storeys and attics with a roughly symmetrical elevation and mullioned windows. The gardens of the house seem to have occupied the W part of the main moat. Much moulded stonework including door jambs and window mullions of 16th and 17th-century date has been used to fill the N ditch of the moat.

The moated outer court still survives, though only the S arm is water-filled. The infilled E and N arms are only just traceable. Slight and amorphous hollows in the interior may mark the site of a building which is shown on the 1794 Enclosure Map. This E moated enclosure overlies abandoned ridge-and-furrow which also occupies the closes to the N and E.

Other features outside the moat include a large bank ('a'), about 1.8 m high and about 60 m long, whose purpose is unknown. It certainly existed in 1794. It may simply be spoil from clearing or widening the moat, and perhaps significantly matches the widest section of the ditch. A more positive function may have been, tree-

[**122**] *South Kelsey (4) Moated Site, (5) Enclosure and Platform.*

covered, in screening the SW aspect of the house and gardens from the adjoining road – certainly its present effect. It could just possibly be associated with a small earthwork to its S (5).

The original E–W way along the S side is marked by a flat area bounded on the S by a slight ditch cutting through earlier ridge-and-furrow and marked as a hedge in 1794. The 1591 survey indicates that this track ran on beyond the E end of the moat and then turned N to become *Sorrylesse Lane* which passed between closes into the *East Field* of South Kelsey St Mary. The lane still existed in 1794.

1. *Book of Fees* II, 1018, 1074; Owen 1975, 19; Davis 1914a, 12; monuments in church; *Feudal Aids* III, 138, 214, 269; Maddison 1902–6 I, 58–68, II, 455–6, 680–4.
2. Trollope 1861–2, 148; LAO South Kelsey Parish Deposit; A530; Monson MS CVII (at South Carlton); OS 1st edn 1 in sheet 86.
3. Gibbons 1928, 33–4; *Lincs Life*, 12/2/52.

(5) Enclosure and Platform (TF 04429754 and 04399748) [122] may be a 17th-century gun position. They lie at 22 m above OD on a low ridge of Boulder Clay.

The remains are not directly documented or diagnostic in form, but Sir Edward Ayscough was a leading local Parliamentarian in the Civil War. In 1642, anticipating Parliament's intention to secure and occupy the county, local Royalists singled out his residence at South Kelsey for an attack and looting. These circumstances may have given rise to his house being fortified and garrisoned.[1]

The field evidence consists of two features, one a surviving earthwork, the other levelled by ploughing, sited on either side of the pre-1794 N–S road and facing S, thereby commanding at least 500 m of road on falling ground and beyond that more than a similar distance again to the next rise. The earthwork ('b') forms a three-sided enclosure, open to the N, with a broad external ditch matching its bank, and a slight counterscarp or irregular line of spoil on the W. On its highest, S side, the bank stands 1–1.5 m above the surrounding ground and over 2 m above the ditch bottom. It was present but abandoned by 1794.[2] The bank ('a') might possibly form part of this earthwork.

On the W side of the modern road and evidently cut through by its realignment, large-scale OS plans portray a sub-rectangular platform about 30 m across ('c') and marked by a curving scarp against the slope.[3] Now under the plough this shows only as a soil-mark and apparently overlay abandoned ridge-and-furrow. While it might be no more than a tree ring it is just possible that it was associated in function with the embanked earthwork to the N.

1. Holmes 1980, 107, 109, 143, 159, 165; Maddison 1902–6 I, 65.
2. LAO South Kelsey Parish Deposit.
3. OS 25 in sheet Lincs 37.6.

SPRIDLINGTON

(1) Settlement Remains (TF 008845) [123], formerly part of the village of Spridlington, lie on a low N–S limestone ridge at 20 m above OD. Though the surviving remains are limited in extent, when supported by the evidence from the existing pattern of streets and properties and by the documentary record, they reveal a complex development from an early polyfocal settlement through late medieval decline to a 19th-century estate village.

Documentary evidence suggests that there were two distinct but contiguous early medieval settlements, which subsequently merged to form the present village. Two manors are listed in Domesday Book with minimum recorded populations of 18 and 24 respectively and both can be traced through the Middle Ages and later.[1] In 1774 the two major landowners each claimed to be lord of a separate manor. This tenurial distinction was still clearly defined at the end of the 19th century, when Hutton wrote that 'there are, and apparently always have been, two estates in Spridlington, each conferring manorial rights. They are about equal in extent, and roughly may be said to lie respectively to the N and S side of the mill-road.'[2]

Two medieval churches are documented, with dedications to St Hilary and St Albinus, presumably one belonging to each settlement. St Albinus is associated with the S manor and St Hilary with the N one. The parishes were united in 1417, because of lack of revenue arising from the small number of parishioners, sterility of the land, crop failure, pestilence and disease beyond the norm, and licence was given to demolish St Albinus. This church clearly stood immediately S of St Hilary's church.[3]

Other documentation confirms the decline of Spridlington from the mid 14th century onwards and perhaps earlier. As a double settlement it appears substantially larger than the average in 14th-century tax returns: the 57 and 50 taxpayers recorded in 1327–8 and 1332–3 fell to only 48 inhabitants over 14 in 1377. The assignment of dower to the widow of Sir John Chaumont in 1372 shows the reduced state of the S manor. It was reckoned to include 14 messuages, 23½ cottages and 3 tofts, but of the 5 messuages assigned to the dower, only 3 had tenants. Two further plots had a single tenant but none of the 8 cottages had any. The demesne was 'unoccupied for lack of tenants'.[4] These vacancies may well explain large areas of abandoned settlement at the S end of the village. In 1273 the N manor included a capital messuage and a total of 16 other messuages, tofts and tenements. In 1428 Spridlington St Hilary was exempt from the parish taxes having less than 10 households and in 1617 the same estate comprised 3 messuages, 6 cottages and 4 tofts.[5] This apparent decline is reflected in the continuing high rate of reliefs in the 15th century. With only 80 communicants recorded in 1603, 76 in 1676, and 23 to 31 households in the period 1705–23, clearly Spridlington did not see any substantial recovery in population until the end of the 19th century.

In 1841–2 H. F. Hutton, rector and lord of the N manor, built a new rectory, now Spridlington Hall, at the N edge of the village. At the same time the curving road running N from the church, shown on the map of 1775, was realigned to the E and lined with trees. Hutton also enlarged the church and built a new village school. His work shows the impact of a resident 'squarson' on a settlement previously deemed 'a poor lost place'.[6]

Indeterminate earthworks occur in four main groups around the periphery of the village. A battered hollow-way S of Spridlington Hall represents the former road realigned during the early 1840s. Before reaching the garden of the Manor House, it is joined on the W by another hollow-way defining the N end of the village, which has been cut through on the N by a long pond divided into two. Two former closes, bounded by low scarps and ditches containing ridge-and-furrow, are visible to the S.

Another group of earthworks appears N and E of Church View Farm, where a hollow-way ('a') runs approximately E–W, and is shown as a lane on the 1775 map. Earthworks occur on either side of it. Those on the N seem to include the sites of former buildings and perhaps represent expansion away from the main core of the settlement associated with the N manor. This idea is supported by the fact that they are cut through broad N–S ridge-and-furrow. A linear hollow, probably a former lane, forms the N boundary. Medieval sherds were picked up in this area during the Commission's survey.

The remains immediately S of the hollow-way ('a') have been mutilated, though a dry pond is still well preserved. Another ('b') has been filled-in with topsoil containing substantial amounts of medieval pottery, derived from the site of a barn to the W. Between the ponds and the Faldingworth road on the S, fragmentary earthworks indicate former properties.

A third group of remains lies SE of Elms Farm where slight earthworks blurred by relatively recent ploughing indicate former properties arranged on either side of the old lane running S. Their relationship to ridge-and-furrow indicates that they represent expansion of the settlement associated with the S manor over earlier arable. If, as the documents suggest, Spridlington started to decline from the mid 14th century onwards, it is likely that this expansion took place earlier. Medieval pottery was recorded in some quantity here too during the Commission's survey.

The most prominent feature of the fourth group of earthworks which lies off the ridge, S of Glebe House Farm, is a roughly rectangular moat ('c') whose interior stands about 1 m above its ditch. Indeterminate earthworks lie outside it with mole up-casts on the W producing 17th to 19th-century sherds. Traces of at least two rectangular buildings are visible and one was still marked on the 1775 map as a standing structure. To the S, the earthworks are now bounded by a drain with a broad S bank whose line is continued up the slope to Elms Farm by a hollow-way ('d'), also shown as a road on the Enclosure Map of 1775. The field to the N of the hollow-way has been levelled and any earthworks linking this group with the area around the church have been destroyed. It is therefore difficult to assess the true significance of the moat but it may represent the site of the S manor house.

A linear hollow ('e'), possibly a former lane, runs SW of Elms Farm and is represented on the 1775 map by a field boundary. This map also shows a significant bend where the boundary joined the present road to Hackthorn. The road pattern which can be constructed from the Enclosure Map and the earthworks suggest that at some stage Spridlington may have had an E–W grid plan with the N–S ridge road as its spine. It is uncertain whether this could have been a consequence of gradual expansion or the result of deliberate

Spridlington
Hall

line of old road

Manor
House

a

b

Church View
Farm

St Hilary's
Church

Grange

Glebe House
Farm

d

c

Elms Farm

e

Metres
0   100   200

0   600
Feet

[123] *Spridlington (1) Settlement Remains.*

planning either in early medieval times or when the two parishes were united in the early 15th century.

1. *Lincs DB* 12/42, 26/25; *LS* 2/11, 18; *Cal IPM* XIII (1954), 149; *Cal IPM* 2nd ser II, 321; LCL Ross MSS IV, 101.
2. LAO Lindsey Encl 68; Hutton, A. W., 'Notes on Spridlington, Lincolnshire', compiled 1893-7, unpublished typescript, 15.
3. Lunt 1926, 252; *Taxatio Ecclesiastica*, 75b; LAO Bishops' Registers, *passim*; Stenton 1920, nos 3 and 4; *Cal IPM* XIII (1954), 149; *Book of Fees* II, 1072; Foster 1920, 206; Davis 1914a, 154; Davis, F. N. *et al* 1925, 88; Archer 1963-82 III, 159-64, 225-6, 249.
4. *Cal IPM* XIII (1954), 149.
5. Foster 1920, 206; Nevile Deeds (Auburn Hall, Lincs, handlist in LAO), 3/11.
6. Hutton, as note 2, 25-7, 30, 31.

STAINFIELD

(1) Site of Benedictine Priory (TF 111732) [24, 124] lies around Stainfield Hall and St Andrew's church on the S side of a small stream on sand and gravel at 6 m above OD, spreading on to the rising ground to the S on Till.

When investigated in 1977, the earthworks around Stainfield Hall constituted among the most complex and informative remains in West Lindsey, since they revealed the interrelationships between a monastic site, a village (2) and a post-medieval great house, its gardens and parkland (3). All except the S side of the village remains and the surrounding ridge-and-furrow survived at that date as well-preserved earthworks. In 1979 the greater part was destroyed leaving only the N area close to the stream in pasture.

In or before the reign of Henry II a priory of Benedictine nuns was founded at Stainfield, the only one in Lincolnshire, probably by Henry son of Henry de Percy, who held the manor. It was well endowed for a nunnery, the principal temporal holdings being in Apley and Stainfield. The nunnery was dissolved in 1536.[1]

The former monastic precinct is marked out by the stream on the N, a water-filled ditch on the E, a broad bank cut by later hedge ditches ('a'-'b') on the S, and the road on the W. Within the SE quadrant lies the church and Stainfield Hall, its gardens and outbuildings presumably occupying the site of the conventual buildings of the priory. Along the stream lies a complex array of fishponds. The principal pond is broad, flat-bottomed, long and curving, with a low island ('c'); both the elevation of the island and the slight damming arrangements at the W end indicate a design for shallow water only. This pond is most probably the old course of the stream, made available by digging the present stream course as an avoidance channel. On the island area between the two ('d') lie three rectangular breeding or sorting tanks of different sizes, and probably the remains of a small building. Three further interlinked sub-rectangular ponds ('e'), with an outlet channel to the W, are arranged around the footings of a large stone building; a small depression on the NE side may be a further breeding tank. The sites of at least three further stone buildings or walled enclosures along the S side of the main pond may relate either to fish management or to other agricultural activities of the priory.

On the hillside S of the precinct on Till, a series of large closes overlying ridge-and-furrow lies along the precinct boundary, though the ditches are continuous with the village property divisions described below. A set of four ponds ('h'), arranged in a tight rectangular configuration set into the rising ground and previously described as a moat, appears to be contemporary with the layout of closes. The ponds lack a reliable running water supply, and their form is quite different from medieval fishponds and more akin to later retting or tanning pits. If this interpretation is correct, such a semi-industrial activity is more likely to belong to the priory than to the village. The suggestion also reduces the village tofts to a more typical clayland and regular scale.

1. VCH *Lincs* II (1906), 131-2; PRO E242/113; Owen 1971, 66; LAO FL Deeds 1295; *VE* IV, 82.

(2) Deserted Village of Stainfield (TF 113729) [24, 124] lies at approximately 16 m above OD on Till, on the crest of rising ground above and alongside the site of Stainfield Priory (1). The earthworks, together with those of the priory, give a clearer picture of the history of the village than does the surviving documentation.

A settlement at Stainfield was recorded in Domesday Book with a minimum total population of 23, and in the Lindsey Survey. Perhaps surprisingly, according to figures that can be obtained from national tax returns, neither the creation of the monastery nor the great house that replaced it, nor the demise of both, had any considerable effect on the crude level of population of Stainfield, unless it was in stifling growth in the 12th and 13th centuries. Certainly there is no record of either what could be seen on the ground as an established fact, that the village remains are those of a planned settlement, or of the likely role of the priory in re-siting it in the 12th century, or even of its later complete clearance. In 1377, 109 individuals paid the Poll Tax, there were 15 taxpayers in 1542-3, 21 households in 1563, 55 communicants in 1676, 12 households in 1705-23, and 14 rising to 30 through the 19th century. In the survey of depopulations of 1607, Sir Philip Tyrwhitt is recorded as enclosing 80 acres of land in Stainfield, and Robert Mellers as occupying the land of a destroyed farmhouse and Charles Metham as letting land and turning its farm into a cottage, and it may well be that the 17th century did see a trough in population resulting from enclosure and emparking that is masked in the general trends. It is the analysis of the earthworks in their topographical setting, however, that gives an important insight into the mobility of settlement and its variety of form that is otherwise quite hidden.[1]

The village remains consist of a broad hollow-way ('f'-'g'), running SW-NE along the brow of the rise, with house sites and closes along its NW side and with further closes, now only visible on air photographs, together with a spread of medieval pottery in the arable land, along the SE. One principal close division runs from the main hollow-way to a gap in the precinct bank and may have provided a subsidiary access to the precinct. The main hollow-way is almost parallel with the precinct boundary; the village tofts and closes are markedly regular, especially for a clayland site, about 50 m in width, and run down to that boundary. The whole layout is placed on top of earlier arable land, as evidenced by the survival of ridge-and-furrow in the closes. These factors combine with the unlikely location in relation to soils, water supply and the church, to argue that the village remains are those of a planned 12th-century settlement re-sited when the priory took over its earlier location. The village must have been finally cleared by Sir Philip Tyrwhitt's emparking and the creation of formal gardens in the first decade of the 17th century. The survey of depopulations may reflect part of that process, though relocation of settlement in scattered farms, in roadside encroachments and on the edge of Stainfield Common rather than crude depopulation appears to have been the effect.

1. Everson 1983, 14-26.

Park Cottages

Stainfield Beck

e

d

c

St Andrew's Church

Stainfield Hall

k

a

b

h

i

j

g

f

Top Houses

Metres
0   100   200

0
Feet   600

[124] *Stainfield (1) Site of Benedictine Priory, (2) Deserted Village, (3) Garden Remains.*

(3) Garden Remains (TF 112731) [24, 124, 125] lie S, E, and W of Stainfield Hall on river terrace sands and gravels and Till at between 6 m and 16 m above OD. They relate to the occupancy of Stainfield by the Tyrwhitt family between the mid 16th century and the late 18th century.

In 1538 the site of the former priory came into the hands of Robert Tyrwhitt, one of the Dissolution Commissioners for the county. Sir Robert does not appear to have occupied Stainfield and family tradition seems to identify his third son Philip (d 1588) as the builder of the first hall, though it was his son Edward, High Sheriff of the county in 1583, who first styled himself 'of Stainfield' and was buried there.[1]

Edward's son Philip (d 1624/5) aspired still higher. He was High Sheriff in 1595–6, waited on James I at Belvoir Castle where he and his son were knighted and quickly availed himself of the newly created rank of baronet in 1611. He obtained a licence to empark at Stainfield in 1607 and the house is believed to have been rebuilt in 1611. The second and third baronets maintained the family's position in the county through tenure of high office and careful marriage. The fourth baronet's support for the Royalist cause and the Catholic faith reduced the estate, but Sir John Tyrwhitt, eighth baronet from 1688 (d 1741), restored earlier tradition, serving as MP for the city of Lincoln and overseeing a major refurbishment of Stainfield Hall. His only child died unmarried in 1760 and in 1766 the estate was finally settled on Thomas Drake of Shardlow and his descendants who for much of the 19th century leased the Hall.[2]

Stainfield Hall at its greatest extent, together with its contemporary gardens, is shown on a plan of 1766 [125].[3] A tentative analysis of the building phases of the house suggests that a 16th-century E-shaped arrangement facing W was extended in the early 17th century to the E at its S end by a new wing giving a S-facing facade. Later, perhaps in the early 18th century, the large block to the N was added as a service quarter to the house.[4] The earlier two phases fit well the work ascribed to the first baronet in 1611 and to his predecessors, while the early 18th century phase can be related to Sir John Tyrwhitt. The brick buildings with stone details of the former stable court have surviving date-stones of 1707 and the walled garden to the E goes with them in material and detailing. The brick church, similarly though more elaborately detailed, is dated 1711; the service wing of the former house fits convincingly into this programme of work and it was certainly in existence by 1726. After 1760 the unoccupied house fell into disrepair and was pulled down in 1773 except for the S wing which was repaired in 1777. The remaining building was reduced to a shell by fire in 1855 and was rebuilt the following year but with a W-facing aspect.

Overlying the S monastic precinct boundary, the large closes and the E end of the village remains, and arranged askew to them, is the rectangular layout of a post-Dissolution formal garden spreading up the hillside from the S facade of the Hall. The most obvious feature is an L-shaped terrace ('i') up to 1.5 m high, designed to carry a raised walk which flanks a square level area named *Bowling Greens* in 1766; a slightly raised N–S path crosses this area. The *Kitchen Garding* to the E appears to have been slightly terraced. Upslope from these formal features the garden extended in a rectangular embanked enclosure ('j'), not shown on the 1766 plan, within which traces of ridge-and-furrow and village closes and a hollow-way survive. This absence of intensive cultivation suggests a formal *Wilderness*. Further ditched closes attached to the W, on its rather than the village alignment, are presumably other contemporary compartments for the garden. This garden is integral with the

position of the S facade of the early house and its style suits perfectly the early 17th-century date suggested by the analysis of the plan of the house and more specifically Sir Philip's documented building work in 1611.

Much of this early garden layout survived in use when the focus was shifted to an E–W axis at the beginning of the 18th century. On the E of the house a brick-walled garden with pilastered piers and stone ball finials was constructed at an angle to the earlier layout. It included an arrangement of rectangular ornamental ponds, one of which ('k') survives in part as a filled-in earthwork. This arrangement not only broke the enclosed nature of the earlier garden and gave a view out, but also allowed a subtle transition from the alignment of the earlier garden and integration with it. This is all depicted on the 1766 plan, but the plan ignores a further area of formal emparking which is presumably also of early 18th-century date. This lies to the W of the house, where two low banks, each broad enough to have been planted with a double row or avenue of trees, form a splayed Bridgemanesque design overlying the SW corner of the monastic precinct. They open out a Romantic vista W over low-lying land to the ruins of Barlings Abbey in the near distance and Lincoln Cathedral on the horizon. There are traces of at least one cross-bank within the splay, if this is not a feature of the monastic precinct, as well as a terminal bank along the modern roadside. The date of about 1710 for these modifications is provided by date-stones and contemporary evidence already cited in connection with the house, but most strikingly by the dated rebuilding of the church, 90 degrees out of liturgical alignment. The church thereby forms a landscape feature integral to the design of parkland and house by presenting a symmetrical façade to the approaching visitor.

1. *Cal LPFD Hen VIII* XIII, pt 1 (1892), 141; Hodgett 1975, 55; LCL Ross MSS, X, *ad loc*; LAO LCC Wills 1590, 445; Maddison 1902–6 III, 1021–2.
2. Maddison, as note 1; LCL ROSS MSS, as note 1; Holmes 1980, 147, 149, 220.
3. LAO TYR 1/5/8.
4. LAO TYR 1/5/1.
5. Marrat 1816, 62; LCL Ross MSS, as note 1.

STAINTON LE VALE

(1) Settlement Remains (TF 170944) [126, 127], formerly part of the village of Stainton le Vale, extend for 1.6 km along a chalk valley draining E between 76 m and 91 m above OD.

The complexity of the surviving earthworks show that Stainton is similar to other Wolds villages, in that it is not always clear what the individual details mean. Yet in the wider context there may be some connection between the overall pattern of earthworks and the medieval tenurial arrangements of four major manors.

Like many of the villages of the Wolds valleys, Stainton had a higher recorded population in 1086 at a minimum of 39 persons than at any time until the later 20th century. This had fallen by the early 14th century to 21 and 16 taxpayers, between half and three-quarters of the wapentake average. Post-Black Death relief in 1352 was 98.1 per cent, the Poll Tax of 1377 listed 60 individuals over 14 years of age and there were at least 10 households in 1428. Reliefs in the 15th century of about 20 per cent perhaps indicate little change, and certainly the settlement emerges in the mid 16th century with only 13 taxpayers in 1542–3 and 16 households in 1563, even after the release of some monastic property. The survey of depopulations in 1607 recorded no major conversion of arable or

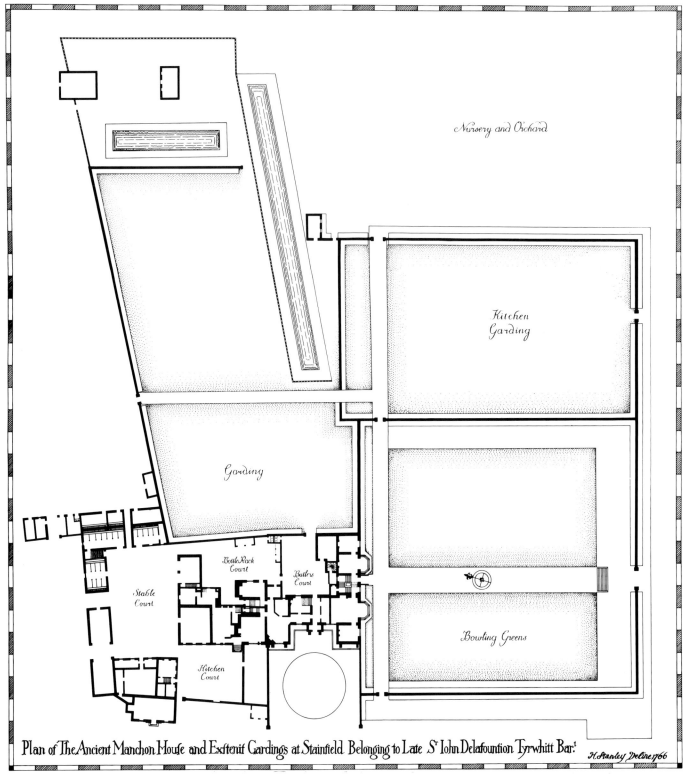

Plan of The Ancient Manchon House and Extensif Gardings at Stainfield Belonging to Late S.r John Delafountion Tyrwhitt Bar.t

H.Stanley Deline 1766

Nursery and Orchard

Kitchen Garding

Garding

Bowle Rack Court

Butlers Court

Stable Court

Kitchen Court

Bowling Greens

[125] *Stainfield (3) Garden Remains 1766.*

engrossing, but piecemeal change involving the abandonment of four farms.[1] The effects of this are still visible in the numbers of communicants in 1676, 65, and of households in the period 1705–23, being about 11 and 12. When in 1780 the parishioners petitioned to reduce their ancient church to a single cell, they claimed the population comprised 'only...two farmers besides cottagers and families'.[2]

Domesday Book and the Lindsey Survey show Stainton shared between four holdings, each reckoned a manor. Of these one came into the hands of Thornton Abbey and when Thornton College was

178

[**126**] *Stainton le Vale (1) from the N. The remains of Stainton le Vale village are probably one of the most extensive medieval earthwork complexes in the country. They stretch for almost 2 km along a narrow chalk valley. They seem to represent the results of a complex tenurial pattern combined with a relatively high 10th to 11th-century village population.*

dissolved in 1546 it was granted to Robert Tyrwhitt. Another late 11th-century manor was held by the Scotney family until the early 14th century while the largest of the Domesday manors was held by the Alnetos in the 12th and 13th centuries and then by the Buslingthorpes. In 1374 the holding in Margaret de Buslingthorpe's hands was 'a messuage and a carucate of land called Westhall'. The Percys' holding that formed the fourth Domesday manor became part of the division of the Percy barony known as the Morers fee. In the later medieval period the three secular manors passed to non-residents.[3]

The settlement earthworks were arranged around and cut into by a series of roads or former roads, which are clearly the result of a number of long-term changes. It seems likely that there has always been a road along the N side of the valley on or near the line of the modern road. A slightly hollowed terrace in the area of natural slips within Tunnel Plantation, for example, suggests that the road has moved around slightly and its earlier exit eastwards from the settlement is marked by multiple hollowing NE of the church.

On the S side of the valley, the settlement is contained within a continuous but irregular boundary, which is apparently made up of sections of road giving access to various settlement elements and linked together by lesser bank or ditch features. Thus what may once have been a hollow-way ('a'–'b') aligns with a surviving lane ('c'–'d') which leads to an extant farm and is shown as a road in use in 1824. At its W end ('d') it gave access on to the top of the Wolds. Its line is now blocked by a bank crossing the N-facing slope of the S branch of the valley. A further lane still in use in 1824 struck N at right angles from the existing lane ('c'–'d') crossing the valley to meet the lane E of the Old Rectory. Its course is not clear in the earthworks but is marked by a field boundary. The abandonment

of these roads by the mid 19th century was balanced by the creation of the present road S, past South Farm, that slices through settlement remains to the S of the lane ('c'–'b').

The valley's NW branch had a prominent terraced way ('i') leading towards Stainton Hall along the length of its SW lip, in addition to a disjointed series of features on the slope. From the roadside spring ('e'), a ditch with a bank on the downslope, possibly a hollow-way, continues the course of the bank ('d'–'e') along the contour towards a large spring head ('h') and forms the SW side of a well-defined settlement block ('f'). To the W of this a block ('g') was first defined by a way or boundary of similar form, later superceded by water channels surrounding the same core area.

Roads crossing the valley at right angles are also in evidence. At the E end of the village a deep hollow-way ('j') may once have continued to link up with the road on the N side of the valley. The deeply cut N–S lane by the church may have crossed the valley to link with the E–W hollow-way ('a'–'b') which coincides with a bridle road shown on early OS plans. The present road (N of 'c') may have formerly crossed the main valley less obliquely and be represented by the earthworks resembling a causeway ('k'). The modern road down the S branch valley too may enter the settlement on an old alignment since it is deeply cut near the spring ('e'); it defines the SE side of the block to its NW ('f') and has abandoned buildings and property plots fronting on its SE. It too probably crossed the valley to join the northern terrace-way directly, for where it now turns E by the Old Rectory to head straight to the church, partly as a road in use and partly as a sharply scarped hollow-way on the same alignment, it cuts through and truncates settlement closes.

These closes, that occupy the strip between the northern terrace-

179

way and the stream and run from the church in the E probably to the point W of the Old Rectory ('l') where the narrowing of the valley squeezes them out, form one recognizable element in this early settlement layout.

Other elements identified as compact blocks without the close divisions and house sites typical of village remains raise the possibility of identification with the four medieval manorial holdings and of a settlement pattern of distinct nuclei which may have been joined by infill to produce what is superficially a long single village. Four manorial blocks may be tentatively recognized.

First, the fields N, E, S and SW of Manor Farm may represent paddocks associated with the manor here. The close containing Manor Farm had the name 'Old Hall' in 1854. In the field to the SW, the complex foundations of large stone buildings arranged around a courtyard ('m'), with access from the W now blocked by modern housing, clearly marks a manorial site. It is defined on the S by a deep straight hollow, perhaps a leat formerly leading from a spring in the hillside; a branch of this leads into the area of buildings, perhaps to a mill site on the E side of them, while the main channel turns N ('b') to feed a strongly embanked contour leat ('n'). Taken with the hollow-way ('a'–'b') these arrangements create a long oblong close – perhaps divided into two by a low bank, but otherwise without sign of buildings or cultivation – and a further embanked close nearer the buildings. Parallel with the stream are at least two pairs of large and small fishponds, and actually on the stream, although more difficult to interpret because of its straightening and the extended farmyard, there may have been two or three further ponds created by low dams and perhaps containing small islands. Continuity of features between this field and that to the E may mean that the two formed a single unit. This whole group of earthworks might be identified with the Scotney holding as the latter originally held the larger part of the advowson of the church which lies at the N corner of the block.

The earthworks SW of the Old Rectory ('f') form another well-marked block bounded by the hollow-way and a bank on the hillside, and by the stream in the valley bottom. The inside is divided into long closes, in the E half arranged along the contour and in the W half across the slope. These could be village closes rather than divisions of a larger unit and there are hints of buildings fronting the hollow-way, but the only clear group is a well-preserved courtyard farm ('f').

To the W another block ('g') is apparently defined on the W by a loop of a hollow-way. However, this extraordinarily deep and anomalous feature is almost certainly a later alteration designed to channel water from the spring ('h') along the contour back up the valley to the pond ('o') perched on the slope, and thence down into the upper of the two mill ponds on the stream. This arrangement cuts clearly across the early neatly rectangular block of properties, that extended SW up the valley side and which contains traces of ridge-and-furrow overlain in one place by a building. Below these closes, in the valley bottom, the foundations of numerous buildings lie adjacent to two large dams on the stream ('p' and 'q'). These dams are over 2 m high. They are now breached, but the outlines of their long oval ponds, probably to power mills, are clearly marked by scarps.

The fourth manorial unit may be represented by those earthworks around and SE of Stainton Hall and can be tentatively interpreted as the site of the Alneto holding of 1086. The group of large closes lying immediately E of the Hall garden ('r') may belong to this settlement block whose core is represented only by slight indeterminate earthworks discernible on the green NE of the Hall,

around a former spring. The earthworks of a small farm in the SW corner of the surviving closes and the prominent terrace-way serving it may mark the fringe of this settlement or a late intrusion into the closes.

In the centre of the earthwork remains, S and SE of the Old Rectory and separating the first and second manorial units, are earthworks more typical of former village closes and buildings. The latter are particularly well marked ('s', 't', 'u' and 'v') and are arranged around central yards. Along the S of the hollow-way ('a'–'b'), and continuing E into the next field are a series of amorphous earthworks perhaps forming closes along the valley side but with no clear traces of buildings; they may in part overlie former arable and represent village growth around the manorial block to the N.

Overall, a pattern of four nuclei of manorial type does emerge in these earthworks, with, in the centre, to the S and SE of the Old Rectory and along the N and S sides of the E nuclei, indications of properties which perhaps represent areas of peasant holdings associated with these manorial blocks.

1. BL Add MS 11574, ff79, 86, 91.
2. LAO Additional Register 3, f115r; FAC 4/1/A–B.
3. *Lincs DB* 22/32, 28/5, 30/17, 40/5; *LS* 7/1, 7/11, 7/12, 7/17; Dugdale 1817–30 VI, 326–8; *Cal LPFD Hen VIII* XXI pt 1 (1908), 378; Gibbons 1888, 67; *VE* IV, 58, 78; Foster and Major 1931–73 IV, 215–6; *Book of Fees* I, 158, 212; II, 1019, 1074, 1095; *Feudal Aids* III, 172, 226, 357; Nottingham University, Middleton Deeds, 3519/2, 3519/7, 3522, 3523; *Cal IPM* I (1904), 233, 255; II (1906), 137; X (1921), 21; XIV (1952), 6; Davis 1914b, 106, 161; Davis 1914a, 20, 43; Davis, F. N. *et al* 1925, 76, 84; Hill 1948, 18, 208, 246; Clay 1963, 284–5.
4. OS 1st edn 1 in sheet 83; LAO TSJ 12/9.

(2) Deserted Village of Orford (TF 198946) [128] lies towards the E end of the parish, on the N side of the valley of the E-flowing beck, on chalk, between 60 m and 70 m above OD. The village was formerly the centre of a separate parish. It may have been deliberately relocated in this position after the Premonstratensian priory (3) had been established on its earlier site.

Two holdings occur in the Lindsey Survey of the early 12th century, both of which may then be identified with Domesday manors recorded under Binbrook. No estimate of population is possible.[1] Orford appears as a member of Binbrook in 1316 and in the early 14th-century subsidies 6 named taxpayers represent barely 20 per cent of the average for the wapentake, presumably because of the extent of monastic land. Even on this low level, reliefs of 75–85 per cent occur not only immediately after the Black Death in 1352, but throughout the 15th century, and in 1563 only one household is recorded. Yet because of Orford Priory's dominant interests, which lay outside these returns, they may be a poor guide to the population represented by the settlement remains.

By the second half of the 12th century there was certainly a parish church at Orford, which was then granted to Orford Priory. A church is listed in 1255 and 1342 but not taxed on either occasion and there is no entry in the parish tax of 1428.[2]

The remains of the village are in good condition, but the surviving earthworks have an apparently curious arrangement. The main feature of the site is a line of well-preserved house sites ('a'–'b') extending along the NW of the site with, in most cases, small closes or paddocks bounded by low scarps extending down the hillside behind them. This layout suggests that these houses once lay along a street immediately to the NW but no trace of this exists in the present arable field and indeed parts of at least two house sites extend NW under the modern cultivation lynchet which forms the boundary of the site. It is probable that there was once a street, being part of a valley-side road between Stainton and Swinhope, but that it was abandoned after the desertion of the village and its area incorporated into the adjacent arable land. Slight traces of a former headland, now a low spread ridge extending SW–NE, indicate that the present arable was once part of the common fields.

If this presumed street did once exist, then it might be assumed that other houses and closes lay on its NW side. Although the sites of any houses themselves would now be buried by the hill-wash and soil-creep of the present arable, some archaeological material should be expected from the area of their attached closes, especially as the modern ploughing is now cutting into the upper layers of the underlying chalk. Yet no finds, except for three sherds of 13th or 14th-century pottery, have been made. It thus appears that the houses at Orford were confined solely to the SE of the supposed main street and that the village had a plan of a type recognized elsewhere in Lincolnshire and Northamptonshire.[3] At all these places, an element of conscious planning may be envisaged; in this instance it may have arisen from the relocation of village properties taken into the priory's precinct, like the *mansura* called 'Colecroft' given for the sisters' cemetery.[4]

Extending SE down the valley sides are two subsidiary hollow-ways, once presumably connected with the main street. That to the SW ('c') extends almost to the stream where it meets a much larger curving hollow-way ('q') which divides the village site from that of Orford Priory to the SW. The former hollow-way has at least five building platforms on its SW side, associated with small closes. The second hollow-way, near the centre of the village, ('d'), extends only a short distance down the hillside but it too has building platforms near it.

To the SE of the latter hollow-way and extending SW is a block of very slight ridge-and-furrow. This appears to post-date the main village earthworks for it overlies an earlier bank and curving scarp and may well have destroyed closes once belonging to some of the houses lining the main street in the area between the subsidiary hollow-ways ('e').

Towards the NE end of the site a more irregular arrangement of closes, including some large building platforms and former ponds may be the site of a late medieval courtyard farmstead ('f').

1. *Lincs DB* 18/7, 57/6; *LS* 7/5, 7/8.
2. Stenton 1920, 236; Lunt 1926, 236; *Nonarum Inquisitiones* (1807), 258.
3. See Croxby (Thoresway (3)); RCHME 1975, Raunds (19); 1981, Braunston (3), Stanford-on-Avon (4).
4. *Cal Chart R 1300–26* (1908), 386.

(3) Site of Premonstratensian Priory and post-medieval House and Garden at Orford (TF 195945) [128] lies immediately S of the now derelict Priory Farm on the NW of the valley, on chalk, between 60 m and 74 m above OD.

The site is that of a house of Premonstratensian nuns, an off-shoot of Newsham Abbey, whose history is largely unknown.[1] Its foundation here may have led to the relocation of the village of Orford (2). There were a prioress and seven nuns when the house was dissolved in 1539, and the site was granted to Robert Tyrwhitt.[2] The Tyrwhitts let the estate, as did their successors, and it seems likely that a series of residences occupied the site. This latter occupation has obscured much of the earlier monastic layout.

Though the site of the priory itself is confined to the NW side of the present stream, its associated fishponds extend across it. This situation is the result of complex technical and administrative alterations in medieval times. The parish boundary between Orford

and Binbrook follows the line of the stream along the whole of the valley except in the section opposite the priory. Here, the Orford boundary extends SE of the beck, thus including in Orford parish a small area of land which must have originally been part of Binbrook. Why this transfer took place is unknown, though it may have been connected with the early gift of land to the priory by the de Aubigny family, some of whose land lay in Binbrook parish. The land on the SE side of the valley is largely covered by lobes of soliflucted material. There are no traces of ploughing or any other activity in this area beyond recent drainage ditches. Traces of ridge-and-furrow, presumably the remains of the common fields of Binbrook, lie above these landslips.

The modern stream, cut in a deep straight channel, is clearly a recent alteration. The earlier line is shown on OS 25 in plans of the county series and earlier estate maps, flowing in a meandering course to the NW of the modern one ('l'–'k'). However, this stream was not in the valley bottom and must itself have been an artificial cut. The original stream course can just be detected SE of the present stream and S of the fishponds ('g') as a low marshy area. It is likely that the old stream to the NW of the fishponds was cut as an intake channel for the ponds themselves and that water entered the ponds at their NW corner and perhaps returned to the original stream in the SE corner.

In addition there are two other watercourses associated with the priory. The larger, which can be traced as an artificial channel SW into the Stainton valley, was, up to the mid 20th century, the intake leat for a water-mill, the remains of which occupy the NW corner of the buildings of Priory Farm. The water approached the mill in the broad channel running parallel to the contours ('h'), passed through it and flowed via a culvert into a broad channel ('i') running SE to join the present stream. Though these leats were certainly used by the 18th or 19th-century mill, their origins are much older. The contour intake channel has been cut through an older leat, the remains of which lie on its NW side, while the outflow channel extends further NW than the mill culvert. This suggests that both inlet and outlet leats were merely reused by the mill and that they were once part of the priory's water supply. However, the original outlet leat probably followed a different but parallel course slightly to the SW ('j'–'k') since the present channel cuts through earthwork features which continue to the NE.

Another watercourse, now a shallow embanked ditch, notable for its straight alignment ('l'), also approaches the site from the SW. It is no longer clear how this leat entered the site, as its NE end has been cut by a ditch which is probably modern. No date or function can be assigned to it, though it may have served a range of buildings ('p') and therefore be part of the priory's water supply.

The majority of surviving earthworks occupy a roughly rectangular area SW of the existing farm buildings. A large mound ('m'), overlying earlier foundations, incorporates a series of rectangular depressions or rooms, and scraps of tile and brick confirm that this is the site of a post-Dissolution house. Other features may be associated with it, including immediately to the NE ('n') a flat rectangular platform, bounded on three sides by a broad ditch, in the centre of which is a rectangular flat-topped mound 0.5 m high. On the unditched SE side, on land falling to the position of the old stream, are some very slight features including a low bank. It is possible that these earthworks represent a garden feature associated with the post-Dissolution house. Mounds and platforms just N of the house site may also be associated with it since they block the line of the channel-like feature ('j'–'k') which, as noted above, may have been a monastic leat. To the W are some

[**128**] *Stainton le Vale (2) Deserted Village of Orford, (3) Site of Premonstratensian Priory at Orford.*

rectangular and curved depressions ('o') up to 1.5 m deep, which are likely to be former fishponds, fed from the leat at their NW ends. There are also the foundations of several large barn-like structures on the N side of the depressions.

Within the SW quadrant two ranges of stone buildings ('p'), in part visible only as a rectangular pattern of parch-marks, are probably part of the conventual arrangement of the priory, the rest of which is obscured by reuse of the site by the later house.

Since the outlet channel of the mill ('i') slices through earthworks, it seems possible that the precinct of the priory extended NE to encompass the area of Priory Farm and the paddock to its SE. The degraded earthworks here confirm this by defining the limit of the precinct. For within the paddock, apart from a low bank and some indeterminate scarps, the only feature is a broad hollow-way ('q') which runs NW from the modern stream and separates the land to the SW from the remains of the village of Orford to the NE (2). The N end of this hollow-way is now blocked, but further N and NE of the farm buildings it reappears as a terrace-way ('r'). It may once either have run on N, or turned NW as the existing earthworks indicate, and continued towards Stainton village.

The S part of the site, in the valley bottom, is occupied by a group of fishponds ('g'). The modern stream has been cut across the centre of the group and spoil from this cutting has been dumped over the N part of the ponds and has almost obliterated their form except for external ditches on the SW and NE. On the S side of the modern stream at least four rectangular or L-shaped ponds up to 1.5 m deep are linked to each other and an outer perimeter ditch by shallow channels.

1. Colvin 1951, 328–30; Colvin 1954, 83ff; *LS* 7/5.
2. VCH *Lincs* II (1906), 209; *Cal LPFD Hen VIII* XIV pt 2 (1895), 298.

(4) Garden Remains (TF 203947) **[129]** lie around Orford House on chalk at about 60 m above OD.

Nothing is known of the early history of the site but the earthworks suggest that a 16th or 17th-century house of some pretension stood here. The first clear evidence for the house is not until 1740 when a substantial residence with a symmetrical façade is shown on the fringe of the Binbrook Enclosure Map.[1] By 1854 the house had been substantially remodelled and was further enlarged later in the century.[2]

The earthworks are the remains of a former garden whose layout suggests a late 16th or 17th-century date. In plan these remains form a series of rectangular compartments which lie together in a square block aligned on the house, which is located in the N corner. The NW compartment is defined by very low broad banks on the SW and NW cut at the NE end by a ha-ha of the same date as the later 19th-century extension of the house. A low circular mound in the angle of the banks might be a tree mound or could mark the site of a small garden house. A hollow-way or ditch to the SW, alongside the modern road, while possibly an earlier road alignment, may be a ramp giving external access from the upper to the lower garden. The northern or upper part of the garden is separated from the southern part which lies on the flood-plain of the stream by a steep natural scarp now partly wooded. Below this scarp a straight, sharply defined canal-like feature, 1 m deep and now dry, runs the width of the lower garden and divides it into two sections. Water was fed into its SW end by a leat from the stream, and controlled by a sluice in a dam at the NE end, with an outlet channel into the stream beyond. The standing walls here are in local yellow brick,

presumably replacing earlier walls. Along its S edge and turning down along the side of the leat is a broad raised walk only 0.3 m high, with a semicircular platform protruding precisely half-way along. A similar almost square platform at the E end of the walk is overlain by the foundations of later buildings.

The linear scarps in the field to the SW are probably medieval and later tracks.

1. LAO Binbrook Parish Council 9.
2. LAO Binbrook Council 13, TSJ 12/9; White 1842, 406; 1856, 474; 1882, 713, 770.

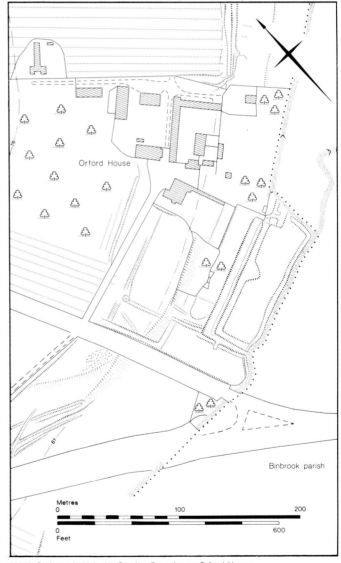

[**129**] *Stainton le Vale (4) Garden Remains at Orford House.*

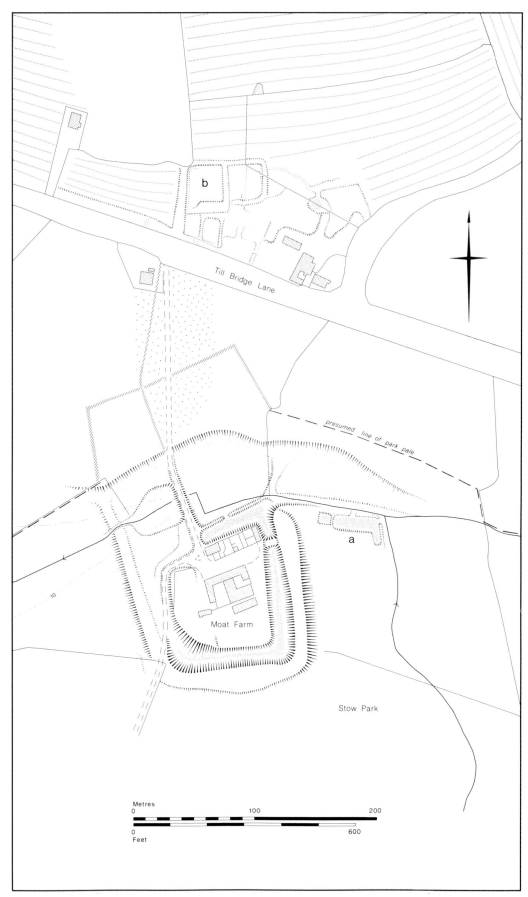

b

Till Bridge Lane

presumed line of park pale

a

10

Moat Farm

Stow Park

Metres
0   100   200

0   600
Feet

[**130**] *Stow (3) Moated Site of Bishop's Palace, (4) Deer Park, (5) Deserted Settlement of Stow Park.*

(3) Moated Site of Bishop's Palace (SK 867809) [40, 130] lies at about 13 m above OD on clay with limestone, on the S side of a shallow valley draining W. The residence with its attached deer park (4) is well documented as a place of retreat, entertainment and centre of episcopal administration throughout the Middle Ages and particularly in the 13th and 14th centuries.[1]

The site is first clearly documented in 1170–1 and about 1186 it forms the setting for Giraldus Cambrensis's tale of St Hugh's pet swan, when it is described as 'delightfully surrounded with woods and ponds'. Giraldus knew the site personally and the flight of the resident flock of swans in the face of the marvellous newcomer of the tale may accurately reflect the part function of the fishponds as a swannery.[2] King John stayed here in 1200, presumably one of many distinguished visitors.[3] In 1336 the King gave Bishop Henry Burghersh licence to crenelate the dwelling-house of his manor at Stow and this has, probably correctly, been taken to refer to this site at Stow Park rather than a manorial residence in Stow village.[4] The residence remained in the bishop's hands until its alienation with much of the other property of the see by Bishop Holbeach at the beginning of the reign of Edward VI.[5] It may then have been used at least partly by the grandson of the Bishop but by the late 18th century Armstrong's map marks the site as 'ruins'.[6] An estate map of the first half of the 19th century and the Tithe Map of 1838 both show much of the complex suite of ponds that is now so degraded by ploughing. Centrally within the inner enclosure at that date stood an L-shaped building.[7]

The site of the palace is represented by a moat whose interior is masked by an abandoned 19th-century farmhouse and outbuildings. This internal area is bounded by a massive ditch surviving to a depth of 3.0 m, that has provided material for an equally impressive outer bank, well preserved on the E but denuded by ploughing on the S. On the W, the bank diverges from the main enclosure and forms a dam across the valley, but has been lowered to a height of 0.75 m by ploughing. Ploughing has also severely damaged a similarly sited bank, now only 0.5 m high, opposite the NE corner of the moat. Between these earthworks, a causeway, 2 m high and probably an original element, carries the track from Till Bridge Lane and gives access into the inner enclosure. It is likely that these three barriers were constructed to create a series of broad ponds on the N side of the palace, the effect of which would have been strikingly ornamental, flanking the entrance, as well as productive. The W pond has had a later and smaller pond cut through its bottom. Two further ponds ('a'), by contrast, are small, neatly dug and linked to the stream, and may have served as fish-breeding or sorting tanks. The detailed relationship of the moat with the associated park pale is now unclear as a result of ploughing.

1. *Cal Chart R 1226–57* (1903), 185–6; *Cal Fine R 1327–37* (1913), 103, 371; LAO Bishops' Registers *passim*.
2. *Pipe Roll Soc* XVI (1893), 122; Dimock 1877, 73.
3. *Rot Obl et Fin*, 100.
4. *Cal Pat R 1334–8* (1895), 330; Thompson 1912, 301.
5. *Cal Pat R 1547–8* (1924), 184.
6. LCL Ross MSS I Well wapentake, 61 and pedigree between 70–71.
7. LAO K184; BRACE 19/2.

(4) Deer Park (centred SK 864798) [40, 130] occupies the whole of an almost rectangular SW projection of the parish and covers some 275 ha, all on clay with limestone or Till at 7.5 m to 15 m above OD. Closely associated with the moated Bishop's Palace (3),

it is first documented at the end of the 12th century but undoubtedly existed earlier. It is thereafter mentioned regularly in documents until the 18th century.[1]

The E and W boundaries of the park survive as large tree-covered banks following the parish boundary, up to 1 m high and 8 m across with water-filled dykes on either side giving an overall dimension of about 15 m. The S boundary also coincides with the parish boundary, and the modern road following it is markedly raised, perhaps from lying on a former park bank. On the NE and N the details of the circuit are less clear but it is most likely that it followed the parish boundary to the point in the NE where the stream that feeds the moat springs westwards.

1. BL Cott Ch II.14 (1-6); Queen's College, Oxford MS 366; Massingberd 1898, 304; Varley 1951, 71–2; *VE* IV, 6; Cole 1915, 151–2; Cole 1917, 120–2; *Cal Pat R 1367–70* (1913), 154; LAO LCC 1630–1, 467.

(5) Deserted Settlement (SK 867808) [40, 130], site of the hamlet of Stow Park, lies to the N of the moated site of the Bishop's Palace (3), on either side of Till Bridge Lane.

A named settlement of Stow Park is recorded from at least the early 14th century and in the 15th century as an ancillary to Stow, without any estimate of its size. In an early 13th-century survey of Stow Manor nine men holding ten tofts are listed under Stow Park, at least three of them with names – William son of Hugh 'gardinar', Swein 'novus carpentarius' and Geoffrey 'kocus' – that suggest specialized skills perhaps associated with the bishop's service. Wills and inventories continue to identify inhabitants of Stow Park throughout the 17th and into the 18th centuries, though by that date it is perhaps more likely that scattered farms rather than a hamlet are in question.[1]

On the N side of the shallow valley N of the moated site the farm track probably runs slightly E of the original medieval approach to the palace, the course of which may be represented by linear marks on a 1946 air photograph.[2] Field-walking in 1977 and 1981 produced a spread of medieval pottery of 13th to 14th-century date, building material and animal bone on either side of the farm track, and there are hints on air photographs that part of this occupation area may have lain in an outer enclosure or forecourt N of the surviving moat. A 19th-century newspaper report of excavations in the field adjoining the moat recorded that extensive foundations of buildings had been discovered.[3] The Bishop's lease of Stow Park in 1534 draws a clear distinction between 'the scyte of the said manor wythe all inner howses ther' and 'alle oute howses to the same scyte belongynge'.[4]

To the N of Till Bridge Lane the line of the farm track is continued by a hollow-way, with small closes ('b') attached to its E side. It is uncertain whether the origin of this settlement was wholly dependent on the palace as it appears, or whether the moat was built on the edge of a pre-existing settlement.

1. Massingberd 1898, 299–343: now dated 1206 × 1230 in Varley 1951, 69–70; LAO wills and inventories dated 1641–1725.
2. RAF VAP CPE/UK1880/2285.
3. *Stamford Mercury,* 18 March 1853.
4. Cole 1917, 120–1.

(7) Deserted Village of Coates (SK 911833) [25, 131, 132] lies at about 10 m above OD on clay with limestone and Till. Though now administratively within Stow, Coates was formerly a separate parish.

Coates has a minimum recorded population of 6 in 1086 and its

Fox Covert

Grange Farm

Hall Farm

St Edith's Church

Coates Hall

a

Metres
0   100   200

Feet
0   600

[**131**] *Stow (7) Deserted Village of Coates.*

[132] *Stow (7). The deserted village of Coates from the NE. The well-marked hollow-way or former main street is clearly visible. Coates was depleted by the Black Death and appears to have been finally abandoned in the late 14th or early 15th century.*

13 taxpayers in the early 14th century were only about 40 per cent of the average for the wapentake. A high level of relief in 1352 suggests the serious impact of the Black Death, and this is confirmed by only 17 persons over 14 years of age recorded in 1377 and exemption from the parish tax with less than 10 households in 1428. Thereafter Coates is commonly recorded with its neighbour Ingham rather than separately. Only 20 communicants were returned in 1603, barely 16 per cent of the rural average for the archdeaconry, and 18 in 1676. The record of 11 taxpayers listed in 1640 is an anomaly, perhaps related to the residence of substantial landowners. There were only 4 and 2 households at the beginning of the 18th century, which rose to no higher than 10 households throughout the 19th century. Most of these post-medieval figures presumably relate to people living in dispersed farmsteads.

During the late 12th century the church and land at Coates was given by Peter de Coates to the Premonstratensian abbey of Welbeck, Notts, which retained possession until the Dissolution. Whether this monastic holding could ever properly be termed a grange it nevertheless may have effectively secured the survival of the settlement, albeit much reduced, through the later medieval period.[1]

A complex history emerges from analysis of the settlement remains suggesting a development from an early nucleus near the church with a regular single-row extension on one side of the former main village street and with later additional or replacement properties extended over former arable on the other.

In detail the field evidence suggests that the W end of the settlement may have been later occupied by a manorial block now partly covered by Coates Hall and possibly Hall Farm. An L-shaped moat up to 1.5 m deep, and perhaps a remnant of a feature that originally surrounded the block, survives SW of the church, which would then have lain within this manorial enclosure. In view of the documentary evidence the moat may rather be part of the enclosure of a monastic grange, or even an ornamental feature belonging to a post-Dissolution residence. There is no evidence that the medieval settlement ever continued W beyond the moat, and field-walking of this area has produced only a few abraded sherds of medieval pottery. This possible western block may have caused the curious bend ('a') in the hollow-way of the former village street. To the NE medieval pottery, animal bones and dark earth visible in the plough soil, show that the road was flanked by former properties. As the hollowed village street continues E into pasture it is similarly flanked by properties, here surviving as well-defined and regular ditched closes. Their interiors contain platforms and hollows representing former buildings and yards. The backs of the closes on the S side of the street, though blurred by ploughing, seem to terminate along a line parallel to the street itself, whereas those closes on the N side finish on a ditch which converges eastwards towards the street.

Church Farm

Manor Farm

St Edward's
Church

The Manor House

Sudbrooke House

Metres
0   100   200
0   600
Feet

Sudbrooke Park

[**133**] *Sudbrooke (1) Settlement Remains.*

These differences may reflect a development from a single row on the S side of the street with additional and later properties on the N side. Attached to the back of the latter, and at the E end possibly extending to the street itself, is a series of small fields or paddocks, defined by narrow ditches and apparently laid out, like the closes, on top of ridge-and-furrow.

1. LCL Ross MSS IV, 135; PRO E 242/113; *VE* V, 170–1; Lunt 1926, 252; VCH *Notts* II (1910), 131, 135.

SUDBROOKE

(1) **Settlement Remains (TF 033758)** [133], formerly part of the village of Sudbrooke, lie at 17 m above OD on Cornbrash.

Sudbrooke was held at least from 1086 by Peterborough Abbey as part of its estate centred on its manor at Fiskerton.[1] No figure for the minimum recorded population in Domesday Book can be arrived at because of shared entries and because almost all the subsequent population records for Sudbrooke include Holme, a small settlement deserted well before the 17th century (2). The parish was apparently populous in the pre-Black Death period since 31 and 30 taxpayers are named in 1327–8 and in 1332–3, one-fifth above the wapentake average. The impact of the Black Death seems to have been marked and to have been followed by a long period of population stagnation and perhaps decline. Relief of a third was allowed in 1352, but only 71 persons paid the Poll Tax in Sudbrooke and Holme in 1377. Nevertheless there are at least 10 households in 1428, reliefs in the mid-century were less than 20 per cent and in 1539 9 names from Sudbrooke were produced for the Lindsey Musters. There were 14 taxpayers for the 1542–3 subsidy, while 8 tenants, not necessarily all resident, are named in a mid 16th-century rental of Peterborough's estate. There were only 40 communicants in 1603, less than one-third of the rural average for the archdeaconry, and 42 in 1676. In 1662, 11 persons paid the Hearth Tax, but by the early 18th century the parish had increased to 18–20 households.

The village of Sudbrooke may have been made up of two distinct elements of which only the N one survives as a focus for dwellings. These are arranged on both sides of an E–W street, which bends at the W end to skirt the churchyard. The Tithe Map of 1838 shows a regular pattern of properties on the N side of the street and running E from the church; this is now obscured by modern development. Some of the boundaries were still visible on air photographs taken in 1947.[2]

The area of earthworks to the S was surveyed in 1978, immediately before its destruction. While some followed existing field boundaries, a N–S ladder pattern of about six closes contained some traces of buildings. They may represent a S extension from the focus around the church. Alternatively there may have been a separate focus here which may have expanded and linked up with the other. This interpretation might account for the fact that on the N the earthworks cut through broad ridge-and-furrow.

Field-walking in 1981 produced pottery ranging in date from medieval to modern. Much of the later material may have been brought from elsewhere to fill former ponds, but in at least two areas this seemed not to be the case and indicated that the village properties may have survived here into the the post-medieval period.

1. *Lincs DB* 8/2; *LS* 3/14; Baker (nd), 26–7, 34.
2. LAO A41; RAF VAP CPE/UK2012/4155-7.

SWALLOW

(1) **Moated Site and Settlement Remains (TA 175030)** [134], formerly part of Swallow village, lie on either side of a broad chalk valley at 50 m above OD. The place-name evidently refers to the behaviour of the E-flowing stream which emerges from an underground source to the W of the settlement and disappears again immediately to the NE. The remains indicate a highly complex village, the analysis of which is obscured by much surviving or modern housing covering vital areas. However, the village was clearly in some sense a polyfocal settlement with at least two or probably three principal nuclei which may be related to the medieval tenurial arrangements.

As at Cabourne (1), documentary evidence for Swallow shows considerable tenurial complexity in the late 11th century with seven entries in Domesday Book, perhaps three of them reckoned as manors. By the early 13th century a manor in Swallow had been granted to the Augustinian abbey of Wellow in Grimsby, and a second estate to the Cistercian nuns of Nun Cotham Priory. Both were apparently organized as demesne manors or granges which appear to have lain within the village rather than elsewhere in the parish.[1] Three other monastic houses, the Yorkshire Cistercian nunnery of Nun Appleton, Thornton Abbey and the Priory of St Leonard in Grimsby, also held small amounts of land in Swallow.[2]

Swallow's Domesday population of at least 35 households does not appear to be matched in recorded sources until this century. Nevertheless the 26 and 31 taxpayers of the 14th century are close to the average numbers for the area. There is a hint of the importance of grazing, however, in a purchase in 1338 of two and a half sacks of wool from the rector of Swallow. In 1372 Wellow Abbey's manor had been reduced from two ploughs in tillage to one, as at Cabourne, but the Poll Tax count of 110 persons over 14 years of age perhaps indicates some recovery from the 75 per cent relief in 1352, and the settlement must have been comfortably above the level of exemption for the parish tax in 1428. Some reliefs continued in the 15th century, and in about 1480 Robert Burgh and his son leased two tofts lying waste and 14 acres in Swallow from Wellow Abbey.[3]

The settlement emerges in the 16th century with 17 and 18 taxpayers in 1524 and 1525, 12 taxpayers in 1542–3 and 20 households in 1563, a figure which had only increased slightly by the beginning of the 18th century. The survey of depopulations in 1607 records a conversion of a total of six farms into cottages and occupation of their lands by three individuals, but apparently no outright decay of property or new conversion of arable. Taken with the figures of only 76 communicants in 1603 and 45 in 1676, however, it may indicate a trough in population contemporary with similar indications elsewhere.[4] A considerable slump in population in the early 19th century was reversed from 1831 onwards.

In general the village earthworks follow the limits imposed by the valley, but on the E they spill over into a subsidiary valley. The N nucleus includes the church and thus may be connected to the Domesday manor of Count Alan later held by the Lascelles family who were patrons of the church. Of the earthworks surrounding the church, those to the W are the most clearly defined. They consist of narrow closes with yards and former buildings at the S end where they front the modern street. The road running NW to Great Limber, shown on the Enclosure Map of 1806,[5] crosses the village earthworks obliquely and is therefore later than those earthworks. Despite the sharp drop from the terraced roadway, the S side of the

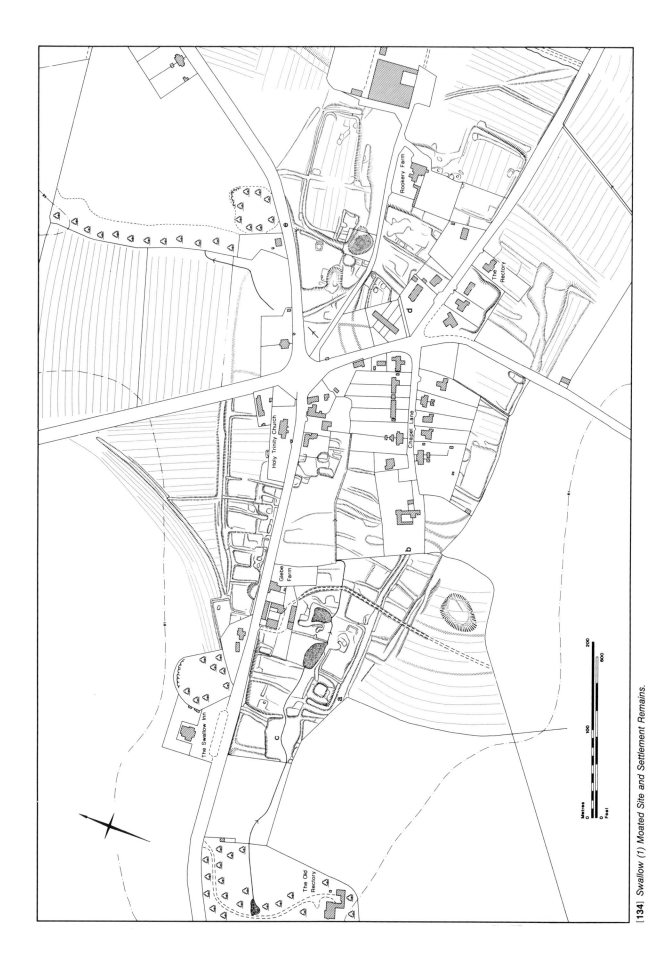

[1134] *Swallow (1) Moated Site and Settlement Remains.*

street was similarly fronted at least in the post-medieval period by buildings lining closes running S and terminating at the stream. Evidence survives for this in both the earthworks and existing buildings. On the N, this settlement block is bounded by a series of scarps, probably representing a narrow back lane and a former headland. The headland probably developed after the shortening of ridge-and-furrow, since battered broad ridges occur in the larger close N of the church which also contains parts of a yard and a small building. A mixture of broad and narrow ridge-and-furrow running N from the headland is truncated by a later NE–SW ditch, possibly an old lane.

Earthworks S of the stream forming the second nucleus focus on an E–W hollow-way ('a'–'b'), perhaps the Cabourne to Beelsby road shown on Armstrong's map of Lincolnshire of 1776–8. This is flanked on either side by closes of former properties, abandoned before 1806. Those on the S side, although damaged by ploughing, survive sufficiently to show that they converge slightly on the street at the W. They may have been added to an original single-sided village street with the earlier properties running back from the hollow-way to the stream. On the NW, and shown on the Enclosure Map, is a dry pond ('c'), 1 m deep, formed behind a dam crossing the stream. Below it, a small moat ('a') may be the site of a former manor house.

The close E of the moat may form an outer enclosure of this moat and thereby give it the aspect of a manorial complex. Further E are village closes which continue NE in the pasture behind the modern housing. This settlement backed on to the stream and therefore is quite separate from the N nucleus. A large depression (SSW of 'b'), apparently overlaid by ridge-and-furrow, is probably a quarry abandoned at an early date. The main hollow-way presumably changed direction at its E end ('b') to survive as Chapel Lane. On the S lip of the valley behind the present houses, closes or small paddocks containing ridge-and-furrow may indicate later expansion over arable. This would support the evidence for the properties on the S of the hollow-way being later additions or, in this area, late infill.

Earthworks on the E side of the valley may represent a third nucleus or simply a continuation of the S nucleus. Their alignment differs from those of the S nucleus but, as they are situated where the valley changes direction, this may reflect the influence of the topography or, alternatively, the old road pattern. A N–S hollow-way ('d'–'e'), partly shown on the Enclosure Map, may be the continuation of Chapel Lane. Former properties on its W side once contained buildings facing the hollow-way. In some of the closes (NW of 'd'), are the remains of broad ridge-and-furrow which pre-dates the properties. This relationship indicates that the settlement remains represent either expansion away from the main focus or infill between the separate nuclei.

On the E side of this hollow-way, a very large block with Rookery Farm as its centre is defined on the N, NE, and SE by a low bank and ditch. This area is divided into a series of closes containing the remains of earlier arable with, here and there, traces of individual buildings overlying it. Irregular earthworks including the sites of buildings W and N of Rookery Farm correspond with groups of buildings shown in 1806, and a particularly well-marked structure SSE of the farm may be its former outbuildings. However, the block itself closely resembles medieval monastic granges or demesne manors, such as those at Collow (Legsby (4)) or Cabourne (1), for example, with their attendant paddocks taking in earlier arable and limited areas of buildings. It may be that this block represents the

holding in Swallow of either Wellow Abbey or Nun Cotham Priory.

Although severely damaged by ploughing, the remains of other earthworks apparently overlying ridge-and-furrow are just visible S of The Rectory. Scatters of medieval pottery and animal bones were located here during the survey. It is possible that this block between the roads SE to Beelsby and to Cuxwold was yet another monastic holding, and an additional distinct element in the settlement morphology.

1. *Lincs DB* 12/15, 17, 27/6; *LS* 9/7, 16; *Book of Fees* I, 154; II, 1019–20, 1072, 1081; *Feudal Aids* III, 134, 150, 237, 276, 362; *Cal IPM* II (1906), 216, 218, 424; III (1912), 87; VIII (1913), 192; XII (1938), 296; *Cal Inq Misc* I (1916), 70; II (1916), 110; LAO Typescript list of incumbents; Davis, F. N. *et al* 1925, 35; *Cal IPM Henry VII*, I (1898), 261.
2. *Book of Fees* I, 222, 226, 596; II, 1019; *Placita de Quo Warranto* (1818), 404; *VE* IV, 67, 68, 75; *Cal LPFD Hen VIII* XVII (1900), 29, 394.
3. *Cal Inq Misc* II (1916), 400; III (1937), 323; LCL Ross MSS V, 413.
4. BL Add MS 11574, f87.
5. PRO MPL/83.

SWINHOPE

(1) Deserted Village of Swinhope (TF 218961) [135] suffered a decline in the medieval period which is well evidenced by documents, earthworks and material finds. This decline was already far advanced by the early 14th century, from a minimum recorded population of 37 in 1086 to 15 and 12 taxpayers in 1327–8 and 1332–3. It was exacerbated by the Black Death. In 1353–4 land belonging to the manor was undervalued 'on account of the pestilence and want of tenants' and in 1384 the site of the manor itself was valueless. In 1428 there were less than 10 households and only 6 in 1563. The limited increase in population since then has been housed in scattered farms and cottages.

There were formerly extensive settlement earthworks around the parish church and up the side of the valley to the E, so well preserved that a transcription of the general layout can be attempted from air photographs.[1] This shows a regular pattern of long tofts and crofts along a small side valley, bounded on the S by a way that survived partly as an earthwork hollow-way, partly as an existing road at Crow Halt and partly as a field track on the same alignment. This pattern, as at Kirmond le Mire (1), contrasts with the remains both surviving and destroyed around the church which form a separate element perhaps marking or including a manorial complex.

The remains were completely destroyed in 1969. Consequent field-walking identified concentrations of cobbles and building materials of flint and chalk. Associated pottery was almost entirely of 11th to 15th-century date.[2]

1. CUAC AHC 99–102, ANK 13–15, AQC 52; RAF VAP CPE/UK 1746/1036–7.
2. *LHA* 5 1970, 14.

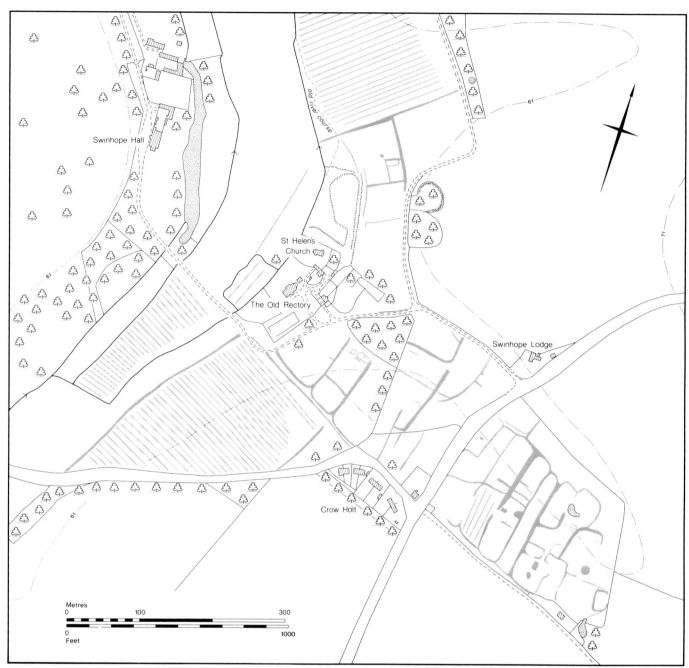

[135] *Swinhope (1) Deserted Village.*

TEALBY

(3) Moated Site (TF 130894) [136], known as Chapel Hill, lies at the extreme W end of Tealby parish, just over 3 km from Tealby church. It is situated in woodland at 35 m above OD, on the S edge of a slightly elevated area of Cover Sands over clay, flanked on the S by low-lying carr land.

The origins and purpose of the site are unknown and the earliest surviving documentation perhaps reflects only events towards the end of occupation there. In 1336 the King gave protection for one year for Roger de Staunford and Richard de Burle, hermits of the chapel of St Thomas at Tealby, and their attorneys, to collect alms.[1] 'A messuage called St Thomas's Chapel' with '12 acres in the Carre' formed part of a quitclaim of right in Tealby in 1638; an early 19th-century list of lands in Tealby that were free of tithe includes *Chapple Hill*, which is shown as a block of old enclosures on the Enclosure Map of 1795. No building is shown on the site at that date.[2]

The earthworks consist of a rectangular area enclosed by a single ditch 1.5 m deep. At the N end of the enclosure, an oblong platform may represent the position of former buildings. Scarps, possibly former boundaries, run ENE away from the E side of the moat.

1. *Cal Pat R 1333–8* (1895), 302.
2. LAO Td'E/BRA 747/Tealby xxxii/C/8 and Tealby xiv/23; Td'E A Misc 1/3; Owen 1975, 20.

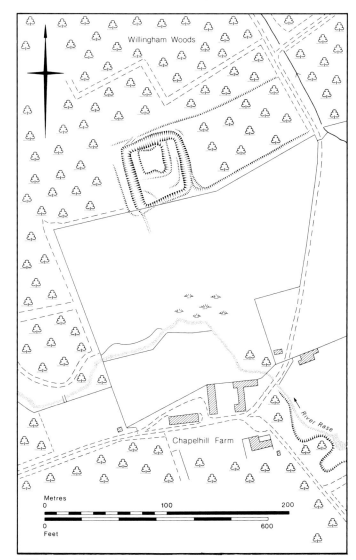

[**136**] *Tealby (3) Moated Site.*

THONOCK

(1) Ring and Baileys (SK 818915) [**137**], known as Castle Hills or Danes' Camp, are situated at 30 m above OD in woodland at the point where the predominantly W-facing Keuper Marl escarpment N of Gainsborough swings away from the R Trent, here about 1 km distant to the W. The site is notable as an early military stronghold, a lordly residence and a major estate centre.

It seems likely that the 'castle of Gainsborough' which, together with the royal manor of Kirton in Lindsey was granted by Stephen before 1146 and probably in 1142, to William de Roumare, Earl of Lincoln, is to be identified with this site.[1]

The tactical and strategic position of the castle is very strong. The E–W road, on its S side, followed by the parish boundary, may be part of an early route leading to a Trent crossing at Morton. The castle stands at only the second point on the Trent above its confluence with the Humber where the river makes contact on its E bank with the solid lands of Lindsey, and from its elevation commands a long stretch of the lower Trent. This overtly military aspect, though again significant in the mid 12th century, perhaps

makes it likely that the origin of the castle in its present form belongs to the immediate post-1066 period. In 1068 William I returned from York to Lincoln to found the castle there and in 1069 Edgar the Aetheling joined with a Danish force in plundering Lindsey and was defeated by Robert Count of Mortain (also styled Earl of Cornwall) and Robert Count of Eu. In the same year William himself came to Axholme, and in 1070 a Danish king named Swein (Estrithson) again entered the Humber under arms.[2] On the other hand it is also possible that the castle was erected or at least enlarged or altered in the mid 12th century when Stephen concentrated much military effort in the county as a result of the adherence of Ranulf Earl of Chester and his half-brother William de Roumare to the Empress Matilda.

In 1086 Thonock was held by Roger de Poitou and around 1115 by the Count of Mortain. Only in the later 12th or 13th century, as part of the Honour of Lancaster, does the site appear to become a principal residence, notably of Edward I's brother Edmund Earl of Cornwall, and the centre of a barony.[3]

The manor remained as a holding of the Duchy of Lancaster until 1563 and its capital messuage remained in residential use into the 15th century.[4] In the mid 16th century Leland described the site as 'a great motid manor place', evidently abandoned for some time.[5]

The earthworks were replanted with trees in 1815–16 and finds made then included a key, a dagger, a battle axe and a horseshoe. In one place reputed to be a burial ground, large building stones were discovered. This may have been the southern bailey which was known as *White Chapel Garth* in the 19th century.[6]

The earthworks consist of a substantial ringwork flanked on both the N and S by outer baileys of more than one period. The first phase was probably the ringwork and the N bailey. The former consists of a steep-sided circular rampart standing up to 5.5 m above the bottom of the surrounding ditch. On the N where the ditch separates the castle from the bailey, its bottom is made up of a series of deep pits separated by low causeways. It is uncertain whether these pits were caused by the method of digging the ditch or resulted from partial infill or a later unfinished refurbishing. The surfaces of both the broad summit of the rampart and the central area are uneven, perhaps partly due to the demolition of former masonry structures. A large hollow on the NW side of the central area may be the site of a substantial building.

The tongue-shaped bailey, lying on sloping ground, is surrounded by a ditch. At the E, unlike on the W, the topography affords no natural defence and a broad inner bank standing 4 m above the bottom of the ditch provides reinforcement. At the NE the bank is interrupted by a narrow entrance, possibly original. Opposite and beyond the ditch, a hollow-way runs W to the foot of the natural slope. Within the bailey and following its outline a scarp, if not wholly natural, might mark an earlier defensive line or have been caused by scraping up or quarrying material for the bailey bank.

An additional line of defensive earthworks along the S side of the ringwork is perhaps contemporary. This consists of a crescentic outer ditch flanked on either side by a bank. The N bank stands about 4 m above the inner and outer ditches while the S bank stands 3 m above the outer ditch. These earthworks were either constructed to give additional protection to this side of the castle, where the land is level, before the addition of the later bailey, or as part of a second phase of development.

The second principal phase was the addition of a bailey S of the ringwork. Here a kidney-shaped area was enclosed by a massive bank still standing some 2.75 m above the interior of the bailey and

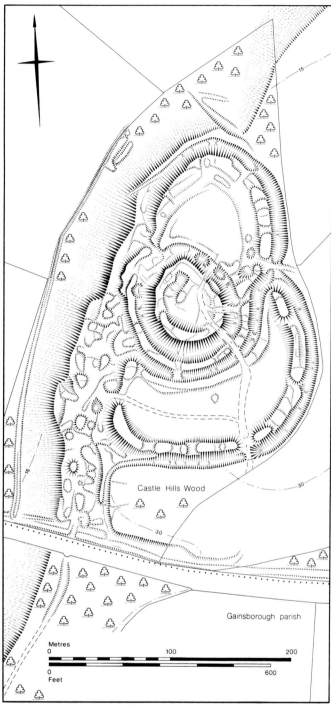

[137] *Thonock (1) Ring and Baileys.*

pale relating to a documented park in this area, to which the low flat-topped E–W bank N of the road probably belongs (2).

On the SW the edge of the spur is highly irregular and characterized by a series of mounds and hollows. Much of this probably results from former quarrying for gypsum, an industry documented in association with the manor in 1303[7] and represented by a large area of quarrying earthworks on the scarp on the S of Castle Hills, known as the *Pitt Hills*.

1. Davis *et al* 1913-69 III, p 184, no 494; Renn 1973, 194; Hill 1965, 180.
2. Stenton 1947, 592–7.
3. *Lincs DB* 16/23; *LS* 4/8; *Book of Fees* I, 596; *Rot Hund* I (1812), 381; *Cal IPM* III (1912), 316.
4. *Feudal Aids* VI, 567, 613; *Cal Pat R 1370–4* (1914), 295; *Cal IPM*, 2nd ser, II (1915), 358, 579; LCL Ross MSS I, 25–6; *Cal Inq Misc* V (1962), 59–61.
5. Toulmin Smith 1964 I, 33.
6. Stark 1817, 312; White 1872, 296; Owen 1975, 18.
7. PRO C133/97 (58.4).

THORESWAY

(1) Settlement Remains (TF 169967) **[29, 138]**, formerly part of Thoresway village, lie in a steep-sided chalk valley at about 76 m above OD. Both this and the side valley to the S are dry above the settlement. The arrangement of the present settlement suggests a gapped two-row street village of fairly regular form – an interpretation superficially reinforced by the earthworks lining both sides of the main valley, in part forming closes laid out from both sides of the street. The proved complexity of the Wolds villages, together with the detailed intricacies of the earthworks at Thoresway, rule out any such simplistic interpretation and combine to present a highly complex settlement whose morphology cannot be readily interpreted. The problems are compounded by ploughing, which in 1962 destroyed a substantial group of earthworks recorded on air photographs in a large field SE of the church.[1] It is possible to indicate certain elements of the site which illustrate the difficulties of interpretation, but all that can be concluded is that Thoresway has had a long history of change and alteration, the details of which are perhaps beyond recovery.

In the post-Conquest period there were two main manors in Thoresway both of which can be traced until the 15th century when they were finally joined together, though both seem to have been extensively sub-infeudated in the 13th and 14th century.[2]

The population indicators for the settlement show that the highest level was in 1086 with a minimum recorded population of 62. While this level may have been carried through the 12th and perhaps 13th centuries, the 29 and 32 taxpayers of the early 14th-century subsidies are a considerable drop. Relief of 88 per cent in 1352 shows the sharp impact of the Black Death and though more than 10 households were present in 1428, reliefs of 30 to 40 per cent throughout the 15th century paint the same picture of restricted population that is revealed in the 22 and 21 taxpayers to the lay subsidies of 1524 and 1525 and the 15 taxpayers of 1542–3. The 26 households of 1563 and 225 communicants of 1603 represent an unexpected up-swing, but this was of limited duration, for in 1676 there were only 30 communicants and at the beginning of the 18th century only 10 or 11 households were returned, and the number did not increase until the mid and later 19th century. Indeed already in 1607 the survey of depopulations reported that two farms and a cottage had recently been 'decayed'. Mid 17th-century records of

5 m above a wide outer ditch. Irregularities in the ditch bottom and on the bank top may largely reflect later damage. Masonry structures could well have been removed from the bailey bank and mounds at its NW and NE corners could represent the sites of former towers or turrets.

At a later date a ditch was dug leading out of the S bailey ditch on the SW towards the present E–W road. Near the road the ditch narrows to a single scarp, which changes direction to run E and may represent an additional outer enclosure. Alternatively it could be a extensive sheep-walks in the parish perhaps suggest much conversion to sheep probably in the 15th and early 16th century.[3]

To the SE of the church an area of earthworks, now destroyed, contained a well-marked E–W hollow-way ('a'), parallel to the present street with occupation on both sides. Closes on its N side appear to have had buildings lining the hollow-way and are therefore likely to have extended N down to the stream. On its S there was certainly a major building complex, with large embanked closes arranged along the slope. The form, size and proximity to the church of the complex suggest a manorial site, perhaps the centre of the larger medieval manor. It is certainly in this area that Lord Culpeper's post-medieval residence formerly stood. Medieval pottery from the area, including Stamford and early shelly ware, is in the Scunthorpe Museum.

It may be significant that the enclosures and the remains of former buildings immediately to the S ('b') are known locally as 'The Castle', for they could form part of this manorial complex. Alternatively they may represent one of the capital messuages of the sub-manors documented in the 13th and 14th century. The hollow-way which surrounds them on the SE and W cannot be seen on air photographs to extend into the ploughed area to the N. Neither can any continuation for the hollow-way ('c') be found. Both features may have been overlain by late medieval or later growth of the main manor, following its consolidation.

To the W of the possible main manorial site and SW of the church is a large roughly rectangular area, bounded on the N by the village street and on the S by a hollow-way ('c'). The W part of this area is roughly L-shaped in plan and may represent two stages of development. The N part of the L, nearest the street, contains the footings of stone buildings with embanked closes extending S and thus probably part of the main village. To the S are the remains of a courtyard farm ('d'), set within an enclosure which could be a later extension of the area to the N. This farm and the small building immediately to the N of it are serviced by a narrow N–S lane extending from the village street. The N end of an identical lane is visible to the E in the E section of the area, but its continuation and any other ancient features have been largely obliterated by a pond, leat and other associated earthworks. The pond provided power for the nearby water-mill, a 19th-century standing structure on the edge of the street. The possibility that the whole area occupied by the mill pond and its associated earthworks was an extension of the manorial complex which destroyed earlier village closes lying along the street, is strengthened by the documentary evidence for a water-mill and pool – perhaps an arrangement similar to that which still exists – appurtenant to the main manor at the end of the 13th century.[4]

On the N side of the street, behind and between the existing buildings is a series of closes which extends from the modern crossroads in the E to a point where the present road swings SW leaving a slight hollow-way ('e') at the W end of the village. The W closes are large and rectangular, but further E there are a whole series of narrow ones which may be either of a different date to those further W and E, or the later subdivisions of earlier closes. Further E the pattern of large closes re-emerges with at least two well-marked building sites within them ('f' and 'g'). At the rear of these easternmost closes is a hollow-way cut into the hillside above them.

The E end of the village has a complex area of earthworks which suggests that this part has also undergone considerable changes. The existing street as far as the present crossroads seems to form one side of a triangular area whose S side is marked by a hollow and terraces, N of the Old Rectory. These are undoubtedly both the original course of the stream and the line of an abandoned way, and they perhaps suggest that the triangular area may once have been a 'green' or funnel-shaped area giving access to the E. If this was so it was certainly built over later; it is now divided by banks into small closes with the remains of at least three building sites at their NW end. Later changes, perhaps caused by the creation of the small park around the rectory, include the realigning of the main N–S road from its old course ('h') to its present position, and the moving of the stream to the N, where it cuts through at least one former close boundary. Indeterminate earthworks on either side of the stream E of the rectory may represent former squatter occupation outside the village.

Though a tentative interpretation of specific parts of the village earthworks has been attempted, the understanding of the overall arrangement is much more difficult and it is possible to suggest a variety of theories. These are made more complicated by the documented tenurial complexity. The village could have originally had two separate parts, one to the W of the church, later replanned in regular form, and the other around the 'green' at the E. The gap between them could have been filled in at a later date, on the N with houses and closes and on the S by the manorial complex which later expanded over part of the village. Further expansion could then have occurred at the W end of the manorial extension and at the E over the 'green' and to the S of it.

Alternatively the village could have been replanned around an existing focus near the church and given a neat rectangular plan with a central valley-bottom street with houses and closes on either side and with back lanes at the rear. Subsequent alterations would then have included the establishment of the manorial complex just outside the village and its later extension over part of it, the subdivision of closes on the N side of the main street and expansion at the E and W end.

A further possibility is raised by the fact that at several villages in the Wolds, notably Croxby (Thoresway (3)) and Stainton le Vale (1) it is clear that the valley bottom was not utilized by the main streets which instead followed the contours well up the valley sides. At Swallow (1) the valley bottom acted as a division between the two principal settlement units relating to streets along the valley side. It is possible that the same is true at Thoresway with the former prominent hollow-way ('a') acting as one of its principal streets with the church on one side and the manorial complex on the other. Only post-medieval changes then may have resulted in the development of the S side of the valley-bottom street in its central section.

1. RAF VAP CPE/UK1746/1046; *LAAS* **10** pt 1 (1963), 10.
2. *Lincs DB* 14/14, 27/10; *LS* 7/4, 7/16; *Book of Fees* I, 158; II, 1018, 1021, 1081, 1088; *Feudal Aids* III, 150, 161, 175, 220, 237–8, 261, 268, 289, 299, 357; *Cal Chart R 1226–57* (1903), 30; *Placita de Quo Warranto* (1818), 405; *Cal IPM* I, (1806), 86; *Cal Pat R 1317–21* (1903), 71, 351, 354; Massingberd 1904–5, 46–9.
3. BL Add MS 11574, f79; LAO RADCLIFFE 6/7b and 8.
4. *Cal IPM* IV (1913), 164.

(2) Site of Monastic Grange (TF 168963) [29, 138] of Revesby Abbey lies at about 80 m above OD, on chalk, in a side valley S of Thoresway village (1).

The grange was created by Hugh de Baiocis's 12th-century grant of 840 acres (350 ha) to Revesby Abbey.[1] In 1288 it consisted of a capital messuage and 185 acres (77 ha) of arable in demesne. It was included as a farm or grange at the Dissolution in the grant of Revesby and its possessions to the Duke of Suffolk.[2] Surveys of 1652 and just prior to that date show from field-names that the grange lay in a valley S of and separate from the village closes. It

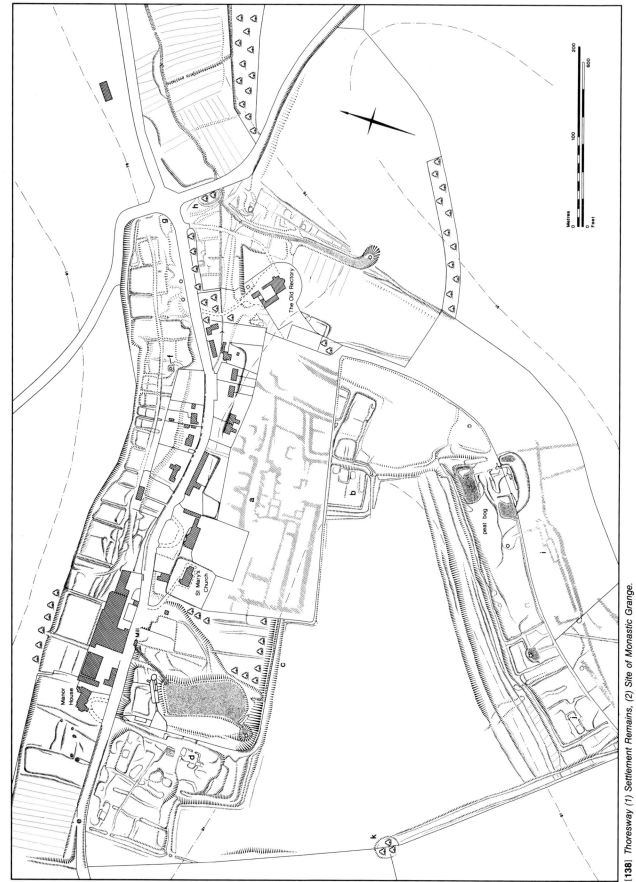

The Old Rectory

peat bog

St Mary's Church

Manor House

Mill

[138] *Thoresway (1) Settlement Remains, (2) Site of Monastic Grange.*

196

may then have been occupied by one of the four farms in the parish, but was vacant by the early 19th century.[3]

The earthworks are linked to Thoresway itself by a short length of hollow-way at their NE end. The remains lie on the SE-facing slope and at the bottom of the valley and have been partly destroyed by modern ploughing. The 1946 air photographs show that the levelled area originally contained large rectangular buildings ('i'). As well as medieval pottery, field-walking here has produced very large quantities of roof tiles, perhaps indicating the presence of a former tile-making centre using clay extracted from the crescent-shaped pit at the NE end. The site of a courtyard farm is visible immediately NW of the clay pit, lying in boggy pasture on the SW side of the hollow-way running N. A series of low banks and scarps shows that the SW end of the site was divided up into a number of blocks with the remains of a rectangular building ('j') still visible. The site was bounded on the NW by a hollow-way running along the side of the valley and which joined the hollow-way from Thoresway at its NE end. Upslope strip lynchets have the ends of earlier ridge-and-furrow laid out in the opposite direction emerging from under them indicating that a complete revision of an earlier field system has occurred. On top of the spur is a battered tree ring ('k'), SE of which a bank runs down the hillside to cross the end of the strip lynchets and the settlement earthworks.

1. *Book of Fees* I, 158; PRO E179/242/113.
2. Massingberd 1904–5, 83; *VE* IV, 44–5; *Cal LPFD Hen VIII* XIV pt 1 (1894), 263.
3. LAO RADCLIFFE 6/7a and 8; OS 1st edn 1 in sheet 86.

(3) Deserted Village of Croxby (TF 192983) [139] lies in the bottom and along the sides of a narrow chalk valley between 50 m and 70 m above OD. Though the earthwork remains of the settlement are relatively well preserved their interpretation is difficult and no obvious pattern of development has emerged.

Croxby's minimum recorded population of 36 in Domesday Book outstrips by a factor of at least two any level recorded subsequently. The number of taxpayers in the early 14th-century subsidies, at 11 and 12, are well below half the average for the wapentake. Grants to religious institutions clearly contributed to this. Before 1300 grants to Louth Park Abbey gave rise to a grange, Orford Priory also had some land here and Newsham Abbey in the late 12th century received the advowson of the church, a dwelling, land and the profits of a mill.

Despite the fact that these monastic holdings may have led to a recording of less than the full population of Croxby, a grant in 1162–72 to St Mary of Lincoln of 'one bovate with one mansion made out of two mansions' at least suggests some early contraction of the settlement.[1] The immediate impact of the Black Death was 100 per cent relief in 1352, but recovery was such that there were at least 10 households in 1428, and with low reliefs in the 15th century and with 13 and 15 taxpayers to the lay subsidies of 1524 and 1525, 10 persons returned for the Lindsey Musters of 1539, 9 taxpayers in 1542–3 and 11 households in 1563, the population has evidently returned to or maintained a level similar to those of the early 14th century. The survey of depopulations of 1607 reported only the decay of the parsonage house[2] and there were reckoned to be 44 communicants in 1603 and 37 in 1676. Yet a sharp decline at the end of the 17th century is evident from the 3 and 4 households recorded in the first decades of the 18th century.

In Domesday Book and the Lindsey Survey, four estates are listed for Croxby.[3] These four secular estates can be traced, but little diminished by grants to religious institutions, into the 15th century with an increasing tendency for more than one to be held in the same hands.[4]

The main village earthworks are in good condition although the NW part of the site has been ploughed over and destroyed. A remarkable feature of the site is the relationship between the village closes and the small stream flowing down the valley. The remains are defined by an abandoned main road system. The present roads consist only of a roughly E–W road crossed by a N–S road to the W of the church. An earlier road system, however, survives as earthworks or crop-marks. To the W of the village remains two older and roughly parallel roads are visible. One left the modern alignment a little NE of the Croxby crossroads and can be traced on air photographs as a former hollow-way running approximately parallel to, but SE of, the present road. Another loop road seems to have turned off the modern road near the crossroads and passed along the W side of the churchyard. To the N of the church it is still visible as a hollow-way and then crosses the shallow tributary valley on an artificial embankment which still survives up to 2.5 m high. It then becomes a hollow-way once more and runs on to join the previously mentioned road.

On the SE side of the valley is another through road. To the SW of Hall Farm Cottages this remains as a modern terraced field track. It once, however, continued NE and its line is marked by two parallel and narrow terrace-ways immediately NE of the farm buildings. The upper terrace-way runs along the crest of the valley and then into the valley bottom and continues as a hollow-way. The lower terrace-way runs into the valley bottom and passes behind the village closes until it joins the previous terrace-way as it reaches the valley bottom. The remains of the village with its own internal street system lie between these main through roads, and are connected to it by various tracks and hollow-ways.

One possible analysis is that the earthworks seem to have distinct parts which may reflect a difference in origin. Perhaps the oldest part is the area E of the church ('a'). This is bounded on the NW by the church and the Old Rectory while the NE side is edged by a hollow-way which runs SE across the stream and then climbs the valley side to join both the eastern terrace-ways in turn. Within this block the village remains to the NW of the stream lie in a field which has been ploughed and reseeded. As a result the surviving earthworks are poorly preserved, ill-defined and difficult to interpret. At least four rectangular platforms, all probably building sites and all but one close to the stream, are identifiable. On the SE side of the stream the earthworks are better preserved and three possible closes are visible. The central one has a terraced platform on the hillside at its SE, on which there is at least one building platform.

The hypothesis that this part of the village is the older, rests on its disjunction with that part to the NE, the less regular nature of the earthworks and the proximity of the church. The latter is now only a small structure but was once much larger: a late 12th-century S aisle, a late 14th-century N aisle and a N chapel have all been removed and the arcades blocked.

The presumed later part of the village extends NE from the supposed original village, along the valley bottom and sides. It consists of a terrace or hollow-way, apparently the main street which runs NE along the valley side and then turns SE and disappears under a modern lake. On the SE side of the lake what is probably its continuation reappears and joins the main through road on the opposite side of the valley.

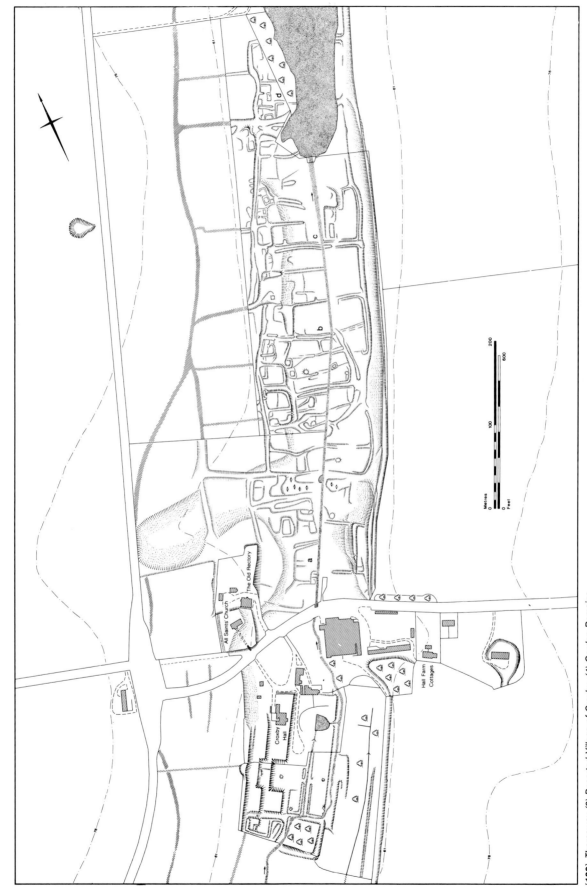

[139] *Thoresway (3) Deserted Village of Croxby, (4) Garden Remains.*

198

Most of the NW side of the street is now under cultivation and only a series of closes, bounded by low banks and completely destroyed by ploughing are visible on air photographs. There is no indication that buildings were associated with these closes and only one possible building platform is visible on the NW side of the street. On the SE this street is lined by at least sixteen embanked paddocks or courtyards, most of which have traces of former buildings within them. Behind these courtyards are long closes, the majority of which extend across the valley bottom, over the stream and terminate against the lower of the two terrace-ways. Some of these closes have cross-banks or scarps subdividing them and other minor features include at least one pond and two circular mounds. Building platforms are few on the SE side of the stream and only one is clearly identifiable.

Within this layout of courtyards and closes, a larger pattern is detectable and may be operating at two levels. At one, the closes themselves seem to be subdivisions of an earlier arrangement of at least six and possibly once eight larger closes roughly 60 m–65 m wide, all of which have been later subdivided by the insertion of intermediate banks, not all of which extend across the stream. This pattern suggests that this part of the village was a consciously planned addition of large plots laid out on one side of the single street and without regard to the existence of the stream. Presumably later population pressure could have forced the apparently subsequent subdivisions.

At another level two principal embanked divisions ('b' and 'c') together with an E–W hollow-way ('d'), now partly obscured by the modern lake, divide the earthworks into large sections. This may reflect late amalgamation of properties. The N part of this area (between 'd' and the northernmost hollow-way) appears in 1804 to have the name *Grange Close*, presumably a reference to Louth Park's property.

The earlier tenurial situation of several manors with none predominant and the population trends perhaps suggest an alternative interpretation to that of outward expansion from a single core. The settlement may always have been strung out for some distance along the valley, becoming filled in and more regular and formalized only in the limited period of maximum population. Indications on early air photographs show that the road system extending northwards was probably accompanied for some distance by settlement remains now under the lake. There may also have been some occupation W of the church.[5]

1. *Feudal Aids* III, 220; *Cal Close R 1354–60* (1908), 516; Dugdale 1817–30 V, 416; *VE* IV, 57, 78; *Cal Chart R 1300–26* (1908), 386–7; Foster and Major 1931–73 IV, 223-8.
2. BL Add MS 11574 f79.
3. *Lincs DB* 14/15, 18/10, 32/9, 49/2, 70/9; *LS* 7/3, 4, 5, 7.
4. *Feudal Aids* III, 268, 283, 296, 299, 302; LCL Ross MSS IV, 33; Maddison 1902–6 III, 869-71; LAO Probate Inventories.
5. RAF VAP CPE/UK1746/3043.

(4) Garden Remains (TF 189981) [139] lie immediately S of Croxby Hall, on both sides of a narrow, steep-sided valley, on chalk, between 53 m and 60 m above OD.

The gardens were clearly associated with the Hall, which sits on the lower principal terrace and is a red-brick structure of late 17th-century date. The arrangement of the garden, too, would suggest a late 17th or early 18th-century date for its construction.

In 1665 Christopher Sheffield, then under age, inherited Croxby. In 1685 he sold the estate to Robert Snoden of Horncastle. Snoden's daughter and heiress, Jane, married Charles Dymoke of Scrivelsby,

and in 1688 he released the manor of Croxby to the couple. Although Jane survived to be buried at Horncastle in 1743/4, Charles Dymoke died without issue in 1702/3, and it is to this brief period that the creation of the house and garden probably belongs.[1]

The N half of the remains now lies within the modern gardens of Croxby Hall, where the faces of the terraces are flower-beds or shrubberies and have almost certainly been extended N from their original terminations. The SW side of the garden consists of two flat terraces cut into the rising ground. The centre of the rear terrace has a slight semicircular recess, above which are the remains of a low curving scarp. This may have originally had an arbour or piece of statuary within the curve. The upper terrace has traces of steps in its centre and the wings project forward, as does the second terrace below, although the ends here project further down the slope. A circular depression below this terrace in the centre may be the site of a water feature. Below the S projection of the second terrace, in the valley bottom, is a slightly raised rectangular platform with a low mound in its SW corner. There may once have been a matching platform to the N but no trace of this now exists in the modern garden. Below this again, a narrow diversion of the main stream flows between two low and flat-topped banks. In the original arrangement the stream would have been dammed to produce a shallow rectangular pond or 'canal' between the banks or walkways, a feature typical of late 17th or early 18th-century gardens.

Beyond the stream is a large rectangular area, featureless except for another shallow circular depression placed axially in the centre of the garden layout. This area is bounded on the S and E by the modern stream, but the latter is edged by straight scarps and again must once have formed a long 'canal'. On the E side of this stream is a large paddock, on the steep slope of the valley and extending the full width of the garden. It is now crossed by the leat of a 19th-century hydraulic ram but apart from this there are no features except for two overlapping long scarps near the stream and a well-marked low bank extending along part of the E side. In a typical garden of this period this area would have been a 'wilderness' planted with trees or shrubs and perhaps with intersecting paths. The existing isolated trees appear to date from a later period, though a few rotting tree-stumps are scattered over the area.

Along the S end of the garden is a series of other features, also part of the formal arrangement. In the SW, continuing the line of the main terraces, is a small trapezoidal area, its upper part subdivided by scarps into three small flat terraces, all presumably for flower-beds. These terraces were perhaps linked by a broad and flat-topped ramped walk along the W and S sides, while the lowest level is occupied by a small steep-sided pond, dammed against the slope, that may be been fed along the modern hedge line from the high-level leat above. The area is bounded on the W and N by a narrow channel which has a steep drop of 2 m–3 m elevation within it towards its SW end. This slope is presumably the remains of a waterfall or cascade. Water was introduced into the garden in the SW corner by means of a high-level leat, which ran off the main stream almost 1 km to the SW and passed along the valley side until it reached the garden. This leat still survived in 1946[2] but has since been destroyed. The water passed round the W side of the trapezoidal area, turned SE and over the waterfall and thence along the channel into the 'canals'.

Below the trapezoidal area, in the valley bottom, is a roughly square ditched or moated enclosure. A modern stream cuts across the NW corner, but is shown on an early 19th-century estate map as entering the W corner of a larger enclosure whose S side has now been lost in arable. The Tithe Map of 1838 shows a stage in its destruction.[3] The present S side appears to have been a linear water feature within the enclosure, parallel and close to that S side, and the earlier map marks what are presumably paths crossing the surviving square area from corner to corner and a third axially N and S. The interior, though now featureless, was once perhaps planted with shrubs or flowers.

There was probably a matching 'moat' on the NE in the area now occupied by the present gardens and a shallow pond. The outfall ditch of this pond, where the water returns to the stream, may mark its S side and the low scarp on the SE and NE may be the remains of the ditches on these sides.

1. Maddison 1902–6 III, 871, 905–6.
2. RAF VAP CPE/UK1746/3043.
3. LAO B11; YARB 4/10/1.

THORGANBY

(1) Deserted Village of Thorganby (TF 208978) [44, 45, 140] lies in the valley of the N-draining Waithe Beck on chalk at between 47 m and 60 m above OD.

It first appears in 11th to 12th-century documentation as a settlement with a multiplicity of tenure, with five or six holdings recorded in 1086 and 1115, but perhaps of no great size. A small number of taxpayers, 10 in 1332–3, perhaps represents a further drop in population but a contributory factor may have been the endowment of monastic interests in the settlement. Wellow Abbey held one of its largest temporal holdings in Thorganby, as well as the parish church, while Bardney Abbey also possessed a smaller manor here.[1]

Despite its small size Thorganby was still a viable community in the 16th century, containing 15 households in 1563. Some depopulation was reported in the 1607 survey[2] and it is perhaps especially significant both that the population was halved in the mid to late 17th century and that the mid 17th-century Thorganby Hall was built, unusually for the area, away from the old village centre. Both may be connected with enclosure which took place between 1606 and 1671.[3] During the 18th and 19th centuries the population of the parish rose to its mid 16th-century levels.

The formerly very extensive and well-preserved earthworks were destroyed before 1966 and the plan [140] is largely based on the evidence of air photographs taken before this date [44].[4] Three distinct elements can be recognized. To the S of the church a block of substantial earthworks appears to have contained two moated features, surrounded and integrated with broad ditches and a complex network of rectangular closes. There is no sign that the closes were served by any streets or tracks and there are few traces of former buildings visible within them. This block, therefore, in form and in its association with the church, is likely to have been manorial in function and perhaps represents the Wellow Abbey holding. However, in detail the N 'moat' and broad ditches may be the remains of a post-medieval house and garden, overlying an earlier manorial site. The old hall at Thorganby, the seat of the Royalist Willoughby family, is said to have been plundered by Parliamentary forces in 1643.[5]

To the NE of the church and E of the stream a smaller moat was set within a row of large paddocks with no other interior features. This is likely to be another manorial block, perhaps that of Bardney Abbey.

Only the remains around Thorganby House Farm had the appearance of former village properties, principally in the way that they formed an E–W row N of the farm with signs of an access-way or street along their S side and with traces of former buildings at that end of the plot.

1. *VE* IV, 67, 81; PRO SC6/Henry VIII/2006.
2. BL Add MS 11574, ff79, 87, 91.
3. Johnson 1962, 143.
4. CUAC ANK 9–12; RAF VAP CPE/UK1880/1503, CPE/UK1746/3039–40.
5. Cox 1924, 314.

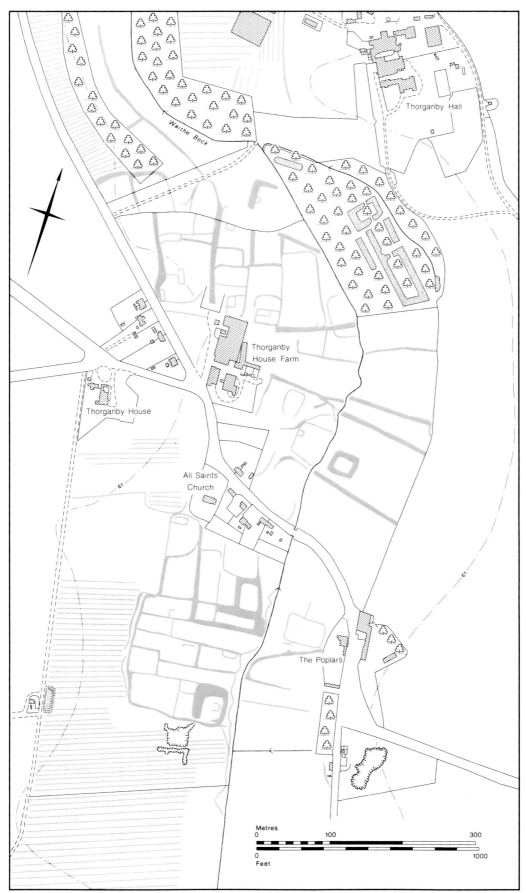

Walthe Beck

Thorganby Hall

Thorganby
House Farm

Thorganby House

61

All Saints'
Church

61

The Poplars

Metres
0   100   300

0   1000
Feet

[**140**] *Thorganby (1) Deserted Village of Thorganby.*

201

medieval pottery

b a

Clandon House

medieval pottery

The Lodge

Roman pottery

Metres
0   100   200
0
Feet   600

[141] *Thorpe in the Fallows (1) Deserted Village of Thorpe.*

THORPE IN THE FALLOWS

(1) Deserted Village of Thorpe (SK 912807) [141] lies at 13 m above OD on an island of clay with limestone amidst Till.

Thorpe is documented from 1086 onwards as a small settlement. No estimate of its population at that date is possible because of combined entries. Early 14th-century subsidies list numbers of taxpayers which at 14 and 10 are only a half or less than the average for the wapentake. A moderate relief in 1352 tallies with only 35 individuals named in the Poll Tax in 1377, and the settlement is apparently omitted completely from the parish tax in 1428. Yet in 1463 the relief is 'nil', for the Lindsey Muster in 1539 Thorpe produced 9 men, and in subsidies in the 1540s, 13, 12 and 9 taxpayers are severally listed. In 1588-9 the manor of Thorpe included four messuages, five cottages and seven tofts. Some decline from these levels is evident in the later 17th and throughout the 18th century, undoubtedly associated with the consolidation of farms and accelerated by the private enclosure of the parish in or about 1727, which also drew farms out of the village on to the former open fields.[1]

The survival of a small, ostensibly secondary settlement through decline in the later 14th century to stability if not growth in the later medieval and post-medieval period is perhaps surprising. An important factor was the multiplicity of tenure, in that there were until the Dissolution four estates in the parish, not one of them predominant and with no major residence. It was not until the second half of the 16th century that the parish came into single ownership.

A church at Thorpe certainly existed in the mid 12th century. The last separate institution was in 1557 and the building was demolished in the early 17th century. Its site, described in a Glebe Terrier of 1638, lay to the NW of Clandon House ('a').[2]

The earthworks lie on either side of a road running E-W. Those S of the road have been ploughed with a consequent loss of detail while on the N there are indications that at least three closes overlay ridge-and-furrow. This may indicate that the whole settlement was superimposed on earlier arable. A map of 1809[3] shows a small open area and pond ('b') which could represent the remains of a green, the full extent of which is uncertain. Documentary support for the existence of a former green comes from the 1580 will of Richard Simpkinson of Aisthorpe in which he left 4*d* 'unto the poore in the house of the greene in Thorpe'.[4]

During field survey, substantial amounts of medieval pottery were found in the arable S of the road where the earthworks survive as slight scarps. In addition, on the E edge of the village, large quantities of Roman sherds and building debris were discovered.

1. *Lincs DB* 68/28; Foster 1927, 12-17, 59, 156ff.
2. Foster 1927, 6-8, 53-60, 81-109, 114-16, 144-55; Dugdale 1817-30 VII, 825, 836.
3. Foster 1927, 153-4.
4. Foster 1927, 171.

TOFT NEWTON

(3) Settlement Remains (TF 043882) [142], formerly part of the village of Toft, are situated at 10 m to 14 m above OD on a low island of Oxford Clay or Kellaways sand and clay. The earthworks fall into at least three discrete blocks, though the exact interpretation of them is uncertain.

The modern civil parish comprises the separate settlements of Toft and Newton and their associated townships. They have always been closely associated and were normally returned as one for most medieval taxation purposes. Yet both had medieval churches and their own field systems from at least the late 12th century.

Toft was recorded as a single manorial holding in 1086 which in 1279 was granted to the Gilbertine priory of Sixhills. The estate remained a valuable possession of the priory, perhaps run from a grange farm, until the Dissolution.[1]

There is no record in the population figures that there has ever been any marked decline at Toft, though reductions are obvious in the late 14th century and in the 17th century. The manor in 1086 had a minimum recorded population of 14; in 1258 out of a total of 30 tenants 20 paid for a toft as well as land and 1 for a house. With Newton in 1327-8 and 1332-3, 29 and 27 taxpayers are named, jointly amounting to about the average for the wapentake but individually clearly already marking a decline. The Black Death brought reliefs of just under 50 per cent in 1352 and a total for the two settlements of only 70 persons over 14 years old in 1377, but neither community was exempt from the parish tax in 1428 so both must have had more than the minimum of 10 households. It is unclear whether reliefs of nearly 20 per cent in the mid 15th century reflect a greater impact on Newton or Toft. In 1524 and 1525 there were 12 and 13 taxpayers in Toft compared to 10 and 8 in Newton, in 1542-3 18 paid tax in Toft against 9 in Newton, and there were 18 households in Toft compared to 16 in Newton in 1563, 80 communicants against 50 in 1603 and 45 against 31 in 1676. A drop to 13 households by the early 18th century may have arisen from enclosure. Already the survey of 1607 found in Toft Newton (undifferentiated) that one farm stood empty and two persons had engrossed the land of a total of five farms, letting the houses to cottagers.[2]

Despite their extent, the earthworks do not allow a fully convincing analysis perhaps because any original settlement plan has been modified by the activities of the monastic grange and by the post-medieval farmsteads which now make up the bulk of the village. The church lies within a rectangular block defined on the N by a ditch or hollow-way ('a'-'b'). At its W end the hollow-way turns S and runs down the slope to the edge of the flood-plain of the small stream. The E side may be marked by a N-S street of which only a short section along the E of the churchyard now survives. The further section to the N was still in use in 1956 and a link to the E-W street seems to be shown in 1824. Across the centre of the block another E-W hollow-way parallel with that to the N seems to have formerly continued E along the S side of the churchyard to link up with the surviving stub of the street ('c'). The closes within this block for the most part are very regular and orientated N-S. Those S and SW of the church were hedged plots until recently, and there was a house (at 'c') at least until the mid 19th century.[3] Between the ditched S boundary of this block ('d') and the stream, at least four E-W ridges seem to be cut through by an L-shaped pond.

Along the N side of the main block is an elongated close with traces of buildings and a yard at its E end. The hollow-way that fringes it on the N serves an E-W row of closes to the N ('e'), also with traces of buildings.

To the E of the modern N-S through road, the fragmentary earthworks around the handful of village properties appear principally to define a large square block centred on The Limes and sliced through by the existing E-W road. A right angle of scarps defines its NE corner and a hollow-way ('f') marks its E side and turns at right angles to the W to be blocked by the dam of a large beast pond ('g') cut into its S side. Although now obscured by a

tangle of successive late hedge-banks and boundaries the hollow-way may have turned S (at 'h') to the stream. To the E and SE of this hollow-way is a patchwork of perhaps as many as seven or eight rectangular ditched closes, few showing definite traces of buildings but nevertheless possibly village closes.

Along the S side of the stream to the W and NW of Field Farm are further closes. Some appear to overlie ridge-and-furrow. If these are not solely paddocks associated with the farm, the earthworks might be those of a monastic holding since they bear a resemblance to those identified elsewhere at Cabourne (1), Riseholme (2) and Collow (Legsby (4)).

Other boundaries overlying ridge-and-furrow to the NE of the settlement also form small enclosed fields and a building platform ('i') may mark an associated structure similar to those identified as sheep-folds at Riseholme (2) and at West Firsby (1).

Because of its definition by a boundary-way, the regularity of the closes within it, its association with the church, and the manner in which other elements in the settlement seem to group around it, the block W of the church suggests itself as a manorial centre. It nevertheless has some features, perhaps principally the axial central hollow-way, which suggest rather a planned village layout. The block centred on The Limes might also be interpreted as a manorial centre and later grange; alternatively the enclosures around Field Farm might be the site of the monastic holding.

1. Walker 1954, 81; *Lincs DB* 4/40; *LS* 7/20; *Book of Fees* II, 1017; *Cal Inq Misc* I (1916) 85–6, 442; Davis 1914b, 160; Davis, F.N. *et al* 1925, 35; Stenton 1922, 15; *Feudal Aids* III, 243; *VE* IV, 83; PRO SC6/Hy8/2018.
2. BL Add MS 11574 ff86, 91.
3. OS 1st edn 1 in sheet 83; LAO Toft Parish Deposit; PADLEY 2/1; OS 25 in Lincs 45.13 and 14.

WALESBY

(1) **Settlement Remains (TF 138923)** [143, 144], formerly part of Walesby village and associated with the now isolated church, are situated at about 100 m above OD on top of a shelf of Tealby Limestone which protrudes W from below the crest of the main Wolds scarp. Downslope, some 500 m W is the centre of the present Walesby village, topographically separate from the earthworks and lying at 65 m above OD on a low spur on the edge of the Lincoln Clay Vale. The village was therefore formerly a polyfocal one and this is borne out by the documentary evidence. The settlement is a good example of contraction as a result of early 17th-century depopulation.

The medieval population for Walesby is difficult to ascertain, as the village is usually included with Risby (2) and Otby (3) in the records. In Domesday Book two of the entries for Walesby are shared with the adjacent settlements and there were 26 and 19 taxpayers in 1327–8 and 1332–3 respectively, presumably including Otby and Risby. The 1377 Poll Tax is lost, but there were at least 10 households between the three settlements in 1428. The 100 per cent relief of 1352 was reduced to 11.2 per cent in the 15th century. A hundred years later there were 22 and 26 taxpayers in 1524 and 1525 respectively, 22 names under Walesby in the Lindsey Musters of 1539 and 22 or 24 taxpayers in 1542–3. These inadequate figures suggest a considerable reduction in population in the 14th century, followed by recovery.

These sources appear to conceal what the tenurial history and the archaeological evidence combine to show, an ancient division of Walesby into two distinct but adjacent nuclei. The two manors of Domesday Book can be traced through the 12th to the 15th centuries as holdings of the honours of Lancaster and of Richmond.[1] The advowson of the church belonged to the Lancaster manor, which may suggest that the upper settlement block represented by the earthworks under discussion equates to that manor.

The lively land market of the later 16th century apparently broke the earlier tenurial pattern. By the end of the 16th century, certainly the Lancaster manor and perhaps the whole township had been purchased by the Conyers family.[2] The survey of depopulations in 1607 alleged that Thomas Conyers 'owner of the whole towne in which there were xiii farmes hath depopulated all the towne'. Conyers sold two farms with the result that they were pulled down. In addition Robert Dearne pulled down another farmhouse, and William Skelton turned 13 farmhouses into cottages and occupied their lands and commons for himself and perhaps let the buildings stand empty.[3] This reads like the same action seen from the point of view of owner and occupier rather than two independent occurrences.

These events befell a settlement that boasted only 22, 26 and 22 taxpayers in 1524, 1525 and 1543 respectively, 20 households in 1563 and 100 communicants in 1603. In 1676 there were 89 communicants. A Glebe Terrier of 1638 records that 'about two and thirty years since [ie 1606] a great part of the manor of W by Mr Thomas Coniers esquire hath been inclosed and in it the parsonage glebe exchanged and alienated by him as lord and patron'. In lieu Conyers allotted a large compact block of land around the church (enclosed by a line of circles in [143]). Though slightly extended before 1626 by Conyers' more sympathetic successor, Frances Dowager Countess of Exeter, it appears on the Tithe Map with only a single dwelling within it and that apparently the rectory ('a').[4] This allotment contains the whole uphill settlement block now represented by earthworks and pottery scatter, thereby segregating it from later reoccupation, and perhaps effectively marking the topographical distinction between the two early manors.

The early 17th-century depopulation was apparently so severe at Walesby that the effects look very similar to cases of village migration. Support for believing otherwise and seeing an earlier polyfocal pattern can be found in the earthworks ('b'), believed to be one arm of a manorial moat, and in the excavation of a medieval building with associated pottery of 13th to 14th-century date ('c').[5] The arrangement of property boundaries along the S side of the village, opposite St Mary's church of 1914, is highly suggestive of post-medieval development overlying an ordered medieval layout.

The earthworks and pottery scatters imply that the NE part of Walesby was never large, much of it lying S of the old church and contained within the curve of its main street. The latter appears to form the only physical link between the two parts of Walesby and its highly irregular course may mean that it has a pre-medieval origin. It leaves the E end of the surviving village as a lane and ascends the natural slope, changing direction on the steepest part and then running out on to the top of the shelf W of the church. The Tithe Map of 1847 marks its continuation along the E edge of the glebe ('d'), where it is now represented by a well-marked hollow-way curving across the shelf. It is interesting that it should form the glebe boundary for this suggests that the village did not extend S of its street. Ploughing has destroyed any upstanding evidence in the field to the NE although its continuation northwards is suggested by the line of the glebe on the Tithe Map and by a mark on air photographs.[6] Slight scarps and low banks divide the area within the curving road into linear closes, which, where ploughed, have

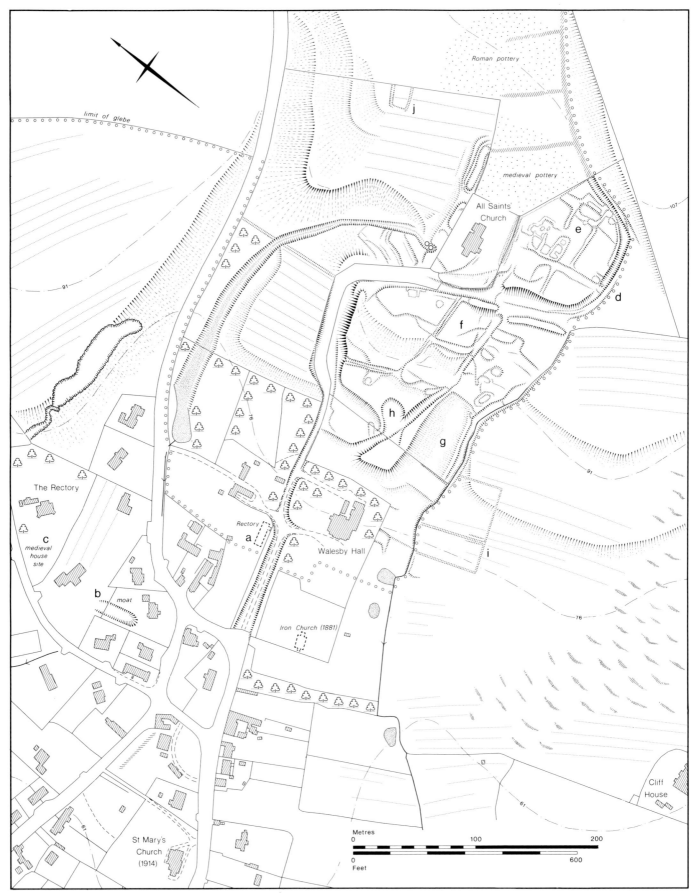

All Saints'
Church

Roman pottery

medieval pottery

j

e

d

f

h

g

i

limit of glebe

The Rectory

c
medieval
house
site

b moat

Rectory

a

Walesby Hall

Iron Church (1881)

Cliff
House

St Mary's
Church
(1914)

Metres
0   100   200

0   600
Feet

[143] Walesby (1) Settlement Remains, formerly part of Walesby.

[**144**] *Walesby (1) from the NE, 13 November 1969. The isolated church stands alone amongst former settlement earthworks, ridge-and-furrow and massive natural landslips, E of the present village. It once lay in the centre of a separate part of Walesby, cleared for sheep in the early 17th century. (Cambridge University Collection: copyright reserved)*

produced large quantities of medieval pottery with Roman pottery beyond. A complex of banks and hollows ('e') represents former buildings. A large hollow to the E, below the former street ('f'), is probably an old road. To the NE of the church, a long rectangular dry pond has a marked external bank on the N.

To the W and SW of the church and street few of the earthworks are clearly man-made except closes immediately along the street and a sinuous enclosure bank and ditch ('g'). The ground falls away sharply in this section and many of the scarps are probably landslips. A small quarry ('h') lies on one side of a prominent hollow-way which crosses the hillside. On the S side of a stream, shown as the glebe boundary on the Tithe Map, are two contiguous ditched enclosures ('i') on top of earlier ridge-and-furrow, which presumably had an agrarian function.

To the N of the church the natural shelf has been cut into by a steep-sided valley containing a stream fed by springs rising below the church. Blocks of ridge-and-furrow exploit the steep slope on either side of this valley. Above it and on top of the ridge-and-furrow is a small ditched enclosure ('j') from which good views can be obtained of the immediate locality. It is tempting to equate these remains with a habitation for the shepherd appointed in the 17th century to manage the sheep-walks.[7]

1. *Lincs DB* 14/13, 16/11, 40/6; *LS* 7/15, 21; *Book of Fees* I, 159; II, 1003, 1017, 1072, 1074; *Feudal Aids* III, 134, 138, 214, 242, 267, 269, 276, 279, 357.
2. Foster 1926, 327; Maddison 1902–6 I, 265.
3. BL Add MS 11574 f76, 79, 82, 86, 91.
4. LAO Walesby Terrier Bundle; A506.
5. Trollope 1861–2, 158; *LHA* **4** (1969), 110; NAR.
6. Air photographs in NMR.
7. LAO Walesby Terrier Bundle.

(2) Deserted Settlement (TF 146918) [9, 145] of Risby is situated at 110 m above OD on the side of the W-facing main scarp of the Wolds. Its long narrow township is delineated on the Tithe Map of 1852.[1] The settlement is remarkable for its location on unstable ground. Its apparently fluctuating population may have been a direct consequence of this situation.

The detailed history of Risby is difficult to ascertain, in part because of its association with Walesby and in part because of the complication of other settlements of this name in Lindsey. In 1086 the single holding here was occupied by the notably high minimum recorded population of 18. From the early 14th century onwards Risby is subsumed, with Otby, within returns for Walesby (1) except on three occasions. In 1463 a relief of 4*s* 8*d* was granted.

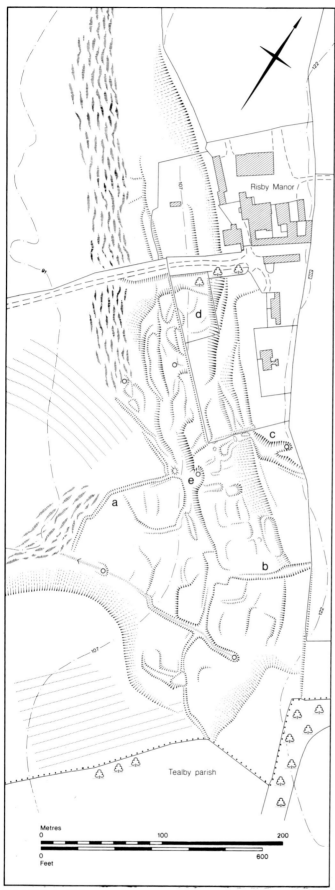

There were 8 households in 1563 and in the census of 1841 6 houses with a population of 49 are recorded. A note, appended to a copy of the 1831 census in the Walesby parish deposits in LAO, shows how tenuous occupation of the settlement was. It says 'no return made for Risby, it being at this time unoccupied and uninhabited; had it been inhabited it would have probably contained twenty-five inhabitants'.

These figures do not allow certainty about timing or reasons for loss of population except in so far as it may have contributed to Walesby's moderate return in the early 14th-century subsidies and the 100 per cent relief in 1352. The 19th-century returns presumably relate to the present Risby Manor Farm complex situated above the earthworks on the scarp edge.

The earthworks lie on a narrow unstable and waterlogged terrace which runs NW–SE of ('e') and interrupts the fall of the scarp. Evidence of former settlement is difficult to disentangle from mud flows and landslips, although a sinuous ditch ('a'), which looks relatively late in date, and two blocks of ridge-and-furrow, are clearly visible. The terrace acts as the main street of the village: at the SE end a hollow-way ('b') leaves the main terrace to run NE up the slope, and on either side of it some small sub-rectangular ledges which interrupt the hillside are probably building platforms. A few medieval and 19th-century sherds were associated with them. Just S of Risby Manor Farm the hillside is crossed obliquely by terrace-ways and by a hollow-way 2 m deep ('c'). Below these terrace-ways, a scatter of medieval sherds ('d') and earlier finds of 13th-century pottery in an area centred about 70 m to the SE, where a small building, possibly a barn, is marked on the 1852 Tithe Map, give direct evidence for habitation. Springs occur throughout the settlement and may have contributed to its origin. Further medieval or Saxo-Norman sherds were noted during the survey on the edge of the main terrace ('e').

1. LAO E687.

(3) Deserted Settlement (TF 138936) [146] of Otby is situated on a shelf below the crest of the W-facing scarp of the Wolds at about 100 m above OD. The front of the shelf is deeply indented by spring erosion which has produced flat-topped short spurs, projecting from the rear of the shelf, which fall steeply at their W ends and are separated by boggy clefts in an area affected by landslips. The earthworks are situated around a prominent cleft with its attendant spring and stream. A few earthworks also occur on the spur S of the cleft around the periphery of Otby House and its farm buildings. As at Risby (Walesby (2)) the location is inhospitable. The earthworks are therefore all the more notable for their apparent evidence of planning.

The documentation of Otby is almost inextricably bound up with Walesby (1). A settlement is named in Domesday Book although its population cannot be ascertained. In the Lindsey Survey it is recorded as a single holding but was later split into two parts, a division which may be reflected in the apparent duality of form of the settlement on either side of the major cleft.[1] With Risby (2), it is subsumed under Walesby in all medieval taxation returns and in 1563 had only 3 households. The 1841 census records it with 7 households and 44 inhabitants, but the Tithe Map of 1847[2] reveals that this small hamlet then lay within or was attached to the curtilage of Otby House and that no buildings stood amongst the main spread of earthworks to the N. Since the Second World War, Otby House has been abandoned and the only dwellings still inhabited are the cottages some 130 m E of the house.

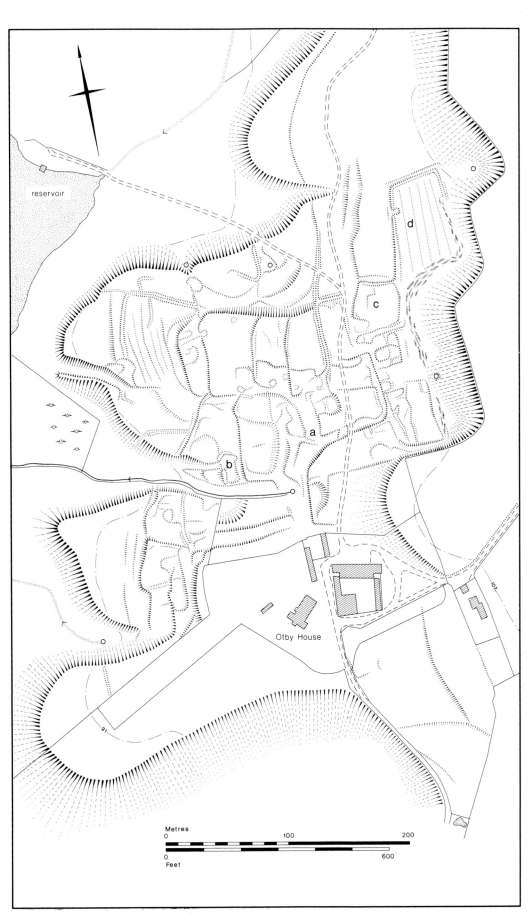

reservoir

d

c

a

b

Otby House

Metres
0   100   200

0   600
Feet

[**146**] *Walesby (3) Deserted Settlement of Otby.*

Although closely associated with Walesby, Otby seems once to have had its own township and field system.[3] This township may be represented by the single holding based on Otby House and shown on the Tithe Map.

The earthworks on the main S spur around Otby House are difficult to evaluate. The N, outer, face of its brick garden wall shows much alteration and provides evidence that structures were formerly attached to it. It is possible that some of the scarps are related to these installations while others immediately to the W and N may represent settlement remains of a village area once set around Otby House.

The earthworks further N over the cleft, perhaps once the centre of a separate part of the village, are of more interest in that they appear to have been arranged in an ordered manner. This is surprising in that the area is both topographically restricted and undulating, factors which would normally militate against formal planning. A terrace-way emerges from under Otby House farmyard and runs N above the spring for about 70 m and then bifurcates ('a'). One branch curves W and is flanked on both sides by a series of carefully laid out village closes. Those on the S run down to the stream and appear to have contained buildings at their N end. A deep rectangular pond ('b') has an exit channel and a dam on its W side. On the N and E sides of the terrace-way are particularly well-marked narrow rectangular enclosures surrounded by low banks or scarps. Immediately alongside the terrace-way, small mounds and depressions probably represent the remains of former buildings and are associated with large hollow areas which may be the remains of rectangular farmyards. At some stage the settlement may have extended almost to the W ends of both spurs. A number of parallel scarps which cross the spurs N–S and must represent either former ploughing or the results of soil-creep on sloping ground have obscured the area.

The second branch of the main terrace-way climbs the shelf as a narrow hollow-way. It runs first E and then N around the perimeter of closes served by the first branch, and gives access to properties arranged on its S and E side. The rectangular building remains associated with these are more regular, better defined and more numerous than those on the spur to the W and could therefore be different in date and function or may simply reflect the more amenable topography. Hollows and building remains ('c') seem to represent a single farmstead. On the NE edge of the village a slightly trapezoidal area ('d'), partly enclosed by a bank and ditch, contains broad N–S ridge-and-furrow. The E and S sides of this feature have been engulfed by landslips which may have also buried the boundary of the building remains to the SW ('c').

1. *Book of Fees* I, 156, 158; II, 1017–18, 1095; *Feudal Aids* III, 138, 160, 172, 214, 219, 226, 267, 298, 307; LCL Ross MSS IV, 244, 253.
2. LAO A506.
3. *Rot Hund* I, 382.

WELTON

(4) Fishponds (TF 009796) [147] lie on the N side of a shallow E-draining valley at 20 m above OD.

No direct documentary reference has been found to the fishponds but they lie within one of the three closes that together made up the medieval prebendal manor of Westhall as shown on the late 18th and 19th-century maps[1] and whose boundaries are depicted by lines of circles on [147]. These closes were *West Yard*, where excavations in 1971 revealed part of a pagan Anglo-Saxon cemetery

of the 6th century, plus pottery and structural evidence spanning the later medieval period,[2] *Chapel Yard* where medieval pottery has been recorded and 13 skeletons were found in 1963,[3] and *Dove Yard*, containing the fishponds.

The ponds are well preserved in old pasture but details of their operation are unclear because of alterations to the adjacent fields and the straightening of the stream. A high-level channel ('a'–'b'), cut into the natural slope, was presumably fed by seepage. It supplied three rectangular ponds, each approximately 1 m deep, arranged at right angles to it to the S. A parallel broad channel S of the ponds, itself embanked against the slope, may have acted as a single long pond.

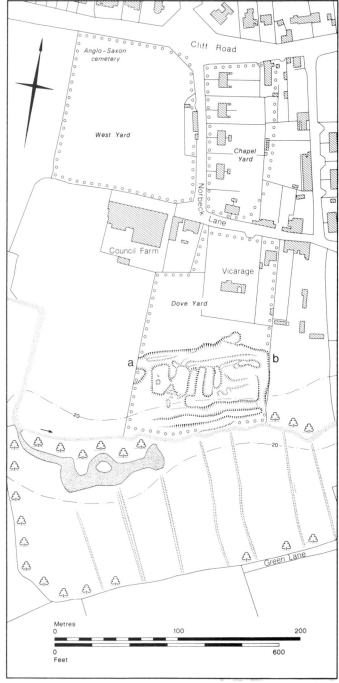

[147] *Welton (4) Fishponds.*

An irregular pond with an island on the S of the stream has been created since 1956. The same field is divided by slight banks into regular rectangular plots.

1. LAO Lindsey Encl 95; 2CC 62/352.
2. *LHA 7* (1972), 11; LM records.
3. LM records.

WEST FIRSBY

(1) Deserted Village of Firsby (SK 990852) [22, 25, 32, 148] lies around and just below the sources of the R Ancholme, on the dipslope of the Jurassic Limestone escarpment at around 35 m above OD. The remains of the village are extremely well preserved in pasture, although its extremities have been partly destroyed by modern cultivation. They include a large number of virtually complete house sites whose limestone rubble walls still stand up to 1 m high. Perhaps the main interest in the site, however, lies in the fact that the remains indicate a complex sequence of development which may plausibly be related to the documentary evidence.

The highest recorded population for Firsby is in Domesday Book with a minimum of 22 persons. It was barely half the average size for the wapentake in the early 14th-century subsidies with only 14 and 17 taxpayers, and though post-Black Death relief in 1352 appears low at about 20 per cent, only 25 persons over 14 years of age were returned in the 1377 Poll Tax and the parish was exempt from the 1428 tax with less than 10 households. Relief grew more substantial during the 15th century in contrast to the normal trend; in the mid 16th century the settlement was returned in the subsidies with neighbouring Saxby (1) and perhaps two taxpayers only belonged to it. It made no contribution to the Lindsey Musters in 1539 and no return of communicants was made in the survey of 1603, though in 1705–23 two households, presumably associated with the existing Manor Farm, were recorded.

The decline of Firsby, already evident in the earlier 14th century and exacerbated by the Black Death, continued through the 15th century probably with conversion to sheep-grazing, and apparently complete by the 16th century, is supported by the documentation of the manor. In 1086 the manor of Firsby was held by the Bishop of Bayeux though it had been two holdings in 1066. The Domesday Book manor can be traced as a single holding throughout the medieval period. Before the end of the 13th century it was reckoned to comprise 36 bovates of land of which precisely one-third used to be held in demesne but which had since been leased out to bondsmen who also held the remainder. The income from the whole 36 bovates was £18. The same arrangement pertained in 1324–5.[1]

Forty years later the picture was radically different. In the hands of Sir William de la Pole in 1366–7 the manor's land was said to be 'poor and sandy and lies in common and uncultivated'. In 1388 his son, Michael, Earl of Suffolk, had the site of the manor with 12 bovates (as of old) worth only 24*s* and only 5 bovates were held by tenants, worth 10*s*, and only 6 'toft garthys' were occupied. The manor's 56 sheep 'in poor condition worth 12d each' are elsewhere the same year recorded as '54 sheep worth 8d each, whereof many are at the point of death by the common murrain'.[2] Following the Earl of Suffolk's attainder the King granted Firsby into various hands until by 1428 it came to William Tyrwhitt. Judging by the family's actions at, for example, Kettleby and Kettleby Thorpe (Bigby (3, 4)), the result was presumably conversion to sheep-grazing. In 1548 the manor contained only three messuages.[3]

A church is listed as a manorial appurtenance in Domesday Book. Already by 1447 William Tyrwhitt as patron of both Firsby and Buslingthorpe petitioned for the union of the two livings on the grounds of their poverty and vacancy for some years past. By 1526 it had been reduced in status to a parochial chapelry, attached to the vicarage of Ingham, a link also recorded in 1535. The last recorded institution was in 1640.[4]

The earliest evidence of occupation actually on the site is that of a small Roman settlement on the N side of the later village whose presence has been revealed by the discovery of large quantities of pottery over a limited area. Roman pottery as well as medieval wares were noted over the whole spread of earthworks in the mid 19th century.[5] There is no indication of the site of the earliest medieval village, though it may have lain around the present derelict Manor Farm, where most of the springs which form the river are located.

The existing earthworks fall into several well-defined parts. An axial road ('a'–'b'), now a hollow-way and terrace-way, was perhaps part of an ancient route along the spine of the parish. Its line is continued W as an existing farm track from the point where it would have passed through the assumed site of the early village.

A rectangular embanked area ('c'), on the N side of the river and partly occupied by the modern farm buildings and subdivided by very slight scarps, banks and ditches, is likely to be the site of a manorial complex. Below it in the valley bottom are the damaged remains of possibly two ponds, one with a small island. Further E, also in the valley bottom, is another, larger pond again with two islands within it ('d'), which may well be the site of the water-mill of which the manor in the 13th and 14th centuries held a moiety.[6] A prominent raised area ('e'), separated from the manor by the stream and lying on the axial road which twists S to skirt it, contains rectangular stone foundations, orientated E–W. These were sketched in 1849 as a two-cell structure and identified as the medieval church foundation. Part of a foot of a cross and fragments of tombstones were also then visible.[5]

To the E of the manorial complex ('c'), between it and the large block of earthworks to the NE ('g') is a compact area of paddocks and house sites with no clear layout ('f'). These earthworks appear to have been laid out over an earlier block of ridge-and-furrow whose truncated ends project to the N. The largest part of the site lies further E again, extending along both sides of the river, and appears to be a coherent and perhaps planned unit ('g'). It is bounded on the S by the main E–W hollow-way, on the W by a small hollow-way which extends across the river and on part of the N by a bank and scarp. It is subdivided internally by four N–S hollow-ways, all but one of which extend across the river. That part S of the river is characterized by groups of stone-walled structures, set against the main hollow-way, each with closes extending N downslope to the river. On the N side of the valley are much more extensive remains of stone buildings and yards, although here the overall pattern is less clear, except that access is provided by the cross-valley ways.

It is not obvious what the E boundary of this area was, if indeed it ever had one. On the NE, a hollow-way running to the river edge appears to mark its limits, but the land to the E is under cultivation and within it a mutilated bank immediately to the E of the hollow-way might be a remnant of the NE limit. Neither the hollow-way nor this bank are linked to any feature to the S of the river.

The relationship of this unit to the ridge-and-furrow is complex and not clear. Three mutilated ridges within the area on the N side, separated from the ridge-and-furrow to the N by a headland,

[148] *West Firsby (1) Deserted Village of Firsby.*

212

suggest that the whole unit may have been laid out over earlier fields. Yet, further E the existing ridge-and-furrow appears to cut into and thus to overlie the assumed boundary. In the SE corner there are slight traces of former ridges within the main trackway which must pre-date the latter. Further ridges lie to the E again. These, though slight, are clearly earlier terminations of the block of ridge-and-furrow to the S which now ends on a secondary headland. Despite the former ridges lying within the trackway and its assumed W continuation, there is no indication of damage by traffic to the ridge-and-furrow in that area.

The SW of the site is occupied by a roughly rectangular area ('h') bounded on the N by the main axial terrace-way and on the other three sides by a loop road or track, partly hollowed. This runs off the axial road in the NE corner and returns to it in the NW corner, though on the SW corner and in the centre of the W side three other trackways, not all contemporary, run on further NW and W. The area contained by the looped track is divided into three or four unequal closes by very low banks running N–S. At the N ends of the closes are the remains of well-preserved stone-walled structures and sunken yards. To the S are slight traces of ridge-and-furrow. The relationship between these structures, the low banks, the S boundary scarp and the ridge-and-furrow is complex. A number of ridges have been cut through at their N ends by the stone structures. At least one of the N–S banks, as well as a short cross-bank, overlie the ridge-and-furrow. In addition, in the E half of the area, the ridge-and-furrow rides over the S boundary scarp, while in the W it terminates well short of this boundary. Further, though not provable on the ground, it is possible that the ridge-and-furrow to the S formerly extended over the whole area as far N as the main E–W road.

Other minor features of the site include two small rectangular embanked enclosures ('i' and 'j'), possibly sheep-folds, both overlying ridge-and-furrow just beyond the N limits of the village.

A tentative chronology of the remains can be suggested from the foregoing account. An early village perhaps lay around the existing Manor House while to the E the ridge-and-furrow of its associated fields may have extended down the valley side, ending close to the river on the N and against a river-edge trackway on the S. If the pre-Conquest manors which made up the Bishop of Bayeux's 1086 holding had any topographical significance, a second nucleus may have existed to the E, providing a focus for a later development.

At a later date the village was replanned on a very large scale. The manorial complex ('c') may have been one element of this planning and the large E unit ('g') is also likely to have been laid out as a coherent block, though with two distinct arrangements, and partly on top of earlier fields. The formal and duodecimally-based division between demesne and bondsmen's land, current in the mid 13th century, may reflect this planning and may go back to the 12th century. A later addition is the small area of structures between these two elements ('f'), also on older ridge-and-furrow and apparently squeezed into the area separating the manorial complex from the planned village. This area has no appearance of unity and may mark uncontrolled expansion, perhaps when the demesne arable was let to the bondsmen to farm in the later 13th and early 14th centuries.

The same context may possibly have seen the framework of the SW block ('h') created, too, but this has a more complex development which may take in earlier and more probably later features. These include walled closes for earlier small-scale demesne sheep-farming documented from the late 14th century onwards, and possibly the latest forms of the settlement clinging alongside its

church. The sheep-folds out on the former arable to the N may mark a final phase of total pasture.

1. *Lincs DB* 4/11; *LS* 2/13; *Book of Fees* I, 190; *Cal IPM* III (1912), 174, 232; VI (1910), 346.
2. *Cal IPM* XII (1938), 56; *Cal Inq Misc* V (1962), 48, 88.
3. LCL Ross MSS IV, 13–14; *Feudal Aids* III, 255, 309, 356.
4. *Lincs DB* 4/11; LAO Bishop's Register (Alnwick) 18, f70; Owen 1975, 19; *VE* IV, 133; Beresford 1954, 309.
5. Notes of Rev E. G. Jarvis, reproduced in LCL Ross MSS IV, 18.
6. *Cal IPM* III (1912), 174, 232; VI (1910), 346.

WEST RASEN

---

(1) Settlement Remains (TF 064893) [149], formerly part of West Rasen, lie on river terrace sands and gravels on the N side of the R Rase and alluvium, Oxford Clay and Kellaways sands and clays, on the S side, at 15 m above OD. The tenurial arrangement in 1086 suggests that West Rasen was originally two separate settlements and this hypothesis is supported, not only by the remains of a former settlement, but by the shape of the parish and by topographical details recorded in later documents.

In 1086 Ralf Paynel held a large manor that included a mill, and the Bishop of Bayeux held a smaller manor with two mills. It is likely that the larger manor included the E half of West Rasen and that the Bayeux manor occupied the W part. By the early 12th century the whole vill was in Ralf's hands[1] and it remained in the possession of the Paynels until 1327. In the later 14th century it was again divided into two for a short while but was then united and remained so until the 19th century.[2]

In 1218–19 Hugh Paynel obtained the grant of a weekly market and soon afterwards an annual fair; both were confirmed in the early 15th century. The 'curia of the hall of West Rasen' had within it a water-mill in 1268–75 and in 1336 this mill is referred to as 'west of a certain island, with stanks and watercourses and a piece of pasture called Riskholm, east of the stanks'. The buildings and appurtenances of this manorial complex in the hands of Paynel and his successors are well documented and continued as a residence until the end of the 15th century.[3]

West Rasen was a large settlement in the early medieval period with a minimum recorded population of 62 in 1086. The number of taxpayers in the early 14th-century subsidies – 43 in 1327–8 and 44 in 1332–3 – though 50 per cent above the average for the wapentake, must already represent a decline from earlier levels and perhaps a sharp one. Over 75 per cent relief was allowed in 1352, but 123 people still paid the Poll Tax in 1377. Reliefs of 20 per cent and 25 per cent were allowed in 1448 and 1463 which suggests no recovery. However there were 27 and 34 taxpayers to the lay subsidies of 1524 and 1525, 40 names appear in the Lindsey Musters of 1539, 33 taxpayers in 1542–3, 50 households in 1563 and 160 communicants in 1603. No enclosure or depopulation was reported in 1607, but the overall population fell by about one-fifth from the mid 16th century to the early 18th century and by the same again over the century to 1801, perhaps reflecting prolonged neglect by the absentee landowners. Following enclosure in 1803–4, the population rose to exceed 40 households by the mid 19th century, these being principally located in new farms and cottages outside or on the periphery of the old village.[4]

The very extensive settlement remains are confined within the old enclosures as defined in the early 19th century and are completely surrounded by well-marked furlongs of ridge-and-furrow. The extent and complexity of the remains reflect the settlement's early

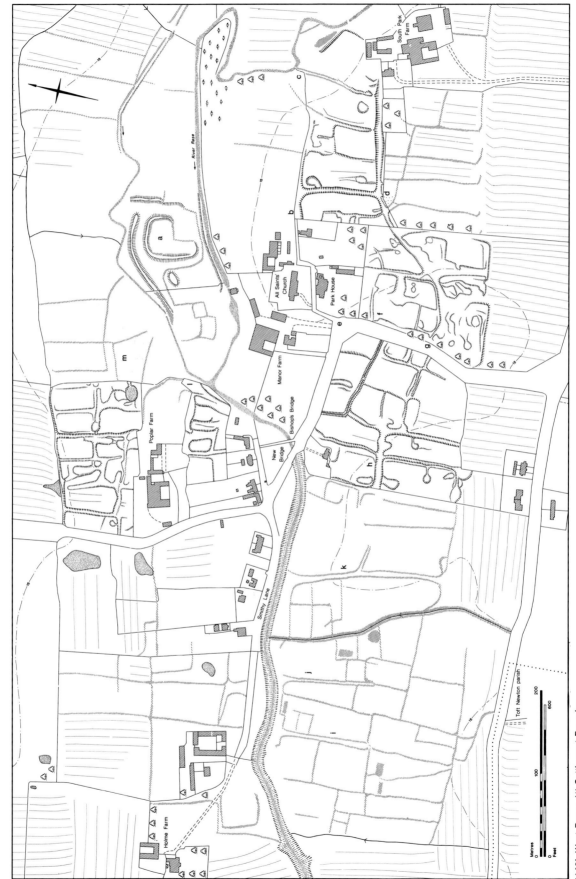

[149] *West Rasen (1) Settlement Remains.*

214

size and chequered history. Traces of ridge-and-furrow overlain by settlement closes appear to indicate expansion or movement before the 14th-century and later decline.

Convincing analysis of the settlement's morphology is hampered by the levelling of more than half of the former earthworks in the 1960s and early 1970s. Their principal features can be reconstructed from early air photographs and OS records, but their interpretation and the relationship to the surviving earthworks are uncertain. Nevertheless, a number of distinct elements can be picked out which may relate to the early development of the village.

The principal manor and the site of the Paynel residence occupied land around the church, certainly on the documentary evidence extending to the N of it and presumably including the present Manor Farm and the site of a group of embanked earthworks ('a') lying between the two streams of the R Rase. These enclosures have previously been described as a moat and more recently as being connected with the adjacent modern water-mill, but there is no doubt that they are medieval fishponds. They were presumably the 'stanks' and associated features documented in 1336 and the meadow to the E equates with the pasture called *Riskholm*. Since the S stream of the river is an artificial mill leat, water was presumably led from it into the SE corner of the complex, and ponded against the long dam along the N side so forming an area of water around a low-lying and perhaps marshy centre island. The whole complex was destroyed in 1965 and only a few sherds of medieval pottery were found.[5]

To the S, E and SW of the church are the remains of a settlement, presumably associated with the principal manor. Though now partly destroyed, at least the overall and relatively regular layout can still be recovered and its relationship with this manorial *curia* indicated. The existing track running between the church and Park House is continued E as a fragmentary hollow-way ('b'–'c') which was still marked as a road in the early 19th century. Mirroring this is a second well-developed hollow-way which leaves the existing road S from the village ('g'), runs NE roughly parallel to the Park House/church track and then turns E ('d'), where it is almost exactly parallel to the N hollow-way ('b'–'c'). Along the latter section, former closes, some containing recognizable house sites, lie between the two hollow-ways and on the S side of the southern one is a further series of closes which, though now ploughed out, appears to overlie earlier ridge-and-furrow. To the S of Park House, other former closes still exist on both sides of the hollow-way ('g'–'d'), all showing evidence of former buildings within them, but less regular and more disturbed than those to the E. This may be, at least in part, the result of the occupation of this area until a relatively recent date. At least two buildings (at approximately 'f' and 'g') are depicted on the Enclosure Map of 1772 and on the 1st edn OS map of 1824.[6] To the W of the existing road is an area of similar closes. At the W end is a short section of an E–W hollow-way ('h').

The interpretation of these features is not entirely clear and there are at least two possible hypotheses. The existing road from Bishop's Bridge, a 14th-century stone structure,[7] with its continuation W first as a track and then, beyond Holme Farm, as a path, is likely to be an ancient route. This road may well have once continued E as a hollow-way leading to South Park Farm and beyond to Middle Rasen. Such a road would have then bisected a rectangular and perhaps planned block of village properties on the S and N with the manorial *curia* in the NW, and the subsequent expansion of the *curia* southwards would have then led to the development of the circuitous route to the S ('e'–'g'–'d'). The main road S (from 'e'), possibly in origin an access lane through the village properties as the one to the E is ('b'–'d'), might then be viewed as a later development.

Alternatively, the settlement block may have originally consisted of a skewed area based on two parallel streets (Bishop's Bridge–'e'–'b'–'c', on the N and 'h'–'g'–'d'–South Park Farm on the S) with properties and cross-lanes between them and the *curia* in the NW, with further properties to the S. Later alterations would have then included the development of the main road S and the obliteration of the S street (between 'g' and 'h'). Whatever the original form of this part of the settlement, it was likely that it was planned and that much of it overlay earlier arable.

To the W, and almost completely separated from the settlement remains described above, is another compact group. The discontinuity between the two nuclei is perhaps marked by the abrupt double bend in the W hollow-way ('h'). The earthworks here have now been entirely destroyed, though the main features can be recovered from early air photographs. These indicate that the second settlement area was made up of a series of rectangular ditched closes, set at right angles to the river, and in part served by three lengths of hollow-way ('i', 'j' and 'k'). The S edge of these closes appears to truncate ridge-and-furrow, but whether this indicates only an expansion of an earlier nucleus, or is because the whole layout was a new development, is unclear. As a distinct focus it may have its origin in the smaller late 11th-century manor held by the Bishop of Bayeux.

On the N side of the river, where the greater part of the present village now lies, are two further areas of former settlement earthworks. To the N of Smithy Lane and now destroyed by modern agriculture are fragmentary closes, all largely developed over former arable, and perhaps to be connected with former and existing buildings along the lane itself. On the E side of the Glentham road, around Poplar Farm, are other earthworks. These, and the farm, lay in the angle between the road to Glentham and a track running NE along the side of the river, whose line is now only marked by a fragment of a hollow-way ('l') but which, in 1824, led on to a group of buildings NE of the farm ('m'). The latter is also depicted on the Enclosure Map of 1772, and air photographs show a group of former closes in this area. These closes extended W as a block of extant earthworks forming a series of paddocks apparently fronting an E–W hollow-way on the N. The whole area may represent a further regular planned element of the village.

All these elements of former occupation are linked by and focused on a small triangular green NW of Bishop's Bridge which then extends W as an elongated strip or broad street, along the N side of the river, now represented by Smithy Lane. This open space may also have originally extended E of the river for the whole area is treated as road on the Enclosure Map of 1772, despite at that date containing two blocks of encroaching properties within the triangular green, which have since been removed. It is possible that this green is the result of the provision of a market area, following the early 13th-century grant, a feature already noted elsewhere.

1. *Lincs DB* 4/38, 35/6; *LS* 7/13.
2. *Book of Fees* I, 156; II, 1004, 1017, 1095; *Feudal Aids* III, 172, 226, 244, 268, 306, 357; *Cal Pat R 1370–4* (1914), 368; *Cal Close R 1337–9* (1900), 246–51; *Cal IPM* VIII (1913), 91–2; IX (1917), 174; XIII (1955), 155; *Cal IPM* Hen VII pt 1 (1916), 475; LCL Ross MSS IV, 178 and pedigree facing 182; monuments and glass in church recorded by Holles, Cole 1911, 108–111; National Register of Archives, duplicated list of Maxwell-Constable (Everingham) deposit, East Riding County Record Office.

3. *Cal Chart R 1226–57* (1903), 237; *Cal Pat R 1408–13* (1909), 162; NRA Maxwell-Constable deposit, DDEV/44/3 and 17; PRO C133/14/1, C135/52/11; *Cal IPM* II (1906), 112; III (1912), 412; VI (1910), 370; Archer 1963–82 I, 33.
4. LAO West Rasen parish deposit; NRA Maxwell-Constable deposit, DDEV/44/162–3, 164, 170, 171; OS 1st edn 1 in sheet 83.
5. OS 1st edn 25 in sheets Lincs 45.10 and 11; NAR TF 08 NE 3; *EMAB 7* (1964), 20.
6. PRO CP 43/884; OS 1st edn 1 in sheet 83.
7. Jervoise 1932, 56.

(2) Windmill Mound (TF 05618886) [39, 150] lies SW of the village, against the parish boundary with Toft Newton on Till at 17 m above OD. There is no documentary evidence for a windmill before the early 19th century when the 1st edn OS 1 in map of 1824 shows a wooden post-mill here, but the furlong name *Milnehill* lying in the West Field and recorded at least from the early 13th century, may relate to this.[1] No mill is shown here on Greenwood's county map of 1830.

The mound is 3 m high, circular, with a surrounding ditch and with a flat top 12 m across. There is a steep ramp on the N side. It is situated on a small triangular piece of land between blocks of ridge-and-furrow, now destroyed, but visible on air photographs,[2] in such a way as to indicate that it has been inserted into an earlier pattern of furlongs.

1. NAR TF 08 NE 18; *Cal Close R Edw III 1337–9* (1900), 247; PRO CP 43/884; OS 1st edn 1 in sheet 83; LAO MCD 579/DDEV/44/8 and 14.
2. RAF VAP CPE/UK1880/2462; CPE/UK2012/2068.

WICKENBY

---

(3) Settlement Remains (TF 090820) [151], formerly part of Wickenby village, lie at 20 m above OD on the S side of a low ridge of Till. Despite considerable destruction the field remains, together with the evidence from existing road alignments and property boundaries, indicate that the village has undergone at least one major change of plan. This involved not only the diversion of the main street and the establishment of a regular pattern of closes, but also the extension and perhaps the reorganization of the manorial *curia*.

The two Domesday manors held by William de Percy had both passed to the Chamberlain family by the mid 13th century and remained in their possession until at least the mid 15th century. The family appears to have been resident at Wickenby for most of that time.[1] It is possible that the Chamberlains were responsible for an extension of the manorial *curia* which disrupted the earlier village arrangements.

No church is recorded in 1086, although its location in the earthworks suggests an association with the manor and perhaps a proprietorial origin. A monastic interest in Wickenby was a holding of Stainfield Priory, presumably based on gifts of the Percys' estate, since that family were the founders of the priory. By the mid 15th century this holding was let.[2]

With occasional exceptions, Wickenby's population indicators generally include returns for Westlaby (Wickenby (2)). In 1086 they can be separated with a minimum of 15 persons recorded for Wickenby. In 1316 the manor took rents of 24 villeins and one *nativus* each holding a toft and land, plus 20 'coterells'.[3] In the subsidies of 1327–8 and 1332–3, 29 and 26 taxpayers listed constitute rather over the average for the wapentake. No relief is

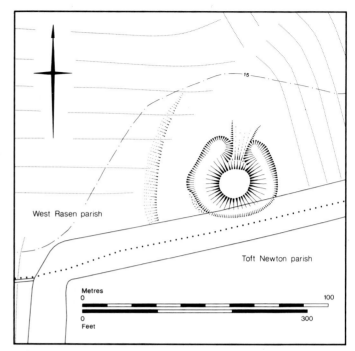

[150] *West Rasen (2) Mill Mound.*

recorded in 1352 but only 66 persons paid the Poll Tax in 1377, which may mark a reduction of up to half through the Black Death period. There were at least 10 households in 1428 and although reliefs of over 15 per cent persisted in the mid 15th century, a hundred years later Wickenby produced 9 men for the Lindsey Musters in 1539, 15 taxpayers in 1542–3, 17 households in 1563 and 83 communicants in 1603.

Some depopulation was reported by the survey of 1607, the land of one farm being engrossed and the farmhouse left empty. The parish was enclosed between 1625 and 1638 but there is no clear evidence for a related decline in population. In 1662 18 persons paid the Hearth Tax, there were 65 communicants in 1676, and by the early 18th century there were 26 households in the parish.[4] After some fall to 21–25 houses in the first four decades of the 19th century, the population more than doubled in the later 1840s, principally with new buildings outside the old settlement nucleus.[5]

The field remains are partly surviving earthworks immediately N and E of the church and the Manor House, and a greater area of levelled earthworks principally to the E, whose overall plan is recoverable from early air photographs taken before their destruction.[6]

Surrounding the Manor House is a rectangular substantially ditched enclosure, probably defining a manorial block that must formerly have encompassed the church also. A chain of hollows running downslope ('a') may have been a set of rather slight fishponds. This manorial *curia* has clearly disrupted the road pattern and remodelled it by expanding across it. The road from the W enters a dog-leg ('b') taking it round the S side of the block and it only resumes the direct alignment of the through road to the E well to the E ('c'). Physical remains of the earlier direct road alignment are not obvious in the earthworks although the estate map of *c* 1800 appears to show just a fragment of surviving road running W from the E bend ('c'). Indeed the remodelling of the settlement seems to have extended to the village closes E of the manor. Their overall pattern of rectangular ditched plots containing, where the earthworks survive, traces of building platforms and hollow yards,

Manor House

St Peter and
St Lawrence's Church

Rectory

a

b

c

d

Metres
0   100   200

Feet
0   600

[151] *Wickenby (3) Settlement Remains.*

217

suggests a degree of regularity with an N–S depth of three or four plots perhaps served by narrow lanes running N from the diverted through road as at ('d').

At the E end (E of 'c') and coinciding with the resumption of the early road alignment, the settlement properties form a further distinct block that is less deep N–S than the village remains to the W but overlaps the road. This block might be a later extension of the settlement, or, perhaps more plausibly, represent Stainfield Priory's holding which acted as a constraint on the realignment of the road. The field-name *Grange Close*, however, occurs 200 m to 300 m further E.[7] Properties at the W end of the settlement (W of 'b'), shown on the early map but removed by 1886, lay on top of ridge-and-furrow. The field-name was *Town End Close*.

1. *Lincs DB* 1/37, 22/10, 34, 28/28; *LS* 16/3, 13; *Book of Fees* I, 172; II, 1062, 1093; *Feudal Aids* III, 169, 223, 269, 303, 360; *Cal IPM* I (1904), 99; II (1906), 24; V (1908), 416; VI (1910), 56; X (1921), 491; XII (1938), 222; PRO C134/57/10; *Cal Pat R 1547–53* (1926), 369–70.
2. LAO FL Deeds 1295; *VE* IV, 82.
3. PRO C134/57/10.
4. BL Add MS 11574, ff80, 83, 88; Johnson 1962, 141; PRO E179/140/806.
5. LAO A262; OS 25 in sheets Lincs 53.11 and 15.
6. RAF VAP 541/185/4134–5 and 4193–6.
7. LAO 3 BNL 10; A262.

WILLOUGHTON

(1) Moated Site (SK 932931) [152], once the site of a grange of an alien priory, lies on the SE edge of Willoughton village on Upper Lias clay and shale at about 40 m above OD.

Before about 1115 Waldin the Engineer's Domesday manor at Willoughton formed the basis of a grant to the Benedictine house of St Nicholas at Angers.[1] It seems unlikely that a priory of monks was ever created here. In all detailed references it is described as the manor belonging to the abbot and convent of St Nicholas and its demise with other English holdings in 1392, confirmed in 1396, was in the name of the abbot and convent directly.[2] The manor was granted to King's College, Cambridge in 1441.[3] In the 14th and 15th centuries a distinct part of Willoughton village is named as 'the hamlet of *Helpesthorp*', whose tithes formed an adjunct to the manor held by St Nicholas at Angers.[4] It is likely that this settlement is to be identified with a rectangular block of properties on the E side of the village, now broken up by the gardens of 19th-century villas but clear on the Enclosure Map of 1769, which flanked a lane running due S from the moated site.[5] It is possible that this block represents a planned settlement created by the alien grange and associated with it.

The field remains consist of a rectangular moat up to 2 m deep surrounding a small platform which is almost completely occupied by what appear to be foundations of a large building. The platform has been artificially raised by up to 1 m above the surrounding land, in part levelled against a slope. The large external bank on the N up to 0.75 m high might have functioned as a dam. A channel leads NW from the moat into a small pond and then at right angles into a large pond surrounded on its sides and downslope end by broad banks. A slight channel at the NW corner allows overspill into the village beck. Local information asserts that the large supposed fishpond was a retting pit for flax: this use may nevertheless have

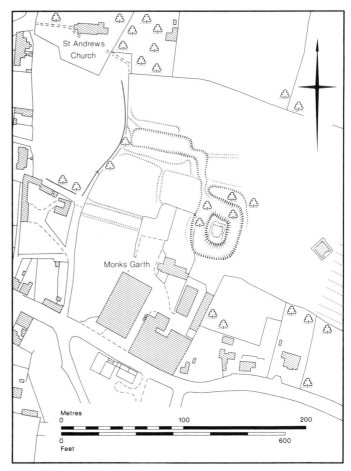

[152] *Willoughton (1) Moated Site.*

taken over or enlarged earlier fishponds. A series of narrow ditches, in part relating to surviving close boundaries, mark out paddocks or closes around the moat. Those to the E and the ridge-and-furrow upslope of them have been largely obliterated by a cricket pitch.

1. *Lincs DB* 47/1; *LS* 2/15; Dugdale 1817–30 VI, 1056; Lees 1935, cxci, cxciv.
2. *Cal Rot Chart et Inq AQD*, 33; *Cal Pat R 1367–70* (1913), 234; *1391–6* (1905), 722.
3. *Cal Pat R 1436–41* (1907), 557; *1461–7* (1897), 74.
4. *Cal Pat R 1367–70* (1913), 234; *1388–92* (1902), 19; *1413–16* (1910), 164–5.
5. LAO Willoughton Parish Plans.

(2) Site of Preceptory of the Knights Templars and Hospitallers (SK 927932) [153] lies on the SW edge of Willoughton village on Middle Lias clay and shale at approximately 35 m above OD. The complex remains mark the site of the richest of the English properties of the Templars.

The preceptory was founded between 1135 and 1154 jointly by Simon de Canci and Roger de Bussei, with the former making the larger contribution to the endowment which in 1185 is recorded as 23½ bovates and 24 tofts with 23 tenants. This estate was the greater part of a Domesday manor, with a minimum recorded population of twenty-four, which had passed to Anfrid de Canceio in the early years of the 12th century.[1] Through its extensive early endowment Willoughton Preceptory became an economic and administrative centre of Templars' estates throughout northern Lincolnshire. When the Templars were suppressed in 1312, the

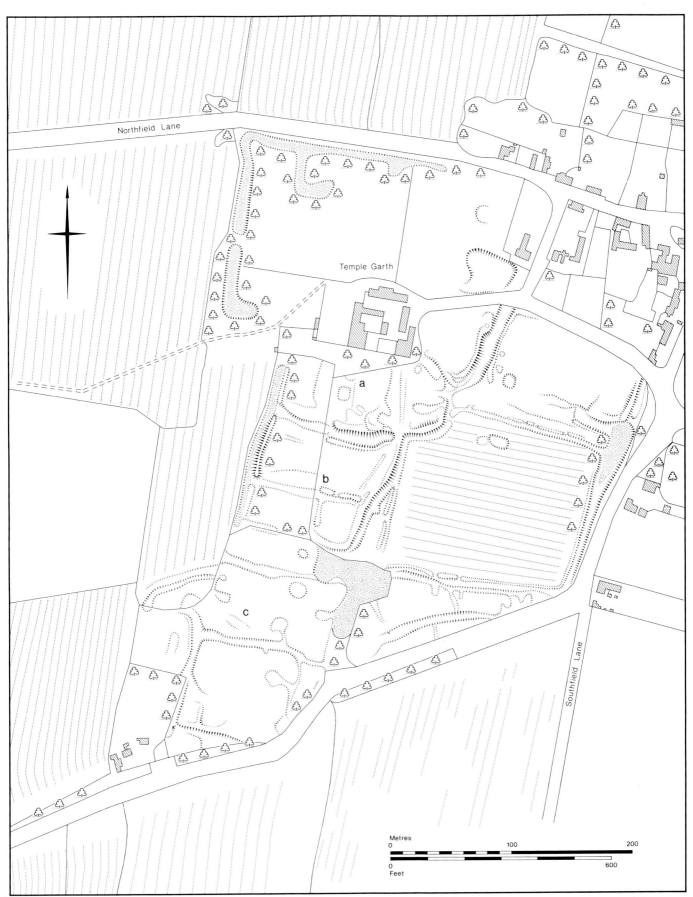

Northfield Lane

Temple Garth

a

b

c

Southfield Lane

Metres
0   100   200

0
Feet
600

[153] *Willoughton (2) Site of Preceptory of the Knights Templars and Hospitallers.*

219

estate passed to the Hospitallers and Willoughton continued its role as the centre of a network of member estates in central and northern Lincolnshire.[2]

The preceptory was dissolved in 1540 and in 1545 'the site and chief messuage of Willoughton Preceptory with its gardens etc' were granted to John Cokke and John Thurgood, who in the same year alienated the property to John Sutton and his heirs.[3]

The preceptory buildings may have included a chapel, named in 1392. A dovecote worth 6s 8d in 1338 appears in 1535 and still formed part of the estate in 1575–6. Similarly the garden attached to the capital messuage in 1338 appears in 1535 as 'ortis, pomeriis, gardinis', which in 1575–6 extended to ten gardens and six orchards.[4]

The main precinct of the preceptory occupied a roughly rectangular enclosure around Temple Garth farmhouse. It is defined on the W and N by a deep water-filled moat, protruding elements of which shelve up to give access as drinking places for stock. On the SE and S a similar moat is dry, with a marked inner scarp up to 2 m high. Within the precinct ('a') S of the house, slight earthworks perhaps including the site of a building aligned on the standing building are as likely to mark post-Dissolution as earlier features.

To the S of the inner precinct, a possible extension ('b') of the moat is slighter in scale but similar in form. It has a dry ditch and an inner stony bank on the E and a water-filled pond with an upcast bank on the W. It defines an area divided into two rectangular closes and perhaps further subdivided. The regular pattern is continued S by three further plots or closes ('c') marked out by ditches. These have been cut through by a large pond, perhaps resulting from digging clay for bricks. To the E of the pond an irregular hollow-way may mark an earlier line of the lane to the S. Two large closes to the N of the hollow-way, marked out by embanked ditches and one of them full of ridge-and-furrow, may also form part of the preceptory complex.

The interpretation of the five closes S of the main precinct is problematical. As earthworks they are not dissimilar to settlement tofts, though large, and there are traces of shallow hollows within them such as mark crewyards on clayland sites. They might include the five tofts of Roger de Bussei's endowment that alone out of the early grant were identifiable in 1185, perhaps just because they were topographically distinct from the main village. Alternatively they might, with the closes to the E, be the gardens and orchards that are named in such numbers in the 16th century. The alternatives are not mutually incompatible, and they serve to underline the physical scale of this important religious house.

1. *Lincs DB* 48/1; *LS* 2/14; Lees 1935, cxci–cxciv, 100–1.
2. *Rot Orig Abbr* I (1805), 184, 197; *Cal Pat R 1307–13* (1894), 465; *Cal Close R 1307–13* (1892), 527; *1323–7* (1898), 108; *1327–30* (1896), 234, 246; Larking 1857, 144–9.
3. Knowles and Hadcock 1971, 301, 308; *Cal LPFD Hen VIII* XX, pt 2 (1907), 224, 303.
4. *Cal Pat R 1391–6* (1905), 152; Larking 1857, 144, 150; *VE* IV, 137; HMC Lumley MSS, 736.

SELECT BIBLIOGRAPHY
AND ABBREVIATIONS

Acts of the Privy Council XII, XIII (1896) ed. J.R. Dasent

Addyman, P. and Whitwell, J.B., 1970 — Some Middle Saxon pottery types in Lincolnshire, *Antiq J* **50**

Allen, T., 1834 — *The History of the County of Lincoln* II

Allerston, P., 1970 — English Village Development, *Trans Inst Brit Geog* **51**

Ancient Deeds — *Catalogue of Ancient Deeds* IV (1902)

Anderson, C.H.J., 1880 — *The Lincoln Pocket Guide*

Andrews, C.B., ed., 1934–6 — *The Torrington Diaries. A Tour Through England and Wales of the Hon. John Byng 1781–1794* 3 vols

AP — Air Photographs

Archer, M., ed., 1963–82 — *The Register of Bishop Philip Repingdon 1405–19* 3 vols, LRS 57, 58, 74

Armstrong, A., 1776–8 — *Map of Lincolnshire*, surveyed 1776–8 (1779)

Aston, M.A., 1985 — Rural Settlement in Somerset in D. Hooke, ed., *Medieval Villages: A Review of Current Work*

Baker, F.L., 1956 — *The History of Riseholme*

1957 — *The History of Nettleham*

nd — *Scothorne*

Beastall, T.W., 1978 — *Agricultural Revolution in Lincolnshire*, History of Lincolnshire VIII

Beckwith, I., 1972 — *The History of Fields and Farms in Gainsborough*

Beresford, G., 1975 — *The Medieval Clay-Land Village: Excavations at Goltho and Barton Blount*, Society for Medieval Archaeology Monograph Series 6

1977 — *The Excavations of the Deserted Medieval Village of Goltho, Lincolnshire*, *Chateau Gaillard* **8**

1982 — Goltho Manor, Lincolnshire: The Buildings and their Surrounding Defences c. 850–1150, *Procs Battle Conference on Anglo-Norman Studies 4 1981*, ed. R. Allen Brown

Beresford, M.W., 1954 — *The Lost Villages of England*

Beresford, M.W. and St Joseph, J.K., 1979 — *Medieval England: An Aerial Survey*

Binney, M. and Hills, A., 1979 — *Elysian Gardens*

BL — British Library

Blair, J., 1981 — The Buslingthorpes and their monuments, *Trans Monumental Brass Soc* **12** (1975–9) pt4

Book of Fees — *The Book of Fees* pt1 (1921), pt2 (1923)

Brace, H.W., ed., 1948 — *The First Minute Book of the Gainsborough Monthly Meeting of the Society of Friends 1669–1719* I, LRS 38

Brakespear, A., 1922 — Bardney Abbey, *Archaeol J* **29**

Britton, J., 1807 — *The Beauties of England and Wales* 8

Cal Chart R — *Calendar of Charter Rolls*

Cal Close R — *Calendar of Close Rolls*

Cal Docs Preserved in France — *Calendar of Documents Preserved in France 918–1206* (1899)

Cal Fine R — *Calendar of Fine Rolls*

Cal Inq Misc — *Calendar of Miscellaneous Inquisitions*

Cal IPM — *Calendar of Inquisitions Post Mortem*

Cal LPFD Hen VIII — *Calendar of Letters and Papers, Foreign and Domestic, Henry VIII*

Cal Pat R — *Calendar of Patent Rolls*

Cal Rot Chart et Inq AQD — *Calendarium Rotulorum Chartarum et Inquisitionum ad quod Damnum*

Cal State Papers Dom — *Calendar of State Papers, Domestic*

Camden, W., 1695 — *Britannia*

Cary, J., 1787 — *New and Correct English Atlas*

Catalogue of Antiquities 1848 exhibited in the museum formed during the Annual Meeting of the Royal Archaeological Institute held at Lincoln in July 1848

Clay, C.T., 1939–47 — The family of Amundeville, *LAASRP* **3**

ed., 1955 — *Early Yorkshire Charters X* Yorkshire Archaeol Soc Record Series, extra series, **8**

ed., 1963 — *Early Yorkshire Charters XI, The Percy Fee* Yorkshire Archaeol Soc Record Series, extra series, **11**

1966 — Hugh Bardolf the Justice and his Family, *LHA* **1**

Cockayne, G.E.C., 1910–59 — *Complete Peerage* 13 vols

Cole, R.E.G., ed., 1911a — The Manor and Rectory of Kettlethorpe, *AASRP* **31** pt1

1911 — *Gervase Holles: Lincolnshire Church Notes 1634–42* LRS 1

1913 — *Speculum Dioeceseos Lincolniensis Sub Episcopis Gul Wake et Edm Geibson 1705–23* LRS 4

1915, 1917, 1920 — *Chapter Acts of the Cathedral Church of St Mary of Lincoln AD, 1520–36* LRS 12; *1536–47* LRS 13; *1547–59* LRS 15

Colvin, H.M., 1954 — A 12th-century Grant to Irford Priory *LAASRP* **5** pt2

1951 — *The White Canons in England*

Cox, J.C., 1924 — *Lincolnshire*

CUAC — Photographs held by Cambridge University Committee for Aerial Photography

CUL — Cambridge University Library

Dalton, C., 1880 — *History of the Wrays of Glentworth 1523–1852*

Davis, F.N., ed., 1914a — *Rotuli Robert Grosseteste Episcopi Lincolniensis AD 1235–53 necnon rotulus Henrici de Lexington Episcopi Lincolniensis AD 1254–9* LRS 11

1914b — *Rotuli Hugonis de Welles Episcopi Lincolniensis AD 1209–35* III, LRS 9

221

Davis, F.N., et al, eds. 1925 — *Rotuli Ricardi Gravesend Episcopi Lincolniensis 1258–79* LRS 20

Davis, H.W.C., et al, eds., 1913–69 — *Regesta Regnum Anglo-Normannorum* 4 vols

Dimock, J.F., ed., 1877 — *Vita S Remigii* in *Giraldus Cambrensis Opera* 7 (Rolls Series 21)

DOE, 1978 — Department of the Environment, *List of Ancient Monuments in England 3: East Anglia and the Midlands*

Dugdale, W., 1817–30 — *Monasticon Anglicanum* 8 vols in 6

Dyer, C., 1985 — Power and Conflict in the Medieval Village in D. Hooke, ed., *Medieval Villages: a Review of Current Work*

Ellison, A., 1976 — *Village Surveys,* Committee for Rescue Archaeology in Avon, Gloucestershire and Somerset, occasional paper I

EMAB — *East Midlands Archaeological Bulletin*

EPNS — English Place-Name Society

Everson, P., 1979 — Pagan Saxon Pottery from Cherry Willingham and Middle Carlton Villages in A.J. White, Archaeology in Lincolnshire and South Humberside 1978, *LHA* **14**

1983 — Aerial Photography and Fieldwork in North Lincolnshire in G.S. Maxwell ed., *The Impact of Aerial Reconnaisance on Archaeology*, CBA Research Report 49

1986 — Occupation du sol au Moyen Age et a L'époque Moderne dans le Nord du Lincolnshire in *La prospection archéologique. Paysage et peuplement,* A. Ferdière and E. Zadora-Rio, eds, Documents d'Archéologie Française No. 3

1988 — What's in a Name? 'Goltho', Goltho and Bullington, *LHA* **23**

Fellows-Jensen, G., 1978 — *Scandinavian Settlement Names in the East Midlands*

Feudal Aids — *Inquisitions and Assessments relating to Feudal Aids, with other Analogous Documents, 1284–1431.* Vol. III: Kent to Norfolk (1904). Vol. VI: York and Additions (1921)

Field, F.N., 1981 — Cherry Willingham in A.J. White, Archaeology in Lincolnshire and South Humberside 1980, *LHA* **16**

1983 — Rand Church, *LHA* **18**

Foster, C.W., 1902 — *Calendar of Lincoln Wills I, 1320–1600*

1912 — *Lincoln Episcopal Records in the time of Thomas Cooper, STP, Bishop of Lincoln, 1571–84,* LRS 2

1920 — *Final Concords* II 1242–72, LRS 17

1921 — *Calendars of Administrations in the Consistory Court of Lincoln, 1540–1659,* LRS 16

1926 — *The State of the Church in the Reign of Elizabeth and James I* I, LRS 23

1927 — *Aisthorpe and Thorpe in the Fallows*

1930 — *Calendar of Wills and Administrations at Lincoln,* IV, British Record Society

1932–3 — Lincolnshire PCC Wills, *AASRP* **41**

Foster, C.W. and Longley, T., eds., 1924 — *The Lincolnshire Domesday and the Lindsey Survey,* LRS 19 (reprinted 1976)

Foster, C.W. and Major, K., eds., 1931–73 — *The Registrum Antiquissimum of the Cathedral Church of Lincoln* 10 vols, LRS

Fox, H.S.A., 1986 — The alleged transformation from two-field to three-field systems in medieval England, *Econ Hist Rev* **39**

Fuller, H.A., 1974 — *Land ownership in Lindsey c. 1800–1860,* unpublished M.A. thesis, University of Hull

Fuller, H.A., 1976 — Land ownership and the Lindsey Landscape, *Annals of the Assoc of American Geog* **66**

Gibbons, A., 1883 — *Early Lincolnshire Wills 1280–1547*

1888 — *Liber Antiquus Hugonis Wells 1209–35*

1898 — *Notes of the Visitation of Lincolnshire 1634*

Gibbons, E.J., 1975 — *The Flora of Lincolnshire*

Gibbons, G.S., 1928 — South Kelsey Hall, *LNQ* **20**

Green, H. — Lincolnshire Town and Village Life: newspaper articles contained in 8 vols, *Lincolnshire Gazette and Times,* 1901 onwards

Hall, H., 1896 — *Red Book of the Exchequer,* Rolls Series 99, vol I

Harding, N.S., ed., 1937 — *Bonney's Church Notes*

1940 — *W.B. Stonehouse, A Stow Visitation*

Hart, C.R., 1966 — *The Early Charters of Eastern England*

Harvey, P.D.A., 1982 — Custom and Lordship in the Medieval Village *MVRG 30th Annual Report*

1989 — Initiative and Authority in Settlement Change in M. Aston, D. Austin and C. Dyer, eds, *The Rural Settlements of Medieval England*

Hill, J.W.F., 1956 — *Tudor and Stuart Lincolnshire*

1965 — *Medieval Lincoln*

1966 — *Georgian Lincoln*

1974 — *Victorian Lincoln*

ed., 1939 — Sir George Heneage's Estate Book 1625, *LAAS* NS **7**

Hill, R.M.T., ed., 1948, 1954 — *The Rolls and Register of Bishop Oliver Sutton 1280–99,* LRS 39, 48

HMC — Royal Commission on Historical Manuscripts

Hodgett, G.A.J., 1975 — *Tudor Lincolnshire*

Holmes, C., 1980 — *Seventeenth-century Lincolnshire*

HSL — Hunting Air Surveys Limited

Hunter, J., 1850 — Henry the Eighth's progress in Lincolnshire, *Proceedings of the Archaeological Institute at Lincoln in 1848*

Hutton, A.W. — Notes on Spridlington, Lincolnshire, compiled 1893–7, unpublished typescript

Illingworth, C., 1810 — *Topographical Account of the Parish of Scampton*

Jackson, C. ed., 1869 — *The Diary of Abraham de la Pryme,* Surtees Soc **54**

Jarvis MS — Copy in Lincoln Museum, original at Doddington Hall near Lincoln

Jervoise, E., 1932 — *The Ancient Bridges of Midland and Eastern England*

JBAA — *Journal of the British Archaeological Association*

Johnson, S.A., 1962 — Some aspects of enclosure and changing agricultural landscapes in Lindsey from the 16th to the 19th century, *LAASRP* **9** pt2

Jones, D., 1987 — North Lincolnshire Transect Survey: a summary, *LHA* **22**

1988 — Aerial Reconnaisance and Prehistoric and Romano-British Archaeology in Northern Lincolnshire – A Sample Survey, *LHA* **23**

Kimball, E.G., 1962 — *Some Sessions of the Peace in Lincolnshire 1381–96* II, LRS 56

King, D.J.C., 1983 — *Castellarium Anglicanum*

King, E., 1986 — Review of P.D.A. Harvey, ed., *The Present Land Market in Medieval England, Eng Hist Rev* **101**

Knowles, D. and Hadcock, R.D., 1971 — *Medieval Religious Houses of England and Wales*

LAAS — Lincolnshire Architectural and Archaeological Society

LAASRP — *Lincolnshire Architectural and Archaeological Society Reports and Papers*

LAC — Lincolnshire Archives Committee, *Archivists' Report*

LAO — Lincolnshire Archives Office

Larking, L.B., ed., 1857 — *The Knights Hospitallers in England*, Camden Soc **65**

LCL — Lincoln Central Library

Lees, B.A. ed., 1935 — *Records of the Templars in England in the 12th century*

LHA — *Journal of the Society for Lincolnshire History and Archaeology*

Lincs DB — *The Lincolnshire Domesday and the Lindsey Survey*, trans. and ed. C.W. Foster and T. Longley, LRS 19 (1924 reprinted 1976)

Livingstone-Bleven, S.F., c 1930 — *The Dowager Minster of Lincoln, or the Story of Stow-in-Lindsey*

Lloyd, C.M. ed., 1973 — *Letters from John Wallace to Madam Whichcot*, LRS 66

Lloyd, L.C., and Stenton, D.M. eds., 1950 — *Sir Christopher Hatton's Book of Seals*

LM — Lincoln Museum

LNQ — *Lincolnshire Notes and Queries*

LRS — Lincolnshire Record Society

LS — see Lincs DB

Lunt, W.E., 1926 — *The Valuation of Norwich*

MHLG — Ministry of Housing and Local Government

Maddison, A.R., ed., 1902-6 — *Lincolnshire Pedigrees*, 4 vols, Harleian Soc

1907-8 — The Tournays of Caenby, *AASRP* **29**

Major, K., ed., 1960 — Blyborough Charters, in *Medieval Miscellany for D.M. Stenton*, Pipe Roll Soc, new ser. **36**

Marrat, W., 1816 — *The History of Lincolnshire* VI

Massingberd, W.O., 1896 — Abstract of Final Concords

1898 — Survey of the Manor of Stow AD 1283, *AASRP* **24** pt2

1904-5 — Survey of the Barony of Bayeux AD 1288, *LNQ* **8**

Micklethwaite, J.T., 1891-2 — On the Parish Church of Knaith, *AASRP* **21**

Moor, C., 1901 — *The History of Scotter*

1902a — *The History of Blyburgh*

1902b — *The History of Lea*

1904 — *The History of Northorpe and Southorpe*

1905 — *The History of Heapham, Pilham and Springthorpe*

MVRG — Medieval Village Research Group

NAR — National Archaeological Record

NMR — National Monuments Record

Newcomb, F., 1937 — *A Short History of St Mary's Church, Knaith* reprinted 1972

Nonarum Inquisitiones — *Nonarum Inquisitiones in Curia Scaccarii* Record Commission 1807

OD — Ordnance Datum

OED — Oxford English Dictionary

OS — Ordnance Survey

Owen, D.M., 1971 — *Church and Society in Medieval Lincolnshire*

1975 — Medieval Chapels in Lincolnshire, *LHA* **10**

Pevsner, N. and Harris, J., 1964 — *The Buildings of England: Lincolnshire*

Phillimore, W.P., ed., 1912 — *Rotuli Hugonis de Welles Episcopi Lincolniensis 1209-35* I, LRS 3

Placita de Quo Warranto — *Placita de Quo Warranto Richard I – Edward II*, Record Commission 1811

Placitorum Abbreviatio — *Placitorum Abbreviatio Richard I – Edward III*, Record Commission 1811

PRO — Public Record Office

Proceedings of the Archaeological Institute at Lincoln in 1848 (1850)

RAF VAP — Royal Air Force Vertical Air Photograph

RCHME 1972 — Royal Commission on the Historical Monuments of England *An Inventory of the Historical Monuments in the County of Cambridge*

1975-85 — Royal Commission on the Historical Monuments of England *An Inventory of the Historical Monuments in the County of Northampton* 6 vols

Renn, D.F., 1973 — *Norman Castles in Britain* 2nd edn

Reynolds, S., 1984 — *Kingdoms and Communities in Western Europe*

Roberts, B.K., 1972 — Village Plans in County Durham, *Med Arch* **16**

Rot Hund — *Rotuli Hundredorum*, Record Commission 1812

Rot Obl et Fin — *Rotuli de Oblatis et Finibus in Turri Londinensi asservati, temp regis Johannis*, Record Commission 1835

Rot Orig Abbr — *Rotulorum Originalium in Curia Scaccarii Abbreviatio, Henry III to Edward III* I (1805), II (1810)

Rotuli Litterarum Causarum — *Rotuli Litterarum Causarum in Turri Londinensi asservati 1224-27*, II, Record Commission 1844

Russell, E., 1974 — Excavations on the site of the deserted medieval village of Kettleby Thorpe, Lincolnshire, *Journal of the Scunthorpe Museum Society*, ser. 3 no 2

Russell, V. and Moorhouse, S., 1971 — Excavation near the Bishop's Palace at Nettleham, 1959, *LHA* 6

Russell, R.C., 1968 — *The Enclosures of Searby 1763-65, Nettleton 1791-95, Caistor 1796-98 and Caistor Moors 1811-14*

1975 — *The Logic of the Open Field System*

Salter, H.S., ed., 1909 — *Pipe Rolls; a subsidy collected in the diocese of Lincoln in 1526*

Schweizer, K.W., 1977 — *A Handlist of the Additional Weston Papers*

Sheppard, J.A., 1976 — Medieval Village Planning Northern England, *J Hist Geog* **2**

SLHA — South Lincolnshire History and Archaeology

Smith, A.H., 1956 — *English Place-name Elements* pt1

Speed, J., 1676 — *The Theatre of the Empire of Great Britain*

Stark, A., 1817, 1843 — *The History and Antiquities of Gainsburgh*

1841 — *An Account of the Parish of Lea with Lea Wood*

nd — *The Visitor's Pocket Guide to Gainsburgh*

Stenton, F.M., ed., 1920 — *Documents Illustrative of the Social and Economic History of the Danelaw*

1922 — *Transcripts of Charters relating to the Gilbertine Houses of Sixle, Catley, Ormsby, Bullington and Alvingham*, LRS 18

1947 — *Anglo-Saxon England*, 2nd edn

Stonehouse, W.B. *see* Harding, N.S. ed., 1940

Strong, R., Binney, M., Harris, J., 1974 — *The Destruction of the Country House, 1875-1975*

Taxatio Ecclesiastica — *Taxatio Ecclesiastica Angliae et Walliae, auctoritate Papae Nicholai IV c. AD 1291*, Record Commission 1902

Taylor, C.C., 1982 — Medieval Market Grants and Village Morphology, *Landscape History* **4**

1983 — *The Archaeology of Gardens*

1984 — *Village and Farmstead*

223

Thirsk, J., 1957 — *English Peasant Farming*

Thompson, A.H., 1912 — *Military Architecture in England*

ed., 1914–29 — *Visitations of Religious Houses in the Diocese of Lincoln* 3, LRS 7, 14

ed., 1940 — *Visitations in the Diocese of Lincoln 1517–31*, I: visitations of rural deanaries by William Atwater, Bishop of Lincoln and his commissioners, 1517–20, LRS 33

Thompson, F.H., 1960 — The deserted medieval village of Riseholme, near Lincoln, *Med Arch* **4**

Toulmin Smith, L., ed., 1964 — *The Itinerary of John Leland* 4 vols (1907, reprinted 1964)

Trollope, E., 1861–2 — Notes on Market Rasen, and other places in its vicinity, *AASRP* **6**

Turner, W.H., 1878 — *Calendar of Charters and Rolls Preserved in the Bodleian Library*

Varley, J., 1945–7 — An Archdiaconal Visitation of Stow, 1752, *LAAS* **3** pt2

1951 — Records of the Manor of Stow, *LAAS*, new ser. **4** pt1

VCH — *The Victoria History of the Counties of England*

VE — *Valor Ecclesiasticus, temp. Henrici VIII auctoritate regia institutus*, 6 vols, Record Commission 1810–34

Venables, E., 1873 — Louth Park Abbey, *AASRP* **12**

Walker, M.S., ed., 1954 — *Feet of fines for the County of Lincoln 1199–1216*, Pipe Roll Soc, new ser. **29**

Weir, G., 1828 — *An Historical and Descriptive Account of Lincolnshire*

Wheeler, W.H., 1909–10 — The Fens of South Lincolnshire. Their early history and reclamation, *AASRP* **20**

White, A., 1979 — *Barlings Abbey*, Lincolnshire Museums Information Sheet, Archaeology Series 5

White, W., 1842, 1856, 1872, 1882 — *History, Gazetteer and Directory of Lincolnshire*

Whitelock, D., ed., 1930 — *Anglo-Saxon Wills*

Whitwell, J.B., 1969 — Excavations of the site of a moated medieval manor house in the parish of Saxilby, Lincolnshire, *JBAA*, 3rd ser. **32**

Young, A., 1799 — *General View of the Agriculture of the County of Lincoln*, (1799, reprinted 1970)

INDEX

Bold numbers in square brackets refer to illustrations.

Abingdon, Earls of, 117
access-ways, 70, 129
Acrehouse, Claxby, 10, 91–3, [**2, 6, 68, 69**]
Aisby, Corringham, 9, 15, [**12, 18**]
Aisthorpe, 9
Aldefeld, Faldingworth, 13
Aldhagh, Saxilby with Ingleby, 12
Alfletby, Willingham by Stow, 12, 27
Alfred of Lincoln, 127
Allerston, P., 14
almshouses, 81–2
Alneto family, 179, 180
Alvingham, Gilbertine priory, 85
Amundeville family, 16, 146, 147, 149
　Lady Beatrice de, 147, 149
　Peter de, 147
Angers, Benedictine house of St Nicholas, 22, 218
animal bones, 162, 185, 187, 191
Anwick, 6
Apley, 3, 35, 36, 47, 63, 175, [**47**]
Apley Grange, 63
Arches, Gilbert de, 164
architectural masonry, fragments of, 68, 70, 82, 91, 118, 127,
　130, 137, 167, 171
Armstrong, *see* maps, county
Aston, M. A., 16
Atterby, Bishop Norton, 9, 38
Audleby, Caistor, 37, 38
Aunay-sur-Odon, Calvados, alien priory of Cistercian abbey of,
　99
avenues, 79, 107, 155, 177, [**79, 80**]
Ayscough family, 49, 73, 136, 171
　Sir Edward, 150, 171, 172
　Francis, 150
　Henry, 39, 73
　William, 150

Baiocis, Hugh de, 85, 195
Bardney, 3, 10, 13, 15, 22, 25, 28, 29, 44, 48, 49, 57, 63–5,
　[**10, 13, 15, 20, 35, 48, 49**]
Bardney, Benedictine abbey, 10, 22, 47, 50, 63, 64, 201; [**10,
　20, 35**]
Bardolf family, 168, 170
　Hugh I, 16, 22, 155, 157
　Hugh II, 157, 159
　Robert, 44, 168, 170
Barketon (Barkeston), North Carlton, 137
Barlings, 6, 7, 22, 39, 44, 47, 55, 66–70, [**20, 50–2**]
Barlings, Premonstratensian abbey, 10, 22, 28, 44, 47, 50, 54,
　66, 67–8, 69, 106, 131, 136, 139, 157, 159, 164, 168, 170,
　177, [**19, 20, 50–2**]
barns, sites of, 68, 75, 78, 101, 103, 105, 113, 130, 131, 149,
　167, 173, 183, 208
barrows, prehistoric, 6, 133, 135

Barton by North Carlton, 137
battle axe, medieval, 193
Bayeux, Bishop of, 159, 211, 213, 215
Bayeux family, 131
　John de, 131
　Ralph de, 127
Beasthorpe, Owersby, 3, 13
Beaumeys, Robert de, 101
Beaumont family, Henry and William, Viscount Beaumont,
　127
Beckett family, Robert senior and Robert junior, 81
Beckfield, Binbrook, 112
Bellowe, John, 99
Berenger, 82
Beresford, G., 38, 42
Bertie family, Earls of Abingdon, 117
Bigby, 7, 8, 9, 12, 30, 38, 39, 41, 48, 49, 53, 55, 56, 70–1,
　211, [**1, 53**]
Billinghay, Walter de, 115
Binbrook, 112, 180, 181, 183
Bishop Norton, 7, 9, 12, 15, 16, 38, [**14**]
bishops' palaces, 47, 48, 50, 53, 54, 129–31, 185, [**18, 96,
　130**]
Black Death, 38, *see also* population statistics
Bleasby, Legsby, 3, 10, 15, 25, 29, 42, 49, 119, 120–1, 122,
　127, [**27, 87, 88**]
Bleasby family, 122
　Joscelin de, 122
Bloet, Robert, Bishop of Lincoln, 129
blood-letting, medicinal, 48–9, 63
Blyborough, 12, 39, 40, 45, 73, [**54**]
Blyton, 3, 7, 17, 25, 29, 38, [**15**]
Blyton Common, 10
Bondemannescroft, Thonock, 12
Bonsdale, Corringham, 12
bowling green, 177
Brampton, 9
Brandon, Charles, Duke of Suffolk, 67, 73, 136, 159, 168
Bransby, Sturton, 10
Braose, John de, 117
Brattleby, 9, 15, 16, 36, 40, 42, 45, 74–7, [**55, 56**]
Brattleby Hall, 77
brickpits, 55
bridge, medieval, 215
Brocklesby, 10, 16, 38, 39, 47, 51, 54, 99
Brocklesby Park, 101
brooches
　Saxon, 7
　medieval, 89
Brooks, George, 91
Broxholme, 3, 15, 17, 35, 39, 40, 76–8, 79, [**57, 58**]
building materials
　brick, 70, 93, 98, 101, 107, 117, 118, 119, 171, 181
　mortar, 70, 117

building materials *continued*
  slates, stone, 78, 113, 118
  stone, 70, 71, 78, 93, 118, 126, 130, 131, 136, 141, 159, 161,
    162, 185, 191, 193, *see also* foundations, stone
  tiles, 78, 95, 113, 131, 136, 161, 164, 181, 197, *see also* tile kiln
    and tile-making sites
  wood, 157, 159
building platforms, 43, 64, 98, 99, 101, 113, 118, 123, 130, 146,
  149, 150, 159, 162, 164, 181, 187, 192, 197, 199, 205, 208,
  216, 218, *see also* houses, sites of small village dwellings
Bullington, 47, 48, 53, 78–9, [59]
Bullington, Gilbertine priory, 47, 78, 106, 153
Burdet family, 16, 153
  John and Stephen, 153
Burgh family
  Robert, 189
  Thomas, Lord Burgh, 122, 161
Burghersh, Henry, Bishop of Lincoln, 129, 130, 185
burials, medieval and later, 113, 153, 171, *see also* cemeteries
Burle, Richard de, 192
Burton, 7, 12, 15, 16, 39, 51, 55, 79–82, [60, 61]
Burton Hall, 82
Burun, Erneis de, 153
Buselinus, 16, 82, 84
Buslingthorpe, 3, 9, 15, 16, 29, 35, 36, 37, 38, 42, 45, 48, 49,
  51, 82–5, 126, 211, [62, 63]
Buslingthorpe family, 82, 84, 179
  Margaret de, 179
  Sir Richard, 84
Bussei, Roger de, 218, 220
Bussy family, 147
Butyate, Bardney, 3, 10, 13, 47, 64, [10]
Byng, John, 117

Cabourne, 1, 7, 9, 30, 37, 41, 43, 44, 56, 85–7, 106, 135, 155,
  189, 191, 205, [64]
Caenby, 10, 41, 146
Caistor, 7, 37, 38, 45, 48, 51, 55
Caistor Canal, 55
Caistor Moor, 10
Cammeringham, 7, 9, 12, 39, 50, 55
canals, navigable and ornamental, 47, 54, 55, 107, 183, 199
Canceio, Anfrid de, 218
Canci, Simon de, 218
Cantilupe, William de, 164
Capability Brown, 99
Carlton Barton, North Carlton, 137
Carlton Mackerel, North Carlton, 137
carriage drives, 82, 105, 107, 155
Castle Carlton, 16, 157
Castle Hills, Thonock, 193
castles and defensive structures
  Saxon, 43
  medieval, 16, 43, 48, 49, 146–7, 149, 157, 193–4, [28, 108, 137]
Catley, Gilbertine priory, 44
cattle, 38, 99, 164
causeways, 67, 68, 69, 107, 118, 119, 127, 136, 139, 141, 153,
  162, 171, 179, 185, 193, 197
Cauthorpe, Owersby, 3, 13, 149, [109]
cemeteries
  Saxon, 210
  medieval and later, 113, 141, 181, *see also* burials
censuses, 19th-century, 34, 136, 164, 208, *see also* population
  statistics
Chamberlain family, 216
Chambers, Bartholomew, 81
Chapel Hill, Tealby, 192
chapels, 55, 117, 126, 131, 146, 161, 192, 211, 220, [93], *see also*
  churches

Chaplin family, 157
Chaumont, Sir John, 173
Cherry Burton, 79
Cherry Willingham, 7, 8, 38, 40, 51, 88–9, [66]
Chester, Earl of, 131, 155
  Ranulf, 193
Church End, Keelby, 28, [16]
churches, medieval, 44–6, 63, 81, 82, 84, 85, 98, 117, 126,
  136, 141, 149, 153, 155, 157, 165, 180, 197, 211, [51]
  Eigenkirche, 153
  isolated, 45, 205
  minster churches, 10, 22, 45, 153
  post-medieval rebuilding, 63, 78, 81, 98, 106, 117, 125,
    136, 139, 165, 177
  redundant, 57
  relationship with manorial sites, 45, 48, 97, 106, 111, 125,
    127, 141, 168, 189, 201, 216
  sites of, 63, 67, 68, 137, 141, 157, 173, 203, 211
  see also chapels
cistern, 130
Civil War, 103, 115, 201
Civil War fortifications, 55, 112, 172, [122]
Claxby, 1, 6, 7, 40, 55, 89–93, 135, [6, 67–9]
Claxby House, 89–91, [67]
Claxby Moor, 3
climatic change, 38
Clixby, Grasby, 40
closes, 14, 29, 30, 48, 63, 64, 69, 70, 71, 73, 77, 78, 81, 85,
  87, 89, 93, 97, 99, 101, 103, 105, 106, 107, 111, 115,
  119, 125, 136, 137, 139, 140, 141, 144, 146, 149, 150,
  155, 157, 159, 161, 162, 164, 171, 173, 175, 177, 179,
  180, 181, 187, 189, 191, 194, 195, 197, 199, 201, 203,
  205, 207, 210, 213, 215, 220, *see also* crofts, paddocks *and*
  tofts
Coates, Peter de, 187
Coates, Stow, 3, 10, 14, 17, 22, 44, 49, 185–7, 189, [25, 131,
  132]
coffins, stone, 161
Cokke, John, 220
Coldecotes, Legsby, 3, 37, 44, 121, 122, 126, 162, [89]
Cold Hanworth, 9, 17, 38, 40, 93, [70]
Cold Harbour, Cammeringham, 12
Coldstead, Newball, 12
Collow, Legsby, 10, 12, 43, 44, 69, 121, 122–3, 191, 205,
  [90]
column, 18th-century, 167
Commission for Depopulations, 77
common areas, 9
communicants, lists of, 34, *see also* population statistics
Conyers family, 205
  Thomas, 205
corbel, medieval, 127
Cornwall, Duchy of, 107, 111
Cornwall, Earls of, 193
Corringham, 3, 7, 8, 9, 12, 14, 15, 25, 36, 38, 48, 53, 70,
  [12, 18]
Cotegarthe, Corringham, 12
Cote Houses, Scotter, 3
Count Alan, 111, 189
Coventry, Warks, Carthusian priory of St Anne, 99
Cracroft family, 106
Crane, Richard, 127
crewyards, 82, 125, 129, 149, 155, 220
crofts, 75, 170, 191, *see also* closes, paddocks *and* tofts
crop-marks
  prehistoric, 6, 7
  medieval and later, 70, 107, 115, 121, 197
Crossholme, Bishop Norton, 9, 12
cross, medieval, 211

Croxby, Thoresway, 12, 17, 34, 35, 36, 38, 55, 56, 195, 197–9, [**139**]
Croxby Hall, 199–201, [**139**]
Culpeper, Lord, 195
cultivation remains
  fields, prehistoric, 6
  fields, post-medieval, 3
  open-field systems, 9, 10, 12, 203, *see also* enclosure of fields
    and wastes
  strip lynchets, 197
  see also ridge-and-furrow
Cumberworth family, 167
  Robert de, 164
  Sir Thomas de, 164, 165, 167
Curci, William de, 129
Cuxwold, Swallow, 9, 36

dagger, medieval, 193
Dallison family, 103, 105
  Sir Charles, 103
  Sir Thomas, 103, 105
Dalton family, Henry and Richard, 117
dams, 77, 85, 88, 89, 111, 119, 121, 139, 140, 141, 144, 157,
    159, 161, 164, 168, 180, 183, 185, 191, 199, 203, 210, 215,
    218, *see also* fishponds *and* ponds
Danes' Camp, Thonock, 193
Danish army, 13
Darcy family, 115
date-stone, 17th-century, 91
Daubney (de Albini, de Albiniaco) family, 161, 162
Dearne, Robert, 205
deer park pales, 53, 99, 117, 161, 185
deer parks, 3, 47, 48, 53, 70, 78, 84, 95, 99, 111–12, 115, 117,
    161, 185, 194, [**40, 41, 73, 85, 130**], *see also* parks,
    landscaped
depopulation, 36–41
  13th-century, 36
  14th-century, 36, 38, 71, 119, 159
  15th-century, 38, 49, 71, 141, 144, 153, 165
  16th-century, 38, 39, 73, 153, 165
  17th-century, 35, 38, 39, 73, 77, 79, 93, 101, 103, 105, 107,
    109, 125, 127, 131, 135, 136, 137, 139, 147, 149, 150, 155,
    157, 165, 170, 175, 177, 189, 194, 197, 201, 205, 216
  18th-century, 40, 136
  19th-century, 40
  20th-century, 40
depopulations, survey of, 39, 73, 77, 79, 93, 101, 103, 107, 125,
    127, 131, 135, 149, 155, 157, 165, 175, 177, 189, 194, 197,
    201, 205, 216
Despenser, Philip le, 103
destruction of earthworks, 56–7
Dickinson, John, 77, [**58**]
Dighton, William, 77
Disney family, 147
Domesday Book, xviii, xix, 9, 10, 13, 22, 34, 35, 36, 37, 43,
    133, *see also* population statistics
dovecotes, 75, 99, 121, 153, 157, 161, 220
Drake, Thomas, 177
Draycote, Nettleton, 9
Drinsey, Hardwick, 12
duck decoy ponds, 55, [**43**]
Dunholme, 29
Dunstall, Corringham, 3, 9, 36, 38
Durham villages, 14, 15
Dyer, C., 16
Dymoke, Charles and Jane, 199
Dyve family, John and William, 147

Earl Hugh, 164
East Ferry, 3, 14, [**11, 15**]
East Stockwith, 14
East Torrington, Legsby, 7, 14, 15, 38, 51, 123–6, [**91, 93**]
Edgar the Aetheling, 193
Edward I, 129
Edward III, 117
Ellison, A., 14
Elsham, 71
Elsham, Augustinian hospital and priory, 147, 149
emparking, 40, 45, 54, 79, 81, 82, 91, 97, 103, 105, 106, 107,
    109, 111, 115, 136, 137, 171, 175, 177, *see also* deer parks
    and parks, landscaped
enclosure of fields and wastes, 3, 6
  15th-century, 39
  16th-century, 71, 77, 93, 155, 159
  17th-century, 79, 101, 103, 121, 125, 127, 136, 139, 150,
    152, 155, 157, 175, 201
  18th-century, 22, 40, 75, 97, 106, 111, 131, 135, 157, 171,
    172, 173, 183, 192, 203, 215, 218
  19th-century, 40, 63, 78, 85, 99, 101, 140, 189, 213
  undated, 63
  see also maps, Enclosure
enclosures
  prehistoric, 6, 7, 133, [**98**]
  medieval and later, 29, 41, 43, 69, 73, 78–9, 99–101, 112,
    119, 121, 126, 131, 146, 153, 172–3, 207, 213, [**52, 59,
    82, 122**], *see also* closes, crofts, paddocks *and* tofts
  undated, 55, 133, 135, [**98**]
Ergun, William, 164
Esethorp (*Esathorp*), Buslingthorpe, 16, 84
Esthalle, Cabourne, 85
Exeter, Countess of, 205

Faldingworth, 3, 9, 13, 17, 29, [**18**]
farmsteads, sites of, 10, 40, 55, 87, 91–3, 106, 118, 131, 136,
    181, 195, 197, 210, [**2, 6, 68, 69**]
Fenton, 111
ferry, 105
field-names, 195
  Acrehouse, Claxby, 91
  Backside, Bigby, 70
  Barton, North Carlton, 137
  Burnt Hall Yard, Tealby, [**17**]
  Castle Dyke, Northorpe, 141
  Castle Hill, Newball, 133
  Castle Hills, Thonock, 48
  Chapel Garth, Northorpe, 141
  Chapel Hill, Legsby, 126
  Chapel House Close, Barlings, 67
  Chapel Yard, Welton, 210
  Chapple Hill, Tealby, 192
  Claxby Stew Ponds, Claxby, 91
  Colecroft, Stainton le Vale, 181
  Collin Croft, Northorpe, 141
  Coney Close, Cabourne, 87
  Cowsey Garth, Barlings, 67
  Cross Homestead, Cherry Willingham, 89
  Dove Yard, Welton, 210
  East Field, South Kelsey, 172
  Elvin Garth, Claxby, 89
  Fountain Garth, Burton, 79
  Grange Close, Thoresway, 199
  Grange Close, Wickenby, 218
  Great Close, Heapham, 111
  Great Lyme Kilnes, Bigby, 73
  Greate Parke, North Carlton, 139

field-names *continued*
  Greens, North Carlton, 137
  Hall Close, Rand, 153
  Hall Field, Heapham, 111
  Hall Garth, Greetwell, 105
  Hall Garth, Tealby, [**17**]
  Hallowed Lands, Harpswell, 107
  Home Close and Moat, Legsby, 126
  House Close, Blyborough, 73
  Lacy Hill Close, Lea, 117
  Little Garth, North Carlton, 139
  Little Lyme Kiln, Bigby, 73
  Little Parke, North Carlton, 139
  Mill Croft, Rand, 153
  Mill Hill, Legsby, 126
  Mill Hill, Saxilby with Ingleby, 161
  Milnehill, West Rasen, 216
  Moat Close, Heapham, 111
  Monks Garth, Willoughton, [**19**]
  Ner Gars, Heapham, 111
  Old Garden, Bigby, 70
  Old Hall, Stainton le Vale, 180
  Old House Close, Blyborough, 73
  Old Orchard, Bigby, 70
  Old Yard, Apley, 63
  Orchard Piece, Lea, 118
  Park, Gainsborough, 95
  Park, North Carlton, 139
  Park Close, Buslingthorpe, 84
  Pitt Hills, Thonock, 194
  Pleasure Ground, North Carlton, 139
  Rectory Field, Brattleby, 75
  Riskholm, West Rasen, 213, 215
  Sand Croft, Bigby, 70
  Temple Garth, Tealby, [**17**]
  The Condyt, Burton, 79
  Town Close, Newball, 131
  Town End Close, Claxby, 89
  Town End Close, Gate Burton, 97
  Town End Close, Wickenby, 218
  West Field, Owersby, 150
  West Field, West Rasen, 216
  West Lime Kiln Close, Bigby, 73
  West Yards, Welton, 210
  White Chapel Garth, Thonock, 193
  Wilderness, Harpswell, 107
  Willow Garth, Bigby, 70
fields, *see* cultivation remains *and* ridge-and-furrow
Fillingham, 7, 12, 46, [**21**]
Firsby, West Firsby, 3, 10, 13, 22, 25, 28, 29, 36, 38, 42, 45, 51, 57, 106, 211–13, [**22, 25, 32, 148**]
fishponds, 29, 41, 42, 43, 45, 47, 48, 50–1, 54, 55, 68, 70, 88, 89, 97, 113, 139–41, 144, 153, 161, 162, 164, 168, 171, 175, 180, 181, 183, 185, 210, 215, 216, 218, [**38, 53, 65, 66, 101, 120, 147**], *see also* ponds
  commercial fish-farming in, 50
  fish-breeding tanks in, 68, 88, 113, 139–40, 141, 175, 185
  islands in, 51, 113, 139, 175, 180, 211, 215
Fiskerton, 189
Fitzpayne, Geoffrey, 155
Fitzwilliam family, 89, 91
flints, prehistoric, 6, 7
flower-beds, 82, 107, 130, 199
Foliot, Edmund, 157, 159
Fox, H. A., 16
Frances, Dowager Countess of Exeter, 205
Fosse Dyke, 3, [**18**]

foundations, stone, 64, 68, 75, 87, 101, 103, 105, 106, 112, 113–14, 117, 119, 121, 126, 127, 130, 131, 137, 139, 140, 141, 149, 153, 155, 157, 168, 170, 175, 183, 185, 195, 211, 213, 218, *see also* houses
Friesthorpe, 9
Fulnetby, 3, 13, 14, 50, 55, 95, 153, [**71**]

Gainsborough, 3, 48, 53, 55, 95, 193, [**40, 41**]
Gant family, 64, 89
  Gilbert de, 64
garden remains, 54–5
  14th-century, 47, 54, 99, 129–31, [**96**]
  medieval, 54, 68, [**37**]
  16th-century, 30, 50, 54, 55, 70, 80, 81, 82, 97–9, 103, 105, 107, 117, 139, 165, 167–8, 183, [**1, 53, 60, 73, 76, 85, 100, 118, 119, 129**]
  17th-century, 30, 47, 50, 54, 55, 70, 89, 97–9, 103, 105, 107–9, 139, 165, 167–8, 177, 183, 199–201, [**1, 24, 53, 73, 76, 78–80, 85, 100, 118, 119, 124, 125, 129, 139**]
  18th-century, 55, 107–9, 137, 167, 199–201, [**24, 78–80, 139**]
  19th-century, 98
  post-medieval, 50, 66, 67, 68–9, 141, 164, 181–3, 201, [**50**]
  water gardens, 68, 70, 117
  see also prospect mounds, summer-houses, terraced walks *and* waterfall
Gate Burton, 40, 97, 117, [**72**]
gates and gatehouses, 68, 130, 131, 149, 171
Gaulton (Galton), John, 99, 101
gazebo, *see* summer-houses
Geoffrey 'kocus', 185
geology, 2–6, [**4**]
Gilbert 'Attepipe', 79
Gilby, Pilham, 15, 40, 152, [**111**]
Gippetoft, Newball, 12
Giraldus Cambrensis, 49, 185
Glebe Terriers, 63, 82, 93, 97, 157, 203, 205
Glentham, 3, 7, 10, 41, 57
Glentworth, 7, 46, 48, 53, 54
Glentworth Thorpe, Glentworth, 7
Goltho, 2, 3, 7, 8, 17, 30, 38, 42, 43, 48, 53, 54, 55, 57, 78, 97–9, [**40, 73**]
Goltho Hall, 98
Gooseman, Robert, 91
Gorwick, Sturton by Stow, 10, 12
Grange de Lings, 10, 43, 159
granges, *see* monastic granges
Grantham family, 97
  Elizabeth, 97
  Robert, 93
  Thomas, d. 1630, 98, 99
  Thomas, d. 1650s, 98
Grasby, 25, 40, 55
grave-slabs
  Saxon, 106
  medieval, 63, 137
  see also tombstones
Grayingham, 7
Great Carlton, 16
Great Corringham, 9, 25
Great Limber, 7, 39, 44, 99–103, [**74, 75**]
Great Torrington, Legsby, 123
Green family, 91
greens, 17, 22, 28, 79, 81, 82, 89, 125, 137, 141, 149, 168, 195, 203, 215, [**15, 17, 18–20**], *see also* infilling
Greenwood, *see* maps, county
Greetwell, 9, 28, 30, 36, 37, 40, 54, 55, 103–5, [**25, 76**]

Greetwell Hall, 103, 105
Grelle (Grellys) family, 121
Grelley, Thomas de, 164
Gresley, Robert de, 162
Grey, Bishop of Lincoln, 129
Gumbald family, 131
gun position, 17th-century, 172

Hackthorn, 3, 9, 10, 44, 45, 93, 106-7, [77]
Haddow, Burton, 12
ha-has, 77, 82, 99, 183
Haia family
    Ralf de, 67, 159
    Robert de, 16, 75, 159
Hall family, 112
Hansard family, 49, 171
Hardwick, Nettleton, 9, 12
hare park, 55
Harpswell, 36, 37, 38, 46, 55, 107-9, [42, 78, 79, 80]
Harpswell Hall, 107, 109, [79, 80]
'Harrying of the North', 15
Harvey, P. D. A., 16
Havercroft, Thonock, 12
Heapham, 14, 15, 28, 39, 45, 46, 110-11, [18, 81]
Hearth Tax, 77, 101, 125, 189, 216
Heighington, 6
Helethorpe, Fulnetby, 3, 13, 14, 95, 153, [71]
Helpesthorpe, Willoughton, 22, 218, [19]
Hemswell, 39, 46, [17]
Heneage family, 121
    Sir Thomas, 112, 162
Henry III, 147
Henry VI, 171
Henry VIII, 70
hermitage, 49
hermits, 192
Heynings, Knaith, Cistercian priory, 47, 50, 112-15, 117, [84]
Hill, J. W. F., 38
Holbeach, Bishop of Lincoln, 185
Hollingworthe, James, 78
hollow-ways, 29, 55, 63, 64, 68, 70, 71, 73, 75, 78, 81, 84-5, 87, 89, 93, 97, 99, 101, 103, 105, 106, 107, 115, 119, 121, 123, 125, 126, 129, 131, 135, 136, 137, 141, 144, 146, 149, 150, 152, 153, 155, 157, 159, 161, 162, 164, 167, 168, 170, 173, 175, 177, 179, 180, 183, 185, 187, 191, 195, 197, 199, 203, 205, 208, 210, 211, 215, 220, [32, 132], *see also* terrace-ways
Holme, Sudbrooke, 189
Holmes, C., 38
Holtham, Legsby, 3, 43, 64, 126, 162, [92]
Holton, Holton cum Beckering, 29-30, 44, [19]
Holton cum Beckering, 29-30, 44, [19]
Holton le Moor, 3, 45
holy water stoup, 161
Hornsbeck, Blyborough, 12
horseshoe, 193
houses, sites of principal dwellings, 67, 68-9, 98, 99-101, 107-9, 155, 159, 180, 181-3, 201, [1, 50, 53, 74, 80, 125], *see also* manor houses
houses, sites of small village dwellings, 63, 71, 78, 85, 101, 103, 105, 106, 115, 131, 135, 136, 137, 141, 146, 150, 173, 175, 179, 180, 191, 195, 201, 203, 207, 211, 215, *see also* building platforms *and* foundations, stone
Huckerby, Corringham, 3, 9
Humet, Sir Richard de, 99
hunting lodges, sites of, 48, 53, 78-9, 133, [59], *see also* keepers' lodges

Hutton family, 97, 117
    H.F., 173
    William, 97

ice-houses, 82, 91
infilling
    of greens, 17, 22, 29, 79, 81, 82, 87, 146, 168, 215, [15, 16]
    of market places, 29
Ingham, 10, 16, 187
Ingleby family, 16
    Robert de, 159
inhumations, *see* burials *and* cemeteries
Insula, Robert de, 82
Iron Age site, 170
iron-smelting furnace, medieval, 89
iron-working, evidence of, 87, 89, 141

James I, 70
John, King, 147, 185
Jones, D., 6

Keelby, 28, [16]
keepers' lodges, sites of, 95, 97, *see also* hunting lodges
Kettleby, Bigby, 7, 9, 30, 39, 48, 49, 53, 55, 56, 70, 71, 211, [1, 53]
Kettleby House, 70, [1]
Kettleby Thorpe, Bigby, 8, 9, 38, 39, 41, 71, 211
Kettlethorpe, 48, 53, 55, 111-12, [40, 82]
Kexby, 9
key, medieval, 193
King, E., 16
Kingerby, Osgodby, 16, 28, 35, 36, 38, 40, 43, 48, 49, 56, 144, 146-9, [28, 106-8]
Kingerby Hall, 146-7, [107, 108]
King's College, Cambridge, 171, 218
Kingthorpe, Apley, 3, 47, 63
Kirkby, 144, 146, [106]
Kirkstead Abbey, 37, 157, 159, 164
Kirmond le Mire, 7, 8, 112, 191, [83]
Kirton, 45, 107, 111, 193
Knaith, 3, 15, 36, 38, 40, 45, 47, 50, 53, 54, 55, 112-17, [26, 84, 85]
Knaith Park, 112, 115
Knights Hospitallers, 43, 44, 47, 85, 99, 101, 106, 136
    Willoughton Preceptory, 22, 43, 44, 47, 48, 49, 50, 85, 99, 218-20, [19, 153]
Knights Templars, 27, 43, 44, 85, 99, 101, 135, 136
    Cabourne *baillia,* 99, 149
    Willoughton Preceptory, 22, 43, 44, 47, 48, 49, 50, 85, 99, 218-20, [19, 153]
Kyme family, 97
    Philip de, Simon de and William de, 78

label stops, medieval, 70, 130
lakes, ornamental, 55, 77, 106, 107, 109, 139, 155, 157, 167
Lancaster, Duchy of, 75, 193, 205
landslips, 10, 39, 179, 181, 207, 208, 210, [6, 9, 30, 144]
Langton, Walter de, 63
Langworth, Barlings, 22, 47, [20]
Lascelles family, 189
Laughterton, 111
Laughton, 3, [21]
lay subsidies, 34, 36, 37, *see also* population statistics
Lea, 3, 7, 29, 42, 50, 112, 117-19, [21, 86]
leats and channels, 47, 50-1, 55, 67-8, 69, 88, 89, 113, 117, 123, 126, 140, 144, 153, 162, 175, 179, 180, 181, 183, 195, 199, 210, 213, 215, *see also* canals

Legsby, 3, 7, 12, 14, 15, 25, 29, 37, 38, 42, 43, 44, 48, 49, 51, 55, 64, 119–27, 191, 205, [**87–94**]
Leland, 95, 193
licence to crenelate, 117, 129, 130, 185
lime-kilns, sites of, 73, 130
Lincoln
  Bishops of, 146, 157, *see also* bishops' palaces
  castle and county of, 75
  cathedral church of St Mary, 106, 197
  Consistory Court, 121
  Dean and Chapter of, 28, 85, 103, 105, 106, 129
  Earl of, 193
Lindsey Musters, 34, *see also* population statistics
Lindsey Survey, xviii, xix, 63, 135, 175, 178, 180, 197, 208
linear ditches, prehistoric, 6, 7
Linwood, 3, 7, 9, 15, 16, 29, 42, 45, 48, 49, 54, 127–9, [**37, 95**]
Lissingleys, 9
Lissington, 8, 9, 10, 29, 39, 122
Little Carlton, North Carlton, 137
Little Corringham, 9, 25
Little Limber, Brocklesby, 38, 39, 165
Little Torrington, Legsby, 123
loom weights, Saxon, 130
Louth Park, Cistercian abbey, 10, 44, 119, 122, 197, 199
Luard family, 73

Mackerel, Matthew, 69
Madgin Moor, 10
Mainwaring family, 97
  Charles and Thomas, 98
Malet family, 16, 129
  Durand, 127
manor houses and sites of manor houses, 22, 42, 43, 45, 48, 49, 50, 53, 81, 82, 97, 105, 106, 111, 117, 131, 136, 139, 141, 146, 147, 161, 162, 167, 168, 173, 191, 205, 213, 215, 216, [**19, 37**], *see also* houses, sites of principal dwellings
manorial blocks, 81, 82, 84, 106, 111, 121, 125, 129, 141, 153, 155, 161, 180, 187, 201, 205, 216, *see also* manorial sites
manorial *curiae*, 28, 29, 42, 45, 48, 75, 97, 111, 127, 129, 153, 165, 168, 213, 215, 216, [**22, 32**]
manorial sites, 28, 29, 30, 41–4, 45, 48, 82, 107, 119, 141, 153, 155, 157, 159, 161, 168, 170, 180, 191, 195, 201, 211, 213, [**17, 28, 120**], *see also* manorial blocks
typology of manorial sites, 41–3
manors, 16, 22, 28, 39, 41, 43–4, 70, 73, 75, 79, 81, 82, 84, 87, 89, 99, 101, 103, 106, 107, 111, 115, 117, 119, 121, 125, 126, 127, 129, 131, 135, 136, 139, 141, 144, 146, 147, 149, 150, 153, 155, 159, 161, 165, 167, 168, 170, 173, 177, 178, 179, 180, 185, 189, 191, 193, 194, 195, 197, 199, 201, 203, 205, 210, 211, 213, 215, 216, 218, [**19**]
  sub-infeudation of, 16, 41, 43, 49, 137, 153, 155, 194
  typology of manors, 43–4
maps, xviii
  county maps
    Armstrong, 70, 91, 105, 107, 118, 152, 167, 185
    Greenwood, 216
    Saxton, 117
    Speed, 117
  Enclosure Maps, 22, 51, 63, 75, 111, 146, 171, 172, 173, 183, 189, 191, 192, 215, 218, [**56**]
  Ordnance Survey Maps and Plans, 51, 70, 73, 77, 84, 85, 93, 97, 99, 106, 107, 112, 118, 119, 125, 127, 131, 135, 136, 146, 149, 150, 152, 155, 181, 215, 216
  Tithe Maps, 10, 44, 51, 63, 73, 77, 81, 82, 84, 89, 91, 93, 97, 105, 115, 117, 119, 121, 122, 125, 126, 129, 135, 136, 137, 141, 164, 185, 189, 201, 205, 207, 208, 210, [**58, 61, 68, 88**]

16th-century, 117
17th-century, 77, 78, 79, 81, 82, 99, 101, 103, 117, [**58, 61, 75**]
18th-century, 68, 70, 77, 78, 79, 81, 82, 131, 133, 140, 171, 210, 216, [**41, 58, 61**]
19th-century, 77, 78, 89, 91, 93, 103, 106, 117, 119, 127, 131, 133, 136, 137, 140, 152, 171, 185, 199, 203, 210, 218, [**58**]
undated, 95
market cross, 101
market places, 22, 28, 29, 101, 103, [**20**]
Market Rasen, 9, 127
markets and fairs, 16, 22, 101, 213, 215, [**20**]
Markham, George, 89
Marmion family, 89
Marrat, William, 103, 105
Marton, 3, 7, 15, 39
Matilda, Empress, 193
Mellers, Robert, 175
Meschin, William, 129
Metham, Charles, 175
Middle Carlton, North Carlton, 8, 136, 137, 168, 170, [**100**]
Middle Rasen, 3, 15, 17, 29, [**17**]
Middle Rasen Drax, 17, [**17**]
Middle Rasen Tupholme, 15, [**17**]
Millecent, W., 18th-century drawing by, 68, [**51**]
minster churches and parishes, 10, 22, 45, 153
moated sites, 16, 22, 29, 41, 42, 43, 47, 48–50, 51, 53, 54, 55, 63, 70, 82–4, 91, 95, 97, 97–9, 107, 111, 117, 119, 126, 127–8, 139, 141, 144, 146, 153, 159–62, 171–2, 173, 185, 187, 189–91, 192, 199, 201, 205, 215, 218, 220, [**1, 19, 27, 28, 37, 48, 53, 62, 63, 73, 81, 86, 87, 95, 105, 107, 108, 112, 115, 122, 130, 134, 136, 152**]
monastic granges, 1, 10, 12–13, 14, 22, 29–30, 37, 41, 43, 44, 47, 48, 50, 56, 63, 64, 69, 85, 87, 91, 99, 106–7, 112, 121, 122, 126, 135, 139, 140, 149, 155, 157, 159, 162, 164, 187, 191, 195, 197, 203, 218, [**10, 19, 29, 38, 52, 77, 90, 100, 101, 114, 120, 138**]
monastic sites, 46–7
  Bardney, Benedictine abbey, 10, 22, 47, 50, 63, 64, 201, [**10, 20, 35**]
  Barlings, Premonstratensian abbey, 10, 22, 28, 44, 47, 50, 54, 66–8, 69, 106, 131, 136, 139, 157, 159, 164, 168, 170, 177, [**19, 20, 50–2**]
  Bullington, Gilbertine priory, 47, 78, 106, 153
  Great Limber, Cistercian alien priory, 99
  Heynings, Knaith, Cistercian priory, 47, 50, 112–15, 117, [**84**]
  Newsham, Premonstratensian abbey, 1, 10, 67, 85, 91, 181, 197
  Nun Cotham, Brocklesby, Cistercian priory, 10, 30, 39, 47, 54, 189, 191, [**36**]
  Orford, Stainton le Vale, Premonstratensian priory of nuns, 15, 47, 50, 180, 181–2, 197, [**128**]
  Sixhills, Gilbertine priory, 30, 37, 44, 46, 47, 50, 51, 112, 119, 121, 126, 162–4, 203, [**19, 116**]
  Stainfield, Benedictine priory, 12, 47, 50, 63, 112, 175, 216, 218, [**24, 124**]
  Willoughton, Preceptory of Knights Hospitallers and Templars, 22, 43, 44, 47, 48, 49, 50, 85, 99, 218–20, [**19, 153**]
  Winghale, South Kelsey, alien priory, 8, 47, 49, 50, 170–1, [**121**]
  see also monastic granges *and* religious houses
Monson family, 39, 49, 55, 77, 79, 81, 82, 85, 136, 137, 139, 150, 159, 161, 168
  Sir John, 16th-century, 39, 168

Sir John, 17th-century, 77, 79
Lady Monson, 17th-century, 136, 139
Lord Monson, 18th-century, 139
Sir Robert, 17th-century, 136, 137, 139
Sir Thomas, 17th-century, 79, 82, 139, 150
William, 16th-century, 85, 168
Morers fee, 179
Mortain, Count of, 170, 193
mottes, 43, 48, 51, 147, *see also* castles
mounds, 6, 82, 91, 130, 135, 157, 181, 183, 199, *see also*
  barrows, pillow mounds, prospect mounds *and* windmill
  mounds

Nattes, C., 18th-century drawings by, 91, 98, 107, 147, [**79,
  107, 119**]
Nettleham, 3, 7, 8, 29, 40, 47, 54, 129–31, 157, [**18, 96**]
Nettleton, 6, 9, 13, 17, 25, 39, 40, 43, 55, 131, [**19, 30, 69**]
Newball, 3, 6, 12, 14, 41, 55, 131–5, [**97, 98**]
Newsham, Brocklesby, 16
Newsham, Brocklesby, Premonstratensian abbey, 1, 10, 67, 85,
  91, 181, 197
Newton, Toft Newton, 7, 203
Newton on Trent, 15, 40, [**14**]
'new' towns, medieval, 3, 22, 37, [**20**]
Nocton Park, Augustinian priory, 44
Nomina Villarum, 63, 84, 125, 152
Normanby, Stow, 10
Normanby by Spital, 39
Normanby le Wold, 6, 8, 10, 27, 36, 43, 44, 46, 89, 91, 135–6,
  [**99**]
Northamptonshire, 13, 14, 15, 181
North Carlton, 8, 17, 39, 40, 44, 54, 55, 136–9, 170, [**26, 100**]
North End, Keelby, 28, [**16**]
North End, South Kelsey, [**16**]
North Ingleby, Saxilby with Ingleby, 14, 16, 25, 29, 34, 48, 49,
  50, 53, 56, 159–61, 170, [**26, 115**]
North Kelsey, 3, 14, 43, 50, 139–41, [**10, 38, 101**]
North Kelsey Grange, 14, 43
North Ormsby, Gilbertine priory, 14, 43, 139, 141, [**38**]
Northorpe, 8, 15, 25, 29, 34, 38, 41, 141–4, [**102–4**]
North Stainton, Stainton le Vale, 84
Nun Appleton, Yorks, Cistercian nunnery, 189
Nun Cotham, Brocklesby, Cistercian priory, 10, 30, 39, 47, 54,
  189, 191, [**36**]

orchards, 70, 81, 82, 84, 95, 99, 118, 121, 131, 220
Orford, Stainton le Vale, 15, 16, 38, 47, 50, 51, 180–1, 183,
  [**128, 129**]
Orford, Stainton le Vale, Premonstratensian priory of nuns, 15,
  47, 50, 51, 180, 181–2, 197, [**128**]
Orford House, 183, [**129**]
Osgodby, Bardney, 3, 10, 13, 44, 47, 64, [**10, 49**]
Osgodby parish, 16, 25, 28, 35, 36, 38, 40, 41, 43, 48, 49, 51,
  56, 57, 144–9, [**28, 105–8**]
Otby, Walesby, 6, 10, 15, 28, 34, 135, 205, 208–10, [**146**]
Owersby, 3, 13, 25, 35, 36, 38, 39, 40, 79, 149–51, 170, [**109,
  110**]
Owersby Moor, 3
Owmby, 38, 39
Oxeney, Oxney, 67, 69

paddocks, 29, 41, 42, 48, 70, 71, 81, 84, 87, 93, 95, 126, 127,
  131, 139, 146, 150, 161, 164, 168, 171, 189, 199, 201, 205,
  211, [**1, 53**], *see also* closes, crofts, enclosures, paddocks *and*
  tofts
parishes as administrative units, 9–10, 41
parish tax, 84, 85, 187, 203, 211, 216

parks, landscaped, 40, 42, 55, 73, 82, 89, 91, 97, 106, 115,
  117, 127, 155, 157, 195, [**24, 31, 67, 85**], *see also* deer
  parks
parterres, 82, *see also* flower-beds
Payne, Geoffrey, son of, 153
Paynel family, 16, 168, 213, 215
  Hugh and Ralf, 213
Pelham family, Earls of Yarborough, 85, 89, 91, 101
  Sir William, 16th-century, 99, 101
  Sir William, 17th-century, 39
Percy family, 179
  Henry de, 175
  William de, 164, 216
Peterborough Abbey, Northants, 22, 189
Pickering, Sir Thomas, 147
Pilgrimage of Grace, 129
Pilham, 15, 40, 152, [**111**]
pillow mounds, 139
pit alignments, prehistoric, 7
place-names, Scandinavian, 8–9, 152
Pole, Sir William de la, 211
Poll Tax, 34, *see also* population statistics
ponds, 29, 55, 67–8, 69, 70, 79, 85, 87, 97, 98, 99, 101, 113,
  117, 119, 121, 125, 135, 136, 139, 141, 149, 162, 164,
  168, 173, 175, 177, 181, 185, 189, 191, 195, 199, 201,
  203, 207, 210, 211, 220, [**1, 62, 63**], *see also* fishponds
Poor Laws, 40
population change, 28, 34–41, *see also* depopulation,
  farmsteads, sites of, population statistics, settlements,
  deserted *and* settlements, shrunken
population statistics, xviii, 28, 34, 35, 36, 37, 39, 63, 64, 71,
  73, 75, 77, 78, 79, 84, 85, 93, 97, 101, 103, 106, 107,
  111, 115, 119, 121, 122, 125, 126, 127, 129, 131, 135,
  136, 137, 141, 146, 147, 149, 150, 152, 153, 155, 157,
  161, 164, 165, 168, 170, 173, 175, 177, 178, 180, 185,
  187, 189, 191, 194, 197, 201, 203, 205, 208, 211, 213,
  216, 218
pottery
  Iron Age, 170
  Roman, 71, 103, 126, 129, 130, 131, 149, 150, 162, 170,
    203, 207, 211
  Saxon, 8, 71, 89, 129, 130, 135, 149, 150, 170, 210
  Saxo-Norman, 112, 130, 137, 144, 150, 208
  medieval, 28, 38, 63, 69, 78, 82, 84, 87, 89, 95, 99, 101,
    103, 106, 107, 112, 113, 115, 129, 130, 131, 135, 137,
    140, 141, 144, 149, 150, 157, 161, 162, 164, 173, 175,
    181, 185, 187, 189, 191, 195, 197, 203, 205, 207, 208,
    211, 215
    Humber ware, 103
    Stamford ware, 195
  post-medieval, 69, 99, 103, 112, 129, 131, 137, 141, 146,
    150, 161, 162, 173, 189
  19th-century, 78, 208
prospect mounds, 54, 55, 70, 107, [**42, 79**]

quarries, 105, 106, 135, 136, 191, 207
  gypsum, 55, 194

Rabayn family, 127, 129
  Elias de, 129
Rand, 3, 10, 16, 29, 38, 42, 45, 48, 49, 50, 57, 153–5, [**25,
  112**]
Rand family, 81
Randy Lea, Thorpe in the Fallows, 12
Ranulf, Earl of Chester, 193
Reasby, Stainton by Langworth, 3, 50, 54, 131

Reepham, 28
religious houses, 22, 34, 37, 43–4, 46–7
  Alvingham, Gilbertine priory, 85
  Angers, Benedictine house of St Nicholas, 22, 218
  Aunay-sur-Odon, Calvados, Cistercian abbey, 99
  Catley, Gilbertine priory, 44
  Coventry, Warks, Carthusian priory of St Anne, 99
  Elsham, Augustinian hospital and priory, 147, 149
  Grimsby, priory of St Leonard, 189, see also Wellow
  Kirkstead Abbey, 37, 157, 159, 164
  Louth Park, Cistercian abbey, 10, 44, 119, 122, 197, 199
  Nocton Park, Augustinian priory, 44
  North Ormsby, Gilbertine priory, 14, 43, 139, 141, [38]
  Nun Appleton, Yorks, Cistercian nunnery, 189
  Peterborough Abbey, Northants, 22, 189
  Revesby Abbey, 195, [29]
  Sées, Normandy, abbey of St Martin, 170
  Thornholme Priory, Yorks, 106
  Thornton Abbey, 85, 178, 189
  Torksey, Augustinian priory of St Leonard, 47
  Tours, abbey of St Martin of Marmoutier, 170
  Welbeck, Notts, Premonstratensian abbey, 22, 44, 187
  Wellow, Grimsby, Augustinian abbey, 30, 85, 155, 189, 191,
    201, see also monastic granges and monastic sites
retting pits, 175, 218
Revesby Abbey, 195, [29]
Reynolds, S., 16
Riby, 28, 38, 40, 43, 56, 155, [31, 113]
Richmond, Honour of, 205
ridge-and-furrow, 14, 69, 82, 85, 87, 91, 93, 99, 106, 111, 115,
    117, 123, 126, 135, 136, 144, 146, 147, 152, 164, 170, 175,
    197, 213, 218
  in deer parks, 95, 117, 161
  headlands, 64, 78, 87, 111, 113, 144, 146, 159, 162, 164, 171,
    181, 191, 211, 213
  on landslips, 181
  narrow, 191
  reversed-S, 146
  settlement remains beneath ridge-and-furrow, 63, 113, 162, 181
  settlements on top of ridge-and-furrow, 13, 14, 16, 22, 28, 30,
    43, 44, 47, 49, 50, 64, 70, 78, 85, 87, 95, 99, 103, 105,
    111, 112, 115, 119, 121, 125, 126, 131, 135, 139, 140, 146,
    149, 150, 152, 153, 155, 157, 159, 161, 164, 167, 171, 173,
    175, 180, 189, 191, 203, 205, 207, 211, 215, 220, [11, 15,
    22, 32]
ring, 130
ring and baileys, 193, [137]
ring ditches, prehistoric, 6, 7
ringwork, medieval, 43, 147
Risby, Walesby, 1, 6, 10, 28, 34, 135, 205, 207–8, [9, 145]
Riseholme, 3, 10, 14, 16, 36, 38, 43, 44, 45, 46, 106, 155–9,
    205, [114]
Riseholme Grange, 159
Robert 'ad pipe', 79
Robert, Count of Eu, 193
Robert on the Grene, 141
Roberts, B. K., 14
Robinson family
  Frederick, 78
  Captain George, 77
Robinson, John, 127
Roger of Poitou, 155, 170, 193
Roman period
  Fosse Dyke, 3 [18]
  pottery, 71, 103, 126, 129, 130, 131, 149, 150, 162, 170, 203,
    207, 211

settlements, 6–7, 28, 79, 203, 211, see also pottery
    continuity into Saxon and medieval periods, 7, 8, 9
  villas, 7, 79
Rossiter family, 54, 167
  Sir Edward, 167, [119]
  Richard, father and son, 39, 165
Rotherham, see Scot, Bishop Thomas
Rothwell, 45
Roumare, William de, Earl of Lincoln, 193
Ryland, Welton, [14]

Sallie Bank, Kettlethorpe, 53, 111
Saxby, 211
Saxilby, Saxilby with Ingleby, 25, 27, 49, [18]
Saxilby with Ingleby, 12, 14, 16, 25, 27, 29, 34, 42, 44, 48,
    49, 50, 53, 56, 159–62, [18, 26, 115]
Saxon period
  brooch, 7
  cemetery, pagan, 210
  defensive site, 43
  documents, 13
  estates, 17
  grave-slabs, 106
  hut-site, 89
  minster churches, 10, 45
  pottery, 8, 71, 89, 112, 129, 130, 135, 137, 144, 149, 150,
    170, 208, 210
  settlements, 8–9, 36
  trading centre, 3
Saxton, see maps, county
Scampton, 40, 43, 44, 45, 54, 55
Scandinavian
  army, 13
  invasions, 9, 16
  place-names, 8–9
  settlement, 28
Scot, Bishop Thomas, 103
Sothern, 9, 25, 28, 51, [19]
Scotney family, 179, 180
Scotter, 3, 7, 14, 15, 17, 22, 25, 29, 41, 44, 45, [15, 20]
Scotter Common, 10
Scotterthorpe, Scotter, 3, 14, 15, 41, [15]
Scotton, 7, 28, [16]
Scotton Common, 10
Searby, Searby cum Owmby, 39, 165
Searby cum Owmby, 39, 165
Sées, Normandy, abbey of St Martin, 170
Seney (Senex) Place, 63
settlement change, 28–33, [24–6], see also depopulation,
    settlements, deserted and settlements, shrunken
settlements, deserted, 12, 15, 36–41, [8]
  Audleby, Caistor, 37, 38
  Beasthorpe, Owersby, 3, 13, 149, [109]
  Beckfield, Binbrook, 112
  Bleasby, Legsby, 3, 10, 15, 25, 29, 42, 49, 119–21, 122,
    127, [27, 87, 88]
  Buslingthorpe, 35, 36, 37, 38, 42, 45, 84–5, [62, 63]
  Butyate, Bardney, 3, 10, 13, 47, 64, [10]
  Cauthorpe, Owersby, 3, 13, 149, [109]
  Clixby, Grasby, 40
  Coates, Stow, 3, 10, 14, 17, 22, 44, 49, 185–7, 189, [25,
    131, 132]
  Coldecotes, Legsby, 3, 37, 44, 121, 122, 126, 162, [89]
  Cold Hanworth, 17, 38, 40, 93, [70]
  Crossholme, Bishop Norton, 9, 12
  Croxby, Thoresway, 12, 17, 34, 35, 36, 38, 55, 56, 195,
    197–9, [139]

Draycote, Nettleton, 9
Dunstall, Corringham, 3, 9, 36, 38
East Torrington, Legsby, 7, 14, 15, 38, 51, 123-6, [**91, 93**]
Firsby, West Firsby, 3, 10, 13, 22, 25, 28, 29, 36, 38, 42, 45,
    51, 57, 106, 211-13, [**22, 32, 148**]
Gilby, Pilham, 15, 40, 152, [**111**]
Goltho, 2, 3, 7, 8, 17, 30, 38, 42, 43, 48
Greetwell, 28, 30, 36, 37, 40, 55, 103-5, [**25, 76**]
Hardwick, Nettleton, 9, 12
Helethorpe, Fulnetby, 3, 13, 14, 95, 153, [**71**]
Holme, Sudbrooke, 189
Holtham, Legsby, 3, 43, 126, 162, [**92**]
Huckerby, Corringham, 3, 9
Kettleby, Bigby, 7, 9, 30, 39, 49, 53, 55, 70, 71, 211, [**1, 53**]
Kettleby Thorpe, Bigby, 7, 9, 38, 39, 41, 71, 211
Kingerby, Osgodby, 16, 28, 35, 36, 38, 40, 43, 49, 56, 144,
    146, 147-9, [**28, 106, 108**]
Linwood, 3, 42, 45, 48, 49, 54, 127, 129, [**95**]
Little Limber, Brocklesby, 38, 39, 165
Middle Carlton, North Carlton, 8, 136, 137, 168, [**100**]
Newball, 3, 14, 131-3, [**97**]
Newsham, Brocklesby, 16
North Ingleby, Saxilby with Ingleby, 14, 16, 25, 29, 34, 48,
    49, 50, 53, 56, 159-61, 170, [**26, 115**]
Orford, Stainton le Vale, 15, 16, 38, 47, 50, 51, 180-1, [**128**]
Osgodby, Bardney, 3, 10, 13, 44, 47, 64, [**10, 49**]
Otby, Walesby, 1, 6, 10, 15, 28, 34, 135, 205, 208-10, [**146**]
Rand, 38, 45, 153-5, [**112**]
Reasby, Stainton by Langworth, 3, 50, 54
Riby, 28, 38, 40, 43, 56, 155, [**31, 113**]
Risby, Walesby, 1, 6, 10, 28, 34, 135, 205, 207-8, [**9, 145**]
Riseholme, 3, 10, 14, 16, 36, 38, 45, 46, 155-9, [**114**]
Snarford, 3, 35, 38
Somerby, Corringham, 7, 8, 9, 14, 38, 53
Somerby, Somerby parish, 37, 38, 39, 164-7, [**118**]
Southorpe, Northorpe, 15, 25, 29, 34, 38, 41, 141, [**102**]
South Ingleby, Saxilby with Ingleby, 14, 25, 29, 34, 42, 56,
    161-2, [**26, 115**]
Stainfield, 12, 14, 15, 16, 38, 175, [**24, 124**]
Stow Park, Stow, 10, 129, 185, [**130**]
Swinhope, 191, [**135**]
Swinthorpe, Snelland, 3, 37, 44, 164, [**117**]
Thorganby, 44, 201, [**44, 45, 140**]
Thorpe, Thorpe in the Fallows, 3, 9, 29, 40, 41, 203, [**141**]
Walesby, 10, 15, 25, 28, 34, 38, 46, 205-7, [**143, 144**]
Wharton, Blyton, 38
Wykeham, Nettleton, 9
see also settlements, shrunken
settlements, medieval, 9-12, [**8**], *see also* farmsteads, sites of,
    settlements, deserted, settlements, shrunken *and* villages
settlements, prehistoric, 6-7, 170, *see also* barrows
settlements, Roman, 3, 6-7, 8, 9, 28, 79, 203, 211, [**7, 18**], *see*
    also pottery, Roman *and* Roman period
settlements, Saxon, 3, 7, 8-9, 10, 36, 43, 106, 210, *see also*
    pottery, Saxon *and* Saxon period
settlements, shrunken, 12, 36-41, [**8**]
    Apley, 3, 35, 36, 63, [**47**]
    Atterby, Bishop Norton, 9, 38
    Bardney, 3, 22, 28, 29, 57, 64, [**20, 49**]
    Blyborough, 39, 40, 45, 73, [**54**]
    Bransby, Sturton, 10
    Brattleby, 15, 16, 36, 40, 42, 45, 75-7, [**55, 56**]
    Broxholme, 3, 15, 17, 77-8, [**57, 58**]
    Burton, 7, 15, 16, 79-82, [**60, 61**]
    Cabourne, 1, 30, 37, 41, 43, 44, 56, 85-7, 106, 135, 155, [**64**]
    Caenby, 41
    Cammeringham, 39

Claxby, 6, 89-90, [**67**]
Cuxwold, Swallow, 9, 36
Dunholme, 29
Faldingworth, 3, 17, 29, [**18**]
Fillingham, 46, [**21**]
Gate Burton, 40, 97, [**72**]
Glentham, 3, 41, 57
Great Limber, 7, 39, 101-3, [**74, 75**]
Hackthorn, 3, 44, 45, 106-7, [**77**]
Harpswell, 36, 37, 38, 46, 107, [**78**]
Heapham, 14, 15, 28, 39, 45, 46, 111, [**18, 81**]
Helpesthorpe, Willoughton, 22, [**19**]
Hemswell St Helen, Hemswell, 39, 46, [**17**]
Holton, Holton cum Beckering, 29-30, 44, [**19**]
Holton, Holton le Moor, 3, 45
Kettlethorpe, 111, [**82**]
Kirmond le Mire, 112, 191, [**83**]
Knaith, 3, 15, 36, 38, 40, 45, 115-17, [**26, 85**]
Linwood, 3, 7, 15, 16, 29, 127-9, [**95**]
Lissington, 8, 29, 39
Middle Rasen Drax, Middle Rasen, 17, [**17**]
Nettleton, 6, 9, 17, 25, 39, 43, [**19, 30**]
Newton, Toft Newton, 7
Normanby, Normanby le Wold, 46, 135-6, [**99**]
Normanby, Stow, 10
North Carlton, 17, 40, 136-7, [**26, 100**]
Northorpe, 25, 34, 141-4, [**103, 104**]
Osgodby, Osgodby parish, 25, 57, 144-6, [**105, 106**]
Owersby, 3, 25, 35, 36, 38, 40, 149-50, [**109, 110**]
Riby, 28, 38, 40, 43, 56, 155, [**31, 113**]
Scampton, 40, 43, 44, 45
Sixhills, 162-4, [**116**]
Snelland, 44
South Carlton, 14, 22, 28, 44, 168-70, [**120**]
South Kelsey, 3, 25, 46, [**16**]
Spridlington, 3, 25, 37, 38, 40, 46, 173-5, [**123**]
Stainton le Vale, 6, 34, 36, 41, 44, 56, 57, 177-80, 195,
    [**126-9**]
Sturton, 10
Sudbrooke, 41, 189, [**133**]
Swallow, 6, 9, 30, 34, 38, 48, 56, 149, 155, 189-91, 195,
    [**134**]
Tealby, 6, 25, 28, [**17**]
Tealby Thorpe, Tealby, 12
Thoresway, 17, 28, 36, 57, 194-9, 201, [**29, 138, 139**]
Thornton le Moor, Owersby, 149, [**109**]
Toft, Toft Newton, 15, 44, 45, 203-5, [**142**]
Torksey, 3
West Rasen, 3, 14, 16, 29, 51, 213-16, [**149**]
Wickenby, 42, 45, 216-18, [**151**]
Yawthorpe, Corringham, 3, 9
see also settlements, deserted
Sexty, John, 75
sheep-farming, 10, 30, 37, 38, 43, 44, 63, 67, 84, 85, 87, 99,
    112, 141, 157, 159, 161, 162, 164, 165, 195, 207, 211,
    213
sheep-folds, 205, 213
Sheffield, Christopher, 199
Sheppard, J. A., 14
Simpkinson, Richard, 203
Simundescroft, Thonock, 12
Sixhills, 162-4, [**116**]
Sixhills, Gilbertine priory, 30, 37, 44, 46, 47, 50, 112, 119,
    121, 126, 162-4, 203, [**19, 116**]
Skelton, William, 205
slag, 87, 141
slates, *see* building materials

Smyth, Thomas, 99
Snarford, 3, 9, 35, 38, 50
Snelland, 3, 7, 44, 164, [**117**]
Snitterby, 12, 36, 38
Snoden, Robert, 199
Somerby, Corringham, 7, 8, 9, 14, 38, 53
Somerby House, Somerby parish, 165, 167-8, [**118, 119**]
Somerby parish, 12, 27, 28, 37, 38, 39, 54, 164-8, [**118, 119**]
sources, xviii-xix, 1, 34
South Carlton, 14, 22, 28, 39, 44, 55, 137, 168-70, [**43, 120**]
South End, Keelby, 28, [**16**]
South Ingleby, Saxilby with Ingleby, 14, 25, 29, 34, 42, 49, 56, 161-2, 170, [**26, 115**]
South Kelsey, 3, 8, 25, 39, 46, 47, 48, 49, 50, 53, 55, 170-3, [**16, 121, 122**]
Southorpe, Northorpe, 15, 25, 29, 34, 38, 41, 141, [**102**]
Southrey, Bardney, 14, 15, 17, 25, 63, [**13, 15**]
Speed, John, see maps, county
Spridlington, 3, 25, 37, 38, 40, 41, 46, 173-5, [**123**]
Springthorpe, 9, 14, 15, [**15**]
squatter occupation, 63, 195
Stainfield, 6, 12, 14, 15, 16, 38, 39, 47, 51, 54, 55, 56, 175-7, [**24, 124, 125**]
Stainfield, Benedictine priory, 12, 47, 50, 63, 112, 175, 216, 218, [**24, 124**]
Stainfield Hall, 67, 175, 177, [**124, 125**]
Stainton by Langworth, 3, 50, 54, 131
Stainton le Vale, 6, 7, 15, 16, 34, 36, 38, 41, 44, 47, 50, 51, 54, 55, 56, 57, 84, 177-83, 195, [**126-9**]
Stallingborough, 171
Stark, 19th-century writer, 117, 118, 119
Staunford, Roger de, 192
Stephen, King, 193
stone heads, medieval, 70, 130
Stonehouse, 19th-century writer, 78
Stow, 3, 10, 14, 17, 22, 29, 44, 45, 47, 48, 49, 50, 53, 54, 184-9, [**20, 40, 130-2**]
Stow Park, 10, 129, 185, [**40, 130**]
St Paul family, 85, 157, 159
Straw, Mr, 103, 105
street-names
    Grainge Lane, North Kelsey, 140
    Ingleby Lane, Saxilby with Ingleby, 161
    Park Lane, South Kelsey, 171
    Sorrylesse Lane, South Kelsey, 172
    South Green Lane, Saxilby with Ingleby, 161
    Town Street, Brattleby, 75
    Town Street, Gate Burton, 97
strip lynchets, 197
Sturgate, Springthorpe, 14, 15, [**15**]
Sturton by Stow, 7, 10, 12
Sudbrooke, 9, 41, 188-9, [**133**]
Suffolk, Dukes of, 67, 73, 122, 136, 159, 168, 195
Suffolk, Earl of, 211
summer-houses, 55, 105, 107
sunken hut, Saxon, 89
Susworth, Scotter, 3
Sutton, Robert, 93
Sutton family, 220
    John, 220
Swallow, 6, 9, 30, 34, 36, 38, 41, 48, 56, 149, 155, 189-91, 195, [**134**]
swannery, 185
Swein Estrithson, King of Denmark, 193
Swein 'novus carpentarius', 185
Swinhope, 6, 191-2, [**135**]
Swinthorpe, Snelland, 3, 37, 44, 64, 164, [**117**]

Swynford family, 48, 53
    Katherine, 111

Tailboys (Tailbois) family, 78, 97
    Sir Geo, 78
tanning pits, 175
Taylor, C. C., 14, 22
Tealby, 6, 12, 25, 28, 49, 192-3, [**17, 136**]
Tealby Thorpe, Tealby, 12
temple, ornamental, 97
terraced walks in gardens, 54, 55, 82, 167, 199
terrace-ways, 87, 115, 130, 136, 167, 179, 180, 183, 197, 199, 208, 210, 211, 213
Terry, John, 101
Thislewood, 18th-century map by, 82
Thonock, 3, 12, 43, 48, 53, 193-4, [**137**]
Thoresway, 6, 12, 17, 28, 34, 35, 36, 38, 43, 55, 56, 57, 194-201, [**29, 138, 139**]
Thorganby, 44, 200-1, [**44, 45, 140**]
Thorganby Hall, 201
Thorncroft Farm, Snitterton, 12
Thornhagh family, 171
Thornholme Priory, Yorks, 106
Thornton Abbey, 85, 178, 189
Thornton College, 178
Thornton le Moor, Owersby, 149, [**109**]
Thorpe, Thorpe in the Fallows, 3, 29, 40, 41, 203, [**141**]
Thorpe in the Fallows, 3, 9, 12, 29, 40, 41, 202-3, [**141**]
Thurgood, John, 220
tile kiln, 164
tile-making sites, 95, 164, 197
tiles, see building materials
Todeni, Robert de, 82, 161
Toft, Toft Newton, 15, 44, 45, 203-5, [**142**]
Toft Newton, 15, 44, 45, 203-5, [**142**]
tofts, 77, 87, 106, 139, 140, 141, 152, 175, 191, 220, see also closes, crofts and paddocks
tombstones, medieval, 63, 211, see also grave-slabs
Tomline family, 155
topography, 2-6, 10-12, [**3**]
Torksey, 3, 9, 13
Torksey, Augustinian priory of St Leonard, 47
Torrington, Legsby, 10, 122, see also East, Great, Little and West Torrington
Tournay family, 25, 144, 146, 152
Tours, abbey of St Martin of Marmoutier, 170
Tours, Gilbert de, 85
tower, 16th-century, 171
townships as economic units, 9, 10, 25, 41, 44
tree features
    avenues, 79, 107, 155, 177, [**79, 80**]
    bank, 159
    mounds, 77, 183
    rings, 55, 127, 173, 183, 197, [**89**]
Trehampton, John de, Ralph de and Roger de, 117
Trinity College, Cambridge, 171
Trussebut, Robert and William, 153
Tupholme, Middle Rasen, 15, [**17**]
Turpin Farm, Fillingham, 12
Tyrwhitt family, 36, 38, 39, 49, 63, 68, 70, 71, 85, 177
    Edward, 177
    John, d. 1741, 67, 177
    Philip, d. 1588, 177
    Philip, d. 1624-5, 175, 177
    Robert, d. 1428, 39
    Robert, d. 1548, 39, 63, 70, 71, 177, 179, 181
    Robert, d. 1617, 70, 127

William, active _c._ 1400, 39
William, active 1431, 82, 84, 127, 211
William, active 1538, 22
William, d. 1591, 70

Umfraville family, 97
    Gilbert de, 99
Upper Walesby, 135
Upton, 9, 15, [**14**]
Usselby, 144, 146

Viking, _see_ Scandinavian
villages, deserted and shrunken, _see_ settlements, deserted _and_
    settlements, shrunken
villages, origins of, 13–28
    estate villages, 73, 106, 137, 173
    influenced by communication patterns, 29
    influenced by ecclesiastical institutions, 1, 10, 12, 16, 22, 28,
        37, [**19**]
    influenced by markets, 16, 22, [**20**]
    influenced by rivers, 3, 10, 14, 15, 39, 115, [**5, 11, 15**]
    influenced by topography, 3, 6, 10
villages, planned, 14–25, 41–2, 45, 49, 75, 77, 78, 81, 93, 99,
        111, 115–17, 123, 125, 136, 146, 147, 149, 153, 170, 175,
        181, 205, _see also_ 'new' towns
    replanned, 14, 16, 36, 75, 78, 81, 82, 119, 125, 129, 136, 153,
        155, 157, 159, 161, 162, 170, 195, 213
    unplanned, 28–30
villages, plans of, [**14–21, 24–6**]
    greens, 17, 22, 28, 29, 79, 81, 82, 87, 89, 125, 137, 141, 146,
        149, 168, 195, 203, 215
    grid plans, 15, 22, 25, 173, [**14, 16**]
    nucleated, 1, 10, 13, 64
    polyfocal, 14, 22, 25, 27–8, 37, 44, 46, 111, 127, 129, 135,
        141, 149, 150, 164, 173, 189, 205, [**15–18, 21**]
    single-row, 15, 40, 71, 187, 189, [**14**]
    two-row, 15, 17, 39, 40, 112, 137, 146, [**14–17, 19**]

Waddingham, 13, 25, 38, 46, [**16**]
Waldin the Engineer, 218
Walesby, 1, 6, 10, 15, 25, 28, 34, 38, 46, 135, 205–10, [**9,
    143–6**]
Walkerith, 29
Wallace, John, 109
Warre, Thomas de la, 121
warrens, 48, 85, 139, 153, 162, [**100**]
Warton, Ricardus, 152
Washingborough, 6
water cults, 46
waterfall in garden, 199
Water House, Burton, 79
water-mills, sites of, 29, 43, 45, 47, 51, 77, 85, 117, 123, 126,
    153, 162, 180, 181, 183, 195, 197, 211, 213, 215
Welbeck, Notts, Premonstratensian abbey, 22, 44, 187
Wellow, Grimsby, Augustinian abbey, 30, 85, 155, 189, 191, 201
wells, 78, 87, 130, 149
Welton, 3, 7, 15, 17, 28, 29, 51, 210–11, [**14, 19, 147**]
West Firsby, 3, 10, 13, 22, 25, 28, 29, 36, 38, 42, 45, 51, 57,
    205, 211–13, [**22, 25, 32, 148**]
Westhall, Welton, 210
Westlaby, Wickenby, 3, 216
Weston family, 167
    Edward, 167
West Rasen, 3, 14, 16, 29, 51, 213–16, [**39, 149, 150**]
Westrum, Bigby, 9, 12
West Torrington, Legsby, 123, 125
Wharton, Blyton, 38
Wheatbear, Corringham, 12

Whichcote family, 107
    Colonel George and Frances his wife, 109
    Sir Hamond, 107, 109
    Robert, 109
    Thomas, 109
White's _Directory,_ 152, 161
Whitworth, George, 91
Wickenby, 3, 9, 42, 45, 216–18, [**151**]
Wickham, Bishop of Lincoln, 129
Wigot of Lincoln, 161
Wildeker, William, 139
wildernesses in gardens, 82, 107, 177, 199
wild-fowl, 51, 55, 79, [**43**]
Wildsworth, 3, 15, 29, [**5, 15**]
Wilkinson, William, 125
William I, 193
William, Count of Mortain, 170
William, son of Hugh 'gardinar', 185
Williams, Bishop of Lincoln, 129
Willingham by Stow, 12, 25, 29
Willoughby of Lincoln, Robert and William, 153
Willoughby of Parham, Lords, 97, 112, 115
    Frances, 5th Baron, 115
    William, 1st Lord Willoughby of Parham, 115, 117
Willoughby of Thorganby, family, 201
Willoughton, 8, 22, 36, 43, 44, 48, 49, 50, 51, 218–20, [**19,
    152, 153**]
Willoughton, Preceptory of the Knights Templars and
    Hospitallers, 22, 43, 44, 47, 48, 49, 50, 85, 99, 218–20,
    [**19, 153**]
wills and inventories, 71, 99, 127, 152, 162, 165, 185, 203
windmill mounds and sites of windmills, 51, 73, 126–7, 133,
    161, 216, [**39, 94, 150**]
Winghale, South Kelsey, alien priory, 8, 47, 49, 50, 170–1,
    [**121**]
Witherwicke family, 89, 91
Wlvedale, Bullington, 78
Woodhouse, Corringham, 9, 12
woodland banks, 78, _see also_ deer park pales
woodland management, 3, 47, 64, 68, 78, 99, 133
wood-names
    Black Plantation, Goltho, 99
    Cocklode Wood, Bullington, 78, 97
    Great West Wood, Bullington, 78
    Hermit Dam, Lea, 112, 117
    Holt, Legsby, 126
    Lea Wood, Lea, 117
    Les Laundes, Goltho, 99
    Newball Park Wood, Newball, 68
    Newball Wood, 133
    Short Wood, Bullington, 78
    Spring Wood, Bullington, 78
    West Wood, Goltho, 78
Wragby, 10, 45, 121, 125, 153
Wray family
    Albinia, wife of Sir Christopher, 68
    Sir Christopher, 54, 68
    Edward, 68
    John, 69
Wright, Edward, 75
Wykeham, Nettleton, 9

Yarborough, Earls of, 85, 89, 91, 101, _see also_ Pelham family
Yawthorpe, Corringham, 3, 9
Yorkshire villages, 14, 15, 16
Young family, 91, 147
    John Joseph, 91